ISBN 978-1-330-72056-1
PIBN 10096738

1 MONTH OF
FREE
READING

at
www.ForgottenBooks.com

By purchasing this book you are eligible for one month membership to ForgottenBooks.com, giving you unlimited access to our entire collection of over 1,000,000 titles via our web site and mobile apps.

To claim your free month visit:
www.forgottenbooks.com/free96738

English
Français
Deutsche
Italiano
Español
Português

www.forgottenbooks.com

Mythology Photography **Fiction** Fishing Christianity **Art** Cooking Essays Buddhism Freemasonry Medicine **Biology** Music **Ancient Egypt** Evolution Carpentry Physics Dance Geology **Mathematics** Fitness Shakespeare **Folklore** Yoga Marketing **Confidence** Immortality Biographies Poetry **Psychology** Witchcraft Electronics Chemistry History **Law** Accounting **Philosophy** Anthropology Alchemy Drama Quantum Mechanics Atheism Sexual Health **Ancient History** **Entrepreneurship** Languages Sport Paleontology Needlework Islam **Metaphysics** Investment Archaeology Parenting Statistics Criminology **Motivational**

TRAVELS

IN

VARIOUS COUNTRIES OF THE EAST;

BEING A CONTINUATION OF

MEMOIRS

RELATING TO

EUROPEAN AND ASIATIC TURKEY, &c.

EDITED BY

The Rev. ROBERT WALPOLE, M. A.

LONDON:

PRINTED FOR LONGMAN, HURST, REES, ORME, AND BROWN,
PATERNOSTER-ROW.

1820.

Printed by A. and R. Spottiswoode,
Printers-Street, London.

Of the numerous works recently published by travellers in different provinces of European and Asiatic Turkey, and other countries of the East, the parts which afford the least gratification are those relating to the civil and political condition of the inhabitants. They refer us to no improvement in art or science; no disposition in the people to profit of the acquirements of the more enlightened states of Europe. The fear that the Emperor Selim the Third would introduce some changes in the government, suggested by the practice of Christian countries, was among the causes which led to his deposition and death. The Constantinopolitan press is not more actively employed now than it was when Mr. Browne gave his first account in 1798. No alteration has taken place in the mode of conducting the administration of the provincial governments; numbers are annually destroyed by the plague, because no means are used to resist its progress; the communication between different parts of Asia Minor and Syria is interrupted by hordes of robbers; the chiefs of neighbouring districts are engaged in warfare with each other; and extensive districts, once celebrated for their luxuriant fertility, are abandoned, or badly cultivated.

The traveller, therefore, directs his attention to other objects; and these countries abound with many of great and varied interest, sufficient to repay him for the difficulties and dangers to which he is exposed. The comparison of the antient and modern geography; — mineralogical, botanical, zoological pursuits; — the examination of the remains of antient art; — observations on the manners and customs of

the mixed population of the provinces which he visits, present to
him an extensive field of research. The success with which his enquiries are carried on, depends on
the quiet or disturbed state of the country through which he passes,
and on the disposition of the ruler of it. The protection afforded by
the present governor of *Egypt* to those who have recently visited that
province, and part of *Nubia*, has given them favourable opportunities
for collecting much valuable information. Without his consent, the
interesting researches of Burckhardt, Bankes, Salt, Belzoni, Beechey,
and Caviglia * could not have even been attempted.

An examination of some of the emblematical representations on
the walls of the temples of *Egypt*, had induced an intelligent traveller † to consider them as confirming the opinion advanced by antient
writers, that arts and civilizations were received by that country from
Ethiopia. From the recent researches of Burckhardt, we find that
many temples of Nubia are of a higher antiquity than those in Egypt.
It is probable, that a more minute observation of the remains of sacred
buildings in Nubia would throw light on the hypothesis of Sir William
Jones, " that Ethiopia and Hindustan were peopled or colonized by '
the same extraordinary race." ‡ Characters have been found in
Ethiopia which have an astonishing resemblance to those of antient
Sanscrit, and particularly to the inscriptions in the caves of Canára,
in India. §

From an examination of the paintings in the interior of the sepulchres, and of the alabaster, marble, and granite figures and bas-
reliefs lately found in Egypt and Nubia, we may learn more accurately
the state of some of the arts in these countries in very remote ages.

* See the extracts from Mr. Salt's Letters. Quarterly Review, vol. xix.
† Hamilton's Egyptiaca, pp. 42. 51. See also Diod. Sic. l. iii.
‡ Works, i. 30. Our *Indian* followers (says Captain Burr, in an account of a visit made
to a temple in *Egypt*) who had attended us, beheld the scene before them with a degree of
admiration bordering on veneration, partly from the affinity they traced in several of the
figures to their own deities, &c. As. Res. vol. viii. See also Burckhardt's Travels, p. 108.
§ Note by Langlès to Norden's Travels, vol. iii. 299.

.The meaning which was conveyed in *antient* times by the various and symbolical figures depicted on the walls of the temples and tombs of Egypt cannot now be easily explained ; but we may, by the assistance of Mr. Salt and Mr. Beechey, who have bestowed the utmost attention in delineating them, as well as in copying the *colours* (1) of the paintings, understand the sense and allusions which they contained, according to the interpretation of the *later* Greeks.

- It is stated by Vansleb and Greaves *, that they observed hieroglyphical characters on the stones of one of the Pyramids. The positive assertions of Abdallatif, and other writers, and a remarkable passage cited by Holstein (2) from an antient author, appear to prove that a casing or covering had been applied to part of these buildings, and that characters had also been engraved on them. From the observations of Captain Caviglia, who saw on the stones of the mausolea, in the vicinity of the Pyramids, sculptures in an inverted position, it has been reasonably inferred that these might have formed a portion of the covering of the Pyramids. " The numerous characters found on the obelisks and cornices of Egyptian temples may not contain truths of much importance. This consideration however, though just, ought not to lead us to neglect the study of symbolic and sacred letters ; as the knowledge of them is intimately connected with the mythology, the manners, and individual genius of nations." † Some very singular documents have been procured in Egypt ‡, which have contributed to explain the nature and meaning of the sacred and popular § language of that country. (3) By the researches of future travellers, many valuable additions may be made to the materials already obtained. A fragment of black granite, larger than the Rosetta-stone, and bearing a trilinguar inscription, is described in the

---

* " On the north side of the second Pyramid I observed a line, and only one, engraven with sacred and Egyptian characters." Greaves. See also Vansleb, p. 137.
† De Humboldt. Pers. Narr. ii. 152.
‡ By Denon, Lord Mountnorris, Mr. Bankes, Mr. Legh, Dr. Merion, Lord Belmore.
§ See the Archæolog. xviii. Mus. Criticum. No. VI. and VII., and the article *Egypt*, in the Supplement to the Encyclo. Britann. vol. iv.

Courier de l' Egypte, and was seen by Dr. Clarke in Cairo; and Coptic monasteries preserve works of considerable antiquity. (4)

The nature of the fatigues and dangers experienced by Mr. Burckhardt in his journey through some regions of *Nubia* *, hitherto impervious to European travellers, may be collected from his valuable journals lately communicated to the public. Nothing but extraordinary patience, perseverance, strength of body, fortitude of mind, the utmost prudence, an intimate knowledge of the language, manners, and religious customs of some of the Eastern nations, could have conducted him with safety through the arduous situations in which he was frequently placed. Great difficulties and obstacles appear also to oppose themselves to those who examine *another* part of *the East*, of which our knowledge is at present very scanty and imperfect ; — the countries extending from Antilibanus, along the east side of the Jordan, to the south of the Dead Sea. " Travellers never venture across Jordan ; and rivers, mountains, provinces, are for the most part delineated, not according to mensuration from real accounts, of which we have almost none ; but marked at random on the empty space, according to the caprice of the designer." † Our defective information respecting this district will be supplied in a great degree by the numerous and important facts collected by Mr. Burckhardt. Some of the remarks made by the late Dr. Seetzen ‡, in his journey in these parts, were communicated by him to his friends. His route led him through the provinces of Ituræa, Auranitis, Gaulonitis, Batanæa, and through the territory of the antient Moabites, Amorites, and Midianites. These countries abounding with " fenced cities" in

---

* Mr. Burckhardt regrets that he was not able to examine the temple near Soleb, in Nubia, in Dar-el-Mahass. " It appeared to have been of the size of the largest of those found in Egypt." p. 74. Is not this the temple described by Abou Selah, as standing in *Dermes* ? (or Dar-Mahass, as it is written in Col. Leake's map of Egypt and Nubia.) " On voit dans ce *Berba* des peintures magnifiques et des colonnes énormes qu'on ne peut contempler sans être frappé d'étonnement." Mémoire sur la Nubie, Quatremère, p. 34.

† Michaelis on the Laws of Moses, Art. 23.

‡ A brief Account of the Countries adjoining the Lake of Tiberias, the Jordan, and the Dead Sea. 1810.

the time of the Israelites, and well peopled and flourishing under the, Romans, and in the first ages of Christianity, are now either deserted, or overrun with Nomad Arabs. The site of many towns was ascertained by Dr. Seetzen and Mr. Burckhardt, retaining under a corrupted form the names which they bear in the sacred writers. They discovered remains of the public works of the Romans,

> Temples and Theatres, Baths, Aqueducts,
> Statues, Triumphal Arcs. — (Par. Reg. iv.)

and some of the ruins appeared to rival in extent and magnificence those of Balbec and Palmyra. The testimony borne by Mr. Burckhardt to the qualifications and talents of Dr. Seetzen, leaves us no room to doubt, that if his papers had been preserved, they would have afforded very valuable materials for the illustration of the geography, mineralogy, and botany of this unfrequented country.

An eminent writer and theologian * of the last century expresses a belief, that the stones on which Moses ordered the law to be engraved † may be found in some future time in Palestine. No where in the Bible is any mention made of the discovery of these stones ; nor indeed any further notice taken of them than in Joshua, viii. 30., where their erection is described. Many curious illustrations of the antient connection between Egypt and Phœnicia may be reserved for future travellers. An intercourse subsisted at an early period between them ; some of the religious ceremonies of the latter were derived from the former ; the monument of Carpentras ‡ shows in a striking manner the connection between the two countries ; Phœnician characters are there written under figures strictly Egyptian ; and the first letter § of the Phœnician alphabet is found intermixed with the cursive writing of Egypt on some of the linen teguments of mummies. Mr. Wood thought it not improbable that he might dis-

---

* Michaelis on the Laws of Moses. Smith's Translation, Art. 69.
† Deut. xxvii. 1—8.   ‡ Acad. des Inscr. vol. xxxii. 725.
§ Barthelemy, Œuv. Divers, part ii. p. 392.

cover (5) *hieroglyphics* in the part of Syria which he visited.   The use
of these characters was not confined to Egypt; they were observed by
De Haven and Niebuhr * in the desert, on their route to Sinai; and '
they were employed by the *Israelites*, in the sixth century before the
Christian æra, in representing the idolatrous rites which are described
by the prophet. †

No one is ignorant how much light has been thrown on many parts
of the Holy Scriptures from the works of different travellers in the
East.   The illustrations which may still be derived from the same
source are very numerous ; but the value of them will be proportioned '
to the opportunities of observation possessed by the traveller, and to the
knowledge which he obtains of the customs, institutions, and languages ·
of the East.   " The sacred historian of the children of Israel,"·
Mr. Burckhardt ‡ observes, " will never be thoroughly understood, ·
so long as we are not minutely acquainted with every thing relating to
the Arabian Bedouins, and the countries in which they move and
pasture."   Syriac is still spoken § in some parts of the government of·
Damascus ; and Niebuhr was informed, that Chaldaic was the language
in use among the Christian inhabitants of many villages in the neighbourhood of Merdin and Mosul; and he supposes that a person
properly qualified would derive much benefit from residing for the
space of a year with the monks of the convents, situated near these
towns.   " But in order," says Michaelis, " to understand properly
the writings of the Old Testament, it is absolutely necessary to have
an acquaintance with the natural history, as well as the manners, of
the East.   We find in that volume nearly three hundred names of
vegetables ; there are many also drawn from the animal kingdom,
and a great number which designate precious stones."   The questions'
which this great Biblical scholar proposed to the Danish travellers,

---

* See Niebuhr, vol. i. p. 189.   Amst. 1776.   The inscriptions are given in Plates 45, 46.
† Ezek. viii. 10.·
‡ Life and·Memoirs of Lewis Burckhardt, p. lxxxiv.
§ See p. 299. of this volume.

relate almost entirely to the illustration of the Scriptures. " In a word," he adds, " while we think we are only occupied with under-standing the most antient book in the world, we find ourselves in-sensibly engaged in studying the greatest part of the natural history, the geography, and manners of the East. I cannot, in fact, name any other book, (at least where the subject is moral,) which is able to render, in this respect, the same service to science." *

It appears from the life of Bruce, that he had been informed, during his residence in Crete, of some remarkable ruins on the opposite coast of *Asia*. He procured a letter to a powerful Turkish governor, whose influence would have given him access to many of the Aghàs of Caramania; but an illness by which he was attacked at Castel Rosso, prevented him from undertaking this journey. The dissensions between the different Aghàs are among the great obstacles to a traveller's progress in Asia Minor; he has also to contend with the mistrust and jealousy of the governors of many of the different provinces. We know, therefore, little of the interior of the country, of its natural productions, of the various remains of antiquity, of the situation of towns celebrated in Sacred and Profane history. A very interesting route was pursued by General Koehler and his com-panions in the year 1800, through Bithynia, Phrygia, and Pisidia. From the bearings and directions noted in that journey, and from comparing the testimonies of antient writers with the observations of modern times, Col. Leake has been enabled to construct a map † far superior in accuracy to any we have yet possessed. A valuable addition to our geographical knowledge of the southern part of Asia Minor has been derived from the survey made by Captain Beaufort, of the Cara-manian shore, so erroneously laid down in our charts. In the course of his observations he was led occasionally to visit the extensive ruins

---

* See the Preface to his Questions addressed to the Danish Travellers.

† This is published by Mr. Arrowsmith. The small map inserted in this volume, edited also under the care of Col. Leake, illustrates the route of Mr. Browne, and his own, and that of General Koehler on his return to Constantinople.

of cities which once flourished on that coast. The illustration of different passages in the writers of antiquity is one of the advantages resulting from researches carried on in Greece, Asia Minor, and Syria. We are now able, by Captain Beaufort's assistance, to understand the meaning of the different expressions applied by them to the *Chimæra*. He describes his visit to this Flame ; the Everlasting Fire, as it has been sometimes termed, AΘANATON ΠYP, which burns on Mount Olympus, in Lycia. (6)

The correction of some of the errors which prevail respecting the geography of Asia Minor, was among the objects of enquiry which Mr. Browne had proposed to himself in his journey through that country. " I at first intended, (he observes in his manuscript papers,) to have taken my station at several different points, and to have directed my investigation at leisure, and as occasion should offer from each of them; the only way, I am convinced, of forming a correct idea of the country." His progress, however, through Asia Minor, was hastened by a desire " to return to Egypt, in consequence of the success of the campaign, and the contemplation of the advantages which it seemed to offer to the traveller." He refers, in his papers, to various geographical observations made in his route ; and states the reasons that led him to consider some of them of less authority than others, and the nature of the obstacles that prevented him from conducting his researches in a manner more satisfactory to himself. *

---

* " Of several of the latitudes I think myself certain ; and these are inserted. Those of which circumstances have rendered me doubtful, whether justly or not, I have suppressed. They were taken with a seven-inch sextant, which, being fond of practical astronomy, was in my hands as often as occasion would permit. In Anatolia, few meridian altitudes were taken, being at a season when the sun was too high. They were chiefly of two altitudes, and the elapsed time of a star, or of the moon, in Meridian.

" I had a chronometer, which failed very early after I received it; and was never afterwards of any use ; and I had a telescope by Dollond proper for observations of satellites ; but which I was fearful of carrying with me through Anatolia, as it had narrowly escaped out of the hands of a Douanier, who wanted to purchase it; and I wished especially to preserve it for the use I hoped to make of it in the neighbourhood of Egypt. I had also some lunar observations ; but most of them were made in places remote from habitations, and not repeated in the same spot, so as to be of less authority than might be wished."

From Mr. Browne's MSS.

In his travels through Asia Minor, Mr. Browne assumed the dress of a Musulman. His acquaintance with some of the languages of the East, which was more perfect in his second journey than in the first, enabled him to appear in that character without much fear of being discovered. In consequence also of this disguise, he had more frequent and intimate communication, than travellers in general, with the people of the country. During his residence at Constantinople, his attention seems to have been directed to the Manners, * Customs, Government, state of Literature, and Education among the Turks; some interesting remarks on these subjects are printed in this volume, extracted from "Miscellaneous Observations" found among his papers.

The talents, character, and general acquirements of Mr. Browne;— the nature of the qualifications which rendered him well fitted † to explore the countries of the East;— the motives which induced him to undertake his last journey; — and the circumstances attending his death; — are described in the biographical memoir of that traveller, inserted in the present work. I have received this valuable contribution from the same gentleman to whom we are already indebted for the Life of Mr. Mungo Park.

In comparing the state of our knowledge of the different provinces of the Turkish empire, we find that our information respecting *Greece* is more copious than that which we have obtained concerning other parts. It is not difficult to assign the reason of this. The population consists, in a great proportion, of Christians; and the intercourse, therefore, with the inhabitants is more frequent than any which can be carried on with a people under the influence and prejudices of Mahometanism. We derive great assistance in conducting our researches in Greece, from this circumstance; and much more would have been done towards obtaining an accurate account of many se-

* The illustration of part of the system of Police adopted in Constantinople forms the subject of a valuable paper in this volume, communicated by Mr. Hawkins; see p. 281.

† " The talents and perseverance of Mr. Browne were such as will seldom be found united in the same person. His friendship for me I can never forget; and to his excellent advice I owe much of my success." — Burckhardt's Travels, p. 349.

a 2

cluded districts, if difficulties had not arisen from the insecurity of travelling through them. But, notwithstanding the inconveniences and privations to which all travellers are subject in countries ·where the civilization is imperfect ; and the consequènt disadvantages under which they labour in carrying on their observations, the information obtained concerning it is very great. The materials, collected with considerable labour by Mr. Hawkins, Col. Leake, and Sir W. Gell, will remove many defects from our maps of Greece. Important enquiries * relating to the Architectural antiquities of the country, to the state of the art at an early period, as well as to the improvements of a later age, when it had reached a great degree of perfection, have been made since the days of Stuart. The works of Dr. Holland, Mr. Hobhouse, and Dr. Clarke, have supplied us with much valuable information. The papers of the late Dr. Sibthorp (which I have been permitted to consult again) were not prepared in any manner for·the press † ; but the extracts printed in the present volume, and those already before the public, reflect the highest credit upon him. His researches have greatly advanced our knowledge of the natural history of Greece, and of some of the islands of the Archipelago ; his list of birds, fishes, animals, and plants, is more complete than any which had been ever made ; and many of his remarks on the productions of the soil, and on various subjects connected with the Agriculture and Statistics of the country, are entirely new.

Three papers are inserted in the present volume, relating to parts of the East not connected with the Turkish empire. An addition to the title ‡ enabled me to insert, consistently with the enlarged plan of the work, these contributions, which will be found to increase

---

* I allude to the excavations in Ægina, and at Phigaleia, conducted by Messrs. Forster, Cockerell, Linck, and the late Baron Haller. See also the " Antiquities of Attica," published by the Dilettanti Society; the introduction to Wilkins' Vitruvius: Wilkins' Atheniensia; and particularly the paper in this volume communicated by Mr. Hawkins, relating to a temple in Eubœa.

† The reader is requested to apply this remark to the Journal also of Col. Squire.

‡ The second edition of the first volume is entitled, Memoirs relating to European and Asiatic Turkey, and other Countries of the East.

the interest of it; they contain an account of some Greek and Armenian settlements in Little Tartary; — a notice of some remarkable monuments found on the site of the antient Susa, in Persia; — and a narrative of a Journey from Suez to Mount Sinai. It has been properly suggested, that the different Memoirs in this work might be better arranged by placing those together which refer to the same country or subject. But unless all the papers intended for publication were in my possession at the same time, this classification could not be made. I was desirous of attending to it in the present instance; but those who have kindly assisted me with their communications were prevented by various causes from sending them at a time when they might have been inserted in parts of the volume which I intended to appropriate to them.

---

(1) " The throne of some of the deities, when chequered with *black* and *white*, was emblematical of the variety of sublunary things. The sun being a body of pure light, his garment, according to Plutarch, was to be of the same colour, uniformly *bright* and luminous; though Macrobius clothes the winged statues of the sun, partly with a *light*, partly with a *blue* colour. Isis being considered as the earth strewed with a variety of productions, her dress was to be spotted and variegated with divers colours. The tresses of her hair, when they are of a dark *blue* colour, denote the haziness of the atmosphere." — Shaw's Travels. 362.

(2) " De marmorea Pyramidarum incrustatione conjectura verissima mihi videtur, qua lapides postea sublatos et in alium usum conversos suspiceris. Nimis enim securus, ne dicam supinus, auctor ille fuisset (Philo Byz).si tam clarâ in re tam turpiter errasset." Holstenii. Epis. ed. Boissonade, p. 469. The passage in Philo is found in Gronov. Thes. G. A. viii. τὰ μὲν ἐστὶν ἡ πέτρα λευκὴ καὶ μαρμαρίτις. See also Abdallatif, Version de S. de Sacy, and Goguet's remark (tome iii.) on the description of the Pyramids by Herodotus.

(3) Before the discovery of the Rosetta stone, and the collection of numerous Papyri, made by different travellers, inquiries relating to the Egyptian language, and its connection with the Sacred character, must have been comparatively vague and uncertain; I shall therefore note, as briefly as possible, some opinions relating to this subject.

" The Egyptians," says Warburton, " carried the *picture* through all the stages quite down to *letters*, the invention of this ingenious people." Works, i. 401. " L'Alphabet de la Langue Egyptienne émanoit des Hieroglyphes." Caylus, t. 1. " M. Barthelemy avoit mis cette excellente theorie de M. Warburton dans un plus grand jour, en plaçant sur une colonne diverses lettres Egyptiennes en correspondance avec les hieroglyphes qui les avoient produits." See also Goguet. t. i. 190.

The Chinese language has also, according to some writers, been considered as a modification of hieroglyphics; but a different account is given in the clear and able statement made by Barrow. (Travels, 245.)

The authors to whom we have referred, consider the Egyptian language as derived from hieroglyphics; but the learned Heeren questions the possibility of such a derivation. See p. 427. of this volume. " The difficulty is, to conceive how marks which are signs for *things* should become signs for *words*." " Comment aura t-on passé des hieroglyphes aux caractères alphabétiques? C'est ce qu'il n'est pas aisé de concevoir." Goguet. i. 190. Warburton endeavours to explain the process.

De Pauw pronounces, on the subject of the Egyptian language, in his usual positive manner. " Les Egyptiens ont eu un caractère alphabétique, à peu-près semblable au nôtre; mais il ne s'ensuit pas qu'il eussent inventé ce caractère en perfectionnant leurs hieroglyphes, comme quelques savans l'ont prétendu." See also Larcher, Herod. Liv. ii. note 125.

According to the laborious investigation printed in the fourth volume of the Supplement to the Encyclopædia Brit., and the Remarks in the Museum Criticum, No. VI. the common or popular writing of Egypt was not " purely alphabetical." p. 54. It contained characters of this kind connected with *others* derived from *hieroglyphics*, as prototypes.

(4) J'ai appris d'Ibrahim Ennasch un des plus savans Coptes de Kahira qu'il avoit vu dans les couvents Coptes des livres écrits en langue de Pharaon et indéchiffrables à ceux de leur propre nation. — Forskal quoted by Niebuhr.

(5) " We had been in Egypt a few months before, and by comparing the linen, the manner of swathing, the balsam and other parts of the mummies of that country with those of Palmyra, we found their methods of embalming exactly the same. The Arabs had seen vast numbers of these mummies in all the sepulchres; but they had broken them up in hopes of finding treasures. We offered them rewards to find an entire one, but in vain; which disappointed our hopes of seeing something curious in the Sarcophagus, or perhaps of meeting with hieroglyphics." — Wood's Palmyra.

(6) Pliny alludes to the singular phænomenon in the reference made by Captain Beaufort; but there are two passages, one in Photius, and another in Maximus Tyrius, which deserve to be transcribed. " I saw," says Methodius, " on Olympus, a mountain in Lycia, fire rising spontaneously near the summit of the mountain, from the earth below. Around the fire grew the Agnus, a plant so flourishing, green, and shady, that it appeared rather to spring from a fountain." Photii. Bib. p. 924. ed. Schotti.

" Trees, brush-wood, and weeds grow close round this crater." Beaufort's Caramania, p. 48.

" Olympus sends out a fire, not like that of Ætna, but quiet and regular." Max. Tyr. Diss. viii.

" It was never accompanied, the guide told Captain Beaufort, by earthquakes, or noises; and it ejected neither stones, smoke, nor noxious vapours." p. 49.

TABLE of CONTENTS.

* The Editor is indebted to the Rev. Mr. Blakeway, of Shrewsbury, executor of Mr. Browne, for permission to print these extracts.

---

* Printed by permission of the Rev. E. Squire. Mr. W. Hamilton and Lieut. Col. Leake were the companions of Col. Squire in this journey in Syria.

† Owing to the discovery of an immense Soros of one integral mass of rock-crystal in Peru, Dr. Clarke was led to conjecture that Belzoni's Soros might be of the same nature (see p. 360.); but he has since received letters from Egypt, written by persons who have seen this Soros, and they describe it as a mass of Alabaster.

* The Editor returns his thanks to the Hon and Rev. G Neville, late Vice-chancellor of the University of Cambridge, for permission to use the types of the University-press, in representing the very perfect and valuable inscription in the Appendix.

DIRECTIONS TO THE BINDER

FOR

PLACING THE PLATES, &c.

* The impression of these three plates has been presented to the work by J. Lee, Esq. The Marble Head was purchased by him in Syria; the Votive Tablet at Athens.

The reader is requested to notice the following errata; as well as the corrections pointed out by Col. Leake in the subjoined letter, addressed to the Editor.

Page 6. l. 15. for *Schmemer*, read *Schmeisser*
113. l. 3. *note*, for *Blumenback*, read *Blumenbach*
160. l 17. for *costs*, read *cost*
288. l 18 for *Cipolino*, read *Cipollino*
384. l. 17. for *race-horse*, read *cart-horse*
390. l. 29. dele *under ,˙*
l 30. after *draught*, insert, *of pure water,*
391. l. 1. for *water*, read *stuff*
450. l. 2. for *Cephrenes*, read *Chephrenes*

Dear Sir ;— As the sheets of my paper upon Asia Minor passed through the press without my having an opportunity of revising them, some inaccuracies of style have inevitably been left, which the reader will detect, but there are also a few errata, of which it seems necessary to take more particular notice. I send you, therefore, the following

CORRECTIONS: I am, Dear Sir, Yours sincerely,
                                        W. M. L.

Page 189 l. 10. for *and Mottraye*, read *de la Mottrave*
193. l. 24 to the names of travellers in this line, add that of *Choiseul-Gouffier*
199. l 15. 18. for *Ghénza*, read *Ghinza*
203. l 17. read Shughut was bestowed upon Ertogrul, the father of Osman, *by* the Sultan of Konia
238. In contents of Chap. IV. for *Satalia (Catarractes)*, read *Satalia — river Catarractes*
243. l. 9. for *Ermerek*, read *Ermenek*
276. l. 22 25. for *Salassis*, read *Lalassis*
278. l 23 fill up the blank with *Ghuhoun*, and l. 4. from the bottom, for *Rhegmis*, read *Rhegmi*
279. l 4. for *Koryhos*, read *Korghos*, for *Lames*, read *Lamos*, l. 9. for *the latter name*, read *the name of Sebaste*
280. l 25. for *lying between Cremna and Sagalassus*, read *lying in the country about Cremna and Sagalassus*
280. last line, for *Sagalassa*, read *Sagalassus*

TRAVELS

IN

VARIOUS COUNTRIES OF THE EAST.

ON THE TAR SPRINGS OF ZANTE.

[COMMUNICATED BY MR. HAWKINS]

Situation of the Tar Springs. — Nature of the Hills which surround the Valley and Morass where they are found. — Remarkable Insalubrity of the Spot. — Luxuriance of Vegetation on the Western Border of the Morass. — The Northern Spring the most abundant in the liquid Mineral. — Attempt to discover whether the Bitumen issues out of the Rock, or oozes out of the Peat of the Morass. — Nature and Appearance of this Substance when first taken out of the Water. — Uses to which it is applied. — Bitumen also found to arise from the Bottom of the Sea in an adjoining Bay. — Analysis of some of the Saline Water from the Northern Spring. — Result of an Experiment made by Distillation of the Tar.

THE celebrated tar springs of Zante are situated in a morass at the head of a bay called Cheri ($\chi^{\epsilon}\rho\iota$), near the south-eastern extremity of the island.

This morass is of an oval form, and appears to be about one quarter of an English mile in its longest diameter. It is closely invested by hills on all sides, except on the south-east, where a narrow bar of shingle, about three hundred yards in length, separates it from the sea. This bar, by damming up the waters, has probably converted the area within into a morass, the surface of which has now nearly risen to the same level.

The surrounding hills consist of a calcareous free-stone called pori (πούρι) by the natives, containing no organic remains : the same stone occurs in all the maritime parts of Greece, and along the shores of the Adriatic.

With respect to the morass, it is composed of a perfect peat to a great depth, which has no bitumen in its composition ; not even in the vicinity of the tar springs.

The soil of the hills is light and of a ferruginous colour to the very borders of the morass, where it quickly changes into a black vege-table mould. This mould has been found to be so remarkably favourable to vegetation, that the whole western part of the morass at the head of the vale has been converted into vineyards, interspersed with fig, peach, quince, and pomegranate trees, which produce an abundance of fruit of a superior size and flavour. This spot, how-ever, is distinguished not less for the shortness of vegetable life, than for the luxuriance of its vegetation : for whereas in other parts of the island the currant vines do not begin to bear fruit in any quantity before the fifteenth year after they are planted, and continue to flourish during one hundred years, or more ; they here yield fruit in the third year, and become barren and exhausted after the fiftieth.

The intelligent native who favoured me with this information added, that the vines on the slopes of the neighbouring hills were observed to be slower in attaining perfection, and in arriving at the period of their decay, in proportion to the distance at which they grew from the morass, until they reached a point where the usual laws of maturition and longevity took place.

The lower and uncultivated parts of the morass are overgrown with sedge, rushes, reeds, and other aquatic plants, which give it the appearance of an English swamp.

On the borders of this morass rise several small springs of water, the collected streams of which, after being carefully conducted through the cultivated grounds, have opened a passage through the bar of shingle into the bay.

It is in consequence of this redundancy of water, of the heat concentrated by the surrounding hills, and the want of a free circulation of air, arising from the crateral form of the vale, that this spot is remarkably unwholesome during the summer and autumn; when a stay here of one day is not to be made with impunity; and a night's sleep proves fatal. On this account every habitation is far removed, notwithstanding the labour, and the frequent attention which are required for the cultivation of the vineyards.

Such is the situation of the celebrated Tar Springs of Zante, which were visited and described by Herodotus above two thousand years ago. No material change seems to have taken place here since his time, except that which is the natural consequence of the neglect in which they have long lain; the progressive growth of the peat having choked up the small lakes or pools described by that author.

The two springs which produce the bitumen are situated on the two opposite borders of the morass. The northern, which produces the greatest quantity of the mineral, has a less copious discharge of water than the other. It is distant about thirty yards from the border, and rises out of a small circular excavation in the solid peat, which has been made for the purpose of collecting the bitumen. This substance gradually oozing out of the earth below settles at the bottom of the pit, which serves as a reservoir for collecting it. Here the traveller is conducted to view this curious phænomenon; and here, as in the days of Herodotus, he may still dip his myrtle-bough into the water, and draw out the liquid mineral.

Some vestiges are observable of an old wall, which seems to have enclosed a space of some extent around the spring. The depth of the pit, which I measured with a rod, proved to be about six feet; but in order to ascertain whether the bitumen really issued with the other stream out of the rock below, or merely oozed out of the peat in which it originated, it was necessary that the pit should be so completely drained as to expose the bottom to view. This was an enterprise which required more than ordinary exertions; nevertheless, I had the satisfaction of witnessing its execution, during my residence at Zante in the year 1795, when the Venetian Admiral Corrèr, who felt the same desire of satisfying his curiosity in regard to the origin of the tar spring, selected for this purpose the most able-bodied men from his ship's crew : these he divided into gangs, who, relieving each other by turns, worked with such spirit and perseverance, that at the end of two hours we had the satisfaction of seeing the bottom of the pit nearly empty.

The spring of water was then observed to issue from the peat at the depth of four feet only from the surface, unaccompanied with bitumen. The bottom of the pit was nearly three feet deeper in the peat, and no signs appeared of the rock beneath it. Here some gallons of the bitumen were found collected; but still no fissures were perceivable, from which it issued; nor could the smallest particle of the mineral be observed in the substance of the peat, which was fresh broken at this depth for examination. It is, therefore, probable, that the bitumen oozes in very minute portions out of the rocky substratum which, in spite of all our exertions, it was not possible to clear entirely and expose to view. If a judgment can be formed from the inclination of the nearest ground on the borders of the morass, the solid rock could not be at the depth of many feet below this level; and here, if any inference may be fairly drawn from observations on the other tar spring, it is probable that the bitumen first rises.

The quantity of bitumen annually extracted from this pit is said to be about twenty barrels; and its faculty of re-production is reported to increase with the quantity taken out. The water has a strong saline taste, and the usual temperature of the springs in the neighbourhood.

The southern tar spring, which lies at a short distance from the sea on the opposite side of the vale, issues out of the stratified rock on the edge of the morass.

Here a more copious discharge of water takes place, and this is perfectly fit for drinking. Its temperature measured 65° of Fahrenheit, which is about the mean temperature of the climate.

The bitumen in like manner stagnates at the bottom, but on account of the shallowness of the water is very distinctly perceivable, and affords a most amusing spectacle; for when agitated by the least motion of the water, it assumes a variety of forms that are given to it by the impulse and whirling direction of the stream; while the small particles of bitumen which are successively detached from the rest of the mass, and rise up to the surface of the water, spread into a fine cuticle, that reflects all the iridescent colours observable on the smooth faces of some sorts of fossil coal. In this state they are borne away by the current, and quickly succeeded by others.

It is said that the bitumen boils up plentifully with a south or a south-easterly wind.

This substance, when first taken out of the water, has the same degree of fluidity as honey. It differs little in colour, lustre, opacity, and smell, from melted pitch, but hardens a little on exposure to the air.

The two springs are usually farmed by an inhabitant of the town, who disposes of the bitumen at a low price, for the use of boats, to which, when thickened by an admixture of pitch, it is said to be well adapted; but it has a corrosive quality when applied to ropes, which renders it unfit for the purposes of rigging.

In calm weather, this liquid bitumen is observed to rise from the bottom of the sea, in several parts of the adjoining bay, particularly between the small island of Marathonisi and the cape of Cheri, at the distance of one quarter of a mile or less from the land. The depth of water is here from twenty to thirty feet; and the bottom is composed of a whitish clay. This phænomenon is particularly striking in the calmest summer weather; the bitumen spreading like oil over the surface of the water. On hawling up the anchor of an English privateer here during the American war, it was found smeared over with bitumen, intermixed with a greyish coloured clay. This circumstance was communicated to me by an eye-witness.

Although in the present advanced state of geological science the tar springs of Zante have ceased to excite astonishment, yet they may still be classed with propriety among the rare phænomena of the earth. They are indebted however for their chief importance to their classical celebrity, having been visited and described by Herodotus, and noticed by many other writers of antiquity. *

I find some mention of them in the earliest of our modern travellers through the Levant; and to the end of Marsigli's Account of the Bosphorus, printed in 1681, there is annexed a small and very inaccurate map of their situation. The particulars given by Wheler, Spon, and Chandler are short and unsatisfactory; and the works of more recent travellers convey no better information.

In the year 1792, an analysis was made, at my request, of two pounds weight of the saline water from the northern spring, by Mr. Schmeiner, who found the contents to be as follows:

Sulphate of magnesia	-	90 grains.
Sulphate of soda	-	- 40
Selenite	- -	- 10
Muriate of lime	-	- 28
Muriate of magnesia		- 24
Muriate of soda	-	- 172
Resinous matter	-	- 8

372. loss 4 grains.

According to the report of the same able chemist, eight ounces of the tar yield by distillation two ounces of oil, similar to that which is known under the name of Petroleum. During the distillation a sulphureous smell is perceived. The residue of the distillation was a black bitumen, which, when dissolved in linseed oil boiled over oxyd of lead, yielded a fine varnish.

---

* The historian Eudoxus; vide Antig. Caryst.; also Dioscorides, Vitruvius, Pliny.

VOYAGE IN THE GRECIAN SEAS.

PRINCES ISLANDS. — DARDANELLES. — CYPRUS. — ISLANDS OF LERO,
PATMOS, STENOSA, ARGENTIERA, EUBOEA. — MOUNT ATHOS. — ISTHMUS
OF CORINTH.

[*FROM THE PAPERS OF THE LATE DR. SIBTHORP.*]

CHAP. I.

The Princes Islands. — Mines of Chalke. — Plants. — Fishes. — Departure from Constantinople. — Arrival at Abydos. — Asiatic and European Coasts of the Dardanelles. — Anchorage at Karabaglar on the Coast of Anatolia. — Birds and Fishes. — Rhodes. — Cyprus. — Favourable Situation at Larnaka for examining some of the Plants and Birds of Cyprus. — Excursion to the Mountain of the Holy Cross. — Plants and Birds observed on the Mountain. — Famagusta ; neglected State of the Fortifications ; desolate Appearance of the Country. — Visit to the Convent of Antiphoniti. — The Lignum Rhodium. — Arrival at Nicosia. — Mountains of Troados ; Plants and Birds. — Descent into the Vale of Soulea. — Immense Beds of petrified Oysters, Pectines, Balani.

THE Princes Islands are seven in number, and about six leagues distant from Constantinople : two of them are uninhabited rocks, called from their shapes Oxeia and Plateia. The first of the islands is named from its position, Protos ; that which is opposite to it, Antigone ; the third, famous for its copper-mines, Chalke ; another is called Prinkipos. These islands are extremely pleasant during the summer ; at which time they are visited by the Greeks of the Fanal *, and the Frank merchants who have here a temporary residence. Chalke is particularly beautiful ; the island breaks into mountains of irregular form, and of no great elevation ; they are of

---

* The Byzantine Greeks were accustomed to retire to the islands of the Propontis, as the Romans to the shores of Campania. Pro Campaniæ ora fuit iis Propontis vicina, et Princeps, Prota, aliæque adjacentes insulæ. Casaub. in Sueton. 260. — E.

an argillaceous soil, strongly impregnated with iron and * copper: the copper-mines are found on the south side of the island, close upon the shore. We observed some pieces of stone incrusted with a plumose malachite; and portions of the rock strongly tinted with a copper colour. The ore, however, did not appear rich; and from its little produce was probably neglected on the discovery of more valuable mines. The rocks on the northern part of the island are red. The heath, Erica multiflora, is the predominant plant; the Pinus Pinea is seen in many different parts of the island; and a wood, through which we walked to the Agia Triáda is entirely composed of it. Arbutus, Myrtle, and Phillyrea are spontaneous shrubs; and the smooth and prickly broom, with the Cassia of the poets, grew in great abundance. Of the three monasteries, those of the Agia Triáda and Agios Georgios are extremely fine, commanding rich and extensive sea views. Under the Agia Triáda, descending by vineyards through a pine grove, we arrived at a fine bay for fishing and bathing; and here were the ancient copper mines. Under the monastery of St. George, there are evident appearances of ponds which formerly communicated with the sea. A great variety of good fish is caught on the shores, particularly the mullet. † We paid five piastres for drawing the net; but unfortunately it broke; and the capture was not large: we procured only a few mackerel, Scombri, and different species of Labri. Very fine lobsters are caught here; large oysters, scallops, κτένες, and muscles, which are called μύδια. ‡ I observed some birds now on their passage : Upupa Epops, a small species of Motacilla, the red and black butcher-

---

* " The soil of Chalkis presents every where indications of a volcano : on the hill nearest the village is found a hard brittle rock, which appears ferruginous." Olivier, 1. — E.

† " We were every day served (says Olivier, speaking of one of the neighbouring islands,) with oysters, muscles, and several fishes; such as mackerel, bonito, turbot, and particularly the bearded mullet." See also Busbequius's account of the fishery of these islands. Epis. iv. — E.

‡ Κτένες is the ancient word, see Aris. H. A. and Athenæ. l. 3. Μύδια is a corruption from the antient Μῦς. See Eustathius quoted by Du Cange in v. όμύδιον. — E.

bird were common. We saw the Merops apiaster in the vineyards ; some cormorants flew along the shore; and the Larus nævius watched our net while we were drawing it. A very small part of the island is cultivated with corn, vineyards, and Melon grounds ; the olive does not seem to flourish in its cultivated state. I observed some Jujube trees in the gardens, which are here called Ziziphi. There is no Turk resident at Chalke ; and singing, dancing, drinking, occupy and amuse the Greek, unawed by the presence of his oppressor.

March 14. 1787. — At four in the afternoon we sailed from the port of Constantinople in the Bethlehem, a Venetian merchant ship, bound for Cyprus ; the weather stormy ; the wind north, with snow.

March 16. — We anchored the preceding evening at Lampsaki, and left it at eight this morning ; and at eleven, cast anchor before Karagaria, on the Asiatic shore, about two miles distant from the Dardanelles. The country is bare, rising into hills covered with Poterium spinosum ; and here and there a few plants of the Astragalus Tragacantha. Some divers, particularly the Colymbus cristatus of Linnæus swam near our ship, and different species of sea-gulls, particularly the Larus ridibundus, flew screaming along the shore. I observed on the beach different species of Confervæ and Fuci.

March 17.—Having visited the town of Abydos, and received some civilities from our consul, we ferried over to Sestos. I mounted the hill which commands the town, and had a distant view of Tenedos and the Straits, as well on the Asiatic as on the European side. The mountains of the Asiatic shore, rising higher than those of Europe, were still covered with snow: those of the latter were skirted with the Pinus pinea. The soil clayey, lightly covered with sand, but poorly cultivated, produced nearly the same plants which I had observed on the Asiatic shore, with the following which I had not seen there :

Daphne Tartonraira
Anemone hortensis

Crocus vernus fl. luteo
Cerastium pentandrum
Fumaria spicata.

I saw several cranes crossing in large, but regular companies from the Asiatic side to the European. In a grove of Planes in the outskirts of Abydos, the Sturnus Cinclus was not unfrequent, of which I shot a male and female.

March 18. — Our captain stopping to take in wine at the Dardanelles, we went on shore at Abydos. Leaving the town, we walked along the banks of the Rhodius ; and penetrating three or four miles into the country we found it well cultivated with corn and vineyards. The Rhodius is a mean inconsiderable river, whose supplies at present were derived from the melting of the snow in the neighbouring mountains. Sand-banks here and there interrupted its course; and the sides were skirted with osiers, not yet in flower. The Ardea cinerea stalked majestically along its banks ; one of which I shot ; and a small species of Motacilla, the M. trochilus, flew from willow to willow.

March 19. — At seven in the morning we dropped down from Caragaria ; at eight past by the Dardanelles ; and shortly after took in our captain, who had been to the custom-house to clear the ship. We sailed with a fresh breeze, passing Cape Janissary ; and were abreast, of the island of Tenedos, opposite to the Trojan shore, at twelve o'clock.

March 20.—At daybreak we were off the north-west part of Mytilene; we coasted along the island the whole day with a fresh easterly wind ; and at sunset were between the main land of Asia and the northern extremity of Scio.

March 22. — The wind had changed to the north in the course of yesterday ; and blew now from the east ; and threatened us with a fresh gale, which soon quickened into a storm. The sea ran very high ; lashed our vessel with relentless fury ; and we shipped the waves with sufficient frequency to alarm us. A considerable quantity of corn belonging to the sailors was damaged by the entering of the sea-water. In vain we attempted to stretch over to the port of Mycone; but having gained the entrance of the great Bogaz, between Samos and Nicaria, we were in some measure sheltered from the fury of the wind by the neighbouring mountains of Samos; these are of considerable height; one of them in the north-west extremity of the island was still covered with snow. The wind which had somewhat sunk at noon now rose upon us with greater fury than in the morning. The timidity of the captain had prevented us from carrying sufficient sail; and at the approach of evening we found ourselves exposed to a wild sea with a furious wind. The sun set, and left us at some miles distance from a port on the Asiatic shore, whose mouth barricadoed with rocks rendered our entrance both difficult and uncertain. The wind whistled wildly along the ropes; confused the cry of the mariners; the steersman heard indistinctly the report from the shrouds; irregular flashes of lightning glimmered faintly before us; and with the white foam at the prow rendered the horrors of our situation visible. After some moments of uncertain existence, having passed several small rocks, we anchored in the evening at Karabaglar, about fifteen miles distant from Boudroun, the ancient Halicarnassus.

March 23.—In the morning the wind blowing hard, with a great sea, we were prevented from going on shore. It moderated in the evening, and we launched the boat, and went to a few scattered houses on the beach, called by the sailors the Capudan Pasha's watering place. Here a fountain of excellent water, a Turkish burying ground, and some white-washed buildings formed a picturesque scene. A rising hill on the left is commanded by an old castle, now in ruins, built by the Genoese. The mountains are composed of Grünstein (of which Nos. 1. and 2. are specimens); and near the beach we found great quantity of pumice. (No. 3.) I was surprised at the number of plants we observed in flower.

March 24. — In the morning we went on shore, and coasting along the beach I collected towards the north point several plants, which I had not seen in my walk of the preceding day. We returned to the watering place over some low hills from which the eye surveyed a rich highly cultivated vale planted with fig-trees. We shot a species of 'swallow, peculiar to the southern parts of Europe, the Hirundo melba; the Fringilla cyanocephalus, and the Strix passerina.

'March 27. — I went on shore to herborise; on my return to the boat I found our sailors had been dragging the net; but had caught few fish. I observed the following species; Sparus Sargus, Chromis, Zeus Faber, and Mullus Barbatus. In our walk we noticed a species of Land Tortoise, Testudo Græca *: and very frequent on the banks of a rivulet, Testudo lutaria; and we shot the female of the Tetrao rufus; and the Motacilla flava. In my different herborisations I collected the following plants. †

' ¨ March 28. — We got under weigh, and doubled Cape Petera. We observed some high mountains of Asia still covered with snow; and passed by at a considerable distance, on the Asiatic shore, Boudroun; and stood for Cape Crio, which we were abreast of at seven o'clock. The following morning we were becalmed between the coast of Asia and the island of Rhodes; about mid-day a light breeze sprung up from the east; as it was contrary, we put into Port Cavaliere on the Asiatic coast, where we dropt anchor at four in the afternoon. Craggy rocks of grey marble veined with white rising to a considerable height walled in the shore; the ruins of an ancient town, perhaps Cressa, and plots of cultivated ground, furnished a diversity of plants whose beauty was not less striking than their variety.

March 30. — Our sailors having drawn the net early in the morning, caught a considerable quantity of the Coryphæna Pompilus; among the smaller fishes, I observed the Sygnathus Hippocampus, Typhle

---

* The Testudo lutaria is sometimes eaten in Lent by the Christians of the East: but the Land Tortoise is preferred, as more wholesome. Russell's Aleppo, ii. 222. — E.

† A list of 182 plants is given in the MS.

and Acus; the Sparus Boops, Dentex, the Labrus Iulis, and the Muræna Conger. Captain Emery walking among the ruins of the town, found a Porcupine's quill, from which we imagined the Porcupine was an inhabitant of this country. * There were also several species of the crab kind.

March 31.—At seven o'clock in the morning we left the harbour of Port Cavaliere, and at ten anchored in that of Rhodes. After dinner we went with a letter from M. de Choiseul to the French consul ; as he was absent, his dragoman attended us in a walk through the town. The streets appeared almost deserted and forlorn ; the principal one, called the Knights' Street, offered a melancholy view of the remains of those houses defended with so much bravery by their valorous tenants. The arms of several of these knights are observable on the walls ; and the ruins of the grand master's palace are covered with the golden Henbane. Leaving the town, we walked along the beach on the south-west side, and among the rocks, which were formed of a congeries of quartz pebbles cemented with ferruginous sand, we observed impressions of Serpulæ not uncommon.

April 1.— At five in the afternoon we raised our anchor. We saw under the shelter of the shore of Rhodes an immense number of Pelicans; this was probably a stage of repose in their way from Egypt, where Hasselquist informs us they winter.

April 3.—Early in the morning we had a very distant view of Cyprus. Our sailors caught a small species of lark, the Alauda spinoletta of L., which probably lighted upon our vessel in its passage. We were becalmed in sight of Cyprus the whole of the next day: We shot the Charadrius spinosus flying near our ship; this singular bird Linnæus makes mention of, as an inhabitant of Egypt ; Wheler saw it in Greece. We caught also two species of Motacilla, the sylvia and trochilus of Linnæus.

---

* The Porcupine is found in Syria, near Aleppo. Russell's Aleppo, ii. 159.

April 8.—We anchored in the bay of Larnaka in Cyprus; the consul being absent, we engaged lodgings at the house of Sr. Natali, an Italian, pleasantly situated on the beach at the Salines.

April 9. — I walked out to botanise, along the eastern coast, and returned by Livadia. The crops of corn had been much hurt by hail and a severe winter; the orange groves or gardens were quite destroyed.

April 10, 11. — I staid at home that my painter might have time to design the plants collected in my walk to Livadia, and several birds that were shot by a Chasseur whom we had employed as a guide. Our situation at the Salines was one of the most favourable in the island for the botanist and ornithologist. Several little pools invited a number of Grallæ to its neighbourhood. Near Larnaka was one of considerable extent, and the salt lake was scarcely a mile distant. Cyprus, situated between Asia and Africa, partakes of the production of both; sometimes we noticed the birds and plants of Syria and Caramania; sometimes those of Egypt. Many of the Grallæ we saw were probably birds of passage.

April 12. — We made an excursion to the mountain of the Holy Cross. We passed by the aqueduct of Larnaka, and after four hours ride over an uneven plain enlivened with varieties of the Ranunculus Asiaticus, now in flower, we dined under a carob tree. Several little rivulets crossed the road, skirted with the Oleander. These were frequented by the beautiful Merops apiaster, one of which we shot. Numerous Jack-daws burrowed in the holes of the free-stone rock near the rivulet; and the Roller, which after short flights pitched frequently before us, rivalled the Merops in the splendour of its colours. After dinner we lost our way in the mountains covered with the Pinus pinea; we arrived late at a hamlet belonging to the convent; and about an hour distant from it. The ascent was steep and difficult; and the sun set soon after our arrival. Disappointed at finding the convent quite deserted, and no habitation being near, we resolved upon attempting an entrance by force. The different instruments we had brought with us for digging were employed;

but without success. At length a Caloyer arrived with the key, and having opened the door of the church, we discovered some straw mattresses; these were drawn before the altar, and we lay down to repose.

The mountain, a bluish grey argillaceous rock thinly covered with earth, furnished but a few plants; a species of Astragalus, which I do not find mentioned by Linnæus, called by the Greeks ἀγριόκυτζος, grew in great abundance. I saw the Valeriana tuberosa, which is certainly the Mountain-nardus of Dioscorides, on the summit, with the Ziziphora capitata, and a species of Cucubalus and Thymus, neither of which I find described. On the walls of the convent I observed the golden Henbane growing plentifully.

April 13.—At eight we left the convent; the Pinus pinea was less frequent as we advanced in our descent. I observed a new species of Gladiolus, G. montanus, and Thymus tragoriganum, frequent. Arrived at the bottom, we stopped at a village to refresh ourselves; we then passed through a more level country covered with different species of Cistus, the Onosma Orientalis, and Lithospermum tenuiflorum. I observed among the scarcer plants the Brassica vesicaria and the Salvia ceratophylloides. Swarms of locusts in their larva state often blackened the road with their numbers, and threatened destruction to the crops of corn now almost ripe. Near the aqueduct we observed several hawks hunting in troops; Falco tinnunculus was the most frequent species in the island, called by the Greeks κύτζος. We shot two other species; one with a blue tail, named Mavromati, and another, something like a buzzard, called φαλκόνι.

April 17. — We set off at eight in the morning for Famagusta; after riding four hours through a rising plain we reached Armidia, a village pleasantly situated about half a mile from the sea. Near the road side I observed the Scabiosa prolifera, and a species of Arum, unnoticed by Linnæus, called by the Greeks ἀγριοκολοκάσια, and a rare species of Linum with a red flower, the Linum viscosum of Linnæus. The low hills round Armidia were covered with the Cistus

incanus now in flower.   On the beach I gathered the Scorzonera
Tingitana and a new species.of Geranium.   We shot also a bird of
the Gralla kind, the Hæmatopus Ostralegus of L.   After a ride of
four hours over an extensive plain, we reached at sunset a small
convent in the outskirts of Famagusta.

April 18. — Early in the morning we walked to Famagusta, a
melancholy place now almost depopulated: . in the time of the
Venetians the fairest city in the island; and renowned for the brave
defence they made in it against the infidels.   The lines of the fortification which are very considerable are still sufficient to show the
extent and former strength of this place : they are now suffered by
the Turks to moulder away in ruins.   Some cannon, with the arms
of Venice, were lying dismounted on the ramparts; the Lieutenant
of the fortress pointed· to them with an air of triumph.   In the
enceinte grew among the rubbish the Aloe vera, the Iris Ger-
manica, and Florentina in great abundance.   Leaving the fortress
we passed through the streets now deserted, a melancholy picture
of Turkish desolation; the gateway by which we returned to the
convent was paved with cannon balls.   At noon after a ride of five
hours we arrived at Upsera.   About a mile from Famagusta, we
observed some small lakes to our right and left : these were frequented by different species of Grallæ : we had shot the Ardea
alba, which flew over the convent, in the morning.   The desolation
we had observed at Famagusta extended itself along the country we
now traversed.   We passed by the mouldering ruins of several
Greek villages, and slept at a Greek cottage at Upsera.   This like
other villages we had passed seemed by the desertion of its inhabitants to be hastening to ruin : it was pleasantly situated on the
side of a hill : a fertile vale stretched beneath it, bounded by the
approaching mountains of Antiphoniti.

April 19. — At eight in the morning we left Upsera, and passing
through the vale below, gradually ascended into the mountain of
Antiphoniti.   At noon we arrived at the convent, most romantically
situated, having a view of the sea and a distant sight of the high

land of Caramania. I was come here on the authority of Pococke to see the Lignum Rhodium; this the Greeks called Xylon Effendi. The Hegoumenos of the convent, a very old man, offered himself as my conductor, and leading me a few paces below the convent into a garden now covered with rubbish, pointed out a tree which on examination I found to be the Liquidambar Styraciflua. The trunk of it was much hacked, and different bits had been carried off by the curious and superstitious, as an ornament to their cabinets and churches. This was probably the same tree that Pococke had * seen. To ascertain the Lignum Rhodium has been much wished by the naturalists. An American tree growing in the swamps of Virginia seems to have little claim to be considered as that which should produce it. The name of Xylon Effendi and the tradition of the convent testify the reputation in which this tree had long been held in the island; it was probably at first introduced by the Venetians during their possession of it. I could not discover, either from observation or enquiry, that it was to be found in any other part of Cyprus; nor do I recollect that the Styrax liquidambar has been mentioned by any botanist as an oriental tree. Whether the Lignum Rhodium of the shops is the wood of this tree, or not, I am doubtful; the Aspalathus primus of Dioscorides I think is certainly the Lignum Rhodium of the ancients; he describes it as a thorny shrub, probably a species of Spartium, which the Cypriotes still call Aspalathi; his Aspalathus secundus, which also grows in the island, is certainly the Spartium spinosum. The Pinus pinea, the Cypress, the Andrachne are the principal trees that grow in this mountainous track. In the crevices of the rocks I found a few curious plants, Scutellaria peregrina, Ononis Ornithopodioides, Polygala Monsp.; and a species of Valeriana † with an undivided leaf, which seems distinct from Val. Calcitrapa. In the environs of

---

* See a paper in the Linnæan Transactions, (read Feb. 1815,) respecting the Lignum Rhodium of Pococke, by the President.

† Valeriana orbiculata of Flora G. F. 3 f.

the cloister we shot two species of Loxia ; one which I have called
L. Varia ; the other L. Cinerea.

April 20. — At eleven we left the convent of Antiphoniti and
descended the mountain to the sea-coast. In our journey I observed
the Papaver somniferum with a small blue flower growing in great
abundance : the plant which we find sometimes in waste ground and
in corn-fields in England has probably escaped there from the
garden. We now coasted along the shore, rocky, and much indented. I here observed several curious plants, Arenaria Cerignensis,
Scabiosa Cerignensis, Cheiranthus littoreus, Teucrium Creticum.

Leaving the shore, we entered into a more difficult tract of
country called Bel Paese ; a ridge of mountains running from north
to south, terminated some rising hills, which, sloping towards the
sea, were richly cultivated with corn. Near Cerignes, where we
arrived rather late in the evening, I discovered a beautiful species of
Salvia, S. Cerignensis.

April 21. — Having employed the morning in drawing, and putting our plants in paper ; we rode out after dinner to the monastery
of Lapasis, a fine remain of an old Gothic structure. In the court
below was a sarcophagus ; but of bad workmanship. We were
told, that on the summit of the mountains to the left of Lapasis
were the ruins of an ancient temple : our guides who had excited
our curiosity refused to satisfy it, by risking their mules on the
steep road which led to them. Captain E. and myself attempted on
foot to reach the summit of this distant mountain. The sun shone
with uncommon force ; nor did the least breeze mitigate the fervour
of its rays. After a very hot and fruitless walk, we came back,
finding the summit too distant to reach it, and return before night.
We joined our companions at the monastery of Lapasis, situated in
a beautiful recess, surrounded by corn-fields and vineyards, and
shaded by trees, whose foliage is kept green by several purling
rills, that watered the environs of this romantic spot. I collected a
few plants in this excursion : the Hedysarum saxatile grew on the

mountain; and the Styrax officinale was frequent in the hedges near the monastery.

April 22. — We left Cerignes at nine, a paltry town with a port, which carries on a small commerce with Caramania: we passed the mountains of Bel Paese by a narrow defile; on the sides of which grew the Moluccella fruticosa; descending, we entered the plains of Messaria; and about two arrived at Nicosia. On the mountains we observed several large birds which our guides told us were Eagles, 'Αετοί; I was not so fortunate as to procure one of them during my stay in the island; but from their flight I should suppose them to be Vultures; near Nicosia, I observed the Salvia Argentea. In the evening, we visited a small convent of Spanish friars, under the protection of France and Spain; and slept at the house of the Danish dragoman, for whom we had brought a letter.

April 23. — The governor of the island being informed of my arrival, sent a message, that he wished to see me; he was a vener-able old Turk, with no other complaint than that of age, and its companion, debility and loss of appetite. He received me with great politeness : our ambassador, Sir R. Ainslie, had procured me letters for him. Having felt his pulse, and prescribed for his com-plaint, he offered us his firman ; and ordered his dragoman to prepare a magnificent dinner. A Gazelle, a species of Capra called by the Greeks, Αγρεινο * was brought to me for my painter to take a drawing of. I was assured it was an inhabitant of Mount Troas; though this animal had been sent to the Governor as a present from the coast of Syria. There was nothing in the palace which indicated the magnificence and dignity of the Governor of so large and rich an island; but unfortunately for Cyprus, it is the appanage of the Grand Vizier; who obliges the Governor by mea-sures the most oppressive to remit an annual revenue much ex-ceeding the force and strength of its inhabitants under the present

---

* Probably 'Αγρίμι. Αγρίμια, λάφια, και λαγούς.   Ano. de N. Th. in Du C. v. A. — E.

distressing circumstances.* The poor Greeks pay a charatch of forty or fifty piastres ; and annual emigrations of large numbers are the consequence of this oppressive despotism. The Greeks have at first, perhaps, from necessity been induced to practise some low tricks of lying and knavery; and from frequent repetition, these may at length have become habitual among many of them. One of our guides had secretly made an agreement with a Turk, that two of our horses should carry his corn to Larnaka ; tempted to this dishonest proceeding with the hopes of gaining a few paras. Had I mentioned the circumstance to the Governor, the poor fellow would have lost his head ; I hinted it only to the dragoman, who immediately sent an officer to inform him, he should answer for his conduct in the most exemplary manner, in case of any further complaint from us. The fellow frightened became, from the most obstinate, the most docile creature in the world on our journey to Mount Troas.

Onr dinner was served after the Turkish fashion ; a great variety of dishes well dressed, gave us a favourable idea of the Turkish cookery, and the Governor's hospitality. I had counted thirty-six, when the dragoman made us an apology for the badness of the dinner ; and that he had not assistance enough to prepare it. The Governor expressed an anxious wish that I should see the medicine prepared, which I had prescribed for him, expressing a great want of confidence in his physician at Larnaka. Upon my making my promise to him, and wishing that it might relieve him, all the persons in waiting exclaimed, Ish Allah. † It was late when we left

---

* A curious and forcible contrast presents itself to us, when we read the accounts of the modern poverty and wretchedness of Cyprus, and the following passage of Ammianus Marcellinus : — " Tanta tamque multiplici fertilitate abundat rerum omnium eadem Cyprus, ut nullius externi indigens adminiculi viribus a fundamento ipso carinæ ad supremos usque carbasos ædificet onerariam navem, omnibusque armamentis instructam mari committat." — E.

† Properly, In Sha Allah, " If God will." 'Εὰν ὁ Κύριος θελήσῃ. James, iv. 15. Breviter, Ish Allah. — From Mr. Usko.

Nicosia, and after eight hours we arrived at our lodgings at the Salines.

April 27. — We set out on an excursion to Mount Troas. Leaving the Salines of Larnaka, we passed through a vale in which were some ruins at a place called Cetti ; being alarmed at the appearance of a thunder storm, we stopped at a small village, Magado, to dine, four hours from Larnaka. In our way to Mouni, I observed the Linum Nodiflorum, and shot a beautiful species of Fringilla with a yellow breast, and a black head, called by the Greeks Σκάρθαλις. this bird sings delightfully, rivalling the Nightingale in its note; we observed it frequently in the evening perched on the top of some bush or tree.

April 28. — We left Mouni eleven hours from Larnaka, and after four hours' ride arrived at Limesol. On the road we passed the ruins of the ancient Amathus ; I observed the Scabiosa Syriaca growing among the corn, and on the sea-sand a species of Anchusa· Limesol is an inconsiderable town, frequented only on account of its corn, and the neighbourhood to the vineyards of La Commanderia. The bay is deeper than that of Larnaka, and ships approach nearer the shore to take in their lading. Our vice-consul, a Greek, treated us handsomely ; and uncommon for a Greek, lodged us in his house without making a bill. At Nicosia, the Danish dragoman brought in a most shameful charge for a supper, to which he himself had invited us. We here found our companion Mr. Hawkins, who had been to Soulea, and the Panagia of Cicci.

April 29. — At seven we left Limesol ; having travelled two hours in a plain, we passed a little rivulet; the country was covered with Cistus and Mastic ; among these we heard the frequent call of the Francoline. Having crossed the rivulet, we entered into a wild mountainous country, and stopped to dine at a Turkish fountain, five hours from Limesol. After dinner, we soon entered into a more cultivated district : the sides of the hills were planted with vineyards ; little brooks watered the vales below, which were sown with corn, yet green. The mountains of Troados covered with the Pinus pinea stretched themselves out, and terminated the vale. I observed the Styrax tree frequent in the hedges; and the Anagyris fœtida in the outskirts of the villages. At sun-set we arrived at the convent of the Holy Cross: this is regarded as the second monastery in the island, and was probably more flourishing under the pious care of Maria Theresa. It is situated in a Greek village, where we observed an appearance of greater affluence than in most of those we had yet seen. Mountains are indeed generally the last retreats of liberty.

April 30. — At seven we set off from the convent of the Holy Cross for Troados. Our road led us through a steep tract of country, well wooded. The Pinus pinea, the Quercus Ilex, and Arbutus Andrachne covered the higher part of the mountain; in the vales below grew the plane, the Cretan maple, the black poplar, the white willow, and the alder. After two hours of very difficult road, we arrived at the convent of Troados; a Greek Papas, whom we had taken as a guide to conduct us to the snow on the summit of the mountain, brought us to this miserable cloister. As we were now told it was impossible to reach the snow, and return, we passed our day with much disappointment at the convent. I picked up but few plants: Smyrnium perfoliatum, Imperatoria Ostruthium, Alyssum campestre, Cheiranthus Cyprius; and among the rocks, Euphorbia Myrsinites, and Turritis glabra. We discovered the jay by hoarse screams, hopping among the branches of the Pinus pinea; and we shot the Parus ater, picking the buds of the fruit-trees below the convent; and the Muscicapa atricapilla busily employed in catching the flies.

May 1. — Having taken a goat-herd for our guide, at seven we began our ascent from the convent. After two hours' climbing with our mules over steep and dangerous precipices, we arrived at the summit, where we found a small quantity of snow lying on the northeast side: the pine-tree and the cypress grew on the heights with the Cretan Berbery. The mountain, composed of grünstein, with large pieces of hornblend, and but slightly covered with earth, disappointed my botanical expectations. A species of Fumaria, an Arabis, A. pur-

purea, with the Crocus vernus growing near the snow, were almost all the plants I observed on the mountain. We now descended rapidly over rocks of serpentine veined with amianth, and in three hours arrived at the bottom. The trunks of the old pine-trees were covered with the Lichen purpuraceus.

We now entered the vale of Soulea, the most beautiful we had yet seen in the island ; well watered and richly cultivated. Green meadows contrasted with the corn now ripe, hamlets shaded with mulberry-trees, and healthy peasantry busily employed with their harvest, and the care of their silk-worms, enlivened the scenery. Having travelled two hours in this delightful vale, I stopped at a Greek village. My guide conducted me to the house of the Papás ; a bed was prepared for me in the vacant part of a chamber, where silk-worms were kept. In a little morass, in passing through the vale, I had picked up the Lobelia setacea, and Pinguicula crystallina. My draughtsman stopping to sketch these plants was the cause of my losing my companion, who slept at a neighbouring monastery.

May 2. — We left the village at six ; the country now became more barren ; the hills were covered with the Cistus Creticus, from which they collect the Ladanum * : some land was sown with corn ; but this was almost devoured by the locusts, which had now their wings, and flew in swarms destroying every green plant. No vegetable escaped their ravages, except some prickly cartilaginous plants of the thistle tribe. After five hours we arrived at Peristeroani, where I found my companions waiting for me. I had collected some grasses in my road ; Poa aurea, Cynosurus durus, and Avena Cypria. Leaving Peristeroani, we travelled over a plain for five hours, and at sun-set arrived at the convent of the Archangel, at a small distance from Nicosia.

---

* " Ladanum is extracted from a species of rock-rose, and gathered in Greece ; in the islands of the Archipelago, in Crete and Cyprus. Among other preservatives from the plague, Ladanum is used ; an aromatic substance, which heat softens and renders more odoriferous : they smell to it from time to time, and especially when they fear any dangerous emanations." Olivier. Cistus Ladan. is the Κίστου εἶδος λήδων of Diosc. See Sprengel, His. R. H. i. 177. — E.

Near the convent I observed the coriander and the garden-cress growing wild among the corn.

May 3. — At seven we left the convent of the Archangel, and after
a ride of eight hours through an undulated plain arrived at our lodgings at the Salines; near Agios Georgios we observed immense beds
of petrified oysters *, Pectines, and Balani. Our chasseur shot a very
rare bird of the Tetrao kind, T. Alchata, called by the Greeks
παρδαλός. † This is a bird of passage, visiting the island in the spring
and retiring in the autumn. We shot also on this plain the stone
curlew, Charadrius Oedicnemus.

CHAP. II.

*Sail for Rhodes ; anchor near Bafo ; the Diamond Hills. — Use of the Leaves of Cistus
Monspeliensis. — Departure from Cyprus ; land on the Coast of Asia Minor. — Testudo
Græca, Testudo Lutaria, Rana Esculenta. — Arrival at Rhodes. — The Island of Lero ;
active Labours of the Peasantry. — Patmos ; Dress and Appearance of the Women ;
Birds. — Island of Stenosa ; Plants. — Beautiful Species of Scarus caught off the Island.
— The Lunaria of Tournefort. — Argentiera ; Lead, Copper, and Iron Oies. — Sail for
Athens ; singular Appearance of an Eclipse of the Sun.*

MAY 8. — At six in the evening, embarked on board the Providence,
a small vessel, for Rhodes. There were upwards of twenty passengers, Turks and Greeks, from different parts of the Levant ; a Latin
bishop, from the environs of Mount Libanus, after being six years
patriarch of the Maronites, had been dethroned by the cabals of his
brethren, and was now on board, with a chaplain and interpreter, on

----

* " A quelques milles de Nicosie," says Le Brun, " il y a une petite montagne, qui
n'est que d'huitres petrifiés." See his description of them, vol. iii. p. 376. — E.

† Found also in Syria, and called by the natives of Aleppo, Kata. See a plate and
description of this bird in Russell's Aleppo, ii. 194. — E.

the way to Rome, hoping by the interference of the Pope to be re-instated in the patriarchate.

May 11. — We anchored about eight in the morning, about five miles to the east of Bafo. The town now presents a melancholy ruin; few of the houses being inhabited. In walking through it, we entered the inclosure of a modern Greek church, where we discovered three pillars of the most beautiful Egyptian granite : at four feet from the ground, they measured ten feet four inches in circumference; and from the present surface, which evidently had been much raised, fifteen feet in height. At the distance of about forty yards were two smaller pillars; one of them was fluted. This was probably the site of an ancient temple of Venus: near it stood the ruins of a small Gothic chapel, probably Venetian. From Bafo we passed over some fields to a beautiful village called Iftinia, where the Governor of the district resided. We produced our firman; and his dragoman, full of promises, offered his services. The bishop, who had been informed of my arrival, wished to consult me. Like the Governor, I found him with no other complaint than that of old age and a weakened vis vitæ. We were offered pipes, and entertained with coffee, liqueurs, and perfumes. From Iftinia we walked to what our guide called the Diamond Hill: these diamonds we found to be nothing but common quartz crystal. Hence we descended to the beach, to some ruins under ground. We found there several buildings; and from the architecture we were led to suppose them catacombs, or repositories for the dead. They occupied a very considerable tract of ground; and offer a curious and interesting field of research to the antiquary. On removing some stones, I discovered two species of lizards; the Lacerta Chalcides, and Lacerta Turcica: on the sand I observed the Sea Eryngo, the Sea Samphire, and the Prickly Cichorium: the Silene fruticosa, the Cyclamen Cyprium, and the Ruta graveolens grew on the rocks : on the road from Bafo to Iftinia, and upon rub-bish ground on the outskirts of the town, the Aloe vera, the Semper-vivum arboreum, and the Physalis somnifera: the Galium Cyprium on the diamond rocks : the Crucianella Ægyptiaca, the Teucrium pseudo-chamedrys, and the Teucrium pseudo-polium on the plain below. It was late when I returned to the ship, where I found a Turk, to whom I had offered a suitable reward, waiting for me, with a specimen of the formidable Κούφι.

May 12. — We went on shore, and after waiting three hours at Iftinia for horses, set off at eleven on an excursion to Fontana Amorosa. Riding three hours through a fine cultivated corn country we crossed a rivulet, and dined under an olive tree; among the corn I had observed the Bupleurum semicompositum and Ruta linifolia. After dinner our road led us over a rough steep·mountain whose sides were cultivated with corn; we then traversed a stony plain, and in three hours' time arrived at a large Greek village. We now descended towards the beach, having a view of the distant coast of Caramania. The Cistus Monspeliensis was frequent on different parts of the road: the leaves of this species are used by the Cypriots as a substitute for the Mulberry leaf: we met frequently with peasants conveying home horse loads of this plant for their silk worms. After riding for some time in the dark, we arrived at Poli; the Aga of the village, a venerable man, received us with much politeness, and having spread before us a frugal repast of Yaourt and rice milk, he left us and retired to his Harem.

May 13. — At six we set out for Fontana Amorosa, which our guides informed us was little more than an hour distant from Poli. We descended towards the coast; and passing near the shore by a narrow and difficult road, and having turned a considerable mountain, arrived in four hours at a small spring: this we were informed was the famous Fontana Amorosa, which had so greatly excited our curiosity. Among the stones of a ruined village we observed the Lacerta Stellio, the same which Tournefort had found among the ruins of Delos; and on the sides of the mountain I gathered the Centaurea Behen, and the Cynara acaulis, and the Thapsia fœniculifolia; and under the shade of some trees hanging over a rivulet the Osmunda Cypria. Our guides, who had contrived to mislead us, after eight hours brought us back to Poli; they now refused to set forward for Bafo, alleging, their -horses were tired. The Aga of Poli was absent when we came back : and a black slave supposing us hungry brought a bundle of bean stalks, and threw them down before us, saying, *there* was something to eat. As we had promised our captain to return, we continued our journey with our guides. The little owl, Strix Passerina, hooted mournfully among the rocks ; and at sun-set, we were left in an unknown and dangerous country. We arrived at a Greek village about an hour from Poli in the dusk of the evening ; and the Papas having furnished us with a guide, we travelled all night, and reached the shore of Bafo at daybreak.

May 14. — We embarked at six in the morning: on the 21st we passed Cape Chelidoni, and immediately after, were becalmed at a small distance off the bay of Myra; about twelve, we came to anchor in the bay ; and went on shore in a Greek boat. · The sides of the mountain skirted a sandy vale; part of which was covered with a river now almost stagnant : here I collected several plants I had not noticed in Cyprus. We killed a beautiful species of Coluber, which I have called Coluber Caramaniensis: I observed a great number of rock pigeons, Columba Oenas rupestris. In the evening we raised the anchor and set sail.

May 22. — We sprung our bowsprit and were obliged to put before the wind ; at twelve we dropped our anchor in the bay of Finica.

May 23. — I went on shore to botanise. An aqueduct to the left continued for five miles into the interior of the country. We saw several scattered hamlets, whose inhabitants, living a wandering pastoral life, had retired into the mountains to milk their goats, and make their cheese. · A rich fertile vale was watered by the * Limyrus. The Pomegranate, glowing with its scarlet colours, ornamented the thicket ; while the Vitis Labrusca, stretching over the rivulet, per-

---

* For the situation of Myra, and the Limyrus, see Beaufort's Caramania.—E.

fumed the air with the most fragrant odours. Oranges and lemons grew in wild luxuriance; crowded around the house of the untutored peasant; and in vain solicited his art to prune and improve them. Fatigued with our walk we sought a retreat under a spreading plane; the Limyrus glided softly at our feet; a singular grotesque view of a Caramanian cottage heightened the scenery. I returned highly satisfied with my walk, and richly laden with curious plants. We met the Testudo Græca frequently on the road side, and the Testudo Lutaria with the Rana Esculenta in the little rivulet which watered the plain: we heard the Potamída frequently, flying on the banks of the Limyrus; but it artfully concealed itself from our view. It was late in the evening before we returned to our vessel.

May 28. — We dropped anchor in the port of Rhodes at five in the morning, and went on shore to visit the French consul; in the afternoon I walked out to botanise; among the rocks to the west of the town we observed a Pelican. Though the season for botanising was too far advanced for the lower grounds, I yet picked up several curious plants, among some corn not yet reaped, which skirted some hills about three miles distant from the town; in the valleys beneath, and among the briars on the margin of the fields. The port of Rhodes is much frequented; it supplies however a few articles only of commerce; among these are oranges and lemons; the best I recollect to have seen. The limes were abundant; and we bought a basket full of them, paying only a para for thirty.

May 29. — The morning was employed in embarking our baggage on board of the boat which we had engaged to carry us to Canea : our intention was to have sailed early, but we were detained partly in waiting for the arrival .of the Sou Basha or officer of the customs, and partly for the leave of. the Aga, who was sleeping at his villa some distance from the town. We sailed at nine o'clock; the wind being westerly we tacked over towards the coast of Asia, and working along the shore dropped anchor at Port Cavaliere at three in the afternoon. This place that six weeks since appeared a beautiful garden enamelled with some of the most curious plants of

the East now presented a dry surface, and furnished me only with
the opportunity of collecting some seeds from the parched skeletons
of those plants which I had formerly collected in flower. On my
return from fishing, one of our Greek sailors met me on the beach
with some Scari, which he had caught among the rocks.   Our
classical curiosity was much raised to taste a dish which.held so
distinguished a place with the ancient Greek and Roman epicures * :
we found the Scarus better flavoured than most of the species .of
Labrus, though not superior to the huge Rhombus, or the spotted
Muræna.

May 30. — Rowed out of Port Cavaliere at day-break, the wind
still contrary in the channel of Rhodes.   During the afternoon, we
stood along the western coast of the island of Symi, and at sun-set
anchored in a small creek on the Asiatic shore.

May 31. — We doubled Cape Crio at nine, and were soon after
becalmed ; at mid-day we passed by the island of Cos, directing our
course to Lero ; in the port of which we anchored in the evening.

June 1. — I walked out at day-break to botanise ; the corn-fields
and the crevices of the hills furnished me with some curious plants.
The port of Lero is singularly beautiful, walled in with picturesque
rocks ; on these stand the mouldering ruins of some old fortifications,
above which is placed the town.   A peasantry lively and active, now
busied with their harvest, furnished a pleasing contrast to the wild
and desolate scenery we had lately left on the Asiatic shore.   At
eight, quitting Lero with a fair wind, after four hours' sail we arrived
at Patmos.

We walked out to examine the island † : leaving the road which
led from the port to the town, we turned to the right to a salt pool,
where we shot the Scolopax Glottis, called here Soueli.   In climbing

---

* Non me Lucrina juverint conchylia,
    Magisve Rhombus aut Scari. — Hor. — E.

† An account of some recent discoveries made in Patmos by Mr. Whittington is
given in an extract from his journal, printed at the end of this division of Dr. Sibthorp's tour.

the rocks above the salt pool we killed two species of serpent; one having a back waved with black on a greyish ground, and a flattened head, appeared to have all the marks of a species highly venomous. The islanders called it φίδι, corrupted from ὄφις; another, which from its long slender form, I judged to be perfectly innocent, they called σαίττα, or arrow, from the manner in which it shoots or darts itself; we were told of a third species πορδοκολόγος; this was represented to us as of enormous size; we were not however able to find it. From these rocks we passed over to the monastery of the Apocalypse, where we were shown a dark church with a chancel or cell excavated in the rock, crowned by the monastery of St. John. Having waited on the Hegoumenos, and admired the extensive view which we commanded from its height, we descended to the house of an Italian physician, an itinerant empiric; he showed us some ancient medals and precious stones. In walking through the town, we were much struck with the beauty of the women. A form sufficiently elegant, and a black sparkling eye heightened the charms of a fair complexion; and we seemed to trace in these Grecian beauties the charms which her poets in the better days of Greece have described with so much warmth. Tournefort accuses these nymphs of want of address in putting on their *fard*; at present however they have greatly improved their art; and the few who we observed to be painted were much more skilful than the Parisian matrons in laying on their pigments. Patmos, like most of the Greek islands at this season of the year, presented a brown sun-burnt surface, forbidding the botanist to hope for a plentiful harvest. Notwithstanding its arid state I still discovered a few scarce plants.

June 2. — Tempestuous weather, with a strong blustering north wind, detained us in the port of Patmos. We walked out after dinner; and near the beach observed the Pelecanus Onocrotalus; we shot a species of Sterna, S. Hirundo. The island furnishes a very inconsiderable number of land birds; some of the swallow tribe and the wheat-ear were almost the only small birds we saw in the island;

the Partridge, the rock Pigeon, the hooded Crow, and the little Owl, were the only larger land birds.

June 3. — We walked to the convent of St. John to visit a learned monk whose name was Gregorio Zeno: he understood the ancient Greek, and had a large library for a man in his situation. Among the botanical works he showed me an old copy of Paul of Ægina and Matthiolus's Commentary on Dioscorides. He furnished me with the Greek names and superstitious uses of several of the plants of the islands.

June 5. — We left Patmos, and arrived by the force of our oars at Stenosa. I observed a sea bird flying near the surface of the water, and seldom settling; the sailors called it Μήκω.

June 6. — The island is very rocky, but furnished a variety of curious plants: among these I observed the Achillea Ægyptiaca described by Tournefort, one of the most frequent plants in the island, now in flower. During my herborisation the Greeks had caught a beautiful sort of Scarus, of a fine blood-red colour, and a golden spot a little above the caudal fin; its form was that of the species which I have described taken on the shore of Cyprus; but the one was of an uniform dusky green; the other glowed with a deep red. My draughtsman has fortunately made a drawing of it, while the colours were yet vivid. In sailing out of the harbour, I observed the Brassica Græca growing on a little islet in the mouth of it. I landed to gather it, and picked up several curious plants which grew near the same spot.

June 7. — We stood over for Naxia, where we put into a small creek to look for water; but not finding any we changed our course; we turned back to a bay where fortunately we discovered a well. We here killed a serpent, whose eyes were singularly small, called by the Greeks Tuphlites: this we were told was a species highly venomous; and that the bite of it would prove fatal to a man in a few hours. We killed also a small species of lizard, whose back was of a deep green; and I saw another, the Lacerta Aurea of Linnæus. I picked up some few plants, and collected several seeds: among the plants

were the following: — Lycium barbarum, Amygdalus communis
spinosa, Allium parviflorum, Sonchus Græcus, Cynara Græca,
Silene Græca.

June 8. — As I anxiously wished to determine whether the Lunaria
of Tournefort was not a distinct species from the genus Cheiranthus,
where Linnæus has arranged it, I prevailed on our Carabokiri to put
back to Caloyero, where I had found it abundantly in seed the preceding year. We sailed from Naxia at day-break ; at eight we
arrived at Caloyero, laid down in the maps as Antichero : we
found the Lunaria in great abundance, but unfortunately at present
in seed. The heights of the rocks, and the cavities formed by them,
gave me hopes of finding some late flowering plants on the eastern
side. I embarked on board of our boat, and was carried to that
part. The wind blew fresh from the island ; and we were nearly
overset in the attempt ; however, getting under the cover of a rock,
we with difficulty made good our landing. I spent two hours in
coasting along the island ; and examined it with the greatest
attention ; but though I found some thousand plants I could not
meet with a single specimen in flower. At eleven we left Antichero,
and in an hour made the island of Nio. It was our intention to
steer directly for Crete, but a considerable swell of the sea coming
on, obliged us to put into a harbour on the south extremity of
Nio.

June 9. — We sailed at one in the morning : a calm, with a great
swell coming on in the night, prevented us from making much
progress ; at eight we changed our course, and stood for Sikino,
where we landed about ten o'clock on the beach, near a chapel
dedicated to Saint John. The fatigue of my walk in Caloyero, and
my sleep disturbed during the night by the great swell of the sea,
with the extreme heat of the day, brought on a considerable degree
of fever. Before dinner I had collected from a peasant the names
of several plants growing round the chapel ; and it was my intention
with this untaught botanist to have made an herborisation after
dinner, but my fever increasing prevented me. I ordered my bed

to be brought on shore, and having laid it before the altar in the chapel, reposed tolerably until midnight, when our Carabokyri pressed our departure for Candia.

June 11. — We sailed over to Argentiera, where we anchored at twelve: the next day, being much indisposed, I remained on shore in my tent. My draughtsman walked out to collect some seeds with Captain Emery, who returned with a few specimens of lead ore. We met with some of copper and iron, with manganese and dendrites beautifully formed from it. We discovered the two species of Cimolian earth * mentioned by the ancients; amethysts, and other curious fossils. I gathered the seeds of several annual plants, and found some few in flower; though the season now far advanced prevented me from making a large collection.

June 14. — At seven o'clock we rowed out of Argentiera to a small island with a monastery upon it; among the rocks I observed the solitary sparrow, and on the higher part of the island, the Stone Curlew, Charadrius œdicnemus, which seemed to make it its breeding-place. The rock opposite to Monastery Island was covered with the Medicago Arborea, and near the sea I picked up a new species of Statice. At eleven o'clock we crossed over to the N. E. point of Milo, where we observed great quantities of Cimolian earth. At two in the afternoon, the wind coming more easterly, we put off for the island of Candia. It soon sunk into a perfect calm, and we rowed back to Argentiera.

June 15. — The wind continuing contrary, we changed our plan of voyage; and determined to proceed to Athens. In the evening we were becalmed off Siphanto. An eclipse of the sun was singu-

* The following remark, relating to this earth, is taken from Brogniart, Mineralogie, i. p. 519.: — " Les anciens, employoient cette Argile à dégraisser les étoffes; les habitans s'en servent encore à présent pour cet usage et elle leur tient lieu de savon pour laver le linge. Mr. Hawkins en a rapporté de cette ile; il a constaté qu'elle blanchissoit les étoffes, aussi bien que la meilleure terre à foulon. Mr. Klaproth à analysé les échantillons que lui a remis ce voyageur; il y a trouvé, silice 0.63; alumine, 0.23: oxide de fer, 0.01; Eau, 0.12." — E.

larly beautiful: it seemed to expand itself; then sinking gradually in the middle to push out from its sides two horns; these rapidly diminished, and appeared like two tapers burning out. We observed it at a quarter before eight by our watches. *

CHAP. III.

Passage between the Main Land of Attica and Negropont. — Composition of the Rocks and Mountains on the Eastern Coast of Attica. — Immense heaps of Schlag, and Vestiges of Mines. — Arrival at the Town of Negropont. — Excursion to Mount Delphis in Euboea. — The Verd Antique of the Ancients. — Return to Negropont; Nature of the Rocks in the Vicinity of the Town. — Magnetic Iron Ore. — Sail for Athos; Excursions to different Monasteries; Ascent of the Summit of the Mountain; Plants and Trees. — Departure for Salonica; and Arrival at Cenchris on the Isthmus of Corinth. — Sail for Patras.

JULY 25. — We left the promontory of Sunium at one in the morning, and having tacked frequently between the main land of Attica and Long Island, we anchored at four in the afternoon in Port Mandri, anciently Thoricus, now Therico. Among some low Mastic trees, we observed the ruins of a temple; and in the plain below, the remains of the ancient town. I walked out with my gun, and shot a small species of Motacilla. The water being brackish, we crossed over to Macronesi: this place is uninhabited except by a few goat-herds, who receive an uncertain subsistence from the neighbouring islands. Among the rocks I observed the Wild Pigeon, and the Cornish Chough, but no small birds, except the Wheat-Ear, the most common bird through Greece and the Archipelago. The

---

* Dr. S. and Mr. Hawkins arrived at Athens, June the 19th; from this place several excursions were made to the neighbouring parts of the continent of Greece. See the first volume of this work.

Conyza candida, the Stæhelina dubia, the Verbascum Græcum, grew high among the rocks.

July 29. — We made different tacks during the preceding days, between the main land of Attica and the Island of Negropont: the gale increasing obliged us to lower down our main-sail; and with a small square sail to run before the wind. We now lost way considerably, and with difficulty gained a small port on the coast of Attica called Seraphina.

July 30. — The storm continuing, we remained the whole day under the lee of a small uninhabited island in Port Seraphina. I collected on it the seeds of the Echinophora spinosa, and a beautiful species of Atriplex with a laciniated leaf, downy underneath. We passed, with some difficulty, the wind blowing very fresh, over to the main land. I shot a small species of Fringilla with the head, back, and tail brown; the breast and belly underneath, yellow. I saw the Sterna Hirundo, and a smaller species of Sterna flying along the shore. The rocks and mountains of the eastern coast of Attica are composed of glimmer slate in the higher regions, and saline marble: they contain lead-ore, with probably a considerable quantity of silver. We observed immense heaps of Schlag; and the appearance of mines that had been once worked were yet evident.

July 31. — We sailed at one in the morning from Port Seraphina, and tacked over to Negropont. The wind rising at four, we dropped anchor under a rock of one of the smaller islands, called Petalion. I rambled over a considerable part of the island, but found no inhabitants; it was rough, uncultivated, rocky; in winter, visited by some herdsmen who come over, with their goats and swine from Negropont. The higher parts of the mountains are covered with wild olives; the vales below with mastic bushes. I saw hares, but no other quadrupeds. At three in the afternoon, the wind coming more off the land, we tacked for the coast of Attica; at sunset, we were before the plains of Marathon.

August 1. — We continued to advance slowly up the Gulf; the coast of Attica is rocky, and rising into low hills covered with the Pinus pinea. We passed by Calamo, Macropoli, and then a village an hour distant from the sea; on the opposite shore of Negropont was Leucadia, with a fertile plain of olives; above which, towered some lofty cypresses. At ten at night, we dropped anchor under the walls of Negropont.

August 2. — We called early in the morning at the French consul's: he was absent in the country, but his dragoman accompanied us to the Governor's, whose kinsman, Osman Aga, received us with much politeness, and gave us a letter for Steni.

I set out, with Mr. Hawkins, on an excursion to Mount Delphis: after a ride of nearly two hours, through an undulating plain highly cultivated with olive grounds, and vineyards, and fruit-gardens, we arrived at Philo, the country residence of the French consul; we then proceeded towards Steni, riding two hours along a torrent bed, now dry, fringed with Oleanders and the Agnus Castus. We reached Steni, a small Greek village at the foot of Delphis; and soon after our arrival, some Turkish guards entered our cottage; we delivered the letter of Osman Bey; the whole village was now at our disposal; the guards offered us as many Greeks as we should have occasion for, to carry our baggage, and accompany us up the mountain. A basket of mulberries was brought; some chickens were caught; and a lamb was seized, slaughtered, and roasted. The guards, having charged the Greeks to procure us every possible accommodation, fired a salute, and returned to a neighbouring village.

August 3. — We mounted our horses at six o'clock, and began to ascend Delphis. After riding two hours through a thick wood of chesnut trees, forming the lower region of the mountain, we arrived at a mandra or sheep-fold. The morning lowered; and it began to rain before we could reach the mandra. The north-wind made us more sensible to the change of climate. The shepherds kindled a fire, and milked their flock for us. The doubtful appearance of the weather detained us some time at this place; we then ascended gradually over a rising plain for an hour. The road now became steep, rugged, and difficult; the rain increased; and a thick mist collected us close together, with the fear of losing one another. We had observed, on leaving Steni, rocks of serpentine in beds of saline marble, forming the Verd-antique of the ancients. The higher region of the mountain was composed of beds of argillaceous slate of various colours, upon which a primary black marble lay superincumbent. I found several of the more rare plants of Parnassus growing among the clefts of the rocks near the summit of the mountain, and some which I had not before observed in Greece. The goats and sheep had cropped the choicest flowers, and left me half-bitten imperfect specimens. The storm increased, and prevented us from examining further. We took shelter in a natural grotto immediately under the summit of the mountain : some alpine plants, now in flower, hung pendant in festoons from the walls of it. Near us, the snow was lying in the deep depressed parts. The storm now increased to a hurricane; the wind raged; the hail drove furiously along the mountain; we with difficulty kept our feet on the declivity of the rock; loose stones covered the road, and made our progress dangerous and uncertain. We arrived at the mandra deluged with rain; a fire was kindled that restored to us the use of our feet and hands; and, in less than a quarter of an hour, we set forward for Steni. It still continued raining; but we were sheltered, in great measure, from the wind, by the thick shade of the chesnuts. In two hours, we arrived at Steni.

August 4. — My portfolio was quite wet, and we spent the morning in changing the plants, and drying the papers. At mid-day, the clouds broke, and the weather clearing up, we set out for Negropont. The torrent-bed, which we had lately passed quite dry, was considerably swollen. On our arrival, we sent our compliments to the Pasha, thanking him for our kind reception at Steni, requesting the further favor of his firman, as we expected to touch at different parts of the island, on our way to Mount Athos, being informed there were pirates in the Gulf of Negropont.

August 5. — We walked out on the shore to the'north of the town; the rocks are composed of serpentine stone, with veins of asbestos, and soap-stone intermixed. On the sands, we collected some magnetic iron-ore, with beautiful crystallizations. The houses of Negropont have a mean appearance; are mostly ill built; and inhabited by Turks. The Greeks are here more oppressed than in the other Greek islands; and the Turks are said to have a bad character; though we were assured, by the French consul that we might travel through the island with the greatest security. The shore of Bœotia, on the contrary, was said to be dangerous, and infested by pirates. We spent three days in working through the straits with a contrary wind; we were becalmed off the island of Scopelo; and on the 10th of August, by the assistance of the oars, we reached the peninsula of Athos, and dropped anchor a little to the eastward of a bay called Daphne. I set out, with Captain Emery, for the village of Caryes, the residence of the Turkish Aga, to show our passports, and demand a guide to attend us during our stay on the mountain. We then proceeded to the monastery of Ivero. On our arrival, we were received by the monks with much distinction; a dinner, composed of different sorts of fish, was immediately provided for us. We were much struck with the splendour and magnificence of this monastery, superior to any we had yet seen in Greece.

August 11. — We went again, early in the morning, to the monastery of Ivero; winding along the shore for half an hour, we passed the port of Daphne; and mounting by a steep ascent, we gained soon the monastery of Xeropotamo, a large magnificent cloister of a quadrangular form. In the middle stands the church, a sumptuous building, paved with different coloured marbles, and ornamented with daubings of strange bizarre figures of saints, with much tinsel and finery, in the taste of the modern Greeks. Leaving the convent, we continued our walk to Caryes, shaded from the sun by some venerable old chesnuts, which composed here the principal part of the sylvan scenery. Near half way from Caryes, the prospect was uncommonly rich and beautiful; ·a vale stretched out into a verdant lawn,

with cattle feeding in it, diversified with habitations, and adorned
with trees, whose foliage was marked with various tints. Caryes,
though only a village, is the market of Mount Athos: here live the
different artisans and mechanics who supply with their ware the numerous monasteries. The name of Caryes is taken from the nut
trees which I observed growing abundantly near it. As we approached this place, another beautiful scene presented itself. The town appeared as it were pendant on the side of the mountain ; some lofty
pine trees towered above it; below, were hanging vineyards and
fruit gardens contrasted with the monasteries and the sombre hue of
the cypress. Leaving Caryes, we descended to Ivero through beautiful sylvan scenery, where we arrived in two hours. Ivero appeared
to us a Grecian Elysium ; from our windows, we commanded a fine
view of the sea; a short lawn intervened between it and the monastery ; to the right, passing a torrent bed shaded with planes, were
vineyards, that broke the roughness of the approaching mountain.

August 12. — The mules belonging to the convent were offered to
us by the Hegoumenos ; and after riding six hours over a mountainous rocky road near the coast, we arrived at the monastery of Laura,
the largest and most considerable of the numerous convents on the
Holy Mountain. It contains six hundred caloyers, and has several
cells or small convents dependent on it. As soon as we arrived we
were waited upon by the exiled Archbishop of Athens, who had
reached this place a few days since. He was full of schemes to obtain
his enlargement, and the see from which he had just been dethroned :
his agent set off for Constantinople during our stay on the mountain.
Notwithstanding the grandeur of Laura, we met with indifferent fare:
a strict fast for the Panagia, or the Virgin, prescribed at present to
the monks of Monte Santo the use of fresh fish ; and the arid environs of Laura ill supplied so numerous a convent with vegetable
products ; and we with difficulty procured some pickled sprats and
olives. Here superstitious folly reigns in full force. The cocks crow
only to wake the sleepy caloyer. Eggs are brought from Lemnos and

other islands. Oxen graze in the valley ; but neither cows, ewes, or she-goats are suffered to pollute this holy spot. In the library, which contains two small rooms, one for the printed books, the other for manuscripts, I was shown an ancient copy of Dioscorides, written in small ancient characters, with illuminated figures, but ill executed. We took leave of the unfortunate Archbishop of Athens, and mounting our mules set forward for the summit of Athos. After riding three hours we passed by the monastery of Keratia, on a rocky steep to the left far below us : our road led us over precipices difficult and dangerous to pass. In two hours, winding by a woody ascent, consisting of Ilex, Andrachne, and other shrubs, we arrived at a small chapel dedicated to the Panagía. Trees now became scarce ; and the higher regions of the mountain rose naked above us ; the summit being about an hour distant, and crowned with another chapel. After dinner, leaving our mules below, we ascended by a road formed by large pieces of marble placed upright on each side of it. Athos is certainly inferior in height to many of the Grecian mountains : we found no snow on its summit ; nor did I observe any of those plants characteristic of an alpine region. The mountain is rich in Plantæ sylvaticæ ; and I observed on it all those trees which I had found in different parts of Greece, and some which I had not seen elsewhere. Descending from the summit of Athos, we mounted our mules at the lower chapel of the Panagía ; and having passed through the higher parts of the wooded region we came, by one of those roads which art had laboured with uncommon ingenuity and difficulty, to the convent of St. Anne, where we arrived in three hours. Gneiss and argillaceous slate compose the lower bed of the mountain ; the superincumbent mass is a grey primitive marble, more or less inclined to white ; near to the summit I observed some almost wholly white. The site of the convent is uncommonly picturesque and beautiful : hermitages excavated in the rock to the number of fifty or sixty, with their tops of argillaceous slate, glitter round it ; several waterfalls, brought down from the upper region of the mountain by wooden conduits, irrigate numerous little vineyards. Above the convent, rises the mountain, breaking into rocks that pierce through the thick foliage, now of various hues ; and high above these towers.the naked summit of Athos: below, the sea extends itself in ₁a. wide expanse.

August 14. — We left the convent of St. Anne in the morning, and descended by hanging vineyards and hermitages cut out of the rock to the beach, where a boat waited for us. The scenery of the south coast of the promontory is very beautiful and various : as we rowed softly along, we had time to admire it. The shore was bold and rocky, with ravines, each presenting the romantic site of a monastery. We passed first a cluster of hermitages ; then the small monastery of St. Paul ; then that of St. John ; afterwards one of St. Nicholas, which appeared new ; and lastly, that of the Panagia, situated on the rounded top of an insulated rock, high on the mountain. We now turned the western point of the promontory, and in somewhat less than three hours arrived at our vessel ; and at seven in the morning, a favourable breeze springing up, we set sail for Salonica.

August 30. — We parted with our friend and fellow-traveller Mr. Hawkins, who intended to make some further excursions in the Archipelago ; and bidding adieu to the hospitable house of our consul Mr. Moor, embarked on board of the Poriote that had brought us from Athens, agreeing for one hundred piastres to be carried to the port of Cenchris, on the isthmus of Corinth.

August 31. — The wind being contrary we dropped anchor about seven o'clock in the small bay of Cassandra, where we were detained the whole day : walking out to herborise, I observed on the shore the Bupleurum fruticosum, and the Convolvulus Soldanella.

Sept. 2. — During the night the Exocætus volitans of Linnæus leaped into our vessel. Sept. 4., at noon, we dropped anchor in the port of Cenchris : a small hut near the port serves as a custom-house, the only remains of the antient Cenchreæ : around it grew corn ; and some plantations of cotton were intermixed with the Panicum Miliaceum, still called by the Greeks κέγχρι. Might not the original cul-

tivation of this plant here in preference to other places have given
name to the port and village? After dinner, I walked out to botanise
on some high and steep rocks on the left. On my return, near the
shore I observed a new species of Cuscuta twining round the branches
of some low Mastic trees ; and on entering our boat, one of the sailors
brought me the Coryphæna Pompilus.

Sept. 5. — We left the Poriote vessel, satisfied with the captain
and his crew, who had served us with fidelity and attention in both
our voyages ; and we crossed the isthmus, about eight miles over, to
a port or scala, consisting of a few straggling warehouses on the beach.
We stowed our baggage in the lower part of one of these warehouses,
belonging to a Greek, who sat at the receipt of custom ; and became
common tenants with a Georgian bishop, our host, and an Albanese
of the upper. We found only a small Zantiote boat lying in the
port ; and agreed with the owner to carry us to Patras, stopping five
days at Asprospiti.

Sept. 6. — Walked out along the beach on the side of the Peloponnesus. Among some low ground covered with bushes I discovered a
new species of Scirpus, and shot a small minute bird which I do not
think is mentioned by Linnæus, of the Motacilla tribe.

Sept. 7. — I traced some of the remains of antiquity on the Grecian
side of the isthmus. The Pancratium Maritimum, now in flower,
ornamented a low sandy beach ; I observed also a species of Clypeola
now in seed ; several Curlews flew along the shore: and in a small
pool near the port I shot the following Grallæ : the Charadrius Hia-
ticula, Scolopax, and Tringa.

Sept. 8. — We embarked on board of the Zantiote at four in the
morning, and by gentle breezes and the use of our oars anchored at
three in the afternoon in the harbour of Asprospiti. At five I procured horses, and set out for Livadia.

We sailed from Asprospiti Sept. 14., and arrived at Patras. On
the 19th I made an excursion to Olono, the highest mountain in the
Morea. After riding three miles through the plain of Palouria, richly
cultivated with vineyards and olive grounds, we entered into a rocky

country, and in six hours' time arrived at Cumano, a small village consisting of a few hamlets on the roots of Olono. The 20th I began my ascent of the mountain ; at the end of nearly six hours we reached the base of the higher summit; and having refreshed ourselves we prepared to climb the remaining part : a thick mist that rose at mid-day obscured the view, and hastened my return. The mountain is a rock of secondary marble : the base is covered with a thick deep soil of a brownish blackish earth, in which were frequent pieces of Jasper and indurated soap-stone. Near the summit I shot a new species of Motacilla : Cornish choughs in great abundance were now very noisy with their young in the caverns of the rock : the mountain naked except where some fir trees were scattered on the base, was much exposed to the wind that had shorn its sides and summit. There were few plants in flower : I saw the Amaryllis lutea, and a new species, which I do not find mentioned by Linnæus. The mist gradually became thinner as we descended ;. and we arrived much fatigued late in the evening at Cumano.

Sept. 2. — Leaving Cumano, I changed my route and returned by Anakaia to Patras ; the former is a small village situated in a fertile vale cultivated with rice, cotton, and India corn. Among the. rice, now nearly ripe, I found some curious plants.

Extract from Mr. Whittington's Journal referred to in p. 29.

PATMOS, February 16. 1817. — In consequence of the enquiries we had made for ancient remains, we were this day directed to a hill which rises precisely on the narrow isthmus, which unites the two divisions of the island, and separates the principal harbour from Port Merica. The present landing place is situated at its foot ; and we were obliged, in going from the monastery, to descend nearly to the magazines, before we could begin the ascent of the hill. We were gratified by finding on the summit very considerable remains of a

Greek fortress.   The   rock   is   not   so   lofty   as   that   on   which   the

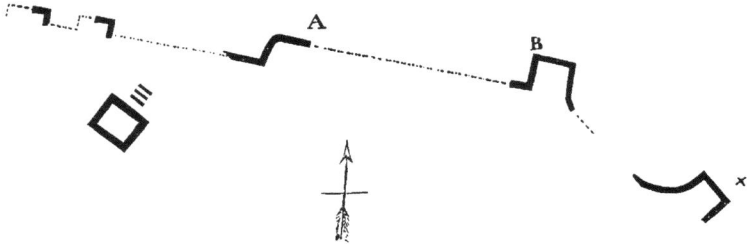

88 paces from A to B.

modern town and monastery are built ; but its singular situation, between two ports, renders it even more commanding.   The remains
are almost exclusively on the northern edge of the hill, and lie between
two of those small churches which are so numerous in the
island. *   The wall and towers on that side are very distinct and easy
to be traced, consisting of solid and regular Greek masonry, resembling exactly that of the Acropolis at Samos, excepting that, in this
instance, the blocks, with which it is constructed, are not of limestone, but of the coarse porphyry of the island.   The annexed is a
ground-plan of the wall as far as we could trace it, and I have marked
in it, with a broad black line, those spots in which the ruins are most
considerable, distinguishing, by a dotted line, others in which the
traces are less perfect.   The wall, when continued at either extremity,
must have made an angle to the southward, for it now finishes in a
precipice at each end ; and though no further traces are distinguish-
able†, it appears, from the nature of the ground, that the fortress
must have covered an irregular triangle.   The thickness of the wall
is seven feet, and the towers measure fourteen feet in front, and seven-

---

* Patmos contains not fewer than 240 churches, of which, however, many are only
used on the feast days of their respective saints.   There is but one town or village in the
island, which consists of 589 inhabited houses.   The stately monastery (which more resembles a castle than a convent) supports fifty-two monks, including the Hegoumenos.   Its
revenue is computed at 200 purses, and it pays annually to the Porte from 3 to 4000
piastres, being one-third of the whole impost furnished by the island.

† At a subsequent visit to the spot, we observed a few remains on the S. W. edge of
the hill, but of so doubtful a nature, that I have not ventured to add them to the plan.

teen feet at the sides. There are the remains of a tower thirty feet square near the western extremity, which seems to be unconnected with the outer walls, between which and it there are traces of a few steps hewn in the rock. The surface in its neighbourhood is much heaped with piles of ruin, and the whole area is thickly strewn with fragments of ancient pottery. I saw no marble remains, of any kind, in any part of the ruins; but I found in the soil a small bronze medal,· I believe of Chios, having a Sphinx on one side, and an Amphora on the other. The view from this spot, as from all the summits of this island, is of remarkable beauty; and from hence, perhaps, is best seen its peculiar and curious form.

February 25. — We descended from the town to Port Sapsala, where we saw near the beach three fragments of columns of common grey granite about seventeen inches in diameter. From thence, we walked to Porto Greco, where we were told, that we should find a remarkable rock, from which a part of that port takes the name of Τὸ Πόρτο τῆς Πέτρας. It is an insulated mass of coarse red and white *breccia*, about forty feet in height, and is covered all over with traces of excavation. On the side next the sea, we found a flight of steps, cut in the solid rock, by which we mounted to the top, where we found the surface artificially flattened, having a slight elevation at one end, to which there was an ascent of a few steps from two opposite sides. Where the rock slopes towards the land, we found two wells cut in the stone, not far from the summit. One was of considerable depth, and both were neatly cut. There was not much water in either, but it was well tasted and clear. On every side, we found the rock excavated into small caverns or niches, worked with much neatness and precision; and all over the surface innumerable traces of stairs leading in different directions, many of which (from the circumstance of parts having fallen) now end in nothing. It is difficult to determine with what intention these caves were formed, as there is nothing to denote them sepulchral chambers, and as the greater number of them, from the smallness of their size, are manifestly unfit for that purpose.

SECOND VOYAGE IN THE GRECIAN SEAS.

[*FROM THE PAPERS OF THE LATE DR. SIBTHORP.*]

CHAPTER I.

Departure from Constantinople. — Beautiful and striking Appearance of the City and neighbouring Coasts. — Marmora. — Substance and Composition of the Rocks. — Unhealthy Situation of the Town at the Dardanelles. — Plants. — Marine Conchylia. — Birds. — Arrival at Imbros. — Shells. — Vegetable Productions of the Island. — Festival in honour of the Panagia· or Madonna. — Porphyry, Pitch-stone, Jasper, Iron-stone, and yellow Earth of Imbros.

SEPTEMBER 9. 1794. — We embarked at Top-khanà, and sailed under the walls of Constantinople, which extended along the eastern shore of Thrace to the Seven Towers. The light wind and the little way our vessel made gave us time to contemplate, at our leisure, the magnificent scene * that presented itself to our view. The gay light buildings of the Seraglio were contrasted with the sombre cypresses which rose among the splendid domes and taper minarets of the mosques and public buildings. The ports were filled with shipping, and boats of canoe-like forms, some gilt and carved, were traversing it in all directions. The waters of Kat-khanà, running into the Pro-

---

* The reader will be pleased to see in what manner a Turk expresses himself when he is expatiating in praise of the capital of the empire: " Constantinople est la crème des capitales de l'univers; il n'y a rien après le Paradis de pareil à Constantinople, ni de semblable à ses agrémens, à sa verdure et à ses promenades; mais surtout voit on quelque chose qui approche du canal ou se joignent les deux mers, qui est orné des deux côtés de maisons, si magnifique, qu'il semble être une portion de l'Irem et même un modèle du Paradis ?" — Relation de Dourry Effendi, translated by Langlès, from a MS. in the Royal Library. — E.

pontis, constantly scoured the canal of Constantinople; on one side of which, with its crowded buildings, rose the northern part of the city; on the opposite shore appeared Galata and the arsenal Top-khanà with its casernes for the artillery. Extensive cemeteries, filled with groves of cypress, rose on the western shore of the Bosphorus. Opposite to it were Scutári and the coast of Asia covered with towns; beyond which were mountains of considerable height [*]: the sea was further encircled with islands interspersed in the Propontis. The points of Asia and Europe, which we had left behind us, appeared to join, and the mouth of the Bosphorus to form a grand and magnificent bay. I felt a gloomy pleasure in viewing these scenes, as I was probably surveying them for the last time, and various political speculations arose from the objects before us. At sunset we had made but little progress: St. Stephano on the Thracian coast, which was low and naked, was nearly opposite to us. The moon rose veiled by a thick mist, which rendered it of an opaque red colour; it gradually, in its ascent, changed to an orange, and then into a clear yellow; rising above the mist, it acquired a bright silver colour. We had now a dead calm, and the vessel would scarcely work. I observed in our boat specimens of Sygnathus acus which had been caught by our boys: our Greek sailors called them Belóni. I perceived some of them, as we embarked, pursuing the small fishes in the port of Top-khanà.

September 10. — Light winds during the night carried us gently along. In the morning, we had a distant view of Marmora covered with a thick haze, which is very frequent in the Propontis during the summer months. At sunset, the island of Marmora bore right ahead, distant about fifteen miles, presenting high and elevated land with rough unequal points. The continent of Asia was about the same distance, more elevated and pointed. We caught the Blatta orientalis, called by our sailors Κατζουρίδν, flying upon our decks, and

---

[*] A media Constantinopoli jucundissimus est in mare, albentemque perpetuis nivibus Olympum Asiæ prospectus. — Busbequius, Ep. 1. — E.

the Gryllus domesticus, ἀκρίδα, chirped incessantly in our cabin through the night. Our sailors, in the morning, looked at their compass ; it had eight points which they distinguished in the following manner: The North, Tramontano ; N. E. Greco ; East, Levante ; S. E. Sirocco ; South, Noteià ; S. W. Garbe ; West, Ponente ; N. W. Magistral.

September 11. — I went on shore at Marmora, and climbed the rocks, which were composed of serpentine-stone traversed with veins of Asbestos and Amianthus. In the ravines, I observed detached blocks of marble rolled down from the higher parts of the mountain. These rocks were covered with Arbutus, the Cerris oak, the Tree heath, the Spanish broom, and the Anthyllis Hermanniæ. The Crithmum maritimum grew abundantly out of the fissures : on the shore Statice Limonium, Cucubalus fabarius, and Bunias Cakile. I saw but few shells : 1 picked up a stone, cast on the shore, perforated by Pholades ; and two or three sorts of Serpulæ encrusted the rocks. From this island, Constantinople is supplied with abundance of white granulated marble for the mosques, fountains, and other public buildings.

At five P. M. we were opposite to Gallipoli : the Hellespont straightened as we advanced : we passed Chardac andLampsaco on the Asiatic coast. The shores of the Hellespont, though inferior in beauty to those of the Bosphorus, offer various inviting points of situation for towns and villages. The soil appears also much richer ; and be_ tween Rodosto and Gallipoli we observed large tracts of cultivated ground in extended stubbles. We noticed beyond them a conical mound of earth of artificial origin ; a tumulus or cairn commemorative of a battle*, or the interment of some celebrated chieftain. It was eleven o'clock when we dropped anchor on the Asiatic side of the Dardanelles.

---

* Busbequius saw some of the tumuli in Thrace, "quos Turcæ de industria excitatos fabulantur, ut essent monumenta pugnaium hominumque quos belli fuioi hausit se_ pulcra." Ep. 1. — E.

September 12. — The house of Tarragona the Jew, where we lodged, was at the farther extremity of the town : we walked through several narrow streets almost overflowed with gutters of putrid water, exhaling strong deleterious effluvia. The great heat of the summer, the want of rain, with the vicinity to marshy land, had made the Asiatic town of the Dardanelles very unhealthy this year. At the house of our consul, the Jew, we found his brother sick in bed, a youth of eighteen years of age; he was attended by his pregnant wife, who appeared about seventeen. Large copious bleedings, improperly made in a typhus or low fever, had greatly weakened him ; and the long neglect of the Peruvian bark, and then the large inconsiderate use of it, continued to protract the disease. Greatly unfortunate are the miserable patients of this country, the object of ignorant empirics who, without medical skill, treat them with superstitious ceremonies. The practice of the most enlightened parts of Europe, founded on the study of physic, is here unknown.

Our consul accompanied us in a walk along the Marina to the north of the town : we passed by numerous potteries, in some of which were manufactured vases and pots of no inelegant shape. We. observed at the Dardanelles the artist very adroitly painting them, but the paint was not burnt in. The clay was dug out of some low flat ground at the end of the town. * On a rushy marsh grew some maritime plants, Salicornia, Salsola arenaria, and Chenopodium maritimum: Statice Limonium was in flower. Leaving the marsh, we walked up a rising ground on which I collected the seeds of some curious plants, as Ruta linifolia and a species of Convolvulus, from which I conceive the celebrated Scammony of Mysia was made. The dead stalks of the Leontice Leontopetalon were blown over the fallow fields with its round black pea-shaped seed inclosed in its inflated capsule, the reticulated case of which only remained ; few plants, except Echinophora tenuifolia, were in flower ; even the Syngenesian, the latest

---

* Dardanelli. Uno in loco Terra cretacea et Argilla Porcellana. Forskal. — E.

flowering plants, were mostly in seed, as Carthamus corymbosus and Creticus, Carlina lanata and corymbosa, and Cnicus Acarnas. The Astragalus tragacantha and Satureia thymbra covered the higher part of the hill, which was a kind of calcareous sand-stone with petrefactions of oysters* and other shells. On the Marina, a quantity of Zostera marina was driven on shore, and this is collected by the inhabitants of the Hellespont, who call it φύκια, for covering their houses. After dinner, we walked to a vineyard, belonging to the consul, at the south end of the town, situated in a vale watered by the Dardanus, which was very shallow, and appeared more like a torrent bed than a river. Pebbles of Jasper and Quartz were brought down by it from the neighbouring mountain. The bitter Willow, the Tamarisk, the Agnus castus fringed its banks. Several Egrets, Ardea Garzetta, were waving in its shallow streams ; and I shot a species of Tringa piping along its shore. On the side next the town, was a fine grove of Planes, on the trunks of which the Picus major ran, with a loud shrill shriek, and a little Flycatcher darted backwards and forwards from its branches.

September 17. — We put into a small bay of the island of Imbros where we found ourselves but ill sheltered, by some projecting rocks, from the wind. We went on shore, but saw no traces of cultivation ; the island was a rough porphyry rock, of considerable extent, broken into irregular masses. Near the spot where our vessel anchored was a large Saline, which extended more than a mile over a flat sandy tract. Several pieces of pumice were driven on shore ; some shells and Zoophytes, Arca Noæ, Mytilus flavus, and several species of Venus, Tellina, Nerita, Buccinum, and single species of Bulla. I found a large species of sponge resembling pumice, called Σφόγγο: the most common plant along the coast was Centaurea spinosa.

---

* On the shore of the Dardanelles, near Sestos, Olivier observed a tolerably thick bank of marine conchylia, ostrea edulis, venus chione, venus cancellata, solen vagina, buccinum reticulatum, cerinthium vulgatum. — E.

Sept. 18. — Early in the morning, we made sail for Lemnos; but the sky appearing very stormy, our carabokyri* dropt anchor again at the eastern end of a little bay on the south side of Imbros. We went on shore to examine the island: on the beach, I met with two or three species of the sponge kind I had not seen before. The rocks were principally composed of porphyry, very barren in plants; near the coast, grew Centaurea spinosa in great plenty, which the inhabitants called Ασπροστόιβη, from its white colour and resemblance to prickly Burnet, which was common all over the island, and named Στόιβη. The Nerion, αγρ.οδάφνη, grew in the furrows between the mountain, and with the Agnus.castus, λυγειὰ, marked the course of the torrent bed. I saw very few trees or shrubs; the Quercus Cerris, Δρῦς, Qu. coccifera, Πρίνο, the Rhamnus Paliurus, ἀπαλιύρι, the wild olive, ἀγριόέλαια: the berries of the broad-leaved Phillyrea, ἐλαιόπρινο, were turning black, and I tasted some of the ripe fruit of the wild Pear, αχλαδιὰ, which had a rough austere taste; this, however, did not prevent the islanders from eating it: the caper shrub grew amongst the rocks, κάππαρις: the Carthamus corymbosus retained its ancient name in χαμαιλέο, and probably the Atractylis of Dioscorides may be found in the Centaurea solstitialis, the name given to this plant by the islanders being ἀτρακλύδα: besides these, I noticed the following plants: Onopordum Illyricum, . ἀγαιδουράκανθα, Asparagus aphyllus, σφαράγγια, Ononis villosa, ἀνονήδα, Hypericum crispum, ἀγουθόυρο, Cichorium intybus, πικρολίδι, Satureia capitata, θυμάρι, Asphodelus ramosus, ασφουδέυλο, and the common bramble, βάτον, the Osyris alba, and the Spartium junceum, φροκαλίδα. The Lichen ventosus, and several species of lichen, encrusted the rocks. The islanders called them ὄβρυα†, but our carabokyri, who was a Poriot, λειχήνι: some sea weeds, which I collected, were promiscuously termed φύκια. On returning from my walk, I met one of the islanders, who was sent by my companion to invite me to the village fête in honour of the

---

* Καραβοχύρης. — Du. C. in v.　　　† The ancient Βρύον, Muscus.. — E.

the Panagia. I was conducted to a few scattered hamlets surrounded by a grove of olives; here two priests officiated, surrounded by a numerous band of peasants: five lambs had been sacrificed, and they were now preparing them for dinner. I was introduced to this rural groupe in a little chapel, and received a benediction from the hands of one of the Papádes; ate of the consecrated bread; and, having made my offering, we sat down to partake of the village fête. The company were disposed in two groupes, men, women, and children promiscuously; when a rustic host distributed, from a wooden scewer, cabobs made of the sacrificed lamb; next was brought in a course of boiled meat; then cheese, and a soft curd, called misitra; and, lastly, a wheat soup, something like our furmenty, kourkouss. After dinner, grace was said with many signs of the cross; bread and wine were consecrated; and a dish with boiled wheat, preserved olives, and raisins, being brought to the Papás, he distributed the contents to the surrounding groupe; then taking a small piece of bread, he dipped it in the wine, when each of the men came, and devoutly received it from the hand of the officiating priest, who put it into his mouth, crossing his upper lip with the back of his finger. The women did not partake of the bread and wine, but only of the consecrated dish of wheat: each time a handful was distributed, a small wax taper was put over it. The ceremony was performed in true rural simplicity, and a gratified look was strongly expressed in the cheerful countenance of the peasantry. One of the priests had an intelligent appearance: he was not discomposed at our entrance: he had, he told us, a little library, consisting of fifty books, and was easy and communicative; the other looked proud and sullen, and said little. We were told by the former, that the island was sixty Turkish miles in circuit; that it had six towns, and about 1000 houses; that the produce of the island was chiefly corn; and in favourable seasons a quantity of it was exported; it has a small race of sheep and goats. The island has no port, and was seldom visited; of course, the few provisions it furnished were cheap: we purchased a lamb for forty-five paras, about twenty-pence of English money. On our return to our vessel, we sprung a covey of red-legged partridges, πέρδικες, and killed a large·serpent ˙we found sleeping by the road side, called Τυφλίτι : we were informed that the island produced five sorts of serpents, and one venomous, called ὄχενδρα ; the others, which, as well as the Tuphlites, were innocent, are called λαφίατι, σάιττα, and νεροφίδι. The most common bird I saw on the island was the Royston crow, κορόυνι. The inhabitants were not much acquainted with the medicinal or economical uses of their plants ; a decoction of the seeds of Vitex agnus castus was used in the diarrhœa. Their pigs were fed with the acorns of the Kermes oak ; and brooms were made from the Spartium Scoparium, called φροκαλίδα: they cut also the herb Origanum, (Riganos) and sprinkled it as a grateful aromatic on their meat.

Sept. 19. — Although the wind of yesterday had abated, our carabokyri still expressed his fears˙about sailing. We went again on shore in the morning. The rocks were exceedingly barren ; and the goats had browsed upon the few vegetables which they produced. Besides the varieties of Porphyry of which the mass was principally composed, we found specimens of different coloured Pitch stones ; pieces of Jasper and Hornstone occurred also near the shore, and white indurated clay in a loose kind of breccia: We found also a bed of the yellow earth of Werner, which is used as a colouring material, and brought to the bazar of Constantinople. We observed also a portion of a rock, a mass of yellow argillaceous stone, but which had no colouring quality. ˙The wind sunk considerably during the morning, and in the afternoon our carabokyri expressed his inclination to sail. As we were raising the anchor, the benevolent Papás, whom we had seen yesterday celebrating the feast of the Panagia, came down to the shore to visit us, bringing a present of bread, melons, and grapes. His village, where he resided, was at the distance of three hours ; this mark of attention was the more pleasing, as it was unexpected ; we added to our thanks some little presents, and the vessel getting under weigh, he was put on shore. We sailed, with a gentle·wind, along the coast of Imbros. Several little bays appeared which might easily be made places of safe anchorage for shipping, especially for small craft. Clearing the island, we had a fair view of the elevated land of Samothrace, and we were not far distant from the south point, when the sun with a glowing tint sunk behind Athos, forming a grand conical figure with an insular appearance.

[The islands of Samothrace and Lemnos are contiguous to Imbros : the former has been seldom visited: of Lemnos, some account is introduced in this place, extracted from the journals of Dr. Hunt, who, with the late Professor Carlyle, spent a few days on the island in the course of their voyage to Athos.] — E.

LEMNOS.

Samothrace. — Anchorage at Lemnos. — Character of the Turkish Governor. — Dress of the Female Inhabitants. — Hot Springs. — Terra Sigillata. — Anecdotes of the celebrated Hassan Pasha. — Volcanic Appearance of the Island. — Duties and Taxes. — Prices of various Articles. — Return to Castro. — Visit to the Didascalos. —Excursion to Palaio Castro.

MARCH 22. 1801.—We regretted not being able to touch at Samothrace : our boatmen assured us that its forests and valleys are very beautiful, not inferior to those of any other island in the Archipelago, and that many remains of ancient buildings are to be found in it. There is now but one town in the island containing about three hundred Greek families, and a few Turks. Some of the women pretend to a knowledge of sorcery and divination ; and it is not uncommon for superstitious Greek sailors to buy a favourable wind from them, or for a fair maid of Scio to consult them on the composition of a philtre to bring back a faithless lover. The woods furnish some ship-timber which is exported, as well as about fifteen thousand bushels of fine wheat, more than their annual consumption, and some goats' milk cheese. On our left, we saw the island which is called, in our charts, Stratia : its ancient name was Nea, but it is now called by the Greeks Ἅγιος ςρατηγὸς, *agios strategos*, the holy warrior, *i. e.* St.Michael. It has a small port, with a village of about fifty families, all Greeks. Here the wind failed us ; but, by dint of rowing all night, we reached Castro, a port on the west side of Lemnos, about eight o'clock next morning. Castro is the ancient Myrina.

March 23. — On landing, we found a servant of the Aga, or Turkish Governor, waiting at the Mole to conduct us to his master. The Aga received us very hospitably, and added that he would cheerfully supply us with any thing we might want, and that could be procured in the island. He spoke Greek with as much fluency as Turkish, and seemed as affable to some Greeks of the island, who were visiting him, as to the Turks ; Καλὸς Ἀνθρωπος εἶναι ὁ Ἀγας, "our Aga is an excellent man," was the expression the Greeks used to us when speaking of him. We could hear of no antiquities nor ruins in the island ; but the Aga offered us one of his guards to accompany us in any excursions we might wish to make. At a house near the shore, we saw a broken Greek inscription on a block of marble. We procured horses, and set out to a place called Palaio Castro, where we were told some ruins remained, and which we hoped might be those of the famous labyrinth of Lemnos with its one hundred and fifty columns, its massive gates, and numerous statues, and described by ancient authors as more extensive and splendid than that of Crete or Egypt, and of which Pliny says there were ruins remaining in his time : " *Extantque adhuc reliquiæ ejus.*" — Plin. xxxvi. 13. Our road, at first, lay through a valley cultivated with corn and a few vineyards, but without any wood on the rising ground. The general appearance of this island is far from picturesque or fertile : the pastures were profusely covered with Anemones of the most vivid and various hues ; and the sides of the hills were white with the large towering Asphodel, which the islanders look upon as an omen of a fruitful year. The ground, we were told, ·was just recovering its verdure, after having been a

prey, for three successive years, to the ravages of the locust, which
had devoured the shoots and leaves of the corn, grass, and vines.
On looking back from an eminence towards the town and Port of
Castro, we had a striking view of the fort or citadel. It covers the
top of a lofty promontory which divides the bay into two parts;
both of these may be defended by it.

The dress of the Turks is nearly the same in all the islands; but
that of the Greek women in Lemnos deserves to be remarked. It
consists of a short corset or jacket of scarlet cloth, with long sleeves,
loose in front, and only reaching a few inches down the back; the
petticoat is very short; the wide trowsers, which are drawn tight
round the ancle, and then hang over, are of callico with coloured
sprigs: they have slippers of yellow Turkey leather, but no stock-
ings; a long shawl-shaped white handkerchief is gracefully tied, like
a turban, round the head, and hangs down the back ready to conceal
the face at the approach of any Turks. To us, they did not think
that ceremony necessary, but civilly accosted us with " Καλῶς Ὁρίσατε—
Καλὴ Ἡμέρα — Ὧρα Καλὴ, and other expressions of civility. Four
miles from Castro, we passed a Greek village, called Chorous, where
there is a hot spring, still called Thermia, and over which the great
Hassan, the Capudan Pasha, had built a commodious bath, and a
chan or lodging house for strangers who frequent it for its supposed
medicinal qualities. A number of people were bathing when we arrived; the process is similar to that used in the Turkish Hummaums,
by first bringing on a profuse perspiration, and then using severe
friction, with mohair gloves, to open the pores, and relax the joints.
The water, which we tasted at the source, was very warm and soft, but
seemed to have no sensible mineral impregnation. This spot also
produces a kind of argillaceous earth, known in the old school
of physic under the name of Terra *Sigillata*. It is still sold here in
small balls, and stamped with *a seal* containing Arabic characters,
and its virtues in fevers and other diseases were much praised by the
natives. Hassan Pasha, who built this bath and chan for the gratuitous accommodation of the sick, is still called the Great Capudan

Pasha, and is always spoken of in terms of high admiration by the islanders of the Archipelago. He seems to have been one of the few Turks, in late times, who possessed, in any eminent degree, either courage, talents, or public spirit. In the year 1770, he hastily collected a handful of volunteers on the Asiatic shore of the Dardanelles, and secretly took them over, in open boats, and during the night, to Lemnos, where, falling unexpectedly on the Russians, who had landed from their fleet, he compelled them, after great slaughter, to evacuate the island. The Turks at Castro assured us that if the Russian Admiral, Elphinstone, had not manœuvred his fleet with a skill truly *English*, the ships, as well as the land forces, must have fallen a prey to this bold attack of Hassan Pasha.

Without the slightest knowledge of letters, this great man, who was master of a Candiot merchant-ship, rose to the supreme command of the Turkish navy, and was invested by the Sultan with absolute power over the islands and shores of the Archipelago : he possessed great penetration in detecting crimes, and always showed inflexible justice in punishing the delinquents, whatever their situation might be. He was fond of presiding in his own courts of justice; and many of his decisions are still quoted by Turks, Greeks, and Jews, which would do credit to more enlightened and impartial tribunals. Before his appointment as High Admiral, the Turkish marines, or Galeongees, used to commit the greatest excesses with impunity, whenever they were ordered to embark on a cruize, breaking open the houses at Galata and Pera; and plundering every Raya they met, whether Greek, Jew, or Armenian. He determined to abolish this· licentious practice, and succeeded in compelling the Galeongees to go unarmed, whenever they were allowed to be on shore, and even then only in small parties; a regulation which his successors have been unable to enforce. He often went amongst them disguised, and more than once has inflicted capital punishment with his own hand on his disorderly troops. A Mussulman, or Christian, in his fleet, who drank wine, was considered by him as guilty of a heinous crime. He ordered the doors of all taverns and wine-shops to be sealed during the time his fleet was in any port; if he then found a. Galeongee drunk, he first made him confess (by torture, if necessary,) where he had procured the liquor : he then punished the wine-seller either with death or condemnation to the galleys. The excesses I saw committed by the present Capudan Pasha's troops, when under sailing orders for Egypt, even in Pera, Galata, and Constantinople, convince me, that no ordinary severity could have kept such a lawless set in order. Whenever he walked out, he was accompanied by a lion which he had tamed, and which had become so docile as to be allowed to go unmuzzled; and Hassan seemed to be pleased at witnessing the terror of the Mufti, the chamberlains, or the effeminate eunuchs of the seraglio, whenever they were forced to pay him and his lion a visit of ceremony. This beast, however, at last became ferocious, and showed a disposition to spring upon Europeans, to whose dress he was a stranger, when he met them during his master's walks in Constantinople. This occasioned some unavailing remonstrances from the foreign ministers; but one morning the vicious beast sprung upon Hassan himself, drew blood with his fangs, and would soon have destroyed him, if some attendant guards had not rushed forward, and overpowered the lion ; some of whom, however, fell victims to their zeal. The Sultan then ordered him to be confined in the Royal Menagerie, where I saw him. Hassan Pasha had some disposition to encourage the arts : his palaces, particularly one still remaining at Cos, are among the most elegant specimens of Turkish architecture, undebased by the gaudy and flimsy decorations now so prevalent at Constantinople.

While our guide was relating to us some traits of Hassan's history, we reached the foot of the mountain on which Palaio Castro is situated. The ascent was steep and rugged : the valley which extends from its base to the sea is very well cultivated : we counted six villages on it, and saw the bay in which Hassan landed when he came unexpectedly on the back of the Russian forces.

From the summit of this hill, two thirds of the island are distinctly seen, with rivulets intersecting the valleys in numerous directions.

A granite column, a few blocks of white marble, and fragments of Grecian pottery, are the only remains of antiquity on this spot. The mountains over which we had passed were barren and rocky, and often without even brushwood on them. The whole island bears the strongest marks of the effects of volcanic fire: the rocks, in many parts, are like the burnt and vitrified scoria of furnaces.· The climate is too cold to ripen lemons or oranges well; they, therefore, are brought from Scio. It produces, however, good grapes and figs. At our return to Castro, we supped with a Greek, to whom we had been recommended, and who is Πρωΐόγερος, or chief Greek magistrate of the island. He told us that the government of their Aga, who is a native of Lemnos, is very mild, and that the Greeks are not much oppressed. The island is about 130 Italian miles in circuit. In the forty villages of the island, he calculates about 3000 families, not above 200 of whom are Turks. The·Aga farms the Sultan's tribute, for which he gives 17,000 piastres, and is supposed to collect about 21,000, leaving him a profit of 4000 piastres. The ossour is fixed at one-tenth of the produce of the·soil equally for Turks and Greeks. The duty paid for all the wine of the island is only 1000 piastres. The extraordinary contributions levied during the war have been considerable. A little pier has been built at Castro, at the expense of the inhabitants; to reimburse which, every ship that enters the harbour pays according to its size: our little sacoleva was charged fifteen paras (about eight-pence). Large merchant-ships are built here; and we saw a fifty-gun ship on the stocks for the Turkish navy: the keel was of fir, but the knees and ribs and other parts of oak from the island of Thasos. From that island, they also get masts for small merchant-ships, but those of large size come from the forests of the Black Sea. Thasos also exports some honey, bees' wax, silk, and olive oil. It has seven villages, all of Greek Christians. The wine of Lemnos is of two sorts: both are black; for one kind, six paras an oke is paid, and eight for the other, about two-pence and three-pence a bottle. Wheat was selling at four piastres, or six shillings the bushel. Wheat-flower seventeen paras, or eight-pence halfpenny

I 2

the oke *; barley eight paras. Cheese, sold wholesale, was seven paras an oke; mutton eight paras an oke; and we gave one hundred paras, or four shillings, for a lamb. The island produces more than sufficient grain for its own consumption, and exports the remainder, as well as some wine, to Mytilene; but its principal exports are ewe-milk cheese, some silk, cotton, and wool. We saw the process of making a new vineyard. It was the season for pruning the vines: this is done close to the stock, leaving the old vine not more than ten or twelve inches above the ground. Of the shoots of the former year, they take cuttings of about three feet long, and plant them deep in the ground, at the distance of a yard square from each other, watering each plant profusely, and leaving a little dam round it to retain the moisture. The third year after planting, a vineyard is in full bearing.

We were anxious to reach Athos; and, notwithstanding the remonstrances of the master of the vessel, we sailed on the 27th of March, at four o'clock in the morning, with a strong breeze from the north. Towards sun-rise the wind increased to a gale; and in about half an hour such a storm came on, as made our situation seem desperate: we shipped three seas successively, and dreaded that the next wave which might break over us would fill our undecked boat, and sink us. Our little crew seemed to hesitate whether they should run before the wind to the island of St. George di Skyro, at sixty miles' distance, or make an attempt to regain the port of Lemnos: they took the latter resolution; and after an hour and a half's tempestuous tossing, we got our little bark into a creek, near the port which we had left. The storm continued to increase during the whole of the day, and towards noon it blew a perfect hurricane; we therefore walked over to Castro, and were accommodated with a room, in a ruinous Khan, now converted into a school for teaching ancient Greek to the boys of the island. We found the Διδάσκαλος, or master, a well-informed man: he had received his education at Jöannina, in Albania, the most celebrated seminary for Greek litera-

* The oke is two pounds and three quarters.

ture in Turkey. He had a good knowledge of history and geography, but seemed inclined to laugh at our eagerness to discover ancient ruins or inscriptions; saying, it seemed to him to be equally uninteresting to discover in an ancient Greek building proofs that it had been erected to Jupiter or Minerva, by a certain sovereign or people, as to find that an old mosque or castle had been built by a Suleyman, an Achmet, a Mustaphá, or any other Sultan. The progress of his pupils in ancient Greek was not extraordinary: we found his headboy reading the Psalter. This schoolmaster's salary was 500 piastres, nearly 40l. sterling, paid by the Greek community of the island.

Next day we made a second attempt to discover the ruins of the Labyrinth of Lemnos: but after every possible enquiry both of Greeks and Turks, we could only hear a confused account of a subterraneous stair-case in an uninhabited part of the island, near a bay called Porniah, containing, as they said, forty steps, and a number of marble columns. To this place we therefore set out; and after twenty miles riding, twelve of them along the road by which we had gone to Palaio Castro, we came to a bay where we saw extensive ruins of an ancient and strong building that seems to have had a foss round it communicating with the sea. The edifices have covered about ten acres of ground: there are foundations of an amazing number of small buildings within the outer wall, each about seven feet square. The walls towards the sea are strong, and composed of large square blocks of stone. On an elevated spot of ground in one corner of the area, we found a subterraneous stair-case, and, after lighting our tapers, we went down it. The entrance was difficult: it consisted of fifty-one steps, and about every twelfth one was of marble, the others of common stone. At the bottom is a small chamber, with a well in it, by which probably the garrison was supplied: a censer, a lamp, and a few matches, were lying in a corner, for the use of the Greek Christians, who call this well an Ἁγίασμα, or *Holy Fountain*, and the ruins about it, *Panagia* Coccipée. The peasants in the neighbourhood had no knowledge of any sculpture, or statues, or medals having ever been found there. I could not coincide with my companion in thinking that these ruins have any relation to the Labyrinth mentioned by Pliny. The place bears also the name of Παλαιὸ Καςρο, *the Ancient Fortress*, and may probably have been the citadel of the town Hephæstias.

We had now traversed Lemnos in various directions, little gratified either with its antiquities, or its natural scenery: for though the mountains are bold, and the valleys sometimes verdant and fertile, yet the total want of wood, and even of shrubs, gives the island a look of desolation and dreariness.

It is not easy to describe the mortification we felt at thus leaving a place so celebrated from the fabulous ages down to the time of Strabo, without our having discovered one valuable vestige of ancient art. We could not ascertain the caverns where mythology had placed Vulcan and his Cyclops, nor could we trace one Pelasgic fortress, nor an Ionic or Doric edifice, the work of Athenian or Carian colonists; not even could an ancient medal be found in the possession of any of the islanders. How is this desolation to be accounted for? Have volcanoes and earthquakes been the true Λήμνια κακὰ, and destroyed that part of the island where these buildings stood?

The 1st of April the master of our boat waked us, to say that the wind seemed favourable for our voyage to Mount Athos: we therefore once more embarked, though not without apprehensions that the equinoctial gale was not yet over — and unfortunately we found our fears too true. The wind rose with the sun, and quite against us; so that after vainly endeavouring to beat some time against it we were again forced back to Lemnos, and anchored at an uninhabited bay, where we could only gather a few limpets from the rocks, and a few Echini or Sea Urchins. This bay was called Cas Pakà. The rocks which rise perpendicularly above it appear volcanic: the shore is covered with pumice-stone. Towards evening the wind fell, and the moon shining very bright, tempted us a third time to try the formidable passage between Lemnos and Athos: — again, we suffered all the terrors of a storm in an open boat. The waves often broke over us in a most alarming manner; the high sea made the vessel pitch so much, that we sometimes thought the mast would go; and at other moments that the planks would start. The wind now prevented our return to Lemnos; and the breakers all along the iron-bound coast of Athos rendered our approach to the monastery of Santa Laura impossible. All the sails were now taken down, and nothing but a small piece of canvas put forward to steer by; letting the wind therefore drive us, we luckily reached a little creek, at the foot of the monastery of Batopaidi, on the peninsula of Athos.

———————

CONTINUATION OF SIBTHORP'S JOURNAL. See p. 54. line 5.

Plants on the Beach and Rocks of Athos. — Ascent to some of the Hermitages. — The Convent of St. Paul. — Nature and Form of the Building. — Servian Monks. — Departure from Athos. — Thessalian Mountains. — Anchor at Skiatho. — Greek Inscription. — Nature of the Rocks of the Island. — Depredations committed by the Albanians. — Voyage continued. — Gulf of Volo. — Shores of Negropont. — Monastery. — Miraculous Legends. — Coast of Bœotia. — Arrival at Negropont. — Fishes. — Plants. — Shells.

Oct. 4th, 1794. The continuance of the calm still prevented us from quitting the peninsula of Athos. A pebbly shore rising into a steep rock of primitive marble, on which appeared a variety of curious plants, made me impatient to land. I could discover from our vessel Erica multiflora in full.flower empurpling spots of the rock. On landing, I found near the beach the beautiful sea-lily, Pancratium maritimum. The Arbutus Andrachne grew on the hanging cliffs on which I gathered from low procumbent shrubs specimens of Globularia alypum, and under its shade, entwined by the rough smilax, the sweet-scented coronilla: on the more exposed and steeper part of the rocks grew the wild cabbage, of whose leaves our sailors gathered large quantities to boil with Stæhelina Chamæpeuce, and Conyza candida. From the beach we ascended by a flight of marble steps to a cluster of hermitages belonging to the monastery of St. Paul: these are called Σκάθια; and in one of them we found a caloyer that had been four-and-twenty years on Athos; who addressed us with a rap-

ture of joy in English : he was a native of Epirus; had been seven
years a sailor in our fleet; tired with the fatigues and danger of the
sea, he sought a retreat in this delightful spot : he was not, however,
consuming his time in the indolence of monastic life ; we found
him very busy in manufacturing a coarse kind of woollen cloak, for
which Athos is famous. His hermitage was exceedingly neat, and
consisted of a hall and two rooms ; before his door was an arbour entwined by a vine from which hung rich clusters of purple grapes ; a
garden formed on the pending rock furnished a plentiful supply of
kitchen herbs and esculent fruits. With a gratified look, he said,
" This is all mine." He commanded from his arbour a fine view of
the sea, which afforded a constant subject of meditation to one who
had been tossed about for seven years on its uncertain waves. Our
stock of provisions being nearly exhausted from the length of our
stay at Athos, we visited the convent of St. Paul, where Nicholas
Andrea, our Epirote hermit, said we could obtain a fresh supply.
The way which led from these skathia to the monastery was along
the ridge of the mountain through a beautiful shrubbery of Kermes
oaks mixed with Arbutus and Andrachne. Those trees now laden
with ripe fruit made a most beautiful appearance, and with the
smooth polished bark, and shining laurel-like leaves of the Andrachne,
were highly ornamental. We descended the rock by a precipice
which led into a wide valley formed by a torrent bed : we observed
among the large blocks of marble hurled down from the mountain,
the narrow-leaved Epilobium, and the Pinaster. Passing the torrent
bed we ascended another rock, which led us to the romantic site of
the monastery of St. Paul, about two miles distant from its skathia.
A wild looking caloyer with a large club appeared as the porter, and
conducted us up stairs through a gloomy chamber to the Hegoumenos, who received us with hospitable kindness. While the dinner
was preparing, we had leisure to examine the monastery : it was one
of those ancient buildings which the writers of romance would have
been happy to have copied : it was consecrated as a spot visited by
St. Paul in his journey in Macedonia. The building was large and

massive, but there appeared little regularity in its form. It was surrounded by balconies; a refectory in which the caloyers assembled was the best sized room; here was a wooden pulpit, like the reading desk in our halls at Oxford, and large oak tables along the side; one of these was covered with pewter porringers, in which the scanty and miserable fare of the caloyers was measured out. The chapel was small, and some few figures of saints, done in the earlier ages of the Greek church, ornamented the walls. We mounted up several stories; at the top of these, we passed to a tower of considerable height: it had from neglect fallen into decay; the stairs were broken, and the floors and partition walls gone: here, as our Hegoumenos informed us, was the very dwelling-place of St. Paul. The entrance to this tower was secured by a strong iron door, and under it was a deep well, a reservoir of good water. The roof of the convent was covered with lead, but its timbers and floors so decayed, that we trod with a kind of fearful caution. The whole building showed either a want of funds or the proper application of them to its support. It was a Servian foundation; but the oppression of Servia by the Turks cut it off from the supplies which the first founders hoped it would receive. The store-rooms of these caloyers offered to our view scenes very different from what the well-supplied cellars of our convents would have afforded before their dissolution. We saw only a few skins with oil, bags of flour, and dried fishes. Some of the caloyers were busy in cutting into slices melongena and tomatoes to dry; these, with preserved olives, furnish a winter provision for the convent. When dinner was ready, we went into a room furnished with a divan in the Turkish fashion, and were first served with a dish of mushrooms stewed in oil; some turnip radishes were brought in at the same time, both of an oblong and orbicular form; to these, succeeded an omlet composed of eggs, with cheese, parsley, and butter: the concluding dish was a pilau, with a dessert of grapes and honey, which was of a brown colour, and had a heathy flavour. The caloyers here were Servians; and our Hegoumenos informed us the library contained several Servian manuscripts.

·· The monastery of St. Paul is distant only five hours from the summit of Mount Athos. I was informed that the road was so rocky, and the precipices so steep, that the mules could not convey me there. My botanical ardour strongly pressed me to visit it: I had before ascended it from Laura, and noticed some of its plants; but I promised myself from this excursion an additional harvest; and though I had suffered so much from the heat of the day on our return from the convent of St. Paul, I formed the plan of executing this scheme, in case our vessel was detained. The hermitages of St. Ann were on the road, and about half-way was a chapel of the Panagia where I could repose. On arriving at our vessel, the boat had procured us a plentiful supply of fish, and one of our sailors had dived, and brought up for me a pinna: it contained within its shell two shrimp-like animals: these were probably the watchful cancri so beautifully described by Oppian.

Oct. 5.—At one in the morning, a light breeze springing up, we steered across the gulf of Athos: we continued our course slowly towards Scopelo; and at sunset we were about thirteen leagues to the S. W. of Cape Drepano: Olympus and the Thessalian mountains appeared very distinct.

Oct. 6. — Our cabin was small and offensive from the smell of the bilge water; and the vermin swarming in every part of it, I preferred sleeping in my bed-gown on the deck. During the night, we had ·a very heavy dew which I found, in the morning, had made my upper blanket quite wet: our sailors protected themselves from these dews by a thick brown coarse woollen cloak with a hood to it. As we advanced in the morning, we saw distinctly the mountains of Thessaly, Elympo, Kissavo, and Zagora, formerly known by the renowned names of Olympus, Ossa, and Pelion. At sunset, the wind freshened, and for two hours it blew hard from the south; at eight A. M. it sunk. We were at a short distance from the coast of Thessaly, and could distinguish the solitary light of a monastery, or Kelli, on the nearest mountain.

. Oct. 7. — At sunrise, we were not ..more than six leagues·distant from Skiatho : we ran along its northern shore which was rocky, but indented with bays towards Castro, or the town, singularly situat̃ed upon a precipice projecting into the sea. We sent out our boat· to make enquiries respecting the pirates. Near the shore was a small Albanian guard keeping watch on the mountain : they fired a musket, and we hailed them from our vessel. We dropped anchor in a fine port on the south side of the island. The scenery was beautiful and striking ; a bay, nearly circular, with islets interspersed in it ; the shore formed by rough rocks covered with mastic, and a warm vale, with a south-east exposure, planted with vines. On the eastern point rose the village consisting of a few houses irregularly scattered over the rock, and a new church on the more elevated height. · We went on shore, and found that the village had about a month since been burned by banditti : a number of· Albanians, as guards, were dispersed in it, and the frightened inhabitants had scarcely more than a month returned to their ruined dwellings : the women still expressed much fear in their countenances, and were extremely reserved : they would scarcely suffer us to enter their houses, and our enquiries ·for provision met with little success. We with difficulty procured some eggs and grapes. The wine, the principal produce of the island, was all new, and the inhabitants were now busily engaged in their vintage. We had heard that there was a fragment of antiquity in the church : we went to visit it, and found an inscribed stone which formed the pedestal of the communion table. The Papás who gave us admittance seemed extremely unwilling that we should see it : he first denied it was there ; at length he was induced, with reluctance, to show it, but violently opposed our taking a copy * ; at last we prevailed over his scruples. Our ignorant Papás could neither read nor understand it : he had, however, sufficient cunning to teach the superstitious islanders that it was something sacred and mysterious.

---

* The inscription is published from Mr. Hawkins's copy in the first volume of this work.

Near the village were the ruins of an ancient church containing four sarcophagi. From this spot, I wandered among the rocks which were composed of a fine grained saline marble, of a snowy whiteness, covered with Lentisc mixed with the Daphne Gnidium, which, bearing at the same time its flowers and fruit, made a gay appearance. The mastic retained, in sound, the ancient name Σχίνο, but the Gnidium was now called Σφλόμο. The Caper bush, κάππαρις, hung from the rocks; and on the more exposed parts near the sea, among the mastics, rose the Sea-quill with a long naked scapus loaded with ripe seed. The Erigeron graveolens, ἀκούζα, flowered near the beach, which was a coarse calcareous breccia.

Oct. 8. — The wind being still contrary, we remained at Skiatho : in the afternoon, we climbed a high hill, on the south side of the island, to the east of our port, covered with Pinasters mixed with Arbutus, Myrtles, and Andrachnes. The whole region had been lately burned by some Albanian incendiaries who had set fire to the olive grounds, which had spread and consumed almost the whole southern side of the island. The vicinity to the main land of Greece brings many an unwelcome visitor to it, and keeps the inhabitants in continual alarm. We heard, near the summit of the hill, the tinkling of the bell of the goats; but our appearance being discovered by the herdsman, he precipitately drove his flock down the steep, and, with vociferations of fear, pressed them towards the village. The Erica multiflora, a grateful flower to the bee, diffused its odour, which, with some aromatic plants, were scattered over the hills : the Thymbra of the ancients, θρούβη, and the Thyme, θυμάρι, were in seed. Mixed with these were the thorny plants of the prickly broom, and a species of Spartium which consisted of a mass of thorns, called ἐχινόποδι. In the ravine formed by the torrent bed from the mountain, some flourishing trees of the Cretan maple had escaped the flame. The sky was tolerably clear, and we commanded a fine prospect from the summit of the hill : on one side, we saw Athos distinctly ; on the other, the eye stretched over Eubœa, and had a distant view bounded by Parnassus, and discriminated clearly the outline of Scopelo. The rock which composed the hill was of glimmer slate; of a grey, fine-grained saline marble, and that beautiful snow-white variety which I had observed in my walk the preceding day.

Oct. 9. — As the season was so far advanced, and we had been considerably detained in our route by the southerly winds, calms, and the fear of pirates, we determined to proceed to Athens. The wind was now north, but it blew too fresh for us to venture out to sea. In the afternoon I walked to a shallow fresh-water lake on the west of our port; it afforded nothing to gratify my botanical researches. On the mud of it grew the Salicornia herbacea, and thickets of the Agnus Castus, a common plant throughout Greece. The shore presented nothing to amuse the conchologist: a few cockle-shells and spiny oysters were all I could find. On our return to our vessel we observed a number of swallows, which seemed to be collecting for their migration.

Oct. 10. — The north wind continued blowing hard through the day. I walked in the afternoon across the island, and found the soil in general thin, covering rocks of glimmer slate: the mastic the predominant tree, with kermes oak, Phillyrea, olives, Spanish and prickly broom, with a thick thorny species of Spartium; the tree and many flowery heath, with Daphne Gnidium. I observed in the exposed part the prickly Acanthus with Cnicus Acarna, Carlina corymbosa and Scolymus Hispanicus: the vales and declivities cultivated with vines, which on the northern side were frequently accompanied with habitations. I saw no cattle, except asses: the flocks of sheep and goats seemed few. With difficulty we procured a meagre kid at a very high price; the islanders were anxious to increase their stock, which had been greatly injured by the late plunderers, and unwillingly parted with any thing. The island is of very irregular shape, and is said to be about thirty-six miles in circuit: it has two towns, and is supposed to contain about five hundred houses. The vineyards form its principal support: we were plentifully supplied with grapes of a good quality, and found some excellent melons.

Oct. 11. — Preparations had been made the preceding evening for our departure; the boys had tied the sails with rush, or βούρλα*, a plentiful supply of which grew on the shore near the lake (Juncus acutus). Early in the morning we weighed anchor; at sunrise we left the small island of Pondiconesi; about a league to the southward, we opened the gulf of Volo, the celebrated Pelasgian gulf; on a hill above we saw the town of Trichiri; the sea was now straightened by the land, having the northern coast of Negropont on our left, and that of Thessaly, with the gulf of Volo, on our right. The coast of Negropont, at first rocky and uncultivated, sunk into the rich vale of Oros: we saw distinctly with our glasses the walls of an ancient town, Syrochoro: having passed Cape Stavros, we sailed by the small barren islands of Argyronesi: the coast of Thessaly appeared high, rough, and barren: as we opened the gulf of Zeitun we saw some cultivated spots, and observed a town obscurely at a distance from the coast. From the vale of Oros rose the rocks of Vlicada; having turned the north-west point of Negropont, we sailed by the islands of Vlicada: the inbat carried us gently down the straits: we saw upon the hills some vineyards, and corn-land dotted over with wild pear-trees, and the town of Vlicada screened by a rock: opposite to us was the bold shore of Thessaly, with the famous pass of Thermopylæ, Oeta, and a ridge of mountains on the back ground. In the evening we anchored opposite to a small dilapidated monastery, surrounded by a grove of olive and pine trees, a mile distant from Vlicada, dedicated to St. George; here miracles, it was said, were still performed; a taper was burnt to the Saint; and we were told by our sailors, that if the man who had the care of it suffered it to go out, he would be punished with blindness; and that if any one cut of the wood which composed the sacred grove, he would either die or cut himself with the instrument he made use of. † The straits of Negropont are here

---

* See Du C. in v. βρȣ̃υλον.
† The reader will recollect the passage in Lucan, l. 3.
            Motique verenda
      Majestate loci, si robora sacra ferirent,
      In sua credebant redituras membra secures.—E.

scarcely a league in breadth ; and a phoca, or sea-calf, passed by our vessel swimming from one shore to the other.

Oct. 12. — Having filled our casks with brackish water from a small spring near the beach, we weighed anchor at sunrise, and with a fair wind proceeded down the gulf. The shore of Negropont rose bold and rocky, covered with low shrubs, and dotted with the soft light green of the Pinus pinea. We passed by Yalta, about six miles distant from Vlicada ; near the shore was Lipso, and about a mile above it, we were told, were thermæ * or warm baths : the coast was now mountainous, rough, and naked, and offered only the solitary site of some monastery : about seven miles from Lipso was a convent dedicated to St. John, and another about a mile from it, consecrated to St. Elias : then followed among barren rocky lands, the towns of Robi and Lymni, and another monastery under the protection of St. Nicholas. A chain of mountainous land formed the opposite coast of Bœotia, which rising gradually, left a narrow tract of cultivated ground along the beach. Above those mountains, Parnassus reared its lofty naked many-headed summit : along the shore we first saw Architza ; then, on a low elevation, close to the sea, appeared the ruins of a town called Levana ; under the mountains, about six miles distant from these ruins, we saw Talanda embosomed in trees. The Opuntian gulf now opened, and the island of Talanda appeared in view : opposite to it, on the coast of Bœotia, were some Salines, where salt was collected. Leaving the Opuntian gulf, we passed by Larymnes ; then a small island not laid down in the maps : somewhat lower down another, named Manetta ; this is probably the island marked in Faden's map as Gaithronesi. We observed with our glasses the ruins of a castle upon it. Below Manetta was a low tract of land running into the straits called Gaithouri : the water near it is very shallow, and our sailors assured us that close to the shore were to be seen the remains of buildings : behind it was

---

* Probably the spot mentioned in Plutarch. Symp. iv. L. Ques. 3. τῆς Εὐβοίας ὁ Γάληψος, ὃυ τὰ θερμά. — E.

72   NEGROPONT.

the high land of Ktypo. We discovered from our vessel mandras (sheep-folds) upon it, and descending farther down the straits, we saw Politico. The huge mountain of Delphis rose with a naked truncated summit high above the rest; and as we continued our course, dolphins played around our vessel. Our Carabokyri, who was no Arion, whistled to them. We were now before the fortress of Carababa, and dropped anchor at seven in the evening at Egripo or Negropont.

· Oct. 13. — Our vessel was obliged to haul down its mast to pass the bridge of Negropont: it has five arches; adjoins a fort which, with a drawbridge, connects the town and island of Egripo with the continent of Greece. We sent our servants early on shore in the morning for provisions: they brought back, with other things, different sorts of fish, Luphari, (Perca Lophari,) Red mullet, Barbouni, and two sorts of Spari ; one I suppose to be the Erythrinus of the Greeks : it is now called Lythrinari, or Rythrinari *, the Coral fish, from its red colour, and in Turkish Mertzan ; the other I suspect to be the Dentex of Linnæus, the Synagris of the Greeks, now Synagrida, and Mouskada. We landed on the quay, which was very much out of repair. I observed the Sertularia halecina attached to the stones in the water. On the return of our servants we went on shore. The town of Egripo is composed of narrow streets, and appeared thinly inhabited. We walked about a mile along the shore to the north of the town. The rock was composed of Serpentine stone, traversed with Asbestos and Steatite: we picked up several shells. We had formerly collected here some crystals of magnetical iron ore; at present we searched in vain without discovering the least traces of it. The Charadrius Spinosus was running along the shore. The rock was thinly covered with soil: but Passerina hirsuta, which was now in flower, grew on it in great abundance, κολλαρουσα, with the two asphodels, fistulosus, and ramosus : goats' rue, Peganum Harmala, was also very common, with a species of Euphorbia, and the

* See the Schol. on Oppian, L. 1. Hal. v. 97. ξάνθοι τ' ερυθίνοι. — λυθρινάρια is the explanation given.—E.

Thyme of the ancients. · On our return from our·walk, our ¡vessel had passed the bridge, and we were obliged to walk'round the fortress, to the south of the town, to arrive at it. In the outskirts, Physalis somnifera, with its coral red ·seeds in their inflated calyces, made a pretty appearance. As we passed by some Turkish·cemeteries, we noticed graves made gay with a covering of the Amaryllis lutea, which had been planted there probably by some friend of the deceased. The distinction of rank is preserved in·Turkey even after death ; and the capitals of the tomb-stones were cut into·various forms marking the situation of life, and character of the deceased. The fortress was of considerable extent, with a deep foss : from the walls of it Capparis spinosa grew in great abundance, and near it some plants of Salsola fruticosa. No place in the world seems, from its situation, to lay so fair a claim to commercial advantages as Egripo ; but a little Hydriote vessel or two were all we observed in its harbour.

On our return on board, we found the bottom of the main-mast, which was made of the silver fir, so completely decayed, that our carabokyri was obliged to call in the assistance of a ship-carpenter : this detained us the whole day at Egripo. ·In the afternoon, I landed in our boat, and walked along the shore on the west of the town on the continent of Greece. I saw here no traces ·of·the serpentine rock : a grey limestone formed the hill, which gradually' sloped towards the sea. Among the rocks, I observed several stones pierced by pholades, which they inhabited·jointly with crabs and sea onisci. Some of these crabs were so little, that they tenanted the deserted shells of Voluta tornata *, and a small species of Medusa, with purplish green·tentacula was fixed· so· close to the rocks, that I separated it with difficulty. · A clustered Sertularia and Tubularia Acetabulum adhered to the shells of Cardium echinatum : the Fucus pavonius was also common in the harbour ; and I scraped from the rocks under water a small brown Conferva : the Conferva rupestris I found on

* Qu. Tornatilis ?

the keel of our vessel: it was called by our sailors Malia. I observed the same plants I had noticed to the north of the town, with the addition of the sea Squill which was in flower, and the Cichorium spinosum ; Verbascum Tournefortii and Phlomis fruticosa both in seed. The Alcedo hispida flew along the shore : this, then, must be considered among the birds that frequent the sea-coast. A prodigious number of Jackdaws, Καρɣα, inhabited the walls of the fortress, and were very clamorous. When I returned on board, I found our mast repaired, and at sunset we weighed anchor, and proceeded down the straits. From the port in which we lay under the fortress, the sea seemed entirely inclosed by the land. The current here changed very much ; and we had noticed it three times in the course of the day. It was now in our favour, and we proceeded with a light breeze ; and in something more than an hour,. our carabokyri ran us aground on the shore of Bœotia opposite to Vathi, and soon after cast anchor. The Greeks are, in general, timid sailors ; and it is almost impossible to prevent them from anchoring during the night, except when they are in the middle of the ocean.

Oct. 14. — A light breeze from the west springing up before sunrise, we weighed anchor. Above Carysto rose, to a considerable height, the mountain of Elias. From the plains of Leucada, on the opposite coast of Bœotia, the country was broken into low hills with cultivated plains, and several towns were interspersed. We now sailed along the shore of Attica, rough, mountainous, and dotted with the Pinus pinea. On a projecting point, we discovered some ancient ruins called by our sailors Tavro Castro, perhaps the site of the ancient Rhamnus ; then followed the cape and bay of Agia Marina : the bay was a remarkably fine one. A wind from the north-east now sprung up, and at sunset we were between the main land of Attica and Macronesi. A small boat came off from the latter with some goatherds, who informed us, that the preceding day a corsair had taken a great vessel : our captain's eyes now pierced every creek ; and a considerable alarm arose on seeing two small vessels in the port of Therico. This part of the shore of Attica is extremely well supplied with harbours: our carabokyri enumerated them in the following order: Dragona, Rafti, Thaskalio, Mavro Mazzine, Agio Nicholas, Therico, Ergastéri *, Mandria, and last of all, nearest to Cape Colonna, Scouria, probably so called from the Scoria of the ancient silver mines of Attica, which were principally worked here, and traces of which we had seen in a former tour. In the dusk of the evening, we passed the celebrated Cape, and through a dim light distinguished the columns of the beautiful temple of Minerva Sunias; and turning round the promontory with a side-wind, we kept between the shore of Attica and the small island of Gaidaronesi: we were again alarmed, discovering a light coming out from the Cape: our candle was extinguished, that it might not direct the pirate to pursue us.

Oct. 15. — We dropped anchor at noon in the Port of the Piræus.

EXTRACT

FROM THE

JOURNAL OF THE LATE DR. SIBTHORP,

RELATING TO

PARTS OF THE ANCIENT ELIS, ARCADIA, ARGOLIS, LACONIA, MESSENIA, AND THE ISLANDS ON THE WESTERN SHORES OF GREECE.

Departure from Zante. — Arrival at the Harbour of Pyrgo in the Morea. — Alarms of Banditti. — Soil. — Plants. — Pyrgo. — Greek Physicians. — Lalla. — Military Appearance and Character of the Lalliotes. — Deveri. — Scenery of Arcadià. — Tripotamo. Arrival at Tripolizza. — Visit to the Pasha. — Argos.

FEBRUARY 26. 1795. — We embarked at Zante from the Mole, and with the wind in our favour, after a short but pleasant passage, anchored in something less than an hour in the harbour of Pyrgo, in

* The word Ergastéri has also a reference to the mines once worked in this spot.

the ancient Elis. We proceeded from our boat along a sandy beach covered with the shells of the Arca Glycymeris and Cardium edule, mixed with the spoils of other testacea, to the convent of the Panagía, about an hour's distance from the landing place. We found there few inhabitants; and the convent, whatever were its revenues, bore no marks of opulence: the frequent but unwelcome visits of the Turks and the fear of banditti kept it in constant alarm. We had scarcely laid ourselves down to repose, when we heard the firing of guns. A hut in the village, a few paces from the convent, consisting of about twenty wigwams of circular form, was attacked, and the first villager who came to its assistance was wounded with small shot. Every body was immediately under arms; and the alarm being given, the robbers made off with only some inconsiderable booty.

Feb. 27. — We waited in the morning expecting horses from Pyrgo. A caloyer attended me in a herborisation, and furnished me with the Greek names and the medicinal and superstitious uses of nearly 200 plants. Among the rocks composed of sandstone, abounding with petrifactions, in which the exuviæ of the greater Scallop and other pectines were very evident, we gathered the Globularia Alypum, highly ornamental with its lively blue flower : the Ricinus palma Christi grew by the walls of the convent. At the edges of the garden flowered the Iris tuberosa ; and we observed also crops of flax, objects of ancient cultivation in Elis. The Flora, though rich in the number of vernal flowers, was not so far advanced as at Zante. The amorous thrill of the green finch was now heard distinctly. The little owl hooted frequently round the walls of the convent. In the river below, otters were frequently taken. On the sides of the banks were the holes of the river crabs ; and the green-backed lizard was sporting among the grass.

At noon, horses and guards arrived from the Aga of Pyrgo ; and having dined upon a roasted lamb which was prepared for us by the Hegoumenos, we set forwards, and traversing a rich plain of argillaceous soil, reached Pyrgo in two hours. The depressed part of this plain was whitened over with the flowers of the Tazetta ; and our guides gathered nosegays of Manousáki, the name by which they distinguished this plant. Some marsh birds, the Curlew and the Moor Buzzard flew along the plain ; and the Magpie, which had not yet travelled so far as Zante, round the mud-built walls of the villages. Pyrgo is situated on a low hill : the town is new, and consists of 600 houses. We were received in a friendly manner by Georgáki; a steward of Said Aga, chieftain of Lalla. In the evening, we visited Husám Husaim, the Aga of Pyrgo. His principal favourite was a Zantiote, who, having tried various trades, was become the physician of the district of Pyrgo. A Moriote physician is, as it were, the privy counsellor of his Aga, and is most frequently the agent of his money matters. Contracts of marriage have been sometimes conducted by the mediation of these persons. A wild looking figure, but possessed of considerable powers of rustic eloquence, the physician to the Aga of Arcadià had just stopped the feuds between two most powerful chieftains in the Morea by planning a marriage between their families; and made them as warm friends as they had been inveterate enemies. The continent of Greece is principally furnished with physicians from Cephallonia ; and there is scarcely a town of note or an Agalick that is not supplied with one of these adventurers. In some places, the physician is paid the fixed salary of so many hundred piastres from the city chest : in the smaller Agalicks, he receives a certain sum from the district ; that of Pyrgo consists of ten towns and villages, and the physician is paid four hundred piastres; but his profits principally arise from presents, and his good offices with the Aga in favour of malefactors. The deportment of the Turks is lofty and imposing ; and the physician, from his constant attendance in the little court of the Aga, acquires some portion of the manner of his chieftain : to this he adds a confidence to which his medical skill certainly gives him pretensions. The physician of Arcadià had been a druggist's boy at Zante : he could neither read nor write : he had brought with him some empirical knowledge, and was highly extolled for the marvellous cures he had performed.

Mr. Hawkins had in a former tour acquired the friendship of the Aga, and he received us with marks of distinction : he proposed to us a party of hunting, and promised to entertain us with an Albanian dance.

Feb. 28. — I walked out with my gun, and crossed a rich plain towards the sea, over a flat tract of land. The lapwing and several grallæ flew piping along the marsh. On the banks of the river Milavla, I shot a ferruginous headed duck called by our host κοκκινοκέφαλο. I observed several water tortoises in the ponds of the pool. The season appeared here at least a fortnight less advanced than at Zante. Near the pools, the Salicornia grew plentifully ; and the gnats were so numerous, that I do not wonder the inhabitants of the banks of the Alpheus, from which we were not a mile distant, sacrificed to Jupiter the Fly-driver.

March 1. — We accepted the invitation of the Aga of Pyrgo to course with him : his greyhounds were of the Turkish breed, with long hairy curled tails. Some village curs, collected on the way, served as spaniels and finders ; and the Aga, with a long pole beating the bushes, supplied the want of vivacity in his dogs. On finding the hare, we crossed the plain to the village of St. George, situated on a low hill covered with mastic and prickly broom. The Greek frog perched on the branches of the mastic, and huge tortoises, of the size of those that Pausanias (in Arcad.) describes as employed by the ancient Greeks in the manufacture of musical instruments *, crept under the boughs. The high ground was not abundant in game ; and we started only a single hare. Changing our direction, we proceeded along the banks of a small rivulet covered with Asphodels ; the water hen flew frequently from under the bushes.

One of Said Aga's guards informing us of the return of his master to Lalla, we determined to set out the next morning for that place. In the evening we went, accompanied by our fat host Georgáki, to

---

* " The ancients might take promiscuously the land or river tortoise for this purpose." Phil. Trans. Ab. iv. 476. — E.

take leave of Husam Husaim: we were courteously received, but Husam expressed his chagrin at our leaving him so abruptly. He was attended by his secretary, his physician, and a Pyrgiote. Having drank coffee and smoked our pipes, Husam introduced wine; and the dragoman taking up his guitar, the physician and the Pyrgiote, warmed by drinking, leaped up to a mimic dance. The doctor showed considerable address with his heels, and raised them sometimes so high that they reached the ears of his partner. The dance, displaying the lowest buffoonery, was applauded by the Aga, who not having the fear of Mahomet before his eyes, took large draughts of wine. A French clerk to a mercantile house at Corone, entered and joined the dance. Georgáki now pulling off his upper tunic added himself to the number, and shaking his fat sides, increased the ludicrous appearance of the groupe. The Aga thought we participated with him in the pleasure of the dance and the music, which was accompanied with Turkish songs, forcing horrid screams and hideous faces. I could not help reflecting on the barbarism and ignorance that now reigned over a country once the most enlightened; and on the difference between these sottish orgies, and the noble games that attracted the ancient states of Greece to the plains of Olympia.

March 2. — We left Pyrgo at ten in the morning; and travelling over a rich plain, cultivated with vines, passed in about an hour by Berbasina, a village belonging to Said Aga. In something less than another hour we crossed the Arvoura, emptying itself into the Alpheus, which glided on our right through a rich plain enlivened with a profusion of various coloured Anemonies: leaving the plain, we entered a mountainous country, covered with the Sea Pine. We were detained some time by the breaking down of a bridge at Cracouchi; and from the obstinacy of our mules had considerable difficulty in fording a shallow stream that flowed along the torrent bed. As we advanced towards Lalla, the size of the mountains increased, and the Pine trees rose to a majestic height: many of them were disfigured by incisions made to draw forth the turpentine. The Pine added much to the beauty of the sylvan scenery, and was mixed

with Phillyrea, Heath, Arbutus, Kermes oaks, and Mastic. About
an hour's distance, under a round hill to our right, we left Olympia,
purposing to visit it at a future opportunity. A rising piece of
ground, near a hanging pine, opposite to a verdant knowl, on which
were the scattered huts of Stravokephalo, afforded us a dining place.
It was late in the evening when we arrived at Lalla. The military
appearance of the house of Said Aga was striking. A number of his
warriors * were reposing on the Divan, when we were introduced.
On the entrance of Said Aga they bow before their chieftain with the
greatest respect. Said received us with warm hospitality.

March 3. — Said, when we visited him the next morning, was
seated upon a carpet that was spread in the gallery of his house,
which was extremely mean, as the habitation of a powerful chieftain,
who could lead into the field of battle upwards of a thousand armed
men. The room in which we slept was the principal one in the
house : it had not even the comfort of glass in the windows : there
were only wooden shutters of such rude work that they were ill
calculated to resist the cold winds that swept the high, exposed plain
of Lalla. During the day we had severe storms of snow and hail,
and we crowded round the hearth, which was warmed with a good
fire. We visited Mustapha, the elder brother of Said, whose house
was now repairing, and were received in almost an open chamber.
Some of the principal Lalliotes were present, whose figure and dress
made a most martial appearance. Mustapha had a darker and more
saturnine complexion than his brother Said : the latter had an open
countenance, and more popular manners, and was supposed to possess
considerable personal courage, a character for which the Lalliotes are
in general renowned. Said had, a few years since, with four-and-forty

---

* In a letter to Mr. Wenman, Dr. Sibthorp mentions " the martial but ferocious life
of the Lalliotes. Lambs roasted whole are served on the table, and every one has his
fingers in the dish. The Lalliote is always clad in armour : when he dances he does not
lay aside his arms. His feet and legs are naked to the knees, which are covered with large
plates of silver. A breast-plate with embossed buttons protects his body. His pistols and
his dirk, richly ornamented, form constantly a part of his dress, being stuck in his girdle.".

of his followers, taken sixty Albanian rebels, and sent them to. Tri_
polizza, where they were executed ; and Ali Aga, one of our party,
a first cousin of Said, had, about a fortnight since, cut off the head of
a robber, and sent his straw-stuffed scalp to the Pasha. .The terror of
these people keeps the Morea in subjection : they were originally
little better than a band of robbers ; who adding to corporal strength
great courage, and inhabiting a country strongly fortified. by. nature,
resisted successfully the precarious and unequal attempts to subdue
them. In the invasion of the Morea, their services in repelling the
Russians were· rewarded with the grants of the lands.of the unhappy
Greeks : they were now increasing in opulence, which, by softening
the ferocity of their manners, will, perhaps, at the· same. time di-
minish that hardy courage for which these mountaineers have been
distinguished.

March —We set out at noon from Lalla, and in the evening
arrived at Deveri, five hours distant, and situated on the confines. of
Arcadia. Leaving Lalla, we traversed a high elevated plain, or rather
forest of oaks, Qu. Ægilops. Many of the young trees were lopped
for the goats to browse on, and the.beauty of the forest.was. sacrificed
to the care of the flock. The Polypody of the oak was no rarity : on
the faith of the ancients it was preserved for medicinal purposes: with
us it is seldom found growing on that tree ; but here it abounded.
The trunks of the oaks, besides the Polypody, furnished me with
some curious Lichens ; and a Boletus, whose under surface was tinged
with a fine violet colour. We arrived at Deveri by a mountainous
descent over rocks of slate covered with. Kermes oak and shrubs,
under whose shade blossomed the starry hyacinth. The Aga had
sent with us a guard of four Lalliótes : the appearance of an European
dress was new and striking, and the peasants collected round their
hóvels to gaze at us. We entered a low hut where we saw an .aged
woman, who had gathered some wild herbs for her supper : among
them I observed the leaves of the Dock, λάπαθο : the wild Poppy :
and the Charlock, λαπσάνα.

March   — We were detained at Deveri by waiting for horses.
I walked out with my gun, ascending some high mountains whose
sides were covered with the silver Fir.   On my return, I found the
Sturnus Cinclus on the banks of a rivulet fringed with willows.
Leaving Deveri, we descended a rocky precipice, crossed a stream,
and proceeded along a narrow glen, walled in by high mountains
covered with forest trees; and from the sides of which issued forth
cascades and purling rills.

The season was not sufficiently advanced at present to exhibit this
sylvan scenery in its full ornament.   The dead leaves which hung
upon the oaks, and the tops of the brooms, and other plants, were
cropped by the goats.   The violet and primrose flowered under the
hedges.   The vegetation was still backward : the pear tree, which in
Elis we had left in flower, scarcely yet opened its blossoms. *   The
early almond was covered with its rosy bloom.   Winding along a
narrow rocky road we arrived, in three hours, at Tripotamo : a junction
of two clear streams here formed three branches.   That this remarkable situation had not escaped the notice of the ancients was evident
from the ruins which we saw on its banks.   These were fringed by
huge Plane trees and Sallows, whose yellow catkins were now intermixed with the lively green of the tender leaf.   We crossed a stone
bridge of a single arch, and traversing a rich plain, occasionally interrupted by a mountainous tract of wooded land, in four hours arrived
at Xeropotamo.   About a mile to our right, was a high mountain
called Carsi.   In half an hour from Xeropotamo, we arrived at the
banks of the Alpheus, which ran violently with its muddy stream
along a rocky bed, and sometimes overflowing its banks, fertilised the
bordering plain.   Indian corn was the principal object of cultivation.
Over the Alpheus was a bridge.   Our road now lay through wooded
scenery and a well watered country.   It was said to be frequently infested by robbers ; and we were shown pits, in which they occasionally

---

* The " cold and heavy" climate of many of the cantons of Arcadia is mentioned by
Polybius, L. iv. 31. — E.

concealed themselves for the purpose of attacking the travelling mer-chant. It was late in the evening before we reached the khan destined for our lodging. We had frequent showers during the day, and towards the evening, settled rain; so that we arrived wet and cold. The khan presented to us a most comfortless aspect : a long chamber was lighted by the door-way, and a window pierced with numerous crevices ; and the failure of the stairs made the ascent both hazardous and difficult.

March —The guard furnished by Said Aga now took their leave, not before we were heartily tired of their company. Like savages, they wanted every thing they saw, and frequently disturbed us with their intrusive impertinence. We made them an offer of 20 piastres : this they refused with disdain ; and we were obliged to add to our present. Near our khan flowed a rivulet which abounded with trout: they were caught in the summer season with Cocculus Indicus, called ψαροβοτάνι, which was sold for this purpose in the bazar of Tripolizza. Leaving the khan, we entered the pass of Dara, and having travelled about three hours, left a lake a mile to our left. Proceeding over some rocky ground covered with low wood (under which the vernal crocus was blowing), we crossed the plain of Lebetha. The plough was now preparing the ground to receive the Indian corn, and turned up a rich loamy soil.

March 10. — Signor Marco, a Cephallonian, who was the city phy-sician, waited on us at Tripolizza ; and we arranged with him the plan of visiting the Pasha. Our consul, Strani, had sent us a letter of introduction ; and we carried one also from the dragoman of the Porte to the dragoman of Tripolizza. We proceeded to the palace of Mustapha Pasha ; and having first presented ourselves to the dragoman, and delivered him our papers, we were introduced to the Cacayabe, or prime minister of Mustapha. He received us with much politeness, sitting upon his divan in great state. From the Cacayabe's we proceeded through a long gallery to the Vizier, by whom we were also received in the most affable manner : we were invited to sit near him upon the divan, and were presented with coffee and sweetmeats. Mustapha, Pasha of the Morea, who is now about 50 years of age, has had the good fortune, from being a Georgian slave, to arrive at this high distinction. Being taken to Constantinople, he was brought up in the seraglio : was made a Pasha of three tails ; and, being a favourite, was married by the Grand Signor to his sister. His various attendants and officers are said to amount to a thousand persons. We had scarcely left the room of the Vizier, when numbers of them crowded round Signor Marco, and desired not to be forgotten : we sent our servant to distribute some money among them : in the evening the city musicians came for their Backshish.

March 11. — We made an excursion to Palaiepiscopi, the ancient Tegea, about five miles to the south of Tripolizza. A church of the early Greek architecture was built of brick, intermixed with the ruins of ancient temples ; among which we observed some inscriptions. Several excavations had lately been made to supply materials for a new mosque that had been erected at Tripolizza. Pieces of columns were scattered over the plain. The rain which had fallen very heavily during the night continued the greater part of the morning ; and prevented our further investigation : but the appearance of the ruins promised a productive field of research to the antiquary. Nothing, however, remained of that temple described by Pausanias as the most beautiful in the Peloponnesus. The plough was now furrowing up its foundation ; and green corn, among which flowered the Leontice, covered its ancient site.

March 13. — We went in the morning to take leave of our friend the dragoman ; when the Cacayabe, hearing that we were there, desired to see us. We were received in the most gracious manner ; and understanding that we were going to Argos, he ordered us to be furnished with horses at the Pasha's expense. We declined the offer, from the idea that it would occasion an Avanía on some poor Greek : the Cacayabe insisted on it ; and I had the pleasure of learning from Signor Marco that these horses were really paid for out of the Pasha's purse. While we were drinking coffee with the Cacayabe, the windows being opened, some swallows entered and flew round the room.' These birds arrive at the same time with the stork ; and if we may credit the observations of the modern Greeks, are even brought on the wings of these birds. How far this is true I know not; but a merchant at Zante, whose veracity I have no reason to suspect, assured me that in an early morning walk to the Acroterion, or promontory, near the town, he observed the approaches of a large white bird, which was covered with smaller ones ; and that as soon as it came near to the shore, he saw the small birds take wing and fly away. On our return home we were struck with the beauty of a remarkable fine steed, that was carrying water through the streets. He had been the favourite horse of the Pasha, but started one day while he was riding, and his turban falling off, the Pasha considered this as a bad omen, and punished the animal by degrading him to the office of water carrier. Though we had already given money to the servants of the Cacayabe and Vizier, we were beset again by the hungry satellites of the court; among the foremost of them was the buffoon of the Vizier. We felt very desirous to rid ourselves of their troublesome intrusion, and having taken leave of Signor Marco, who overwhelmed us with compliments, and added a hope that his services might be made known to the nation, we mounted our horses. The street was lined at our departure with female figures : among the youngest were some pretty faces ; but the decay of beauty in Greece, from the warmth of the climate and relaxation of the bath, is very rapid. Leaving Tripolizza, we crossed a fertile plain ; and having passed along a dry river bed on our right, we entered on a rough mountainous country, whose surface was covered with the thorny plants of the prickly spurge, the barnet, and the broom. We descended from this tract by a steep paved road cut out of the rock. On our left were the ruins of an ancient town, called by our guides Palaiomycle, in a high and almost inaccessible situation. About three hours from Tripolizza, we descended into a fruitful plain, and in about an hour more, found ourselves in a miserable khan. The room that had been accustomed to receive the weary traveller was now untenantable : the tiles were off the roof. We descended into a kitchen, but it was so pierced with air holes that we in vain attempted to keep our candle lighted. We retired into an adjoining chamber, where onions hanging in festoons formed the ornaments; and here we passed the night. A couple of guards, whom we met on the road, came to this place to spend a few paras, which we had given them. They lamented to us, in pathetic language, the severity of the Charatch, and the oppression of the Turks.

March 14. — We left our weather-beaten khan, and by a rough mountainous road continued our journey towards Argos. The country was barren, thinly wooded, and afforded some prickly shrubs for the goats to browse on: among these were interspersed Cretan-maples, and the Kermes oak, with scattered trees of arbutus, and a few andrachnes, which now began to open their flowers. We had a fine view of the bay of Argos, its island, the watch-tower, and port of Nauplia. Descending into the plain, we seemed to have passed into a new climate: the corn which grew rank in the rich soil was ready to produce its spikes; and a number of vernal plants were now flowering under its shelter. We passed a stream, the Kephalo, whose banks were decked with asphodels; and after five hours' ride we arrived at Argos.

March 15. — We waited the next morning on the Aga. In the court-yard the Turtur risorius was cooing: from the note, the Greeks have given this bird the name of Decoctouri, as the French have *Dix-huit* to our Lapwing. The Kirkenási, a hawk, very like our Kestril, flew screaming round the house; and the stork was busy in repairing his nest, to which he had returned about eight days since. We proceeded from the Aga's to a Greek church, to the south of the town. The walls were covered with Chrysanthemum coronarium, which began to open its golden blossoms: the Hypecoum, several species of toad flax, one of which adorns our parterres, and a number of Diadelphous plants, were flowering among the corn. It was a warm still day, and a number of insects were sporting in the air. I caught a beautiful species of Cantharis on the rich blue flower of the Alkanet; and a Chrysomela, with two spots, was feeding on the leaves of the wild pear.

The church being shut, we examined only its external walls, but found no inscriptions. Passing over a field covered with asphodels, we proceeded to the ruins of the theatre, under which are the remains of a temple supposed to have been that of Venus, mentioned by Pausanias. We were struck with the immense size of some of the stones that had formed the walls. The thick haze, which so frequently obscures the view in these climates, induced us to defer going up to the Acropolis: this place my friend intended to make a station for his geographical observations. On our return, being market-day, a number of villagers, bringing in the produce of their labours, had collected together: the women were sufficiently homely, and the men were simply clad with an outer garment lined with sheep's skin, the fleece turned inward. Argos had taken an active part in the late Russian war; and the ruins of numerous houses testified the resentment which the Turks had taken on the unfortunate town. Many of its inhabitants had fled, and others concealed themselves. This place shared, with the rest of the Morea, the general calamity of the plague, and lost, three years since, a great part of its population. It is one of the smaller Villaettis, and contains only twenty-four towns or villages within its district. If the Aga is oppressive, by means of money the Argians procure his removal; and the hope of a better master occasions frequent changes at the expense of the people. The small-pox was in the house where we lodged; and two children infected with it, were committed to the care of a Papás, and an adventurous son of Æsculapius, who had just emerged from a shop in Cephallonia. We counselled them to an exposure to the air, and the avoiding an accumulation of heat. *

---

* Dr. Sibthorp, in a letter to Mr. Wenman, mentions " his crossing the Bay of Argos from Napoli di Romania; and finding the famous lake of the Lernean hydra: this is composed of a number of mouths or sources, which are extremely clear and transparent. Like our blow-wells in the marshes of Lincolnshire, they are said to have no bottom. The white water lily, with the Riccia fluitans, was floating on the surface."

CHAPTER II.

Mistia. — Unsettled State of the Country. — Political Speculations of the Greeks. — Visit to Sclavo-chorio. — Singular Representations in Bas., elief. — Sparta. — Excursion to Ithome. — Wood of the Holy Cross. — Crown of Thorns. — Remains of Messene. — Beautiful Structure of some of the ancient Gates. — Corone. — Confinement and Concealment of the Turkish Women. — Turkish Wedding. — Embark at Corone. — Stations of the Turtle Doves. — Zantiote Sportsmen. — Cephallonia. — Marine Exuviæ. — Plants. — Coast of Ithaca. — Channel of Leucada. — Santa Maura. — Prevesa. — Fishery. — Anecdote of Count Carburi. — Ruins of Nicopolis. — Sail from Corfu. — Island of Fanno. — Plants and other Productions. — Mode of Farming in Zante. — Depraved State of Society in the Island under the Venetian Government.

APRIL 19. — We were hospitably received in the house of a Dutch Barratlee, who was preparing, from the unsettled state of property at Mistra, to proceed to Patras. We were here at something more than an hour's distance from Sparta ; but it was necessary to have a guard ; and that composed of Turks. It was the great Turkish festival of the first day of the Bairam : we were obliged therefore to defer our excursion to Sparta, and to engage the Vaivode to furnish us with a guard for the purpose the next day. We were visited by the Bishop and the Archons, deploring the miserable state of the subjugated Greeks : they persuaded themselves we were sent on some political mission, and formed various hopes from our arrival. The Proto-archon squeezed us cordially by the hand, and said he ventured now to raise up his head ; and felt a new beam of life. The Bishop had some learning ; a rare circumstance in a Greek diocesan. Hearing that the Vaivode had granted us an escort to conduct us the next day to Sparta, he begged he might be permitted to take advantage of it, and visit one of his parishes ; and such was the insecure state of property, that our host, who had lands in the neighbourhood of Sparta, had been deterred by the fear of robbers, for six months past, from visiting them ; while his property was suffering from the abuse of his tenants. Among the robbers the name of Zacharias stood first on the list : he had long bid defiance to the Turks, and either eluded or defeated the different troops which had been sent to take him prisoner. He treated the Turks who fell into his hands with great severity, murdering most of them. A sort of armistice took place between him and the Vaivode of Mistra; but this was insufficient for the safety of travellers who were not protected by a guard. of the Vaivode. In the evening I took a walk in the outskirts of the town, our host, who was my guide, not thinking it prudent to venture far beyond the walls. On the side of the road the water was conducted in wooden troughs, usefully serving a number of mills. I added to my herbarium an Antirrhinum, resembling Cymbalaria, but with woolly leaves, elegantly entwining the rocks.

April 20. — We set out for Sparta with ten guards, well armed, and attended by our host : the Bishop was prevented from accompanying us by some visits of ceremony he was expected to pay to the first Turkish families, making to their servants a kind of Easter-offering, the usual present at the Bairam. At something more than an hour we arrived at Sclavochorio. In a Greek church, near the altar-piece, were preserved two curious specimens of ancient sculpture*, representing the different articles relating to the dress of a Greek lady. Our Proto-archon recollected the Abbé Fourmont at Mistra : described his researches as expensive, and engaging a number of workmen. Many of the inscriptions which were dug up were covered again and left. The government of the town was then in the hands of the Greeks, who gave every assistance to the Abbé in his enquiries : the unfortunate success of the insurrection of the Morea had now enslaved them, and they possessed scarcely a nominal power. On our arrival, in a wall near the road, we observed several ancient fragments : one represented a chase, in which was the figure of a wild goat or Ibex. One of our guards, though a Turk, was well acquainted with the modern Greek names of several plants. From Sclavochorio we proceeded to Sparta, about two hours' distance. In addition to the theatre, we observed the remains of numerous build-

---

* Now in the possession of the Earl of Aberdeen. See the first volume of this work, p. 452. 2d edit.

ings on the low hills that rose on the plain, which was partly sown with corn : a ploughman with two lean steers, with difficulty turned up the soil, covered with stones and the ruins of buildings. The walls of several of them, raised of brick, were still remaining: we saw, however, no columns. The river which glided through the plain had frequently shifted its bed: willows and the Agnus Castus skirted its sides. We returned and spent the day at Mistra. I greatly regretted that I was not able to extend our tour throughout Maina : it was our intention to have visited the promontory of Tænarus, so famous for its marble; but it was infested by a lawless tribe of banditti, whose force is so formidable as to set even the orders of the Bey at defiance.

April 23. — We determined on making an excursion to Mount Ithome ; and setting out from Kutchuk Maina in the afternoon, after a ride of something more than three hours over a rich plain, watered by the Pamisus, now called Agio Florio, we ascended the mountain of Vulkano, and arrived at the convent. The Hegoumenos, who had read Meletius, offered himself as our guide, and promised in the morning to conduct us to the ruins of Messene. He was a great polemic ; and to show his knowledge of theology, contended that our Saviour's cross was made of three sorts of wood, of cypress, of cedar, and of pine. * This idea was probably founded on the Greek verse of the octoechos, ἐκ κυπαρισσιας καὶ πευκη, καὶ κεδρο, κ.·τ. λ., which is chanted in the Greek churches on Good Friday. The thorny crown, according to this sage monk, was formed of the Smilax aspera : I shall leave the botanical theologists to contend with him in favour of the Paliurus and the Spina Christi. I herborised in the evening, round the monastery, in the garden rank with weeds. The sides of the mountain offered me some curious plants : among others, the little Anthyllis figured by Girard in his Flora Gallo-provincialis ;

---

* Sandys records another opinion held on this subject by some of the Christians of the East. " The cross was formed, as they report, of four several woods, the foot of cedar, the bole of cypress, the transome of palm, and the title of olive." 144. — E.

but botany slept; and such was the profound ignorance of the caloyers, that they were unacquainted with the most common names of the most common plants.

April 24. — We proceeded from the convent up the mountain, conducted by our Hegoumenos : in half an hour we came to the ruins of an ancient gateway : ascending higher up, on the summit of Ithome we found the remains of the walls of the ancient Acropolis. From this height, we commanded a rich and extensive view of the fertile plain of Messenia, watered by the Pamisus, and walled in by Taygetus and a high range of mountains. The descent to the city walls was extremely rough; and Ithome, though far from the highest, is one of the steepest and most rugged mountains of the Peloponnesus. The purple flax, and the red Crepis which is the ornament of our parterres, with the Catananche lutea, were flowering on its summit. The silver fir, characteristic of the higher regions of Greece, was wanting; the rocks were covered with mastic, broom, and low shrubs, browsed by the goats. The Wheat-ear, a bird of passage, flew among the ruins. The small village of Mavromati is within the enceinte of the ancient walls. While we roasted a lamb, a number of squalid female figures, who were washing at the fountain, assembled round us, offering a number of coins that had been found in the ruins. Having dined under the shade of a huge walnut-tree, we proceeded to a gateway composed of immense stones : it was extremely well preserved, and of a circular form : one on the road, leading to the Acropolis, may be considered among the finest remains of the architecture of the ancients, and a proof of the extraordinary mechanism with which they moved enormous masses of stone to their buildings. These stones formed by the chissel were accurately fitted to each other ; as no mortar was used in the walls, this exactness of position was more strictly attended to. We saw no inscriptions; but a number of fragments of columns were scattered over the area of the ancient town, now sown with corn. Among the marbles was an alto relievo representing a chase, in which the figure of a lion was preserved. Several fragments were found in the walls of the Greek churches. From

N 2

Mavromati, we proceeded to Nisi, leaving Andrusa, a Turkish town, about half a mile on our right, and met with a very hospitable reception at the house of the Venetian consul. I was here ·visited by a Corsican physician, who pressed me to several consultations.· A basket of Truffles was brought to me, in which my host distinguished three sorts. Lent, is ·the season when· the greatest numbers are found. The diet of the Greeks at that season is very generally drawn from the vegetable kingdom, and the Truffle becomes then an object of considerable importance.

April 25.. — .When advice is to be had gratis, invalids are always found. My good host had consulted me the preceding evening : I was in the morning drawn into a consultation for the wife and daughter. Female complaints are more frequent in Greece than in the rest of Europe ;· much of this is owing to the confinement of the women, and that want of exercise which enervates the system. The hysterical complaints of my two patients were owing to these causes. From Nisi, we had a journey of seven hours to Corone : our road conducted us chiefly along the beach : the rocks were covered with Cistus : patches of corn were spread over the vales, and rich olive grounds·extended to Corone. On our way we passed by some ruins at Petalida. We had been warmly recommended to the Bey, who received us on the beach in an elegant kiosk built in the Chinese fashion. The Bey himself was learned for a Turk : he had some knowledge of Astronomy, Mathematics, and Architecture : his brother was Disdar or commander of the castle. The kiosk was at our disposal, and the Bey had provided ·for· us 'an elegant supper. It was served in the European manner, with tables, chairs, and Staffordshire ware, luxuries we had not seen before in a Turkish house. The' waves beat gently along the walls of our kiosk, and brought on a soft and comfortable repose.

April 26. — In the morning, the approach of the Venetian brig was announced to us : it was returning from an unsuccessful·cruise against the pirates on the coast of Maina. A reward of 1000 piastres, was offered to a Mainote chief, who promised ·either to shoot or secure the person of the pirate. The wind was contrary; and notwithstanding our impatience to embark, we were detained at Corone. We were visited by the bishop and by Mr. Thibaut, who, attached to the royal cause, had disdained to accept his office under the Republic, and sought protection from the British embassy. The violence of party disturbed the repose, and broke the union which should subsist between merchants of the same nation in a foreign country. The Bey was extremely anxious to receive my advice for his son, a youth of eighteen, and for his wife. The latter wished personally to consult me; but the jealousy of the Bey was an objection not to be overcome. She sent me the account of her case by a lady of her acquaintance, and the physician·was charged .by the Bey to give me the details : his information, however, was very imperfect: he had not seen the lady, and felt her pulse only through a piece of muslin thrown over the hand. The Turkish women carefully conceal the face : none but the husband has the privilege of seeing it : the exposure of it would be considered as the prostitution of the person. The Turkish women, whom we saw on the roads, had their faces muffled up ; and when they met us, they either turned themselves away, or stood behind a tree until we passed.

The residence and society of the French merchants at Corone had a considerable influence in softening the manners of the Turks. We went in the evening to visit M. Thibaut, who with his lady, a Parisian, bore their adverse fortune with a resignation which did them honour. M. T. had been consul in Egypt, and made a small collection of gems : among them was a Leander, much admired by the author of Anacharsis; and a Leda, which he parted with to my friend Hawkins. M. T. had extracted from Lemery the names of some simples and drugs ; and his knowledge placed him at least upon a level with the Greek doctors. He expressed himself at a loss, not being able to get the Hypocistis : I consoled him by giving my opinion, that the composition would not be hurt by the omission of that ingredient. We passed our evening pleasantly at his house; his lady, with much vivacity, entertaining us with an account of the buffoonery she had seen at a Turkish marriage. Indecent dancing, and music performed by women, furnished the principal parts of the entertainment ; when the bride veiled, and crowned with sequins, was led into the room, and kneeling before the mother of the bridegroom, receives his presents and those of his friends. It was already midnight, when the Captain of the Merope summoned us aboard: the janisaries of the Bey were waiting to conduct us to the shore, where we found the launch, and embarking in it, we went on board the brig. We looked in vain for the comfortable neatness of the English cabin ; and our sleep was disturbed by the numerous insects which preyed upon us.

April 27. — We had in the night advanced so far out, that we had cleared Cape Gallo, and the appearance of the weather, which was thick and hazy, flattered us with the hopes of a Sirocco wind. The haze, however, went off as the day advanced, and instead of a Sirocco, the calm was succeeded by a contrary wind from the west.

April 28. — We steered our course towards the Strophades : it was our intention to have landed and spent a day here ; but it now blew so fresh, that the landing in our boat would have been difficult and dangerous. A nobleman of Zante, Count Nicholas Logotheti, was considerably alarmed : his fears produced frequent vows to the Panagia to favour our escape. We left the island of the Harpies about a mile distant, and proceeded in our course towards Zante ; but the wind falling in the evening, we found ourselves at about five leagues from that island at sunset. In the course of the day several turtle-doves flew by the vessel ; and a species of Motacilla, pitching upon the cordage, was caught by the hands of one of our sailors. The islands of the Strophades are low and flat; peopled by a monastery of Caloyers : they are occasionally visited by Zantiote sportsmen, as they are a noted station for the turtle-doves in their passage. The Count Nicholetto was here to have joined a party who came with that intention from Zante.

April 29. — Early in the morning we were near the shore of the island ; when a contrary wind springing up, we went in the launch to Cape Basilico : here Anthonio Camouta Cornaro, and Count Antonio

Logotheti, and a party, had collected for the purpose of shooting turtle-doves. We dined with our friends at the convent ; and in the evening, procuring mules, we proceeded to the town. Zante now appeared with extraordinary beauty : the olive-trees were covered with flower ; the corn already producing its spike, promised a rich and speedy harvest. The chase was not here the reward of indefatigable labour ; the Zantiote nobleman enjoying luxurious ease, had his arms carried by a servant ; and softly reposing in an elbow-chair, under a spreading olive-tree, expected the arrival of the turtle-doves. Books of amusement, the social conversation of friends, gentle exercise, provoked an appetite which all the science of Apicius was employed to satisfy. The liver of the Scarus * was not forgotten ; and the critical moment of sacrifice was strongly and eagerly debated. The philosophy of Epicurus finds here many disciples ; and the pursuit of the Summum Bonum is only occasionally arrested by the alarming reports of earthquakes and apoplexies.

May 1. — I took an affectionate leave of the house of our worthy consul, who accompanied me at day-break with my friend Hawkins to the Caique. As we rowed along the beach, we were saluted by them with many Καλὰ κατεβόδια †, and I contemplated with pleasure the shore where I had experienced the warmth of so much hospitality. We had made little way with our oars, when the wind, which was contrary, strengthening, obliged us to put into a small port, distinguished by the name of Gaidaros. Our bark lay here sheltered from the westerly winds. We landed, and walking along the shore I made some additions to the Zantiote Flora. The olives were now covered with blossoms ; and the fruit well formed on the stalk of the asphodel, promised an abundant harvest. At sunset the wind sunk, and after a few hours, our sailors having reposed, ventured on with their oars.

May 2. — A light westerly wind springing up in the morning, we advanced considerably before our gun-boat, by which we had been

---

* See the first volume of this work, p. 286.
† Κατεύοδια, ." buon viaggio." Sommavera. — E.

escorted, on account of the alarm of pirates.   At ten we dropt anchor in a small port called Scala, in the island of Cephallonia.   On the fragments of sand-stone, separated from the rock, I noticed the exuviæ of Pectines, Gaideropi, and other shells.   Above the port was the town of Scala, and behind it rose Mount Eláto, thinly clad with pines.   It was formerly covered with wood; but the Venetian government exacting much gratuitous service from the inhabitants, in felling and drawing the timber for public service, excited such discontent, that to rid themselves of the onus, certain persons set fire to the wood, and consumed a considerable number of the trees.   We landed near a watch-tower, which served in time of plague as a guard-house.   The rocks on the shore were covered with cistus and the flowering heath, and the thyme of the ancients.   Among these shrubs I noticed the Emb. Melanocephalus, which arrives with the turtles : it is confounded with the ortolan called Ampelourgos.   I picked up but few plants on the beach : the rarer ones were the night-flowering Silene, and a species of Ononis ; and a little Gypsophila was in flower among the bushes.   In the evening we weighed anchor, and advanced with our oars along the shore, bold, naked, and rocky.   The Magistral wind blowing strong, we dropped anchor under the lee of some projecting rocks.

May 3. — We proceeded slowly in the morning under the shore with our oars, taking in water on the stony beach of Port Poros : our sailors dug a hole in the sand, and the water, with a slight brackish taste, rose within a few feet of the sea.   The chasm in the rocks served as a passage to a vale, on which, according to the tradition of our mariners, once stood a large and populous city.   At two in the afternoon, we doubled Cape John, the south-east point of Ithaca.   The island affords several good ports : we dropped anchor in that of Skino.   To our left was the harbour of Vathi, which is the chief town in the island.   The rocks on the shore make the navigation dangerous : they appeared to be composed of a white friable lime-stone.   I saw a number of maritime plants : the Cineraria maritima, the Stæhelina chamæpeuce, &c.   The hills were white with the flowers of the

Caucalis : I gathered on them another umbelliferous plant, with a five-divided leaf, which appeared a species of Athamanta.

May 4. — We weighed anchor in the morning, the weather being calm, and continued our course with our oars : we passed by Chione, a village situated in a recess near the shore. Several islands were in view : among these Calamo, renowned for the excellence of its corn, which is esteemed the best in the Levant. We passed by a narrow entrance into a channel formed by the main land of Romelia and Leucada. In the evening, the wind being contrary, we dropped anchor under the small island of Madoura. I was pleased to see the garden lily growing, abundantly, wild among the rocks ; but I suspected it was not the original habitat ; and upon enquiry I found that it had been planted by the proprietor of the island about forty years since ; but alarmed with the fear of robbers from its vicinity to Turkey, he had left the place. The island offered a rich crop of corn, intermixed with flourishing olive trees now abounding with flowers.

May 5. — It being calm in the morning, we proceeded with oars to Santa Maura : a number of Monoxyla, the hollowed trunks of an oak, called Δρῦς *, and small boats laden with fish were rowing to the town. We hailed several of them, and made different purchases : they had caught a sort of Scomber, called by the Greeks γοπέω, by the Italians goplico; plenty of soles, and grey mullet. From the fishermen I procured a kind of crab with a large caudal spot, called Carrochio. The muddy bottom of the canal furnishing a favourable feeding-place, Santa Maura is well supplied with that article. We visited on our arrival the Proveditore Extraordinary, who gave us a polite reception. Leucada contains about 16,000 inhabitants, and 34 inhabited towns. Santa Maura, the capital, has the air of a Turkish town : the streets narrow, and the little attention paid by

---

* " Le nom que l'on donne à ces bateaux exprime bien l'étoffe et la manière dont ils sont batis ; car Monoxylon en Grec veut dire qu'ils sont faits d'une seule pièce de bois. Ce nom de Monoxyla n'est pas inconnu à Hesychius, qui dit que les Cypriots appelloient aussi ces bateaux ἄδρυα. Α. πλοῖα μονόξυλα, Κύπριοι." Spon. Voyage 1. — E.

the police to cleanliness, the offensiveness of the stagnant water in the canals of the street, joined to its low situation, and the salines, must render it unhealthy, particularly during the summer season. A strong fortress commanded the channel; and a bridge of upwards of 300 arches connects the town to the citadel. The bridge, which is narrow, is of Turkish structure, originally intended for an aqueduct. The principal produce of the island is oil and corn : it is larger than Zante ; but greatly inferior in point of population and produce. The cultivation of the currant-grape has in vain been attempted. The salines near the town are an important object of revenue ; and several vessels were taking in cargoes of salt. The produce of a fishery in the vicinity of the town is considerable. Near it women were busy in collecting marsh-samphire : they eat it both raw and as a· pot-herb ; and call it armoríthra. Baskets of the heads of wild artichokes were standing in the street for sale ; and were sold thirty for a para.

May 6. — Our boat having been unloaded, and pushed over the shallows with the aid of men, who waded in the water, we embarked in another of a lighter construction, and joined it. The water in several places was not two feet deep, and the distance from shore to shore in some places not half a mile. The Magistral blowing fresh, we were induced to put into Prevesa, about ten miles distant from the town of Santa Maura. On our landing we were struck with the bizarre appearance of the mixture of Venetian and Turkish manners. A considerable quantity of shell-fish were taken in the bay for sale : amongst them were Pinna marina, πίννα ; Gaideropus, γαιδερόπος ; Arca Noæ, σπεττονίκιας ; Solen, σουλινάρι, and the large Scallop, or *Capo Santa.* At Santa Maura I saw several of the exuviæ of the Venus, called Pιx- τίαις. Prevesa is said to consist of 3000 houses, without any par- ticular manufacture : the population is large ; and the place serves as the port of exportation for much of the produce of Romelia. The situation of the town is flat, low, and particularly during the summer season must be considered as unhealthy.

May 7. — A contrary wind detained us at Prevesa. Intending to see Nicopolis, we visited in the morning the captain of the guard, requesting the favour of an escort. He was the cavalier servente of a French lady who had been married to Carburi, one of the most active and enterprising spirits of modern Greece ; and who had fallen an untimely sacrifice to the jealousy of the Cephallonians, by the hands of some Albanians, whom he employed as labourers. He had eminently distinguished himself by his knowledge of mechanics ; and by the conveyance of that immense mass of granite *, out of which the famous statue of Peter the Great was worked. Influenced by a strong desire of improvement, he had obtained from the republic of Venice the grant of certain lands in Cephallonia, and had here successfully introduced the culture of indigo ; and was naturalising the products of India, when the resentment of certain persons, stimulated by other Cephallonians, who had formerly enjoyed the feed of the waste granted to Carburi, occasioned his massacre. The reformer in this unhappy country, where the person is not sufficiently protected by the laws from the knife of the assassin, is a character attended with much danger. On our return from Nicopolis, we passed by the warehouse and the docks of a French merchant, who, favoured by Ali Pasha, was carrying on the exportation of timber to Touloñ on a large scale, when he was sacrificed by some Albanians to the jealousy of the inhabitants of Prevesa. We made an excursion in the afternoon to the ruins of Nicopolis : the road was over a plain of rich loamy sand, with patches of corn and olive grounds ; but the culture of it, in general, much neglected. The territory of the republic is here very limited, not extending more than an hour beyond the town. Arriving at Nicopolis, we were shown an oak tree, which is in this place the boundary mark. The ruins are very considerable and

---

* The foundation of the statue of Peter the Great, erected at Petersburgh by Catherine II. is composed of a boulder or detached block of granite, found in a bay of the gulf of Finland, whence it was transported to the capital. *Relation par le Comte Marin Carburi de Cephallonie.* Brande's Lectures. — E.

extensive; and the broken walls, built of brick, encompass a large circuit, now covered with luxuriant crops of corn. There are considerable remains of a theatre, with the arched way or piazza round it. I gathered on the walls of it the Asplenium Hemionitis: within the enceinte of them, and near the gateway, I observed the Celtis australis, called Μελικόκκυα. We saw remains of aqueducts and baths, but observed no inscriptions. I was shown some granite pillars, with Ionic and Corinthian capitals; and a large frize, which serves at present as the decoration of a fountain. The situation of Nicopolis, on a gentle rise approaching the mountains, commanding Actium and the Gulf of Arta, is beautiful and striking; and the extent of the remains are evidence of its former magnificence. The plough is continually turning up ancient ornaments or memorials. I saw several gems; and large collections of coins have been made within its ruins. Palæocastro is not more than an hour from Prevesa. We returned along the beach to the house and garden of the unfortunate Frenchman. The want of personal security is such, that the republic permits the general use of arms here to all its subjects. The sword of justice is kept sheathed; and every man depends on the strength of his own arm, or that of his friend, for protection. Even the immediate vicinity of the town is considered as insecure; and the neighbouring Turks are characterised as bands of robbers.

.We left Prevesa before day-light, and dropped anchor two hours before sunset in the port of Corfu. The approach to the town was very striking: the coast covered with groves of olive trees. Oil is the principal produce of the island, and both the quantity and quality of it are superior to that made in the other islands. The produce of last year's oil was valued at 500,000 pounds sterling. Corfu, in point of soil, is the richest of all of them: it is peculiarly suited to the culture of the olive; but the Corinthian grape does not succeed here. The olive is left to maturate upon the tree; nor is the juice expressed until the fruit is fully ripe. At Zante the olive is gathered green, and preserved with salt, which communicates to the oil a bad flavour.

May 11. — We sailed. in the morning with a favourable wind: it freshened, and obliged us to make for the little island of Fanno. In approaching the shore, we were stranded among the rocks : a small boat, fortunately lying at anchor in a cove, rowed to our assistance. We lightened our vessel by embarking in it our baggage ; and the sailors wading in the water, with the assistance of the crew of the other boat, at length cleared our caïque, and brought her into the cove. It blew hard in the evening ; and we accepted the invitation of a Greek Papás to sleep at his dormitory, a large cheerless magazine near the shore ; a table and a few broken chairs its only furniture ; the roof in many places untiled.

May 12, 13, 14, 15. — We made various attempts to leave the island, but the Magistral wind forced us to return. We disembarked our beds again, and sought our miserable magazine for shelter. I amused myself with shooting some turtle-doves and rock-pigeons that were now on their passage. The evening was still. The Melba, the Marten, and the house Swallow were sailing in the air in pursuit of insects. A number of the Scarabæus Solstitialis buzzed round the olive-trees which were now covered with flowers : a goatsucker, hovering over them, caught several ; and a little flycatcher, darting frequently, preyed upon the lesser insects. The island of Fanno is mountainous, and the rocks are composed of a white dense marble : the vales present a light sandy soil : the circuit is about twelve miles, and contains about 114 scattered houses. A noble Venetian, of the name of Cornaro, is the proprietor. Wine is the principal produce, and barley, which is of that species called by the botanists Hexastichon, and by the Greeks Hexagono ; of this they make their bread. A few olive-grounds, with the culture of oats and leguminous plants, supply the wants of the inhabitants. It is distant about eighty miles from Otranto ; and small boats are frequently obliged to wait here several days for a favourable wind. Another vessel, the companion of our misfortunes, that was laden with tortoises, and steeiing the same course, was obliged to return back, and seek for shelter in the port.

. May 16. — The Magistral blew fresh. I lessened the pain of confinement by herborising and reading. The rocks were covered with the Asperula Calabrica, which the inhabitants called Αλεπουπόυρδι, and with its elegant purple flowers made a showy appearance. The Stæhelina chamæpeuce, the Conyza candida, and saxatilis, the Campanula pyramidalis and Gnaphalium Stœchas angustifol., grew on the rocks along the coast. Low Mastics and Myrtles, mixed with wild Thyme and Cytisus, covered the uncultivated hills, and on the side of the torrent bed grew the Agnus castus : it is here called ἄγνος, one of its ancient names ; and in Zante, λυγεια, corrupted from λύγος ; and at Athens, κανναπίττα. The best illustration of the ancient botanists would be by a vocabulary of the provincial or insular names used in the different parts of Greece : this is a work of time, and demands a long residence in the country. Near our miserable dormitory grew a great quantity of the Coch. Coronopus ; the islanders collected it as a pot herb, and called it κουρουνοπόδι. Dioscorides informs us it was eaten, and that it grew in situations, similar to that where we found it. Among the leguminous plants, I observed the cultivated Pea and the Pisum ochrus : the one is called μπίσι, the other ἄυχος * ; the Lathyrus, λαθώρι, and the Lentil, φάκι.

. May 17. — The Magistral wind continued to blow with violence, and we were still obliged to bear the ennui of Fanno. Our rest was disturbed by a small gnat, called by the Greeks τζουκτήρα, the co-inhabitant of our miserable granary, and which inflamed our hands and face with prurient tumours. In the afternoon, I ascended one of the higher mountains, and descried the coast of Italy covered with a thick haze. On some rocks at a distance from the sea, I observed the Lichen Roccella †, and growing in such abundance, that it might form a valuable article of commerce. In the evening, my com-

---

* περὶ φασόυλου καὶ ἄυχου.　An. Med. Du. C. App. ad. Gl. in v. A. — E.

† The φῦκος θαλάσσιον or πόντιον of Theophrastus and Dioscorides. It grew also on the rocks of Crete. It was used in their time for dyeing wool. Tournefort found it in Amorgos. Beckmann Hist. Inv. 1. — E.

panions made their supper on boiled fennel. The Greeks temperate their salt diet with the copious use of wild herbs, and in the Greek pottage enter a number of vegetable ingredients neglected in the rest of Europe. * We had supped before on the leaves of the Picris Echioides, called χοιροβοτάνον, and some sailors on the beach were preparing their mess composed of charlock, λαπσάνη. Scorp. Picroides, τοῦ λάγου τό ψωμὶ, and πικρολίδι, Succory. At Zante, a number of women gain a subsistence by collecting the ἄγρια λάχανα, and bringing them to market.

May 18. — My companions were now become outrageous with the obstinate continuance of the Magistral, and talked of returning to Zante: one, almost despondent, made frequent vows; another, who bore his exile with more philosophy, favoured me with his system of farming at Zante. He had a flock of sheep, a vineyard, olive grounds, a fruit garden, more arable acres than supplied his house with corn. His flock of sheep, which consisted of 200, were let to a tenant or colléga, who was (whatever accidents might happen) to be responsible, and to keep up the number of his flock, and pay to the proprietor 600 pounds weight annually of cheese, 100 pounds weight of wool, and 16 lambs, besides two fat lambs, one at the Carnival, the other at Easter: these were to be fattened with more than common care, by being fed on milk. He had a certain number of cows that were kept for breeding: the milk of these was, however, entirely destined for the nourishment of the calf: half of the profits of this calf belonged to the proprietor; the other half was that of the colléga for his care and attention in feeding it. He had also several labouring oxen which were worked by the colléga, on condition of his

---

* Extract from a letter of Dr. Sibthorp to Mr. Wenman: — " I wish to tell our poor people that they may collect many a dish from our corn fields. Our charlock will furnish them with an excellent pot herb called by the Greeks λαπσάνη: that Tordylium which grows in the parks is, I believe, the ancient Caucalis, as it is now called καυκαλίνα, and the leaves of it are eaten both raw and boiled; and to quiet the fears of our good people about the water parsnep, mistaken for water cresses, I have often seen the Greeks eat whole bunches of it (Sium nodiflorum) as a sallad, with impunity."

paying three baccilli or measures of wheat for each ox. The corn was divided into equal shares, half to the proprietor, the other half to the colléga. The olives were estimated by two appraisers chosen, the one by the proprietor, the other by this colléga. The valuation was then made, and three-fifths of the olives allotted to the former. My Zantiote acted candidly, and allowed his tenants to make the full value of their portion : other landlords have a most iniquitous way of obliging them to sell their oil to them at an under price, which is sometimes so low as to take away all the profits of labour : others ruin the colléga again by advancing him money at a high interest. The expense of preparing the crop is made by the colléga ; and to supply the wants of his tenant, our Zantiote furnished him with the necessary money at ten per cent. This, in an island where the interest of money is high, at twenty or even thirty per cent., may be considered as moderate. The oil of Zante, being pressed from green olives, is of an inferior quality : the reason assigned for this practice is, that if the olives were left to ripen on the trees, they would be stolen, and justice here is only procured by expenses, and seldom fairly administered. He who pays the proveditor best is almost sure of a decision in his favour ; and though there are appeals from his decision, the distance from Venice, the chicanery of lawyers, and the length of the suit, are circumstances of a most forbidding kind, and the defendant frequently sits down consoling himself with his first loss.

The great object of the republic of Venice is to provide for its poor nobility. Some are sent as proveditors or governors to the different islands and colonies belonging to the republic. The proveditor of Zante exercises his office for three years, and at the end of this period carries off a sum from six to twenty thousand sequins : part of this is made by fines or liberation money ; that is, the money paid in order that a criminal may escape from prison ; and the Zantiote, not finding the sword of justice lodged in the hands of an active government, becomes his own executioner, and ferocious with a vindictive spirit, makes no distinction in the measure of crimes ; hence the number of massacres that disgrace the island, and carry off the flower of the

Zantiote youth.   So low is the estimate of murder, that thirty piastres are considered as the price of blood.. . " I would shoot you," said one Zantiote to another, " had I thirty piastres to pay for your skin." During my stay at Zante, a notorious bravo of the name of Gallani, who had fouled his hands with ten murders, walked the street with impunity.   Some of these murders he had committed in the public square at noon-day.   I had seen him a temporary fugitive in the Morea, just escaped from the hands of the Lalliotes; who were going to murder him : he was then in a penitential mood, vowing to leave his wicked courses, and to turn monk, and pass five years as a caloyero at the Strophades.   I said to him that the least he could do was to spend as many years in repentance as he had committed murders. " I must then double the time," said Gallani, very coolly.   These vows were, however, soon forgotten ; and on my arrival at Zante, I learned that Gallani had returned, and committed a fresh murder. During my stay at Zante, I heard frequently the discharge of fire-arms in the streets, and was informed of several murders.   The idea of consumption being contagious, is very prevalent at Zante.   A sick person accidentally discovered that his brother had died of a con-sumption, and the malady had been carefully concealed from him by the doctor.   The patient enraged at the supposition of his having caught the disorder from his brother, in consequence of not being advised of it, loaded his pistols, and when the doctor, in one of his visits, approached the bed-side of his patient, the latter discharged the contents into his body.   This happened while the philanthropic Howard was at Zante, who was shocked with horror at the scene.

May 20. — The Magistral sinking in its force during the night, we were tempted early in the morning to row out of the harbour.   The attempt was ineffectual : the wind beginning to blow fresh, we turned our helm, and sheltered ourselves under the lee of some rocks, which were broken into steep and craggy precipices, affording a breeding-place to the falcon.   A pretty Dianthus, now in flower, grew in the cleft ; and great abundance of Samphire, which our sailors gathered as a pot herb.   The waves of the sea, beating against the rocks, had worked out a number of subterraneous cells, the lodgings of the phoca, or sea calf. In the evening we returned to the port.

May 22, 23, 24. — A cloud that rose from the island augured a sirocco wind; and having paid our Papás for his prayers and miserable cell, all joyous at the favourable omen, we embarked for Otranto. ,A light gentle sirocco carried us out of the port, but gradually sinking into a calm, our mariners took to their oars: we continued rowing with little intermission; but it was not till two hours after midnight that we anchored at Otranto.

JOURNEY FROM CONSTANTINOPLE, THROUGH ASIA MINOR, IN THE YEAR 1802.

[FROM THE PAPERS OF THE LATE WILLIAM GEORGE BROWNE, ESQ.]

CHAPTER I.

Nicomedia. — Kara Mursal — Journey thence to Broussa. — Lake of Nicæa. — Bazarkué. — Description of Broussa. — Baths. — Environs. — Character of the Inhabitants. — Conflagration in 1801. — Population of the City. — Silk. — Armenians and their Bishop. — Mount Olympus. — Journey to Toushánlu; thence to Kutaieh. — Afiún-kara-hissar. — Ak-shehr. — Elghin. — Koniéh. — Mewlawi Derwishes. — Manufactures.

I LEFT Constantinople early in the month of June, and proceeded to Nicomedia. The towns of Scudar, Cartal, Gebisé, and Nicomedia, being so near the Capital, and on a very frequented road, are populous, and supplied with various kinds of provisions, and all articles of ordinary consumption. The soil between Scudar and Ismit is light and productive; furnishing large crops of barley, (some of which was then ripe, 20th June,) and also of rye, onions, and lentils : but there was no appearance of wheat. I observed some fruit-trees near the towns and villages. Part of the soil is rocky; part consists of clay, with chalk at intervals.

Nicomedia is governed by a Pasha of two tails. Being on the high road to Kutaieh, the caravans from the east and south-east are continually passing through that city: but I found it difficult to procure a conveyance to Broussa, with which Nicomedia has no regular or frequent communication. I therefore proceeded in a boat to Kara Mursal; a small town, containing two moderately-sized mosques, on the south coast of the gulf, and agreeably situated under a ridge of hills. Its vicinity abounds in fruit-trees, which furnish large supplies to the markets of Constantinople.

Kurûn-kué, and some other villages, are seen on the coast a little east of it: a few miles to the west is Hersek, a wretched place, but frequented by travellers between Broussa, Yenishehr, and the Capital, on account of its ferry; this being the narrowest part of the gulf. The price of the ferry, whether for one person or for a large company, is six piastres and a half. We were about three hours in reaching Kara Mursal from Nicomedia. The conveyance from the former place to Broussa was far from convenient; for though the animals on which we were mounted were active and well fed, yet the horses and mules were furnished indiscriminately with a pack-saddle and halter, and were without bridles. Having advanced along the coast for nearly three hours, we ascended the mountain by a ravine or narrow road, a little to the east of the principal route, which leads through Kezderbend and Nicæa, but which is reckoned somewhat longer. From the summit of this ridge, which is calcareous and pretty lofty, we enjoyed, soon after sunrise, an extensive and commanding view of the country on both sides of the gulf of Nicomedia, almost to its mouth; and on the other, of the still snow-capped Olympus and the lake of Nicæa.

It is from these elevations that the traveller may observe how small a proportion the cultivated soil bears to that which lies waste. Yet in this quarter the motives that excite to activity, industry and good cultivation, are more powerful, and the tracts of neglected surface much less extensive than in other parts of Anatolia. The soil seems well adapted to the growth of corn; and the mountain is covered with low-wood, extremely luxuriant in foliage, and altogether very beautiful. The wood consists, for the most part, of oak, intermingled with beech, chesnuts, walnuts, and other trees; and occasionally there are vines in great profusion, and very flourishing. The whole scenery of this mountain-pass was truly enchanting. A long and steep descent brought us into a fertile plain, now called Is Nik, which extends to the lake of Nicæa, and is beautifully watered by the clear streams that gush out from the naked summits of the mountain.

On reaching the plain, we came to a few villages, from whence, in about three hours, we arrived at Bazarkué, a town of some extent, but apparently not populous, the houses being thinly scattered. About five miles beyond it, we rested on the bank of a small river, flowing among fields of barley, and bearded wheat, which were now enlivened by the voice of the reaper. In passing the mountain, I observed some villages of Armenian Christians.

: We employed about six or seven hours in going from Bazarkué to Broussa. The road is of various levels, and we passed one steep hill : low wood and corn-lands diversified the scene. The situation of Broussa is delightful: it is wooded on three sides, and enclosed on the fourth by the opening bosom of Mount Olympus. The meaner parts of the city, in this approach to it, are completely concealed; while the mosques, and superior buildings, are seen emerging from the widely-spread verdure of lofty trees. Small streams descend from the mountains behind, among the extensive and numerous gardens, vineyards, and mulberry trees adorning the face of nature, and exhilarating the mind with the prospect of never-ending plenty. Some trees of extraordinary size, particularly walnuts, adorn the approach to Broussa, which is almost as celebrated as Damascus for its beauty, its waters, and the abundance of its fruits.

The distance from Scudar to Nicomedia is fifteen hours; and we employed about sixteen and a half more in our journey from Kara Mursal to Broussa.

: The baths of Broussa are noted : several warm springs are seen in the vicinity; some are chalybeate, others sulphureous. That which is called Kaplutcha Hammam, is situated north-west, or north-west by north, of the city, at the distance of nearly a mile and a half from the gate : it is but slightly impregnated with sulphur, and the heat of the water does not exceed 100° of Fahrenheit. A very spacious and commodious apartment, not much less, probably, than a hundred feet long (though I had not an opportunity of measuring it) and proportionably wide, forms the anti-chamber to a second room, almost equally spacious. The temperature of the latter is warmer. The center of each is occupied by a sumptuous marble fountain, yielding a copious stream of pure and cold water, for the purpose of drinking. A third apartment, which is circular, and of smaller dimensions, though still very spacious, and of higher temperature, is appropriated to bathers. It contains a circular *piscina*, or pool, not less than twenty-five feet in diameter. Two marble steps are continued round it, and the water is about four feet and a half deep. The cupola, which forms the roof, is lofty ; and there are six niches, with large marble basins, in the sides : the walls are lined with coloured tiles, but the pavement is of marble. The whole is sumptuous, and commodiously disposed ; and the attendants are numerous, skilful, and active.

In the pool the youth of Broussa and its neighbourhood divert themselves : some go there to learn to swim ; others to practise swimming ; others merely to amuse or to wash themselves. The water is sufficiently clear, and the building is kept tolerably clean : decency and order are scrupulously observed. The price to Mohammedans is very moderate. * A few paces distant, is a building of the same form, distribution, and dimensions ; and under similar regulations, but attended by women, supplies the same accommodations to the other sex.

Broussa is not well built, but it is populous and extensive. A certain degree of cleanliness prevails in the streets, and the air, unquestionably, is salubrious. Some of the mosques are spacious and

---

* For mere admission, and the use of the water, only two paras aie paid; but twelve oi fifteen if attendance and the use of soap and linen are required.

elegant, though inferior to several of those at Constantinople. Towards the N. W. is an extended plain, bounded N. W., N. and W. by mountains ; which, though not of very considerable height, add greatly to the beauty and grandeur of the scene. This plain, or vale, for it is both, resembles, in some degree, the environs of Damascus, with which those of Broussa may well admit of a comparison. The force of the present impression, or the faintness of that which I retained at the distance of four years, made me doubtful which merited the preference.

Clear and beautiful streams descending from the heights, spontaneously irrigate the trees and flowers, give life and fertility to the plain, and yield to the favoured inhabitants a constant succession of the most delicious fruits, and the richest harvests. Not to be soothed by the scenery of Broussa is to be destitute of all feeling ; or cursed with that of misery and despair. Here indeed it is, and at Damascus, (if any where,) that the destroying frenzy of the race of Othman seems to have been arrested in its career ; and its menaces successfully defied by the productive powers of indulgent nature.

Of the temper and habits of the people more experience would be necessary to enable me to speak with accuracy. They are, comparatively, insulated ; and, therefore, their ignorance and fanaticism cannot be supposed less strong or less general than in other parts of Asia Minor. It is fortunate if they be not greater, which from the report of Christians of the place may reasonably be suspected. Of their persons it may be said, that they are often tall, and that many of them have well formed limbs, a graceful carriage, and regular and interesting features. Many also, it may be observed, appeared to have reached an advanced age : a farther proof, if any were wanting, of the salubrity of the air.

My walks in the neighbourhood of Broussa furnished many fragments of stone covered with sulphureous incrustations. In other places are seen stalactites and stalagmites. Some cypresses are preserved of enormous growth : one of them between the city and the bath, I found by measurement, at one foot above the root, to be nineteen feet in the girth.

Broussa stands in the parallel of 40° 9' 30" N. lat., and is about 9' 30" E. of the merid. of the Seraglio, or 29° 4' 45" E. G. I observed, during my stay there in the month of June, the thermometer sometimes stood at 88° ; but the heat is seldom excessive.

Between my first visit to Broussa in June 1801, and my second in June 1802, a dreadful fire had destroyed almost one half of the city. The natives say that it was the best half, and contained the most elegant and valuable buildings; and they pretend that the stone edifices offered no effectual resistance to the flames, but perished almost as soon as those of timber. The conflagration terminated at the gate of Sarmakesh Khan, a spacious building where I lodged. A considerable portion of the houses had already been rebuilt ; but they were constructed principally of timber, and so slightly and hastily put together, that a stranger might almost imagine it was the intention of the builders to facilitate the return of a similar calamity.

The inhabitants of Broussa are said to exceed sixty thousand souls ; and it is reported, on some foundation, that the Mohammedans are in number nearly fifty thousand. The Armenians are about seven thousand, of whom a hundred and twenty families are rich, and carry on a valuable trade ; indeed, none of that nation are absolutely poor at Broussa. There are three thousand Greeks, and eighteen hundred Jews.

A great quantity of silk is produced in the environs of Broussa, and is manufactured into articles of various kinds.

I visited the Armenian bishop, who is a very distinguished personage, and exercises despotic power over those of his own nation ; many of whom dwell around him in a fauxbourg of the city, in which their church is situated. The bishop had an intelligent countenance, and a most reverend beard. His demeanour was civil, with some mixture of hierarchical importance. He conversed with me on the present situation of Egypt, and the policy of several European states with regard to Turkey. His questions were, many of them, pertinent, and some of his observations sensible and just. He could by no means believe that the British intended to evacuate Egypt; " which," he said, " would expose that country to evils much greater than it before suffered, and, ultimately, to a repetition of invasion."

The Armenian church narrowly escaped the conflagration before mentioned. It was saved by demolishing all the private houses near it. They assert, that it would have been impossible to rebuild it, on account of the Mahometan women of Broussa being particularly furious against Christians. On some late occasion, when it had become necessary to repair the church, a party of these amazons, together, it is said, with some men dressed in female apparel and instigated by a fanatical saint, tumultuously assembled. The saint declared, " that every nail which was driven, operated as a new wound in the body of the prophet;" and the mob destroyed all the repairs that had been made. The same spirit of insubordination in the inhabitants curbs the government. An attempt was made to establish a new custom-house; but the *Ghiumrukji*, or douanier, was obliged to seek his safety in flight.

I have already observed that the appearance of the people is unusually healthy. A medical practitioner, however, informed me that dropsies, and pulmonary complaints are not unfrequent; and that there are even some instances of scurvy. But his observations may have been made among the Christians, who are intemperate in the use of spirits, and salt provisions. Most of them, he says, make three regular meals in a day, and, consequently, are always in a state of repletion. The air, however, it may be remarked, must be keen, and is probably favourable to digestion. I saw scarcely a cripple or deformed person : no instance of leprosy; and but few of cutaneous eruptions. Wine is not allowed to be publickly sold; and the Mussulmen are not accused of intemperance in drinking.

The snow was still visible in many parts of the ridge of Mount Olympus *, on the 29th June, when we advanced towards Kutaieh,

---

* Called in Turkish كشيش ظاعي or mountain of the *religious*, from كشيش, a monk or priest.

by a road running at the foot of it, for about three hours; it then gradually leaves towards the right the chain of mountains, which takes a course more S. E. * Several small streams, descending from Olympus, cross the road. The ground at first, for some distance, is rocky and unproductive; but as we advanced farther it was better cultivated; and wheat and barley overspread the surface. On the banks of a small stream, near which we rested for the first time, about four hours from Broussa, I observed several plants of Papyrus, or, at least, of a Cyperus so much resembling it as not to be distinguished in its then nascent state. Early on the second day we passed a large village, whose name I have not accurately recorded, and soon after came to a smaller, called Ortakué. The road here lay through a wood, where I observed the largest flocks of sheep that I have ever seen in Turkey. The shepherds told me that the number there collected exceeded seven thousand: they were driven to this spot for the advantage of being sheltered by the trees from the sun.

---

* It is to be feared that there is little chance of recovering the valuable papers which the Oriental traveller, Seetzen, left behind him. The Editor has lately met with extracts from one or two letters addressed by him to M. Blumenback. They are published in a work not common in England, and may therefore be properly introduced here, as illustrating part of the Journal of Mr. Browne; a man, who, like Seetzen, possessed many of those qualifications so necessary to a traveller in the East. " Itineris Orientalis Spartam inire, tueri, complere," says the editor of Forskal's papers, " non cujusvis genii et ingenii est."

" De Bursa nous fimes une petite excursion sur l'Olympe Mysien, montagne célebre, couverte de neige. La region moyenne est composée de granit; la région superieure de marbre salin sans la moindre trace de pétrification. Le sommet le plus elevé, au pied duquel nous fimes des observations astronomiques, n'offre presque point de végétation; cependant j'y ai trouvé assez frequemment la myosotis scorpioides arvensis."

The following remark also respecting the Mineralogy of Asia Minor, is worthy of observation.

" Dans cette course j'ai eu occasion d'enrichir mon journal de plusieurs observations interessantes relatives à la mineralogie. Prés de Chanissa, l'ancienne Magnesia ad Sipylum, j'ai trouvé beaucoup de porphyre vert. Les montagnes des environs de Smyrne sont pour la plupart de porphyre brun, approchant quelquefois d'une nuance bleuâtre; il n' étincelle que fort peu sous le briquet. J'ai été fort surpris de n' avoir pas encore trouvé une seule trace bien determinée de petrification dans toute la partie de l'Asie Mineure que j'ai parcourue."

The soil in this wood has a red, ochreous appearance in some places; but the greatest part is a deep vegetable mould. Soon afterward begins the ascent of the mountain, which is covered with a forest of various foliage; consisting chiefly of large and luxuriant beeches. Our course the first day was due E., then S. E. by our compass.

After a long and difficult ascent of nearly four hours, we reached the summit, near to which is a plot of verdant grass, and a spring flowing down on the south side of the mountain. This point is very elevated : the wind blew strong, and the thermometer stood at nearly thirty degrees lower than it had been in the plain; a change of temperature produced partly by the elevation, and partly by the approach of night.

At sun-rise we began to descend. Few beech trees are visible after having passed the summit, but their place is supplied by firs and oaks. This ridge appears to be principally calcareous : I did not observe any granite. Near the end of the descent, we came to the banks of a swift brook, which runs west, and forms, I understood, a part of the river Mikalizza. One of the scourges of unhappy Asia, the wide-wasting locust, had already overspread and destroyed all the vegetables within its reach, to the south of the mountain's summit. Some fields of poppies, however, were not yet ravaged. The wood we passed through was formerly famed for being the resort of banditti and assassins ; but the Pasha of Kutaieh, who claims it as a part of his domain, had lately rendered it more secure. A great variety of plants and wild flowers enlivens and adorns the earth, within the wood and its vicinity; and the scenery is in a high degree picturesque and romantic.

To this first descent succeeded a forest of pines, at the end of which was a stony, open country ; yielding, however, a moderate crop of barley, wheat, lentils, and other vegetables, a small part of which had escaped the attack of the locust. A large farm, or chiftlick, presented itself on the right, formerly belonging to Toushân Pasha, but then to Kara Osman Oglo. I also observed, near the road, a few scattered columns of small dimensions, and which do not appear to have belonged to any important edifice. Part of the soil is chalky; but some rocks are seen, the superficies of which is perforated and cellular, and they have altogether a remarkable appearance.

Toushanlu, where we arrived on the first of July, is a town containing seven mosques, with minarets. A small castle, situated on an elevation, appears to the N. N. W. The town is somewhat populous : one khan is inhabited principally by Armenians ; but the people are chiefly Mohammedans, as are those of almost all the villages in this road. The stork is very frequent in the whole of this district, and uncommonly domestic.

From Toushanlu to Kutaieh, is a journey of about eight hours, S. E. in which we passed only one village. The soil between them is little cultivated, and covered with low bushes and brambles ; among which wild flowers are interspersed. The soil is various, being in some places stony, in other parts clay, and in other red marl. Near Kutaieh is a plain, tolerably cultivated, but the crops appear at present very backward, perhaps from the coldness of the soil. Through the plain runs a river, which is a branch of the Sangaris. Trees are rare ; and the devastation of the locust was conspicuous far and wide. We met a number of carts laden with salt, which is produced in the interior, and transported to the extremities of Anatolia; commerce, in other respects, seemed almost extinct. The structures in this quarter consist of stone and wood intermingled ; the roofs are of wood, and very rough.

Kutaieh is a city of some extent, but its buildings are neither sumptuous nor beautiful. It is well supplied with water ; and provisions and horses are cheap. The population does not seem to be great. The south side is protected by a mountain on which are the walls of a ruined castle. It furnishes a khan or two with apartments for travellers. Two hours and a half from Kutaieh, on the road to Kara-hissar, is seen a bridge over a small river running north-west, and near which are some trees. The soil is partly stony and partly clay, not favourable to vegetation. Three hours and a half farther, is a ruined khan. The country is open ; and there are no villages. We passed for six hours and a half through a tract overspread with bushes and brambles, though the soil was good. There were many hills, but none of them lofty. We stopped near a miserable village, where no provisions could be procured, except milk. The houses are of unburned brick : the inhabitants told me that the lands near them were divided between five Agas or landed proprietors. A single well supplies them with water. Wood for fuel, from Kutaich onward, is very scarce. At the end of five hours and a half, we came to a considerable hill, the descent of which employed us near an hour. A small river runs east through the vale below ; and near it are seen a hot spring and a bath : one such is found near Toushanlu, and it is said there are several more in this part of Anatolia. Trees and cultivation were here less rare : the locust, however, covered the soil, and had left no verdure between Kutaieh and Kara-hissar. From the bath, near which is a village or two, we reached in three hours Kara-hissar.

In Afiûm-Kara-hissar, the ancient Apaméa, we lodged in a decent khan : part of the building is of stone, part of unburned brick ; great quantities of which are prepared in the neighbourhood, the clay being tenacious and well adapted to that purpose. A whiter and finer argil is found near Kutaich, of which a coarse porcelain is made. There is also a manufactory of painted tiles, used in Turkey for adorning the interior of baths, and for other purposes. Few appearances of commerce are observable in travelling ; and there is little industry in the towns, beyond what is required for the supply of immediate necessaries. The inhabitants are sober, honest, and inoffensive, though their faculties are little developed. Kara-hissar is a mart for opium : it is brought to market frequently by the indigent cultivator in cakes of a few ounces in weight, and purchased cheap * by the

---

* The price at present is from ten to eleven piastres the 250 drachms, which is the oke or weight by which this commodity is sold. The words Opium and Afiûm or Aphiûm of the Orientals are doubtless both derived from the Greek ὄπιον, juice of poppies, the root of

merchants who are somewhat richer, and who having thus collected a quantity, dispose of it to the European factors at Smyrna or other parts of the coast.

The population of Kara-hissar, I have reason to believe, is not inferior to that of Kutaieh, though the town is somewhat smaller. A castle, in which some French prisoners are now confined, is situated to the west of it on an insulated rock. On the N. W. and W. S. W. are also rocks : on the E. and N. the country spreads out into a fruitful plain.

Bread is of indifferent quality : mutton and beef are nine or ten paras the oke; the latter is most common : the other articles in the market appear to be only those of constant and general home consumption. Provisions are supposed to be cheaper at Angora and Konieh than in any part of Anatolia.

The government of Kara-hissar is said to be tolerably good, being administered by a deputy, who dares not be guilty of any glaring excesses. The houses have all flat roofs, resembling those of Arabistan. Nine or ten mosques are seen, each of which is adorned with a minaret. From the exposed situation of the place, the cold of winter and the heat of summer are both excessive. The roads were represented as very dangerous ; being infested by disbanded troops, who plundered in considerable bodies.

Having left Afiûm-kara-hissar, we travelled with a more numerous caravan than before, by the high road, through a plain open country, till we came to Ak-shehr. Three hours from Kara-hissar is seen a coffee-house ; and a little farther on, a village called Ishaklu, which in itself is inconsiderable, but is surrounded by extensive gardens of fruit-trees, particularly pears. The lake on the left was visible at day-break ; and we soon came to another coffee-house, delightfully

---

which is ὀπὸς, "juice," generally. Apaméa has probably quite a different derivation, but the Turks call the place Afiûm-kara-hissar, " the castle of the opium district," without any reference, perhaps, to the sound of the ancient name.

situated on a high ground, near a spring of excellent water, which forms a stream descending into the lake. Some trees beautify this spot, but the face of the country soon becomes again open and uninteresting. About half an hour before entering Ak-shehr, I observed two fragments of a very solid wall, to the right of the road, under the hill, which appear to be ancient. Other fragments of hewn stone are visible about the city, but dispersed and no way considerable.

On entering Ak-shehr, a large mosque presents itself on the right, sumptuously built of marble, but now dilapidated. A wide plain opens itself on the left, of light soil, indifferently cultivated. Locusts still overspread the surface. Not far from Ak-shehr, to the west, a road is seen traversing the mountain to the right, which is said to lead directly to Caramân.*

In this part of Anatolia, the dress of the Mohammedans of the upper class is the same as elsewhere. The males of the lower order wear drawers of cotton, either blue or white, with jackets coarsely embroidered of woollen yarn, of different lengths, but some of them not above five or six inches deep, and consequently covering only the shoulders and part of the arm. The women, as usual, live retired, but are not all covered with veils. The Christians are many of them of the Greek ritual, and are found in the towns where commerce collects them ; but seldom in the villages, which are inhabited by peasantry. Their habits of life, and their morals, resemble those of the Mohammedans, by whom I did not find they were treated with harshness, except it be in affairs relating to the government. They differ materially in features and manner from those of the islands, and of Constantinople ; and while their address is more rude and unpolished, they are at least without the exterior of servility which characterises the latter. They generally wear a turban of blue cloth round a white felt *caouk*, or cap.

---

* Olivier, Voyage, &c. tom. vi. p. 385., finds that the site of Laranda, where there are said to be ancient remains, is a league and a half north of the present town Caramân.

Butchers' meat was scarce at Ak-shehr; and even the bread was of very inferior quality. Burghul is a principal article of food: it is wheat, first dried artificially, the husk removed, and then softened by boiling. The khan is dirty and inconvenient. The market is supplied with a few leather manufactures, smiths' shops, vestments, harness, sadlery, all of the coarsest kind. Three sides of the town are surrounded by a plain country; the fourth is terminated by a mountain. Eight minarets are visible: the edifices are, some of them, constructed of stone, the remainder of unburned brick: many of them are in a state of decay. The town is extensive, but far from populous. From Kara-hissar to Ak-shehr I reckoned twenty-one hours consumed in the route.

Leaving this city, the mountain ridge declines more to the S. E., and the road in an E. by S. direction. The *Katergis*, alarmed at the reports which they had heard of disbanded Delatéa, quitted the high road, and pursued one which is less frequented, and a little to the south of it. Harkut-kué, a village, was the first place we came to; and the second was El-kîn, or El-ghîn: in the last reside an Aga and a Cadi. A few fragments of columns are seen in the neighbourhood. As the country abounds with clay, the structures are chiefly of rude bricks made of clay mixed with straw. From Ak-shehr to Elkin is considered as a journey of nine hours: the same open and extended plain continues from Kara-hissar, with the exception of a few inequalities; and trees are seen only near the villages. The soil is of various kinds; clay, chalk, and stony: but very partially cultivated.

Large flocks of broad-tailed sheep, mingled with goats, were sometimes visible; horned cattle are also numerous. This district, from Elkîn eastward, is within the pashalic of Konieh, which was administered by the son of Seid Achmet, Pasha of Siwas, a name well known in the empire.

From Elkîn onward the face of the country is more diversified by hills and rocks: few villages are seen from the road; and the inhabitants with whom I had occasion to converse, complained of oppression from the government. Some fields of wheat, which appeared to be healthy, and some crops of barley yet unripe, (on the 18th of July,) formed the whole amount of the tillage for several miles. The remaining surface was overspread by the spontaneous vegetation of thorn-bushes, junipers, long coarse grass, and other plants equally unprofitable.

Having passed two small streams, over which are bridges, we encamped in a large grove of walnut trees, at the foot of a ridge of mountains running from S. W. to N. E. The ascent of this ridge employed about three quarters of an hour; and we were five hours more alternately ascending and descending, when at length we gained a distant view of the extensive plain of Konieh. We passed a miserable village on the hill, which a party of soldiers from Konieh had just been plundering; and in an hour and a half more, by a steep descent, reached the large village called Silli; which, however, is poor and destitute of provisions. The caravan passed the night there, and the following day advanced to Konieh: this city, though ruinous, is sufficiently marked by the remains which it still presents, as the ancient Iconium. The whole of this road is rocky until we came to Silli; and employed about eight hours. The air of Silli has the reputation of being salubrious, and the situation is agreeable. The inhabitants of Konieh come occasionally to divert themselves in the gardens around it, which appear to be very extensive. We could only obtain there a few apricots and dried wheat (Burghul). The natives seem to be muscular, and of a fair complexion; but they appear distrustful; and we saw but few of them. They consist of Mohammedans and Christians.

A variety of mineral substances is seen in the mountainous ridge, which we passed. In one place I remarked red and white, in another blue and white marble; in another fluor; in a third pyrites; limestone and a hard blue stone in the highest part. In descending, we saw schistus resembling our slate, the laminæ of which are vertical: near the slate is an appearance of something like coal; and nearer to the village, chalk and other calcareous substances; finally, in some places micaceous sand, and in others clay. Fuel is scarce in this neighbourhood; and not unfrequently the natives have recourse to the same method as in Egypt, of drying the dung of animals on the walls of their houses, and afterwards burning it. The herbs which grow on the mountain afford some food to the beasts of burden; and firs and oaks (the latter of diminutive size) diversify its rocky surface. Among them are scattered a few plants of Cistus, and other flowering shrubs.

We advanced from Silli twenty minutes S. by E.; when at length coming into the high road in an hour and forty minutes more, we arrived at Konieh. The calcareous rocks of Silli terminate in the extensive plain of Konieh, which is very productive, and comparatively well cultivated.

The scanty population and shapeless mud hovels of the present day, the abode of poverty and wretchedness, are strongly contrasted with what still remains of the spacious and lofty walls of the Greek city. The only buildings, which form any exception to the general desolation, are three or four good mosques, but especially the splendid Tekié or Monastery of Mewlawy Derwishes, the first among such buildings in the Turkish empire, and universally celebrated. Its cupola, covered with shining green tiles, is conspicuous from afar. The tomb of the founder is of black marble: it is known by the name of Mulla Hunkiar. Voluntary contributions are brought to the fraternity from all quarters, and from very distant regions : even the Emperor of Morocco, according to their report, annually sends them a hundred pieces of gold. Notwithstanding the celebrity and comparative opulence of this institution, there is reason to believe that it is one of the most decent and respectable of the monastic orders in the Turkish empire.

The order was founded by Jalâl-ed-dîn Mohammed, Ben Moham-med, el Balkhi, el Konawi, (also named Mulla Hunkiar,) who lived at Konieh, where he was regarded as a saint, and visited by Ertoghrûl, the father of the first Othman, who recommended his son to the saint's prayers. He died at that place A. H. 672. (1273.)

The Mewlawis have the tenth place in the chronological enumeration of these orders, which have their date as early as the first century of

Mohammedism. There are, in the whole, not less than twenty-four distinct bodies, each wearing a different habit and observing different rules. The extravagancies of the Rufayis, as well as the dances and music of the Mewlawis, are well known from the descriptions given by many travellers; and the history of the various establishments of Derwishes would be no more than that of many of the monastic orders of Christendom, a disgusting and monotonous history of the deplorable effects of fanaticism, imposture, and credulity.

Some of these institutions, however, boast a few characters respectable for their talents and learning. Jalâl-ed-dîn was the author of the Mithnawi, in which the use of music and the dance is taught. It is written in elegant Persian verse, and contains the rules of the order, with a variety of moral reflections and maxims on several subjects. Many commentaries have been written upon it. The well-known Turkish and Persian vocabulary, in verse, was written by the Mewlawi Shahidi, which, whatever be its other merits, (upon which I do not presume to decide,) is unquestionably well adapted to assist the memory of young persons.

The laws of few or none of these societies oblige individuals to celibacy; and it is only in the Tekié or convent of Mewlawis at Konieh, that such of the fraternity as are married are not permitted to pass the night. Though all the orders of Derwishes may be regarded as mendicant, none of them are expressly permitted to solicit alms, except the Bektashis, and even these are never importunate. The majority are sufficiently instructed in some art or trade to maintain themselves by their own industry. Finally, none of them are bound by an oath to their order for life, but may return to society, and resume any occupation that suits them. Of this last privilege, however, they seldom avail themselves. The general of each order appoints the superior of each Tekié, who is always one of the senior Derwishes. All the orders are under the supreme jurisdiction of the Mufti at Constantinople.

The Tekié at Konieh is known to possess very considerable property in Wakfs; but not even a conjecture can be offered as to the amount. · No external appearance of wealth presents itself to the eye, and the mode of living is in all respects simple and frugal.

The price of provisions at Konieh, though advanced considerably beyond what it was formerly, is still moderate, and even low. Eight paras is the price of an oke of meat (400 drachms). Three paras are paid for an equal quantity of milk. Bread enough for three persons costs one para. The bread is formed into thin cakes of more than three feet in length, and about eight inches in breadth : it is white, and of good flavour. Within about thirty years, it is said that a horse might have been amply fed for a night at one para. Water is obtained from wells alone. Salt may be procured for little more than the carriage.

A considerable quantity of ordinary yellow leather for shoes and other purposes is manufactured at Konieh, part of which is carried to Egypt and Syria. Arms and articles of clothing are sold cheap : our Katerdgis purchased some of each, and slippers and small carpets, with a view of disposing of them with advantage at Aleppo and other parts of Syria.

Without the walls is a bath, formerly a magnificent Saracenic structure, with an octagon chapel, or mosque adjoining it : these are now in ruins. Near the first gate is a large statue without a head ; and higher up, on the wall, a row of figures in alto relievo. The wall itself contains many other ancient sculptures ; and several inscriptions in Arabic characters. It is strongly built ; flanked by numerous square towers ; very extensive and highly ornamented.

The people are rude and uncivilized, and in no degree remarkable for industry. Their dress does not differ from what has been before described. The Armenians and Greeks have each of them a church, and some Jews are found there.

CHAPTER II.

JOURNEY FROM KONIEH TO ANTIOCH.

*Yeshil. — Kara-bignar. — Erakli. — Passage of Mount Taurus. — Turkmans. — Tarsús ;
and thence to the Coast. — Embarkation. — Voyage to Aisus, and thence across the Mountain to Antioch. — Some Account of Antioch. — Remarks. — Pi oductions and Trade. —
Kutchuk Ali Pasha. — Departure fiom Antioch. — Arrival at Ladakié. — Maronite
Farmer of the Mui. — Mischievous Santon. — Passage to Larneka in Cyprus.*

THE Katerdgis at first proposed to themselves to proceed to Caramân,
which they considered as the shortest and best road to the coast : but
having heard that the place was invaded by a large troop of Dellis,
they determined to advance by the straight road to Erakli. We
went from Konieh to Yeshil in nine hours, through a widely extended
plain of excellent soil, in which scarcely a stone is visible, now lying
waste, though not long since extensively cultivated. Yeshil is
inhabited by peasants who till the ground ; without any appearance
of commerce or manufactory. The buildings are constructed of unburned bricks. The plain, in which Yeshil stands, is often overflowed, and the village, which presents a naked appearance, being
wholly destitute of trees, is built on a small eminence, like many of
those in Egypt. We rested here at a private house. From Yeshil
we travelled ten hours, without intermission, to Kara-bignar ; a town
consisting principally of mud hovels. The only remarkable edifices
are a mosque, and the khan in which we rested ; both built on an
uniform plan. They were raised at the expense of an eunuch of one
of the Emperors, with the wealth obtained by plundering his master.
These buildings are spacious and substantial ; the khan is about four
hundred feet long, and a hundred wide ; but is now in a state of
decay. There are some fragments of alabaster columns adjoining to
the mosque.

A manufacture of gunpowder is carried on at Kara-bignar; and the women prepare a kind of socks for the feet, of coarse woollen yarn, which are very strong and warm, and much sought after by travellers in winter: they are sold for nine or ten paras the pair. Apricots and other fruits abound, but of no exquisite flavour. The soil is rich and fertile; and continues to be so till within about two hours' distance of Kara-bignar, when it becomes rocky.

The route from Kara-bignar to Erakli employed us about twelve hours; the road is over a sandy plain, which is little cultivated. Erakli, however, is agreeably situated in the midst of gardens full of fruit and forest trees. About forty minutes from the city, begins the ascent of the mountainous ridge, a continuation of Taurus. It employed us nearly five hours to reach the summit. The Katerdgis, not knowing the road, were obliged to take guides from Erakli to conduct them. A little farther we came to a small village, near which I saw, perhaps, an acre or two of cultivated land. The Turkmans, with their flocks, dwelling under tents, inhabit this almost inaccessible region. A series of stupendous bare rocks succeeds to the first summit. The air is cool and salubrious, even in the hottest season; and pellucid springs give spirit and animation to the scene. The summit of this primitive ridge is composed of a large grained marble; other calcareous substances recline on its ample sides, or are upheaved by its frequent asperities. They are all of them massy rocks, without any appearance of strata. A number of very ancient cedars, whose stunted growth and fantastic branches cast a gloomy shade, diversify the rugged sides of the mountain.

In my visits to the Turkman tents, I remarked a strong contrast between their habits and those of the Bedouin Arabs. With the latter, the rights of hospitality are inviolable; and while the host possesses a cake of bread, he feels it a duty to furnish half of it to his guest; the Turkman offers nothing spontaneously, and if he furnish a little milk or butter, it is at an exorbitant price. With him it is a matter of calculation, whether the compendious profit of a single act of plunder, or the more ignoble system of receiving presents from the caravans for their secure passage, be most advantageous. The Arab values himself on the *hasb we nasb* *, that is, his ancient pedigree ; the Turkman, on his personal prowess. With the former, civility requires that salutations be protracted to satiety ; the latter scarcely replies to a *Salam aleikum.*

The muleteers, who had preferred this devious path to the high road, to avoid the Dellis, were now alarmed at the frequent visits of the Turkmans. They described me to them as an officer of Chappan Oglou's retinue, employed to communicate with the English fleet on the coast ; an explanation which appeared to satisfy them ; and fortunately I was able to support that character. It is to be observed that Chappan Oglou has a large military force at his disposal, and administers justice with a rod of iron. His vengeance pursues, on eagle-wing, the slightest transgression against his authority. Our precautions at night were redoubled ; and I divided the time into two watches, which I ordered my servant to share with me ; but the disposition to sleep having speedily got the better of his vigilance, a pipe, although carefully placed under the carpet on which I myself slept, was stolen unperceived before morning.

The dress of the Turkmans consists of a large striped and fringed turban, fastened in a manner peculiar to themselves ; or sometimes

---

* " حَسَب (Hhasab, or Hasb,) bears in Arabic (among other significations) that of dignity, reputation, estimation, nobility, &c. و wa, is the copulative particle, and ; نَسَب (Nasab, Nasb,) signifies genealogy, lineage, origin of a family, &c. حَسَب و نَسَب Hasb wa Nasb, or Hhasab wa Nasab, as it ought properly to be written and pronounced, 'dignity and noble origin of a family,' as in the following phrase by Saâdud-din, the elegant historiographer of the first Ottoman family : بو سَبَ عالی حسبی حضرت نوحه منسوب اِتمِشلردر Bu Nasabĕ Âalee hhasabee hhaziatĕ Nuhhah mansoob itmishlerdur, i. e. They have derived the origin or genealogy of this most noble family from the patriarch Noah ; or, Mansoob itmishleidur, they have referred ; hhaziatĕ Nuhhah, to the patriarch Noah ; Bu Nasabĕ Âalee hhasabee, the origin of this exalted or most noble family or lineage.

The same author employs the words Hhasab wa Nasab, in the subsequent phrase, and for the same purpose, thus : شرف حسب و سبدن محروم اِیکن Sharafĕ *hhasab wa nasab*-tan mahhroom eeken, " being destitute of nobility and high origin." — Note communicated by Mr. Usko.

of a simple high-crowned cap of white felt. A vest, usually white, is thrown over the shirt; the Aga's superadd one of cloth; and in general, and in proportion to their rank and wealth, they approximate to the dress of the capital. But the common people wear a short jacket of various colours. A cincture is indispensably required, in which are fixed an enormous yatagan *, and a pistol. Many of them wear half boots, red or yellow, laced to the leg: the dress of the women is a coloured vest, and a piece of white cotton cloth on the head, covering part of the face. They are masculine and active, performing all the harder kinds of labour required by the family. Their features are good, but not pleasing. The men are generally muscular, and well proportioned; tall, straight, and active. Their teeth are white and regular; their eyes are often extremely piercing; and there is an air of uncommon boldness in their countenances and mode of address. Their complexions are clear, but sun-burnt. In a word, they have every thing that denotes exhaustless health and vigour of body. A general resemblance is visible between them and the populace of Constantinople; but the latter appear effeminate by the comparison. Every action and every motion of the Turkmans is marked by dignity and grace. Their language is clear and sonorous, but less soft than that of the capital; expressing, as may bé conceived, no abstract ideas, for which the Turkish is indebted to the Arabic alone; but fitted to paint the stronger passions, and to express, in the most forcible and laconic terms, the mandates of authority. Their riches consist of cattle, horses, arms, and various habiliments. How lamentable to think, that with persons so interesting, and a character so energetic, they unite such confirmed habits of idleness, violence, fraud, and treachery! From the rising of the sun till his disappearance, the males are employed only in smoking, conversing, inspecting their cattle, or visiting their acquaintance. They watch at night for the

---

* A sword with a broad painted blade, concave, and cutting with one edge, which is nearly straight, or rather inclining inwards, in a contrary direction to the sabre.

purpose of plunder, which among them is honourable, in proportion
to the ingenuity of the contrivance, or the audacity of the execution.
Their families are generally small, and there seems reason to believe
that their numbers are not increasing. My experience among them
was too short to enable me to point out the checks which operate to
counteract the natural tendency to multiply. They lately surprised
a party of disbanded cavalry, and made themselves masters of the
horses and booty. The riders were many of them killed, and the
remainder left to pursue their march on foot, unarmed and destitute.

The destructive locust has not spared even the solitary domain of
these wandering tribes. An infinity of junipers and cedars over-
spreads the first descent of the mountain, which is long and steep,
and covered with loose stones. Those near the summit are granite
and hornblende : lower down, limestone is the prevailing substance.
The dwarf Elder, whose odour is very agreeable, skirts the mountain
at a certain height. The route from Erakli to Tarsûs occupied in
the whole about twenty-nine hours. On the third day, we rode for
about a mile through the bed of a torrent, now dry, but occasionally
flowing between lofty and tremendous rocks. We soon after ascended
another ridge, inferior in height to the first : having crossed it, we continued our journey through a beautifully wooded valley, in which
there are a great variety of ornamental trees and shrubs. On one
side is a precipice descending to the dry bed of a torrent, and on both
lofty and almost perpendicular rocks, shaded with the most luxuriant
verdure. A few spots might be remarked which were capable of cultivation ; but the valley contained many fragments of granite, micaceous schistus, and limestone. Some of the rocks have a black
unctuous or shining appearance.

From the last resting place, another descent ensued, which at
length brought us into an extensive plain, and shortly afterwards to
Tarsûs, distant about three hours from the sea. Its site in summer
and autumn is deemed so unhealthy, that such of the inhabitants as
are able to remove elsewhere do not choose at that time to reside in

the city. It is a place of some commerce, but the circumstance just mentioned gave it at this time an air of great dreariness.

Myrtles, Oleanders, Cyclamens, and a variety of other beautiful plants, of the most luxuriant growth, overspread the plain from Tarsûs to the sea, excepting where it is cultivated with Hashish or Hemp, Bamia or Hibiscus esculentus, and Tobacco, to which the soil is adapted, and which is at once cheap and of agreeable flavour. The water of all these low lands, if used freely and without purification, is said to produce fevers and dysenteries * ; yet the natives have invented no method to render it salubrious. The fruits are abundant and good.

I proposed to myself to pass into Syria, by way of Adene and Baias ; but the rapine and cruelty of Kutchuk Ali Pasha had long before compelled the caravans to seek another road. I did not readily find a vessel for Cyprus ; and therefore resolved to accompany the Katerdgis to Suadéa and Antioch ; though the assemblage of twenty-five mules and horses in a diminutive and fragile bark (shuktûr), together with the company of a dozen vulgar, dirty, and noisy muleteers, did not promise much satisfaction or security on the voyage. Respecting the latter, I readily anticipated that increasing nausea would speedily terminate their vociferations and insolence ; and my hopes were verified : the most boisterous among them became the most pale, tame, and dejected ; and when landed, each congratulated himself on having escaped from the jaws of death. In fact, off Ras-el-chamîr, a hurricane came on, which suddenly darkened the atmosphere ; and the strong light made by pitch-makers on the mountain above alone saved us from being driven aground, by enabling the seamen to know their situation.

But notwithstanding all the exertions of the crew, who were Greeks, it was impossible to weather Suadéa ; and we found our-

---

* " Probably these complaints arise from an air infected with marsh effluvia, and not from the water. It is a common error." I am indebted for this observation to an eminent chemist.

selves under the necessity of steering for Arsûs, the ancient Rhesus, which is more to the north. Here we were fortunate enough to land on the following morning.

Three hours distant from Tarsûs are situated a few houses near the sea, where resides an officer, who is employed to collect certain duties on exports and imports. The buildings there are narrow, dirty, and every way wretched. Near to each house is an insulated room or kiosk, to which the ascent is by a ladder, and where the natives in summer pass much of their time. They enjoy in them a freer circulation of air than below, and imagine that they in some measure avoid the vapours which are more deleterious in proportion as they are near to the surface of the earth. * Two inconsiderable villages were seen in the plain before we reached the custom-house; and in one of them was a ruined fort seated on a small elevation. I observed also a line of small towers, placed on rising grounds, most of them in a state of decay, extended along the coast.

Advancing westward from the place where duties are paid, for nearly two hours, in which space of time we crossed a small river, we at length arrived at the spot where the boat (shuktûr) was in shallow water. Two Greek ships were receiving cargoes of grain. Many of the natives on this part of the coast speak Arabic.

I have already mentioned our voyage to Arsûs, a miserable village, which is built on a small river descending from the neighbouring mountains. It contains a house for the Soubashi, another for the Sheik, a mesjid or small mosque, and a street consisting of four shops on each side, and about the same number scattered round. Wheat and barley are not exported from thence : the price of the latter was twenty paras the yaum, which is more than our peck, though not amounting to two pecks. Tobacco of good quality was sold at the price of 30 paras for 720 drachms. A Sheik, who administers legal decisions, a Soubashi, and an Aga reside there occasionally. But

---

* This idea is probably correct, and strengthens the conjecture in the preceding note, regarding the innocence of the water.

though the situation be well adapted for trade, the soil rich, and the environs beautiful, such are the noxious qualities of a tepid, humid, and stagnant atmosphere, that the natives have a cadaverous aspect, and constantly complain, as at Scanderoon, of agues and malignant fevers; and a stranger rarely sleeps there with impunity. In the autumn all those, who are able, retire to Beilan, which is distant only nine hours. A small river flows down to the sea, close to the village; and ornamental shrubs grow luxuriantly on its banks : but the water at this season is stagnant and corrupt. The fruits we obtained there, particularly small white figs, were of exquisite flavour.

I had no sooner landed, than I was civilly invited by the Cadi, or Sheik, to partake of some refreshment; and during the remainder of my stay there I lived at the house of the Aga. Without knowing my country or religious profession, they imagined me to be well-informed as to the politics of the Europeans; and were very desirous to learn whether they might not expect English ships to resort there. They were probably the more anxious on this subject, in consequence of the profits resulting to the people of Macri, Moglah, and other places, from their traffic with the English. I answered, generally, in the affirmative; with which they seemed satisfied. At Arsûs, the Katerdgis paid three piastres duty, for the passage of every loaded mule, and one piastre for every empty one.

The plain which we crossed to the foot of the mountain, in our way to Antioch, is about two miles wide : the ascent to a resting place, under the shade of some trees, employed us nearly three hours; and to the summit, which is clothed with pines, intermingled with cedars, two hours more. The sides are covered with useful, ornamental, and rare plants. Towards the west is a widely-extended prospect of the sea, and the plain below; towards the east of Antioch, the country around it, the lake, and the mountains which terminate the horizon. A limpid fountain, near the summit of this lofty ridge, pours forth a copious supply of icy water; a delightful beverage in this spot, and at this season. The paths which lay in our route were some of them

s 2

narrow, abrupt, and nearly impracticable. One of our horses rolled down a precipice, and was much lacerated ; and a mule, by a similar accident, broke his thigh, and could not proceed. At this the owners grew impatient and clamorous ; sometimes weeping, but oftener venting horrible imprecations. Their complaints of the road were not without reason. An arduous ascent, on one side encumbered with a profusion of loose fragments of stone ; a precipice on the other, nearly perpendicular; in some places trees entwining their branches, and denying a passage ; in other places, loosened at the roots, and threatening a tremendous fall : these were objects interesting to the traveller, but in no way gratifying to the muleteer. The ascent employed four hours ; crossing the chain four more ; and in the descent were consumed about three and a half. Equal impediments oppose themselves in the descent, which cannot be safely performed, but on foot. We were two hours and a half on the road from the base of the mountain to Antakie (Antioch). From this place to Beilan the distance is commonly estimated at nine hours ; and from Arsûs to Antioch, at ten hours : but by this must be understood the time required for a single horseman, for we employed full fourteen hours. Not far from the foot of the mountain we came to a village in the plain, near which we reposed for the night, and obtained a supply of fresh bread, figs, grapes, water-melons, and eggs, all excellent in their kind.

Early on the following morning we proceeded to Antioch, once the opulent, the luxurious, the refined mistress of Syria ; now presenting no monument of ancient grandeur, except the skeleton of its ample walls. The plain, over which the road leads to Antioch, is covered with myrtles, and other flowering and odoriferous shrubs. The khans, or caravanserais, at Antioch, are not sumptuous buildings, but they are secure, and adapted to the use of the merchants. The three best are Khan el Nakir, Khan el Beiz, and Khan el Gidid. I had an interview with the Mitsellim, who has been long fixed here. He received me with great politeness. His administration was said to be distinguished by justice and severity. He was very temperate ; and his pleasures were understood to be strictly confined to his harem. He had never indulged in the use of opium or strong liquors.* The Christians of the Greek ritual, now established in Antioch, are about a hundred and fifty families; the Armenians, twenty families; and there are about forty Jewish. The number of Mohammedans is not so easily ascertained. The troops of every description now in the service of the Mitsellim do not exceed four thousand, and are probably not more than three thousand five hundred; these are known under the general name of Tuffenkjié, or " bearers of fire-arms." There are ordinarily four or five hundred Yenktcheris (or Janissaries), who are at present most of them in Egypt with the Vizir.

The staple commodity of Antioch is well known to be silk. The rotal of this city, which consists of 800 drachms, of forty-eight grains each, when I arrived there, sold for twenty-eight piastres; but before I left the place, it had risen to thirty-five piastres. The cantar of Antioch is 100 okes of Constantinople; a bale of silk weighs fifty okes. The cantar of Aleppo is ninety okes. The average quantity produced by Suadéa, and the neighbourhood of Antakié, sold rough in the city, is about 200 cantars. The silk in this district is divided into four kinds; that of Antioch, of Suadéa, of the mountains, and of Beilan. The present year (1801) has been unfavourable to the produce of silk. A large portion of it is demanded for the manufactories of Aleppo. The price of the best wheat is now forty-eight †piastres the shimbul, which is the common measure of capacity at Antioch. This measure weighs one-fourth of the cantar of Aleppo, or seventy rotals, equal to 800×70, or 56,000 drachms, avoirdupois. My informant esteems the ordinary consumption of wheat-flour for bread, for a family of six persons, at about seven cantars. In addition to this, his

---

* His revenues exceed thirty, but do not amount to forty purses; about 1000*l.* or 1250*l.* sterling. The maintenance of troops is not to be included in this estimate.

† 48 piastres may be estimated at 3*l.* 4*s.* The shimbul equals 218 lbs. 12 ounces, or nearly three bushels and two thirds.

own family, consisting of that number, consumes about four cantars of Burghûl.*

A great quantity of grapes is produced in the neighbourhood. They are used for food, converted into Dipse †, (a kind of jelly made of the juice of grapes,) or dried as raisins. Little wine is prepared; but what I have tasted there was perfectly well-flavoured; it may be kept any length of time, and is improved by a period of seven or eight years. It is strong, and perhaps rather too sweet. Of provisions, excellent fish is brought from the lake and the Orontes, and sometimes from the sea; but the encouragement offered to the fishermen is not a sufficient inducement for them to go out frequently in quest of it.

Quarries of free-stone are found in the adjacent mountain; and there is timber at no great distance, but the carriage is somewhat difficult. A convenient house for a family may be built for about 1500 piastres: the interior of the city is, nevertheless, mean and ill-built. The wages of a man-servant are not more than twenty-five piastres per annum, exclusively of food and clothing. The mithkal, or twenty-four karats of pure gold, which are equal to one Venetian sequin and a half, is twelve piastres; yet a single Venetian sequin passes for ten piastres. A firman, from the Porte, was expected to regulate the value of the current coin; but the evil of its inequality was not to be remedied by a simple mandate. The want of intrinsic value in the Turkish coinage, one of the wretched expedients of a bankrupt government, had caused sequins to be received at ten or ten and a half piastres; that coin being more pure, more portable, and pretty generally preferred to others; and those who possess them could not be expected to part with them at eight piastres, which was the legal value, whatever might

* The seven cantars of wheat give for the annual consumption of each person, in bread-corn, about 43,333 drachms, avoirdupois; and these equal 169 lbs. 4 oz. 5 dis., or two bushels and five-sixths.

† See Shaw's Travels, pp. 143. 339. " Carry down to the man a little balm, and a little dipse." Genesis, xliii. 11. — E.

be the terms of the firman. The wages of workmen, and the price of provisions, have nominally increased within the last thirty years, owing to the same cause. The daily pay of a master-mason was, within that period, fifteen paras : ·it is now seventy. That of an inferior mason was six paras ; and is now from thirty to forty.

The natives of Antioch are healthy and vigorous. Bilious complaints, however, I observed to be common. The air is very salubrious ; and, notwithstanding its latitude, and somewhat low situation, the thermometer seldom rises above 84° or 86°. The prevailing wind is westerly, or rather S. 57° W. by the compass : it scarcely deviated from that point during the time I was there. This wind blowing from the sea equally mitigates the cold of winter, and the heat of summer; nor does the breeze remit during the night, but blows steadily during the whole of the twenty-four hours. Perhaps this is the cause why the inhabitants are less incommoded by flies and gnats than in other places. When a different wind prevails, which rarely happens, but for a short interval, both the heat and cold are more severely felt.

The water of the Orontes is very white and turbid at this season : it is not used for drinking until it has deposited its mud. At the bridge of Antioch it flows from south to north. From the strong west winds, Suadéa is an inconvenient harbour for ships; which cannot then get out of the river. The bearing of Suadéa from Antioch is W. S. W. ¼ S.

The rebellious Pasha, Kutchûk Ali, has lately been negociating his peace with the Porte : he was promised, as a condition of his obedience, which the government was not able to compel, that the caravan of pilgrims should this year pass by Baiâs; and that he should have the pashalic of Adene in addition to his own. Neither of these promises having been performed, the Pasha thought himself absolved from the contract, and renewed his former system of plunder, which indeed had scarcely been suspended. The East India Company was obliged to negociate a peace separately from the Porte, that ·their Tatars from Aleppo might be permitted to pass.

On the 21st of August I left Antioch, and took the road to Ladakié, where I arrived on the 23d, having employed about twenty-
four hours in the journey. Three hours from Antakié I observed a
torrent, which descended among rude and broken rocks, covered with
lively verdure, into the Orontes : on the torrent was constructed a mill,
forming altogether a striking and a picturesque scene. Near this point
commences the ascent of a mountain, which is somewhat rugged : between the foot of it and Antioch, may be remarked some remains of
antiquity, such as broken columns; but there was nothing in a tolerably
perfect state. They prove, however, that great public buildings have
extended to this distance. A bridge, over another torrent, now dry, is
seen at about one hour from Antioch. Our course, hitherto, was south-
west. Three hours more brought us to a village on the mountain,
where we slept. Our course afterwards was south. In the plain are
some rocks, which appear to be tufa, perforated and cellular : others
of talc, or large mica, are seen on the mountain : all are soft stones.
Myrtle, oak, sumach, are scattered about in profusion ; but there are
no large trees. The culture, where the ground is plain and productive, consists of maize, vines, and some tobacco. On the second day
we came to a village called Ourdé, by a mountainous road, with much
low wood. Pear-trees, walnuts, and vines adorn this village, which is
said to be two hours short of half-way from Antioch to Ladakié. Before we came to Ladakié, the road led us through a plain for two
hours and a half to three hours, in which our course was S. S. W. This
plain is most of it cultivated ; and it was watered by three small
streams, which we had occasion to cross. The vegetation on the
mountain consists chiefly of pines ; the air at the foot of it is said to
be very unhealthy ; but at Ladakié there is little reason to complain ;
the sea-breeze prevents it from being stagnant.

The small, but agreeable, city of Ladakié is slowly recovering from
the calamity which assailed it in 1797. The greater part of the
buildings then overthrown by the earthquake are reconstructed, but
less substantially than formerly. The singular imbecility of the
Pasha has left the farm of the Miri (and virtually the greatest power

in the city) to a Maronite Christian; intriguing, rich, insolent, and overbearing. The hands, as Volney observes, which the mallet has hardened in beating cotton, are not fitted to wield the rod of authority. The natives execrate his rapacity, while they prostrate themselves before his power; and it is striking to observe the conflicting passions which torture the countenances of the crowds of persons who linger for successive hours at his levee, often without obtaining an audience.

A fatal accident was near happening on the evening of my arrival at Ladakié, from the absurd prejudice which prevails in that country, with regard to persons deprived of reason. * A young Georgian Mamlûk, in the service of a Capigi bashi, with whom I travelled from Antioch thither, sleeping on the terrace of the khan where we lodged, was so forcibly seized by the throat by one of these mischievous ideots, that he had nearly lost all sensation, when his companion fortunately awoke, and discovered his situation. The Capigi, on my remarking, in strong terms, the great absurdity of the popular prejudice, agreed with me perfectly in the conclusion, but did not think fit to make any remonstrance to the proper persons; so that the Shecb was left to strangle with impunity the next person who should unfortunately be exposed to his mischievous attempts.

The rescue of Egypt by the English I had reason to believe was very unpopular in Syria among all who were not immediately attached to the Turkish interests. Present evils are always more intolerable than those which are contingent and remote; and with all that Egypt suffered from the invasion of the French before their eyes, they are incapable of discerning how impossible it would be for a conqueror, however mild and generous, for many years at least, to ameliorate their condition. Besides which, it may be observed that many of the Oriental Christians would be gratified by possessing the power of plundering, even at the expense of being plundered themselves; and

---

* " They hold such as have lost their wits, and natural ideots in high veneration, as men ravished in spirit, and taken from themselves, as it were, to the fellowship of angels." Sandys Travels in Turkey, p. 44. — E.

their little vanity would make great sacrifices even for the gratification of wearing a white or yellow shawl.

The price of wheat at Ladakié was four piastres the kilot; of tobacco from thirty to forty-five paras the rotal; of coffee, from seven to seven piastres and a half, for the same quantity.

The port of this town is at present very small and inconvenient; but there seems good reason to believe that it might be rendered capacious and secure with less labour and expense than any other place on the coast of Syria.

No considerable remains of the ancient city of Laodicea are now visible, yet perhaps enough is found in the neighbourhood to ascertain its extent with tolerable accuracy. Subterraneous works, steps cut in the solid rock, and various other remains are seen to the north, near the sea. A number of petrified pistachio nuts is found in the rocks of the vicinity; but scarcely a single tree of that description now grows there. What can have extinguished this species of tree it is not easy to imagine. Have the frequent earthquakes destroyed them? Scarcely any wine is now made there, and few vines are planted; though tradition informs us that wine was formerly prepared at Laodicea in great abundance. Sulphur and bitumen are seen even on the surface of the soil, near a spring known among the Franks by the name of *Fontaine d'amour*.

I embarked in a small boat with several passengers for Larneka in Cyprus, which in Turkish is called Tûsla from the adjacent salt works. None of the company departed from the rules of civility and mutual forbearance, with the exception of a Derwîsh. The monastic order called Nakshebendi to which he belonged, was one of the strictest; yet many individuals who are members of it may be said to unite great profligacy, vulgarity and ignorance, with pretensions to superior sanctity; and gross worldliness and servility, with extraordinary professions of devotion and self-denial. This man talked incessantly in a very forward and irrational manner; and occasionally threw out hints that he suspected me to be a Christian; declaring at the same time how much he despised and hated infidels. His pointless satire I bore for some time very patiently, reserving my reply for a proper occasion. Being one day together at the table of the Custom-house officer, the Derwîsh suddenly left off eating, and looking directly at me, said, " *La illah ila ullah **;" to which I instantly replied in a cheerful tone, " *We Mohammed abduhu we rasoulouhu*," and I immediately added ; " I congratulate myself, father Derwîsh, on hearing the sacred profession of Islam drop from your tongue ; but I should be still better pleased at learning that the faith had place in your heart. God built the Islam on five things † ; but of the five you possess not one. 'You receive alms and never give : your knees are bent at table, but never on the carpet of prayer : you abstain from food only when no one will give it to you : your ablutions are performed with dust, when they ought to be performed with water : and your pilgrimage has only been from the Tekié to the brothel : you drink no wine, but you are drunk with opium : and your embroidered cap ‡ instead of being a crown of sanctity, is a mark of folly. With such morals, any marriage that you could contract would not be a marriage, but a repetition of the sensuality to which you are accustomed ; and if any one of the true believers in this place should consent to give you his daughter in marriage, I am content to bear all the obloquy that you can utter for a week to come." It may be supposed that 1 did not venture to talk in this strain without having previously ascertained in what degree of estimation the Derwîsh was held by the rest of the company ; and far from taking his part, they acknowledged by their loud laughter the justice of my reproof.

---

* Thus pronounced, La Illāhu illa llāhu; " There is no other God, but God :" wa Muhammedu âbduhu wa rasouluhu, " and Mohammed is his servant, and his messenger or ambassador." From Mr. Usko. — These are the words pronounced from the minarets of the mosques at the different hours of calling to prayer. — E.

† When De la Motraye was at Rama, he had a treatise given him " Of the Five Commandments of the Law of Allah (God); viz. Belief in the Divine Essence and in the Prophet; the Sala or Prayer; Fasting, Charity, and the Pilgrimage to Mecca." The treatise on these five points is given in the Appendix to his Travels. — E.

‡ This cap is called Taj, a crown.

T 2

On the morning of the seventh day from our departure, we landed at Larneka. The heat of this part of Cyprus is very intense; and the north-east wind, which is said to be the most hot and oppressive, blew at the time of my arrival. Caleshes, in other places used as a luxury, are here almost necessary; for though the town be but at a small distance from the sea, yet exposure to the rays of the sun in passing thither, is seldom hazarded with impunity. Agues and complaints of the eyes are common; and none of the natives have the appearance of robust health.

The bread made in private houses in Cyprus is unequalled, except perhaps by that which is prepared for the table of the Sultan, at Constantinople. It is composed of what is called " *fiore di farina*." The flour is divided into three parts, to obtain the kind which is proper for manipulation. The first separated is the coarse and husky part; the next, the white impalpable powder; after which operation remains the *fiore di farina*, which is neither very finely pulverized, nor remarkably white, and is by far the smallest quantity of the whole mass. This is found to contain the purest part of the wheat, and to make the finest bread.

CHAPTER III.

Journey from Smyrna to Constantinople. — Greek Sailors. — Arrival at Smyrna. — Jelembe. — Balikesr. — Kuirdes. — Lake Ulubad. — Yenishehr. — Nicæa. — Kizderbend. — Corrupt Manners of the Female Inhabitants. — Heisek. — Muggrebine Soldiers. — Arrival at Constantinople.

A LAD on board * our vessel having imprudently ventured to swim, when violently heated, was subsequently attacked by a fever, which, as he soon became delirious and buboes appeared, was imagined to

* Mr. Browne was now sailing from Alexandria to Smyrna.

be the plague. This so much alarmed the Greek passengers and crew, that to quiet their fears, they had recourse to strong liquors, and speedily became perfectly intoxicated. About midnight we were disturbed; and going on deck, I observed them all dancing and singing, totally inattentive to the state of the vessel, which was already close to the rocks, north of the gulf. It was with great difficulty they could be quieted; and having laid to until the sun had risen, we at length anchored safely in the afternoon near the new castle of Smyrna.

Having left this city to proceed to Constantinople, we ascended the Sipuli Dag, from which there is a good view of Smyrna, and the neighbouring sea: the remainder of the road towards Magnisa is for the most part a perfect plain, watered by rivulets and cisterns, and wooded in many places: the soil is clay, mixed with stone. In the winter it is moist and deep, but in dry weather firm and smooth. Two Tchutcheks or places where guards are stationed, present themselves: here a few men are employed to watch for the safety of passengers, and exact from Dhummies (Christians), and solicit from Mussulmans, a trifling sum as they pass, in acknowledgment of their vigilance too often remitted. The environs of Smyrna are occupied by gardens; and between it and Magnisa some corn is cultivated. Four or five villages are seen to the right and left, but not very near the road. We encamped about a mile beyond Magnisa *, in the open

---

* The following account of Magnisa (the ancient Magnesia ad Sipylum) and of Cara Osman Oglo, whose character forms so striking an exception to that of the Turkish governors in general, is taken from another part of Mr. Browne's papers.

" Magnisa is situated nearly N. 40° E. of Smyrna, at the distance of about eight hours; it is said to exceed Smyrna in dimensions, but contains fewer inhabitants; many of these are Greeks and Armenians, who carry on a considerable traffic; the latter occupy a large distinct building, in the part of the city nearest to Smyrna, which at night is secured by gates. An ancient castle, on a considerable elevation overhangs the east part of the city. This place is now the seat of one of the richest, the most powerful, and perhaps the most just of the several chiefs, who divide among them the government of Anatolia, under the feeble reign of the Othman dynasty. Originally the holder of a Zaym or Fief, his power and possessions have been augmented by various circumstances beyond what is usually acquired, even by the first order of Pashas; yet he has never accepted that

field.   At that season the Katerdgis rarely enter a town or village ; and thus, feeding their cattle gratis, are able to travel at a cheap rate. Our company together consists of twenty-six mules : the hire of a horse or mule from Smyrna to Broussa is now twenty piastres.   Having passed several villages, we at length arrived at one called Ballage, and hence, after a ride of about eight hours, we reached Jelembé, which is erroneously placed in the maps.   The country we have passed from Magnesia to Jelembé is fertile ;   at first plain, but the latter part more hilly ;   ill cultivated, but not unpleasant.   Between Ballage and Jelembé are several small villages.

Jelembé is a small town, containing, however, several mosques ; the inhabitants I understood to be four or five thousand ; a proportion of them consists of Greek Christians.   Wine, and various articles of provision, abound in Jelembé ;   but it is a town of no manufactures or commerce.   The character of the government, so far as I had the means of observing, seemed to be moderate and lenient.

Cisterns of fine water are every where met with on the road ; the rocks are chiefly of limestone ; vines and fig trees are in abundance. Having procured some provisions at Jelembé, I proceeded to join the caravan, which I found encamped in a pleasant valley, adorned with the agreeably varied green of low trees and bushes, of which the

---

title.   His establishment is splendid without profusion, and his economy exact without being parsimonious.   By observing this just medium, he is enabled to remit annually to the Porte a sum much exceeding his quota ; and he furnishes, whenever called upon, a numerous body of feudal troops.   It is impossible to say what is the exact number of the one, or value of the other.   The surplus of his revenue is sufficient occasionally to repair bridges and roads, and to be applied to other useful objects too generally neglected in the Turkish empire.   Travelling within the limits of his fiefs is perfectly secure; and the administration of justice speedy and impartial.   The Porte, in some measure, conscious of the importance of such a governor, though disregarding the principles of justice, has hitherto abstained from its wonted system of spoliation and perfidy.   It is not, however, to be imagined that Cara Osman Oglo is distinguished by a really elevated or enlightened mind.   To a naturally benevolent disposition, he unites a competent discrimination of character in those he employs.   His education was much better than usually falls to the lot of men of his rank and station ; and, unlike the rest of the great among the Osmanli, he is not one of those who have ' crept to rise, and sunk to reascend.' "

Quercus* forms a prominent part; and watered by a small rivulet which is conducted to a stone reservoir, built by some charitable person; and affording a copious, cool, and salubrious beverage to the wearied traveller.

After passing a Tchutchek, where the guard extorted from some Christians twelve times the sum he was entitled to, we came to a valley where two roads part off, the one leading to Ulubad, the other to Balikesr. The caravan took the former; some of the horsemen, among whom was myself, the latter. In half an hour we arrived at Balíkesr; the road as far as Tchakish is hilly, thence onward, plain and open. The plain of Balikesr is fertile, and though much of it lies waste, a considerable portion of corn is grown there. The barley harvest (6th June) is at its height; and much wheat has already been cut : but that which yet remains unripe is threatened by the locusts, which are now becoming numerous in this part of the country.

Balikesr is a considerable town, in which is annually held a celebrated fair for various kinds of merchandise. It begins about the tenth of the month Safr. The inhabitants are many of them Christians; and have the reputation of being civil and attentive to strangers; a report which I shall not contradict. Proceeding from Balikesr through the plain, north-east, we joined the caravan at its encampment at the end of four hours. The following day we met a large company of Kuirds on the march; they, as well as the caravans, frequently encamp close to the standing corn, which, as there are no enclosures, is exposed to continual depredation : a striking proof of the depressed state of the cultivator of the land, of the defects of the laws, and the blindness of the government!

Two of the chief Kuirds came and sat down in the tent where we were reposing. I was anxious to enter into conversation with them; but one of our company observed, loud enough for them to hear, " those dogs and vagabonds, though so rich in camels and sheep,

---

* The name of the species of oak appears to be omitted. — E.

did not blush to beg bread of us, who were strangers and travellers on the road." At this expression, both the Kuirds * instantly rose, and saying Ullah *Ismerladek* †, mounted their horses and rode off. They spoke Turkish but imperfectly.

The night being serene, two of us left the caravan, and passed onward by a plain open country, for about an hour and a half; and then over rising grounds until we came into the great road to Ulubad, which, for about four hours, runs along the delightful banks of the river Mikalizza, here a beautiful stream, and not of inconsiderable size : romantic and well wooded hills enclose it on all sides, sometimes overhanging the path, sometimes receding in gentle declivities. The verdure and the fragrance of spring surrounded us on all sides, and enlivened the whole of this beautiful scenery.

Having passed through the town of Ulubad, we stopped at a khan near a long wooden bridge, built over the Mikalizza, where Christians are expected to pay a toll of ten or twelve paras each. We had seen three villages before we arrived at Ulubad. Crossing the bridge, a few paces north of it, two roads part off, the one leading to the town Mikalizza, the other to Broussa. We advanced to Chatalor-Kué, which is a village situated nearly due north of the eastern extremity of the lake of Ulubad, or ancient Apollonia. This lake is bounded on the south by a chain of mountains, which seems to terminate in Olympus, whose snow-capped summit is distinctly visible. The lake is fresh, and said to be full of fish. We dismounted, and rested near a beautiful clump of large trees, a little to the right of the road. Broussa, where we arrived the following morning, has been before sufficiently described.

---

* Kuird, according to the Turkish pronunciation, or as they are more commonly termed, Curds. — B.

† Allaha Ismarladuk, We recommend (you) to God. N. B. It ought to be thus written, and not Ullah Ismerladek. The words in Turkish are, اللّه اصمرلدق allaha ismarladuk. The Germans say the same in taking leave : God befohlen. The French : adieu, i. e. nous vous recommandons à Dieu. The verb is اصمرلمق ismarlamak, to recommend, &c. — From Mr. Usko.

I advanced, with only a single muleteer, from Broussa to Yenishehr; the distance is computed at twelve hours, but it employed us rather more. The road, for two hours, lies among gardens and cultivated grounds, particularly those applied to the produce of silk, with flourishing trees in the hedge rows.. Thence we entered a large grove of walnuts, casting around a thick shade, impenetrable to the fiercest rays of the sun. To this succeeds a valley, in which a mill copiously supplied with water, forms an agreeable and picturesque object. Soon after we reached the spot where two great roads diverge; the one leading to Kutaieh, the other to Yenishehr. Having reached the foot of the mountain in about three hours, we commenced the ascent. The top of Olympus and the smaller hills around, presented themselves on the right, while the copious streams which issue from his snow-clad head or oak-mantled sides, rapidly descending among the loose pebbles which form their beds, now delight us with their clear currents and soothing murmurs; but in winter alarm the traveller by their resistless force, and impede his progress by their depth and number. These all run to the north, and are at length discharged into the gulf of Moudania. The plain which I contemplated from near the summit extends from south-west to north-east, in length, perhaps, about four miles; the breadth, on an average, a mile and a half or two miles. It is intersected by small streams, divided into cultivated fields and rich pastures, and adorned with many beautiful and useful trees, particularly walnuts. A small lake, due north of us, enriched the view; above which rises a ridge crowned with sombrous verdure. Before noon we reposed under a lofty tree, and then, after a short descent, coming into a fertile plain, well watered, in which is a small lake, we arrived after thirteen hours at Yenishehr. The plain is in part cultivated, and the peasantry were employed in reaping. The ravages of the locusts have every where been felt; and in some places the corn is cut unripe, to prevent its complete destruction by them. The harvest, however, is on the whole favourable. In going from the foot of the hill to Yenishehr, we were employed nearly five hours. We have to-day passed three villages, and a large chiftlick, which formerly belonged to a pasha, whose oppression caused the plain around to be deserted and left waste.

Yenishehr is an agreeable town: the inhabitants are chiefly Mohammedans : the government is in the hands of a Waywode, who has not more than fifteen soldiers, and whose household consists only of five or six persons. His government is spoken of as mild ; but it may be readily conceived that, with a force so moderate, tyranny could not be carried very far. When it is added, that his word once passed is sacred, and that his manners are simple, the praise is more appropriate, and consequently more valuable. The market is pretty well supplied with provisions ; but the traffic is small, the city not being on a high road. The Katerdgis do not pass from Yenishehr to Scudar more than once in fifteen or twenty days. I therefore obtained a horse from the Menzilgi to Scudar ; but having been obliged to pay the hire of him before my departure, the man who attended with the post-horse went away twice. The first time, which happened at Hersek, I brought him back by force ; but we were scarcely arrived at Gebisé, when he escaped with the horse, and I never saw him more.

From Yenishehr I arrived at Nicæa, in four hours and a half. In this place the population is small, commerce inactive, and provisions are by no means abundant. The Mohammedans and Christians live in distinct quarters. The city, it is well known, is situated at the eastern extremity of the lake of the same name, on a flat of no very considerable extent. The walls have been massive and extensive; in many parts double, and flanked with numerous towers. Many of them consist of large stones ; and Grecian mouldings, profiles and altars are every where visible. A very small portion of the space surrounded by these walls is now occupied by buildings; the remainder is in part divided into gardens ; and is in part waste. The road from Yenishehr to Nicæa lies at first through a plain ; and then traverses the extremity of a ridge extending from east to west, which terminates near the lake running a little to the south of it. During two hours, which we employed in crossing, various forms of overhanging rocks, mingled with verdant foliage, offered themselves to our view. Some streams, after meandering through the vale, fell into the lake. On emerging from the hills, we came by a descent of some length into the plain of Nicæa. The view of the city, at a distance, is imposing. One of the first objects which attract the sight, is a spacious white kiosk, belonging to the governor of Yenishehr, a little to the right of the road, on a small elevation.

In about five hours and a half from Nicæa we arrived at Kizderbend, and in four hours more at Hersek. The mountain which we ascended after leaving the lake, is of no great height; but in many places steep, and the passes narrow: low wood covers much of its surface. The rocks are of limestone, from which issue some small streams. The villages are few, and the population scanty. This land between the two gulfs is called Dillan, or Tongue, by the natives. The village Kizderbend consists of Greek Christians, whose situation appears in no degree enviable. Like Mart-rawan, in Syria, the place is remarkable for the facility with which the inhabitants give up their females to strangers. We obtained a scanty supply of eggs, bread, and sour milk: wine they had possessed in the preceding winter, but it was long since exhausted. The women were wishing that the Vizier might pass that way on his return; " as they should then get some money." This anecdote alone describes the character of the people; their wishes being in such direct opposition to those of all other Christian villages, who never fail to deplore the visits of Turkish soldiery. Hersek is also a wretched place, containing a single mosque, about twenty-five houses, two places called khans, and one coffee-house: no provisions or forage are to be obtained. Having crossed the ferry, for which an extravagant price is here paid, I proceeded to Gebisé, leaving Mallum, a populous village, on the right. Gebisé is a cheerful and much frequented town, nearly a mile in length. It furnishes a good market for all kind of provisions, and various other articles. The inhabitants are chiefly Mussulmen; there being only four or five Christians who keep shops. There are several mosques; and, as I was informed, fourteen khans.

Having passed several hours at Gebisé, a Muggrebine whom I had seen before accosted me: he had been dangerously wounded in the right side, while in the Vizier's army, by the explosion of a bomb. I found he had exhausted the powers of wine, brandy, opium, and hashîsh, until none of them raised his spirits ; and his constitution was entirely, his intellects almost, destroyed. He boasted to me of the number of Frenchmen and Copts whom he and his countrymen (Barbaresques) had killed in Kahira, on the irruption of Nassîf Pasha, and the great wealth they had obtained by despoiling the houses. The heads of those whom they had murdered were put into sacks ; and they received from the Pasha, according to this man's statement, eighty sequins for the head of every Frenchman, and fifty for that of every Copt. When Nassif Pasha's party was obliged to withdraw, my informant left, if he said truly, 6000 dollars in specie or value, in his apartment at Kahira. He spoke very contemptuously of the Asiatic troops ; of whom, he says, one Barbaresque is capable of beating ten.

I arrived at Cartal, through a heavy and continued rain, in something less than five hours. The town is about half a mile long ; not ill built ; has a market for provisions ; but is in other respects only a place of passage. The eastern extremity is inhabited by Christians. In four hours more I arrived at Scudar: the master of the Custom-house, hearing that I came from Egypt, was very inquisitive as to the state of that country. The following day I proceeded to Constantinople.

MISCELLANEOUS REMARKS WRITTEN AT CONSTANTINOPLE,
1802.

Neither science, literature, nor any kind of knowledge is forbidden to a Mohammedan by his religion ; a truth which might be abundantly confirmed by many texts from the Korân, the Hadîth, and other books. Why then are the different branches of knowledge not cultivated ? This is owing to the fatal prejudice which prevents them from being the means of advancement. No man is indebted to his learning or talents even for the humble appointments of Cadi or Imam ; much less can these qualities raise him to any lucrative or honourable office. The same remark applies to the Christians of the empire ; and superior attainments scarcely secure to the possessor the scanty provision of a Papás. As a speculative question (for such only it is), we may be allowed to enquire what would be the readiest way to restore a portion of vigour to this wasted empire? And it will certainly occur, that the first step towards improving the character of the people must be to make them aware of their own defects. No temper of mind can be more adverse to improvement than a calm and undoubting self-sufficiency. A national feeling of their own inferiority, and a disposition to emulate the improvements of their neighbours must first be excited ; and these, if they could once become prevalent, would speedily produce the most salutary effects.

But though this may be regarded as the most certain and effectual method of working great national improvements, it is happily not the only one. Does not the example of the Russians prove that a state may be powerful, and, in a certain degree, civilised, the majority of whose citizens show little disposition to improvement ? The simple circumstance of a change in the succession of the crown, by placing it on the head of a man of talents and enterprise, wrought wonders in Russia ; and perhaps might not operate less favourably on the Turks. In a national view much has been lost to the latter by the succession of four feeble monarchs. A considerable reform might certainly be effected, if the throne were once filled by a man of judgment, experience, and firmness. The feminine and eunuchal cabinet, which has long governed not only the Seraglio but the Empire, would then be speedily annihilated : the army also might soon be placed on a respectable footing : the navy would be gradually organised. Indeed without the adoption of European tactics no reform would be effectual. To accomplish this, strong popular prejudices must be encountered ; but though these are obstinate and inveterate, there is sufficient reason to believe that they would not be found absolutely insurmountable by a wise and energetic sovereign.

After providing adequate revenues for the judges, the will alone of the monarch would be sufficient to purify the administration of justice; and the advantages resulting from this important reform would be immediately felt.

The changes which are here supposed would unquestionably require some increase in the public expenditure; but this would be sufficiently provided for by regulating the public and private revenues of the sovereign, both of which would become far more productive than at present, if a stop were put to some of those abuses which now absorb so large a portion of them in their way to the public treasury. An augmentation of imposts might be difficult in the first instance; but the amount of the revenues would be increased by a better system of collection; and, in due time, the people, whether Christians or Mohammedans, might perhaps be induced to pay an advanced price for additional security and a certain degree of independence.

Among the various causes which have contributed to the ruin of the Turkish provinces, the arbitrary and independent jurisdictions conceded under the names of *Mocatta* and *Iltezim* * hold a conspicuous place: to understand their nature the following remarks may be necessary.

The revenues of a certain district, perhaps ten or twelve villages, are to be disposed of. The person who wishes to farm them, after ascertaining their value with all practicable accuracy, goes to a minister, and offers what he thinks proper for the term of one, two, three, or four years. As the government is always indigent, the offer of ready money is generally accepted; and nothing more is required to enable the farmer to exercise unlimited authority over the district

---

* The word *mocateh* in its simple acceptation answers to the Latin *vectigal*; *Iltezim* to *conductio*: the former is for life; the latter generally for a year. A new restriction has taken place respecting the former: the Mocatteji cannot now sell his interest if the value exceed five purses per annum.

in question, and to augment his revenue by every means of fraud, violence, and extortion. Thus, what was originally supposed to produce fifteen purses, he perhaps makes to yield forty. The peasantry is thereby ruined: but this does not embarrass the Mocatteji or Miltezim, who is concerned only with what the district will yield during the term for which he holds it. A more absurd system for the administration of provinces cannot possibly be imagined : it is adapted only to the possessions of a horde of rapacious banditti, who expected to be expelled in a year or two from the provinces they had overrun.

The farmer must oppress in order to reimburse himself for his enormous expenses; or he must fail. The peasant being rated in proportion to the *gross* produce of the lands he cultivates, cannot possibly do more than glean a scanty subsistence, which may be obtained by slight exertions and the most wretched system of husbandry ; and thus, whilst there is, on the one hand, a strong positive motive to oppress, the stimulus to production, on the part of the landholders, is the most feeble and negative that can be imagined. The practical effects of this system are seen in the depopulation of the country, and the increase of robbers and rebels, the great body of whom, it is known, are composed of peasantry and other subjects of the Porte, who have been thus stripped of their possessions.

Various attempts have been made, with as various success, by European writers on the Turkish empire, to ascertain the amount of its revenues. But as it rarely appears from what data their information is derived, their statements cannot be received with implicit confidence. The registers of what is paid at the capital are simple, perspicuous, and to a certain degree authentic; but it is very difficult to obtain accurate information of public transactions in the provinces. Arrears of revenue occur in some places ; anticipations in others ; and the truth is involved in an inextricable labyrinth of error and obscurity. With a due regard to the various difficulties which surround this subject, the following statement may perhaps be considered as something like an approximation to the truth : — Before the Nizam el gedid or new regulations, the entire revenue of the Porte is said to have been 46,000,000 piastres, which at 15 for the pound sterling, give 3,066,666l. The new regulations of taxes on articles of consumption, importation of corn, &c. &c. are supposed to have doubled it; and the sum is now said to be full 90,000,000 piastres, or 6,000,000l. sterling.

According to the new Nizam, or order, the government purchases all the corn for the supply of the capital. The prime cost is very often not more than sixty paras the kilot; but that quantity is never sold for less than three and a half or four piastres. The pretence for the government taking into its own hands the importation of grain, is, that the city may be well supplied; but the real object was an augmentation of the revenue. The profits of government, on this article alone, amount, it is said, to 15,000 piastres daily; which, at a moderate computation, is equal to 300,000l. per annum. The poor, it is true, have not much fear of corn rising to an exorbitantly high price; but they have, on the other hand, no hope of the commodity becoming cheaper. This, however, is not the only evil; the quality of the grain is bad; many frauds are practised in its passage to the capital, such as causing the grain to swell by wetting it with salt water; increasing the quantity by adding other substances; all which are very practicable, as it is laden, not in sacks, but in bulk. The hopes of the cultivator of the soil are crushed; and the officer who is employed to make purchases in the provinces obtains a lucrative job.

Among the little and ineffectual expedients adopted in a falling empire, the depreciation of the current coinage is generally one. This has been rapidly progressive during the two last reigns in the Ottoman empire. It is superfluous to add that none of the currency goes out of the territory: its value is very various, even within the limits of it. The fendoukli and mahbûl are exchangeable in some parts of Asia for a less number of paras than in the capital; in Aleppo for a greater; but their highest value in exchange is in Kahira: in the Upper Egypt they pass for something less. Foreign coinage, particularly Venetian sequins, Dutch and Imperial gold, and Imperial and

Spanish silver, are sought after with great avidity. In Antioch and Aleppo, in 1801, the Venetian sequin passed for a sum much exceeding what an equal weight of pure gold would have been exchanged for. The gold of Selim III. contains one-fourth part alloy ; but some means are used by which a better colour is given to it than that of other gold ; marine acid probably enters into the wash used for this purpose. Its indented edges are produced by filing, and not by milling. The nominal silver, it is believed, does not contain much more than a third of that metal ; even the paras have been depreciated during the present reign. I was disappointed in endeavouring to obtain more satisfactory details respecting the mint. An English guinea, in 1801, was worth seventeen piastres and a half.

It is perhaps worth remarking that the receipts for the Miri, in Anatolia, were within the last two centuries given in a manner similar to the Exchequer tallies among us. The intendant of a pashalik, at the beginning of the year, caused a number of small sticks to be prepared, exactly resembling each other. One was given to the person of whom the Miri was demanded, and a notch was cut for every payment he made of it. The whole being paid, the second stick was delivered into his hands, which served as an acquittance.

Although the Ottoman government be provided with an arsenal, founderies for cannon and other requisites for carrying on war, such is the supineness, ignorance, or criminal negligence of those who direct that department, that they are quite inadequate to the purposes for which they were intended. Among other instances of the defective state of their ammunition, I am credibly informed that, when the Vizier marched against the French, no bombs were ready, and they were cast and sent off to the army, a hundred at a time, warm from the furnace, to Nicomedia ; that on their arrival before El-Arish, the balls and shot were so bad, that instead of making a breach in the wall, they were shattered into fragments as soon as they impinged on it.

In Constantinople there are now ten offices where the customary duties are received on the following articles, viz. wine, tobacco, dry fruit, green fruit, grain, and various kinds of miscellaneous merchandise. The duty on wine is at present four paras the oke; and the sum collected on that article, in the first year after the duty was imposed, amounted to four thousand purses; almost as much as the whole of the duties on all the other articles of consumption. If there be no misrepresentation, this makes the annual consumption of the city 20,000,000 of okes of wine; forty okes per head for each inhabitant, taking the number at 500,000.

The mode by which the tribute of the provinces is transmitted to the Imperial treasury, may be new to some readers. It is first put into bags, containing each five hundred piastres; and each of these is called a *purse* (kïs). A certain number are then sewed in canvass, and the whole laced together with cords, forming a net-work. One of these is slung on each side of a horse or mule, who carries nothing else. The two together may weigh about two hundred weight English.

At the Tibaa-Khané, or printing-house, which adjoins the Muhendis Khan, I found them, on the 14th of June 1801, preparing to reprint the Arabic translation of Euclid, by Nasned-dîn el Tousi; but without corrections or emendations. An impression of a recent English Atlas was also meditated, with the names in Turkish; part or the whole of which is reported to have been since executed.

The æra of the introduction of printing into Turkey, was 1139 of the Hegira (A.D. 1761): the works then printed, according to the learned author of the book *De Fatis Linguarum Orientalium*, whose report I have since for the most part verified, were the following:

1. Ketab Loghat Wankuli. — An Arabo-Turkish Lexicon, A. H.
   2 tom. in folio,   -   -   -   -   -   -   1141
2. Tuhfat el Kubâr. — A History of the maritime wars of
   the Ottomans,   -   -   -   -   -   1141
3. Tarikhes Seyah. — A History of the wars between the Ag-
   whans and the Persians,   -   -   -   -   1142
4. Tarikh cl Hind el Ghurhi. — History of America,   -   1142

5. Tarikh Timûri. — History of Timur leng, - - 1142
6. Tarikh Misr kadîm we Misr gidîd. — History of ancient and
   modern Egypt, - - - - - 1142
7. Ghiulsheni Chulifa. — History of the Chalifs, - - 1143
8. A Turkish and French Grammar, - - - 1143
9. Nizam el umen. — (Qu. ?) A treatise on government, 1144
10. Feiaz el Maknatissié. — On the load stone, - - 1144
11. Gihan Namé. — An atlas, - - - 1145
12. Tekwimi Tawarikh. — Chronological tables, - - 1146
13. Tarikh Neima. — Ottoman annals, - - 1147
14. Tarikh Rashid Effendi. — Ottoman annals, - - 1153
15. Tarikh ahwali ghazawat Diar Bosna. — History of the war
    with the Austrians, - - - - - 1154
16. Firkenghi Shuri. — A Persian and Turkish Lexicon, - 1155

   In the year 1155 (A.D. 1777), the use of the press was discontinued, in consequence of the death of Ibrahim Mutefarika, the intelligent and active supporter of the institution.

   The war with the Austrians, in 1158, effectually impeded any farther progress.

   Another firman was afterwards issued for its restoration by Abd-el-Hamid, when the only books printed, were,

1. Tarikhi Sami, we Sachir, we Subhi. — Annals composed by these three public historiographers.
2. Tarikhi Yzzi. — Another of the same kind.
3. An Arabian and Turkish Grammar, by Ibnel Hajib.

   In consequence of the subsequent war with Russia, want of expert hands, new types, and other causes, the press was stopped from 1786 to 1797. New types were then cast by an Armenian; since which time there have been printed the following books, according to a list which I received on the spot:

1. Burhani Katé. — A Persian and Turkish Lexicon, published, however, without corrections or improvements.
2. Tehfa Wahbi sherai heiati Afendinin. — A vocabulary.

   x 2

3. Leghé Loght. — Another philological work.

4. Loghat Wancuil, was in the press.

Here let me acknowledge my obligation for various kinds of information to Mohammed Emîn Effendi, better known in Constantinople by the name of Rijani Effendi, who is distinguished by zeal in the acquisition and propagation of useful knowledge; and whose mild and conciliating manners give effect to his patriotism and benevolence. Some such characters still exist in the capital of the Osmanli; but, alas! their number is too small, and their voices too feeble, to awaken their countrymen from the degrading and oblivious slumber in which they have been so long buried.

There are in Constantinople twelve Maddrassés, or public academies, each of which bears the name of its founder. The same regulations and the same course of lectures, with slight exceptions, prevail in all these establishments. The salaries of the professors are not considerable, though more than proportionate to the effect of their labours. Their holidays are Tuesday and Friday in every week; three days of Beiram, which succeeds to Ramadân; and the ten days devoted to Courban Beiram; lastly, part of the month Rajib; and the whole of Shabân and Ramadân. The Mektebs, in which reading and writing only are taught, and which answer to our day-schools, are very numerous. These, and the Maddrassés, or superior academies, may be said to comprehend the whole system of education at Constantinople: if we add the instructions given at the mathematical school at the arsenal and the new marine school at the bottom of the port; instructions, it must be observed, rather nominal than real.

Exclusively of the library spoken * of in the Seraglio, which I have never seen, there are twelve public libraries:

1. That of Agia Sophia.	3. That of Mohammed II.
2. ——— Suleyman.	4. ——— Kiupruli pasha.

---

* See Professor Carlyle's letter, in the first volume of this work, respecting the Seraglio library.

5. That of Walidé.   9. That of Bayazid.
6. ———— Seid ali pasha.   10. ———— Osman III.
7. ———— Ibrahim pasha.   11. ———— Abd-el-Hamid.
8. ———— Atêf affendi.   12. ———— Rughib pasha.

MISCELLANEOUS REMARKS.

It is a ride of about nine miles from Boyuk-dere to the place where the coal appears; the country is picturesque and interesting. The strata, externally, are shallow and unpromising: perhaps at a greater depth better veins might be found. All that is visible has decidedly the appearance of wood, more or less bituminated. The dip, westward, is about 15°, and there is also an inclination inwards. It is long since the coal was wrought; and it appears that the workmen contented themselves with what was to be found near the surface. A supply of it would doubtless be advantageous near the capital, for culinary purposes, blacksmith's work and various coarse arts, as well as for heating the baths, since wood is rising in price. But in regulating the temperature of habitable apartments, it could never be used without a totally different arrangement in the edifices; and it may be doubtful how far the exhalation of fossil coal would be agreeable to nostrils accustomed to the more grateful odour of wood.

At Yeni Capu, the new gate, on the south side of the city, is seen a range of coffee-houses, raised partly on ground recovered from the sea, partly on piles. These were constructed by order of Sultan Mustapha. They are spacious, neat, and convenient; an ample awning of canvas protects the head from the sun, and it is open below to the sea-breeze. This place is much frequented by those whose leisure permits them to. employ much of the day in idleness. On a Thursday, and during the month Ramadân, respectable persons assemble there ; on a Friday, those of an inferior class. Where indolence is considered as happiness, it may be supposed that such a recreation is in no small esteem ; numbers, therefore, consume the day in listening to the mueddahs, or professed story-tellers. A greater variety of musical instruments is observable here, perhaps, than in any other part of the capital. Of the former, the following are the most conspicuous :

1. Tambûr ; an instrument with eight strings.
2. Sheshadâr and Santûr ; a species of harps.*
3. Nei or Duduk ; a flute like the German.
4. Kemân, of two or three kinds, resembling the violin, and viol da gambo.
5. Dairé ; a circle covered with skin, and having jingling pieces of brass round it.
6. Mescal, a Syrinx, i. e. reeds of canes of unequal length, sometimes to the number of twenty-three.

———

An instrument, similar to the bag-pipe, is in use in European Turkey ; it consists of an entire goat-skin, which, when sounded, is placed on the breast of the performer. The sound is far more agreeable than with us ; and the drone is avoided.

———

The mosque dedicated to Aiûb (whom the popular voice at Constantinople reports to have been the prophet's standard-bearer, I know not with what reason,) which had fallen into a state of decay, has been rebuilt by Selim the Third ; and though not among the most capacious edifices, is elegant and richly adorned. The internal structure is composed of marble, and numerous lamps of silver ; some of

---

* " Gitterns, harps, and recorders, are their principal instruments." — Sandys' Travels, p. 56.

which are gilt, and depend from the roof. The floor is spread with sumptuous carpets. The structure is at the bottom of the port; and not far from it is an Imaré, a spacious school and many shops. A vast pile, intended for barracks, and situated at the east end of the arsenal, is also due to Selim the Third, whose buildings seem to be more numerous than those of any former prince who has filled the seat of Othman.

———

There is a kind of fine porcelain, or China-ware, much esteemed in the East, from the prevalent credulity which is common there respecting its supposed properties. It is distinguished by the name of Mir tabân, and is said to indicate poison, if any exist in the food. From this prejudice, a plate or other vessel, composed of this material, is sometimes sold for three or four hundred piastres. The absurdity of the idea is evident; but it might be curious to know how it originated.

———

It is well known that the usages of the country do not admit of the intended bride being seen by the husband before marriage. The woman may, however, more easily satisfy her curiosity regarding the person of the man; though even that is not always possible. This state of restraint gives rise to several practices, tending to facilitate mutual approximation. Among them are to be enumerated the existence of professed *match makers,* who make the occupation profitable to themselves, in a manner not difficult to be understood. The excellent qualities of the future bride and bridegroom are repeated to the persons concerned, of course with great exaggeration. Accordingly, if the parties be credulous or inexperienced, a connection takes place, which, in many cases, is terminated by divorce in a few days afterwards.

Some account of the forms which are observed, with little variation, in matrimonial contracts, may not be wholly uninteresting.

Each of the parties chuses a wakîl, or procurator, and two witnesses, who are to agree before the Imâm, or priest, on the sum to be given by the man, towards furnishing at least one room of the house with cushions, carpets, and other necessary articles; and likewise on the Nikab, which is not paid immediately, but is demandable by the woman in case of a divorce. The paper, setting forth the particulars of this agreement, is drawn up and signed by the witnesses; hence the married woman is called kitabié, *wife by writing*. The Imâm receives a proper present; often a benish, or outer vesture: the other parties are gratified by presents of smaller value. From this time to the day of marriage, a fête is celebrated; and the house of the bridegroom is kept open to every person of the mahhâl, or parish; and even strangers are allowed to enter. Sometimes dishonest persons gain admission, and carry off such portable articles as are exposed to their depredations; they have been known to slip off the amber mouth-pieces of the pipes, and escape with them.

The common expenses of a marriage, in Constantinople, costs a man, on a moderate estimate, a full year of his income, and sometimes more. Thus, to a person of middle rank, they will amount to 2000 or 2500 piastres.

When the day of marriage arrives, the bridegroom is conducted to the apartment of the bride, by the Imâm, and the rest of the company; the Imâm places his back against the door, and commences a kind of prayer, to which, when terminated, the company present reply, Amên; after which they all retire to their own houses.

The bridegroom knocks at the door three times, which is then opened by the Yeni chatun, or bride maid, who replies to the " Salam aleikum" of the bridegroom, conducts him to the bride, and puts her right hand in his. She then quits the room to bring in the Suffra, or eating table, which is placed near at hand; furnished commonly with a roasted fowl and some other trifles.

While she is absent, the husband tries to uncover his wife's face, which is overspread with a long veil; to the removal of which the established rules of decorum require that she should offer some resistance.

He presents to her some ornament, generally of jewellery, which she accepts after proper hesitation; and at length consents to abandon her veil. They sit down at table, and the husband divides the fowl with nis hands, offering a portion to the woman, which she receives. Much time is not consumed in eating, and the suffra being removed, they wash. The Yeni chatûn then brings the bed, which she spreads on the floor. She takes out the bride to her mother and the women, who are in the next room, where she is undressed; after which the Yeni chatûn brings her back to her husband, places her right hand in his, and leaves them together.

The last ceremony is that of the bride being conducted in form to the bath. This takes place at the expiration of six or seven days.

The custom of *throwing the handkerchief* is frequently in the popular mouth, and supposed to be reported from undisputed fact. I have never been able to ascertain that such a practice was in use in the Harems of the Great, or among any other class of women at Constantinople, or in any of the towns of the East. In the West of Turkey, indeed, a custom prevails, which, transmitted by report through the medium of the Germans or Venetians, may possibly have given rise to the prevalent opinion on the subject.

In a part of Bosnia, young girls of the Mohammedan faith are permitted to walk about in the day-time, with their faces uncovered. Any man of the place, who is inclined to matrimony, if he happens to be pleased with any of these girls, whom he sees in passing, throws an embroidered handkerchief on her head or neck. If he have not a handkerchief, any other part of his dress answers the same purpose. The girl then retires to her home, regards herself as betrothed, and appears no more in public. I learned from a Bosniak of veracity, that this is an usual preliminary to marriage, in the place where he was born.

An idea has very generally prevailed in the West of Europe, and has been countenanced by some respectable travellers in the East, that marriages of a temporary nature, termed Kabîn, are in use among the Mohammedans of the Turkish empire, and are deemed valid by

VOL. II.   Y

their public law. I have even been personally assured by an Italian of intelligence and veracity, who had resided many years in the island of Cyprus and in Syria, that in the course of a long conversation with a Mulla, on the comparative advantages and conveniences of the Christian and Mohammedan laws relating to matrimony, the latter had insisted strongly on this valuable prerogative of his countrymen.

I mean not to apply terms either of censure or approbation to the sentiments expressed by the Mulla respecting the advantages of such a practice; but I must remark that after searching for traces of such contracts in books of jurisprudence, and making repeated and careful enquiries among intelligent Mohammedans at Constantinople and in other parts of the empire, I have found no reason to believe that such engagements had any legal validity; on the contrary, passages from the juridical writers have been quoted to me to prove that usufructuary marriages, *nekah el metaat*, and temporary marriages, *nekah el muwokkat*, which are esteemed nearly the same, are decidedly illegal. The English reader will find this confirmed, by referring to vol. i. p. 92. of Mr. C. Hamilton's Code of Mohammedan Laws.

I therefore conclude, notwithstanding the popular and current opinion on this subject, that when such a practice obtains, it has no other sanction than it would receive from the agreement of the parties, as might happen in any other country; and that it cannot be considered as permitted by the jurists, or recognised by the tribunals.

Kabîn is a Persian word, which literally signifies *promissio donorum sponsalitiorum*, (see Ferhenghi Shauri); but has not the import commonly assigned to it.

As a sequel to the foregoing Extracts it will not be deemed improper to subjoin a short Account, derived from authentic sources and, in part, from Mr. Browne's own papers, of the Life of their estimable Author; whose labours have extended the bounds of geographical knowledge, and whose melancholy fate, in the prosecution of further discoveries, cannot but be interesting to the reader of these pages.

WILLIAM GEORGE BROWNE was the son of a respectable wine-merchant in London, the descendant of an ancient family of that name in Cumberland, and was born at his father's house on Great Tower Hill, on the 25th of July, 1768. Being originally of a feeble constitution, his health was, for many years, an object of constant anxiety to a tender and affectionate mother. His education, till he went to Oxford, was entirely private; and was principally conducted by the Rev. Mr. Whalley, known as an editor of Ben Jonson's works; a man of considerable taste and learning, to whom he always acknowledged himself to be under great obligations. At the age of seventeen he was sent to Oriel College, which did not then enjoy that high reputation, which it has since deservedly acquired. He frequently complained in after life, that although, on his entrance at the University, he had a decided taste for literature and a strong desire of improvement, he met with no encouragement and little assistance, in his academical studies. He applied himself, however, with great diligence to a course of classical reading; and went carefully through the whole of the Greek and Latin historians. He also made some progress in mathematics, and took a wide range in miscellaneous and general literature. His industry, at this time, was such, that he used to read from twelve to fifteen hours a day; by which his health was sensibly affected.

After the usual period of academical residence, it was necessary to think of some plan for his future life; and his genuine love of learning, combined with a grave and studious disposition, naturally directed his attention towards the Church; to which indeed he had been originally destined by his family. But the instinct of adventure, and a certain passion for arduous enterprises which he even then secretly cherished, suggested to him the idea of some active employment; and he turned his thoughts for a short time to the Army. A little reflection, however, convinced him of the inexpediency of following a profession, to which he was, in other respects, little inclined, and for which he was not at all suited by his character and habits. Law and medicine remained; and after deliberating a short time between the two, he made choice of the former; and, taking chambers in the Temple, he for some time kept his terms, and attended the courts at Westminster. But, after a certain period, he deliberately relinquished that arduous pursuit; and contenting himself with the moderate competence of which he had become possessed on his father's death, lived afterwards without any profession or regular employment.

The interval between the time of leaving the University and his expedition to Africa in 1791, he devoted principally to general literature. He improved himself also in modern languages, and cultivated, in a certain degree, a taste for the fine arts. What was most important, he acquired some knowledge of the general principles of botany, chemistry and mineralogy, which he found afterwards of the greatest use to him in his Travels. During the latter part of this period, his attention was strongly drawn to the early occurrences of the French Revolution; and he became zealously attached to the principles of civil liberty, which appeared at first to be intimately connected with that event. He adopted, and caused to be engraved on his rings and seals, the motto taken by the learned Selden, " Περι πάντος Ελευθεριαν :" and he entered with the greatest warmth and interest into the political discussions of that eventful period. Extraordinary as this passion may seem in a retired and solitary student, such instances were far from being uncommon among the men of letters of those times. In most of them, indeed, the enthusiasm was only temporary, and passed away with the events which had given it birth : in others, it changed its direction, and, without any abatement of its original violence, went over to the opposite extreme. As Mr. Browne's opinions were more reasonable, they were more permanent; and his zeal, being tempered by knowledge and founded on conviction, underwent no material change during the remainder of his life.

As the most unexceptionable, and at the same time the most effectual, mode of promoting these principles, Mr. Browne had recourse to the press. He republished, at his own expense, several political tracts, with short prefaces. He also reprinted a part of Buchanan's treatise " De Jure Regni apud Scotos;" and he projected a plan of publishing, in an elegant form, a collection of the best tracts on Government which have appeared since the revival of letters, with a copious introduction and occasional notes. The subsequent events of Mr. Browne's life put an end, shortly afterwards, to this favourite scheme.

From a very early period, he had entertained the hope of signalising himself as a traveller and explorer of remote or unknown countries; and many adventurous projects of this description had floated, at times, across his imagination. Among many others which were much more visionary, he had once formed a plan of making a complete classical survey of

Greece, then comparatively an unknown country. But he reluctantly abandoned this design, from an apprehension that his knowledge of the Greek language and literature was not sufficiently accurate or extensive to justify such an undertaking.

He had been a diligent reader from his early youth of Travels and Voyages; but it was the publication of Bruce's Travels in Abyssinia, which gave the immediate impulse to his ambition, and determined him to lose no further time in carrying his long meditated designs into effect. The style and subject, no less than the contents, of that remarkable and, in some respects, highly interesting work, inflamed his curiosity, and called forth all his enthusiasm; and he became impatient to follow the same course, to struggle with the same difficulties, and to pursue the same victorious career. He read likewise, about the same time, and with similar emotions, the first volume, then lately published, of the Proceedings of the African Association; a book abounding with new and interesting views of the vast continent of Africa, and opening an unbounded field for enterprise and geographical discovery.

The perusal of these works led immediately to Mr. Browne's first expedition, and determined him to attempt a passage into the interior of Africa. His general qualifications for such an undertaking may be collected from the foregoing narrative. His physical and moral qualities he has himself thus shortly and correctly described, in a paper which he has left upon this subject: — " Among the requisites for my journey, of which self-examination " induced me to believe myself possessed, were, a good constitution, which, " though far from robust, was, I knew, capable of enduring fatigue and " change; steadiness to my purpose, and much indifference to personal ac- " commodations and enjoyments; together with a degree of patience which " could endure reverses and disappointments without murmuring."

Having determined on proceeding to the interior of Africa by the Egyptian route, Mr. Browne left England at the close of the year 1791, and arrived early in January at Alexandria. After gratifying his curiosity during a re- sidence in that city of near two months, he took a journey westward into the desert to explore the unknown scite of the temple of Jupiter Ammon. With this view he proceeded, by a very circuitous direction and along the sea-coast, to the Oasis of Siwah; where his attention was attracted to the remains of a remarkable and very ancient edifice of Egyptian architecture. As tradition was entirely silent concerning these ruins, they afforded a ready subject for any hypothesis which the imagination of a discoverer might suggest; and few travellers in Mr. Browne's situation would have found it difficult to satisfy themselves that they had succeeded in the object of their search. He gave, therefore, an unquestionable proof of great candour and sincerity, and of that calm and dispassionate tone of mind which was one of his peculiar characteristics, when he determined, whether rightly or not, that the building in question was *not* the temple of Jupiter Ammon. * After experiencing great difficulty and some danger from the bigotry and violence of the inhabitants, and exhausting all means of enquiry with regard to any other ruins likely to be found in that neighbourhood, he penetrated three days farther into the desert; but finding nothing which bore the most remote resemblance to the object of his enquiry, returned to Alexandria early in April 1792, after an absence of several weeks.

His health had suffered considerably from this journey; and after a month passed in recovering from its effects, he proceeded to Rosetta; where he beheld, for the first time, with the greatest astonishment and delight, the luxuriant fertility of the Delta, and " the unruffled weight of waters of the " majestic Nile." † From thence he went to Damietta, and to the celebrated Natron Lakes, east of the Nile, which he examined with great

---

* Major Rennell, who is justly regarded as the greatest authority upon such subjects, has decided this question in the affirmative. His opinion has been generally followed; and the place, where these ruins were found, is now known by the appellation of the *Oasis of Ammon.* But the judgment of an intelligent eye-witness is entitled to considerable weight; and the question may still, perhaps, be acknowledged to be somewhat doubtful. — The marked and appropriate praise which Major Rennell has bestowed upon Mr. Browne, with reference to the present subject, may be worth transcribing.

" The discovery of the temple itself, and the circumstances belonging to the Oasis
" which contain it, together with the operation of fixing its geographical position to a
" degree of exactness sufficiently critical to admit of a comparison with the ancient de-
" scriptions, could not perhaps have been accomplished otherwise than by the zeal, per-
" severance, and skill of an European. Mr. Browne is therefore entitled to great praise
" for his spirit of enterprize, which bade defiance to the hardships and dangers consequent
" on an undertaking similar to that which has been so much celebrated in the history of
" the Macedonian conqueror; and which was unquestionably performed with much more
" *personal risk* on the part of our countryman than on that of Alexander," — *Geographical System of Herodotus by James Rennell.* 4to. 1800. p. 603.

† See Mr. Browne's Travels in Africa. 4to. 1799. p. 31.

accuracy; and after visiting the Coptic Convents, embarked on the Nile, and arrived at Cairo on the 16th of May.

He established himself for some time in that city, where he resided at different periods, for the space of eleven months; and where, as he had before done at Alexandria, he applied himself with great diligence to the study of the Arabic language and of Oriental customs and manners, in which he afterwards became so remarkable a proficient. He also acquired a very accurate and detailed knowledge of the different classes of which the Egyptian population is composed, and of the remarkable system of usurpation then established by the Beys, which had superseded the ancient Turkish government.

On the 10th of September he left Cairo, with the intention of travelling into Abyssinia, and sailing up the Nile as far as Thebes, employed some days in surveying those venerable ruins, probably the most ancient in the world, which extend for three leagues on each side the river, and shew the circumference of the city to have been about twenty-seven miles!

Proceeding farther up the Nile he came to Assûan (Syene), the ancient boundary of the Roman Empire. Here he visited the famous cataracts of the Nile, or more properly speaking, *rapids;* for instead of deafening the spectator with their sound, according to the fabulous accounts of antiquity, he found their noise scarcely audible.

At Assûan Mr. Browne endeavoured to penetrate into Nubia; but a war having broken out between the Mamlûks of Upper Egypt and a neighbouring chief, no person was suffered to pass from Egypt into that country. After many ineffectual attempts, he was obliged to abandon all hopes of reaching Abyssinia during that season.

Deeply mortified at this disappointment, he reluctantly traced back his steps towards Cairo; when, having proceeded down the Nile as far as Genné, he recollected the striking description in Bruce's Travels of the great quarries situated between that place and the Red Sea, in the direction of Cossîr. It happened from several causes, that a journey from Genné to Cossîr was attended at that time with considerable danger. But, by a successful assumption of the Oriental dress and character, he performed it in safety; and his curiosity was amply rewarded. He passed through immense excavations, appearing to have been formed in the earliest ages; from which many of the great Egyptian monuments were obtained, and which furnished statues, columns and obelisks without number to the wealthy and luxurious inhabitants of the Roman Empire, at its most flourishing period. He viewed with

astonishment those exhaustless quarries of granite, of porphyry, and of verd
antique, (now abandoned and become the abode of banditti or wandering
tribes,) which supplied the most costly materials of ancient art, and to which
modern Rome is indebted for some of her principal decorations.

It may be remarked on this occasion, that Mr. Browne was desirous of
ascertaining from whence the basalt, so much used by the ancient Egyptian
artists, was procured ; but his enquiries on this subject were unsuccessful. He
observed no quarries of basalt either in Egypt or any other part of Africa. *

He returned to Cairo in the month of December 1792, and soon afterwards visited Lake Mæris and the Pyramids ; and in the following Spring
took a journey to Suez and Mount Sinai.

Having now seen the whole of Egypt, it became necessary for him to form
his plan for visiting the interior of Africa. It had been his original intention
to endeavour to penetrate to the source of the great western branch of the
Nile, (the Bahr-el-abiad, sometimes called the White River,) which, from
being considerably longer than the eastern branch, explored by Bruce, was
justly regarded by Mr. Browne as the true and genuine Nile. But the
sources of this river are extremely remote, being laid down by geographers
two hundred leagues farther south than the sources of the eastern branch ;
and, enterprizing and adventurous as our traveller was, he considered the
prospect of accomplishing such a journey, through unknown and barbarous
countries, and in a tropical climate, to be altogether desperate. He had,
therefore, determined to limit his views to Abyssinia ; and to attempt nothing
further than to go carefully, and with geographical exactness, over the ground
already traversed by Bruce, to investigate the accuracy of his statements, and
to take the chance of such farther discoveries as enquiry might produce, or
accident cast in his way.

But the anarchy and desolation caused by the war which had prevented
his journey through Nubia during the former year, still continued, according
to the best information he could obtain, to oppose insurmountable obstacles
to his passage through that country. Another route to Abyssinia by the
Red Sea and Massouah was also stated, upon good authority, to be impracticable at that period ; and Mr. Browne thought he had no alternative left
but to accompany the great Soudân Caravan † to Dar-Fûr, a considerable

* Browne's Travels, p. 142.
† Soudân in Arabic means the Country of the Negroes. — *Browne.*

Mohammedan country, lying west of Abyssinia, and north of the sources of the White River. There was some reason to believe that he might be able to penetrate from thence into Abyssinia; and he might perhaps obtain important information regarding that unknown branch of the Nile, which had engaged so much of his attention. Independently of these considerations, the journey, by a new direction, from Egypt into the interior of Africa and the country of Dar-Fûr, which no European had ever yet visited, were in themselves interesting objects, and afforded a reasonable prospect of gratifying his curiosity and rewarding his exertions.

The caravan which Mr. Browne accompanied left Egypt early in May, 1793, at the hottest season of the year (the thermometer, during the journey, being occasionally at 116° in the shade); and, after inconceivable hardships and fatigues, arrived in Dar-Fûr about the end of July, when the great rains had commenced. It appeared, immediately on Mr. Browne's arrival, that he had been entirely misinformed as to the character of the government, which he had understood to be mild and tolerant. From his first entrance into the country, owing in part to the treachery and intrigues of the servant he had brought from Cairo, but principally from the natural bigotry and violence of the reigning sovereign, he was treated with the utmost harshness and severity; and this circumstance, together with the fatigues of his late journey, and the effects of the rainy season, (so formidable to European constitutions,) produced, very speedily, a dangerous and almost fatal illness, from which he recovered very slowly and with great difficulty.

His first object, after the partial restoration of his health, was to obtain permission to quit the country; for which purpose he attempted a negociation with a principal minister of the Sultan, which was wholly without effect. After this failure, and after having been plundered in various ways of the greater part of his effects, he resigned himself to his fate; and establishing his residence in a clay-built house or hovel at Cobbé, the capital town of Dar-Fûr, he cultivated an acquaintance with the principal inhabitants, and acquired such a knowledge of the Arabic dialect used in that country as to enable him to partake of their society and conversation.

He renewed his applications, however, from time to time; and continued, more than two years, to be a suitor at the Sultan's court for liberty to depart. To attempt to give an adequate idea of his sufferings during this long period of captivity would greatly exceed the limits of the present narrative. In a burning climate, without books or amusements, without society, and almost without resources, surrounded by dangers, and in utter hopelessness of escape,—it is wonderful that he did not entirely sink under such an accumulation of sufferings. That his health and spirits did not altogether desert him ; still more, that he was able to collect much curious and minute information respecting the diseases, the natural history, the agriculture, the manners and language of the country in which he was thus detained, can only be attributed to that force of character, and invincible serenity and firmness of mind, for which he was doubtless very remarkable, and which place him on a level with the most distinguished travellers.

Among the expedients he adopted to relieve his *ennui*, there is one which deserves to be mentioned. He purchased two lions, whom he tamed and rendered familiar. One of them, being bought at four months old, acquired most of the habits of a dog. He took great pleasure in feeding them, and observing their actions and manners. Many moments of languor were soothed by the company of these animals. *

At length, owing to causes not sufficiently explained, possibly from mere caprice, the desired permission to quit Dar-Fûr was reluctantly granted ; and Mr. Browne departed in the Spring of 1796, after a constrained residence of nearly three years. He returned to Egypt, travelling, as before, with the Soudân caravan, during the hottest season. When he arrived at Assiût, on the banks of the Nile, it was four months since he had tasted animal food ; and he was detained there some time by a severe illness, the consequence of hardship and fatigue. Immediately after his recovery he proceeded to Cairo, where he remained till the month of December following.

In January 1797 he embarked at Damietta for the coast of Syria ; and after visiting Palestine, proceeded, by Acre and Tripoli, to Aleppo, and remained there some weeks. From Aleppo he went to Damascus, where he was charmed alike by the excellence of the climate, the fertility of the soil, and the beauties of the surrounding country. He continued at Damascus two months ; and, after viewing the ruins of Balbec, returned to Aleppo, and proceeding through Asia Minor, arrived on the 9th of December 1797 at Constantinople.

---

* Travels, p. 262.

Having resided several months in that capital, he returned by way of Vienna, Berlin, and Hamburg, to England; and arrived in London on the 16th of September, 1798, after an absence of nearly seven years.

———

During the course of his journey, and indeed before he left Egypt, Mr. Browne had lost, by several accidents, some of the most valuable journals and registers which he had kept in Africa, and especially during his residence in Dar-Fûr. But several important papers still remained; and he employed himself for some time in collecting from those materials, and preparing for the press such information as he judged to be new or important. He published his work in the Spring of the year 1800, under the title of " Travels in Africa, Egypt, and Syria from the Year 1792 to 1798."

It was a work of some expectation; and no labour was spared by its author to render it fit, according to his conceptions, for the public eye; but notwithstanding this labour, and the novelty and interest of the information which it contained, it had no success and has never become popular. The causes of this failure are sufficiently obvious. The style is abrupt, artificial, and not without affectation; and the work, considered as a whole, has little that is engaging or attractive. It contains some passages offensive to good taste, and a few that are more seriously objectionable. It is written throughout with a certain coldness and languor; and is altogether deficient, not only in that spirit with which great enterprizes ought to be described, but in those picturesque touches which give life and reality to a narrative, and especially to a book of Travels.

Such faults (and some of them are important) could not be overlooked by the public. But, independently of these objections, the work must be acknowledged to contain much that was new and valuable. It bears indisputable marks of industry, learning, and great accuracy. Many of the details concerning Egypt, although now superseded by the accounts of later travellers, were at that time highly interesting; and the information it supplies respecting the interior of the African Continent can never cease to be of importance.

It is the value and authenticity of this information, which constitute the essential merit of Mr. Browne's work; and whatever may be thought of his talents as a writer, he has certainly acquired a high rank among geographical discoverers. Upon this subject the testimony of Major Rennell is full and

z 2

explicit, and must be acknowledged to be altogether conclusive. The following is an extract from his Geographical System of Herodotus, which was published about the same time as the work in question.

" Since this section went to the press the author has had the satisfaction to peruse Mr. Browne's Travels in Africa; which he conceives will be classed among the first performances of this kind. The aids it brings to geography are great, and will probably lead to further discoveries; as it forms a link between Abyssinia on the east, and Bornou on the west. Moreover, it confirms, in a great degree, two positions advanced in the present system of African geography; first, that the Niger *does not* join the Nile ;. and secondly, that the most remote head of the Nile is *not* situated in the quarter of Abyssinia, but far to the south-west of it." — *Geographical System of Herodotus*, 4to. p. 480.

Mr. Browne had no sooner completed the publication of his Travels than he began to prepare for another journey. He quitted England in the summer of 1800, and proceeded, by Berlin and Vienna, to Trieste. He remained there a short time ; and early in the following year embarked at that port for the Levant, when he visited Athens and Smyrna, and afterwards went to Constantinople ; and from thence, after some stay, proceeded by a land-journey to Antioch, and subsequently to Cyprus and Egypt. Here he remained a considerable time, and passed the greater part of the Winter at Cairo. In the Spring of .the following year (1802) he went to Salonika, and took the opportunity of visiting Mount Athos; and proceeded thence, by Albania and the Ionian islands, to Venice, where he rested for several months.

From Venice, in the year 1803, he went to Sicily, which was then occupied by English troops, and employed a considerable time in viewing the antiquities with which that classical country abounds, and in examining every part of the interior. The neighbouring cluster of Lipari islands next engaged his attention ; and after making a complete survey of that volcanic archipelago, he returned, at length, reluctantly to England.

After his arrival, and as soon as he was settled in London, he employed himself for some time in arranging the materials collected during his last journey, with a view to publication. He made a considerable progress in this undertaking ; but afterwards laid it aside, whether with an intention of resuming it at some subsequent period,· or from feeling the difficulty of throwing any new light upon countries so often described, cannot now be ascertained.— It must be observed that the Extracts from Mr. Browne's papers, contained in this publication, are selected from the manuscript volume which he prepared on the occasion here alluded to.

The intervals between Mr. Browne's journies were periods of bodily repose ; but they were not passed in idleness. Since his last return to London he had resumed his former habits, which were those of a severe student. Oriental and classical, especially Greek, literature furnished regular employment for the greater part of his day ; and his hours of relaxation were dedicated to Voyages and Travels. He mixed little, if at all, in general society, saw few friends, and those men of literature or science ; and led the life of a retired scholar and recluse in the vast solitude of the metropolis.

His friendships, especially those contracted in the latter part of his life, were almost invariably founded upon similarity of studies and pursuits. Among these it may be proper to mention the connection which he formed about this time with the late amiable and excellent Mr. Smithson Tennant, a person much distinguished by his chemical discoveries, his attainments in science and literature, and his general talents for society. Although he had never himself travelled in the East, Mr. Tennant had a singular fondness for Oriental literature, and was remarkably conversant in the works of the best Eastern travellers. This induced him to pay some attention to Mr. Browne, whom he accidentally met in society, probably at Sir Joseph Banks's ; and an acquaintance, thus casually formed, was soon ripened into a sincere and solid friendship.

Some memorial of the intercourse between these two remarkable men has been preserved in an unpublished account of the Life of Mr. Tennant, which was circulated a few years ago among his friends ; and the following extract from that work may be inserted with great propriety in this memoir, as being not uninteresting in itself, and throwing a new light upon Mr. Browne's habits and manners.

" With the tastes and feelings resulting from his fondness for the East, it may easily be conceived that Mr. Tennant had a peculiar gratification in the society of Mr. Browne. He found in that distinguished traveller, not only an intimate acquaintance with those countries which so much interested his curiosity, but a considerable fund of learning and information, united with great modesty and simplicity, and much kindness of disposition. By strangers, however, Mr. Browne's character was apt to be misunderstood. Whether from natural temperament, or from habits acquired in the East, he was unusually grave and silent, and his manners in general society were extremely cold and repulsive. Even in company with Mr. Tennant, to whom he became sincerely attached, he would often remain for some time gloomy and thoughtful. But after indulging himself for a few minutes with his pipe, his eye brightened, his countenance became animated, and he described in a lively and picturesque manner the interesting scenes in which he had been engaged, and to which he again looked forward. Of the impression left on Mr. Tennant's mind by these interviews, some idea may be formed from the following passage of a letter written by him to an intimate friend soon after he had received the account of Mr. Browne's death. ' I recall,' he says, ' with a melancholy pleasure, the *Noctes Arabicæ* which I have often passed with him at the Adelphi, where I used to go whenever I found myself gloomy or solitary ; and so agreeable to me were these soothing, romantic, evening conversations, that after ringing his bell, I used to wait with great anxiety, fearful that he might not be at home.' " *

The habits of Mr. Browne's life during the intervals of his journies, and while he thus resided in London, were extremely sedentary. He seldom, indeed, quitted home, except for short and occasional visits to friends in the country; for he took no delight in travelling in England. The wild and romantic scenes to which he had been accustomed had taken possession of his imagination ; and created in him a certain distaste for that monotony and tameness, which industry, wealth and improved agriculture, are apt to give to the face of a country. He was prevailed upon, however, by Mr. Tennant, in the summer of 1805 or 1806, to make a tour in Ireland ; and he accompanied his friend through a great part of that country, on horseback, equipped with pistols and a long Turkish cloak, as he had been accustomed to travel in the East. He had anticipated little pleasure from this journey ; but he found it very interesting. His curiosity was excited by many striking and characteristic features in the country and its inhabitants ; the results, as he justly inferred, of particular circumstances in the government, and of an inferior state of civilization. He felt himself, he said, upon foreign ground, when he observed, in travelling through the southern provinces, the wild aspect of a great part of the country, the general want of enclosures, the vast extent of fertile and ill-cultivated land, and, above all, the idleness, the

---

* Account of the late Smithson Tennant, Esq. 1815. p. 30.

poverty, and the thoughtless and turbulent gaiety of the vast, overflowing population. *

Mr. Browne likewise expressed himself with great pleasure, and in stronger terms than he was accustomed to use on such subjects, as to the picturesque merit of some particular places which he had seen in his Irish journey; and especially as to the romantic and very peculiar beauties of the Lakes of Killarney.

After several years had been thus passed by Mr. Browne, his ruling passion returned; his present course of life became insipid and irksome, and he began to meditate new expeditions. His imagination naturally recurred to some of those adventurous schemes which he had formed in early life; and he seems once to have had thoughts of applying, at this period, to the Directors of the East-India Company for permission to travel into Thibet. But after due consideration of this and other projects, he fixed at length upon the Tartar city of Samarcand and the central region of Asia around it, as the objects towards which his attention should now be directed.

Having made the necessary arrangements in this country for a long absence, he took his departure from England in the summer of 1812, and proceeded, in the first place, to Constantinople; from whence, at the suggestion of Mr. Tennant, he made a diligent, but fruitless, search for the meteoric stone, which is mentioned by the Parian Chronicle and the Natural History of Pliny to have fallen at Egos-potamos in the ancient Thrace.† From Constantinople he went, about the close of the year, to Smyrna, where he had determined to pass the winter.‡ He established himself for some time in that

* Mr. Browne mentioned these observations respecting Ireland to the writer of this memoir, in conversation, a very short time before he left England in 1812.
† Plinii Nat. Hist. lib. ii. cap. 58.
‡ Before Mr. Browne left England he received from his friend Mr. Tennant a paper containing the heads of some subjects of enquiry to which he wished to direct Mr. B.'s attention. It is a hasty and imperfect memorandum, and the topics are sufficiently obvious; but as the suggestions are very judicious, and contain much information in a small compass, respecting what should be considered as the principal duty of a traveller, it may be deemed worthy of insertion.

" HEADS

city, and was fortunate enough to become intimately acquainted with the Rev. Mr. Renouard, then Chaplain of the Factory, a man of learning, intelligence, and congenial studies, in whose society he passed many happy hours, and with whom he contracted a sincere and cordial friendship.

He left Smyrna in the Spring of 1813, and proceeding in a north-easterly direction through Asia Minor and Armenia, made a short stay at Erzerûm, the capital city of that province, and arrived on the 1st of June at Tebrîz on the frontiers of Persia. No account of this long and curious journey, through a country highly interesting, but at present very imperfectly known, has been found among the few papers of Mr. Browne which have been recovered since his death ; but some particulars may be collected from the following extracts of one of his letters to Mr. Tennant.

Tabriz, July 16. 1813.

" Aware of the little interest which will attach to my own materials, I have prepared a document which I obtained at Smyrna, and which will enable you to form some idea of prices at that place. You may judge of the difficulty of procuring any exact information, when I tell you that it took me three

---

" HEADS OF ENQUIRY.

" Prices of articles : to ascertain, as far as possible, the value of the coin by the weight of the precious metal it contains.

" With respect to ancient prices, to learn the rate of the depreciation of money.

" Price of labour; both rude and skilful, in country and in town.

" Rent of land ; to be careful in ascertaining the measure, and to recollect that an English acre contains 4840 square yards.

" Rate of interest for money, and how often payable, whether at the end of one or two months, &c.

" Tenure and state of property in land and houses.

" Details of the modes of living and kinds of food, in the country and in towns.

" Extortion, what kinds practised upon different orders of persons; what degree of security of property.

" Moisture of the air to be ascertained by swinging the thermometer ; first to get the temperature quickly, then again with a wet paper on the bulb ; observing the degree each time.

" Pearl-fishery in Persia ; numbers employed; season; diving, how long under water; colour of the pearls; price by weighing or gauging; amount of annual produce.

" Nitre, whether made in Persia, and how ; and to enquire whether ashes are added to the impure nitrous solution," &c. &c.

months to obtain this; and that it was completed only the day before my departure. † * * * *

---

† For the information of the reader, a copy of the document here alluded to is inserted. It was procured by Mr. B. at the desire of Mr. Tennant, who to his other acquirements added a considerable knowledge of political economy. He had found reason to believe that the rise of prices, so remarkable in Europe during the last fifty years, was universal throughout the world; and that it was probably occasioned by a general and permanent cause, namely, a gradual and continued increase in the quantity of the precious metals; the fact of such an increase appearing very probable, as he thought, from other circumstances.

" PRICES OF COMMODITIES AT SMYRNA IN THE YEARS 1780, 1790, 1800, AND 1812.

1780.	1790.	1800.	1812.
Beef, per oke, 6 paras - - -	16 paras.	26 to 28 paras.	36, 40, 44 paras.
Mutton, per oke, 8 paras - - -	18 paras.	34 paras.	42 paras.
Butter, per oke, 36 to 40 paras - -	66 to 70 paras.	2 piastres.	$4\frac{1}{2}$ to $4\frac{3}{4}$ piastres.
Olive-oil, per oke, 12 paras - -	16 to 18 paras.	36 to 44 paras.	60 paras.
Wheat of Asia Minor, per kilot, 60 paras -	$3\frac{1}{2}$ to 4 piastres.	$5\frac{1}{2}$ to 6 piastres.	$14\frac{1}{2}$ to 15 piast.
Fine flour, per oke, 4 paras - - -	6 to 8 paras.	18 paras.	24 to 25 paras.
Ordinary flour, per oke, $2\frac{3}{4}$ paras - -	5 paras.	16 paras.	23 paras.
Black grapes for making wine, per quintal, $1\frac{1}{4}$ to $1\frac{1}{2}$ piastres - - -	3 to $3\frac{1}{2}$ piastres.	$4\frac{1}{4}$ to $4\frac{1}{2}$ piastres.	$5\frac{1}{2}$ to 6 piastres.
Red wine, per oke, 3 paras - - -	6 to 8 paras.	14 paras.	15 to 16 paras.
Six eggs, 1 para - - - -	2 for a para.	1 para each.	3 to 5 paras each.
A good fowl, 14 to 15 paras - - -	25 paras.	35 to 40 paras.	70 to 80 paras.
Chickens, 4 to 5 paras each - - -	11 to 12 pa. each.	25 to 30 pa. each.	40 to 50 pa. each.
Smoked tongues from Adrianople, 5 for a piastre - - - - -	3 for a piastre.	1 piastre each.	60 to 70 pa. each.
Fresh fruit: grapes, 2 paras, figs, 4 paras, apricots, 6 paras per oke - - -	4, 8, 12 paras.	6, 12, 15 paras.	8, 16, 20 paras.
Herbs worth 2 paras were sufficient for a soup for 5 or 6 persons - - -	4 to 5 paras.	8 to 10 paras.	10 to 12 paras.
A salad which cost 1 para, sufficed for 6 persons - - - - - - -	4 paras.	5 to 6 paras.	7 to 8 paras.
Egyptian rice, 2 piastres the kilot of 10 okes - - - - - - -	$4\frac{1}{2}$ to 5 piastres.	$5\frac{1}{2}$ to $5\frac{3}{4}$ piastres.	$7\frac{1}{2}$ piastres.
Fish, from the smallest to the largest, 8 to 14 paras per oke - - -	18 to 36 paras.	24 to 50 paras.	50 to 80 paras.
Hire of a boat for 2 hours, 15 to 20 paras -	20 to 40 paras.	40 to 60 paras.	2 to $2\frac{1}{2}$ piastres.
A good horse for 2 or 3 hours, 30 to 40 paras - - - - - - - -	50 to 60 paras.	60 to 80 paras.	$2\frac{1}{2}$ to 3 piastres.
A labourer, per day, 20 paras - -	40 to 50 paras.	50 to 60 paras.	70 to 80 paras.
Rent of a fire-proof warehouse 120 to 150 piastres per annum - - -	200 to 250 piast.	350 to 400 piast.	500 to 800 piast.
A dwelling on the Marina, 4 to 500 piastres per annum - - - -	1000 to 1500 pi.	2000 piastres.	2500 to 3000 pias.
A female servant, 20 to 30 piastres per annum - - - - - - -	50 to 60 piastres.	100 piastres.	120 to 150 piast.
A nurse, per month, 4 piastres - -	8 to 10 piastres.	15 to 16 piastres.	18 to 20 piastres.
A cook, per annum, 70 to 80 piastres -	150 piastres.	250 to 300 piast.	350 to 400 piast.
Any other domestic, 40 to 50 piastres -	100 piastres.	150 piastres.	200 piastres.

" I left Smyrna on the 16th of March. From that moment to the present I have been employed in traversing Asia Minor, the borders of Armenia and Kiurdistan, and I arrived here on the 1st of June. My progress has not been attended with more than the usual impediments ; and fortunately I have preserved a tolerable share of health. The immersion of my papers in crossing a river was the worst accident I met with, and has caused me some inconvenience. The Spring, in most places through which I passed, was more backward than it generally is in England at the same period of the year. * * *

" My eyes have been very much opened in this journey to the volcanic nature of certain parts of Asia Minor and its confines. At Kôlah, near the Hermus, only three days from Smyrna, may be seen an unquestionable scite of volcanic eruption. It is one of the most recent, though still probably of a very remote period. Carabignar is another; but this probably may have been noticed by others. Kôlah, I imagine, has not hitherto been observed. I shall have something to say of Afiûm Karahissar. The neighbourhood of Konié, and still more of Kaisairié, is overspread with fragments of lava, some of it almost in the state of scoria. The quantity of lava in the district of Erzerûm is immense, and the whole country about Mount Ararat is volcanic. The eruptions in those places appear to be of the highest antiquity.

" I hope to send you some water of the lake Urmia, and some fossil salt which may not have been examined; but the difficulty of conveyance across so wide a part of the continent is very discouraging. The only conveyance which may afford a prospect of their safe arrival will be, when the Ambassador's baggage is sent down to the Persian Gulf; which I suppose will be next year.

" Water boils at Erzerûm at 200° and 200½° * ; and at Tabrîz spirits of wine begin to boil at 164°, and water at 204°. The thermometer, when moistened, at Tabrîz sinks 23° ; viz. from 81° to 58°.

N. B. For properly understanding the above Table, it is necessary to apprize the reader of a circumstance not mentioned by Mr. Browne ; viz. that the value of the Turkish piastre fluctuated at the periods specified in the Table ; the piastre having been equal to 1s. 3d. sterling in 1800, and equal only to 11d. in 1812. What was its value in 1790 the writer has not been able to ascertain ; probably it was somewhat higher than in 1800. It is to be remarked that the piastre consists always of 40 paras.

* These observations of the temperature of boiling water were suggested to Mr. Browne by the correspondent whom he here addresses, as a ready and convenient mode of calcu-lating elevations. From the above statement, the height of Erzerûm above the level of the sea, may be estimated at about 7000 feet, and that of Tabrîz at about 4500 feet.

" If you see Sir James Mackintosh, have the goodness to inform him that the Chalfah and principal clergy of the monastery called Aitalmiazin, near Erivan, desire to offer him their most respectful salutations. They remember with gratitude the numerous benefits which their church and nation have derived from his integrity as a judge, and his benevolence as a man, during his residence in India; and they implore him to continue his protection to them in an affair now agitating, which menaces their interests in that country with considerable danger. The fact is, that one of their principal dignitaries has embezzled a large portion of their property, which they entertain hopes of recovering by legal process. *

" I am here only till I can make the necessary preparations for proceeding further; and I have hitherto seen no occasion to alter or to despair of the execution of my plan. The Ambassador is at present at Hamidân; but I am in hopes that he will be here in a few days, as it is very desirable that I should see him. Major D'Arcy, an intelligent and active officer, who is his agent here, has received me with great politeness and hospitality. I shall soon be as much at home in Persia as in Turkey; and I look forward with great hope to the future. * * * *

" This had been written for some days, but no means of forwarding it occurred. Sir Gore Ouseley is now here; and I flatter myself with being able to advance shortly. The accounts I have recently received of the state of Tartary are very discouraging; but I am not given to yield or to despond. I hope to make my next letter more interesting. Adieu! All well to the 24th of July."

Writing upon some of the same subjects to another friend, he expresses himself thus: — " In endeavouring to reach my destination, it will probably be necessary to take a circuitous route, first to Meshed, and then to Herat; but if I can contrive to get into Tartary before the inclemencies of winter commence I shall deem myself fortunate. I do not fear the snows of Bactriana and Sogdiana, when stationary; but reposing in the open field, I should not find them acceptable.

" I was gratified with much romantic and beautiful country in passing the confines; and indeed most of the route from Arzerûm hither is sufficiently

---

* This probably alludes to some appeal from the Courts of India then depending in England.

interesting. It is all classic ground; and almost every spot is connected with historical records. Volcanic matter is so widely diffused, that I am disposed to acquit Sestini of exaggeration in his route to Diarbekîr. Trap and pudding-stone and black granite prevail in this neighbourhood. Iron-ore also is common in various places : probably coal might be found. Nearer Turkey, besides the calcareous and schistose and porphyritic rocks which occur every where, I noticed volcanic glass and pumice. There is a considerable variety of plants near that confine ; but my catalogue must be imperfect, for Turkish travelling is unfavourable to botanical research.

" It seems to me that the sublime Ararat himself must owe a part, at least, of his grandeur to subterraneous fires. I was well inclined to attempt reaching his summit, discrediting the fables related of failures in that attempt. It would no doubt be difficult ; as the trackless ascent of a lofty and snow-capped mountain always is. But why should it be more so than that of Mount Perdu or some of the Andes, which have been visited ? One side at least is not very steep, but what ravines there may be I know not. The real difficulty, if I am not misinformed, consists in the lawless tribes from both confines, who inhabit the lower and middle parts of it. No guide is to be had ; and if any know the way, they would not encounter the risk of being stopped by these mountaineers. The robbers, it seems to me, must be the guides, if any one is to attempt this ascent, which would surely be desirable.

. " There is a British officer commanding horse-artillery at Erivân ; four serjeants with the men they have drilled at Nakjewân ; and Major D'Arcy has the chief command here (at Tabrîz), having with him an officer from India. The hospitality and kindness of Major D'Arcy have been a great resource to me. He is an accomplished draftsman, and has a large collection of interesting views, taken in different parts of the Persian Empire. It is to be hoped that our mission will promote literary and scientific enquiry, and procure us a complete survey of the country."

Mr. Browne continued several weeks with Major D'Arcy at Tabrîz, in expectation of Sir Gore Ouseley, who at length arrived. He experienced from both those gentlemen the most marked and friendly attention ; and received every assistance towards the prosecution of his journey from the latter which the influence of his public situation could afford. It is gratifying to record these proofs of esteem and attachment, which accompanied Mr. Browne through every part of the present journey. His name was well known, and the object of his expedition had greatly interested his fellow-countrymen in the East. They received him every where with the greatest kindness; and the partiality, which it was natural for them to feel in favour of such a traveller, was justified and confirmed by their experience of his character and manners. Towards the end of the Summer of 1813, having completed the preparations for his journey, he at length took his departure from Tabrîz, accompanied by two servants, for Teherân, the present capital of Persia; intending to proceed from thence into Tartary. He passed on the second day through a part of the Persian army which was encamped at the distance of 36 miles from Tabrîz. What subsequently happened can only be known from the testimony of those who accompanied him. After some days, both the servants returned with an account that, after advancing to a place near the river Kizil Ozan, about 120 miles from Tabrîz, the party had been attacked by banditti; and that Mr. Browne had been dragged a short distance from the road, where he was plundered and murdered, but that they were suffered to escape. They brought back with them a double-barrelled gun and a few other effects, known to have been in Mr. Browne's possession. At the instance of Sir Gore Ouseley, soldiers were immediately dispatched to the spot described; with orders to bring back Mr. Browne's remains, and to make a strict search for the murderers. On their return, they reported to the government that they had failed in both these objects; but that they had fully ascertained the fact of Mr. Browne's death, and had found some portions of his clothes, which, having been made at Constantinople, were very distinguishable from those generally worn in Persia. They added, that they had been unable to discover any traces or remains of the body, which was believed to have been abandoned to beasts of prey. Notwithstanding this report, the search for his remains appears to have been afterwards continued; and some bones, said to be those of Mr. Browne, were brought to Tabrîz; which, having been deposited in a cedar chest, were interred, with due respect, in the neighbourhood of the town. The spot was happily chosen near the grave of Thevenot, the celebrated French traveller, who died in this part of Persia about a century and half before. *

---

* The traveller here alluded to is " the accurate Thevenot," mentioned by Mr. Gibbon (Hist. vol. iii. p. 17. 8vo.), who has been sometimes confounded with the well-known compiler and publisher of Travels of the same name. He is said to have introduced the use of coffee in France. He died in Persia in 1667.

Every exertion was made by the English Ambassador to ascertain the circumstances of this melancholy transaction, but wholly without effect. Considerable doubts were entertained with regard to the fidelity of the servants; and some suspicion appears to have fallen on the Persian government. It is certain that Mr. Browne's appearance at Tabríz had excited great attention; and that enquiries had been made by persons in authority, respecting his objects and destination; and, in particular, whether he was a military man or engineer. The Persians also, at this time, were at war with the Turcomans, and would naturally view with great jealousy the commencement of any European, and especially any English, intercourse with nations east of the Caspian. But these circumstances are too slight to give any colour to so serious a charge as the above suspicion implies; nor can any particular hypothesis be required to account for the commission of an act of outrage and cruelty by the lawless tribes who inhabit the Persian frontiers. Mr. B.'s preparations for his journey at Tabríz were very public; he was reported to be possessed of considerable property; and the Turkish dress which he wore, rendered him particularly obnoxious to the bigotry and violence of the Persians.

––––––

It remains only to give a short view of Mr. Browne's character, the leading parts of which have been already anticipated in the events and transactions of his life.

In his person he was thin and rather above the middle size, of a dark complexion, and a grave and pensive cast of countenance. His manners towards strangers were reserved, cold, and *Oriental;* but he could occasionally relax from this gravity, and his society and conversation had great charms for the few friends with whom he would thus unbend himself.

His moral character was deserving of every praise. He was friendly and sincere, distinguished for the steadiness of his attachments, and capable of acts of great kindness. Though far from being affluent, he was liberal and generous in no common degree. He was perfectly disinterested, and had high principles of honour; and (what is very important, with reference to his character as a traveller and geographical discoverer) was a man of exact and scrupulous veracity.

He had no brilliancy or quickness of parts; but he was a great lover of labour, and cultivated his favourite studies with intense and unremitting assiduity. He was a man of erudition, and may be ranked among the learned Orientalists of modern times.   But that which principally distinguished him, and in which he was certainly unrivalled, was a familiar and intimate acquaintance with the manners and customs of Eastern nations, and the minute details of their domestic life, extending even to their prayers and ablutions. It was this knowledge, the result of long and patient observation, which enabled him to personate the Oriental character with an exactness and propriety which has rarely, perhaps, been equalled.

Although a good classical scholar and an admirer of the best writers, he was certainly deficient in taste; a circumstance, which has detracted from his literary character, and been injurious to his general reputation.   He was betrayed into perpetual faults as a writer by a constant effort to shine, and by an ambition of ornament, very inconsistent with his general character. The affectation of his style formed a singular contrast to the unassuming simplicity of his manners and conversation. *

His sincere and excessive admiration of Oriental life (which was another of his peculiarities) admits of an easier explanation.   It arose partly from long habits of residence in the East, and partly from the natural gravity, tranquillity and *repose* of his character and disposition.   That a feeling of this description should influence his habits and give a peculiar colouring to his system of life was reasonable and naturally to be expected.   But it had a considerable effect on his understanding, and must be said to have warped his judgment; since it produced the extraordinary and paradoxical Dissertation †, at the end of his volume of Travels, in which, after an elaborate comparison between the Eastern and European nations, with respect to wisdom, morality and happiness, he gives his decided preference to the former!

The leading principle of his character was a lofty ambition, a desire of signalizing himself by some memorable achievement.   On opening his will, which was made a few days before he left England, a paper in his handwriting was found enclosed, containing a remarkable passage from one of

---

* It was generally believed at the time of the publication of Mr. Browne's Travels that he had been materially assisted in the composition of the work by a literary friend of very eccentric taste, to whom the peculiarities of the style were attributed.   But it appears from Mr. B.'s papers that the report was without foundation.

† Travels in Africa, p. 425.

Pindar's odes, highly expressive of that generous ambition and contempt of danger and death, which are the true inspiring principles of great enterprizes. Probably his most intimate friends had not been fully aware, before the appearance of this paper, of the real force of his character, and of those powerful and deep feelings, which the habitual reserve and coldness of his manners effectually concealed from observation. *

---

* The following is the passage alluded to : —

'Ο μέγας δὲ κίνδυ-
νος ἄναλκιν ἀ φῶ-
τα λαμβάνει. Θανεῖν δ' οἶσιν ἀνάγκα,
Τί κέ τις ἀνώνυμον γῆρας ἐν σκότῳ
Καθήμενος ἕψοι μάταν, ἁπάντων
Καλῶν ἄμμορος; ἀλλ' ἐμοὶ μὲν ἑτοσὶ
᾽Αθλος γ' ὑποκείσεται.   *Pindari Olymp. Carm.* 1. v. 129.

In the paths of dangerous fame
    Trembling cowards never tread ;
Yet since all of mortal frame
    Must be number'd with the dead,
Who in dark inglorious shade
    Would his useless life consume
And with deedless years decay'd
    Sink unhonour'd to the tomb?
I that shameful lot disdain,
    I this doubtful list will prove.— *West's Translation of Pindar.*

JOURNEY THROUGH SOME PROVINCES OF ASIA MINOR,

IN THE YEAR 1800.

[COMMUNICATED BY LIEUT. COL. LEAKE.]

CHAP. I.

Difficulties experienced by the Traveller in exploring Asia Minor. — Little Knowledge hitherto obtained of the Interior. — Object of the following Journal. — Survey of Part of the Coast by Captain Beaufort. — Nature of the Information furnished by preceding Travellers. — Ancient Authorities respecting the Geography of Asia Minor. — Assistance to be derived from an Examination of the actual Remains of Antiquity. — Departure from Constantinople. — Kartal. — Ghebse. — Temperature of the Climate. — Kizderwent. — Situation of the Lower Class of the Christian Population in Asia Minor. — Lake Ascanius. — Nicæa. — Site of ancient Towns between Constantinople and Nicæu. — Ruins of this City.

AMONG the countries where the traveller, in tracing vestiges of Grecian art and civilisation amidst modern barbarism and desolation, illustrates history, and makes important additions to the science of geography, there is none so difficult to explore as Asia Minor. In European Turkey, the inhospitality of the Mahometan system is somewhat tempered by its proximity to civilised Europe, and its conscious weakness, and the great excess of the Christian population over the Turkish ; but in Asia Minor, the Christian must always feel that he is merely tolerated : the Turks are sensible that the country is still their own, and that they are a step further removed from those Christian nations whose increasing power keeps pace with the decline of their own race, obliging them to look forward to their expulsion from those regions which they usurped from the Greeks when the Christian states were comparatively feeble, as to an event that must some day be fulfilled ; while in the eyes of civilised Europe it is one of the most wonderful political phænomena of the present day, that countries so favoured by nature are still suffered to remain in their hands.

In Asia Minor among the numerous impediments to a traveller's success must be chiefly reckoned the deserted state of the country, which often puts the common necessaries and conveniences of travelling out of his reach ; the continual disputes and wars among the persons in power ; the precarious authority of the government of Constantinople, which rendering its protection ineffectual, makes the traveller's success depend upon the personal character of the governor of each district ; and the ignorance and suspicious temper of the Turks, who have no idea of scientific travelling ; who cannot imagine any other motive for our visits to that country than a preparation for hostile invasion, or a search after treasures among the ruins of antiquity, and whose suspicions of this nature are of course most strong in the provinces which, like Asia Minor, are the least frequented by us. If the traveller's prudence or good fortune protect him from all these sources of danger, as well as from plague, banditti, and other perils incidental to a semibarbarous state of society, he has still to dread the loss of health from the combined effects of climate, fatigue, and privation, a misfortune which seldom fails to check his career before he has completed his projected tour.

Asia Minor is still in that state in which a disguised dress, an assumption of the medical character, great patience and perseverance, the sacrifice of all European comforts, and the concealment of pecuniary means, are necessary to enable the traveller thoroughly to investigate the country, when otherwise qualified for the task by literary and scientific attainments, and by an intimate knowledge of the language and manners of the people. Had Browne or Burckhardt been spared to science, all these requisites might, perhaps, have been applied to the examination of Asia Minor ; at present, of the countries which antiquity has rendered interesting, it is that in which there remains the finest field for the exertion of such talents.

Among modern travellers two only have yet traversed this country in different directions for exploratory purposes: Paul Lucas in the years 1705 and 1706, and Captain Macdonald Kinneir in the years 1813 and 1814. The rest have merely followed a single route in passing through it; and even the travels of the two persons just named amount only to a description of three or four routes instead of one; the state of the provinces and mode of travelling having rendered it impossible to make any of those excursions from the main road, without which the geography of an unknown country cannot possibly be ascertained. It even appears from the journal of Mr. Macdonald Kinneir that the difficulties of travelling in Asia Minor have rather increased than diminished. The principality of Tchappan-Oglu, which offered some security, has been broken up by his death; and there remain only a few dispersed chieftains, most of them in a state of doubtful allegiance to the Porte, in whose districts, by good management and previous preparation, the traveller might, perhaps, be allowed to explore the country in safety. In no other parts can he, unless with all the requisites above stated, and a great sacrifice of time, hope to effect more than a rapid passage along the principal roads, take a transient view of some of the remains of antiquity, and note the distances of places, the general bearings of the route, and the relative situations of a few hills or other remarkable objects on either side of it.

Under such circumstances, it is obvious that the geography of the interior of Asia Minor can only be improved by collecting together the journals of different travellers, and by endeavouring to make a gradual approximation to a detailed map of the country, by combining together the information thus obtained. It is with a view of contributing to this object, that the following journal of a route through the centre of Asia Minor, from Constantinople to the coast of Cilicia, is submitted to the public. The line is one of the most important in the province; and the latitude and longitude of its southern extremity* having been lately ascertained by Captain Beaufort, it may now be laid down on the map with certainty. This, and two or three other lines †, of which the extremities are equally certain, furnish, together with a few observations of latitude in the interior of the Peninsula ‡, a good foundation for the skeleton of a map, where, however deficient we may be in filling up the outline, many points, at least, and the direction of the principal ridges of the mountains, may be fixed in a satisfactory manner. In our further progress, we shall be greatly assisted by the knowledge of the coasts already obtained; for it is observable that this part of the geography of Asia Minor is in a much more advanced state than that of the § interior. By several partial surveys, in the vicinity of Smyrna and Constantinople; by the observations of Beauchamp, in the Black Sea; but, above all, by the surveys made by Captain Beaufort, of the southern and part of the western coast, in the years 1811 and 1812, it may now be said that one half of the coast is accurately known in detail, and that of the other parts, no point of importance is much in error; so that future routes across the Peninsula, between two points of the coast, may be laid down with great accuracy, provided the traveller is attentive in noting his bearings, rates of travelling, and distances in time. It should be observed, that routes in a north and south, or north-east and south-west direction, are now become much the most

---

* The position of its northern extremity, Constantinople, is known by a variety of earlier observations.

† The most important of these are from Satalia to Shughut, by General Koehler; from Satalia to Kassaba, near Smyrna, by M. Corancey; another from Smyrna to Satalia, through Allah-Shehr and Burdur, by Paul Lucas: the two last have the advantage of crossing the routes of Chandler and others in the valley of the Mæander.

‡ The places are, Adana, Tarsus, Erkle, Kónia, Afiom Karahissár, Kutaya, Taushanli, Brusa, Kesaría, Uskát, Kastamúni. The observations were made by Niebuhr, Browne, and by Messrs. M. Kinneir and Chavasse.

§ Of the interior, on the contrary, (after having laid down all the published routes, and some others in manuscript, and after having rejected all the information for which there is not good authority,) I find that five-sixths of Asia Minor are still a blank. The skeleton, or essay, of a map, here alluded to, will shortly be published by Mr. Arrowsmith.

valuable: the frequent passage of travellers from Europe to India, or from Constantinople and Smyrna to Persia and Syria, or in the opposite direction, having multiplied the longitudinal routes, while we possess very few in the transverse direction.

It may possibly assist the labours of the geographer, if I briefly subjoin the several authorities upon which, in addition to those already mentioned, all our knowledge of the geography of Asia Minor rests. The elder travellers may be confined to Tavernier, Tournefort, Paul Lucas, Otter, and Pococke; for Bertrandon de la Brocquiére, and Mottraye, Le Bruyn, and Griffiths and Capper [*], afford no geographical matter that is not contained in the others.

Tavernier informs us, in his introduction, that he began his travels by a visit to England, in the reign of James the First: he died in 1685. Although he crossed Asia Minor several times, in the way to Persia, where his commercial speculations carried him, he affords no geographical matter relating to the central parts of the Asiatic Peninsula, with the single exception of the caravan road from Smyrna to Tokát, which passed by Kassabá, Allahshehr, Afiom Karahissar, Bulwudun, and across the Salt country to the Kizil-Ermak, which he passed at Kesre Kiupri. Though he appears to have travelled the road three times, at least, he has left scarcely any other remarks upon it, than the number of hours between the halting places, of which he has seldom even given us the names.

Tournefort traversed Asia Minor only in one direction, from Erzrum to Angura, by Tokat, and thence passing a little to the north of Eski Shehr, to Brusa.

Paul Lucas was sent out in the year 1704, by the same minister of Louis XIV. who employed Tournefort in a similar tour in the Archipelago, the Black Sea, and Armenia. But, unfortunately for our

---

[*] It should be mentioned that Capper certainly visited the valley of Doganlu, which the reader will find described in the following pages; but his drawing, and account of it, are very incomplete.

geographical knowledge of Asia Minor, Lucas's qualifications were
very inferior to those of his contemporary; nor does he appear to
have been very well adapted, by previous study, even for those
branches of investigation to which his attention was particularly directed by his employers, namely, the collecting of coins and inscriptions.

By assuming the medical character, he secured a good reception at
several of the provincial towns, and protection from the governors, as
far as their authority extended; but the banditti which at this period
infested every part of the country obliged him always to travel in
haste, and often in the night; and he was not qualified to derive as
much advantage from journies made under such circumstances as a
more experienced and more enlightened traveller might have done.
He was generally careful in noting the time employed in each stage;
but the names of places are often disfigured by his careless mode of
writing. His ignorance and credulity made him delight in repeating
the absurd tales which the traveller so often hears in these half-
civilised countries; at the same time that he omits the insertion of
many useful observations which he cannot have failed to make. In
some instances he has repeated the fabulous accounts of the natives
as if he had himself witnessed them, and has thus rendered himself
liable to the suspicion of having wilfully imposed upon his readers.
There can be no doubt, however, that his itinerary, abstracted from his
narrative, is as correct as he was capable of making it. The geographical results, when connected and compared with those of other
travellers, are a sufficient proof of this fact; and Lucas, with all his
faults, has furnished us with a greater number of routes than any
other traveller in Asia Minor. 1. He went from Constantinople to
Nicomedia, Nicæa, and Brusa; 2. from Brusa to Kutaya, Eski-shehr,
Angura, Kir-shehr, Kesaria; 3. from Kesaria to Nigde, Bor, Erkle,
and Konia; 4. from Konia to Angura, Beibazar, Gheive, Nicomedia,
and Constantinople; 5. from Smyrna to Sardes, Allah-shehr, Alan-
kivi, Burdur, Susu, Adalia; 6. from Adalia to Susu, Isbarta, Igridi,

Serkiserai, and Konia; 7. from Konia to Erkle, and over Mount Taurus, by the Pylæ Ciliciæ to Adana and Tarsus.

Next to Lucas, Otter is the most useful of the early travellers. He was a Swede, sent to Persia by the Court of France in 1734; and he passed from Constantinople through Asia Minor, by Isnik, Inoghi, Eski-shehr, Ak-shehr, Konia, Erkle, and Adana. His narrative is chiefly valuable as being composed of the information extracted from some Oriental geographers, whose works are in the Royal Library at Paris, and from one Ibrahim Effendi, director of the press at Constantinople, whose information there is every reason to believe correct, as it accords, in regard to Caramania, with that contained in the works of two other Turkish geographers, who lived about the middle of the seventeenth century : the eldest of these was Mustafa Ben-Abdalla Kalib Tchelebi, better known by the name of Hadji Khalfa; the other was Abubekr Ben-Behren of Damascus. Though little is to be derived from these authors with regard to the exact situations of places, their evidence on the orthography of the names, and their information upon the political geography are important.

Among our own countrymen, Pococke is the only traveller of the last century who has published his route with sufficient precision to be of any use to the geographer, but he has been extremely negligent in noting bearings and distances : his narrative is very obscure and confused; and his journey in Asia Minor is consequently of much less importance than it might have been made by so enlightened, learned, and persevering a traveller. In the year 1739, after visiting a great part of Ionia and Caria, he ascended the valley of the Mæander and its branches to Ishekli and Sandakli, from whence he crossed to Beiad, Sevrihissar, and Angura. From Angura he went to Constantinople, by the way of Boli and Nicomedia.

Niebuhr's route in Asia Minor in the year 1766, an account of which would have formed part of a third volume of his travels, had not a fire, which destroyed all the copper-plates of the engravings, put a stop to the work, was through Erkle, Konia, Karahissar, Kutaya, and Brusa. He made the observations of latitude which have already been mentioned; and Major Rennell is in possession of a copy of the map of his route, struck off from the copper before the fire.

In the year 1797, Browne returned from the interior of Africa by the way of Asia Minor. From Aleppo and Aintab, he traversed the range of Taurus to Bostan, Kesaria, Angura, Sabanje, and Nicomedia. Mr. M. Bruce * travelled the same route in 1812, and has given us a diary of names and distances not to be found in Browne's printed book of travels.

It was in the year 1797, also, that Olivier passed through Asia Minor, from Celenderis by Mout, Laranda, Konia, Ak-shehr, Afiom Karahissar, Kutaya, Yenishehr, Nicæa, and Nicomedia.

Seetzen traversed Asia Minor from Constantinople to Smyrna, and from Smyrna to Afiom Karahissar, Ak-shehr, Konia, Laranda, Ibrala, and across Mount Taurus to Karaduar, (Anchiale, the port of Tarsus,) from whence he passed by sea to Seleucia, the port of Antioch. The distances and the names of the places which he passed through, written with great care, have been preserved; but it is to be feared that the rest of his valuable manuscripts are irretrievably lost.

In the year 1801, Browne again traversed Asia Minor from Constantinople, by Nicomedia, Brusa †, Kutaya, Afiom Karahissar, Akshehr, Konia, Erkle, Tarsus.

---

* See the appendix to M. Kinneir's Travels.

† The following are among some of the observations of the latitude of places on the road from Smyrna to Constantinople, made by Mr. Browne. They are taken from his MS. papers.

				Latitude.	Longitude.
Smyrna	-	-	-	38° 28′ 7″	27° 6′ 48″
Magnisa	-	-	-	38° 41′ 30″	
Demir Kapu	-		-	39° 49′ 0″	
Balikesr	-	-	-	39° 32′ 0″	
Ulubad	-	-	-	40° 9′ 30″	
Michalizza	-	-	-	40° 16′ 30″	
Brusa	-	-	-	40° 9′ 30″	
Yenishehr	-	-	-	40° 12′ 0″	
Kizderbend	-	-	-	40° 32′ 0″	
Nicea	-	-	-	40° 21′ 30″	

Among recent travellers, Captain M. Kinneir has made the most important additions to our geographical information respecting the interior of Asia Minor. His routes were, 1. from Constantinople, by Nicæa, Eski-shehr, and Gherma, to Angura; from Angura, by Uskat, to Kesaria; and from Kesaria, by Nigde, Ketch-hissar *, and over Mount Taurus, by the Pylæ Ciliciæ, to Tarsus, Adana, and Iskenderun. 2. From Celenderis to Mout, Laranda, Konia, Ak-shehr, Afiom Karahissar, Kutaya, Brusa, Mudania. 3. From Constantinople, by Nicomedia, Sabanje, Tereboli, Boli, Kastamúni †, Samsún, Tarabizun, to Erzrum.

Mr. Kinneir was also one of the many persons who, during the latter years of the war, crossed the northern part of Asia Minor from Tokat, by Amasia, Osmangik, and Boli. This route has been laid down upon paper with considerable accuracy, but cannot be of great use in connecting the geography of the northern parts of Asia Minor, until the longitude of some of its points is known; and until we have some other routes intersecting it in a direction from north to south.

Another road which has been still more traversed, is from Brusa or from Maalitch, by Ulubad and Magnesia, to Smyrna; the latitudes of all the principal places on it have been determined by Browne. Of these and of several other routes in the ancient provinces of Mysia, Lydia, and Caria, we have many descriptions in Smith, Wheler, Spon, Chishull, Pococke, Picenini, and Chandler, as well as in manuscript tours which would not be inaccessible to the geographer.

The authorities upon which our knowledge of the *antient* geography of the interior of Asia Minor is founded, are the works of Strabo,

---

* This is probably an error for Kilissa-Hissar, which, according to Hadgi Khalfa, is the name of a castle near Bor. The bearing and distance of Mr. Kinneir's Ketch-Hissar from Nigde proves that it is the same place as the Bor of Hadgi Khalfa and Paul Lucas.

† Mr. Kinneir calls this place Costambol, but the Turkish geographers give it the name in the text.

Ptolemy, Pliny, Stephanus Byzantinus, the curious table or map of roads called the Theodosian or Peutingerian Tables, the Antonine and Jerusalem Itineraries, the Synecdemus of Hierocles, and the following historical narratives of some celebrated military expeditions: 1. The Journal by Xenophon*, of the route of Cyrus from Sardes to Celænæ, and from thence to Iconium ; and through Lycaonia and part of Cappadocia, and over Mount Taurus to Tarsus. 2. Arrian's Narrative of the March of Alexander the Great, from Lycia into Pamphylia and Pisidia, and thence to Gordium in Phrygia, and to Ancyra, and through Cappadocia and the Pylæ Ciliciæ to Tarsus.† 3. The account by Livy, of the marches of Cn. Manlius, in Phrygia, Pamphylia, and Pisidia, and thence into Gallogræcia, and to Ancyra. ‡ 4. The march of the Emperor Alexius Comnenus, from Constantinople to Iconium, in an expedition against the Turks, as related by his daughter Anna Comnena.

To these may be added, with regard to the southern coast, an anonymous Periplus, intituled, " σταδιασμὸς τῆς θαλάσσης," which was extracted from a manuscript in the Royal Library of Madrid, and published in a volume, called Regiæ Bibliothecæ Matritensis Codices Græci MSS. by the librarian Iriarte, in the year 1769. But the best and most numerous evidences of ancient geography are those which still exist in the country itself; in the ruins of the ancient cities, and in the inscriptions and other monuments which may be found there. When these remains of antiquity are thoroughly explored, and the results applied to the explanation of the passages of history just referred to, they will probably lead to a system of Ancient Geography in Asia Minor, much more correct than we at present possess. For while we are still ignorant of the exact position of such important points as Gordium, Pessinus, Synnada, Celænæ, Cibyra, Sagalassus, Aspendus, Selge, Antioch of Pisidia and Isaura, it is a vain attempt to form any satisfactory system ; the several parts of

---

* Ante Christum, 401.   † A. C. 333.   ‡ A. C. 189.

which must depend so much upon one another, and upon an accurate determination of the principal places.

On the 19th of January, 1800, I quitted Constantinople, on my way to Egypt, in company with the late Brigadier General Koehler, the late Sir Richard Fletcher, the late Archdeacon Carlyle, Arabic professor at Cambridge, and Mr. Pink, of the corps of Royal Military Surveyors, and Draftsmen. We were well armed, and dressed as Tatar Couriers, and the whole party, including servants, baggage, Turkish attendants, and postillions, formed a caravan of thirty-five horses. At this time, there were two roads across Asia Minor, used by messengers and other persons, travelling post between the Grand Vizier's army, and the capital; the one meeting the south coast at Satalía, the other at Kelénderi. We deferred deciding as to which we should follow, until we should arrive at the point of separation.

We left Iskiodar* at 11 A.M., and travelled for four hours along the borders of the sea of Marmora, through one of the most delightful tracts in the neighbourhood of Constantinople; its beauty heightened by the mildness of the weather, and clearness of the atmosphere. On our right was the tranquil expanse of the sea of Marmora, as far as the high woody coast on the south side of Nicomedia, surmounted by the majestic summits of the Bithynian Olympus. In the midst of the magnificent basin were seen immediately before us the Princes Islands, with their picturesque villages and convents, amidst pine groves and vineyards. Our road led sometimes through rich pastures, covered with sheep, but, for the most part, through the gardens which supply a large proportion of the vegetables consumed in the city and its suburbs. Already the beans, and other productions of the spring, were in a forward state. The road was in some places muddy, but in general very good. Kartal, where we arrived at the end of four hours, is a small place upon the edge of the gulf, in the midst of a fertile and well cultivated district, and has a harbour for small vessels. Half

---

* In Greek, Σκουτάριον, Skutári.

cc 2

an hour further is a Greek village, which preserves unaltered the ancient name Παντίχιον, pronounced Pandíkhi.

Jan. 20. — From Kartal to Ghebse * five hours, passing through Pandikhi ; and at the end of three hours Tuzla, so called from the salt-works belonging to it. The road winds along the side of the gulf, which, as it narrows, presents a great variety of beautiful landscapes. The soil affords a fine pasture, in some parts of which appear rocks of blue and white marble, projecting above the surface ; and several remains of ancient quarries. We met a Mollah travelling in a Tak-treván, lounging upon soft cushions, smoking his Narghilé †, and accompanied by splendidly-dressed attendants on horseback. His baggage-horses were loaded with mattresses and coverings for his sofas ; valises containing his clothes ; a large assortment of pipes ; tables of copper ; cauldrons ; saucepans ; and a complete *batterie de cuisine*. Such a mode of travelling is undoubtedly very different from that which was in use among the Turks of Osman, and Orchan ; and the articles of the Mollah's baggage are, probably, for the most part, of Greek origin, adopted from the conquered nation in the same manner as the Latins borrowed the arts of the Greeks of a better age. In fact, it is to Greek luxuries, with the addition of coffee and tobacco, that the present imbecile condition of these barbarians is to be ascribed ; and " Græcia capta ferum victorem cepit" applies as well to the Turks, as it once did to the Romans ; for, though Greek art in its perfection may be degraded by a comparison with the arts of the Byzantine Greeks, yet in the scale of civilization, the Turks did not bear a higher proportion to these than the Romans did to the others.

Ghebse, called by the Greeks Κίτυζα, is a Turkish town, having a few Greek houses. The only remarkable object in it is a fine

---

* The rule observed in writing the Turkish names is, that the vowels should be pro-nounced as in Italian, and the consonants as in English. Gh, Dh, and Kh, are intended to express the aspirated forms of G, D, K.

† A kind of pipe in which the smoke is made to pass through water : used in every part of the East.

ASIA MINOR.197

mosque of white marble, surrounded with a grove of large cypresses, both of the pointed kind and of those of which the branches are looser and more spreading. This mosque, and some good baths, were built by Moustafa Pasha, who was Grand Vizier to Sultan Selim the First at the time of the conquest of Egypt. An imperfect Greek inscription was the only indication which I observed of Ghebse being on the site of a Greek city.

Jan. 21.—From Ghebse to Kizderwent, nine hours. Our route for the first three hours was parallel to the shore of the gulf, which here presents, on either side, a beautiful scenery of abrupt capes and woody promontories, with villages upon the sides of the mountains, and corn-fields and vineyards to their very tops. The road then descends to the water-side under the small village of Malsum, where a long tongue of land, projecting from the opposite shore, affords a convenient ferry of about two miles across, to the south side of the gulf. It is called the ferry of the Dil (tongue), and being much frequented is well supplied with large boats and constant attendance. The persons employed in it are lodged in tents by the water-side. We write to our friends at Constantinople by a huntsman of the Sultan, who is returning from the chace loaded with pheasants, partridges, and other game, which he had been killing for the Imperial table in the woods near the gulf. It takes us two hours to unload, cross the ferry, and reload. We then ride three miles along the Dil before we gain the line of coast. Leaving the town of Ersek at no great distance on our right, we proceed up a beautiful valley, watered by a river which joins the gulf near the Dil. This river we cross more than twenty times; passing through the water, or over good stone bridges. In many places the river falls in cascades over the rocks. The sky is without a cloud; and the temperature that of England in April or May. The ground is covered with violets, crocusses, and hyacinths. The road being excellent, we travel nearly at the rate of four miles and a half an hour, and finish our nine hours in seven. We passed the ruins of an old castle of the date of the lower Greek empire, with many towers. On the slopes on either side are seen flocks of sheep and goats; in the valley the peasants are at plough, and we meet long caravans of camels tied together, and preceded by an ass. As we approached Kizderwent, which is situated in a retired part of the valley, near the source of the river we had been following, we enter an extensive mulberry plantation, this being one of the numerous villages in the neighbourhood that supply Brusa with the excellent silk for which it is noted in the commercial world. Vineyards, on the slopes of the hills around, furnish also a tolerable wine. Kizderwent (the pass of the girls) having the misfortune to lie upon the great road from Constantinople to Brusa, Kutaya, and Konia, is exposed to a thousand vexations from passengers, notwithstanding the privileges and exemptions which have been granted to it by the Porte. It is inhabited solely by Greeks. Upon our arrival we found our konakgi, a Tatar courier, who has the charge of riding forward to procure lodgings (konak), seated over a blazing fire in a neat cottage, which formed a favourable contrast to the meanness and want of comfort seen amidst the pretended magnificence of the Turkish houses. To judge from what we have hitherto observed, the lower order of Christians are not in a worse condition in Asia Minor than the same class of Turks ; and if the Christians of European Turkey have some advantages arising from the effects of the superiority of their numbers over the Turks, those of Asia have the satisfaction of seeing that the Turks are as much oppressed by the men in power as they are themselves; and they have to deal with a race of Mussulmans generally milder, more religious, and better principled than those of Europe.

Jan. 22. — We travel in a fine valley, continually ascending. At the end of an hour we came suddenly upon a view of the lake Ascanius. It is about ten miles long, and four wide ; surrounded on three sides by steep woody slopes, behind which rise the snowy summits of the Olympus range. A forest of Ilex, and other evergreens, mixed with oaks, cover the nearer slopes ; while on the left, along the head of the lake, we perceived a rich cultivated plain, at the extremity of which, soon afterwards appears, on the edge of the lake, the entire circuit of the ancient walls of Nicæa, with their massy towers and gates. Nothing is more striking in this magnificent prospect, than that clearness of atmosphere, and brilliancy of colouring, which is so seldom seen in our northern scenery. We make the circuit of the northern end of the lake; passing for ten miles through the plain, where we find the almond-trees already in blossom ; and traverse plantations of olives, mulberries, and vines. We leave, at about two miles on our left, an ancient triangular obelisk, standing single in the middle of the plain. It bears an inscription, which has been published by Pococke, and proves that the obelisk was erected in honour of C. Cassius Philiscus. We pass through one of the ancient gates of Nicæa, and in the midst of the garden ground now inclosed within its walls, we arrive at the wretched Turkish town of Isnik, distant five complete hours, or about twenty miles, from Kizderwent.

Of the ancient places situated between Constantinople and Nicæa, we have sufficient evidence of the situation of Scutarium * and Pantichium †, in the preservation of their ancient names. Ghéviza has generally been supposed a corruption of Libyssa, the name of a small maritime town, celebrated as having been the burying place of Annibal ; but Ghéviza is more probably the successor of Dacibyza ; the word, when written in Greek, (Κίζυζα) being no more than the ancient Δακίβυζα, with the loss of the first syllable. The thirty-six or thirty-nine Roman miles, moreover, placed in the itinerary, between Chalcedonia and Libyssa, will not agree so well with the nine hours from Skutáre to Ghebse, as with the twelve hours to Malsum, which place I take to stand on the site of Libyssa. Plutarch appears to confirm this supposition, for in mentioning Libyssa ‡, he speaks of a sandy place, which answers to the promontory of Dil. Dacibyza is mentioned by several of the historians of the Lower Empire, as a place where, by order of the Arian Emperor Valens, eighty priests, of the

---

* Ορχάνης . . . . ἦλθε πρὸς τοῦ Βυζαντίου τὴν Περαίαν, ὃ Σκουτάριον ἐγχωρίως ὀνομάζεται. — Cantacuz. l. 4. c. 4.

† Antonin. Itin. Wess. p. 19. Hierosol. It. p. 571.

‡ Ἐν δὲ Βιθυνίᾳ τόπος ἐστὶ θινώδης ἀπὸ θαλάσσης καὶ πρὸς αὐτῇ κώμη τις ὀυ μεγάλη Λίβυσσα καλεῖται. — Parall. in Flamin.

opposite sect, were burned with the ship wherein they were embarked.* The river descending from Kizderwent to the Dil, can be
no other than the Draco, which Procopius describes as remarkable for
its winding course. It is singular that I had made the observation,
that we crossed it about twenty times, in our way from the Dil to
Kizderwent, before I was aware that Procopius had made precisely
the same remark with regard to the Draco.† In the first crusade, the
passes of the river Draco were fatal to some of the Normans, under
Peter the Hermit. After landing at Helenopolis, and rashly push-
ing forward towards Xerigordus, on the way to Nicæa, they here fell
into a Turkish ambuscade which awaited them. ‡ Helenopolis,
named after the mother of Constantine the Great, having been near
the Draco, was probably at or near Ersek. We find time, in the
evening, to walk among the ruins of Nicæa. The ancient walls,
towers, and gates are in tolerably good preservation. Their construction resembles that of the walls of Constantinople, with which
they are coæval. In most places they are formed of alternate courses
of Roman tiles, and of large and square stones, joined by cement of
great thickness. In some places have been inserted columns, and
other architectural fragments, the ruins of more ancient edifices. Of
the towers, those on the edge of the lake, and on either side of the
different gates, are the largest and most perfect. We remark, also,
the remains of two walls which projected from the main *enceinte*
into the water, intended, undoubtedly, to exclude, when necessary,
all communication under the walls, along the edge of the lake. Some
of the towers, like those of Constantinople, have Greek inscriptions,
which have been published in the Inscriptiones Antiquæ of Pococke.
The ruins of mosques, baths, and houses, dispersed among the gardens
and cornfields, which now occupy a great part of the space within the

---

* Zonaras, l. 13. c. 16.   Socrates, l. 4. c. 16.   Sozomen, l. 6. c. 14.   Cedrenus, p. 311.
Theophanes, p. 50.
† Διαβαίνειν αὐτὸν πλεῖον ἢ εἰκοσάκις ἐστὶ τοῖς τῇδε ἰοῦσι.   Proc. de Ædif. l. 5. c. 2.
‡ Anna Comnena, l. 10. c. 7.

Greek fortifications, show that the Turkish Isnik, though now so inconsiderable, was once a place of importance, as indeed its history, under the early Ottomans, before they were in possession of Constantinople, gives us sufficient reason to expect. But it never was so large as the Grecian Nicæa, and it seems to have been almost entirely constructed of the remains of that city ; for the ruined mosques and baths are full of the fragments of Greek temples and churches.

CHAPTER II.

Lefke. — Cultivation of the Country. — Dress and Appearance of the People. — Shughut. — Eski-shehr, the ancient Dorylæum. — Seidel Ghazi. — Mode of extracting the Turpentine from the Pine Trees. — Rocks excavated into Sepulchres and Catacombs. — Remarkable and interesting Monument of Doganlu. — Characters inscribed on the Rock. — Attempt to ascertain the Site of Nacoleia. — Opinion respecting the Sculpture and Inscription at Doganlu. — Kosru Khan. — Inscription to Jupiter Papias. — Bulwudun. — Isaklu. — Ak-shehr. — Ilgun. — Ladik. — State of the Climate.

J AN. 23. — From Isnik to Lefke, six hours, and from Lefke to Vezir-Khan, four hours. We rise at two in the morning; but as it takes near three hours for the whole party to breakfast, pack up the baggage, and load the horses, we are not ready till five, and have then to wait an hour and a half for horses. We soon leave the borders of the beautiful lake of Isnik, and proceed up a valley, which we quit after three or four miles, and suddenly ascend to the left a hill of moderate height. Soon losing sight of the lake, we advance along an elevated barren country, until we enter a deep ravine formed by towering cliffs on either side, where a great variety of luxuriant evergreens spring from among the rocks. The ravine leads into a valley, where the same kind of scenery receives additional beauty from the contrast which opens upon us of a fine valley, watered by the Sakaria, a name corrupted from the antient Sangarius, although this seems

not to have been the main branch of the river, but that which was anciently called Gallus. · Lefke, a neat town built of sun-baked bricks, is
situated in the middle of this beautiful valley near the river, which we
crossed by a handsome stone bridge a little before we entered the town.
We find the cultivation in this valley as perfect as that of some of the
most civilized parts of Europe. The fields are separated by neat
hedges and ditches. Extensive plantations of mulberry trees, mixed
with vineyards and corn-fields, occupy the lower grounds, while cultivated patches are seen to a great height in the hills, which in other
parts furnish a fine pasture to sheep and goats. This delightful region
exhibits a most picturesque contrast with the unevenness and grandeur
of the surrounding mountains. We were told there had lately been
an insurrection with the design of expelling an obnoxious Kadi, but
we did not perceive the least appearance of disturbance. We follow
the valley, passing many villages on either hand, for four hours more,
to Vezir-Khan. Since we have left the gulf of Nicomedia we have
seen no marks of wheel-carriages, and we meet with scarcely any
person on the road during this day's journey, except a party of
Turkish horsemen with their dogs, in search of hares. The Turks of
this part of the country are an extremely handsome race: they have
a great variety of head-dresses, most of which are highly becoming
to their fine countenances. The women who appear abroad are invariably dressed in the shapeless ferijé, and the veil so often described
by travellers. At Vezir-Khan we were lodged in a small mud-built
house, and had to wait a considerable time before our attendants could
prevail upon the people to kill the fowls intended for our dinner, and
to send men to the river to catch some fish. The valley around is
covered with extensive plantations of mulberry trees ; and the orchards,
vineyards, and corn-fields, enclosed with hedges, exhibit signs of
neatness and comfort to which there is a great contrast in the misery
of the houses.

    Jan. 24. — From Vezir-Khan to Shughut, eight hours : the weather
still delightfully clear and mild. For the first two hours we continue
to pursue the valley, and then ascend a lofty ridge, a branch of

Olympus. It incloses on the east the valleys watered by the branches of the Sangarius which we have passed, as the heights between Isnik and Lefke do on the opposite side. Our road across the mountain presents some wild scenery of broken rocks and barren downs with little or no wood, and occasionally the view of extensive valleys on either side. At the summit of the ridge we pass a Karakol-hané (guard-house), and at the foot of the mountain on the east side we enter some pleasant valleys, conducting into an open expanse of undulated ground, well cultivated with corn. It gives a favourable idea of Asiatic husbandry, but there is little appearance of inhabitants, only three or four small villages being in sight in the whole of our day's journey. The weather being dry the road is excellent; but in rainy weather must be quite the reverse on account of the rich deep soil. At the further end of this champaign country we perceive the town Shughut, and upon an adjacent hill the tomb of Ali Osman, founder of the Ottoman dynasty. Shughut was bestowed upon Ertogrul, the father of Osman the Sultan of Konia, for his services in war; and became the capital of a small state, which included the circumjacent country as far as Angura on the east, and in the opposite direction all the mountainous district lying between the valleys of the Sangarius and those of the Hermus and Mæander. From hence Osman made himself master of Nicæa and Prusa, and of all Phrygia and Bithynia, and thus laid the foundations of the Turkish greatness. There is another tomb of Osman at Brusa, the most important of the places which he conquered from the Greeks. The Turks, however, of this part of Asia Minor assert that it is a cenotaph, and that the bones of Osman were laid by the side of those of his father Ertogrul in his native town. The tomb is built like some of the handsomest and most ancient of the Turkish sepulchres at Constantinople, and is situated in the midst of a grove of cypresses and evergreen oaks.

The town is said to contain 900 houses, but now exhibits a wretched appearance, chiefly in consequence of a late insurrection of the inhabitants, a party of 300 of whom have put to death, within three months, three different Ayáns sent here by the Porte. At present the government of Constantinople has the upper hand, and the insurgents have been obliged to fly to the mountains, but we find the new governor with all his troops still on the *alerte* to prevent the place from being once more surprised and pillaged. Our situation is rendered still more uncomfortable by the discovery we now make, that our travelling firmahn, in consequence of an intrigue at Constantinople, of which we too well know the original mover, is drawn up in such a manner as to leave it in the power of any of the Turks to obstruct our progress, and the Ayán of Shughut accordingly takes advantage of it to extort a present before he will give us the smallest assistance. We are wretchedly lodged in a ruinous apartment over a stable occupied by the Ayán's cavalry; and cannot prevent the soldiers from coming into the room and examining our arms and baggage. There are large plantations of mulberries around the town, and every house manufactures a considerable quantity of raw silk.

Jan. 25. — It is nine o'clock before we can procure any horses, and then find none to be had but some wretched animals covered with sores, and almost skeletons. At first setting out they are hardly able to walk ; but to our surprise we find, before we have travelled many miles, that most of them have a very easy and rapid pace, perform a journey of ten hours' distance with only a few short halts, and arrived at our konák at Eski-shehr apparently in better travelling condition than when they set out. Our road indeed is dry and level, and the weather still fine. Half the route was over mountains and woody ; the latter half over an extensive plain not less than 30 miles in length and 10 in breadth, but very thinly peopled and not above one-third cultivated. Seven or eight miles short of Eski-shehr were some ancient Greek ruins upon a rising ground in the plain. Amidst a great number of scattered fragments of columns, and other remnants of architecture, we find several pedestals or στήλαι of a clumsy construction, with some almost-defaced fragments of Greek inscriptions, in which we endeavoured in vain to discover the name of the city though the word πόλις was visible. The ruins are called Besh-Kardash (the five brothers); the number of pedestals standing, however, is more than five, but five is a favourite number with the Turks ; to 5, 15, 40, 100, or 1001, all uncertain numbers are generally ascribed.

Eski-shehr is about the same size as Shughut, and is advantageously situated on the root of the hills, which border on the north the great plain already mentioned. The town is divided into an upper and lower quarter, and is traversed by a small stream which at the foot of the hills joins the Pursek or ancient Thymbrius. This river rises to the south of Kutaya, passes by that city, and joins the Sangarius a few hours to the north-east of Eski-shehr. This place is now cele-brated for its hot-baths : we were unable to ascertain whether it pre-serves any remains of antiquity * ; but there can be little doubt that it stands upon the site of Dorylæum. The plain of Dorylæum is often mentioned by the Byzantine historians as the place of assem-blage of the armies of the Eastern empire in their wars against the Turks, and it is described by Anna Comnena † as being the first ex-tensive plain of Phrygia after crossing the ridges of Mount Olympus, and after passing Leucæ. As we have undoubted evidence of the position of Leucæ in the name of the village Lefke, which is exactly the modern pronunciation of the Greek Λεύκαι, there seems to be little doubt that the plain of Dorylæum is that of Eski-shehr.

The site of the town itself is not less decisively fixed at Eski-shehr by the description of Cinnamus (16. c. 14.), who mentions its hot baths, its fertile plain, and its river, as well as by the ancient iti-neraries ‡ : for from Dorylæum diverged roads, 1. to Philadelphia ; 2. to Apameia Cibotus, or Celænæ ; 3. to Laodiceia Combusta, and Iconium ; 4. to Pessinus and Amorium ; 5. to Ancyra : a coincidence of lines which (their remote extremities being nearly certain) will not apply to any point but Eski-shehr, or. some place in its immediate neighbourhood. The position of Eski-shehr accords also with the

---

* Mr. M. Kinneir found some antique remains, and copied Christian Greek inscriptions here. Paul Lucas found some ruins, and transcribed some incomplete inscriptions at an Armenian village an hour and a half from Eski-shehr.

† L. 11. and L. 15.

‡ Tab. Theodos. Segm. vi. Anton. Itin. p. 202.

Antonine and Jerusalem itineraries, inasmuch as we observe in these tables that the road from Nicæa to Ancyra did not pass through Dorylæum ; Eski-shehr being about twenty miles to the south of a line drawn from Isnik to Angura.

The Aga of Eski-shehr was formerly in the government of a town six hours distant, the name of which we neglected to note. He had long been at war with the governor of Eski-shehr, and at length having acquired the preponderancy so far as to carry off all his opponent's sheep and cattle, he followed up his successes last year with such increased energy that he added his rival's head to the other spoils, and has since been in undisturbed possession of both places, and confirmed in his authority by the Porte.

Jan. 26. —From Eski-shehr to Seid-el-Ghâzi, a computed distance of nine hours. We have a sharp wind at east. Our road for the first half of the journey continues to cross the same wide uncultivated plains, but towards the end they are more broken into hill and dale, and appear less wild and desolate. Scarcely a tree is to be seen through the whole day's journey. Upon the edge of the plains we observe in many places sepulchral chambers excavated in the rocks. In these and in the fragments of ancient architecture dispersed in different parts of the plains, we have undoubted proofs of their ancient state of cultivation and populousness. The latter part of our journey is over low ridges; the road throughout is excellent, and fit for wheel carriages. Seid-el-Ghâzi is a poor ruined village, but it bears marks of having once been a place of more importance, even in Turkish times ; as there is a fine mosque upon the side of a hill which commands the village, dedicated to the Mussulman saint, from whom the place derives its name. There are also several fragments of architecture which fix it as the site of an ancient Greek city.

Jan. 27. — From Seid-el-Ghâzi to Kósru Pasha-Khany, the distance is seven hours ; but we make a détour to the right of the direct road, for the sake of viewing some monuments of antiquity, which were reported to us at Seid-el-Ghâzi. We first ascend for some distance, and pass over an elevated stony heath, in a direction to the westward of

ΑΕΓΑΓΑΚΕΓΑΓΟΓΑΓ◦Σ᛬Ι᛬ΔΑΙ᛬ΓΑΓΑΓΤΑΒΙ᛬ΓΑΓΑΚΤΕΙ᛬ΕΔΑ

᛬ΜΕΜΕΓΑΙΞ᛬ΓΡ◦ΙΤΑΓΟΣ᛬ΚΦΙΙΑΓΑΓΕΙ◦Σ᛬ΞΙΚΕΜΕΜΑΝ᛬ΕΛΑ

London, Published May 16th 1824 by Longman, Hurst, Rees, Orme & Brown, Paternoster Row

south; we then enter a forest of pine-trees, from many of which they
had been extracting the turpentine, by making an incision at the foot
of the tree, and then lighting a fire under it. By these means the resin
descends rapidly, and is soon collected in large quantities, but the tree
is killed; and it sometimes happens that the fire communicating de-
stroys large tracts of the forest. We saw several remains of these
conflagrations, as we passed along. After traversing the forest for an
hour, we come in sight of a beautiful valley, situated in the midst of
it. Turning to the left, after we descend into the valley, we find it to
be a small plain, about a mile long, and a quarter of a mile broad,
embosomed in the forest, and singularly variegated with rocks, which
rise perpendicularly out of the soil, and assume the shape of ruined
towers and castles. Some of these are upwards of 150 feet in height,
and one or two, entirely detached from the rest, have been excavated
into ancient catacombs, with doors and windows, and galleries, in such
a manner that it requires a near inspection to convince us that what
we see are natural rocks, and not towers and buildings. We find the
chambers within to have been sepulchres, containing excavations for
coffins, and niches for cinerary vases. Following the course of the
valley to the S. E., we come in sight of some sepulchral chambers, excavated with more art, and having a portico with two columns before
the door, above which a range of dentils forms a cornice. But the
most remarkable of these excavations, is that which will best be understood by the annexed sketch of it, taken by General Koehler, while
Mr. Carlyle and myself were employed in copying two inscriptions
engraved upon the face of the rock. In the upper, a few letters are
deficient at the beginning and end; the lower appeared to us to be
complete. The letters of the first are larger and wider asunder than
those of the second. Both are written from left to right, but in the
lower inscription the letters are written *downwards*, along the edge of
the monument, so that to place the eyes upon the same line with the
inscription, the head must be held sideways. The rock which has
been shaped into this singular monument rises to a height of upwards
of one hundred feet above the plain, and at the back, and on one of

its sides, remains in its natural state. The ornamented part is about
sixty feet square, surmounted by a kind of pediment, above which are
two volutes. The figures cut upon the rock are no where more than
an inch deep below the surface, except towards the bottom, where the
excavation is much deeper, and resembles an altar. It is not impossible, however, that it may conceal the entrance into the sepulchral chamber, where lie the remains of the person in whose honour
this magnificent monument was formed; for in some other parts of
Asia Minor, especially at Telmissus, we have examples of the wonderful ingenuity with which the ancients sometimes defended the entrance into their tombs. There can be little doubt that the
monument was sepulchral; the crypts and catacombs in the excavated rocks prove that the valley was set apart for such purposes, to
which its singularly retired position and romantic scenery, amidst
these extensive forests, rendered it peculiarly well adapted.

The valley bears the name of Doganlu,.from a neighbouring village
which we do not see, but where we are informed are remains of
antient fortifications, called by the Turks Pismash Kalesi. I am inclined to think they mark the site of Nacoleia, named by Strabo
among the cities of the same province of Phrygia Epictetus, in which
were situated Cotyaeium, Dorylæum, and Midaium; for the first of
these places (now Kutáya) is only twenty geographical miles, in direct
distance, to the north-westward of Doganlu; the second Dorylæum
(Eski-shehr) is thirty G. M. D. to the north of Doganlu; and Midaium (as will presently be seen) was somewhere to the north-eastward,
at about the same distance. But a still closer argument, in favour of
Nacoleia, being situated near the valley of Doganlu, is derived from
a comparison of the several routes leading from Dorylæum, as stated
in the Theodosian tables, and in the itinerary of Antoninus. These
routes are five in number; and though little reliance can be placed
upon the distances between the several places, especially in the Theodosian tables, from which four of these routes are extracted, the order
of names seems to furnish evidence that cannot be very erroneous.

The first of the routes, as they are arranged in the subjoined note *, led east, by Germa to Ancyra (the modern Angura); the second led east-south-east, by Midaium to Pessinus, from whence there was another road to Amorium, the site of which last appears from inscriptions found by Pococke to have been not far from Sevrihissar; the third conducted south-east to Synnada, Philomelium, and Laodiceia Combusta (now Yorgan Ladik); the fourth led south to Nacoleia, and by Peltæ to Apameia Cibotus; and the fifth led south-west by Cotyaeium to Philadelphia (Allah-Shehr). Now, although the exact situation of Apameia Cibotus has not yet been determined, we know that it was towards the sources of the streams which form the Meander, and it cannot be doubted that the bearing of these streams from Eski-Shehr is a little to the westward of south. Nacoleia, therefore, bore in that direction from Dorylæum; it was on a route lying between the road leading to Synnada and Laodiceia, and that leading to Cotyaeium and Philadelphia; and it was the first town which occurred on the road to

---

* I. Iter a Dorileo Ancyra.

Arcelaio	-	-	-	M. P. 30.
Germa	-	-	-	M. P. 20.
Vindia	-	-	-	M. P. 32.
Papira	-	-	-	M. P. 32.
Ancyra	-	-	-	M. P. 27. — Antonin. Itiner. p. 202. ed. Wessel.

The total is 141 Roman miles. The real distance upon the map, between Eski-Shehr and Angura, is 100 geographical miles direct.

In the Theodosian Tables, we have the following distances: —

II. Dorileo, 28 Mideo, 28 Triconia, 21 Pessinunte, 24 Abrostola, 23 Amurio. Total 77 M. P. to Pessinus, and 47 M. P. fiom Pessinus to Amorium; the former distance on the map is about 60 G. M. d., the latter about 20 G. M. d.

III. Dorileo, Docymeo, 32 Synnada, 32 Jullæ, 35 Philomelo, 28 Laudicia Catacecaumeno. Total 127 M. P. plus the distance from Dorylæum to Docimia. The distance upon the map is about 130 G. M. d.

IV. Dorileo, 20 Necolea, 40 Conni, 32 Eucarpia, 30 Eumenia, Pella (lege Peltæ), 12 ad vicum, 14 Apamea Ciboton. Total 148 M. P., plus the distance from Eumenia to Pella. The distance upon the map is about 100 G. M. d.

V. Dorileo, 30 Cocleo (lege Cotyæo), 35 Agmonia, 25 Aludda, 30 Clanudda, 35 Philadelfia. Total 155 M. P. The distance upon the map is about 120 G. M. d.

In the Theodosian Tables, the proportion between the real distances, and the amount of the several computed distances in Roman miles, show that the distance from one place to another cannot be relied on to within ten or twelve miles. In some cases the errors are still greater.

Apameia: all which circumstances accord with the position of Doganlu in respect of Eski-Shehr.

On first beholding the great sculptured rock of the valley of Doganlu, and on remarking the little resemblance which it bears to the works of the Greeks, our idea was, that it might have been formed by the ancient Persians, when in possession of this country ; and that the lower part, resembling an altar, might have had some reference to their worship of fire ; but, upon further reflection, there appeared several objections to such a supposition.   In the first place, none of the great monuments of the Persians are likely to be found at so great a distance from Susa and Persepolis, in a part of the country of which they had only a temporary possession, and which could never have been considered by them in any other light than a conquered foreign country of doubtful tenure.   Secondly, the style of ornament does not exactly resemble any known monument of the ancient Persians ; and, thirdly, the characters of the inscriptions, which have every appearance of being coeval with the rest of the work, bear so close a resemblance to the letters of the Greek alphabet, in their earliest form, that the most reasonable conjecture seems to be that this monument is the work of the ancient Phrygians, who, like the Ionians *, Lydians †, and other nations of Asia Minor, in a state of independence before the Persian conquest, made use of an alphabet differing slightly from the Greek, and derived from the same Phenician original.   While the form of the characters ‡, as well as the

---

* Herodot. l. 1. c. 142., l. 5. c. 59.

† We have the remains of the Lydian alphabet in the Etruscan ; for though it is contested by Dionysius of Halicarnassus that the Etruscans were a Lydian colony, Appian, Strabo, Plutarch, Justin, Velleius Paterculus, Dionysius Periegetes, and Marcian of Heracleia, prove that such was the general opinion of antiquity, and the evidence of Herodotus, (l. 1. c. 94.) together with that of the Etruscan alphabet, and of an Etruscan decree reported by Tacitus (Annal. l. 4. s. 55.) seems decisive on the subject.

‡ Besides the F, which is the Greek digamma, and the Ϝ, which is the early epsilon, the reader will observe that there occurs also a Ⅲ, with four transverse lines ; whether the two latter are the same, or different letters, is doubtful, but I should suspect the same, as both inscriptions end with the same word, ϜΑΑϜ; though in the one, the first letter of the word is Ϝ, and in the other Ⅲ.   I particularly observed that both these characters recurred several times in the inscriptions, and endeavoured therefore to distinguish them with accuracy.

vertical ranges of points * for noting the separation of the words, bear a marked resemblance to the Archäic Greek, some of the words are in unison with the sculptured ornaments of this monument, which indicate that the inscriptions are not in pure Greek. Both in the resemblance and dissimilitude, therefore, they accord with what we should expect of the dialect of the Phrygians, whose connection with Greece is evident from many parts of its early history ; at the same time, that the distinction between the two nations is strongly marked by Herodotus, who gives to the Phrygians the appellation of barbarians.

It is further remarkable that the sculpture of the monument of Doganlu, though unlike any thing of Greek workmanship, is very much in the same style, as the elaborate ornaments (equally remote from Grecian taste) which covered the half columns formerly standing on either side of the door of the Treasury of Atreus, a building said to have been erected by the Cyclopes, who were supposed to have been artisans from Asia.

Upon comparing the alphabet of the monument of Doganlu with the Archaic Greek, and with the Etruscan, it is observable that there is no greater difference between the three than might be expected in distant and long-separated branches of the same family. It is to be remarked, however, that the Greek alphabet, and that of Doganlu, resemble each other much more than they resemble the Etruscan, as well in the form of the letters, as in the important circumstance of their being written from left to right, instead of from right to left, as the Etruscan always continued to be.† But this is a distinction which may be accounted for, by supposing that the monument of Doganlu is much less ancient than the migration of the Lydian alphabet to Italy ; that in the interval between that migration and the date of the inscriptions of Doganlu, the Lydians and Phrygians had changed the

---

* See some of the most ancient Greek inscriptions; particularly that given by Montfaucon Palæo, relating to those who died in the Peloponnesian war.

† See Lanzi, Saggio di Lingua Etrusca.

E E 2

direction of their writing, as we know to have been the case with the
Greeks, who at first wrote either from right to left, or indifferently
either way ; then in alternate lines, in the manner called Βουστροφηδὸν,
and at last constantly from left to right ; while the Etruscans may
have continued to employ the original method used in Lydia, according to a practice common among colonists, of adhering to ancient
customs, even after they have become obsolete in the mother country.

It seems a vain attempt to endeavour to explain inscriptions, written
in a language of which we have no other remains ; yet as the characters are themselves a proof that there was a great resemblance between
this dialect and the Greek, it is not impossible that some light may be
thrown upon ancient history by the monument of Doganlu, if other
inscriptions in the same dialect should hereafter be discovered. Upon
this subject there are one or two remarks that cannot fail to occur,
even to a superficial examiner of the inscriptions.

It has already been remarked, that the lower inscription beginning
BABA is complete, and it may be presumed that the upper, though incomplete at either end, wants but a few letters. This seems evident, as
well from its occupying the whole length of a sort of outer pediment,
as from its concluding word, which wants only one letter of being the
same as the concluding word of the lower inscription. This concluding word is very remarkable ; written in Greek it is EΔAE, or
EΔAEΣ. Now εδαε from δαίω, to divide or cut with a sharp instrument,
is precisely such a Greek word as one might have expected to find in
a very ancient *Greek* inscription upon a monument, all the apparent
merit of which is the cutting of squares, lozenges, and other regular
figures, upon the smoothed surface of a rock. In examining the other
words, we find further resemblances of the Greek. The 2d, 3d, and
4th words of the lower inscription, and the first word of the upper inscription (if it be a single word), all seem to end in sigma, and three
of them in ος, thus rendering it not improbable that the words 1, 2, 3,·
4, of the lower inscription, contained the name and title of the person
who engraved that inscription ; that Σικεμεμαν perhaps indicated the
place from whence he came ; and that the long word, No. 1. of the

upper inscription, was the name of the person who placed that inscription. But the most remarkable words of all are the second and fourth of the upper inscription, which, written in Greek, are MIΔAI FANAKTEI, " to King Midas," with some word between them, which, like them, appears to be in the dative case, and may be some title or patronymic of the King ; so that the result of these remarks is a strong presumption that the monument was erected in honour of one of the Kings of Phrygia, of the Midaian family. The situation of the place, the construction of the monument, the tenor of the inscription, and the form of the letters greatly resembling the Greek of the same period of time, all render the supposition probable ; while the names Midaium and Gordium ; the remark of Strabo that the banks of the river Sangarius were the ancient habitation of Gordius and Midas; the observation of Pausanias * that Ancyra was founded by Midas, and that in his time there was a fountain in that city, called the fountain of Midas ; together with the testimony both of Strabo † and Pausanias, that a tribe of Gauls, in seizing the country adjacent to Ancyra and Pessinus, occupied a part of the ancient dominions óf the Gordian dynasty ; are all proofs that the banks of the Sangarius were the central parts of their dominion, and consequently that the valley of Doganlu, which lies between the Sangarius and one of its principal branches, the Thymbrius, was exactly in the part of the country which the dominions of that dynasty must have included. According to this supposition, the date of the monument of Doganlu is between the years 740 and 570 before the Christian æra ; for that such was nearly the period of the Gordian dynasty appears from Herodotus ‡, who informs us that Midas, son of Gordius, was the first of the Barbarians who sent offerings to Delphi, and that his offerings were earlier than those of Gyges, king of Lydia, who began his reign B. C. 715.

---

* Attic. c. 4.   † P. 571.   Paus. *ib.*

‡ Herod. l. 1. c. 14. Eusebius places the beginning of the reign of this Midas in the fourth year of the tenth Olympiad, or 737 B. C.

Phrygia lost its independence, when all the country to the west of the
Halys was subdued by Crœsus, king of Lydia, in or about the year
572 B. C. A few years afterwards Atys, son of Crœsus, was killed
accidentally by Adrastus, who was of the royal family of Phrygia, and
son of Gordius, son of Midas. * This last Gordius, therefore, seems
to have been the king of Phrygia, who was rendered tributary to
Crœsus ; and as he was son of a Midas, and the first Midas was son
of a Gordius, it seems probable that the monarchs of Phrygia, during
the two centuries of their independence, had borne those names alternately, from father to son, according to a custom which has been
common in all nations and ages of the world.

As we are quite ignorant how many monarchs of independent
Phrygia there may have been, it will be impossible to determine to
which of them, or to what period in the two centuries of their independence, the monument of Doganlu is to be ascribed, unless some
further elucidation of the inscriptions should be obtained.

Close by this magnificent relic of Phrygian art is a very large sepulchral chamber and portico, of two columns, excavated out of the
same reddish sandstone of which the great monument and other
rocks are formed. The columns have a plain plinth at the top, and
are surmounted by a row of dentils along the architrave. They are
of a tapering form, which, together with the general proportions of
the work, give it an appearance of the Doric order, although, in fact,
it contains none of the distinctive attributes of that order. It is an
exact resemblance of the cottages still in use in this country, which
are square frames of wood-work, having a portico supported by two
posts made broader at either end. The sepulchral chambers differ only
in having their parts more accurately finished ; the dentils correspond
to the ends of the beams, supporting the flat roof of the cottage.

I cannot quit the subject of this interesting valley without express-

---

* Herod. l. 1. c. 35.

ing a wish that future travellers, who may cross Asia Minor by the routes of Eski-Shehr or Kutaya, will employ a day or two in a more complete examination of it, than circumstances allowed to us; as it is far from improbable that some inaccuracy or omission may have occurred in the inscriptions, from the singularity of the characters, the great' height. of one of the inscriptions above the ground, and the short'·time. that 'was allowed us for transcribing and revising it.

After leaving the great sculptured rock, we follow the valley for a short distance, then pass through a wild woody country, meeting scarcely any traces of habitations till we reach our Konak, at the little village' which is called from the Khan, built there. by a Pasha of the name of Kosru, where we arrive at five in the evening, having, according to our calculation, made ·a. circuit of nine or ten miles more than the direct' distance from Seid-èl-Gházi. We had a sharp shower of hail as we galloped through the wood, but the weather soon cleared again.

Jan. 28. — From Kosru Khan to Bulwudun, twelve hours. We rose at two in the morning; the baggage set off at five; ourselves at six: the weather still clear. The road lay through several small woody valleys, in one of which, at ten or twelve miles from Kosru Khan, we saw near a fountain several inscribed stones; the annexéd is the only inscription I could decypher;

ΔΗΜΑΣΚΑΙ
ΓΑΙΟΣΥΠΕΡ
ΒΟωΝΙΔΙωΝΠΑ
ΠΙΑΔΙ .. ΙΣωΤΗ
ΡΙΕΥΧΗΝΚΑΙ
ΗΡΑΚΛΗΑΝΙΚ
ΗΤ.

It appears to be a dedication of thanks to Jupiter Papias, the Saviour, and Hercules, the Invincible, for the care of the oxen of Demas and Caius. Both these names occur also in the writings of the New Testament; the latter is the more common appellation of the two: a person who bore that name, and belonged to Derbe, was a member

of one of the churches in Lycaonia * ; and Demas sends his salutation
to the Christians of Colosse.†

The inscription we copied is upon a flat slab, surmounted with a
pediment, in the middle of which is a *caput bovis*, with a festoon.
Another large stone was a square stele, surmounted with an ornamented cornice ; on one side was an obliterated inscription, in the
center of a garland. Towards the latter part of our journey, the road
lay across a ridge of hills, with a fine soil, containing a few cultivated
patches of ground, but for the most part overgrown with brushwood ;
at intervals we saw a few flocks of sheep and goats, and in one place a
large herd of horned cattle. We saw many sepulchral chambers excavated in the rocks, some of which were ornamented in the exterior ;
others were plain. In several parts of our route, also, were appearances of extensive quarries, from some of which was probably
extracted the celebrated Phrygian marble, called Synnadicus, or Doci-
mitis, from the places where it was found.

This marble was so much esteemed that it was carried to ‡ Italy,
and such was the force of fashion or prejudice, that Hadrian placed
columns of it in his new buildings at Athens §, where the surrounding
mountains abound in the finest marble. At about ten miles from
Bulwudun we came in sight of that town with a lake beyond it, to
the southward of which was the high range of mountains called
Sultan-dagh, and parallel to it, on the northern side of the plain of
Bulwudun, Emír-dagh.

From hence we descended by a long slope to Bulwudun, which is
situated in the plain. It is a place of considerable size, but consists
chiefly of miserable cottages. There are many remains of antiquity
lying about the streets, and around the town, but they appeared to
be chiefly of the time of the Constantinopolitan empire. At Bulwudun we had to make choice of two roads to the coast ; one leading

---

* Macknight, Epist. ³ John. Preface.   † Coloss. iv. 14.
‡ Strabo, p. 577.   § Paus. Att. c. 18.

to Satalia, the other, .by Konia and Karaman, to Kelenderi. We prefer the latter on account of the uncertainty of the long passage by sea from Satalia to Cyprus at this season of the year; and we are in-formed that all the Grand Vizier's Tatars now take the Konia road.

Jan. 29. — From Bulwudun to Ak-shehr, eleven hours. For the first two hours the road traversed the plain which lies between Bul-wudun and the foot of Sultan-dagh, crossing near the latter by a long causeway, a marshy tract, through the middle of which runs a consi-derable stream. It comes from the plains and open country, which extend on our right as far as Afiom Karahissar, and joins the lake which occupies the central and lowest part of the plain lying between the parallel ranges of Sultan-dagh and Emir-dagh. Our road con-tinues in a S. E. direction along the foot of Sultan-dagh; it is perfectly level and, owing to the dry weather, in excellent condition. On our left were the lake and plains already mentioned. The ground was every where covered with frost, and the hills on either side of the valley with snow; but these appearances of winter vanished as the day advanced, and from noon till three P. M.•the sun was warmer than we found agreeable; our faces being exposed to it by that most inconvenient head-dress, the Tatar Kalpak. Our Surigis (postillions) wore a singular kind of cloak of white camels' hair felt, half an inch thick, and so stiff that the cloak stands without support when set up-right upon the ground. There are neither sleeves nor hood; but only holes to pass .the hands through, and projections like wings upon the shoulders for the purpose of turning off the rain. It is of the manufacture of the country. At the end of six hours we passed through Saakle or Isaklu, a' large village surrounded with gardens and orchards in the midst of a small region well watered by streams from Sultan-dagh, and better cultivated than any place we have seen since we left the vicinity of Isnik and Lefke. Yet the Aga of Isaklu is said to be in a state of rebellion; and this is not the first instance we have seen of places in such a state being more flourishing than others; whence we cannot but suspect that there is a connection in this em-pire between the prosperity of a district and the ability of its chieftain to resist the orders of the Porte. This is nothing more than the natural consequence of their well known policy of making frequent changes of provincial governors, who purchasing their governments at a high price are obliged to practise every kind of extortion to re-imburse themselves, and secure some profit at the expiration of their command. It seems that the Aga of Isaklu having a greater share of prudence and talents than usually falls to the lot of a Turk in office, has so strengthened himself that the Porte does not think his re-duction worth the exertion that would be required to effect it, and is, therefore, contented with the moderate revenue which we are told he regularly remits to Constantinople. In the meantime he has become so personally interested in the prosperity of the place, that he finds it more to his advantage to govern it well than to enrich himself rapidly by the oppressive system of the other provincial governors. The territory of Isaklu contains several dependent villages in which fer-tility is insured by the streams descending from Sultan-dagh. We observe a greater quantity and variety of fruit-trees than in any place in Asia Minor we have yet visited. Their species are the same as those which grow in the middle latitudes of Europe, as apples, pears, walnuts, quinces, peaches, grapes ; no figs, olives, or mulberries. * The climate, therefore, though now so mild, and exposed undoubtedly to excessive heat in summer, is not warmer upon the whole than the interior of Greece and Italy.

We follow the level grounds at the foot of Sultan-dagh until we come in sight of Ak-shehr (white city), a large town, situated, like Isaklu, on the foot of the mountains, and furnished with the same natural advantages of a fertile soil, and a plentiful supply of water. It is surrounded with many pleasant gardens, but in other respects exhibits the usual Turkish characteristics of extensive burying-grounds, narrow dirty streets, and ruined mosques and houses. At a small distance from the western entrance of the town we pass the

---

* Strabo, however, informs us that anciently it bore olives; he describes the plain of Synnada as ἐλαιόφυτον πέδιον.

sepulchre of Noureddin Hogia, a Turkish saint, whose tomb is the object of a Mussulman pilgrimage. It is a stone monument of the usual form, surrounded by an open colonnade supporting a roof; the columns have been taken from some ancient · Greek building. The burying-ground is full of remains of Greek architecture converted into Turkish tombstones, and it furnishes ample proof of Ak-shehr having been the position of a Greek city of considerable importance. The only apartment our Konakgi could procure for us at Ak-shehr was a ruinous chamber in the Menzil-hané (post-house); and the Aga sending insolent messages in return to our remonstrances, we resolve, though at the end of a long day's journey, upon setting out immediately for the next stage. While the horses are preparing, we eat our *Kebáb* in the burying-ground, and take shelter from the cold of the evening in the tent of some camel-drivers, who were enjoying their pipes and coffee over a fire. On our arrival, we observed the people fortifying their town, by erecting one of the simplest gates that was ever constructed for defence. It consisted of four uprights of fir, supporting a platform covered with reeds, in front of which was a breastwork of mud-bricks with a row of loop-holes. These gates and a low mud-wall are the usual fortifications of the smaller Asiatic towns. In one place we saw the gates standing alone (honoris causâ) without any wall to connect them.

The lake of Ak-shehr is not close to the town as D'Anville has marked it on his map; but at a distance of six or eight miles: it communicates by a stream with that of Bulwudun, and after a season of rain, when these lakes are very much increased in size, they form a continued piece of water, thirty or forty miles in length. It is probable that D'Anville was equally mistaken in placing Antioch of Pisidia at Ak-shehr: for if Sultan-dagh is the Phrygia Paroria of Strabo, as there is reason to believe, Antioch should, according to the same authority, be on the south side of that ridge; whereas Ak-shehr is on the north.

At six in the evening we set out from Ak-shehr, and at one in the morning of January 30. arrived at Arkut-khan: our pace was much slower ‚than by day. The road lay over the same open level country as before, and towards the latter part of the route, over some higher undulations of ground, which separate the waters running into the lake of Ak-shehr from those which flow into the lake of Ilgun. The weather was frosty and clear, but very dark after eleven o'clock, when the moon set. Several of our party then became so oppressed by sleep as to find it difficult to save themselves from falling from the horses. After two or three hours' repose at Arkut-khan, we pursue our route for three hours to Ilgun, a large but wretched village, containing some scattered fragments of antiquity, where we procure some eggs and Kaimak (boiled cream) for breakfast, and then continue our route to Ladík. Since we left Ak-shehr, the loftier summits of the range of Sultan-dagh have appeared to recede from our direction towards the S. E., and our route has continued through the same wide uncultivated champaign, intersected by a few ridges, and by torrents running from Sultan-dagh to the lakes in the plain. At two hours is a more considerable stream, crossed by a bridge, and discharging itself into the lake of Ilgun. Six hours beyond Ilgun we pass through the large village of Kadún-kiúi, or Kanun-haná, said to consist of 1000 houses, and three hours farther we come to Yorgan-Ladík, or Ladik-el-Tchaus, another large place famous throughout Asia Minor for its manufacture of carpets; and advantageously situated in a well watered district, among some low hills to the north-ward of which lies a very extensive plain.

Our road throughout the open country we have passed has been wide, well beaten, fit for any carriage, and owing to the late dry weather in an excellent state. We continue to enjoy a sky without a cloud : there is generally a slight breeze from the east in the day : in the afternoon the sun is hot ; and at night the sky is perfectly calm and clear with a sharp frost, which in the shaded places generally continues to a late hour in the afternoon.

CHAPTER III.

THE plains between Arkut-Khan and Ladik are traversed by several low stony ridges, and by streams running towards the lake of Ilgun. The country is bare and open; not a tree nor inclosure was to be seen, nor any appearance of cultivation, except in small patches around a few widely scattered villages. The country to our right forms the district of Dogan-hissar, a town belonging to the Sangiac of Ak-shehr. To the left is seen the continuation of the series of long narrow lakes which began near Bulwudun : they receive the torrents running from the surrounding mountains, and are greatly enlarged in winter, but in summer are entirely dried up.

Jan. 31. — From Ladik to Konia, nine hours ; the road excellent, and weather very fine ; the sun even scorching, and much too glaring for our exposed eyes. At Ladik we saw more numerous fragments of antient architecture and sculpture than at any other place upon our route. Inscribed marbles, altars, columns, capitals, frizes, cornices, were dispersed throughout the streets and among the houses and burying-grounds ; the remains of Laodicea κατακεκαυμένη, antiently the most considerable city of this part of the country. At less than an hour's distance from the town, on the way to Konia, we met with a still greater number of remains of the same kind, and copied one or two sepulchral inscriptions of the date of the Roman empire. The following fragment appears to be part of an impre-

cation against any person who should violate the tomb upon which it
is inscribed.

TON βωMON AΔIKHCEI
H KAI ΠEPI TON TAΦ
ONTI OPΦANA TEKNAΛIΠOI
. . . .
TON XHPON BION OIKONE
PHMON

Soon after we had quitted this spot, we entered upon a ridge branching northwards from the great mountains on our right, and forming
the western boundary of the plain of Konia. On the descent from
this ridge we come in sight of the vast plains around that city, and of
the lake which occupies the middle of them, and we saw the city with
its mosques and antient walls, still at the distance of 12 or 14 miles
from us. To the north-east nothing appeared to interrupt the vast
expanse* but two very lofty summits covered with snow, at a great
distance. They can be no other than the summits of Mount Argæus
above Kesaría, and are, consequently, distant from us, in a direct line,
more than 150 miles. To the south-east the same plains extend as
far as the mountains of Karaman, which to the south of the plains of
Konia are connected with the mountains of Khatoun-serai, on the
other side of which lies Bey-shehr and the country of the antient
Isaurians; and these bending westward in the neighbourhood of
Konia form a continuous range with the ridge of Sultan-dagh, of
which we have been following the direction ever since we left Bulwudun. At the south-east extremity of the plains beyond Konia we are
much struck with the appearance of a remarkable insulated mountain,
called Karadagh (black mountain), rising to a great height, covered
at the top with snow, and appearing like a lofty island in the midst

---

* The immense extent of some of these plains and pastures of Asia mentioned in this
journal illustrate well the *Magnitudinem Pastionis* in the following passage of Cicero.
Asià tam opima est et fertilis, ut et ubertate agrorum et diversitate fructuum et Magni-
tudine Pastionis et multitudine earum rerum quæ exportantur facile omnibus terris ante-
cellat. Pro lege Man. — E.

of the sea. It is about sixty miles distant, and beyond it are seen some of the summits of the Karaman range, which cannot be less than ninety miles from us; yet it is surprising with what distinctness the form of the ground and of the woods is seen in this clear atmosphere. As far as I have observed, the air is much more transparent in a fine winter's day in this climate than it is in summer, when, notwithstanding the breeze of wind which blows, there is generally a haze in the horizon, caused probably by the constant stream of vapour which rises from the earth. The situation of the town of Karaman is pointed out to us exactly in the line of our route, a little to the right of Mount Karadagh. After descending into the plain we move rapidly over a road made for wheel-carriages; the first we have met with since we left the neighbourhood of Skutári.

At Konia we are comfortably accommodated in the house of a Christian, belonging to the Greek church, but who is ignorant of the language, which here is not even used in the church-service: they have the four Gospels and the Prayers printed in Turkish. At the head of their community is a Metropolitan bishop, who has several dependent churches in the adjacent towns. As it is now the moon Ramazan, when the Turks neither take nourishment nor receive visits till after sunset, we are obliged to defer our visit to the Governor of Konia till the evening. He is a Pasha of three tails, but inferior in rank to the Governor of Kutaya, who has the title of Anadol-Begler-beg, or Anadol-Valesi, and who has the chief command of all the Anatolian troops when they join the Imperial camp. Our visit, as usual among the Turks, was first to the Kiaya, or Deputy, and afterwards to the Pasha. The entrance into the court of the Serai was striking; portable fires of pinewood placed in a grating fixed upon a pole, and stuck into the ground, were burning in every part of the court-yard; a long line of horses stood ready saddled; attendants in their gala-clothes were seen moving about in all directions, and trains of servants, with covered dishes in their hands, showed that the night of a Turkish fast is a feast. The building has little in unison with these appearances of gaiety and magnificence, being a low shabby wooden edifice, with ruinous galleries and half-broken window frames; but it stands upon the site of the palace of the antient sultans of Iconium, and contains some few remains of massy and elegant Arabic architecture, of an early date. The inside of the building seemed not much better than the exterior, with the exception of the Pasha's audience-chamber, which was splendidly furnished with carpets and sofas, and filled with a great number of attendants in costly dresses. Both the Pasha and the deputy, in the previous visit, received us with haughtiness and formality, though with civility. The Pasha promised to send forward to Karaman for horses to be ready to carry us to the coast, and to give us a travelling order for Konaks upon the road. After passing through the usual ceremony of coffee, sweetmeats, sherbet, and perfumes, which in a Turkish visit of ceremony are well known to follow in the order here mentioned, we return to our lodging. Nothing can exceed the greediness of the Pasha's attendants for Bakshish. Some accompany us home with Mashallahs (the torches above mentioned), and others with silver wands. Soon after our return to our lodgings we are visited by a set of the Pasha's musicians, who seem very well to understand that after our fatigues we shall be very glad to purchase their absence at a handsome price; but no sooner are they gone than another set make their appearance; the Kahwegi, the Tutungi, and a long train of Tchokadars; and these being succeeded by people of the town, who come simply to gratify their curiosity, it is not till a late hour that we are at liberty to retire to rest.

The circumference of the walls of Konia is between two and three miles, beyond which are suburbs not much less populous than the town itself. The walls strong and lofty, and flanked with square towers, which at the gates are built close together, are of the time of the Seljukian kings, who seem to have taken considerable pains to exhibit the Greek inscriptions, and the remains of architecture and sculpture belonging to the antient Iconium, which they made use of in building their walls. We perceived a great number of Greek altars, inscribed stones, columns, and other fragments inserted into the fabric, which is still in tolerable preservation throughout the whole extent. None of the Greek remains that I saw seemed to be of a very remote period, even of the Roman Empire. We observed in several places Greek crosses, and figures of lions, of a rude sculpture; and on all of the conspicuous parts of the walls and towers, Arabic inscriptions, apparently of very early date. The town, suburbs, and gardens around are plentifully supplied with water from streams, flowing from some hills to the westward, which to the north-eastward join a lake varying in size according to the season of the year. We are informed that after great rains, and the breaking up of the snows upon the surrounding mountains, the lake is swollen with immense inundations, which spread over the great plains to the eastward for near fifty miles. At present there is not the least appearance of any such inundation, the usual autumnal rains having failed, and the whole country labouring under a severe drought. The gardens of Kónia abound with the same variety of fruit trees, which we remarked in those of Isaklu and Ak-shehr; and the country around supplies grain and flax in great abundance. In the town they manufacture carpets, and they tan and dye blue and yellow leather. Cotton, wool, hides, and a few of the other raw materials which enrich the superior industry and skill of the manufactures of Europe, are sent to Smyrna by the caravans. The low situation of the town and the vicinity of the lake seem not to promise much for the salubrity of Kónia; but we heard no complaint on this head; and as it has in all ages been well inhabited, these apparent disadvantages are probably corrected by the dryness of the soil, and the free action of the winds over the surrounding levels. The most remarkable building in Kónia is the tomb of a saint, highly revered all over Turkey, called Hazret Mevlana, the founder of the Mevlevi Dervishes. His sepulchre, which is the object of a Mussulman pilgrimage, is surmounted by a dome, standing upon a cylindrical tower of a bright green colour. The city, like all those renowned for superior sanctity, abounds with Dervishes, who meet the passenger at every turning of the streets, and demand paras with the greatest clamour and insolence. Some of them pretend to be ideots, and are hence considered as entitled to peculiar respect, or at least indulgence. The bazars and houses have little to recommend them to notice.

Before we pursue our route from Kónia it may be right to offer a few remarks upon the situation of the ancient places on the road from Eski-shehr to Kónia. Of two of these there can be little doubt. The modern name of Ladik is decisive of its being upon the site of Laodiceia Combusta, and the sound of Πολυβωτὸν as pronounced by the modern Greeks so nearly resembles that of Bulwudún, especially as the accents in both are the same, that there can be little doubt of the latter name being the Turkish corruption of the former. The position of Bulwudún, moreover, agrees perfectly with that ascribed to Polybotum in the narrative of Anna Comnena *, where the name occurs. Polybotum, however, is mentioned only in the history of the Lower Empire, and although from the 6th to the 12th century it appears to have been with Philomelium and Iconium the chief place of these vast plains †, its name is not found in the earlier periods of history, when Synnada, Philomelium, and Iconium seem to have been the principal places. ‡ The position of Polybotum affords us no assistance, therefore, in tracing the other ancient places on the main route between Dorylæum and Laodiceia.

Of these places the most important to determine is Synnada, which indeed is in some measure the key to the ancient geography of the central parts of Asia Minor. It appears from the Theodosian tables that Synnada was on the great road from Dorylæum to Iconium by Laodiceia Combusta, and from Livy that Synnada was in the way from the neighbourhood of Apameia Cibotus towards the frontiers of Galatia. The crossing of these two lines will fall not far from the modern Bulwudún, as sufficiently appears from the route of Pococke in his way from the upper valley of the Mæander to Amorium and Ancyra. It may safely be concluded, therefore, that the extensive quarries which we saw on the road from Khosru-khan to Bulwudún

---

* L. xi. c. 4, 5.   L. xv. c. 5.   † Procop. Hist. Ar. c. 18.   Anna Com. ib.
‡ Cicero ad Att. l. v. ep. 20. ad Divers. l. iii. ep. 8.

indicate the vicinity of Synnáda and Docimia, for these two places were only sixty stades apart, and were equally famous for their marble.

· Santabaris, a place of the Lower Empire, from whence Alexius Comnenus * is mentioned to have sent detachments of his army against the Turks, in one direction towards Polybotum, and in the other towards Pœmanene and Amorium, seems to have been at Seid-el-Gházi.

Though the proportionate distances do not exactly agree with the numbers in the Theodosian tables, it may be inferred from the remains of antiquity at Ak-shehr and Ilgún, that these were the Jullæ and Philomelium mentioned in the itinerary. Strabo describes Philomelium as being in a plain on the north side of the hills of Phrygia Paroreia; his description † of which region agrees exactly with Sultan-dagh; and it appears from the narrative of Anna Comnena ‡ that the territory of Philomelium was at no great distance from that of Iconium; for as soon as the Emperor Alexius had taken Philomelium from the Turks, his troops spread themselves over the latter territory. The lake of the Forty Martyrs mentioned in this narrative corresponds also with that of Ilgún, so that it will probably be found that Ilgún stands upon the site of Philomelium.

Jullæ in the Theodosian tables seems to be a false writing for Julia, a name which became so common in every part of the Roman world under the Cæsars; and it may also be the same place as the Juliopolis placed by Ptolemy § in the part of the country where stood Synnada, Philomelium, &c. But if Ak-shehr was Julia, there can be little doubt that so fine a situation was likewise occupied by some

---

* Anna Com. l. xv. c. 4.

† Ἡ μὲν Παρωρία ὀρεινήν τινα ἔχει ῥάχιν ἀπὸ τῆς ἀνατολῆς ἐκτεινομένη πρὸς δύσιν· ταύτῃ δὲ ἑκατέρωθεν ὑποπέπτωκέ τι πεδίον μέγα καὶ πόλις πλησίον αὐτῆς· πρὸς ἄρκτον μὲν Φιλομήλιον, ἐκ θατέρου δὲ μέρους Ἀντιόχεια, ἡ πρὸς Πισιδίᾳ καλουμένη, ἡ μὲν ἐν πεδίῳ κειμένη, ἡ δ᾽ ἐπὶ λόφου, ἔχουσα ἀποικίαν Ῥωμαίων. It is evident from this passage how greatly the discovery of Antioch of Pisidia would assist the comparative geography of all the adjacent country.

‡ L. xv. c. 5. § L. v. c. 2.

earlier city *, which on its being repaired or re-established may have assumed the new name of Julia or Juliopolis.

Of the cities mentioned by Xenophon †, on the route of Cyrus, through Phrygia into Lycaonia, Tyriæum and Iconium are the only two which occur in later authors. Tyriæum is named both by Strabo and Hierocles, and appears from the former ‡ to have been between Philomelium and Iconium, consequently at no great distance from Laodiceia.

The hills which bound the plain of Iconium on the north, seem to be those naked downs of Lycaonia mentioned by Strabo. § The highest part of them is now called the mountain of Sheik Fudul Baba. I did not hear of the wild asses which Strabo mentions, but the want of water is noticed by Hadgi Khalfa, who, in confirmation of Strabo's observation on the fineness of the sheep pastures, adds that there is

---

* Major Rennell thinks it was Caystrus.

† The following was the route of Cyrus, according to Xenophon : —

	Stathmi.	Parasangs.
From Celænæ, afterwards Apameia Cibotus, to Peltæ,	2 or	10
Ceramorum Agora, at the end of Mysia,	2 —	12
Caystri Campus (a city),	3 —	30
Thymbrium, where was the fountain of Midas,	2 —	10
Tyriæum,	2 —	10
Iconium,	3 —	20
Through Lycaonia	5 —	30
Through Cappadocia to Dana (Tyana),	4 —	25
Total parasangs,		92

In Major Rennell's work on the retreat of the Ten thousand, the reader will see the extreme difficulty of fixing the places on this route. Indeed there seems no mode of reconciling it with other geographical authorities than by supposing great errors in the numbers; for it is difficult to believe that the plain of the Caystrus is not the same as that placed by Strabo (p. 629.) to the east of Mount Tmolus, or that Thymbrium, where was the fountain of Midas, was not upon the river Thymbrius, that being exactly the situation of the dominions of Midas, and not the plains between Ak-shehr and Ilgun, where we must place Thymbrium, if we follow the evidence of Xenophon's numbers.

‡ (A Caruris) ἐπὶ τὸ πρὸς τῇ Λυκαονία πέρας τοῦ Παρωρείου τὸ Τυριάιον διὰ Φιλομηλίου, μικρῳ πλείους τῶν πεντακοσιων, p. 663.

§ Τὰ τῶν Λυκαόνων ὀροπέδια ψυχρὰ καὶ ψιλὰ καὶ ὀναγρόβοτα· ὑδάτων τε σπάνις πολλή. - -
- - - - - - - - ὅμως δέ καίπερ ἄνυδρος οὖσα, ἡ χώρα πρόβατα ἐκτρέφει θαυμαστῶς.
— Strabo, p. 568.

a breed of wild sheep on these mountains, which are considered sacred
to the saint from whom the mountain takes its name.

Feb. 1. — Our journey of this day is from Kónia to Tchumra,
reckoned a six hours' stage. We have remarked that since leaving
Ak-sher the post-horses are of an inferior kind. They are larger and
not well formed, often broken knee'd, and frequently falling, which
seldom happened in the first part of our journey. Those supplied
from Kónia for this day's journey are very indifferent, and we did not
get them till ten o'clock, nor till after we had paid some high fees to
the post-master and Tatár-aga. The plain of Kónia is considered the
largest in Asia Minor ; our road pursues a perfect level for upwards
of twenty miles, and is in excellent order for travelling. In such
roads the journey, even with loaded horses, may be performed in two-
thirds of the computed time. A rough kind of two-wheeled carriage,
drawn by oxen or buffaloes, is used in this plain. It runs upon
trucks, ingeniously formed of six pieces of solid wood, three in the
center, and three on the outside, the outer joints falling opposite to
the center of the inner pieces, and the whole kept together by an iron
felloe, and by fastenings connecting the outer pieces with the inner.

Tchumra is a small village with a scanty cultivation around it. We
are lodged in a Turk's cottage, consisting of two apartments on the
same floor, and separated only by a rail, and two or three steps. The
largest of the two is for his horse ; the other is occupied by the passage
into the stable, and a small raised apartment, in which is just sufficient
breadth for the fire-place, and a sofa on either side of it. This is the
whole of his habitation, and here we are just able to find room enough
to lie down at night.

Feb. 2. — From Tchumra to Kassabá, nine hours, over the same
uninterrupted level of the finest soil, but quite uncultivated, except in
the immediate neighbourhood of a few widely dispersed villages. It
is painful to behold such desolation in the midst of a region so highly
favoured by nature. Another characteristic of these Asiatic plains is
the exactness of the level, and the peculiarity of their extending,
without any previous slope, to the foot of the mountains which rise

from them, like lofty islands out of the surface of the ocean. The Karamanian ridge seems to recede as we approach it, and the snowy summits of Argæus are still seen to the north-eastward. We passed only one small village in this day's route. It was called Alibey Kiui, and was situated at one hour's distance short of Kassabá. We observed, however, some ruins of villages, and in several places fragments of antient architecture, particularly about half way, at a bridge constructed almost entirely of such remains, which traverses a small stream running from the mountain on the south to the lake of Kónia. At three or four miles short of Kassabá, we are abreast of the middle of the very lofty insulated mountain already mentioned, called Karadagh. It is said to be chiefly inhabited by Greek Christians, and to contain 1001 churches; but we afterwards learned that these 1001 churches (Bin-bir Klissa) was the name given to the extensive ruins of an antient city at the foot of the mountain. Since we left Kónia we have experienced more civility from the inhabitants than before; a change to be ascribed to our being now upon a less frequented route. On approaching Kassabá, the people met us in great numbers. One person threw a pair of pigeons, with the legs tied together, under the feet of the General's horse; others wrestle and dance. On arriving at our lodging they bring us presents of water-melons, dried grapes, and other fruits. Kassabá differs from every town we have passed through, in being built of stone instead of sun-baked bricks. It is surrounded with a wall flanked with redans, or angular projections, and having some handsome gates of Saracenic architecture. It has a well supplied bazar, and seems formerly to have been a Turkish town of more importance than it is at present. The dry clear weather which has been so propitious to our travelling, has been very unfavourable to agriculture. At Kassabá we are informed that there has been neither snow nor rain for two months, and that the drought is very distressing. Khatun-serai is four hours to the westward of Kassabá, in a pleasant situation in the mountains.

Feb. 3. — From Kassabá to Karaman, four hours: the weather cool and overcast; the road still passing over a plain, which towards the mountains begins to be a little intersected with low ridges and ravines. At one hour from Kassabá we pass on the outside of Illisera, a small town with low walls and towers, built of mud-bricks, and situated upon a rising ground half a mile from the foot of the mountains to the southward. Between these mountains and Kara-dagh there is a·kind of strait, which forms the communication between the plain of Karaman and the great levels lying eastward of Kónia. Having passed this opening we enter the plain of Karaman. Our course from Kónia has been more southerly than it was before we reached that town, or upon an average S. by E. ¼ E. by compass. We are told that the mountains above Illisera produce madder in great abundance, partly used in the dyeing manufactories of Kónia, and partly sent to Smyrna. The plain of Karaman and the foot of the surrounding mountains are in general well cultivated; and as they present a more bounded prospect, and are intersected with frequent streams, and varied with swelling grounds, they are much more pleasing and picturesque than the immense unbroken levels we have for so many days been travelling over.

Advancing towards Karaman I perceive a passage into the plains to the N. W. round the northern end of Kara-dagh, similar to that of Illisera, so that this mountain is completely insulated. We still see to the north-east the great snowy summits of Argæus. It seems to be the highest point of Asia Minor, and is probably about 6500 feet above the level of the sea. As we approached the town of Karaman two horsemen met us, and conducted us to our Konák, at the house of the Vekil of the Bishop of Iconium, who is at the head of the Christian community of the place. Karaman is situated at a distance of two miles from the foot of the mountains. Its ancient Greek name, Laranda, is still in common use among the Christians, and is even retained in the firmahns of the Porte. The houses, in number about 1000, are separated from one another by gardens, and occupy a large space of ground. There are now only three or four mosques, but the ruins of several others; and the remains of a castle show that the place was formerly of much greater importance. It was the

capital of the Turkish kingdom, which lasted from the time of the
partition of the dominions * of the Seljukian monarchs of Iconium
until 1486, when Caramania was reduced by the Ottoman Emperor
Bajazet the Second. Karaman derives its name from the first and
greatest of its princes, who made himself master of Iconium, Cilicia,
Pamphylia, and the interior of Asia Minor from Philadelphia (Alah-
shehr) as far southward as Antioch in Syria; the other chief officers
of Aladin seized upon different parts of Asia Minor; and it was at
this time that the great Turkish divisions of Sarakhan, Karasi, and
Aidin received their names from those persons. The Ottomans upon
obtaining possession of Karaman divided it into Itsh-il, the part
towards the sea, and Kharidj, the interior country. These were subdivided into seven Sandjaya: Iconium became the seat of the Pashalik;
and the decline of Karaman may be dated from that period. The
appearance of Karaman indicates poverty. The only manufactures
are some coarse cotton and woollen stuffs; but they send the produce
of the surrounding mountains, consisting chiefly of hides, wool, and
acorns, used in dyeing, to the neighbouring coasts and to Smyrna.

The houses are built of sun-baked bricks, with flat roofs. The
chimneys being very wide, and much exposed to violent winds from
the surrounding mountains, have a trap-door on the top, which may
be raised or lowered at pleasure, by means of a cord, communicating
through the roof into the house. The women of Karaman when
passing through the streets conceal their faces with unusual care. In
the other parts of Asia Minor a veil covering the upper and lower
parts of the face has been the utmost we have remarked, but here I
see several women with only a single eye exposed to the view of
passengers. The rest of the person is in the usual shapeless form of
Turkish drapery.

We could not find any Greek remains at Karaman, with the sole
exception of a stone in a wall near the entrance of the castle with the
words IωANNHC ΔOMECTIKOC upon it.

---

* On the death of Aladin the Second, about the year 1300.

The chief antient towns lying between Iconium and Laranda, were Derbe and Lystra, rendered celebrated by the sacred writer of the Acts of the Apostles. Lystra being ascribed by different authors both to Lycaonia* and to Isauria †, must have been on the frontiers of the two provinces, probably at the foot of the mountain which borders the plain of Laranda on the south-west; for at these mountains we may suppose the rugged region to have commenced. The resemblance of the modern name Illisera to Lystra might lead one to suppose that Lystra was there situated, more especially as in one of the copies of Ptolemy instead of Λύστρα we find Λίσυρα : but in Hierocles both Lystra and Ilistra are named, so that it seems more probable that Illisera is the latter place, which has preserved its ancient name slightly changed.

Derbe having been at no great distance from Laranda towards the frontiers of Cappadocia ‡, seems to have been about Mount Kara-dagh. The ruins now called the Thousand and One Churches will, perhaps, be found to be those of Derbe; they have never yet been visited, or at least described, by any modern traveller. Nothing can more strongly show the little progress that has hitherto been made in a knowledge of the geography of Asia Minor, than that of the several cities rendered interesting to us by the journey of St. Paul, the site of one only (Iconium) is yet certainly known ; Perga, Antioch of Pisidia, Lystra, and Derbe remain to be ascertained.

Feb. 4. — Such is the poverty of Karaman that we cannot procure the number of horses necessary for our party, and are obliged to perform the remainder of the journey to the coast, reckoned at thirty-six hours, with camels for carrying our baggage, although the intervening track, being almost entirely mountainous, is the kind of country the least adapted to that animal. It requires all this day to procure a

---

* Act. Apos. c. 14. Hierocl. Synec. p. 675. † Ptol. l. v. c. 4.
‡ Τῆς δὲ Ἰσαυρικῆς ἐστὶν ἐν πλευραῖς ἡ Δέρβη, μάλιστα ἐν Καππαδοκίᾳ ἐπιπεφυκὸς, τὸ τοῦ Ἀντιπάτρου τυραννεῖον τοῦ Δερβήτου· τοῦ δ᾽ ἦν καὶ τὰ Λάρανδα. Strabo, p. 569.

sufficiency of camels and horses; and we are under the necessity of deferring our departure.

Feb. 5.—The arrival of Captain Lacy from Constantinople produces a further delay this morning, an addition to our cattle being necessary. It was eleven o'clock before we set out from Karaman though we rose at two, and were ready to start at four. At the distance of two or three miles from the town we began to ascend, and entered the mountainous region which extends all the way to the coast, and anciently formed part of the division of Cilicia called Cilicia Trachea, or Tracheotis. Our caravan now consists, besides saddle-horses, of thirteen camels, one of which is laden with provisions for the rest. On account of the difficulty of the road, their burthen is light; they carry no more than the usual load of a horse, yet with this light weight they do not move quicker than two miles and a half an hour. They step a yard at a time, and make about seventy-five steps in a minute. The post-horses laden with baggage in the former part of the route moved at the rate of three miles and a half an hour in the plains. Entering the hills we see rocks excavated into a great number of chambers, anciently sepulchral, but now inhabited by peasants and shepherds. As we leave the plains the climate changes. At four hours from Karaman, in the lower region of the mountains, we pass a village where the snow beginning to fall heavily, and there being no habitation beyond for the next fifteen hours, our guides and attendants are much inclined to remain for the night; but our delay at Karaman makes us impatient to proceed, and we advance four hours further to a Khan in the wildest part of the mountain. During the ascent the road presented some magnificent views of mountain-scenery. We leave on the left a very lofty peaked summit, one of the highest of the range of Taurus, probably between 6 and 7000 feet above the level of the sea. In the lower regions of the mountain we passed through woods consisting chiefly of oak, ilex, arbutus, lentisk, and junipers of various species. As we ascend, we enter the region of pines; and through the latter part of the route do not see a living creature, though we are told that

the woods abound with deer, wild boars, bears, and wolves. The Khan
where we take up our lodging for the night is deserted, and partly in
ruins. As we resolve not to unload the camels, they are seated on
the outside of the Khan in a ring round the door. We break some
branches from the fir-trees, covered with snow, which grow near the
Khan, select a part of the building where the roof is still entire, and
make a fire on one of the hearths, which are ranged in a line along
the inside of the wall. Here we cook some meat which we had
brought with us; and then sleep round the fire till midnight: soon
after which we send off our camels in advance, and at six o'clock
(Feb. 6.) pursue our journey to Mout, distant eleven hours. The
weather is again fine. The road lies over the highest ridges of the
mountains, where, amidst the forests of pines, are several beautiful
valleys and small plains, forming with the surrounding rocks and
woods the most beautiful scenery. In several places we trace the
footsteps of the wild animals, and observe spots where wild boars
have been rooting up the earth. The soil is fertile in the intervals
of the woods, and the climate cannot be very severe during the
greater part of the year, there being no permanent snow, now in the
middle of winter, upon any but the highest summit. There appears,
however, no trace of cultivation, though there is ample proof that
these mountains were antiently well inhabited, as we meet with
scarcely a rock remarkable for its form or position that is not pierced
with ancient catacombs. Many of these rocks present at a small distance the exact appearance of towers and castles. At a Khan half
way between our last night's Konak and Mout, we begin to descend
into the valley where that town is situated. This Khan seems to
stand upon the site of an antient temple or other public building,
there being many fragments of antient architecture in its walls, and
lying around it, and among the latter a handsome Corinthian capital.
Not far beyond the Khan we stopped to examine a tall rock which,
partly by its natural form, and partly by the effect of art, represented
a high tower. At the foot of it was a niche with a semicircular top,
the lower part forming a coffin, cut out of the solid rock: the lid of

this sarcophagus, which is a separate stone, lies at the foot of the rocks; upon it is the figure of a lion seated in the middle with a boy at either end; the boy facing the lion has his foot upon the paw of the animal. The sculpture is much defaced, and the heads have been purposely destroyed. We found also many entire sarcophagi, with their covers; but they had all been opened; in some instances by throwing off the covers, in others by forcing a hole through the sides. The usual ornament is the *caput bovis* with festoons, but some have on one side a defaced inscription on a tablet: on either side of this are ornaments varying on different sarcophagi. We observed on some a garland on one side of the tablet, and a crescent on the other: some had emblems which seem to refer to the profession of the deceased. These, and all the other monuments of antiquity we have met with, excepting those of Doganlu, are evidently of the time of the Romans. Not far from the spot where we see these remains is the village of Mahile: it is not in view from our road, and may, perhaps, have been the site of the antient town to which the sepulchres belonged. From hence we begin to descend through woods of oaks, beech, and other timber-trees, growing amidst an underwood of arbutus, andrachne, ilex, lentisk, and many other of the shrubs cultivated with so much care in our gardens. As we approach the valley, we meet with the wild olive in considerable quantities, and at length, after a very rugged descent, we enter the valley of Mout. The town and its dependant territory are governed by a pasha of two tails, who in this retired and distant situation seems to care little for the orders of the Porte, for he laughs at our firmahn, and declares, what the desolate appearance of the place tends to confirm, that he has not a horse or camel to furnish us with; but he offers us forage for our cattle, and lodging for ourselves. The latter is a ruinous hut in the castle, where we can procure nothing but some coarse barley-bread to add to the meat which we brought with us. The walls of the castle are surmounted with battlements, flanked by square towers open to the interior. In the middle is a round tower, cased, as it were, in another circular wall, rising to half the height of the tower, and leaving

a narrow interval between them. * On one side of the castle is a
precipice, the foot of which is washed by a river. Mout stands. on
the site of an ancient city of considerable extent and magnificence.
No place we have yet passed preserves so many remains of its former
importance, and none exhibits so melancholy a contrast of wretchedness in its actual condition. Among the ruined mosques and baths,
which attest its former prosperity as a Turkish town under the
Karamanian kings, a few hovels made of reeds and mud are sufficient to shelter its present scanty population. Some of the people
we saw living under sheds, and in the caverns of the rocks. Among
these Turkish ruins and abodes of misery may be traced the plan
of the antient Greek city. Its chief streets and temples, and other
public buildings, may be clearly distinguished, and long colonnades
and porticoes with the lower parts of the columns in their original
places. Pillars of verd-antique, breccia, and other marble, lie half-
buried in different parts, or support the remains of ruined mosques
and houses. Most of the inhabitants whom we saw appeared half-
naked, and half-starved; and this in a valley which promises the
greatest abundance and fertility, and which is certainly capable of
supporting a large population. Its scenery is of the greatest beauty:
the variegated pastures, groves, and streams are admirably contrasted
with the majestic forms and dark forests of the high mountains on
either side: every thing is seen that can be desired to complete the
picturesque, unless it be an expanse of water.

---

* There is a similar keep at Launceston in Cornwall.

CHAPTER IV.

IN leaving this place in the morning, (Feb. 7.) we particularly admire the fine effect of the castle with its round and square towers, the precipices with the river below them, the surrounding trees, the antient colonnades, and, among the most remarkable of the modern buildings, an old Turkish mosque with the tomb of Karaman Oglu, its founder. On quitting the town, we pass along the antient road, which led through the cemetery. Sarcophagi stand in long rows on either side, some entire and in their original position; others thrown down and broken; the covers of all removed, and in most instances lying beside them. The greater part were adorned with the usual bull's head and festoons, and had a Greek inscription in a tablet on one side. The letters were sufficiently preserved to indicate the date to be that of the Roman Empire, but we searched in vain for the name of the city.

The journey of this day is from Mout to Sheikh Amur, reckoned 12 hours for walking horses, and 18 for camels, the proportion of their movements being nearly as two to three. We had wished to have sent off our camels in the middle of the night, and to have followed in the morning, that we might all have arrived at our journey's end at the same time, but the pasha's language and the wildness of the country make us think it more advisable to keep together. Another apprehension of more real magnitude is suggested by our Tatár, that the drivers, having been forced to go beyond their post, would take some opportunity, unless we should send a sufficient force along with them, of cutting off the baggage, leaving it on the road, and,' perhaps, plundering it, and riding away with the horses. We had risen at three in the morning, but could not with every exertion set out from Mout before seven ; from which time we continued travelling, without halting, except occasionally for a few minutes, till eleven at night, having during the last two hours preceded the camels which arrived at a little past twelve. For the first two or three hours the road led us along the delightful valley of Mout. A little beyond a small village, around which are some rice grounds, we forded, by the help of guides belonging to the place, a deep and rapid river, called the Kiúk-su (Sky-blue river). The river of Mout is a branch of this stream, and joins it further down the valley. After passing over a level for a short distance, we crossed another stream rather wider than the former, the water of which runs perfectly clear over a bottom of pebbles. This branch, the principal of those which form the Calycadnus, is called the Ermenek-su, from a town of that name near its sources in the western part of the valley, where we are informed considerable remains of antiquity, similar to those of Mout, are to be seen. More are said to exist also lower down the valley, between Mout and Selefke. The Calycadnus passes the ruins of Seleucia at Selefke, and joins the sea not far below that place. Soon after crossing the Ermenek we began to ascend, and travelled for the rest of the day along a horse-track amidst the forests and mountains. The oaks are not numerous, and are chiefly confined to the lower regions, where they are intermixed with arbutus, ilex, cornel, juniper, lentisk, &c. In the upper parts scarcely any trees were seen but pines of different species : most of these were of a moderate size, but some which we saw in the highest parts of the mountain were straight, large, tall, and fit for the masts of ships of war. Great numbers had been destroyed for the sake of the turpentine, by making an incision near the foot of the tree and lighting a fire under it, which has the effect of making the resin run more freely. The summits in the center of the ridge which we crossed yesterday are higher than any part of this range, but these mountains are more extensive, and of a still wilder and more rugged description. We are told that in addition to the wild animals found in that ridge, the forests of these mountains contain tigers, or at least an animal to which the Turkish name of Kaplan is given. The road sometimes passed along the edge of precipices of immense height; at other times it was a rugged path, climbing amidst broken rocks, where there seemed hardly a footing for a mule; and at others a descent upon banks and slopes so slippery that it was difficult even on foot to avoid falling. The camels, whose footing is so very ill formed for such roads, passed them nevertheless without any material accident; they had no doubt been often accustomed to carry the merchandize of the people of Karaman across the mountains which separate that town from the coast in every direction; and it may be mentioned as a remarkable instance of the force of habit. We met with a very civil reception from the Aga of Sheikh Amur, who presented us with part of a large wild boar which his men had killed in the woods.

This morning, Feb. 8. we are much gratified by the delightful situation of the village perched upon a rocky hill, in a small hollow, surrounded by an amphitheatre of woody mountains. We proceed from Sheikh-Amur to Gulnar, on the sea side, a distance of six hours for horses. At a short distance from Sheikh-Amur we remark several comfortable cottages, surrounded with patches of cultivation, and in-closures of pallisades. These detached habitations, so uncommon in Turkey, indicate a degree of security which gives us a favourable opinion of the Caramanian mountaineers, whom indeed we have found very hospitable and inoffensive. The road is through the most beautiful mountain-scenery. A woody valley between high rocks, with a rivulet of clear water trickling through it, conducted us into a district more open and level, but at the same time more singularly wild than any we had yet seen; for over the whole of it high perpendicular rocks, of the most grotésque and váried forms, stood up among the trees, re-sembling nothing to which we could compare them but some of the representations of scenery on the Chinese earthen ware. From hence we passed along the dry bed of a torrent, which served as a road, between high calcareous precipices, rising close to us on either side. As we advanced, these rocks were fringed with ivy, saxifrage, &c., and mixed with small groves of evergreens: at the bottom, a clear stream ran along a natural groove in the rock. The prospect soon opened upon an extensive forest of oaks upon the slope of the moun-tain, and at length conducted us to a pass between two summits, from whence we beheld the sea with almost as much delight as the soldiers of Xenophon, on the top of Mount Theches. The island of Cyprus appeared in the horizon. We descended into the valley which borders the coast, by a long and extremely steep and rugged mountain-path, often intersected by rivulets running in ravines, shaded by plane-trees. The valley presented a prospect very different from those we had passed. Its meadows and cultivated fields were in all the luxuriant vegetation and brilliant colours of an advanced spring. Among them are dispersed some cottages, with flat roofs and open galleries, like those of the interior country. We followed down the mountain the remains of an antient aqueduct, and as we approached the coast, traced it again leading towards the ruins of the antient town which occupied the cape forming the bay of Celenderis. The road through the valley led along the beds of torrents adorned with oleander and agnus castus, and through groves of myrtle, bay, and other shrubs, produced only in the softer climate of the coast. The ruins, the beautiful curve of the bay, and the distant sea-view on the one side, and on the other the rich valley, contrasted with the steep mountains and dark woods behind, form a most beautiful picture, especially when seen, as by us, with the advantage of the brightest weather.

Gulnar of the Turks, and Kelenderi of the Greeks, is the name applied to the harbour and surrounding district, where the dispersed cottages, already mentioned, and the tombs and subterraneous vaults of the antient Celenderis, are the only habitations; several of the latter were occupied by poor Turkish families. Our lodging was a brick-vault, with a stone-pavement, which seemed once to have been a cistern; a low arch divided it into two equal parts. The roof of the outer had fallen in, but the inner furnished a dry and comfortable apartment. The remains of Celenderis are of various dates, but no part of them, unless it be some sepulchres excavated in the rock, appear to be older than the early periods of the empire of Rome; and there are some even of a late date belonging to that of Constantinople. The town occupied all the space adjacent to the inner part of the bay, together with the whole of the projecting cape. The best preserved remains of antiquity are a square tower upon the extremity of the cape, and a monument of white marble among the tombs; the latter is formed of four open arches, supported upon pilasters of the Corinthian order, of not very finished workmanship; and the whole is surmounted with a pyramid, the apex of which has fallen. I observed some handsome tesselated pavements among the ruins, and a great number of sarcophagi, and fragments of columns and wrought stones.

Although it now preserves remains only of a Roman town, Celenderis, in more antient times, seems to have been the principal place in this part of the country. It gave name to a region called Celenderitis, and coined those silver tetradrachms which supply some of the earliest and finest specimens of the numismatic art. The antiquity of the city is proved by the tradition of its having been founded by Sandocus, son of Phaethon *, and it seems to have received a colony of the same Samians who founded Nagidus.† It is situated about the center of the coast of Cilicia Tracheia.

As this province extended to the boundaries of Tarsus, on the east, of Coracesium on the west, and of Laranda on the north ‡, it seems to have corresponded exactly to the Turkish province of Itshil. The most fertile and the only level part of Tracheiotis is the valley

---

* Apollodorus, l. 3. c. 14.   † Pomp. Mela. l. 1. c. 13.   ‡ Strabo, p. 668.

of the Calycadnus, which district was sometimes called Citis.* The river rising to the north-west, passes by the modern towns of Ermenék, Sinanti, Mout, and Selefke, and joins the sea not far below the last. Olbasa being the only city mentioned in the inland part of Citis by Ptolemy †, and Claudiopolis by Ammianus ‡, it is probable that Olbasa changed its name to Claudiopolis, upon occasion of the colony established there by Claudius Cæsar, and that its situation was at Mout. Philadelphia and Diocæsareia, which were also in this part of the country, may have been at Ermerek, and at the ruins already mentioned between Mout and Selefke.

Feb. 9. — Nothing can more strongly indicate the present desolation of these fine countries, than the fact that as we descended the hills yesterday, towards the coast, only one vessel was visible in the vast extent of sea then open to our view. It proved to be the boat which was to carry us across to Cyprus, and in which we embarked this evening, having delayed until that time, in the hope of profiting about midnight of the land-breeze from the mountains, which seldom fails when the weather is fair.

Feb. 10. — The land-breeze carried us half across the channel, and then left us to be tossed all day by the swell in a calm.

Feb. 11. — We land this forenoon at Tzerína, called by the Italians Cerina, and by the Turks Gherné. It is the antient Ceryneia, and is now a small town with a Venetian fortification, and bad port on the north-eastern coast of Cyprus. It is reckoned by the Greek sailors eighty miles from Kelénderi, probably less than sixty English. The town is situated amidst plantations of oranges, lemons, olives, dates, and other fruit-trees; and all the uncultivated parts of the plains around are covered with bay, myrtle, and mastic. On the west side of the town are extensive quarries, among which some catacombs are the only remains of the antient Ceryneia. The harbour,

---

* Basil of Seleucia, in the Life of Thecla.   † L. 5. c. 8.
‡ Claudiopolis, quam deduxit coloniam Claudius Cæsar.

bad and small as it is, must, upon a coast very deficient in maritime shelter, have always ensured to the position a certain degree of importance. The formation of the eastern part of the north side of Cyprus is very singular : it consists of a high rugged ridge of steep rocks, running in a strait line from east to west, and descending abruptly to the south, into the great plain of Lefkosía, and to the north to a narrow plain bordering the coast. Upon several of the rocky summits of the ridge are castles which seem almost inaccessible. The slope and maritime plain at the foot of the rocks, on the north, possess the finest soil and climate, with a plentiful supply of water, and this is one of the most beautiful and best cultivated districts I have seen in Turkey.

Feb. 12. — Finding it impossible to procure horses in time to enable us to reach the gates of Lefkosía before sunset, when they are shut, we are under the necessity of remaining at Tzerína to-day. I visit a large ruined monastery, in a delightful situation, not far to the eastward of Tzerína, at no great distance from the sea. It contains the remains of a handsome Gothic chapel and hall, and bears a great resemblance to the ruins of an English abbey.

Feb. 13. — From Tzerína to Lefkosía, six hours. At the back of Tzerína the road passes through a natural opening in the great wall I have already described, and descends into the extensive plain of Lefkosía. This is in some places rocky and barren, and is little cultivated even where the soil is good. Like most of the plains of Greece, it is marshy in the winter and spring, and unhealthy in the summer. On the west and south are the mountains which occupy all that part of the island, and the slopes of which produce the wines exported in so large a quantity from Cyprus to all the neighbouring coasts. In the center of the plain is Lefkosía (Λευκοσία), called Nicosia by the Italians, the capital of the island and of the province of Itshili, of which Cyprus is considered a part, though the government is now always administered, like the other Greek islands, by a deputy of the Capudan Pasha. The ramparts of the Venetian fortifications of Lefkosía exist in tolerable preservation; but the ditch is filled up, and there is no appearance of there having been a covert way. There are thirteen bastions: the ramparts are lofty and solid, with orillons and retired flanks. There is a large church converted into a mosque, and still bearing, like the great mosque at Constantinople, the Greek name of St. Sophia: it is said to have been built by Justinian; but this may be doubted, as Procopius, in his work on the edifices of that emperor, makes no mention of it. The flat roofs, trellised windows, and light balconies of the better order of houses, situated as they are in the midst of gardens of oranges and lemons, give, together with the fortifications, a respectable and picturesque appearance to Lefkosía at a little distance, but, upon entering it, the narrow dirty streets, and miserable habitations of the lower classes, make a very different impression upon the traveller; and the sickly countenances of the inhabitants sufficiently show the unhealthiness of the climate. At Lefkosía we are very hospitably entertained by an Armenian merchant, of the name of Sarkés, who is an English baratli, and under that protection has amassed a considerable property, and lives in splendour: he and his relations seem to occupy all the principal offices of the island held by Christians, such as interpreter and banker to the Motselim, or deputy of the Capudan Pasha, collector of the contributions of the Christians, head of the Christian community, &c.

Feb. 14. — From Lefkosía to Larnaka, eight hours. The first half of the distance was a continuation of the same plain as before; the remainder over rugged hills of soft limestone, among which we cross some long ridges of selenite. At Larnaka we found Sir Sidney Smith with his small squadron: he had just signed a treaty for the evacuation of Egypt by the French.

Feb. 15. — We pass the day on board the Tigre, where we find General Junot, afterwards Duke of Abrantes, and Madame Junot and General Dupuy: the latter, next to Kleber, the senior general of the army of Egypt. They were taken by the Theseus, Captain Styles, in attempting to escape from Alexandria.

The town of Larnaka* stands at the distance of a mile from the shore, and has a quarter on the sea-side, called Αλικὶς by the Greeks,

---

* We landed at the sea-port or Marina of Larnaka, called by some authors Salines from the salt-pans in its neighbourhood. It stands at the bottom of the bay: it is a small place; but contains a mosque, a church, baths, coffee-houses, and well filled shops. In these we observed plain and striped cottons, mixed stuffs of cotton and silk, silk purses, tobacco-pipes, hard-ware, books in modern Greek. Some of the streets are rendered cool and pleasant in summer by a canopy of vines. Larnaka is situated about a mile to the east of the Marina, and is a fine village; but owes all its beauty to the delightful gardens in the neighbourhood; the walks of which are overhung with the jasmin, the evergreen rose, and particularly by the nerium oleander, or rose-bay. This grows here with great luxuriance, and is remarkable for the clusters of pale crimson flowers; and forms the chief ornament of the gardens. In the fields adjoining the town, we observed the caper-bush in flower, as well as the lycopersicon, or love-apple.

From the accounts we had received of the unhealthiness of Cyprus we were under considerable apprehensions on our arrival; and were cautious at first: but such is the effect of habit, that in a short time we walked about in the middle of the day. Among the natives not a creature was stirring abroad at that time; but in the morning and in the cool of the evening there is a considerable bustle among them. Except the oppression produced by excessive heat, I remember no unpleasant effect from the air of the island; in summer, however, strangers are apt to be affected by a *coup de soleil*, often the fore-runner of fever or death. The fevers of Cyprus are in general so rapid in their course, that there is little time for remission; but in one case I saw almost an intermission: the patient walked about and said he was in perfect health; but from the appearance of his eyes and hurried manner, it was too evident this was not the case. Those men who died of the fever on board of the Ceres had slept all night on shore. The sick belonging to the Thisbe were landed at Limosol; and kept in a tent during the ship's stay there; and though the surgeon's conduct in this instance appears to have been rash, I did not hear that any bad consequences followed it.

There seemed to be no want of schools at Larnaka. In the courts of private houses, I have seen the elder boys teaching the younger to read; and not from manuscript, but printed books. Of these they have a considerable number; but most of those I examined related to religious subjects: they have also translations from the European languages.

The church of St. Lazarus at the Marina is a large heavy building; instead of a steeple, it has merely a circular rising, or rude dome, on its roof; the use of bells being prohibited to the Greeks by the Turks. The church is large and spacious inside; is ornamented with much carving and gilding; and has some paintings ill executed. A part of the building being more elevated than the rest, and separated from it by wooden lattices, is appropriated to the women: but it has no kind of ornament. From the area, or ground-floor, which at the time of our visit was kept remarkably clean, a flight of steps leads to the relics and pictures, which are all placed in that part of the church opposite

and Marina by the Italians. In the intermediate space are many foundations of antient walls, and other remains, among the gardens

---

to the female lattices. Our guide took care to point out the most valuable relic, the great toe of St. George, who at one time was held in great reverence on the opposite coast of Syria. The grand object, however, of our guide's veneration was the tomb of St. Lazarus. It is in a vault under ground, and said by the Cypriotes to be possessed of sovereign virtue, being able, in their opinion, to restore even the dying to perfect health, if they be laid upon the tomb. In passing to this, our friend cast an approving glance upon a picture of a huge saint, with a dog's head, which had the name ΧΡΙΣΤΟΦΕΡΟΣ written above it. The representation resembled extremely the common figures of Anubis. In the neighbourhood of this church is the burying-ground for Protestants; and here I took notice of the tombs of several Englishmen, who had all died in the summer, when the heat is excessive.

The Mahometan burying ground in this part of the island is full of grave-stones; but inscriptions are not common. When the body is deposited in the grave, an arch is built over it with lath and plaster, and then covered with earth: we saw the grave open in places where this had given way.

In our observations on the domestic habits of the Cypriotes, we found them hospitable and obliging: in whatever house we entered, we were received with kindness. The inhabitants, in general, are well clothed: the shops are well filled; and the women of the middle classes have rich dresses. There seemed to be no want of provisions; they have sheep and fowls in great number; the gardens abound with vegetables, and the vines hang almost every where in the villages with luxuriant clusters. The desserts on their tables consisted of the finest fruits, musk and water melons, apricots, &c. The musk-melons we seldom tasted, on account of their supposed tendency to produce disease, but the watermelons afforded an agreeable beverage, peculiarly grateful in a hot climate.

During the month of July, 1801, we were twice at Limosol: this place is situated in the southern part of Cyprus, in N. lat. 34° 39′, E. lon. 33° 30′. It stands at the extremity of an open bay, and is a long straggling town intermixed with gardens, inclosed, for the most part, by stone walls. It is much cooler in summer than Larnaka. I observed in the fields near the town the wild poppy in flower, a branchy species of hypericum, with small yellow blossoms, a species of orobanche with violet-coloured flowers, and the convolvulus. The gardens seemed to be equally productive with those of Larnaka.

We went to Limosol for the purpose of procuring wood and water: the latter was obtained from a well by means of a Persian wheel of rude construction, turned round by an ass. The well was in a sequestered situation, to the west of the town, overshadowed by a variety of trees, among which were the Palma Christi, or Castor-oil Shrub, and the Morus alba.

The plain of Limosol is perhaps one of the most fertile districts in the island; and where the ground is not cultivated there are clusters of the olive and locust tree, and the evergreen Cypress. No tract of country perhaps affords a finer variety of thorns and thistles; and there, as well as at Larnaka, the caper-bush grows luxuriantly. Some small fields near the town were covered with tobacco and cotton plants; and in this plain the sugar-

and inclosures. The stones are removed for building materials almost as quickly as they are discovered ; but the great extent of these vestiges, and the numerous antiquities which at different times have been found here *, seem to leave little doubt that Citium stood on this spot, the most antient and important city upon the coast.

March 2. — After having remained several days at Larnaka and Lefkosía, we arrive to-day at Tzerina, on our return to Constantinople. The purity of the air on the north coast of Cyprus is very sensibly perceived, after leaving the interior plains and the unhealthy situation of Larnaka. The Turkish troops are already arriving in large bodies, on their way home, in the faith that the war of Egypt is concluded.

We set sail at eight this morning, in a three-masted covered vessel, with latine sails, for Satalia. A halo round the moon last night, and a turbid atmosphere this morning, portend a change of weather. At two or three miles from the port, the land-wind which carried us out falls and leaves us becalmed, but a breeze soon springs up from the eastward, and we steer N. by W. Having come in sight of the coast, we soon perceive the point of Anemur, five or six leagues to leeward of us. As we approach the shore, the wind coming from the westward, and freshening, we are unable to weather Cape Selenti, and are obliged to make for a small cove, called Kalándra by the Turks, and Kharadra (its antient name) by the Greeks. Here we are sheltered under the lee of a high cape, and by the help of six cables, three attached to

---

cane is said to have at one time abounded. I found the olive on the banks of a river, the bed of which was now dry ; and on the borders of other streams a number of trees were in bloom, such as the Mimosa, the Oleander, the Pomegranate, and the Jasmin. The fruit of the locust-tree is very astringent, when green ; but as soon as it ripens, it becomes sweet and pleasant, and in the winter-season constitutes the ordinary food of the sheep and goats. In the hedges, that beautiful shrub, the Palma Christi, is quite common, and its ripe fruit is sometimes used by the natives medicinally; but I do not know that they have ever extracted the oil as an article of commerce. The vine is seen growing in almost every courtyard, and its fruit is of exquisite flavour; but the richness of the red grape brought to Limosol in little hampers, from the interior, is perhaps unequalled.

Extracts from the Journal of Dr. Hume.

* See Mariti, Drummond, and Pococke.

the anchors, and three to the shore, we ride out a most tempestuous night of wind, rain, and thunder.

March 8. — At ten this forenoon, the weather having become serene, we land and spend the day at some huts on the sea-shore, belonging to a village on the hills which we do not see. Here the coast, retiring from the cape under which we were sheltered last night, forms a small bay; around it is a fertile valley; at the head of which a torrent, making its way from high mountains *, between lofty precipices, seems to have given to this place the Greek name of Kharadra. The retired valley, with the bold coast, and the woods and precipices at the back, is extremely beautiful. The only remains of antiquity are part of a mole, just below the huts on the sea-shore. On the side of the torrent, a mile up the valley, is a deserted building, which has every appearance of Venetian or Genoese construction. Kharadra is reckoned by our boatmen ninety miles from Tzerina, twenty or thirty from Cape Selenti, and sixty from Alaia. It has been already remarked that they reckon eighty from Kelénderi to Tzerina; it seems, therefore, that the Greek mile is about two thirds of the geographical. As the word μίλι was borrowed from the Latin, the measure must originally have been the same as the Roman mile, though it is now shorter. It is, however, merely a computed, and not a measured distance, and I could never obtain from the Greeks any accurate definition of it.

March 9. — We sail this forenoon at ten with a fair breeze, which in two hours · brings us abreast of Cape Selenti. Here the wind slackens, and becomes variable, and sometimes contrary with frequent showers and calms, so that we do not arrive at Alaia till eight in the evening. During the first half of the distance from Cape Selenti, we sail under high cliffs and headlands, above which are some very lofty mountains, covered with snow. Further on, the mountains retire

---

* This is the Mount Andriclus which Strabo places above Charadrus.

more inland, and leave upon the coast a fertile plain, which increases in breadth as we approach Aláia.

March 10. — This town is situated upon a rocky hill, jutting into the sea from the outer or westernmost angle of the plain. It resembles Gibraltar, the hill being naturally fortified on the western side by perpendicular cliffs of vast height, and falling in the opposite direction by a very steep slope to the sea. The whole face of the hill is surrounded with high solid walls * and towers, but the lower part only is occupied by the town, which is about a mile in circumference. The ground upon which it stands is so steep that the houses rise above one another in terraces, so that in many places the flat roofs of one row of houses serve for a street to those above them. To the eastward of the town there is an anchorage for large ships, and small vessels are drawn up on the beach. In the middle of the sea-front are some large vaulted structures, on a level with the water's edge, intended for sheltering galleys ; and constructed, perhaps, by the Genoese. They now serve for building the vessels, called by the Turks Ghirlanghitsh (swallow), which are generally formed with three masts and a boltsprit, all bearing triangular sails. Of these and other vessels nearly resembling them, of from twenty to sixty tons burthen, there are several belonging to Alaia. This place is said to have taken its name from its founder Alah-ed-din, son of Kaikosru, who was surnamed Kaikobad, and was the tenth of the Seljukian dynasty, and founder of the Iconian race. It seems to have become the principal maritime fortress and naval arsenal of these sovereigns, and of their successors the princes of Karaman. In the old maps Alaia is called Castel Ubaldo, which may possibly have been the name given to it by the Venetians and Genoese, when in possession of this and other strong holds upon the Caramanian coast, but there is no recollection of the name at present. In the year 1471 the Prince of Karaman, then engaged in a struggle for independence with Mahomet the

---

* In some parts of the modern wall are remains of Hellenic masonry, of the kind often called Cyclopian.

Second, was put in possession of Alaia, and several other places, by the Venetians, who were then in alliance with him against the Ottoman Emperor. From the town, the beach runs eastward, and thence forms a long sweep to the south-east to Cape Selenti, which is seen from Alaia. The level coast extends about half that distance, and ends in an angle, where some trees are seen round a village, at which I was informed that there are remains of an antient city. There are other ruins said to be of great extent at a few hours to the northward of Alaia.

I was detained at Alaia by illness, and while General Koehler, with his two remaining companions, (Mr. Carlyle having left them in Cyprus,) pursued their journey overland to Constantinople, I proceeded thither by sea, touching at the most remarkable places on the coast, as well as at the adjacent islands of Rhodes, Cos, Patmos, Samos, Chios, Lesbos, and Tenedos. Of those places which I visited on the coast, and which deserve to be more thoroughly described, the most remarkable are, 1. The ruins of a large city, with a noble theatre, at Kakava, in a fine harbour, formed by a range of rocky islands. 2. The island called Καστελόρυζον by the Greeks, and Castel Rosso by the Italians. It is a flourishing little Greek town, carrying on a considerable commerce of timber and charcoal with Alexandria. In a plain in the interior of the island, I found the remains of some antient buildings, of Hellenic construction. The importance of the situation must at all times have attracted inhabitants. 3. Antiphellus, on the main land, opposite to Castel Rosso. Here I found a small theatre nearly complete, the remains of several public buildings and private houses, together with catacombs, and a great number of sarcophagi, some of which are very large and magnificent. The greater part have inscriptions, few of which are legible. In two or three, however, I read the name of the city Antiphellus. 4. Telmissus, at Makri, the port of Mei, at the bottom of the gulf of Glaucus.* The theatre, and

---

* On this coast of Asia Minor is situated the harbour or bay of Marmorice, in which part of the English fleet anchored, prior to the landing in Egypt. As there is no

the porticoes and sepulchral chambers, excavated in the rocks at this
place, are some of the most remarkable remains of antiquity in Asia

---

published account of this bay, the reader will peruse with pleasure the following extract
from the journals of Dr. Hume : —
    " On the 1st of January, 1801, about mid-day, the weather being rough and cold, we
came abreast of Rhodes, and thence continued our course towards Marmorice, formerly
the Peræa Rhodiorum, situated on the southern coast of Caria, and near the gulf of
Glaucus, the modern Macri. The entrance to the bay lies between a range of high mountains; and we might have, probably, missed it, had not a sloop of war been cruising off
the coast on purpose to lead us in. Of the mountains that hid the bay of Marmorice,
many were partially obscured with mist, others were overshadowed by a variety of trees,
and streams of the clearest water were falling from the rocks upon this bold shore, which
showed no appearance of inlet or harbour. We perceived, however, as we advanced, the
mountains gradually separating, and at length beheld, over a narrow neck of land, the
masts of our advanced squadron, which had left Malta about a week before us.
    " The entrance to Marmorice bay is so narrow that a line of battle ship, or even a frigate,
is not able to work in with a foul wind. When, however, the projecting point of land
which conceals the bay is once passed, a vast basin of water, presenting an expanse of
about twenty miles, with its shores rising to a great height, and covered with wood, bursts
upon the view. The scene, though sufficiently beautiful in itself, was at this time rendered
doubly interesting by the presence of the fleet and transports intended for the expedition
against the French in Egypt.
    " The form of Marmorice Bay may be represented by a triangle, the sides of which are
nearly equal, and lying east, west, and south. The eastern and western sides are formed
by high mountains, the southern by an island, and a peninsula joined to the eastern continent by a narrow neck of land. Between the island and the peninsula is the principal
entrance; the other, between the island and the western continent, does not appear to be
in use, the passage to it being more crooked, and the water shallower. The main entrance
lies in N. lat. 36° 47′ 45″, and in E. long. 28° 32′ 26″, about twenty miles, almost due
north of Rhodes. It is open to no wind capable of doing any material injury to the shipping in the bay, which may be said to be completely land-locked. But in very high
easterly or southerly winds, the motion of the open sea is communicated to the interior of
the bay, and causes a considerable swell; and the wind sometimes blows in heavy squalls
from the high land.
    " The town of Marmorice is situated near the northern extremity of the eastern side of
the bay, about five miles from the entrance. It stands on a little rocky eminence, and is
very irregularly built, having no street, but merely a few dirty and crooked lanes that
separate the houses. These were very ordinary buildings, and bore a striking resemblance
to the cottages in Scotland, which in barren districts are built of whinstone. In the
highest part of the town is a modern castle, almost in ruins, having a few rusty cannons
planted on its walls, of no great calibre. Behind the town is a small mosque, very plain,
but neat; within, it has no ornament except a few Arabic sentences written on the wall :

Minor. 5. The ruins of Assus, at Behrem Kalesi, opposite to Molivo, the antient Methymna in Mytilene. The ruins are extremely curious.

---

we observed, when we looked in, some of the inhabitants of the place kneeling in prayer. In the cemetery near the mosque were small stones set up in the form of the antient cippi.

" On the arrival of the English, a number of people were soon collected together in the town of Marmorice, from the interior of the country; they formed a market upon stands in the open air, and offered a variety of articles for sale, among which we noticed dried figs, raisins, walnuts, honey, wax, tobacco-pipes of coarse workmanship, and a confection of walnuts and almonds.

" To the north-west of the town is an extensive plain, well watered by a number of rivu. lets, which descend from the adjacent highlands; but in some places near the sea it is very marshy: it is divided into enclosures, mostly in the state of meadow, among which are a few rude cottages. Near the town are some fine plantations of orange trees. On the western side of the bay, beyond this plain, is a considerable tract of ground, nearly level, lying between the sea and the foot of the mountains, covered in many parts with small trees, or brushwood; and along the beach is a road leading to a valley a little further to the south than the entrance of the bay.

" I visited this valley in a shooting excursion, and was much struck with the scenery. It was watered by a rivulet, which, after winding among thickets of myrtle, laurel, willow, and wild sage, lost itself in the bay, or among sedges and sand. Near the centre, and on the border of the rivulet, were a few cottages, of very rude construction; the walls of some were built of mud dried in the sun; others consisted of stones loosely put together, and the roofs were formed by pieces of wood laid across the wall, and covered with sods or straw. In one of the cottages was a woman, sitting at a loom, and weaving. About half a mile higher we came to a water-fall, where the river seemed to force itself through a narrow opening of the mountain; the thickets here were impenetrable, and we were obliged to return. Among some low wood, near the entrance of the valley, I found marble pillars, both plain and fluted, lying on the ground; they were of small dimensions.

" The island at the entrance is very little elevated, when compared to the neighbouring mountains; but it is rugged, precipitous, and covered entirely with thickets. The adjoining peninsula is much higher, but equally rugged; and seems to have no fixed inhabitants. I landed on it at a spot equally distant from the entrance and the neck of land; and though the larger trees had been already felled by our people for fire-wood, it was with some difficulty that I forced my way to the narrow isthmus which joins it to the continent. This isthmus is quite flat; in some places covered with a kind of stunted willow, and in others with sand; and so narrow that the captain of a ship who had come hither through mistake, instead of to Marmorice, made his sailors drag the boat across it, and so proceeded to the flag-ship. The land of the adjoining continent is very high, and is in many places covered with firs. A little way to the south-east of the isthmus is the fine bay of Karagatch, which, though smaller, is as safe, and not less picturesque than Marmorice. The Turks in this part of the country are stout handsome men; with swarthy complexions, and dark piercing eyes. They were all armed either with muskets and pistols, or sabres or long knives stuck in their girdles. The sabres and knives have

There is a theatre in very perfect preservation ; there are also the remains of several temples, at one of which are figures in low relief, in
a very antient style of art, sculptured upon the hard granite of Mount
Ida, which forms the materials of many of the buildings. On the
western side of the city the remains of the walls and towers, with
a gate, are in complete preservation ; without the walls is seen the
cemetery, with numerous sarcophagi, some of which are of gigantic

---

generally silver or plated handles ; and the barrel and wood of their fowling-pieces are
bound together with small circles of brass: but they are, in every respect, of clumsy
workmanship. Of the Caramanian women, the few we saw at Marmorice had no pretensions to beauty; their dress also was unbecoming: the head is enveloped in a large
handkerchief or bonnet; the limbs are concealed by a kind of wide trowsers ; and the
whole body is wrapped in a loose upper robe or garment. Like the women in all countries removed from civilisation, they appeared to be domestic slaves; tilling the ground,
or working at some trade; the husbands being much abroad in pursuit of game.

" Near Marmorice the wild boar has been shot in the woods. Jackals are numerous. I
saw several dromedaries in the vicinity of the town. Sheep were few in number. The black
long-haired goat is quite common ; and so is a small breed of black cattle, like those of
the Scottish Highlands. Partridges with red bills and feet, woodcocks, snipes, wood and
rock pigeons, wild ducks, abound. Near the mouth of the rivulets we found among the
sedge, a number of tortoises.

" Before the arrival of Sir Sidney Smith on this coast, subsequent to Buonaparte's attack
on Acre, the fine harbours of Marmorice and Macri appear to have been entirely unknown; at least their position had been determined accurately by no chart. There are
no remains of the antient Physcus : I found only part of a shaft of a column two feet and
a half in diameter, among some low wood, about a mile to the west of the town of Marmorice ; but probably more remains of antiquity might be discovered in that direction.
On the east side of the valley, I have already spoken of, at the outside of the harbour, the
appearance of the ground rising from near the sea to the foot of the rocks is so singular as
to lead us to suppose it was the work of art. It forms a small segment of a great circle
facing the sea towards Rhodes, and rises by regular terraces like the seats of an immense
theatre, each terrace being about ten feet broad, and elevated by three feet above the one
immediately below it. A tree or shrub is here and there met with; but in most parts the
terraces are covered by a smooth green turf. Neither marble nor inscriptions were discernible ; and hardly any rubbish. The height of the rocks above may be fifty or sixty
feet. In climbing the terraces, I took notice of a prodigious excavation in one part of
these rocks, with a road leading to it from the mountain behind; but though on the
terraces the ascent to this cave seemed practicable, yet in trying to penetrate so far, I
found my way obstructed by a deep ravine, which prevented my proceeding. I hope that
some traveller may be more fortunate than myself in examining this spot. It did not
seem to me to be a natural excavation."

dimensions, still standing in their places, and an antient causeway leading to the gate. The whole gives, perhaps, the most perfect idea of a Greek city that any where exists.

I shall subjoin a brief itinerary of the route of General Koehler and his party from Aláia to Shughút, where he fell into the same road by which we came from Constantinople in January.

March 11.—From Aláia to Alara, eight computed or caravan hours : the road leads along the sea-shore, sometimes just above the sea-beach, upon high woody banks, connected on the right with the great range of mountains which lies parallel to the coast ; at others, across narrow fertile valleys, included between branches of the same mountains. There are one or two fine harbours formed by islands and projecting capes, but the coast for the most part is rocky and without shelter, and after such a westerly gale as we experienced last night, is exposed to a tremendous surf. The equinoctial monsoon occurs very regularly upon these coasts, and the Greek sailors think themselves sufficiently prudent if they remain in port for the first fortnight of March, old style. Alara is two or three miles from the sea, in a valley inclosed between woody hills, and situated amidst gardens and corn-fields, with neat fences. Near the village is a remarkable conical hill, with the ruins of a strong castle upon it in good preservation. It is said by the natives to have been built by the Sultan Alah-ed-din, of Iconium.

March 12. — From Alara to Hadgi-Ali Kiúi, eight hours. The road proceeded at a distance of three or four miles from the sea, crossing several fertile and well-cultivated valleys, and passing some neat villages pleasantly situated. The valleys are watered by streams coming from a range of lofty mountains, appearing at a great distance on the right. The largest of these rivers was a little beyond the fortified hill of Alara, which was traversed by a wooden bridge sixty feet in length. Another large river occurred about three hours further. On the west side of the gulf, a little to the left of the direction of the route, appeared another range of mountains, still more lofty than those on the right, and so distant that nothing but their outline was visible. No remains of Grecian antiquity were seen by the travellers either this day or yesterday.

March 13. — From Hadgi-Ali Kiúi to Menovgát, four hours: weather rainy. Crossed the large river of Menovgat at one hour short of the town, which is situated in the midst of fields and gardens, in a fertile district, watered by many rivulets. The surrounding valleys are well cultivated and inhabited. Distant mountains appear to the north and east; and to the N. W. is the steep range which rises from that side of the gulf, and extends from Cape Khelidóni to Satália. Price of a sheep at Menovgat, eight piastres, equal to twelve shillings sterling; four fowls for a piastre.

March 14. — Detained at Menovgat for want of horses.

March 15. — From Menovgat to Dashashehr, six hours. These two days were frosty, and perfectly clear. The road passes at the same distance from the sea as before, but winds for the most part through deserted valleys, where the rich soil, and the rains which have lately fallen, have made the road deep and difficult. There is seen abundance of the cattle which is brought for pasture in the winter and spring from the mountainous districts of the interior; at intervals are several villages, with a scanty cultivation around them. Dashashehr is situated upon some rocky hills, commanding a view of the sea; and the cottages have gardens, and orchards, and plantations of vines and fig-trees attached to them. The great range of mountains is seen at a distance, twenty or thirty miles to the northward. The whole of this part of Pamphylia seems to be a succession of fine valleys, separated by ridges branching from the mountains, and each watered by a stream of greater or less magnitude.

March 16. — From Dashashehr to Stavros, six hours, through a vast plain of the richest pasture, in which was an abundance of oxen and sheep. At the end of two or three hours they cross a large river, by a bridge built upon the ruins of a magnificent antient bridge, one arch of which, still standing, forms a part of the modern work. They pass several other smaller streams. In the last half of the road a heavy rain had inundated the plains in several places. The villages are numerous, and the population consists entirely of Turks, who are hospitable and inoffensive.

March 17. — From Stavros to Satalia, six hours. The first half over the same kind of road, inundated in many places. At the end of two hours they cross a large and rapid stream by a ferry, a little beyond which, appear on the left the ruins called by the Turks Eski-Kalesi, where are great remains of walls and vaulted buildings. The road passes from thence over a more elevated level, with a dry soil, nearly as far as the walls of Satalia, at one hour short of which it crosses a very deep and rapid stream *, dividing itself into several branches, from which there are artificial derivations for irrigating the gardens and cultivated fields around Satalia. Besides the two principal streams just mentioned, the road crossed several smaller, particularly one between those two, the banks of which are thickly sheltered with trees, and where is a solid antient bridge, its summit level with the banks. Satalia, called Adália by the Turks, is a large and populous town, which, though governed only by a Motsellim, is considered as one of the best governments in Anatolia, the district being large and fertile, and the maritime commerce extensive. The town is situated around a circular port ; behind it, on a height, is a castle, built with battlements and square towers. In the suburbs, the houses are dispersed amidst orange groves and gardens, and thus occupy a large space of ground. Granite columns, and a great variety of fragments of ancient sculpture, found about the place, attest its former importance as a Greek city. Among other remains are those of an aqueduct, extending the whole length of the suburbs, but now

---

* In passing by sea from Alaia to Castel Rosso, I was obliged to follow the coast of the gulf of Satalia, the sailors being afraid, in this season, of crossing directly to Cape Chelidóni. This practice of the Greek sailors has always been common, and was anciently expressed by the word καταχολπίζω. After having been detained three days in the mouth of a river, to the westward of Menovgat, I passed within sight of the mouth of the river of Palea Satalia, and I observed that it discharged itself into the sea by a perpendicular fall over a high cliff. This singularity seems to prove that it was the ancient Catarractes.

quite ruined and overgrown with bushes. These different objects, with the sea, and the stupendous ridge of rugged mountains on the west side of the gulf, render the place extremely picturesque.

March 18. — Halt at Adália.

March 19. — From Adalia to Bidgikli, seven hours, due north. The road passes over a region of rugged rocks, intersected with hollows full of water. No cultivation is in sight ; to the left the same kind of ground seems to extend as far as the ridge of rocky mountains, which borders the west side of the gulf, and to the right as far as the Dudén, or river of Satalia.

March 20. — From Bidgiklí to Karabunar Kiúi, nine hours : the first two hours over the same rugged plain not far from the river. The two great ranges on the west and north of the plains of Satalia now approach each other, and at length are only divided by the passes, through which the river finds its way. The road, however, leaves this gorge to the right, and ascends the mountain by a paved winding causeway, a work of great labour and ingenuity. At the foot of it, in the plain, are the ruins of a castle, and of many towers and gateways of elegant architecture, with cornices, capitals, and fluted columns lying upon the ground. Sarcophagi, with their covers beside them, are seen in great numbers, as well in the plains as for a considerable distance up the side of the hill. Some of them were of large size, many with inscriptions. At the top of this formidable pass, which was antiently commanded by the city, standing at the foot of it, the road enters an elevated level surrounded with mountains, and proceeds along a winding valley amidst rocks and precipices, some of which, being quite detached and perpendicular, appear at a distance like castles and towers. The Konak this evening was a Tchiftlik (farm and country-house) of the Motsellim of Adalia, situated near three small villages on the banks of a rivulet, in a pure air and most romantic situation. The usual spring weather of these climates has now prevailed for some days ; that is to say, showers, often with thunder, in the afternoon and in the early part of the night, with a sky perfectly clear and serene the remainder of the day.

March 21. — From Karabunar Kiui to Tchaltigchi Kiui, five hours and a half. One hour from the place of departure is a Khan, formed out of the remains of an old building, upon which are angels sculptured on either side of a large arched gate. It appears to have been a church of the earliest ages of Christianity. The route continues through valleys of the same description as that of Karabunar Kiui, level and surrounded by barren rocks and mountains. A neighbouring town, called Bidgikli, is said to contain a thousand houses, and has the reputation of refusing quarters to strangers, especially to couriers and persons travelling under the orders of the Porte. This district, however, as has already been remarked in regard to other places having the character of rebellious, exhibits several marks of superior industry, and a better kind of public economy; good roads and bridges are seen, and large clean pieces of wheat surrounded with ditches or fences. In the mountain not far from Bidgikli are said to be ruins of antient buildings with columns, and sculptured and inscribed stones. A hill which bounds the district of Bidgikli to the north is the limit of the command of the Motsellim of Adalia. At the foot of it is a Khan, formed of some large antient building with fragments of architecture, and ruins of walls in various directions around it. The hill is rugged and extensive, and has on the north side a level much lower than all those lying between it and Satalia. A river flows through it, and there are many villages, among which is that of Tchaltigchi. The people appeared simple and hospitable, and welcomed the travellers by presents of fruit and flowers, which they threw down at their feet, and then departed without saying a word. The villages in the valley are surrounded with fruit-trees, but no oranges, nor lemons, nor olives are seen among them; and the season here is a month or six weeks behind that of Satalia. Wheel-carriages are used: the wheels being either solid trucks formed of one piece of wood, or of three pieces joined together, and shod with an iron plate turned up at the edges, and thus fixed on without any nails. They had also iron axles, and a box for them to turn in, exhibiting a neatness of workmanship seldom seen in Turkey.

March 22. — From Tcháltigchi to Búrdur, seven hours and a half: for the first two hours along the valley; then up a high steep mountain, not a mere rock, like the others which the travellers had passed, but having trees, and a soil fit for any vegetation. They passed an insulated valley, where was a rivulet which disappeared in a cavity at the foot of a mountain. The weather was very cold, and four inches of snow lay upon the ground at no great distance above them. After a narrow craggy pass, they entered an open country, which, unlike the level valleys to the southward, was diversified with undulations and slopes. At two hours short of Burdur, they came into a valley full of rocks, thrown about in the wildest manner: some of these were of a kind which looked like bundles of rushes, incrusted with cement, and petrified into a solid mass: in some places the scene around looked like a succession of enormous sand-pits. They passed several water-mills, and saw nothing of the town or lake of Burdur till they were close upon it. The houses are flat-roofed; the town is large and comparatively well paved, and there is some appearance of wealth and industry in the streets. Tanning and dyeing of leather, weaving and bleaching of linen, seemed to be the chief occupations. Streams of clear water flowed through most of the streets. The country around produces good butter. The salt-lake of Burdur begins at a very short distance from the town, and stretches to the N. and N. W., forming a beautiful picture with its winding shores, its shrubby or bare and rocky capes, and the cultivated lands, numerous villages, and woody hills around it.

March 23. — Detained at Burdur by a violent southerly gale and heavy rain.

March 24. — From Burdur to Ketsiburlu, six hours. The road along the edge of the lake having been rendered difficult by the rains, they took another nearer the hills. They passed a good deal of arable land, and many villages with abundance of fruit-trees and vineyards. The walnut-trees grow to a great size : on the 22d they saw poplars of six and eight feet in diameter.

March 25. — From Ketsiburlu to Dómbai-ovasi (the valley of Dombai) five hours : the wind north : a sharp frost, and the hills around. covered with snow : the road very good, leading at first through rocky hills, but afterwards through a rich valley, where are many villages ; Dombai is the chief and one of the largest. Here they received much civility from the Motsellim, whose design in it was to get their interest at the Porte in his endeavours to obtain the Pashalik of Isbarta, a considerable town at no great distance to the eastward. At Dombai they were told of the ruins of an antient town very near, with the remains of columns, inscribed stones, and statues.

March 26. — From Dombai to Sandakli on the river Méinder, distance seven hours, through a fine country variegated with gentle undulations, but bare of wood, except upon the mountains, which are at no great distance on either side. There were several small villages and a good deal of arable land, but the season was still six weeks behind that of the coast : the cold severe with much snow.

March 27. — From Sandakli to Sitchanli, seven hours : north wind, with ice an inch thick : the road was for the most part hilly and stony, but in some places there were villages and cultivated lands. Sitchanli is in a fertile valley, with many villages around.

March 28. — From Sitchanli to Altún-Tash, nine. hours : the country of an undulated form with little wood. They observed several villages, and in many places scattered fragments of antient buildings, but in no one spot any thing that indicated the site of a large town. At Altun-Tash the snow was lying on the ground. The place takes its name, (signifying golden stone,) from some rocks of a yellow colour in the neighbourhood. It stands on the left bank of the river Pursek, the antient Thymbrius, a branch of the Sangarius. Here were 200 horsemen of the Pasha of Kutaya, who had been re-ducing a rebellious chieftain, and were in the act of driving away his fiocks.

March 29. — From Altun-Tash to Kutaya, nine hours : at first over a swampy plain, which had been inundated by the rains and the melting of the snow upon the hills, then across the Púrsek, which

between this place and Kutaya forms an S: a high mountain, at the
foot of which Kutaya is situated, filling up the northern part of the
S. After crossing the Pursek they passed over gentle hills and a
pleasant country. Nearly midway was a fountain and the ruins of a
mosque, and antient Greek church. A good gravel road led in a
winding direction through a delightful scene of lawns of the finest
herbage, adorned with detached trees and clumps of evergreen, disposed in a manner which art could not have improved. From hence,
after passing a tract of wild cliffs and rocks, which formed a remarkable
contrast to the former, they descended a steep hill to the Pursek,
here a very deep and rapid river. Having crossed it by a bridge,
and ascended a part of the mountain of Kutaya, they proceeded along
a dangerous path on the edge of an immense precipice: the mountain with its snow-topped summit rising to a great height on the right,
and on the left the Pursek taking a large sweep round the base of the
mountain. Thus they made almost half the circuit of it before they
arrived at Kutaya. This is a large town with an antient castle, which
stands upon a projecting point of the hill a little above the town.
Being the usual residence of the Beglerbeg of Anatolia, Kutaya may
in some measure be considered the capital of the province, though
much inferior in size to Smyrna, Tokat, and Angura. The Pasha
being absent with the army in Syria, the place was governed by a
Motsellim, who furnished the travellers with a Tchaous to accompany
them to Constantinople, and orders for horses and other necessaries.
Antient coins and gems may be collected in the bazars of Kutaya in
considerable numbers.

March 30.—Halt at Kutaya.

March 31.— From Kutaya to In-oghi, twelve hours : the weather
fine, and the road for the most part good. They soon crossed the
Pursek, and passed at first over a flat swampy road, inundated by
floods from the mountains ; they then ascended a hill, upon the top
of which the rocks appear by their description to have been of a hard
and handsome species of breccia. Thus they proceeded nearly half
the day's journey :' the scenery sometimes very dreary and barren ;

at others grand and picturesque ; but the country no where cultivated. They then descended a steep slope to the Pursek, which they
now crossed for the second time since they had left Kutaya, and proceeded for some distance along its left bank with high steep cliffs on
each side ; among these, and along the river, grew a variety of trees
and shrubs, particularly evergreens. In one part conical and sharp-
pointed rocks arose to a great height, resembling in some places the
spires and ornamented sides of Gothic churches. Here the antients
had excavated crypts, niches, and sepulchral chambers with doors and
windows. After the pass the valley opened into fine meadows, with
the river winding through the middle. Soon afterwards the road
quitted this valley and turned to the right up another, watered by a
small branch of the same river ; then passed through a tract of
country where the road winds amidst clumps of evergreens beautifully
disposed by nature upon a fine turf, with hills, valleys, and lawns, as
in an English park. Here they met a company of Turks coursing
with their greyhounds, who made them a present of a hare. They
then crossed a ridge, the absolute height of which (though apparently
inconsiderable, when compared with the adjacent valleys) was indicated by large patches of snow lying upon the ground. The country
consists of fine pasture-lands, mixed with good timber-trees. On a
long descent from this place they looked down upon an extensive
and well-cultivated plain, at the foot of which they arrived at In-oghi,
a large village situated on the edge of the plains under the vast precipices of a mountain of bare rock, excavated naturally into caverns,
and artificially into sepulchral chambers. Some of these in the upper
part of the heights, are the abode of eagles, which are seen soaring
around them in great numbers. One enormous cavern is shut up in
front by a wall with battlements and towers, and seems once to have
served as a sort of citadel to the town.

April 1. — From In-oghi to Shughut, five hours : the weather very
clear. The road passes over pleasant hills and dales, where appears
a considerable degree of cultivation, interspersed with fine oaks and
beeches, and in one place there is a large forest. Some symptoms

of Spring have begun to appear, but the season is not yet so forward as it was upon the south coast in the beginning of February. Not a tree has begun to bud: the corn is but just above the ground; and primroses, violets, and crocusses, are the only flowers to be seen. At Shughut the appearance was more wintry than when we passed in January; and the broad summit of Olympus was capped with snow to a much greater extent.

CHAPTER V.

Remarks on the antient and modern Geography of Part of the Southern Coast of Asia Minor, and those Districts of the Peninsula traversed by General Koehler.

IT remains to offer a few remarks upon the comparative geography of the southern coast from Celenderis to Castel Rosso, and upon that of the districts traversed by General Koehler from Satalia, until he fell again into our former route at Shughut. In regard to the southern coast little seems necessary to be said after the publication of the Karamania of Captain Beaufort, who by his survey has given us a clearer knowledge of this coast, hitherto the most erroneously described of any in the Mediterranean, than we possess of any part of the countries which antient history has rendered interesting to us. It may be worth while, however, to enter a little more minutely than was consistent with the plan of Captain Beaufort, into the antient authorities regarding this coast, for poor and deserted as it now is, the very numerous remains of antiquity which Captain Beaufort discovered there, are a proof that it was once one of the most opulent regions of the antient world; and it is remarkable that in Strabo, and in the anonymous Periplus already mentioned, there exists a more detailed account of this coast than of any other, which has been distinguished by Grecian civilisation. The easiest mode of putting the reader in possession of the antient authorities upon the southern coast of Asia Minor is to give a translation of the description of it by Strabo, subjoining in the notes the parallel authorities of other antient writers. The following is the account of Strabo, beginning from Patara.

" Patara (1), * * * next to which is Myra (2), twenty stades above the sea on a high hill; then the mouth of the river Limyrus, and twenty stades inland from it, the town of Limyra. On the coast between Patara and Limyra, are many harbours and islands: of the latter the chief is Megiste (3), with a town of the same name. In the interior are Phellus, Antiphellus (4), and Chimæra, of which last we have already spoken. Then the Sacred Promontory (5), and then the three rugged islands, called the Chelidoniæ, equal in size, and distant from each other about five stades, and from the continent six stades; one of them has a port. From hence it is generally thought that Mount Taurus has its beginning. * * * But in truth the mountains are uninterrupted from Peræa (6) of the Rhodians, to the parts about Pisidia, where the mountains are also called Taurus. * * * From the Sacred Promontory to Olbia there remain 367 stades, in which space occurs Crambusa (7) and Olympus: the latter is a large city, and has a mountain of the same name, which is also called Phœnicus (8); next to it is the coast named Corycus (9); then Phaselis, a large city with three harbours and a lake. Above it is Mount Solyma. Termissus, a Pisidian city, is situated at the passes of Mount Solyma, where is the ascent into Milyas. Hence Alexander destroyed Termissus, being desirous of opening the passes. Near Phaselis are the passes on the sea-shore, through which Alexander led his army. (10) The mountain is called Climax; it borders upon the Pamphylian sea, leaving a narrow passage along the shore, which when the sea is calm, is practicable to travellers, but when swollen, is, for the most part, covered by the waves. The road over the mountain is circuitous and difficult. Alexander happening to be here in the winter season, and trusting to fortune, attempted to pass before the waves had subsided; the soldiers in consequence had to march the whole day up to the middle in water. Phaselis is a city of Lycia on the confines of Pamphylia, but does not belong to the community of the Lycians. Thus Homer considers the Solymi as separate from the Lycians. * * * Next to Phaselis is Olbia (11), a great fortress, and the beginning of Pamphylia; then the Catarractes, a large and rapid river, falling from a lofty rock, with a sound heard at a great distance. (12) Then is the city Attalia, founded by Attalus Philadelphus, who also placed another colony in the small city of Corycus, and enclosed a small space around it.   It is said that (the position of) Thebes and Lyrnessus are to be seen between Phaselis and Attalia; and Callisthenes informs us that a part of the Trojan Cilices were driven from the plain of Thebe into Pamphylia.   Next is the river Cestrus (13), in which is a navigation of sixty stades up the river to Perge; near it, in a lofty situation, is the temple of Diana Pergæa, where a religious assemblage is held every year.   Then, at the distance of forty stades towards the sea, is a lofty city, conspicuous from Perge; then a lake of a considerable size, called Capria; and next the river Eurymedon; and a navigable ascent of sixty stades to the populous city of Aspendus, which was a colony from Argos.   Higher up lies Petnelissus. Beyond (the Eurymedon) is another river, with many small islands lying before it. (14)   Then occurs Side (15), a colony from Cyme, and having a temple of Minerva.   Near it is the coast of the lesser Cibyra; then the river Melas (16), and a station for ships; then the city Ptolemais (17), and the boundaries of Pamphylia and Coracesium, the beginning of Cilicia Tracheia.   The whole circumnavigation of Pamphylia is 640 stades.

" Of Cilicia, beyond Taurus, a part is called Tracheia (rugged), and a part Pedias (plain).   Of the rugged, the maritime part is narrow, and has very little or no level country; Mount Taurus rises above it; being badly inhabited as far as the northern flanks, which are near Isaura, and the Omonadeæ, who extend to Pisidia.   It is called Tracheiotis, and the inhabitants Tracheiotæ.   Cilicia Pedias extends from Soli and Tarsus as far as Issus; and although Taurus, on the northern side of which are the Cappadocians, overhangs it, it abounds for the most part in plains, and a fertile land.   Having spoken of the parts within Taurus, we shall now proceed to speak of those without Taurus, beginning with Tracheiotis. The first fortress of the Cilicians is Coracesium, built upon a precipitous rock. (18) Diodotus, surnamed Tryphon, made use of it as an arsenal, when, with varying success, he headed an insurrection of Syria against its kings, but at length was forced to put an end to his own life, upon being blockaded there by Antiochus, the son of Demetrius. Tryphon set the example of piracy to the Cilicians, &c.

" After Coracesium is Sydra (19), then Hamaxia (20), a small inhabited place upon a rock, with a station for vessels below it, from whence ship-timber is exported. The principal is cedar, a wood apparently more abundant in these parts than elsewhere, for which reason Anthony gave this region to Cleopatra, as being well suited for fitting out her fleets. Next comes Laertes (21), a fortress situated upon a hill shaped like a woman's breast, and having a station for ships under it; then the river Selinus; then Cragus, a rock precipitous towards the sea; then Charadrus, a castle, with a station for vessels, above which is the mountain Andriclus; then a rugged shore, called Platanistus, and the promontory Anemurium. Here the continent lies nearest to the coast of Cyprus, at the promontory Crommyon; the distance being 350 stades. From the frontier of Pamphylia to Anemurium, the length of the coast of Cilicia is 820 stades, and the remainder, as far as Soli, 500 stades. (22) In this space Nagidus (23) is the first city after Anemurium, then Arsinoe (24), having a station for ships before it; then the place called Melania, and Celenderis, a city with a harbour. (25) Some consider this place, and not Coracesium, as the beginning of Cilicia. * * * Next occurs Olmi, where the people of Seleuceia first dwelt, but who after the erection of Seleucia upon the Calycadnus, emigrated to that place. For immediately after you have turned the shore which forms a promontory, called Sarpedon, is the mouth of the Calycadnus; near the Calycadnus is Zephyrium, also a promontory, and the river is navigable up to Seleucia, a populous city. * * * Next to the Calycadnus is the rock Pæcile (27), cut into steps leading to Seleuceia. Then is Anemurium, a cape, of the same name as the former, and the island Crambusa, and the promontory Corycus, 20 stades above which is the Corycian cave. * * * Next to Corycus is Eleusa, an island near the shore. The town was founded by Archelaus, and became his residence when he took all Cilicia Tracheia, except Seleuceia, in the same manner as Amyntas had it before him, and still earlier Cleopatra. * * * The boundary of Cilicia Tracheia is between Soli and Eleusa, at the river Latmus, where is a town of the same name. * * * Beyond Latmus is the important city of Soli, the beginning of Cilicia Issensis founded by the Acheans, and the Rhodians of Lindus. To this place, being in a deserted state, Pompey the Great removed such of the pirates as he thought most worthy of clemency and protection, and named the place Pompeiopolis. * * * Next occurs Zephyrium, of the same name as that at Calycadnus ; then Anchiale, situated a little above the shore. * * * Above it is the fortress of Quinda, where the Macedonians formerly kept their treasures. Above this place and Soli are mountainous districts, where is the city Olbus, with a temple of Jupiter, founded by Ajax, the son of Teucer. * * * Next to Anchiale are the mouths of the Cydnus, near the place called Rhegma. In this place, which resembles a lake, were antiently naval arsenals ; it is now the port of Tarsus. The river Cydnus, running through the middle of Tarsus, flows into it. * * * The sources of this river are not far distant from Tarsus.

NOTES.

(1) Patara has lately been visited, and thoroughly exploded, by the Mission of the Society of Dilettanti, under the direction of Sir William Gell.

(2) Myra still preserves its antient name.

(3) The reading which substitutes Μεγίστη for Κισθήνη in Strabo, is supported by the collateral authorities of antiquity, and has been admitted by all the commentators. Taking it for granted, therefore, that the modern Kasteloryzo is Megiste, as being the largest island upon this coast, Rhope, which, according to the Anonymous Periplus, in the passage cited below, was 50 stades

to the west of Megiste, answers to Aghios Georgios. The island of Kákava, by its form and position, corresponds equally to the Dolichiste of * Stephanus.

(4) Strabo is inaccurate in placing Antiphellus among the towns ἐν τῇ με- σογαίᾳ, in contradiction to Ptolemy, Pliny, and the author of the Anonymous Periplus. There can be no doubt of the ruins on the coast opposite to Kastelóryzo being those of Antiphellus, the name being still preserved in the corrupted form of 'Αντίφιλος. Many of the Sarcophagi, moreover, still pre- serve Greek inscriptions, where may be perceived the word 'Αντιφελλείτης, which is found to be the gentile adjective in Stephanus Byzantinus.

(5) The name of the Chelidoniæ insulæ has been transferred to the Sacred Promontory, which is now called Cape Khelidhóni. The following is the description of the coast between Patara and the Sacred Promontory, in the Anonymous Periplus, which travels in an opposite direction to Strabo, or from east to west : —

'Απὸ δὲ 'Ιερᾶς ἄκρας ἐπὶ τὰς Χελιδονίας νήσους σταδ. λ. (30).
'Απὸ δὲ Μελανίππης εἰς Γάγας σταδ. ξ. (60).
'Απὸ δὲ Μελανίππης εἰς Τάμον ἁλμυρὸν σταδ. ξ. (60) · ὑπὲρ σταδ. ξ. κεῖται πόλις 'Αλμυρά.
'Απὸ Μελανίππης εἰς πύργον τὸ ῎Ισιον καλουμενον σταδ. ξ. (60).
'Απὸ τοῦ Ισίου πύργου εἰς 'Αδριακὴν σταδ. ξ. (60).
'Απὸ 'Αδριακῆς εἰς Σόμηναν σταδ. δ. (4).
'Απὸ Σόμηναν εἰς 'Απέρλας (lege 'Απύρας) σταδ. ξ. (60).
'Απὸ 'Ακρωτηρίου εἰς 'Αντίφελλον σταδ. ν. (50).
'Απὸ 'Αντιφέλλου εἰς νῆσον Μεγέστην σταδ. ν. (50).
'Απὸ Μεγέστης εἰς νῆσον Ρόπην σταδ. ν. (50).
'Απὸ Ρόπης εἰς Ξεναγόρου νήσους σταδ. τ. (300). An error.
'Απὸ Ξεναγόρου νήσων εἰς Πάταραν σταδ. ξ. (60).

Of the places here mentioned, Gagæ was of some celebrity. † It is shown by Scylax, and by Pliny‡, to have been in the district to the west of Olympus, and north of Cape Hiera ; and as the Anonymous Periplus places it at 90 stades from the latter, it may be concluded from Pliny, and the Theodosian Tables, that it was in the way from the Sacred Cape to Corydalla, a large town, of which coins are still extant §, and which was 29 M. P. from Phaselis, in the way to Patara, the road undoubtedly leading through the remarkable pass which lies behind Olympus. Andriace, the port of Myra ‖, mentioned

---

* Plinii, l. 5. c. 31., and Ptolem. l. 5. c. 3.
† Stephanus Byzantinus, with the notes of Holstein.   ‡ Lib. 5. c. 27.
§ See Eckhel Doc. N. V.   ‖ Appiani Bell. Civ. l. 4. c. 82.

also by Pliny, is still called Andraki. Apyræ, which appears from Ptolemy and Pliny to have been upon this coast, and from the Anonymous Periplus to have been between Andriace and Antiphellus may have been at the head of the fine bay of Kákava.

(6) The dependencies of Rhodes on the opposite shore of the continent formed a district called Peræa.

(7) Still called by its antient name slightly corrupted, Karabusa.

(8) In the same book Strabo remarks, that all Lycia, Pamphylia, and Pisidia were visible from this mountain, and that it was the fortress of a celebrated pirate, named Zenicetus.

(9) The anonymous Periplus describes the places between Attalia and Cape Hiera as follows:

'Απὸ 'Ατταλείας ἐπὶ χωρίον Τένεδον σταδ. χ. (20.)

'Απὸ Τενέδου εἰς Λύρναντα χωρίον σταδ. ξ. (60.) ὑπὲρ τῆς πόλεως ὄρος μέγα ὑπέρκειται Φασίλις· ἐκ δὲ Φασιλίδος εἰς Κώρυκον σταδ.

'Απὸ Κωρύκου ἐπὶ τὸν Φοινικοῦντα σταδ. λ. (30.) ὑπὲρ μέγα ὄρος ὑψηλὸν κεῖται ᾿Ολυμπος καλούμενον. ᾿Εκ δὲ Φασιλίδος ἐπ' εὐθείας εἰς Κράμβουσαν σταδ. ϱ. (100.)

'Απὸ Κραμβούσης ἐπὶ χώρας Ποσιδαρισοῦντος σταδ. λ. (30.)

'Απὸ Ποσιδαρισοῦντος ἐπὶ Μωρὸν ὕδωρ καλούμενον σταδ. λ. (30.)

'Απὸ Μωροῦ ὕδατος ἐπὶ ἄκραν 'Ιερὰν καὶ νῆσον Χελιδονίαν σταδ. ν. (50.)

Upon comparing this passage with the text of Strabo, it appears that the mountains above Olympus and Phaselis were sometimes known by the same names as the cities; and were sometimes called Phænicus and Solyma, though the latter name more properly belonged to the whole ridge which extended 70 miles to the northward. Captain Beaufort discovered the remains of Olympus at Deliktash, and of Phaselis at Tékrova. It is curious that in the inscriptions which he found at Olympus the name of the people is written ΟΛΥΝΠΗΝΟΙ, whereas on the coins it is constantly written ΟΛΥΜ, with M. Lyrnas marks the site of the antient Homeric city of Lyrnessus.

(10) Arrian relates the same incident in the following words: " Alexander moving from Phaselis sends part of his army through the mountain to Perga, the Thracians pointing out the road, which was difficult; but not long. Those attached to his person were led by himself along the sea-side. This road cannot be used, except when the wind is northerly; when the south wind blows, it is impracticable. When Alexander arrived there, a north wind, succeeding to violent south winds, rendered the passage short and easy, an accident, which by Alexander and his court was considered as the inter-

ference of some deity." These two accounts are well illustrated by the actual appearance of the coast, which rises like a steep wall from the sea-shore, from near Cape Avóva to the western corner of the plain of Satalia. Arrian in saying that the detour of the mountains was not long from Phaselis to the plains where Perge was situated, shows that there was a passage over Mount Solyma not far from Satalia, for Alexander was not yet in possession of Ter. missus, which commanded the principal pass of Mount Solyma, and the detour that way instead of being short would have been very long.

(11) The position of Olbia is still uncertain, but when it is considered that Attalia, like the other foundations of the successors of Alexander, was probably only a renovation of the town, which stood upon the most advantageous position of this part of the coast, and that Strabo's expression of μέγα ἔρυμα, applied to Olbia, will not easily suit any other than the fine situation which Satalia now occupies, it may be conjectured that Attalus built his new town upon the site of Olbia. This conjecture is in some measure confirmed by the author of the Anonymous Periplus, and by Pliny ; the former of whom makes no mention of Olbia, nor the latter of Attalia. Strabo indeed mentions both, but it may easily be believed that his text is incorrect ; for in placing Attalia to the eastward of the Catarractes, he is equally at variance with Ptolemy, with the evidence of the modern name of Satalia, and with the author of the anonymous Periplus, whose description of the coast between Coracesium and Attalia is as follows :

Ἀπὸ Κορακησίου εἰς Αὔνησιν ἐπὶ χωρίον Ἀνάξιον σταδ. π. (80.)
Ἀπὸ Ἀναξιῶν εἰς χωρίον καλούμενον Αὐγὰς σταδ. ō. (70.)
Ἀπὸ Αὐγῶν ἐπὶ ἀκρωτήριον Λευκόθειον σταδ. ν. (50.)
Ἀπὸ Λευκοθειόυ εἰς Κύβερναν σταδ. ν. (50.)
Ἀπὸ Κυβέρνης ἐπὶ Ἀρτεμίδος ναοῦ σταδ. ν. (50.)
Ἀπὸ Ἀρτεμίδος ναοῦ ἐπὶ ποταμὸν πλωτὸν Μέλανον σταδ. θ. (9.)

*　　　　　*　　　　　*

Λοιπὸν Παμφυλία.

Ἀπὸ τοῦ Μέλανος ποταμοῦ εἰς Σίδην σταδ. ν. (50.)

*　　　　　*　　　　　*

Ἀπὸ Σίδης εἰς Σελεύκειαν σταδ. π. (80.)
Ἀπὸ Σελευκείας εἰς ποταμὸν πλωτὸν καλούμενον Εὐρυμέδοντα σταδ. ϱ. (100.)
Ἀπὸ Κυνοσθρίου ἐπὶ ποταμόν καλόμενον Κεστρόν σταδ. ξ. (60.) ἀναπλεύσαντι τὸν ποταμὸν πόλις ἐστὶ Πέργη τοῦ Κέστρου ἐπὶ Ρουσκόποδα.
Ἀπὸ Ρουσκόποδος ἐπὶ Μάσουραν καὶ τοὺς Καταρράκτας σταδ. ν. (50.)
Ἀπὸ Μασούρας εἰς Μυγδάλην σταδ. ō. (70.)
Ἀπὸ Μυγδάλων εἰς Ἀτταλείαν σταδ. ῑ. (10.)

(12) Pomponius Mela gives a similar description of the Catarractes : —
" Deinde duo validissimi fluvii, Cestros et Catarractes: Cestros navigari
facilis ; hic quia se præcipitat ita dictus. Inter eos, Perga est oppidum."
The Anonymous Periplus affords a still more accurate allusion to its present
state, by using the plural τοὺς Καταρράκτας, the Cataracts. The river on
approaching the coast divides itself into several branches, which in falling
over the cliffs that border the coast from Laara to Adalia, form upon their
upper part a mass of calcareous deposition, projecting considerably beyond
the perpendicular line of the cliffs. Through the calcareous crust, the water
makes its way to the sea, and being thus separated into several streams by a
natural process which has been rapidly increasing in its operation in the
course of time, the river has now no determinate embouchure (as it may
perhaps have had in former ages,) excepting after heavy rains, when, as I
saw it in passing along the coast, it precipitates itself over the cliffs near the
most projecting point of the coast a little to the west of Laara. Besides the
natural phænomenon which divides the Catarractes into separate streams, its
main stream is further diminished by the derivations which turn the mills
and supply water to the gardens and town of Satalia. The ruins which
Captain Beaufort observed at Laara seem to answer to the Masura of the
Anonymous Periplus, or the Magydis of Ptolemy.

(13) Although the antient geography of the coast of Pamphylia cannot be
thoroughly illustrated until the position of its chief towns is examined and
ascertained, there seems little doubt that the four rivers mentioned by Strabo,
namely, the Cestrus, the Eurymedon, a third river not named with islands
before it, and the Melas, are accurately fixed by the survey of Captain
Beaufort, and the route of General Koehler, confronted with Strabo, the
Anonymous Periplus, Zosimus *, and Pomponius Mela. † The Cestrus
is that which General Koehler crossed at two hours to the west of Stavros,
and the ruins which he had on his left hand in crossing it seem to be those
of Perge. The Eurymedon is called Kápri-su, a name derived from the
antient city of Capria, which appears to have stood at a distance of about
two miles from the sea, upon the banks of a lake of the same name, which
occupied a part of the maritime region between the Eurymedon and Cestrus.
The name of Kápri has, by a common process, been transferred from the
lake to the neighbouring river Eurymedon. The remains of Aspendus should

---

* Lib. 5. c. 16.   † Lib. 1. c. 14.

be found at six or eight miles from the mouth of the Eurymedon, on a lofty precipitous height on the banks of the river. * Higher up was Petnelissus : but the most important discovery in this part of the country would be Selge, a colony of the Lacedæmonians, situate on the frontiers of Pisidia and Pamphylia, in a very fertile district, difficult of approach, in the upper regions of Mount Taurus, near the sources of the Cestrus and Eurymedon.† Paul Lucas heard of great ruins at Durdan near Isbarta.

(14) There can be little doubt that the river without a name here mentioned, is that which is marked on the map between Side and the Eurymedon, although instead of any islands before it, nothing is now seen but some rocks below or even with the water's surface. In proceeding by sea from Alaia to Castel Rosso, I remained for two or three days in the mouth of this river, in a two-masted vessel of Alaia of about 50 tons. It is the only river which affords shelter, or even entrance to a boat, the Cestrus and Eurymedon, although much larger streams, being now closed by bars. It is very probable that the remains of Sylleium would be found upon the banks of the river, for which we have no name either antient or modern; for Sylleium appears from Scylax to have been situate between Side and the Eurymedon, and from the narrative of Appian‡ to have been at no great distance either from Side or from Aspendus. It appears also from the Anonymous Periplus that half way between Side and the Eurymedon there stood one of the numerous places named Seleuceia, unless this be a mistake for Sylleium.

(15) The fine ruins of Side have been described by Captain Beaufort. Its site is decisively fixed by the inscriptions found there. Though the Turks are so ignorant as to give it the name of Eski Adalia (Old Attalia) the name of Side was not unknown to their geographers 150 years ago, being mentioned by Hadgi Khalfa. The Greeks give the name of Παλαιὰ Σαταλία to the ruins of Perge.

(16) The words of Zosimus, (τοῦ Μέλανος καὶ τοῦ Εὐρυμέδοντος ὧν ὁ μὲν ἐπέκεινα διαβαίνει τῆς Σίδης· ὁ δὲ διαρρεῖ τῇ Ἀσπένδῳ, l. 5. c. 16.) and the distance of 50 stades east of Side, at which the Anonymous Periplus places the Melas, are decisive when added to the evidence of Strabo and Mela, in fixing the Melas at the Menovgat-su.

---

* Pomp. Melæ, l. 1. c. 14.   Arrian Ex. Alex. l. 1. c. 27.
† Strabon. Geog. p. 570.   Dionys. Perieg. v. 858.   Arrian. de Exp. Alex. lib. 1. c. 28.
‡ Appian. Hist. lib. 1. c. 26.

Cape Karaburnu being the only remarkable projection upon this coast, must be the Leucotheius of the Periplus, though the modern name implies *black* and the antient white.

If the Κύβερνα of the Periplus is the same as the Little Cibyra of Strabo, as we can hardly doubt, there is a manifest disagreement between the two authorities in regard to the position of its territory. It is probable that the text of Strabo is in fault, and that the territory of the Lesser Cibyra should follow rather than precede the Melas; for it is difficult to believe any other territory than that of Side should have been interposed between so large a city and a river which was only seven miles distant from it. The vestiges of Cibyra will probably be found removed at some distance from the coast, a few miles to the eastward of Menovgat. Ptolemy * is positive in placing it among the inland towns of Cilicia Tracheia; Scylax names it as a city of Pamphylia, near Coracesium.

(17) As no other author makes mention of this Ptolemais, and as its name is not found in the Anonymous Periplus, it may be conjectured that it did not stand upon the coast, but occupied, perhaps, the situation of the modern town of Alara, where is a fine stream, and upon its banks a steep hill crowned with a Turkish castle.

(18) The testimonies of Strabo, Ptolemy, Scylax, and the Anonymous Periplus, concur in placing Coracesium at Alaia, the extraordinary situation of which town upon a rocky promontory, precipitous on one side, and on the other extremely steep, is well suited to that fortress, which held out against Antiochus the Great, when all the rest of the coast of Cilicia had submitted to him. Coracesium was one of the positions which particularly assisted in supporting the spirit of piracy upon the coast, and it was the last where the pirates ventured to make any united attempt against the fleet of Pompey, before they separated and retired to their strong holds in Mount Taurus. For the history of the pirates the reader may consult Strabo, the Mithridatic war of Appian, who gives an account of their reduction by Pompey, and Plutarch's life of the same Roman commander. But notwithstanding Pompey's triumph, they continued to exercise their trade until a late period, for we learn from Constantine Porphyrogennetus †, that in the tenth century, Side was still the work-shop of the pirates (τὸ τῶν πειράτων ἐργαστήριον). Their success in the time of the Romans was owing to the

---

* Ptolem. Geog. lib. 5. c. 5.   † De Themat. 14.

commodious ports and strong positions of the coast, to the strength of Mount Taurus behind, and to the frequent disputes of the Kings of Cyprus, Egypt, and Syria, among one another, and with the Romans; which made it oc̄ casionally the interest of every party to support the Cilician cities in piracy and independence. Thus, like the Barbary states in the present day, the opportunity was afforded them of collecting plunder and captives from every vessel and shore that was unable to resist them. The sacred island of Delos became the entrepôt of their trade; and the increasing luxury of the Romans gave encouragement to the commerce in slaves.

(19) Lucan * calls Syedra a port. Florus describes it as a desertum Ciliciæ scopulum; yet its copper-coins are not uncommon †; and it shared with Coracesium a fertile district along the coast, which, although narrow, is not to be equalled by any other in Tracheiotis, except the valley of the Calycadnus.

(20) Notwithstanding the apparent precision of Strabo in this passage, the situation of Hamaxia is still doubtful; for in the Anonymous Periplus, where, though there are frequent interruptions, false spellings, and false distances, the order of names is generally more to be depended upon than in Strabo, Anaxion or Anaxia is placed at 80 stades to the westward of Coracesium, thus nearly answering to the ruins upon a hill, near the coast, where Captain Beaufort found remains of antiquity. Unfortunately, Hamaxia is not mentioned by any other author.

(21) The following is the description of the coast between Coracesium and Anemurium, by the Anonymous Periplus: —

'Απὸ δὲ 'Ανεμουρίου εἰς Πλατανοῦντα σταδ· τν. (350). Error.

'Απὸ Πλατανοῦντος εἰς χωρίον Χάραδρον σταδ. τν. (350). Error.

'Υπὲρ δὲ Χαράδρου κεῖται ὄρος μέγα ˝Ανδρόκος καλούμενος ἀπὸ σταδ. λ.

'Απὸ τοῦ Χαράδρου ἐπὶ χωρίον Κράγον καλούμενον σταδ. ρ. (100).

'Απὸ τοῦ Κράγου ἐπὶ χωρίόν ἐπὶ θαλάσσης, Ζεφελίους (lege Νεφελέως) σταδ. κε. (25).

'Απὸ τοῦ Ζεφελίου ἐπὶ ἄκραν Νησιαζούσης σταδ. π. (80).

'Από Νησιαζούσης ἄκρας εἰς Σελινοῦντα σταδ. ρ. (100).

        *   *   *

'Απὸ Λαερτοῦ εἰς Κορακήσιον σταδ. ρ. (100).

The distance between Selinus and Laertes is wanting; but the order of names being the same as in Strabo, and the preservation of the antient appellations, Selinus, Charadrus, and Anemurium, being decisive of those three points, the

---

* Pharsal. lib. 8. v. 259. † Eckhel, Doct. Num. Vét.

whole coast, from Coracesium to Anemurium, is very well ascertained. The
ruins to the westward of Kharadra, upon a hill exactly answering to Strabo's
description of Cragus, leave little doubt either of their being the remains of
the place which Strabo meant, or of its being the Antiocheia super
Crago of Ptolemy, which he mentions next to Selinus. The promontory
Nephelis, rendered illustrious by an antient treaty of the * Athenians
which has not reached us, can be no other than the Cape which lies to the
westward of Antiocheia two or three miles, a distance answering exactly to
the 25 stades of the Anonymous Periplus. With this evidence it can scarcely
be doubted that Ptolemy improperly inserts Nephelis between Antiocheia and
Anemurium.

(22) These numbers are obviously incorrect; perhaps they should change
places, the distance from Coracesium to Anemurium being about 60 nautical
miles, and from Anemurium to Soli 100.

(23) Nagidus, a colony of the Samians †, appears from its silver ‡ coins
to have been antiently one of the chief places of this coast; afterwards
giving way, perhaps, to the neighbouring position of Anemurium, which was
better adapted to be one of the fortresses and ports of the pirates. The two
theatres, the aqueduct, and other ruins at Anemurium, show that it chiefly
flourished under the Romans.

The river Arymagdus, placed by Ptolemy between Anemurium and
Arsinoe, seems to be the same as the Salassis, which, according to
Pliny, flowed from Isauria into the sea of Anemurium. § The latter name
was probably derived (as we so often find instanced in other parts of Greece)
from the region Salassis, upon its banks, in which Ptolemy mentions Nineia,
as the only town. The river is now called the Direk-Ondasi; it joins the
coast five miles north-eastward of Cape Anamúr, at the Castle of Anamúr.
The following are the places between Anemurium and Celenderis, according
to the Anonymous Periplus : —

'Από Κελενδέρεως εἰς Μανδάνην σταδ. ρ. (100).

'Από Μανδάνης ἐπ' ἀκρωτήριον Ποσείδιον καλούμενον σταδ. ζ. (7).

'Από Μανδάνης ἐπὶ τὰς Διονυσιοφάνους σταδ. λ. (30).

'Από Διονυσιοφάνους εἰς Ρυγμάνους (qu. 'Αρυμάγδους ;) σταδ. ν. (50).

'Από Ρυγμανῶν εἰς 'Ανεμούριον σταδ. ν. (50).

(24) This Arsinoe is named by Pliny, Stephanus, and the Geographer of
Ravenna, the last of whom, in giving the names in this order, Anemurium,

---

* Liv. Hist. lib. 33. c. 20.   † Pompon. Melæ. lib. 1. c. 13.
‡ See Eckhel, Hunter, &c.   § Plin. Hist. Nat. lib. 5. cap. 27.

Arsinoe, Sicæ, Celenderis, corroborates Strabo and Ptolemy, and justifies us in fixing Arsinoe at Softa-Kalesi. The name of Syce or Sycea is also found as a Cilician town in Athenæus *, and Stephanus Byzantinus; and if the emendation of Scylax, by Gronovius, may be followed, it was very near the promontory Poseidium, which being placed in the Anonymous Periplus, at about half way between Anemurium and Celenderis, accords very well with the only remarkable Cape in this space, now called Kizliman.

(25) The author of the Anonymous Periplus gives the names and distances between the mouth of the Calycadnus and the gulf of Berenice, which, as he indicates no interval between it and Celenderis, seems to have been the bay in which Celenderis is situated.

(26) The promontory of Lissán-el-Kahpeh being very accurately described in the Anonymous Periplus by the words ἄκραν ἀμμώδη στενὴν, seems to leave little doubt of its being the Cape Sarpedonia, celebrated as being the place beyond which the ships of Antiochus were forbidden to sail, by his treaty with the Romans. We are confirmed in this belief by Ptolemy, Strabo, and the Anonymous Periplus, who all place the mouth of the Calycadnus to the eastward of Sarpedonia. It would appear also that the projection of the coast at the mouth of the Calycadnus was the Cape Zephyrium, of Strabo and Ptolemy; for Appian † in mentioning Cape Calycadnus, evidently means this projection of the coast, and the Anonymous Periplus does not notice any Zephyrium on this part of the coast, naming only the mouth of the Calycadnus at 80 stades to the east of Cape Sarpedonia. Pliny ‡ in like manner omits Cape Zephyrium, stating the order of names as follows: — " Calycadnus, promontorium Sarpedon, oppida Olme, Myle, promontorium et oppidum Veneris, a quo proxime Cyprus insula."

The situation of the city of Venus, here given, agrees with that ascribed to Aphrodisias, by Ptolemy and the Anonymous Periplus, from whom it appears to have been situated between Celenderis and Sarpedon, on the part of the coast which lay nearest to Cyprus, and about north of Cape Aulion, in that island. Aphrodisias, although unnoticed by Strabo, is mentioned by Stephanus Byzantinus, by Diodorus §, and by Livy. ‖ It is difficult, however, to discover the exact situation of this city, from the confused account of the places between Celenderis and Sarpedonia, in the Anonymous-Periplus, but supposing the gulf of Berenice to have been the

---

* Athen. Deipnos. lib. 3. cap. 5.   † Appiani Syriac. lib. 3. c. 39.
‡ Plin. Hist. Nat. lib. 5. c. 27.   § Diodor. Sic. lib. 19. c. 61.
‖ Livii, Hist. lib. 33. c. 20.

same as the bay of Celenderis, it seems probable that Aphrodisias, being marked at 170 stades from the gulf of Berenice, and at 120 from Cape Sarpedonia, (and the sum of these two distances is pretty nearly the correct distance between Cape Lissán-el-Kahpéh and the bay of Kelenderi,) should be sought for at rather more than half way between the two, at the harbour of Porto Cavaliere, the cape on the outside of which, called Cape Cavaliere, is in fact the most projecting point of the coast, and may be said to lie nearly opposite to the eastern extremity of Cyprus, now Cape St. Andrea, and antiently Cape Aulion.

The small stream which joins the sea, between the bay of Kelenderi and the island of Papadúla, being the only stream found in the part of coast under consideration, seems to have been the Melas of the Periplus.

Olmi, which appears from Strabo, Pliny, and the Periplus to have been to the eastward of Sarpedonia, and from the last-mentioned authority to have been at the same distance from Sarpedonia that Seleuceia was, namely 120 stades, will fall at or near Aghalimán. Mylæ, which is placed by Pliny and the Periplus between Olmi and Aphrodisias, was probably on the coast opposite the island of Provençal, for the Periplus informs us that the island of Pityusa was 20 stades from the cape or peninsula of Myla, and 45 stades from Aphrodisias, distances which agree very well with the respective distances of the isle of Provençal from the main land opposite to it, and from Porto Cavaliere.

(27) The following are the places which occur on the coast between the river Pyramus, now the   , and the Calycadnus, according to the Periplus : —

· Ἀπὸ τοῦ Πυράμου ποταμοῦ· εὐθυδρομοῦντι εἰς Σώλους * * * σταδ. φ. (500).

Ἀπὸ τῆς κεφαλῆς τοῦ πυράμου ἐπὶ τὸν Ποταμὸν Ἀρειον σταδ. ϱκ. (120).

Ἀπὸ Ἀρείου ποταμοῦ ἐπι στόματος λίμνης ὁ καλεῖται Ῥήγμοι σταδ. ō. (70).

Ἀπὸ Ῥηγμῶν εἰς Τάρσον σταδ ō (70.)· ῥέει δια μέσης τῆς πόλεως ποταμὸς Κύδνος.

*   *   *   *

Ἀπὸ τοῦ Κορακησίου ἐπὶ τὴν Ποικίλην Πέτραν, ἥτις ἔχει κλίμακα, δι᾽ ἧς ἐστιν ὁδὸς εἰς Σελευκείαν τὴν ἐπὶ Λύκου, σταδ. ο. (70).

Here it will be observed, 1. That the distance of 500 stades from the river Pyramus to Soli, is the same as that given by Artemidorus. *

2. The relative situations of the rivers Areius and Rhegmis how that the Areius is the same as the Sarus of other authors. The lake of Rhegma is now filled up with sand and alluvial soil.

3. That the Periplus exactly confirms the steps in the rock leading from the

---

* Apud Strabonem, p. 675.

rock Pæcile to Seleuceia. Upon the whole, however, the author of the Periplus adds little on this part of the coast to the description of Strabo, and few of his distances correspond to the actual measurement. The modern names of Koryhos (Corycus), Lames (Latmus), and Tersous (Tarsus), with the fine ruins of Soli or Pompeiopolis, at Mezetlu, are the principal landmarks, and render it easy to fix most of the places.

Sebaste, which Ptolemy places between Corycus and the river Lamus, is the same as Eleusa, as appears from Stephanus Byzantinus, and from Josephus *; it received the latter name when it became the residence of Archelaus, king of Cappadocia. Zephyrium may be placed at the small projection of the coast which exists at the mouth of the river of Mersin ; for this falls not very far from the distance of 120 stades from Tarsus, at which the author of the Periplus places Zephyrium : his distance of 70 stades from Tarsus to the mouth of the Cydnus is equally near the truth.

The route of General Koehler, from Satalia to Shughut, traverses a part of Asia Minor, upon which antient history throws little light. Arrian's† March of Alexander from Pamphylia to Gordium, in Phrygia, and Livy's‡ Account of the Progress of Cneius Manlius, in his Expedition from Cibyra into Pamphylia, and from thence by Sagalassus to Synnada and Galatia, are the only historical documents. The itineraries supply little or nothing, and Strabo has scarcely done more than point out the boundaries of the provinces. The passage of Livy, just alluded to, is very detailed, and may hereafter be extremely useful in giving us a knowledge of the antient geography of the country; but while we are still ignorant of the exact sites of Sagalassus, Apameia Cibotus, and Synnada, very little certain information can be derived from it in regard to a single route. There are three points in General Koehler's road that may be considered certain, or at least very nearly so ; these are, Termessus, Tabæ, and Cotyaeium. The great ruins at the foot of the pass, which leads over the mountains, on the north side of the plains of Satalia, seem clearly to be those of Termissus, which, next to Selge, was the largest of the Pisidian towns, and was situated at the passes of Mount Solymus, leading into Milyas, and thence to Sagalassus and Apameia. Milyas being on the confines of Pamphylia, Pisidia, and Lycia, and occasionally assigned to each of these provinces §, agrees exactly with the elevated region traversed by General Koehler and his party, when they had mounted the pass which I

---

* Josephi Antiquitat. lib. 16. c. 4.   † L. 1. c. 27, 28, 29.
‡ L. 38. c. 13, 14, 15.   § Strabo, p. 630, 631. Ptolem. l. 5. c. 5.

supposed to be the Termessian. It is here to be observed, that there can be little doubt that Arrian has improperly called the Termessus of Mount Solymus Telmissus, an inaccuracy which, uncorrected, throws much obscurity on his narrative. On the coins of Termessus, that city is called the greater Termessus, to distinguish it from another Pisidian town of the same name.

It can hardly be doubted that Dombai is a corruption of Tabæ, scarcely indeed a corruption, as it is no more than the broad and rustic pronunciation of the antient word Τάβαι. Tabæ appears from Strabo to have been in the country between the Upper Mæander and Phrygia Paroreius, which is exactly the situation of Dombai. The fertile district now called the Dombai-ovasi, or valley of Dombai, agrees equally well with the Ταβηνὸν πέδιον, which, according to the geographers, lay on the borders of Phrygia and Pisidia. We may suppose, therefore, that the ruins which the travellers heard of near Dombai were those of Tabæ.

It may here be remarked that the enumeration by Strabo of the principal plains in the western part of Asia Minor may be serviceable in deciding the site of several of the cities. These plains were, the Caystrian, the Cilbian, the Hyrcanian, the Peltine, the Cillanian, and the Tabene. The salt-lake of Burdur is evidently the lake Ascania, which Alexander passed on his way to Celænæ, after having reduced some of the strong places of Pisidia: for Arrian observes, that salt was formed spontaneously in the lake Ascania; and Pliny remarks that the upper surface of the water was fresh while the lower was nitrous.

Sandakli seems to correspond in position, as it does in name, with Sandalium, a town lying between Cremna and Sagalassus, which last was one day's journey from Apameia Cibotus. The river called the Meinder-su which runs by Sandakli, may, perhaps, be that branch of the Mæander antiently called Obrimas, the fountains of which were something more than a day's journey from Synnada towards Apameia.

The very remarkable ruins noticed by Paul Lucas, twelve or fifteen miles after he had turned out of the route of General Koehler to go to Isbarta, would be well worthy of a more particular examination. They may possibly be those of Cremna, which is the more likely to have preserved some considerable remains, as having been a Roman colony. The situation of these ruins, on the side of a steep mountain, agree moreover with Strabo's description of the site of Cremna. But it is unnecessary longer to detain the reader with what must be mere conjecture, until some of the sites of the towns, especially those of Apameia and Sagalassa, are decisively determined.

281

SOME PARTICULARS RESPECTING THE POLICE OF
CONSTANTINOPLE.

[COMMUNICATED BY MR. HAWKINS]

Among the various objects of enquiry which merit the attention of travellers at Constantinople, there is none, perhaps, of more importance to an Englishman than the police of that great capital; and the following particulars respecting one of its departments, which I collected there in 1797, may be thought to possess at this period a more than ordinary interest.

Although by the Mahometan law theft is punishable with death, (and it is well known in how summary a manner, according to this law, judgment is pronounced and executed,) yet the government here have thought it more expedient for the good of the public, to connive in some measure at this crime; and with this view they have appointed an officer to superintend this particular department of the police, under the title of Zyndan Hassekisi (keeper of the prison), who in fact is no other than the head or chief of the thieves.

This chief is selected from the corps of the Mumgi (servants of the Aga of the Jannissaries), and his office, which is venal, and costs 2300 piastres, is held so long only as he is considered capable of discharging its duties; his incapacity being deduced from his inability to apprehend any thief whose person is sought after.

The organization of this singular branch of the police is as follows: Every thief on his first apprehension has recourse, through the medium of his friends and of presents, to the Zyndan Hassekisi, who employs all his interest with the higher powers to save his life, and to cause him to be transferred to the Bagnio, or great prison of the Arsenal, from whence after some time he procures his discharge.

In the mean time, the name of this new thief, every particular which is thought to be characteristic of his person, and his favourite mode of thieving, are noted down with great accuracy in the registers of the Zyndan, from which moment he is constituted a regular member of the fraternity. A thief who has not in this manner put himself under the protection of the Zyndan Hassekisi, is sure to be executed the very first time he is convicted.

The thieves who are subject to this sort of superintendance are of both sexes, and of every age and country. They disguise themselves in a váriety of ways, assuming every character from the mendicant to the man of rank; and, in short, exercise their professional talents here as systematically, and with less hazard than in any other great capital, although, as will be seen by what follows, with less profit.

Both the Zyndan Hassekisi and the other officers of the Zyndan, consider themselves as greatly beholden to any person who lays an information before them of his having been robbed; because not only he who has actually committed the robbery is obliged to give them a portion of the effects stolen, but even he who is innocent of it, and is apprehended merely on suspicion, cannot obtain his release without paying for it. As the last case may occur as often as the Zyndan Hassekisi pleases, the thieves carefully avoid falling in the way of this officer, through fear of being detained on the slightest pretexts or grounds of suspicion; well knowing that at all events they would be made to pay for the recovery of their liberty.

It may be proper to observe that the Zyndan Hassekisi from the circumstance of his having been selected from the corps of the Mumgi, is necessarily a person of some experience and ability in this line of employment, and is fully acquainted with his duties. Now as every thief is known to excel in some particular way; for instance, one is noted for his dexterity in forcing a door, another for his skill in picking locks, another for his address in openly entering a house on some pretext or other; the person who comes to the office to give information of his having been robbed, is closely interrogated as to all the particulars. Whereupon the Zyndan Hassekisi summons before him all those thieves who are known to pursue that line of their profession, and the guilty person is soon discovered and brought to a confession. The stolen effects are then recovered; notwith_ standing which, if the person who has been robbed do not fee well the Zyndan Hassekisi, he obtains the restitution of no part of his property;. for the Zyndan Hassekisi, who becomes the depositary of these effects, divides them in reality with the thief and some of the persons in office, particularly the Assas Bashi. It is supposed, for these reasons, that the thieves at Constantinople receive not more than one-fourth of their booty; the remaining three quarters being partitioned among the officers of the Zyndan.

Should any one discover the effects he has been robbed of, it matters not in whose possession they may be, or what time may have elapsed, he is entitled by the law to take possession of them, after proof given of their having been stolen; and the person in whose hands they were found cannot sue him for any compensation; first, because according to the Mahometan law he can claim restitution of the money which he had paid for these effects from no other person than he who sold them; and secondly, because, should he persist in withholding these effects from the reclaimant, he would subject himself to an accusation of his having been an accomplice with the thief.

Nevertheless those who purchase gold and silver for the mint, as well as the venders of copper utensils, are particularly exempted by a firman from this obligation to restore effects stolen. The jewellers and goldsmiths likewise once possessed a similar privilege, although it. was restricted to effects which had been purchased at their, real value. This last-mentioned firman having been little acted upon for many years past, has now nearly lost all its authority, and some endeavours are making to get it renewed, which it is thought will prove successful.

The above is nearly a literal statement of the information which was given to me at Constantinople, and I believe it to be authentic. It follows, that travellers, like De la Motraye, are mistaken in supposing, from the rarity of those cases where theft is punished, that the crime itself is unusual there. *

To what particular nation these privileged thieves mostly belong, I neglected to enquire; and the population of this vast city is so heterogeneous, there is here such a *colluvies gentium*, that it would be difficult to form a conjecture: but I cannot help remarking in this place, that the Turks of genuine descent have been always justly esteemed for their honesty.

Nor is it possible, I believe, to ascertain how long this state of things has subsisted; for the police of Constantinople is scarcely noticed in any of the numerous books of travels which I have consulted. I suspect, however, that the Turks have, in this instance, as well as in many others, adopted the practice of their predecessors; and should this view of the subject be correct, it may not be easy to assign any limits to the antiquity of the system; for we learn from Diodorus Siculus that something very like it prevailed in Egypt. The account which he gives is as follows: —

" The Egyptians have a very singular law respecting thieves. Those who are disposed to follow this way of life, are obliged to have their names entered in the register of the head or chief of the thieves, to whom it is understood that they are to bring directly, and without delay, whatever they have stolen. Those who have been robbed are likewise required to specify to him, in writing, what they have lost, stating the place from whence, and the day and hour when it was taken away. In this manner all the effects are recovered without trouble, and the person who has been robbed, after paying a fourth of their value, gains possession of them. For since it was found to be impossible wholly to put a stop to the practice of thieving, a way was found out by the legislator of recovering what was lost on the payment of a moderate price of redemption."— L. 1.

---

* " As for thieves, there are so few of them, that 1 did not hear of twenty who suffered at Constantinople during almost fourteen years that I was in Turkey." — *De la Motraye's Travels,* vol. i. p. 188.

AN ACCOUNT OF THE DISCOVERY OF A VERY ANTIENT TEMPLE ON MOUNT OCHA, IN EUBŒA.

[*COMMUNICATED BY MR. HAWKINS.*]

Form and Appearance of the Southern Coast of Eubœa. — Object of the Visit to that Part of the Island. — Carysto. — Ascent of the Mountain St. Elias. — Quarries of Carystian Marble. — Remains of a Greek Temple on the Summit of the Mountain. — Observations relating to the Structure and Character of the Building. — Conjecture respecting the Name of the Deity to whom the Temple was dedicated. — Extensive View from the Summit of St. Elias. — Population of the District.

THE navigation of the Archipelago resembles, in many respects, that of the Hebrides; the two seas are equally interspersed with rocks and islands, or intersected by promontories. The land, too, rises on all sides into mountains of great elevation; and the aspect of both countries would be equally uninviting, were it not for the advantage which one of them enjoys, of a superior climate. The scenery of the Grecian Archipelago derives from this circumstance a beauty and charm which are denied to the Caledonian; and it is owing to this cause, perhaps, aided by a more powerful association of ideas, that the descriptions which travellers have given us of these shores, are, upon the whole, so seducing.

The passage northwards through this diversified scenery, in a ship of burden, with the Cyclades on the right, and the shores of the Peloponnesus and of Attica on the left, leads through the straits which separate Eubœa from Andros, the scene of so many disasters in antient times. Here ships are not unfrequently stopped by adverse winds, and constantly assailed by currents of air, which blow round Cavo d'Oro (the Capharean promontory). * This, in fact, is

---

*. Νῦν δὲ ὁ Καφαρεὺς ἰδιωτικωτέρως Ξυλοφάγος καλεῖται. Tzetzes ad Lycophr. v. 373.

regarded by the Levant sailors as the most dangerous part of their navigation: for there is no sheltered retreat at hand; and the horrors of shipwreck are heightened by the inhospitable character of the natives of this mountainous promontory. Numerous stories are related of their rapacity upon these occasions; and the life of a shipwrecked mariner is said to be little regarded if it be an obstacle to its gratification.

The whole appearance of this coast, which forms the southern extremity of Eubœa, corresponds with the savage reputation of its inhabitants. It rises boldly from the sea into a high dorsal ridge; the flanks of which, more especially those on the north, exhibit a frightful succession of chasms and precipices. The summit of the mountain is so elevated as to be usually shrouded in clouds, the broad shadows of which cover its upper region. This was precisely the effect produced by the state of the weather, as I approached Cavo d'Oro from the north on the 11th of September. * The scene was a most striking one, independent of its classical interest : it was nature in her wildest, grandest aspect.

I continued my voyage along this desolate coast, which is swept by every wind that blows, until I reached the bay of Carysto. The object which induced me to visit a place of such evil repute, and so little frequented, was the ascent of the mountain that crowns this great promontory. I had fixed upon this very high point (the Ocha of antiquity) † as a very important station for delineating the contiguous coasts, and combining my larger triangles ; nor had I then a conception of the very interesting discovery which I was destined to make there.

On the forenoon of the 12th I visited the Waivode of Carysto, and made preparations for ascending the mountain ; but the wind

---

* In the year 1797.

† Καρυϛος δὲ ἐϛὶν ὑπὸ τῶ ὄρει τῇ Ὄχῃ. Strabo, lib. x.

Καὶ Ὄχη δὲ εκαλεῖτο ἡ νῆσος· καὶ ἐϛιν ὁμώνυμον αὐτῇ τὸ μέγιϛον τῶν ἐνταῦϑα ὁρῶν. Ibid.

which rose in the evening, just after my return to the vessel, blew a violent gale in the night, and continued, with no abatement, the whole of the next day. In this interval it was impossible to land; and as the vessel more than once drifted from her moorings, we were in imminent danger of being driven on some rocks which lay at a very short distance to the leeward.

The circumstances which occasioned our distress were singular; perhaps unexampled. My Greek captain had evinced some want of confidence in the security of this bay before our arrival here; to which I had paid no attention; for we appeared to be so completely sheltered from the Meltem wind *, then blowing by the ridge of Mount Ocha, and there was so little chance at that season of a wind from any other quarter, that I felt no apprehension of danger. What then could exceed my surprise and consternation, when the whole fury of the Meltem poured down upon us from the ridge above, its force having been concentrated, as I conceive, by the hollow form of the coast on the opposite side of the island? I had often experienced the effect of very violent gusts of wind in sailing along a mountainous coast; but this was a continued blast for the space of 30 hours, which would have tried the strength of the stoutest cable. Had there been a swell we could not have held by our anchors a single minute, so great was the strain upon them. To add to our distress, we had at this critical period a broken rudder; and the Turkish inhabitants of Carysto, who bear a very bad character, were seen assembled on the beach, in momentary expectation of witnessing our destruction.

At six o'clock on the morning of the 14th we took advantage of the first abatement of the gale, to weigh our anchors; and, putting right before the wind, in a few hours we fortunately reached the harbour of Zea. Here a new rudder was procured, and as it was impossible, while the Meltem continued, to execute what I had in

---

* This is the modern name of the Etesian among the Greek sailors, perhaps a corruption of Beltempo; but the term βορέας, Voreas, is universally adopted on the continent of Greece.

view at Carysto, I resolved to proceed to the southward until the
usual change of the season. On the 19th of October, soon after this
had taken place, I once more anchored in the bay of Carysto.

The following day, the weather threatening, I sent my servant
ashore to make the necessary preparations for my expedition. On
the 21st I visited the Waivode, who congratulated me on my escape,
and the Bishop of the diocese, who lamented most feelingly the
barbarous and anarchical state of the country; after which I proceeded, on a mule, to the summit of the mountain (now called
St. Elias). * The ascent from the town was attended with some
difficulty. We had not proceeded far before I descried the marks of
some antient quarries, and on the side of our road lay seven entire
columns, apparently on the spot where they were quarried. One of
these measured 13 feet in length by 4 feet 3 inches at its base, and,
except the last polish; which it had never received, it was in a finished
state, and ready for removal. Here then, without doubt, were the
celebrated quarries of Carystian marble † ; the nature of which I had
thus an opportunity of ascertaining. It proved to be the Cipolino
of the Roman antiquaries. There is a gradual descent the whole
way from this spot to the beach, which is three miles distant; the
columns, therefore, after being incased in wood, to defend them from
injury, might have been rolled to the place of their embarkation.

The principal excavations seem to have been immediately above
the castle hill, and in a direct line between it and the summit of the
mountain. When we had surmounted the rugged heights where
they first occurred, the marble disappeared, and the strata which

---

* This denomination is now given to many of the higher mountains of Greece.

† In the time of Strabo the quarries of Carystian marble were at Marmarium, ἐν ᾧ,
says he, τὸ λατόμιον τῶν Καρυϛίων κιόνων. Stephanus Byzantinus, however, places them
- at Carystus. These entire shafts were probably destined for some building at Rome ; for
Pliny, quoting the account which Nepos gives of Mamurra's house, says that the columns
were of marble, " et omnes solidas e Carystio aut Lunensi." A very great number of
these columns are still preserved at Rome.

Western View of the Temple on Mount Orthax.

Published by Longman, Hurst, Rees, Orme & Brown, Paternoster Row, Feby. 1, 1811.

Interior View of the West Wall with the Door way and part of the Roof

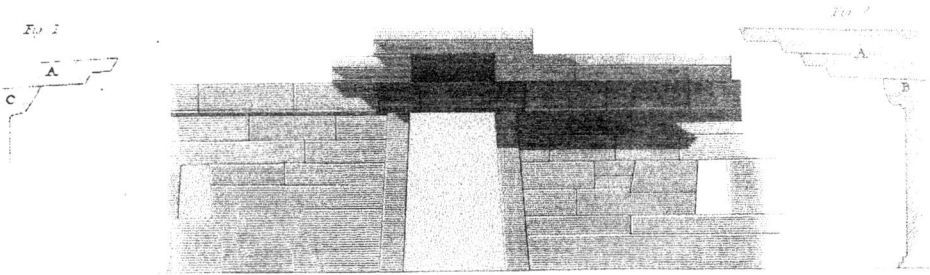

Fig 2

A

C

Fig 1

A

B

A Part of the Roof
B Lintel of the Door way
C General Cornice of the Interior
Fig 1 & 2 Sections shewing the profile of the Roof and Cornice

Ground Plan of the Cell

Plan & Section of the Temple on Mount Ocha

Published by Longman Hurst Rees Orme & Brown Paternoster Row Feb 19 1820

EUBŒA. 289

succeeded, wholly consisted of gneiss. A scanty and withered forest of chesnuts, clothed the mid-region of the mountain.

I now gradually approached the summit, which was composed of several distinct craggs, or rather ledges of rocks ; one of which I soon made choice of as a station for my drawings and trigonometrical operations. In the narrow interval between this and the next ledge, I saw, what at the first view might be mistaken for a ruined Greek chapel ; no unusual object of occurrence in similar situations. But what was my astonishment, when, on a nearer approach, I discovered in this ruin, the remains of a Greek temple, of a most antient and peculiar construction ! I must refer the reader to the annexed engraving for a view of this building, and the character of the wild scenery which accompanied it. It is certainly the very last situation where the ruins of a temple might have been expected.

Pausanias speaks of the altars of Jupiter, which were on the summits of several mountains ; but mentions only one instance of a temple in such a situation, the dilapidated remains of a temple dedicated to the Cyllenian Mercury : nor can. it be said that the temple of Apollo Epicurius was so situated ; although its site is unquestionably a very elevated one. I had visited the summits of so many of the highest mountains of Greece, without meeting with any vestiges of antiquity, and was so little prepared to expect a discovery of this kind in a spot so difficult of access, that for some time I could hardly believe the reality of the venerable object of antiquity which presented itself to my view ; the total absence of columns, and the usual decorations of temples, having occasioned some degree of ambiguity. My doubts, however, vanished by degrees, the more I examined the plan of the ruin, and the various details of its construction. These the reader will find very accurately exhibited in the annexed engravings ; and the information which they convey, will probably suggest to him the following reflections. *

---

* Perhaps I have given my readers credit for more skill in practical architecture than they can be supposed to possess ; and have laid claim myself to more than is my due : but the fact is, that I am indebted to Mr. Robert Smirke for this masterly developement of the construction of the building.

VOL. II.   P P

The roof is simply a covering of stone which is made to support itself, and of which no example is known.

That part of the roof which lies upon the walls, counterbalances the weight of that which is between them; or in other words, is sufficient to counterbalance that part which projects inwards and forms the ceiling.

The eastern wall was probably built a little thicker, in order to counterbalance the slabs, that on this side were not bevilled away and notched, as those were on the west.

The inclination of the slabs answered two purposes; first, to throw off the rain; secondly, to throw the weight more upon the wall.

The opening between the opposite projecting stone must have been about two feet, which was probably covered with a ridge stone; the whole being covered with slab stones, of which there are plain indications in the view.

In short, the whole roof appears to have been an affair of calculation; and plainly denotes a considerable progress having been made in the art of building.

Had Pausanias extended his Itinerary to Eubœa, he would have completed the plan of his invaluable work on the Antiquities of Greece; and we should not now be at a loss for the history of this temple. In the absence of any direct information concerning it, we must content ourselves with conjectures. According to Stephanus Byzantinus, Mount Ocha was the scene of an event in the mythological history of the Gods, the memory of which might have been consecrated by a dedication of a joint temple to Jupiter and Juno. It is however more probable, that the temple here existing has been dedicated to Neptune; for Strabo, speaking of Geræstus, which was almost at the foot of the mountain, says, " It has likewise a temple of Neptune, which is the most distinguished of all those which are * here,"

---

* ἔχει δ᾽ ἱερὸν Ποσειδῶνος ἐπισημότατον τῶν ταύτῃ· upon which the editors of the French Strabo observe, " Strabon n' auroit il voulu parler que de divers temples de Neptune situés dans le voisinage de Geræstos ?"

meaning, I suppose, " in this part of the island :" and I cannot help suspecting, when I consider that the disasters which befell the Grecian fleet on the Capharean promontory, were ascribed to the anger of Nauplius, the son of Neptune ; that the whole of this mountainous promontory was in a peculiar manner consecrated to the same divinity. These, I believe, are all the facts or notices which can throw any light upon the history of this temple ; and it must be confessed that they lead to no very satisfactory conclusions.

I shall now revert to the narrative of my proceedings.   The re-mainder of the day was fully employed in delineating and measuring the ruins, and in the use of the sextant.   At a late hour we descended to a mandria, or sheep-fold, where a quantity of wood being collected, my attendants kindled a large fire, round which we passed the night, wrapped in our capots, and stretched on the bare ground.

Early the next morning I returned to the summit, where I com-pleted the measurement of my angles ; but the clouds which gathered fast on the north side of the mountain prevented me from making an accurate delineation of the line of coast beneath, which comprehended the famous Cœla of Eubœa.   Of all the other interesting objects around, the very elevated point on which I stood, and the clearness of the atmosphere, enabled me to have a distinct view.   Scio was just within the reach of vision ; and by the aid of a telescope annexed to my sextant, I combined its position with that of the islands near me. The form of Andros appeared as if it were delineated on a map, so completely was it overlooked from this lofty station.   In the evening I descended to the beach, where I found my boat's crew waiting to take me on board.

As Carysto is so little known, I shall here add a few particulars re-specting this district, which I collected chiefly from the bishop of the diocese.

It contains 1400 Greek, and 1600 Turkish families.   The inhabi-tants have assumed the right of appointing their Waivode, who is at present (1797) the elder brother of the famous Mustapha Aga. The latter has, in the course of a few years, rendered himself master, by force, of most of the villages on the north side of the town ; and no stranger is suffered to take the farm of a spahilik, or of an excise tax, in the whole district.

Carysto is a simple bishopric, which, on account of the barbarous state of society here, remained unoccupied, from the period of the conquest of the island until the present bishop made a purchase of the see ; of which he heartily repents. The diocese reaches as far as Avlonéro and Petriais.

But the most remarkable circumstance in the history of this district is what I have now to mention. There are five villages on the northern flanks of the mountain, near Cavo d'Oro, the inhabitants of which are branded with the appellation of Acriánides and Burmádes, to distinguish them from the Mahometan and Christian population of the mountain. The men speak Albanian, like the rest, and are of Christian origin, although they profess Mahometanism. This, however, their forefathers appear to have embraced through restraint, or merely with a view to exempt themselves from the Karatch or poll-tax ; for they conform to none of the essential practices of the Mahometan faith. On the other hand, they seem to have lost, by a long disuse of the Christian worship, their belief in Christianity ; and, in fact, with the exception of a few superstitious practices of the Greek church, which they have retained, they are considered as appertaining to neither sect. Their women, however, still profess Christianity, and this is perhaps the reason why the men have each a Christian name coupled with the Mahometan ; by the former of which, alone, they are distinguished among their countrymen.

The names of the five villages inhabited by these semi-apostates, are Kalianù, Platanistòs, Adià, Grámisi, and Kapsúri, each of which contains, on an average, from twenty to thirty families.

These people are said to be of such a savage and inhospitable character, as even to murder those who escape from the wrecks of the vessels that are driven on the coast, in order that they may divide the spoil with more chance of impunity. They chiefly subsist by the care of their flocks, and are a hardy, bold race of mountaineers. I

brought away with me a shepherd's crook, as a memorial of their
muscular strength, as well as of their rude simplicity of manners. It
is five feet ten inches long, by five inches and one half in girth, and
is truly a most formidable weapon.

TRAVELS THROUGH PART OF THE ANTIENT COELE SYRIA, AND SYRIA SALUTARIS.

[FROM THE PAPERS OF LIEUTENANT COLONEL SQUIRE.]

CHAPTER I.

Tripoli. — Situation of the Town. — Roadstead. — Commerce. — Turkish Sepulchies. — Different Routes from Tripoli to Balbec. — Cultivation of the Districts inhabited by the Maronites. — Arrival at Baitroun. — Interview with a Prince of the Druses. — Balbec. — River Chrysorrhoas. — Remains of Sculpture on a Rock. — Damascus. — Structure and Form of the Houses in that City. — Distribution of Water iu the Vicinity of the Town. — Mosque. — Bazars. — Sepulchres. — Departure from Damascus. — Cteifa. — Lake formed by the Orontes. — Termination of the Northern Part of Libanus. — Hems. — Greek Inscription. — Hamah. — Mode of raising Water for the Supply of the Town.

APRIL 15. 1802. — Towards sunset we have a magnificent view of
the mountains in Syria, consisting of an extensive range of lofty hills,
terminated by Carmel to the south; to the north we see Libanus, a
complete mountain of snow; here the form of the land plainly indicates the valley of Coele Syria *, while in the center of the landscape

---

* " The plain of Bekka, is the Cœle Syria Proper, of the antient historians : it is
bounded on the other side by a ridge of mountains, Antilibanus, parallel to Mount Libanus." — *Bruce's Journey to Balbec. See Murray's Life,* p. 191.

the hoary Antilibanus raises itself in the most majestic manner above the whole.

April 16. — At noon, the latitude by observation was 34° 20'. At half-past five P. M., we bring up in the bay of Tripoli, in four fathom water.

April 17. — It blew a heavy gale last night from the W. S. W., with occasional squalls of rain. At four A. M. there was a lunar Iris in the north-east. Yesterday evening a boat came from the shore, and we sent our names to a Greek merchant, who resides as English Consul at Tripoli.

April 18. — The weather became more moderate ; at nine A. M. we receive a note from the Consul, requesting us to come on shore in our own boat, and not to have any communication with the inhabitants ; as seven or eight persons had been lately attacked by the plague at Tripoli. He stated that at Latakía, between which place and Tripoli, there is constant intercourse, 3000 had died in three months ; and that he had put himself in quarantine for fifteen days past. He had sent his secretary, Mr. Laurella, to meet us on the beach with a Janissary, who conducted us to the house of the Consul.

We were told that the inhabitants of Tripoli are in a frequent state of rebellion, disagreeing with the Pashas appointed by the Porte. About two months since Yousuf Pasha was compelled to make his escape to Cyprus ; and at present the town is governed by Mustapha, Aga of the Janissaries. Those who were of the party of Mustapha having gotten possession of the citadel, obliged the Pasha to retire to that quarter of the town which is towards the Marina : he remained in a small house with his troops in the neighbourhood, until he saw there was no safety for his person but in flight ; he therefore, after plundering every house he had possession of, took advantage of a dark night, embarked on board a small vessel, and landed at Cyprus.

April 19. — We told the Consul that we wished to see the environs and situation of the town, and that we would be particularly cautious not to touch any of the inhabitants. The secretary accompanying us with the Janissary, we passed towards the south end of the town, and ascended the hill near the citadel, on the river.

Tripoli is situated along the base of a triangular plain, having for its vertex a flat promontory towards the sea : the base runs nearly in a north and south direction, is about two miles long, and is bounded by a rocky height ; immediately under which the town of Tripoli extends itself three-fourths of a mile in length, and three hundred yards in breadth ; the north side of the triangle is about one mile in its extent ; the southern about three-fourths of a mile ; each of these is bounded by the sea. On the flat promontory, on the north side of which is the place of anchorage, is the Marina, of the size of a small town, where the vessels discharge and receive their cargoes. Between the point of the promontory and the mouth of the river Kadisha (the Holy) are six square isolated towers, placed at irregular distances from each other : they stand immediately on the sea ; appear to be of Saracen construction ; and the lower part of their walls, as at Alexandria, is fortified with fragments of grey granite columns, placed horizontally in the building. The whole of the plain is planted with trees, and chiefly the mulberry, the food of the silk-worm ; for here silk is the principal article of commerce : the nopal, or prickly pear, also abounds. In the plain of Tripoli there is a quantity of stagnant water, and as it is necessary in the summer season that the mulberry plantations be constantly watered, noxious vapours arise, which in the hot months render the situation un-healthy in the extreme. The mulberry trees are planted with the greatest regularity ; and at this season of the year the silk-worms are deposited in the ground in little huts, composed of reeds and the branches of trees. The river Kadisha, which traverses the town and discharges itself into the sea at about the center of the northern side of the triangle, enters into the plain through a beautiful narrow valley : it is a shallow rapid stream at its junction with the sea, and by no means practicable for boats. The citadel, which commands the town, as well as the plain below, is built on the south side, and immediately close to the Kadisha, where it enters the town : it is apparently an old Saracen building, in a wretched state, and mounted with a few guns ; and is commanded by a height on the north side of the river, and only 150 yards distant. Tripoli has no other fortification : the town has gates, but is merely enclosed with the walls of the gardens. A short distance east of the citadel, and on the same side of the river, is a convent of Dervises, in one of the most agreeable situations that can be imagined : it is close to the Kadisha in a deep valley surrounded by orange and mulberry groves, besides poplars and many other trees and shrubs, which render the air fragrant, and the *coup d'œil* exceedingly picturesque.

The road of Tripoli does not afford very safe anchorage for shipping : the bottom is composed of rocks, and large stones, which, when the wind is fresh, rub and wear the cables. It is protected in some degree by a line of small islands, which project more than a league west, from the point of the promontory. These shelter the shipping from the south, and south-west winds, very prevalent during the winter along the coast, and at intervals blowing most tempestuously. Ships coming from the southward are obliged to pass to the westward of all these islands, unless they are acquainted with a narrow passage between them.

The Chameleon, an English sloop of war, when in the road of Tripoli, used to anchor at the mouth of the river, at no great distance from the shore, because the holding ground was preferable to that near the Marina. Northward of the road of Tripoli, the coast runs in a north-westerly direction, as far as the projecting island of Raud, the antient Aradus ; perhaps five or six leagues distant from Tripoli.

Before the war, (for since that period the commerce between Europe and the Levant has been almost ruined,) the exports from Tripoli consisted in raw silk, silk handkerchiefs for turbans, soap, which is manufactured in the town, and a few sponges, found along the shore between this place and Beirout.

Beyond, to the east of the base of the triangular plain of Tripoli, is a valley about three leagues wide, situated at the foot of Libanus, whose tops sometimes emerging from the clouds beneath them ; in other places, boldly prominent to the view, display the snowy dreariness of winter; while the forwardness of the corn, and the agreeable warmth of the valleys, indicate the far advancement of spring.'

With the Turks, the burying places are always without the walls of the city. The Mahometans pay peculiar attention to the tombs of their departed friends. At stated times of the year they make frequent visits to their sepulchres, ornament them with myrtle sprigs, and say prayers for the happiness of the deceased. At Tripoli we observed several tents placed over the tombs in the burial places.

We saw two arched caves near the Kadisha, about a quarter of a mile from its mouth, where the heads of the culprits are thrown, after they have been decapitated by orders of the Pasha.

This afternoon we walked towards the north end of the town, and visited the mouth of the Kadisha; we ascended one of the ruined towers in this part, and took the following bearings:

Convent of Dervises - - N. E. by E. distant 1 mile.
Island of Aradus - - - N. N. E. - - 14
Point of Marina - - - N. N. W.

April 21.— After having completed the preparations for our projected tour into the interior, we took leave of our hospitable entertainer, at Tripoli; and commenced our journey to Balbec. Thence we proposed to cross Anti-Libanus; visit Damascus; and returning by Aleppo and Antioch, to rejoin the Mentor; which was dispatched from Tripoli to the Bay of Scanderoon.·

From Tripoli to Balbec, there are three routes; one passes to the north of Libanus, the other two traverse it; the shortest, and immediately east of Tripoli, is by the way of Cannobine, and the Cedars over the summits of the mountain. The snows, however, were not thoroughly melted, and on this account the route of the Cedars, at this season, was impassable. The road along the sea-shore to Beirout, and then the passage of Libanus, was represented as extremely rugged and difficult; and we were recommended to take the northern, over a plain and easy road, which turns the north extremity of Libanus. At ten A. M. we left Tripoli; our general rate of travelling (the ordinary pace of the camel caravans) was 2¼ miles in an hour; and a day's journey is in general seven hours, though this depends on the distance of villages, or caravanserais from one station to another. The road was along the sea-side, over a flat country; and about two leagues from Tripoli we passed the Nahr-el-Bered, or the Cold river. On our right the mountains were bare, and without cultivation. As the country appeared so extremely dull and uninteresting, and we heard much of the hospitality of the Maronites, who live in the southern parts of Libanus, and the beauty and fertility of their mountains, we decided to return to Tripoli this evening, and to set out on the following day for Beirout, to the southward : half-past one P. M. we returned, and encamped near the river Kadisha, close to the town.

April 22. — At nine A. M. commenced our route for Baitroun, situated on the coast. The road was along the roots of Libanus, which meet the sea in a gentle declivity, though their surface is rocky and uneven. We passed through a beautiful and romantic country, inhabited by the Maronites. The sides of the mountains are interspersed with numerous little villages, around which the ground is highly cultivated, either with corn, vines, olive or mulberry-trees; the earth being supported by terraces, formed of dry masonry, having the appearance of the seats of an amphitheatre. The people are seen without arms, an unusual thing in any part of the Turkish dominions; and an air of liberty and independence * is conspicuous in the inhabitants of these mountains, which we vainly looked for in any other part of the country. We passed through the

---

* Bruce gives a similar account of the state of the country in some parts of Libanus, which he crossed in his journey to Balbec. " The mountains of Libanus, at Zakala, begin to be of rich mould, and are all cultivated. Every valley has a stream running through it into the plain, and every stream on its side a village, where the people live in a sort of independence, under the protection of the Druses, in free exercise of their religion, whatever it is, and out of the reach of the oppressions of the neighbouring Pashas of Tripoli, Seide, and Damascus." P. 191. — Murray's Life of Bruce.

valley of Hora, near the extremity of Cape Capougeè, which forms a promontory in the sea; and close to its summit we observed a Greek convent in the midst of wood, and in a very romantic situation. After having crossed the mountain, which is connected with Cape Capougeè, a rugged and difficult road, we arrived at the head of a beautiful valley, watered by a pleasant shallow stream, well wooded, and chiefly cultivated with the mulberry tree. Towards the south extremity of the valley is an old ruined castle, singularly placed on an isolated rock, rising in the midst of the vale, with perpendicular sides. We next passed well-cultivated grounds; and about half-past four arrived at Baitroun, a small village on the sea. Here there is no port; the rock is cut, as if stone had been once shipped from this place for the purposes of building. The village belongs to the Maronites, who are under the government of the Druses. The Emirs, or Princes pay a small tribute to the Porte. From their mountainous situation they assert their independence, and most parts of their country have never been visited by the Turks. The Druses and the Maronites live on terms of union and intimacy; the latter have a large church at Baitroun; their religion is similar to that of the members of the Latin communion*; their feasts and fasts are different, and more numerous. The Maronite religious books are Arabic, written in the Syriac character. † The Christians, in Turkey, are much pleased to have the use of bells for their churches, and in many places they pay a considerable sum for that privilege. At Livadia, in Greece, there is a church bell, which was not obtained without a high contribution from the Greeks. At Baitroun, instead of a bell, the Maronites, as in

---

* Le pere Michel y celebra la messe en Syriaque, selon leur coutume, laquelle excepté l' idiome ne differe presque point de la notre. Pietro de la Valle. Tra. Fr. 325. 1. — E.

† This language is still in use in parts of the East. On ne peut compter la langue Syriaque parmi les langues mortes; car suivant ce que j'ai appris à Damask, il y' a encore dans la province du Pasha de ce gouvernement quelques villages ou les paysans ne parlent pas que Syriaque. Dans plusieur hameaux aux environs de Merdin et de Mosul, les Chretiens parlent encore Chaldaique, d' autres disent Syriaque. Niebuhr. i. 81. — E.

many other parts of the Turkish dominions, make use of a flat piece of board, held in one hand, which is beaten with a wooden *mallet by the other. We sleep in a sort of public coffee-room, near the sea. April 23. — A quarter before nine, A. M., we left Baitroun ; the road rocky and gravelly ; the soil, though poor, much cultivated in mulberry trees and corn land. The mountains, on the left, whose sides are constantly divided in terraces, present a most beautiful aspect. Our route was along the sea side, and at half-past twelve we arrived at Dgebail, supposed to be the antient Byblus. This place is now a small village on the sea ; here is no harbour, even for the small boats of the country. Dgebail is surrounded by a stone wall towards the land, and in one part is a large square tower of masonry, of Saracen construction. At Dgebail we found a young prince of the Druses, son of the Emir Yousuf, who welcomed us with the greatest hospitality. He appeared of about twenty or twenty-one years of age. He received us in a miserable apartment, in the tower, where he was accompanied by Georgius Bess, his minister, and a large party of attendants. It was our intention merely to halt at Dgebail, but Saad-el-din, our youthful entertainer, and his minister, prevailed upon us to remain at Dgebail that day, and proceed by a shorter route immediately across Libanus to Balbec. We accepted the invitation, and were provided with an apartment in the castle. We had a long interview with Saad-el-din, who was extremely affable. The whole of the company were unarmed. Georgius Bess gave us an account of the stones which contain the exuviæ of small fishes, and are found in the neighbourhood of Dgebail ; he promised to procure some for † us,

---

* Called, by the Greeks, σήμαντρον, and σημαντήριον; the use of it is very antient. Mention of this instrument, as well as of bells, is found in George Pachymer, l. 7. ὡς μηδὲ σημάντροις και κώδωσιν ἠθροισμένοι. Leo Allatius, de templis Græcorum recentioribus. — E.

† Above Bairout there is a bed of whitish stone, but of the slate kind, which unfolds in every flake of it a great number and variety of fishes. They are so well preserved, that the smallest strokes and lineaments of their fins, scales, and other specifical distinctions are easily observed. Shaw, 344. — E.

and immediately dispatched a messenger into the mountains for an ass load, which was afterwards forwarded to us at Scanderoon.

At Dgebail there is a spacious Maronite church ; and we observed a curious cornice in front of the entrance, having Greek ornaments. On the sea-side are several fragments of grey granite columns, and foundations of building. We visit an exiled Mousellim, or governor, from Tripoli.

From Tripoli to Dgebail the coast is extremely rocky ; and, except in the bay of Hora, absolutely inaccessible.

April 24. — At half past seven A. M., after having taken leave of the minister, who ordered an escort to accompany us, consisting of two horsemen, and two men on foot, we ascended the mountains immediately east of the town, which were exceedingly well wooded ; and, wherever cultivation was practicable, cultivated ; the ground being disposed in terraces, and producing mulberry-trees and corn. After a rugged, narrow, stony road, of three hours' continual ascent, we arrived at Kafr-Baal, a village consisting of four or five houses ; half an hour beyond, the scenery becomes rich and magnificent in the extreme : Waadi-el-amid, *the rich valley*, watered by the river Vidar, is on our right, a large and deep stream, and its banks exceedingly fertile ; on the other side of the valley are most lofty mountains covered with snow, the clouds passing beneath their summits. Shortly afterwards, we passed the villages Duziyere and Hameige, on heights below us, but considerably above the bottom of the valley. At two P. M. we arrived at Dgibel-Dgudge, or the Mountain of Fowls, very steep, and covered with holm oaks : the descent was as a sharp-pointed staircase of rock ; and most of us were obliged to dismount. In this part we were embosomed in the depths of snow-topped mountains, wild and horrid in the extreme : *Solinghi e taciturni orrori.*

At the foot of Dgibel-Dgudge is a rushing stream, the ground on either side, being cultivated ; this river is called Nahr-Mehaal, and seems to form part of the Vidar, which flows through the " rich valley," the Mehaal being perpendicular to the Vidar. At the head of the former is a fine waterfall, about 100 feet high, composed of five cascades, the first of which has a descent of 30 feet. After passing a short distance to the eastward, along the bank of the river, we forded it, and ascended the snowy mountains to the southward. Here the snow was very deep, the road difficult, and our horses frequently fell in the hollows. Throughout the winter this route is absolutely impracticable. In about an hour we turned to our left, and after passing a rugged uneven ground, we arrived at the vale, and then at the village of Alcoura, at the head of the valley. Alcoura is a Maronite village, situated at the foot of a very lofty precipice; it consists of about 100 houses, and is tributary to the minister at Dgebail. The houses are merely square stone buildings covered with beams of rough hewn trees and branches, instead of plank; this again is overlaid with a composition of mud, and forms a terrace: the only openings are a door, and two or three square holes to admit the light. Here the silk-worms were still in the egg, while at Tripoli they were already brought into the garden. At Alcoura, indeed, every thing had the appearance of winter; there were no leaves on the mulberry-trees, nor any other marks of spring vegetation.

April 25. — This morning we attended mass at the village church, which seemed to be officiated precisely in the same manner as the Latin. It appears that the only difference between the Maronites and Roman Catholics consists in the former following the Greek calendar, and observing some festivals and fasts, which were omitted by the latter.

At twenty minutes past eight A. M. we took leave of Alcoura: our chief horseman was our host at this village. In the valley of Alcoura is the village Mogeiree: shortly after passing this, we had a view of the sea. The mountains which form the valley of Alcoura are lofty, and covered with snow. In an hour and a half we arrived opposite to Dgibel Mitree. Between us and this mountain is the valley of the same name, with a small stream, and village called Mitree, belonging to the Motoualis; and another called Kafr-Uftar: both these villages are on the opposite side of the stream. At the head of the valley

Mitree, we halt at the Ain-el-Bukhara, " the fountain of the cow;" here the mountains were lofty, wild, and uncultivated; rarely inter. spersed with large juniper-trees. The road led us sometimes over hardened snow; at others, over gravel.

At half-past noon we saw the highest summit of Libanus * ; Anti. Libanus running in a direction north and south; between them ex. tends the plain of Balbec, about two leagues and a half in breadth. From this point we took the following bearings : —

Summit of Libanus - - N. E. by E.
Point of ditto in valley - - E. N. E.
Balbec - - - - E. S. E.
Direction of the valley of Balbec N. N. E. and S. S. W.

Hence we soon began to descend the mountain; and, after traversing a steep road for more than two hours, we arrived at the ruined village Sardac, at the commencement of the plain. Here we crossed the valley, badly cultivated, and with scarcely any trees; the soil of a reddish colour. We soon distinctly perceived the towering ruins of the temple of the Sun. At half-past six P. M. we arrived at Balbec, and pitched our tent south of the temple.

April 26.—After breakfast this morning, we visited the Emir Djugar, of the family of Harfouche, of the race of the Motoualis, the present Governor of Balbec; who was then tributary to Mahomet, the Pasha of Gaza. As we gave him to understand that we had brought him a small present, (a piece of Lyons stuff,) which is extremely necessary to gain the good will of these ignorant plunderers, he received us in a very civil manner; told us we might go where we pleased, and remain at Balbec as long as we wished. After pipes and coffee, we proceeded to visit the temple, accompanied by a minister of the Prince, and a large troublesome suite of inhabitants.

---

* According to Abulfeda, Libanus should receive the name of Shenir only where it begins to run more to the north than Damascus: while it is more south than that city it should be called Gahel Eltalg, or the Snowy Mount, which also is its common name in Chaldee. — Michaelis on the Laws of Moses, i. 92.

The first building that attracted our notice was a beautiful small temple of an hexagonal figure : on the outside four columns of the Corinthian order are still standing, with niches between them for statues, which no doubt were formerly placed there : the cornice was very beautifully executed. Since the introduction of Christianity, this elegant building had been used as a Greek church ; but about 40 years ago, having been very much shook and injured by an earthquake, it is entirely ruined. This little chapel is about 60 yards S. E. of the grand temple. The latter seems to be composed of four principal parts — the entrance ; an hexagonal court ; a large square area, enclosed with walls, and the temple itself. The entrance appears to have been a raised colonnade with, perhaps, a large flight of steps. The hexagonal court is ornamented with niches and beautiful pediments and cornices. The north and south sides of the square court are composed of recesses, two of which are semicircular : in these are niches for statues, pediments, pilasters ; and all the riches of the Corinthian order are displayed in the greatest profusion. Of the grand temple, only six columns remain on their basements, with the architrave above them. The whole place is covered with fragments of columns, friezes, pediments, and of various other ornaments, which once composed this superb edifice. South of the grand temple, and without the line of its terrace, is a smaller temple, whose sides are tolerably perfect ; presenting a striking specimen of the Corinthian order of architecture. The long sides of the temple north and south are about 120 feet in length ; the short sides 70. It is surrounded by a corridor, composed of fluted pillars, supporting a roof 14 feet wide, carved and executed in a most elaborate manner. It is divided into compartments, and ornamented with the sculptured portraits of Princes or of Queens. One of these latter, which has fallen, we observed to be of a colossal size, and nourishing an infant at the breast. The roof on the north side is composed of eight large stones, each 16 feet long, and of the breadth of the corridor : they are cut in a small degree in the form of an arch : the pillars are about 30 feet high, and composed of three stones. On the east side, after creeping through an opening in a wall apparently built by the Saracens, we arrived at the portal of the temple, of magnificent workmanship. This entrance is about 25 feet high, and 20 feet in width : on each side are lines of sculpture, representing small figures intertwined with garlands of flowers and fruits : parallel to these again is a variety of ornaments. On the under part of the architrave of this entrance is the representation, in bas-relief, of an eagle with expanded wings, grasping a sort of caduceus, the emblem of majesty; and holding in its mouth the joined ends of two festoons, each of which at the other end is held by a figure representing a youth with wings : the festoons are enriched with different sorts of fruits and flowers ; and the north side is in the most perfect preservation. This architrave is composed of three stones, the center one of which has fallen at least four feet below the others, in consequence of an earthquake. The roof of this temple is entirely destroyed; the interior, however, surrounded by niches richly ornamented with handsome pediments, sufficiently indicates its former magnificence. From the remains of plaster on the walls, it appears that this building was once used as a church. The columns within, with a rich entablature, produce a fine effect : and they are tinged with a reddish yellow.

Both temples are built on artificial terraces ; and in the wall, to retain the grand terrace at the N. W. angle, are three stones *, occupying a length of 150 feet, and 10 feet in height. The whole of this magnificent ruin is so much intermixed with Saracen building, extremely good and solid, that in many places it is difficult to distinguish the modern walls from the originals. Near the entrance of the small temple on the south side, is a complete square tower, built of the materials of the temple, and of excellent workmanship; indeed the whole building has been converted into a place of defence, and surrounded by high walls pierced with loop-holes ; and in many places are machicoulis. Under the grand temple are two vaulted

---

* Au nombre des merveilles du monde sont, dit Kodhai, les trois pierres de Balbec. Extract from Makrizi. See Abdallatif, S. de Sacy. 503. — E.

subterraneous passages on each side, running E. and W., and connected, about 20 yards from the east entrance, by a similar passage running the breadth of the building : the first are about 370 feet in length ;
the connecting passage 200 feet; the arch is part of a circle, and
20 feet wide.   On the soffit, or under part of these vaulted passages,
are a few heads sculptured in bas-relief: near one of which are these
letters,
                          DIVISIO
                          MOSCH

The workmanship of the buildings at Balbec is excellent: the
stones are large, and so closely joined together without cement,
that the blade of a knife could not be inserted between them : the
stone itself, taken from the quarries, S. W. of the town, is a very hard
limestone, approaching the nature of marble.   Many of the standing
columns have been cut by the barbarous inhabitants to their very
center, towards the bottom, for the sake of the iron, which unites the
pieces, of which each column is composed.

Balbec is situated at the foot of Anti-Libanus ; on the east side of a
very extensive, uniform, plain, in general about eight miles in width.
In the plain scarcely any trees are visible ; but around Balbec there is a
variety : — the walnut, the willow, the poplar, and the ash ; rendering the situation pleasant in the extreme: it is watered by two
small brooks, which have their sources adjoining each other, about a
quarter of a mile S. E. of the town.   Balbec was originally contained
in an enclosure of the extent of nearly four miles ; the Saracen wall,
which still remains, though in a ruinous state, is built in a most solid
manner : perhaps it may have been about 16 feet high, with small
square towers at intervals, of the same height as the wall. Several of the
stones, which compose it, are remnants of inscriptions, friezes, enta-
blatures, and other ornaments in architecture.   On the S. W. side
of the town is a high hill, the lower part of which is enclosed within
the walls of the place.   Immediately near this angle are the different
parts of the column of 18 stones described by Pococke, which is now
thrown down, and destroyed : the capital, the base, the channel for

the water, remain exactly according to his relation. Near this spot is a stone, eight feet long, six wide, and fourteen inches in thickness: it may have served as a canopy to a throne; for at the four angles are evident marks that there were four small columns for its support: it is now standing on one of its edges: the interior is elegantly sculptured with roses and serpents, and divided into four compartments. On this height is a Saracen tomb of very good execution, in a S. W. direction: about one mile from the town is another Mahometan sepulchre, composed of a dome and five low granite columns; this we had no opportunity of visiting. On the north side of the height, commanding the town, are several catacombs. Only one-fifth part of the original enclosure of Balbec appears to be inhabited, and that part is towards the S. E.: the whole town presents a most wretched appearance, as the principal part of the hovels have been destroyed by earthquakes, which it appears very frequently occur. The inhabitants are partly Moutoualis, and partly Maronite Christians: here is a church and a mosque. The place seems to be very unproductive, and to have no trade whatever.

In the afternoon of this day we visited Emir Suldan, the brother of the governor, who is a great sportsman: there was a fine falcon in his apartment; and he told us he was very fond of hawking. He had just built a small hut entirely of plank, as a place of retirement in the event of an earthquake.

April 27. — The Emir informed our companion, Monsieur Laurella, that we had met with more indulgence than any Franks who ever visited Balbec; he had heard, he said, that we had in our possession eight watches, and desired a handsome one for himself. After some consultation, —— offered his own as the most valuable; but the Emir, not sufficiently esteeming it, declined the acceptance; so that we thought, from several hints which had passed, it would be most prudent to depart; we therefore immediately ordered our tent to be struck, and prepared to leave the place. The Emir sent to invite us to remain this evening, and to quit Balbec to-morrow: he sent a second message; and when we were mounted, he solicited, and even pressed, us to stay; this, however, we absolutely refused. The Emir wished to gain as much from us as he could : he repented of having refused the watch. He had asked Laurella for my spying glass ; and perhaps if we had remained much longer at Balbec, we might have been completely plundered. At half-past one P. M., we commenced our journey, and about a quarter of a mile south-west of the town, we observed a range of quarries, from ' which, no doubt, materials were extracted for the temple. There is now lying, in an horizontal position, an immense stone, completely separated and quarried from the rock : it is about fifty feet long, fourteen feet wide, and eight feet in height : here is also another detached from the rock, about twenty feet high, and standing on one of its ends in a perpendicular manner. We observed also in this part several arched excavations, probably catacombs. After passing in a south direction for two hours over the slopes of the mountain, which extends into the plain, we saw on our right the village Betrane ; and half an hour afterwards arrived at a torrent between two heights, called Sarle. The view in this part is extremely singular : not a tree or a house in the plain, which is here bounded by the highest points of Libanus, running in a north and south direction. At the end of four hours we arrived at a wretched Moutoualis village, called Kribe : we stop to rest on the north side near a well. The soil of these mountains appears of a reddish coloured clay, intermixed with rock : near our halting place we observed several vineyards.

April 28. — At six A. M. we commenced our journey, the weather being extremely fine. After one hour's riding across a high mountain, we arrived at a small bridge, over a stream, which waters the valley of Maraboun : a little to the north is a village of the same name. Here we took a south direction, and an hour beyond passed the village Serghey. In this valley are several mulberry grounds, and vineyards, the vines being carefully cultivated *en espalier*, and propped up with small sticks about two feet in height. In three quarters of an hour we passed Din-Hour, on the east of the road, which is watered by a small brook taking its course to the southward. An hour beyond this place, we arrived at Zebdany, in the north-west corner of a beautiful,

well cultivated plain, about nine miles in circumference : the ground
is very neatly disposed, and the enclosures in excellent order. Here
are many vineyards, mulberry grounds, and a variety of fruit trees in
blossom. On entering the plain, Blazel, a village, is to the east. Half
an hour beyond Zebdany we halted at a spring on the road side, with a
weeping willow at its head. On the heights to our left were the two
villages, Buchai and Mozaia. After passing an hour and an half from
the fountain along the slopes of the hills, bounding the east side of the
valley of Zebdany, we directed our course to the eastward : through
this valley flows the river Barrady, the antient Chrysorrhoas. On turning to the eastward we followed the course of this stream, nearly east
and west, as far as the bridge of Suke, which we crossed. Where the
turn of the river makes an angle with its direction through the vale of
Zebdany, there is a very fine cascade, about sixty feet high, composed
of three waterfalls : this being surrounded by lofty poplar trees and
different kinds of shrubs, renders the scenery very picturesque. The
river flows in a narrow rocky vale, and part of the road is through an
artificial excavation in the rock. A short distance before we arrived
at the bridge, we observe on our left the remains of an aqueduct,
communicating with an almost perpendicular mountain, north of the
bridge. There were many excavations in it, forming probably the
catacombs of a large city : in one part we could distinguish with a
glass the remains of sculpture in a square compartment of the rock,
which represented a figure sitting in a chair, with another beside it.
After passing the bridge, we entered the vale of Sukè, about three miles
in length : the river is almost concealed by a variety of trees, but
chiefly the Lombardy poplar : these, intermixed with corn fields, and
the brown lofty mountains above, afford some of the most beautiful
views that can be imagined. We passed the village Sukè, at two
P. M. to the north of the river, and shortly afterwards Kafr-Senaiah
to the south ; we then crossed some low mountains in a N. E.
direction, leaving the village Tsdaidy. on a hill, near the Barrady, and
at half-past five, after traversing Hamè, we halted on the Damascus
side of a bridge across the Barrady : this river, flowing through the

vale of Sukè, takes a direction to the north, then to the east, and afterwards to the south, close to the village Hamè: the banks of it are well wooded, and afford much pleasing scenery.

April 29. — At half-past seven A. M. we struck our tent, and proceeded on our route to Damascus. We soon passed Tseieh on the right, and in three quarters of an hour we left, in the same direction, the village Dommer, situated in the pleasant valley through which flows the Barrady. West of Dommer is a neat, well-built stonebridge, of four arches. After passing Dommer, we began to ascend the heights bounding Damascus to the west: in half an hour we perceived the south part of the plain of Damascus, and, shortly afterwards, when we descended the hill, the city itself burst upon our view, presenting the most striking scene that can be conceived: an extensive plain, for the most part well covered with trees, and interspersed with numerous villages, and, immediately before us, the large city of Damascus, whose minarets, intermixed with the trees, and contrasted with the terraced roofs of the houses, extending nearly three miles in length, produce an effect at once singular and picturesque. On our right, at the foot of the mountain, was the village Mizzee; to the southward, Deriah; on our left, under the hill, was Saheiah. We passed near this place: afterwards, through a number of gardens; and, at the end of two hours and a half, we halted near the gate of the seraglio. The Pasha being absent with the grand caravan of Mecca, (for the office of conductor of the pilgrims is always attached to the Pashalic of Damascus,) we were introduced into the seraglio, with the intention of paying our compliments to the Mousselim, or deputed governor of the city. We were ushered into a large apartment, with a fountain before the Divan. Here we took coffee; and, as the governor was engaged in affairs of importance, we agreed to pay our visit at another opportunity. At the seraglio, we were furnished with two attendants by the Mousselim; and, after passing through a great part of the town, we arrived at a Spanish Catholic convent, where there were six Fathers, who received us with the utmost civility. This convent is well built, large, and the most respectable at Damascus. Here we took up our quarters, in preference to a house which was offered us by the Mousselim. In the afternoon, we visited him : he was seated, with the Mufti, in a kiosk, adjoining the seraglio, and immediately on the rapid current of the Barrady, in this part surrounded by a little forest of fruit-trees. The governor was extremely polite, and said, that whatever we wished should be immediately attended to ; for the Porte had received great obligations from the English. During our conference, the Mufti retired into the anti-chamber, and prayed to Mahomet with the usual prostrations, although the place was crowded with attendants. In the afternoon, we passed through the gate of St. Paul, or, as the Arabs call it, Bab Shirke *, " The Gate of the East ;" and, after walking about half an hour, we were shown the spot where Saul fell, and became blind : it is a small elevation, formed of a mass of stones. Near this place are the tombs of the Christians.

April 30. — This morning, we walked over the greater part of the town, and passed through the various bazars, in which, as at Cairo, the different trades are each in a particular quarter. We entered a sort of public garden, where there were fountains, and an abundance of fruit-trees. We paid our respects to the Aga of the castle, with the hopes of seeing the interior of it, and the antient arms and armour it contains. This, however, was impracticable: we were told that, without an order, there could be no admission ; and, as for the arms, they were locked up, and sealed with the seal of the Vizier. We visited several silk-manufactories; and, after passing through a considerable part of the quarter of the Jews, we arrived at the house of So-lomon, of the family of Haimè, which has been established more than a century at Damascus. This man is a banker, and manages the pecuniary affairs of the Pashalic : he is extremely rich, as, indeed, one

* The seven ancient gates of Damascus, according to Aboulbaka, are Bab-alsaghir; Bab-kisan ; Bab-scharki; Bab-touma; Bab-aldjanik; Bab-alfaradis; Bab-aldjabiyeh. The five modern are, Bab-alsalameh; Bab-alfaradj; Bab-elhadid; Bab-alserr; Bab-alnasr. — Abdallatif, S. de Sacy. 580. — E.

might conclude from the splendour of his mansion. Of these great houses, from without, one sees nothing but walls, badly built, with no windows : all the ornaments and beauty are within. We entered into a spacious square court, paved with marble : a large fountain occupies thé middle, surrounded with orange and lemon-trees. On two sides of the court were open lofty apartments, with a superb Divan, and the walls and ceiling painted after the oriental style, in a very rich and gaudy manner. The chambers, with doors forming the other sides of the square, were fitted up expensively, each having its fountain of water, in a basin of different-coloured marbles. As the proprietor of the house was then at the seraglio, we took leave, after having been regaled with sherbets, sweetmeats, pipes, and coffee, which were served to us by the nephew of Solomon. Towards the close of the evening, we visited the distribution of the waters at the gorge of a valley, immediately westward of the town. This spot is a place of very great resort with the inhabitants of Damascus ; the valley is narrow, well wooded, running east and west, and the rapid stream of the Barrady flows over its bottom. On the south side are two canals, one above the other ; and both considerably higher than the river. On the north side are also two artificial channels, running along the side of the mountain; the highest, after following the direction of the valley, turns off to the northward, and waters the village of Selheiah. The stream of the other, in this part, passes un_ der a rock, and continues in the same direction as the valley. This canal is twenty feet above the level of the river; the former is, at least, sixty feet higher than the Barrady. The division of the waters is one of the most beautiful spots in the neighbourhood of Damascus. We returned to the town through a small part of the village Selheiah, which is at the foot of the high mountains westward of Damascus. Here we observed several Saracen buildings, in a most ruinous state. Between the city and Selheiah there is a paved road of stone, to the extent of half a mile, after passing over a bridge across the Barrady, near Bab-Salam. On this is a large coffee-house. We entered Bab-Touman, and arrived at the convent.

·May 1. — This morning we visited an artificial, arched grotto, which is said to have been the residence of Ananias: it is near Bab-shirke; the descent is by means of steps. The grotto consists of three small apartments, open to each other. In the afternoon, we passed through Bab-shirke: following the walls to the southward, we made a complete tour of the town of Damascus. Having walked through several gardens, near which flowed two streams of the Bar-rady, on different levels, we entered Bab Touman.

May 2. — This morning we visited the castle, having obtained a particular order for that purpose from the Mousselim; and then, after passing through a considerable part of the town, we arrived at our convent.

Damascus is situated on the west side of an extensive plain, bounded, for the most part, by distant mountains; and, towards the eastern side, by part of the Desert. The direction of the town and suburbs, in their length, is nearly north and south, about two miles and a half, and the greatest breadth, three quarters of a mile. The town, properly so called, which is to the north, is not above three miles in circuit. This is surrounded by a double wall, with round towers at intervals, in a very decayed state, apparently built on the foundation of the ancient Saracen fortification. Formerly there was a ditch, but at present it is almost entirely filled up with rubbish; and the mean, ill-built walls afford little defence to the city. The castle is in the south-west angle of the town; it is a good building, of a square figure, each side about two hundred yards long, and flanked by twelve square towers, placed at the angles, and at intervals in the sides. Under the entrance of this castle, are the remains of some ancient armour, a part of a balista, and an instrument, which may have been made use of to discharge stones or darts. We did not see more than five guns in the fortress, and these of a very small calibre, badly mounted on the ramparts; within, is a small manufactory for powder. The height of the walls of the castle exceeds eighty feet; they are extremely well built, most probably by the Saracen Caliphs; and are in very good preservation. The town is watered by the

Barrady, (the Abana of the Scriptures, the Chrysorrhoas of the Greeks,)
which, branching out into several small streams, passes through the
gardens in different parts of the city : every house has its fountain. The
largest, and most frequented of these coffee-houses in Damascus, is
near Bab Salam, (the Gate of Peace,) on the north side of the city ; it
is situated on a bridge, through which flows the principal stream of the
Barrady. Before it passes this bridge, there is a small waterfall, and
its banks are crowded with a variety of fruit trees. These objects,
with the murmuring of the river flowing rapidly over its bed, and the
rich and varied dress of the Turks, who appear the most respectable
merchants of the town, compose a scene extremely gay and enliven-
ing. Indeed, Damascus is placed amidst gardens and swift streams,
and is of itself, without the assistance of art, a sort of terrestrial para-
dise. What a delightful spot it might be rendered in the hands of an
enlightened people, who understood the real value of its situation ! —
what a city might be erected ! — what elegant retirements, amidst
water and verdure, — the principal objects to be desired in these
warm climates !

The houses of Damascus are built principally of mud and wooden
rafters, and sometimes of small bricks hardened in the sun ; and very
rarely, the lower parts are of stone : without, their appearance is poor
and wretched in the extreme ; within, as we saw in the house of the
Jew, Solomon, there is, amongst the higher class, a great display of
riches and magnificence. The principal mosque was formerly a
large Christian church, dedicated to St. John the Baptist, and built
in the early ages of Christianity ; we were not even permitted
to enter the outer court, although it is a thoroughfare for the inhabitants ; they, however, from motives of respect, when passing
from one end to the other, always carry their slippers * in their

---

* Among the Jews and other nations of the Orient especially, that rite of discalceation,
or putting off their shoes, is still used, and continued among them unto this day, when
they come into their temples and sacred places. — Mede's Works, 347. — E.

hands: we looked at the interior of this court through one of the entrances; the gate of which is covered with plates of brass, and the whole court was surrounded by a vaulted colonnade supported by small pillars of different coloured granite, which are surmounted with Corinthian capitals. Within, this mosque appeared extremely spacious *, and paved with various pieces of marble. It appears that most of the mosques in this city were originally churches; there is one towards the south, different from the rest: the court in front is surrounded by a colonnade, the roof of which consists of several cupolas, covered with sheet lead, as well as the grand dome of the mosque. This building has two Minarets; they are built in the style of those at Constantinople; in the middle of the city is a mosque which has a Minaret covered with green tiles. Near the principal mosque we observed the remains of some Greek architecture, which after great difficulty, because it was in the midst of houses and harams, we succeeded in examining. This remnant appears to be part of a pediment over a gateway formed by a circular arch; it is supported by four columns, each four feet in diameter: as it was intermixed with the roofs of houses, we did not see above four or five feet from the capital of the columns. Near it are the remains of an architrave almost entirely defaced, supported by pillars of the same diameter as the first; it is about fifteen feet long: the ornaments are Corinthian; and probably the ruin formed part of a temple built in the latter ages of the empire. Some of the covered bazars at Damascus are well built; and the shops well furnished with different commodities for sale. Each art or trade has its particular quarter: the boot and slipper makers, as well as those engaged in sadlery, occupy a large division; there are, besides, silk bazars, and a large display of rich articles of commerce. In the city are several manufactories of soap, glass, lamps, sattins, cotton-stuffs, and large round

---

* La grande mosquée de Damas est comptée par les écrivains Arabes au nombre des merveilles du monde. — Abdallatif. S. de Sacy. 442.

s s 2

tents; a poor manufactory of cutlery; and on the river are many water-mills and tan-yards. At present the climate is like that of England in June; the trees are in full leaf; the fruit perfectly formed; and in three weeks, we are told, there will be ripe apricots. In our journey from Tripoli to Damascus we have passed through the three climates of winter, spring, and summer; and these changes we experienced in little more than a week; near Tripoli every object was of the spring; on Libanus we met with the chilly dreariness of winter; in the plains of Damascus we were gladdened with the joyous appearance of summer.

It seems that the Barrady, after passing through Damascus, follows a north-east direction, and discharges its waters into a lake in the Desert.

Djebail Sheik, part of Anti-Libanus, lies south-west of the town, and is one of the highest mountains in Syria; the summit and sides are much covered with snow, and with the chain of hills to the westward of the city, forms a striking contrast with the verdant plains of Damascus.

This city is the place of assemblage for pilgrims from the north and east, who undertake the holy journey to Mecca, which is about 45 days distant from Damascus. The caravan is conducted by the Pasha in person; on his return he is joined, near the confines of the desert, by the Pasha of Tripoli, who brings a supply of provisions for the pilgrims. As at present the government of Tripoli is only provisional, the Pasha being deposed by the inhabitants, the Seraglio at Damascus is employed in preparing the usual provision for the caravan; which supply, according to the orders of the Vizier, should have been on its march ten days ago.

Without almost every gate of Damascus is an extensive burying-ground, and it really is the case, that these habitations of the dead appear much more neat and cleanly than those of the living. The women here are extremely punctual in their visits to the sepulchres of their relations; in each tomb is a small earthen pot let in at one of the ends; in this pot there are constantly fresh branches of myrtle *, or some small shrub, over which they frequently pour water, and preserve with the most respectful care and attention; most of these tombs are formed of dried mud in the shape of an oblong pyramid, and surrounded by two steps. Some of the sepulchres are covered with a wooden building ornamented with lattice-work; in many of the burying-grounds we have seen large green tents placed over the tombs.

The convents of Damascus are three; a convent of the *Terra Santa*, in which are six Spanish fathers, with whom we took up our residence; one of Capuchins, and one of the Lazarists: neither of the two latter were inhabited. It seems that the sight of a Frank, in the European dress, presented a strange and novel appearance in Damascus. As we walked through the town, every one was struck with amazement at our hats, and close dress, so different from their own; and we were always accompanied by a numerous suite, gaping widely with astonishment: — the carpenter dropped his hammer, the embroiderer his needle, the coffee cooled in the hands of the idle, the pipe was extinguished; every one indeed neglected his employment, and gazed on us with wonder.

May 3d. — Having made the necessary arrangements for our journey, we this day took leave of the fathers of the convent, and at three P. M., proceeded on our route for Aleppo. Our direction was north-east; at half-past four we passed the village Havistar; then, afterwards having crossed two bridges over the Barrady, we entered the village Dummer; and a quarter before six we arrived at a large Khan, within the outer court of which we pitched our tent for the evening: this Khan is almost east of Damascus, and situated near three streams of the Barrady, on different levels.

May 4th. — At seven this morning we continued our route, and after passing one hour and a half over an ill cultivated plain in an

* They put some green myrtles in little air-holes that are round the tombs, and they are of opinion that their relations are the happier the longer these remain green, and retain their colour. — Rauwolff's Travels, p. 46.

easterly direction, we arrived at the foot of Dgebail Cteifa, where
there is a ruined Khan. From this spot we changed our course to the
north-east, and here we met a caravan of sixty camels from Aleppo,
laden with merchandise. On entering the passage of the mountains,
seven armed men offered themselves as an escort across them, telling
us that seventy mounted Arabs had passed yesterday, and that there
were many robbers in the neighbourhood. These people would most
probably either protect, or plunder caravans, as circumstances might
dictate. At half-past ten, A. M., we saw before us a large plain,
bounded by barren mountains, with little cultivation; in the distant
part towards the east we observed a great part of the plain exceedingly
white; this we afterwards learnt was a salt lake: half an hour before
noon we arrived at a well-built Khan adjoining the village of Cteifa;
here we pitched our feet for the evening. This Khan was built in
the year 1440, by Sinaum Pasha; it consists of two courts, the inner
of which is extremely well-built, and in excellent repair. On entering the south gate of the outer court, the passage is through a vaulted
bazar, about sixty feet long, with shops on each side of it: in this
court is a mosque with a Minaret. The inner court is surrounded by
a raised arched colonnade, adapted for the accommodation of travellers: within this colonnade, and along the sides of the building,
are vaulted chambers for the cattle; in the center of this court is a
large square stone reservoir for water, which is constantly supplied
from a small brook, that flows between the south side of the building
and the village. The outer court, merely a square inclosure, is composed of bad masonry, and mud-bricks. The walls of the inner court
are sixteen feet high, of very good masonry, with counter-forts at
intervals. The village of Cteifa is surrounded with fruit gardens,
which, as at Damascus, are laid out without any taste * or arrangement, and are sown with barley.

---

* A similar observation applies to the gardens in parts of the coast of Barbary. " They
are not laid out with method, or design, the whole being a medley of fruit trees, with
plantations of cabbages, turnips, beans; nay sometimes of wheat and barley, interspersed." 146. Shaw. — E.

May 5. — At five this morning we proceeded in a north direction, to cross the heights which bound the plain of Cteifa to the northward. After riding nearly one hour, we arrived at the foot of these heights, and passing a ruined Khan, followed the road for the most part in a north-easterly direction. About eight o'clock we passed another ruined Khan, near which were some small remains of an antient aqueduct; at nine, on the left of our road was Ain Tenee, a ruined convent in the mountains, and the village Yebroot; an hour after-wards we passed the hamlet of Castal on an eminence, the female inhabitants of which brought us a supply of dried grapes, cheese, milk, and other eatables. As far as Castal the road was across the mountains, though very even and regular, without any rapid falls or ascents; the country in this part was waste and dreary in the extreme, scarcely a single tree relieved the horrid appearance of the mountains. Between Ain Tenee and Castal, we met with an unladen caravan of two hundred camels from Aleppo; it was conducted by about twenty unarmed Bedouins. After crossing an uncultivated plain, with scarcely any natural verdure, at half-past noon we pitched our tent in the inner court of a Khan, adjoining the village Nebbek, situated on the north side of a hill; the Tchocodar who accompanied us, by order of the governor of Damascus, having written commands for the Sheiks of the different villages in the Pashalic, to supply us with whatever we might require, desired the chief of this place to provide us with a dinner, and we were very soon satisfied with an abundance of mutton and rice : in the afternoon we were visited by the Sheik and a long suite of peasants. After passing Carraw, in our next day's journey, he recommended us to take an escort, for there were many Bedouins between that village and Hems. At Nebbek there are a few Greek Christians.

May 6. — At half-past four we commenced our route in a northerly direction, across a barren stony plain, more than an hour in length. At the further extremity, to the east, was the village Deradaiah ; soon afterwards we passed a small eminence, on the top of which were the remains of a square tower ; here we came in view of Carraw, three hours' distant from Nebbek. The gate of the Khan, at this place, appears, from some ornaments that remain, to have been the entrance of a church. At Carraw there are about twenty Greek Schismatics ; the rest of the inhabitants are Mahometans. To the north of the village we were shown the site of a chapel, dedicated to St. Nicholas ; their present place of worship has the appellation of St. Sergius ; the mosque was formerly a church, and, within, tolerably capacious. From a stone in the building we copied the words 'Aθανάσιος 'Επίσκοπος : there were also other letters which we could not decypher. About an hour westward of Carraw is the ruined convent, Dar-Mar-Yacoub. Having dismissed our guard of six peasants, with musquets, we took an equal number from this village, and at eight o'clock continued our route to the northward, across low rocky mountains, and after two hours arrived at the very small village Briedy ; here we observed a sarcophagus of white polished marble, used as a drinking-place for cattle. We could perceive the sand-hills to the east, immediately on this side of Palmyra, a distance of nearly ten leagues. At Briedy we relieved our guard, and continuing in an eastern direction, after three hours we arrived at the Khan of Hasseiah ; instead of pitching our tent, we occupied a good warm room provided for us by the Aga.

After we had passed Carraw, we had the desert to our right, and on our left the sterile mountains eastward of Balbec. Hasseiah is a small village, placed on the confines of the desert, in a most dreary chearless situation. Mussood, the Aga of the place, treated us with marked attention and hospitality ; he told us that his village was five days' journey from Palmyra ; that this was dependent on him, as well as many other places in the neighbourhood, for which he annually paid a certain number of purses to the Porte. He made an offer to conduct us to Palmyra, and added that his father and grandfather had visited those ruins with Englishmen : circumstances, however, compelled us to continue our journey to Aleppo, and reluctantly to decline visiting Palmyra. In Hasseiah are a few Christian families of the Greek persuasion.

May 7. — After we had taken leave of our host, who provides us with an escort of seven horsemen, we continued our route across an uncultivated plain, in a northerly direction, and at eight o'clock arrived at the village Chemor. In the N. W. we perceived the lake formed by the Orontes; and about seven miles distant beyond is the termination of the north part of Libanus. After rather more than an hour, we passed a square stone inclosure to the right, formerly a Khan, now having the appearance of a small village; hence we crossed an extensive plain, capable of cultivation, but neglected. At noon we entered Hems, and took up our quarters in the house of a Christian, (a banker to the government,) who treated us with the greatest hospitality. On the south-west side of the town is a curious Roman monument, which was most probably a sepulchre; it is a square building of three stages, terminating in a pyramid towards the upper; there are the remains of pilastres on the sides, which were faced with small black and white stones, placed alternately in a sloping direction. On the west side is an inscription : as much of. it as was legible, we, with great difficulty, copied. *

- - - - - -
- - - - - -
- - - - - -
- - ΓΑΙΟΥΙΟΥΛΙΟΥ
ΛΕΞΙωΝΟϹΥΙΟΥ
- - ΙΝΕΠΟΙΗϹΕ - -
ΑΥΤωΚΑΙΤΟΙϹ - -
- ΟΙϹΕΤΟΥϹΙ - - -

This sepulchre is a solid building, arched within, and formed of thin burnt brick and mortar.

Hems is situated in an immense plain; and though there is nothing to render its site particularly striking, it is pleasing to observe the great cultivation immediately in the neighbourhood; chiefly of vine-

---

* J'y remarquai encore proche de la ville ce sepulcre ancien duquel Belon fait mention avec une inscription Grecque de Caius Cesar, à ce qu'il dit ; mais après le soin que j'y ay donné à la bien lire et à la copier toute, comme j'ay fait, j'y trouvay un ΓΑΙΩΙΟΥΛΙΩ mais non pas Cesar. Pietro de la Valle. Trad. Fran. 331. 1. — E.

yards and corn.   The town is three miles in its circuit, and appears
well inhabited; the houses are built in general with stone and mud,
mixed up with straw; the streets are paved with a small path-way for
camels and horses in the middle : the walls enclosing the town are in
a very ruinous condition.   This enclosure, of rather a singular construction, consisted of a perpendicular wall, against which was raised
a bank of earth; the slope of it towards the country was faced with
masonry.   The citadel is placed on a lofty eminence, in the south-
west angle of the town, which is in all appearance artificial, as the
site of the castle of Aleppo ; the top of the hill is completely circular,
and 130 feet higher than the bottom of the ditch.   The upper enceinte is about one hundred feet in diameter; the ditch is sixty feet
wide, with a perpendicular counterscarp, thirty feet high : the Saracen
fortifications on this height were of excellent workmanship, but are
now entirely ruined.   As at Alexandria, there are columns placed horizontally in different parts of the walls to strengthen the masonry.   At
Hems we sent a message to the Mufti mentioning our arrival, and
that we wished to see the different antiquities in the neighbourhood ;
and at the same time requesting a ladder to examine the inscription
on the sepulchre.   The Mufti replied, that, without a firman from
the Porte, we could see nothing ; that we must make no remarks on
paper ; and on no account enter the castle.   At present Hems is
without a governor, and all is confusion and disorder.   When we
made our promenade, our guides led us to the citadel, whence we had
an opportunity of making every observation we could wish.   It appears that the Aga of Hems and the neighbouring villages had been
extremely oppressive to the inhabitants, and that in the course of one
year he had levied, by means of Avanías and extortions, 4000 purses ;
his conduct had of course rendered him extremely odious to the
people of Hems ; a party was raised in the town, which showed frequently open marks of hostility against the governor.   When the
Vizier, on his return from Egypt, passed through this place, he arrested the Aga, who was compelled to accompany him as far as
Aleppo ; and they believe he has since been decapitated.   The

brother of the Aga, fearing, at the same time, the severity of the Vizier, and the resentment of the inhabitants, has collected all the treasure possible, and fled from the town.

May 8. — At six o'clock we continued our route to the northward, with an escort of seven horsemen.. Soon after leaving Hems we had a very clear view of the valley of Balbec ;· Libanus on the west side ; Anti-Libanus on the east; the former, running N. W. and S. E., is composed of the high mountains of Aqqar to the north ; to the southward, the Kesraouan ; Anti-Libanus, of the mountains of Balbec, to the north ; and Djebail Sheik to the south. After two hours we arrived at the village of Telbeshee, to the right of the road, which our escort dared not approach, on account of the little war between that place and Hems. We were curious to see Telbeshee, because most of the houses are conical, resembling the large pigeon-houses in Egypt. On our arrival we were entreated by the Aga to dismount, and to take· some refreshment. We were ushered into a small apartment, filled with the grandees of the place, and a large suite of attendants : here we found the brother of the governor of Hems, who had taken refuge at Telbeshee, the inhabitants of which were partizans of his family. Soon after ten. we passed the village Rastan, built on a high hill, at the foot of which winds the river Orontes ; · its modern name is El-asser, (the Impetuous,) so called from the swiftness of its current. Here we crossed the river over a well-built bridge of ten arches, on the west side of which is a large Khan, with a mosque in the center. Ascending the opposite hill, forming the valley which gives passage to the river, we crossed a plain of excellent soil, though with scarcely any cultivation ; at noon we entered a plain, upon a lower level, the village of Ipshereen, of conical houses, being to our left ; soon afterwards, Kafr Arein, a conical village also, to our right ; and at two o'clock we arrived at Hamáh. This day, on our left, we have in view a chain of low mountains, which seem to commence near the lake of the Orontes. Hamah is situated in an oval valley, watered by the Asser, and the houses are built on either side of·the river ; the stream of which, after passing by

T T 2

Rastan, takes its course to the east; then to the northward, and flows through Hamah in a westerly direction. The town appears large, because the houses are intermixed with numerous gardens, and placed in a very scattered manner. Nearly in the center of the whole is a circular hill, which appears to have had a regular slope, and was formerly the site of the citadel; no walls, however, or any remains of building, are to be seen on this eminence. Three bridges, extremely well built, connect the opposite sides of the town. On the north side of the center bridge we observed, in the corner of a wall, a stone about five feet long and two feet high, covered with curious characters. In many parts of the town we saw the capitals of columns, pieces of cornices, and in the court of a mosque a dome supported by eight low pillars of the Corinthian order, which certainly indicate that the good taste for architecture was in its decline at the time of their erection. Under the hill S. W. of the town, we were shown a small catacomb of four chambers, in which was a stone door having an iron ring let into its surface.

The most remarkable object at Hamah is the mode of raising water for the supply of the inhabitants; the town in general being built on ground considerably higher than the level of the river, large Persian wheels are used for the purpose of raising the water; along the banks of the river are several, and one of the largest, from an accurate measurement, we found to be sixty-seven feet in diameter; the circumference of the wheel is hollow, and divided into partitions, with small apertures to admit and discharge the water: by means of a dam across the river, a strong current is forced into a narrow channel along the bank, and thus small projecting pieces of wood being disposed at equal distances along the circumference, the wheel turns round on its axle; the partitions are filled as they pass through the water, and when they arrive at the opposite point above, discharge their contents into an aqueduct: the aqueducts are built of stone, supported by irregularly shaped arches, and of course, where the water is first raised, are as high as the wheel: these aqueducts, intermixed with the trees, the movement of the wheels, and the murmuring of the water, have a very uncommon and pleasing effect. In no place do these aqueducts extend more than 150 yards from the river : there is an Arabic inscription upon them, most probably recording the name of the founder, and the date of their erection. The wheels are formed in a very slight manner, and with little ingenuity ; the aqueducts are also of a bad irregular kind of architecture ; still, however, the idea was noble, exceedingly useful, and, no doubt, reflects much credit on its author. At Hamah we were entertained at the house of Mooser-Yasgèe, or the *Writer*, who treated us with every mark of eastern hospitality : he was a Schismatic Greek. Here, as well as at Hems, all the Christians, who are very numerous, are of that persuasion. Our host, who is one of the most wealthy inhabitants, keeps an open house for the entertainment of every description of strangers who may arrive at Hamah : the court of his house, the day we were his guests, was filled with Sheiks from the Ansarian mountains, Arabs, and other persons, all of whom, more than sixty, were feasted by the liberality of Mooser. In the house of our rich entertainer, we slept in sheets of the finest white silk, which were sewed to a very thin coverlet.

CHAPTER II.

Route to Marrah. — Seraqueb. — Aleppo. — Visit to the Grand Vizier. — Dissensions in that City between the Pasha and Janisaries. — State of the Turkish Government in Syria. — Departure of the Grand Vizier for Constantinople. — Manufactories at Aleppo. — Tur-comans. — Curds. — Elmanas. — Plain of Antioch. — Course of the Orontes. — Towers and Walls of antient Antioch. — Caramout. — Beilan. — Scanderoon.

MAY 9. — As we decided to make two days' short journey to Marrah, instead of one, which would be of twelve hours, we did not leave Hamah till half-past ten in the forenoon. Our route was in a north-westerly direction, having the Orontes on our left : on the west side of the river was the conical village Chasde. Soon after quitting the town, the traces of cultivation began to languish, and we saw nothing but fine pasture land, covered with numerous flocks of goats and sheep, and camels, belonging to the Bedouin Arabs, who had small encampments in the neighbourhood. From Hamah, the Orontes takes a westerly direction; then to the northward, and in less than three hours we again joined the river, its course in this part being to the north-west; here we observed several fragments of walls, which were, we imagined, formerly aqueducts for wheels. At two, P. M., we passed a ruined mill on the river, running here to the south-west, and entered on a fine plain, which only required the plough to render it very productive, then leaving Zuckar, (at some distance on the west side of the river,) and afterwards the conical village of Ziat on the left, we arrived, in a most heavy hail-storm, at Scheikoun, and took up our quarters in a room in the Khan : we were escorted from Hamah by ten Delhi, the regular cavalry of the country. Khan Scheikhoun, about which there are a few houses, is situated on the south side of one of the many circular heights, which we observed this day ; and from their regular appearance, and from the circumstance of their being isolated mounds in an extensive plain, we judged them to be artificial.

May 10. — At seven this morning, with an escort of five horsemen, and in company with five Delhi, who were conducting a sum of money to the Grand Vizier from Hamah, we continued our journey. This treasure, it seems, consisted of five or six purses, which Ali, governor of the province of Aqqar, north of Tripoli, has sent to the Vizier, with the hopes of gaining his interest, and afterwards the Pashalic of Tripoli. Our route was rather to the eastward of north. After ascending a gentle acclivity, we proceeded across a large plain, whose exuberance in wild herbs and flowers sufficiently announced the fertility of the soil. We passed several Bedouin camps with their flocks. On the road we observed many deep cisterns, and near them a small portal with an architrave of Greek work. A little to the eastward of the road, at ten, we passed the well of Mar-Hattar, having deep and excellent water :. half an hour beyond this, was the ruined village Hennach, on the left. A little before eleven, on one side of the road, we saw in a field a sarcophagus, with a lid on the top : in this place were scattered several large stones; and we observed the foundation of buildings, and several deep cisterns. At half-past eleven we arrived at Marrah, and were entertained at the house of the chief writer of the place. Marrah is a large village : the houses are built of stones, badly put together ; but the Khan is really a magnificent building ; it consists of most excellent masonry, with a mosque and bath. The dome of the former is covered with lead, as well as the colonnades, which are on the four sides of the building. Near the Khan is a square minaret, of the same good kind of architecture as the Khan itself. In the court of the mosque, we observed from without, (for admission was refused,) a dome supported by eight pillars of the architecture of the lower Greek empire. Not far from the Khan, is the house of an individual, which has a gate of stone : it is of a grey colour, and on the outside is ornamented with crosses and flowers, in the style of the early ages of Christianity. The projections at the top and bottom are six inches in diameter, and let into sockets made to receive them ; the door itself is eight inches in thickness : this door is in constant use, and easily moved by a single person. The Khan is on the east side of the village.

May 11. — At six we commenced our route, with an escort of three horsemen, and shortly after seven, we passed on our left the ruined villages Edanah and Gezasde : on the right of the road there were fragments of pillars and sarcophagi : in three hours we passed the Khan Sibbit. An hour before our arrival, we were informed by some travellers, whom we met, that there were several Arabs on the road; and that yesterday a horseman from the Vizier's army was killed by them, we therefore waited for the escort of the Khasnè, or Treasure, as they were far in the rear, that we might form a respectable body for our defence . before our arrival at Khan Sibbit, twenty horsemen, armed with muskets, presented themselves from behind ·a small hill, on a sudden, and would no doubt have attacked us, had we not been so formidable a party ; they therefore saluted us, and said, that they were only seeking a camel, which had been stolen from them by some other Bedouins in the neighbourhood. The Khan Sibbit is a square inclosure, and fortified with small round towers at the angles. Instead of following the usual route to Surmeen, we accompanied the Khasnè to Seraqueb. On our left we saw the distant village of Daddeer, chiefly inhabited by Greeks; on our right was Masdebsee and Murdeer: to the westward we saw Kafr Jeubass. Half way between Khan Sibbit and Seraqueh, we passed several large cisterns to the right of the road; and, in five hours from Marrah, arrived at Seraqueb. Our journey this day was over uncultivated ground, the soil of which, in general excellent, was occasionally intermixed with rock, but more so on the left than to the right : a few olive trees varied the dull uniformity of the scene. Before we arrived at Seraqueb, our Tchocodar went forward to provide us with an apartment. Having dismounted, we had no sooner entered the room that had been set apart for us, than we heard a dispute below, between the people of the village and the escort of the Khasnè. We immediately went on the terrace of the building ; the Delhi were abusing, in the Turkish language, and in the most violent manner, the Aga and the people who accompanied us. One of the horsemen presented his musquet to the Aga, exclaiming, " Are the English infidels (Djaourler) to be entertained in the best apartment, and we, the soldiers of the Vizier, with his treasure, to be excluded? Let the English dogs go where they please, we will have the apartment." The chief of the Delhi then ascended, with others ; and, as we saw these ruffians were determined to gain their point by force, we decided to mount our horses, and continue our journey. Surmeen is directly west of Seraqueb, and about two leagues distant. Soon after our departure from Seraqueb, we saw the villages Ervis and Benish at some distance on our left ; and, in two hours, we passed several Bedouin encampments ; one of which, consisting of thirty-five tents, was immediately on the road. From Seraqueb we crossed a long plain, of two hours and a half, in a northerly direction ; then a low ridge, which separates a second plain from the first.

We passed this, and in two hours arrived at Khan Touman, only a short distance from Aleppo. The country between Seraqueb and Khan Touman is of a reddish soil. Near the Khan, which was built by Touman Bey, the last Mamaluke Caliph of Egypt, is a small village of conical houses ; to the south of the little height, on which is the village, runs the river Coick to the west, then to the southward: here there is a canal, on a higher level, to conduct the water from this river into the Khan. We pitched our tent in the village, where we determined to pass the night.

May 12. — At six o'clock we proceeded across some rocky heights, a little to the eastward of north, leaving our baggage to follow us: in an hour and a half we arrived at a small stone building, with a cupola, where we found Mr. Barker, who had come hither to receive us.

May 13. — This morning we proceeded, in a large cavalcade, to pay a visit to the Vizier, who was without the town, in a convent of Dervises, very beautifully situated. We were first introduced to a great personage, (brother-in-law of the Vizier,) who was sitting in the apartment of the Reis Effendi : after pipes and coffee, came the Reis Effendi himself. He speaks French fluently, and had accompanied the first Turkish embassy, in capacity of secretary, to England. In a few minutes, it was announced that the Grand Vizier was prepared to receive us ; and we were ushered, with all due form, into his apartment. He appeared about sixty years old, with a long, grey beard, and has lost his left eye, by a blow from a Djerid, in his youth. It seems that Aleppo has of late been in a continual state of ferment and rebellion ; the Pasha and the corps of Janissaries being constantly embroiled with each other. The Janissaries, though formerly a respectable military body, are a set of persons who, under pretence of forming the garrison of the place, exercise trades and professions, oppose the extortions, and even the just claims of the Pasha. At Tripoli, the Pashas have been frequently expelled by the power of the Janissaries. At Aleppo there are more than twelve thousand Janissaries ; and their chief officers, now the Vizier is arrived, have taken refuge in the Desert, fearing his determination to punish them. When the presence of His Highness is removed, there will be as much tumult and commotion as ever. The weakness of the Turkish government cannot appear in a stronger light than in the province of Syria, almost the whole of which is held by governors, in a state of rebellion; who have the resemblance, or so great a reality, of power, that the forces of the Porte are not deemed adequate to subdue them. The mountains of Libanus, and part of Anti-Libanus, belong to a family wholly independent of Constantinople. Dgezzar, building fortifications, and establishing himself as a little prince, bids defiance to his enemies: the people of Tripoli depose and confirm whom they please, as their governor. Between Damascus and Aleppo one village is at war with another; some, profiting by the extortions of an Aga, espouse his cause; while the body of the people, exhausted by continual oppressions, will not allow him a residence amongst them. This have we seen at Hems, Hamah, and the villages adjacent. On the gulf of Scanderoon, Kutchuk Ali, (Little Ali,) of Paias, (a wretched, inconsiderable town,) with two hundred followers, has been a declared rebel, and the cause of the most serious alarm to the government, for forty years : he allows no one to pass through his territory, without exacting an enormous contribution. If a ship anchors before Paias,· he endeavours to make the crew prisoners, to take possession of the ship, and demands a ransom for the people. The Dutch consul at Aleppo, (Mr. Masseyk,) on his return from Constantinople to that city, while passing through the country of Kutchuk Ali, was seized by order of the tyrant, and confined eight months in chains, until he could procure a sufficient sum for his release. This Pasha is without money, and has but a handful of men ; yet the Vizier, with three thousand troops, on his return through Asia Minor, is obliged to make a great detour, in order to avoid too near an approach to the domain of this rebel. The caravans coming from Asia Minor to Aleppo are compelled to go a journey of fifteen days out of their route, that they may not pass through the territory of Ali.

Saturday, May 14. — This day we made several visits to the Jews and Frank merchants, who have taken up their residence at Aleppo ; and, in the afternoon, paid our respects to Ibrahim, Pasha of the district, an old man, and formerly a farrier in the town.   Yesterday there was much rain, and the climate cold, as in England.

May 15. — This afternoon we were conducted to the castle. There was some difficulty in obtaining admission : the Pasha had said, that, in order to see the armoury, we must make particular application to the Reis Effendi.   The secretary hesitated on this important point, told the messenger he would talk to the Vizier on the subject, who gave orders to the Aga of the castle that we should be received.   It is situated on an artificial height, towards the north-east part of the town, and is nearly of a circular figure.   The outer slope, from the summit of the hill to the bottom of the ditch, has been covered with masonry.   The ditch is about sixty feet wide, and has a counterscarp twenty feet high, formed partly of the natural rock, partly of masonry. The outer circumference along the edge of the ditch is nearly three quarters of a mile.   The entrance is on the east side : the perpendicular height of the hill may be one hundred and twenty feet, from the bottom of the ditch.   The passage is supported by arches, substantial, well-built, though in a very tasteless manner.   After having passed through three gates of solid iron, half an inch in thickness, we arrived at the interior of the castle; and were immediately conducted, to use the words of the Reis Effendi, to " *the inexhaustible treasury of Aleppo.*"

We entered a large well-built hall, arched and supported by pillars, in which we literally saw nothing but a few arrows, damaged sabres and musquets ; a few dusty cuirasses, and some rusty iron helmets, probably used in the time of the Crusades : these, with some other rubbish, and wooden shovels, &c., composed the whole contents of the armoury.   Every thing that relates to fortifications or warlike implements the Turks make of the utmost importance : they imagine that the Franks are spies, that they wish to take plans of their military works, and they show a ruined tower open on all sides, and without

u u 2

any defence, with the greatest caution and jealousy. The walls of the castle are about sixteen feet high; and in a very decayed state: they are certainly mounted with cannon, but there is not a single gun on a carriage in the castle; besides, the Turks have shown the greatest economy; for in many places one cannon has been divided into two, and placed in different parts of the rampart: the old guns scattered about the interior of the castle are in general of a small calibre; and perhaps all of them are not unserviceable. Near the entrance a gun with a bore five inches in diameter, is pointed through a loop-hole two inches in width. The castle is completely filled with houses, and quite a little town of itself: it is supplied with water by means of a well four hundred feet in depth. The water is raised by means of a reel, which raises one bucket, while the other descends: the reel turns round on a pivot, which rests on a small mass of masonry. The horse which works the machine, when the bucket arrives at the top, by a certain word from the driver, turns and continues his labour in a contrary direction. From the fortress is a commanding view of the town. There are many cypresses interspersed through the city, which, with the domes and minarets of the mosques, the neat appearance of the houses, and the gardens without, afford a magnificent prospect to the beholder.

May 16. — This day we visited the Reis Effendi, intending afterwards to pay our compliments to the Vizier: the latter, however, was so much engaged that the Reis Effendi requested us to defer our visit to the following morning. The head of Hussein, Aga of Antab, who was strangled on the fourteenth instant, by order of the Vizier, was exposed on the side of the road through the camp, for the satisfaction of the public. This Aga, it appears, had been extremely tyrannical and oppressive towards the people of Antab, and the town had been almost deserted on account of the avanias of the Aga. The Vizier had decided on his death; and it is curious to observe what methods the Turkish government is obliged to adopt in order to obtain the ordinary ends of justice. The Vizier sends a full pardon to Hussein for his vexatious conduct towards his subjects; he even entreats him to pass a few days with His Highness at Aleppo; the Aga arrives with a train of six hundred followers: the Vizier invests him with a fur; and treats him with every mark of distinction: he is fearful of seeing his victim in the camp, and applies for the interference of the Pasha of Aleppo, who prepares a sumptuous repast in honour of the Aga: the unsuspecting Hussein accepts the invitation, and repairs to the fortress, accompanied by very few of his domestics: in the midst of the entertainment he is seized by the myrmidons of the Pasha; thrown into confinement, and three or four days afterwards is strangled. It was reported that Hussein suffered many torments before his death, with a view to extort a confession where his treasure was secreted; he persisted, however, in an absolute denial of his riches, asserting to the last, that he was poor and greatly in debt. When the executioner arrived to perform his office, the Aga declared that the hour of his death was ordered by God; that he died contented, and only requested that after his execution his face might be turned towards the holy city. Osman, Aga of Hems, is still with the Vizier, and it is supposed that for a large ransom he will obtain his release.

After our visit to the Reis Effendi, we made a pleasant tour on our horses through the gardens to the northward of the town: in the afternoon we walked to Bab-el-Nasr, (the Gate of Victory,) to examine a Greek inscription. It is at the angle of the wall, about five feet from the ground: the stone is so placed, that the writing is perpendicular to the horizon.

May 17. — This day the Vizier, with his army, began his march towards Constantinople. In the forenoon we made our visit of leave to His Highness, and afterwards joined the family of Mr. Barker in a garden close to the road along which would pass the grand procession of the Vizier and his suite: before noon his departure was announced by minute guns from the castle; and shortly afterwards the procession moved forward in the following order:

A few Tatars with two streamers ;
Some Delhi (the native cavalry ;)
Tatars ;
Fourteen led Horses ;
A Corps of Delhi ;
A four-wheeled Carriage drawn by eight horses ;
Six Mules for the Tartrevan ;
The Vizier's Tartrevan (a close carriage) ;
Three Standards and two Tails * ;
Some Horsemen ;
The Vizier.
. Two standards ;
A Corps of Cavalry ;
Four Camels ;
Cavalry ;
The Tartrevan of the Reis Effendi ;
Seven led Horses ;
The Reis Effendi (smoking a pipe).
Cavalry ;
Three Standards ;
A Band of Music ;
Three Mules ;
Tartrevan of the *Defterdar* (Chancellor) ;
Seven led Horses ;
The Defterdar ;
Three Mules ;
Tartrevan of the *Tufekgi Bashi* (Chief of the musqueteers) ;
Tufekgi Bashi ;
Six Standards ;
Corps of Albanian Cavalry.

---

* One of the tails had been sent forward two days before.

The procession moved forward with very little regularity: there were nót more than five hundred persons in the whole ; and, though the Turkish dresses made a pompous appearance, and the fine trappings of the horses, and the horses themselves have great advantage on occasions of this kind, we were not impressed with a high idea of Ottoman magnificence.

May 18. — This day a courier was dispatched to Constantinople : he will arrive there in eight days, an unusually short journey * : the Tatar even said, that he should be there in seven : the couriers are in general twelve days on the road between Aleppo and Constantinople, a distance of more than seven hundred miles : they have been known to reach the capital, several times, on the eighth day from their leaving Aleppo.

On our visit of leave to the Vizier, there was a mean dirty looking fellow sitting beside him and smoking : this man, it appears, was a Santon, and consequently with the Turks privileged to remain with the people of the first distinction, and to act as he pleases : during our conference, this reputed saint was employed in picking off the vermin from his body.

Since the departure of the Vizier, forty-three Janissaries, the principal rebels, having been proscribed, the Pasha has placed some troops in the castle, and is determined to prevent their return to the city.

May 19. — This afternoon we visited some of the best built houses in Aleppo, the property of Christians : they were constructed of a hard stone, and the workmanship excellent : they consist, with very little variation, of a square court with a fountain in the center, and a few trees and shrubs on one side of it. The apartments are on the sides of this court : some of them have fountains ; are painted in very

---

* The reader will compare the journey of Cesarius. " In the time of Theodosius, Cesarius, a magistrate of high rank, went from Antioch to Constantinople, post ; he began his journey at night ; was in Cappadocia, 165 miles from Antioch, the ensuing evening, and arrived at Constantinople the sixth day about noon. The whole distance was 725 Roman, or 665 English miles." Gibbon, i. p. 83. — E.

gaudy colours, and have cushions and low sofas around them: the ceiling is in general extremely expensive, being adorned with a profusion of gilding: one room in particular, in the house of a man named Abdany, was very curiously wrought, and in a very superior style of workmanship: it had been finished fifty years, and the ornaments were as fresh, and in as good preservation, as if they had been the labour of yesterday. The rooms are high, and have a large painted window, at the top of which is a wide shelf, where it was formerly the custom to arrange large bowls with small cups in the intervals, the best workmanship of India: we saw three or four apartments fitted up in this sort of taste, now nearly out of fashion at Aleppo. Many parts of the square court, which in a summer evening is always much frequented, are paved with a variety of marbles, in Mosaic work: among other stones we observed pieces of porphyry, serpentine, and the *breccia verde* of Egypt.

May 20. — This afternoon we passèd through a gate in the south-east part of the town, to the eastward of which are some extensive excavations, which may have been originally quarries : the entrance into them is at the bottom of the side of a rock ; and on a level with the ground there are many intricate turnings within, and in several instances whole chambers have been filled up by the falling of the soil from above : there are circular shafts in different parts communicating with the surface of the ground for the admission of light and air. We returned through the gate of Antioch (Bab Antakie) ; a little above which, from a part of the town called Aggibar (or the Steep), we had a commanding view of the gardens and valley to the westward of the city. Close to this spot is a small mosque with a stone in its walls, having an inscription, much obliterated, yet resembling hieroglyphics.

Each Thursday, being the eve of the Mahometan Sabbath, the principal mosques are illuminated on the outside: the lamps are placed around the gallery of the minaret, and have a very pleasing effect.

May 21. — This day we set out at seven in the morning, and in two hours and a half arrived at. Heilan, a deserted village to the northward of Aleppo : at this place we pitched a tent. Our route was along a narrow valley, through which ran the stream of the Coick, watering a continued garden, chiefly of fruit trees, extending the whole length of the valley : on either side are rocky heights, which form an agreeable contrast with the verdure between them. About an hour from the town, is a small spring called Ain-el Tell.

The river Coick has its rise at Antah, three days' journey from Aleppo, to the northward. After winding through a plain above Heilan, its course is through the gardens along the west side of the town ; then to the eastward, afterwards south, losing itself in a lake. The inhabitants of the city are supplied with water from two springs, about a quarter of a mile south of Heilan, and on the east side of the valley ; and this by means of an aqueduct two feet wide, and running for a long distance parallel to the Coick, and fifteen feet above the level of that river: it enters the town towards the north-east. At Heilan is a small artificial height, and at the further extremity of an extensive plain, of a reddish soil, tolerably well cultivated, are two others, which though not so large, resemble those we have before observed on the road between Damascus and Aleppo. The water of the two springs near Heilan joins the Coick immediately at the head of the valley, about one mile from their source.

May 22. — This afternoon we visited one of the principal manufactories of the finest stuffs that are made at Aleppo : there may be fourteen or fifteen of these buildings in the town, with about one hundred looms in each : these stuffs consist of silk, and India cotton, and are ornamented with flowers worked with gold and bright-coloured silks in a very ingenious manner. Many of the patterns are striped, but though their stuffs are much esteemed by the Orientals, they are not in general well adapted to the taste of Europeans. The looms are worked by a man and two boys: one of the latter sits above the loom, and by the movement of the different threads he regulates the pattern : these three earn about fifteen piastres, or one guinea, in the week: the stuffs are two feet in width ; and the three workmen generally complete thirteen inches of the length of the stuff in a day. The Mahometans, as well as the Christians, are engaged in this manufacture; though the Christian weavers are much more numerous than the others. A kind of velvet is also made here, besides cotton stuffs in imitation of India shawls, and knives and swords of a very inferior description. Not long since there was a glass manufactory at Aleppo, which has now ceased to exist on account of the smallness of the demand for that article: here is also a manufactory of soap.

A little after sunset this day the firing of a gun from the castle announced the execution of a Janissary, one of the proscribed, who had been taken the day before in a neighbouring village: it appears that the Pasha and one of his sons (the receiver of the customs) had made out the list of the Janissaries who had been marked as rebels, consulting, as usual, their own passion and caprice, rather than the real guilt or dangerous character of the individuals. The unfortunate wretch who was executed this day had given offence to the son of the Pasha, because he had offered an asylum to one of his debtors in a coffee-house, of which the Janissary was the proprietor; this exasperated Mustapha (the receiver of the customs), and he was glad to embrace so fair an opportunity of revenge. The principal cause of the disgrace of Achmet Aga (one of the Chiefs of the Janissaries) was his having refused to present a fine Arab horse to the Vizier, which had been demanded from him by His Highness. The Aga was at the Vizier's camp, on the borders of the desert, before the battle of Matarea in Egypt: here the Vizier made the demand, with which the Aga refused to comply; in consequence, the Aga was thrown into confinement, his horse taken from him, and he, no doubt, would have been strangled, had not one of the grandees of the camp undertaken to intercede in his favour: so that, after paying an enormous ransom, and losing his horse, the unfortunate Aga was released from his captivity, and returned to Aleppo. When the Vizier arrived here, Achmet, with several others, who had reason to fear the designs of the Vizier, fled from the town into the villages, and forty-three of the most obnoxious were proscribed: Achmet Aga was amongst them.

At Aleppo there are three different parties, which continually occasion tumults and insurrection in the city: the Pasha and his party; the Janissaries; and the Scheriffs, the pretended relations of Mahomet. With the Turks every thing is decided by force; and according to their strength the Pasha and his troops, or the Janissaries, keep the people in subjection. These last, at Aleppo, amount to nine or ten thousand persons: originally, this body was intended as the regular armed force of the government; most of them, however, exercise trades and professions, and from certain privileges attached to the title they are extremely insolent and overbearing.

May 24. — In the afternoon we made an excursion on the outside of the town; which, including the suburbs, may be four miles in its circuit. The walls, which, from their remains, appear to have been of good Saracen architecture, are so much ruined, and confused with the houses, that in most parts it is not possible to discover them. On the south side is a deep excavation in a chalky soil between the walls of the town and the country, which seems to have been the labour of man: the bottom of this ditch is covered with plantations of artichoke.

Aleppo is surrounded, on all sides, by low rocky heights: the soil, except in the valley, which gives passage to the Coick, is, in most parts, intermixed with rock. The river takes its course west of the town, and the plantations of pistachioes, (a tree peculiar to Aleppo,) not requiring much water, or a rich soil, are, for the most part, to the eastward.

May 25. — The Turcomans are a wandering set of people *, who, in the winter months, migrate from the northern parts of Asia Minor, and, during that period, occupy with their numerous flocks the plains of Antioch. They never pass towards the southward beyond the limits of

---

* The Turcomans live always in the field. Russell, i. 389.

the Pashalic of Aleppo. Their numbers, in Syria, seldom exceed five thousand. They return to a cooler climate at the latter end of April. In the same manner as the Bedouins, they are divided and subdivided into tribes and families. These also claim a right of plundering all, and treating them as enemies, who pass their territory, without seeking their protection, or acknowledging their sovereignty by a present. When their friendship is once gained, they are punctual in their engagements. They are remarkable for a fine, stout breed of horses; and the camel amongst the Turcomans, from the richness of the pasture, is large and fleshy, and very different from the meagre lank appearance of the camel in the Desert. The Turcomans are a numerous race of people : they extend themselves as far as Angora, in Asia Minor. The present chief of those in the neighbourhood of Antioch is called *Heidar Aga*, of the family of Moursal.

The Curds*, like the Turcomans, lead a pastoral life : in Syria they occupy the mountains between Aleppo and the sea ; and never pass farther to the southward than Antioch. Their number amounts to between four and five thousand. The Curds have villages amongst them, though in summer, like the Turcomans, their ordinary residence is under tents. These also exact a tribute from travellers, though their faith once plighted in your favour, you need never suspect their sincerity. Their women make a coarse sort of carpet, which is tinged with different colours. The reigning chief of the Curds near Aleppo is named Cossum Aga, of the family of Ommou.

May 26.— The Arabs, who in general conduct the caravans from Aleppo across the Desert, are of the tribe of the Anizes : their chief, Ali-Abdallah, is of the family of Mehamma-el-Fordal. Mr. Masseyk mentioned a tribe of Arabs, called Sleyle, who are mounted on

---

* The Curds inhabit a great part of Amanus, and the neighbouring mountains; and subsist chiefly by plunder. Some of them are employed as reapers about Aleppo.— Russell's Aleppo, ii. 340.

asses, and carry guns, with matchlocks. They are excellent marks-men, and live almost entirely on antelopes : they eat the flesh of the animal, and clothe themselves with its skin. They follow cara-vans, in their journey across the deserts near Aleppo, and supply them with antelopes.

May 27. — A few days since, we received information from Alex-andretta, that Georgius Bess, the minister of the young prince at Dgebail, had, according to his promise, sent us the stones, which are found in the neighbouring mountains. At Aleppo there is very good fresh butter, which is brought from Armenia. The butter is preserved in *dibs*, or in honey * : the butter is pressed down in the case which contains it, and covered with the liquor ; and, even twelve or fourteen months after its arrival, it is as sweet and well-tasted as if made but yesterday.

There have been some partial attacks of the plague at Aleppo within these few days ; but as yet there are no apprehensions that it will become general.

May 28. Friday. — This afternoon we rode to some very agreeable gardens westward of the city. The river Coick, taking its course in this direction, enlivens the verdure, and renders the little kiosks, or plea-sure-houses, in the midst of them, cool and grateful in the extreme. The Pasha, it appears, not content with preventing the proscribed Janissaries from entering the city, is searching for them in the dif-ferent villages in the neighbourhood. The Pasha's force at Aleppo consists of three thousand horsemen, most of whom are encamped under the walls. The expence of these, with the maintenance of his household, is so great, that it is thought, from his poverty, he will not long hold the government of the city.

May 29. — The streets of Aleppo are paved, for foot passengers, on each side ; and the bazars, in general, are arched with stone, or

---

* Dipse is applied in the East both to date-honey and raisin-honey. Compare Shaw, p. 143. and p. 339. In the latter sense it is used in Genesis, xliii. 11. " Carry down to the man a little balm, and a little dipse." Shaw, 339. — E.

covered with a roof of wood. They are neither so large nor so well built as those at Damascus ; neither is there a display of so much wealth and commerce at this town as at the other. The mosques of Aleppo, though few, are, in general, of a good architecture, consisting of a square court, surrounded by a colonnade. The mosque itself is a square building, having a cupola for its roof, (about forty feet in diameter,) which is covered with lead. The Minaret (or steeple) is light, and of well-constructed masonry. Most of the houses are surmounted with domes, and small cupolas, which, from their disposition, are not elegant, though they give to the interior a noble appearance. The khans, and dwelling-places for the merchants, consist of a large square court, paved, with two arched colonnades, one above the other, along the four sides of the building. The spaces between the arches of the upper colonnade are blocked up with masonry. This part is converted into dwelling-places, while the corridor below furnishes magazines for merchandise. In the middle of these khans there is generally a mosque, surmounted with a cupola. The masonry of the whole is extremely neat and substantial. The Frank merchants and consuls have their houses in khans, which are always shut up in the evening. At Aleppo the shops are closed before sunset : the people retire to their houses ; and, after the evening prayer, not a person is seen, nor a voice heard, to disturb the stillness of night.

June 1. 1802. — Yesterday Mr. Laurella, our late companion, returned from the camp of the Vizier, whither he had been to transact some business with His Highness. When the Vizier approached Antab, the inhabitants, having understood that Achmet Aga, son of the Pasha of Aleppo, had been named, as successor to their late governor, threw stones at some of the messengers of the Vizier, which even reached the tents of His Highness himself. They showed also other marks of discontent : the Vizier, in consequence, ordered several to be imprisoned, loading them with chains, and rewarding their mutinous activity with thirty strokes of the bastinado on the soles of their feet : two of the ringleaders were executed. The

Vizier had contrived to secure the treasures of the Aga, who was strangled at Aleppo, which, for the most part, were sold by public auction in his camp. Even the jewels and trinkets of the women were disposed of. Two of the most refractory rebels of the party of the late Aga, one of them the Tufekgi, or chief of the mus-queteers, were strangled by his order. During his stay at Aleppo, the Vizier sent troops into the mountains to the westward, to seize the chief of the Curds. These fell in with a party of the moun-taineers, whom they attacked, but with little success; for they were soon compelled to retire and fall back on Antah. The Vizier made a second attempt, which was equally ineffectual as the first. At present he is not accompanied by more than one thousand followers.

June 2. — During our stay at Aleppo, the thermometer, in a cool room, was generally at 74°, and the wind westerly, in the day blowing fresh : at present there is no dew.

June 3. — At six this afternoon, after having taken leave of our friends at Aleppo, we proceeded on our journey for Scanderoon. Our caravan consisted of seventeen animals, mules and horses. At nine we passed Khan Touman, W. S. W. of Aleppo, then took a westerly direction across uneven ground, until eleven, when we halted near a well immediately on the road. In this spot were several cisterns, small hillocks of earth, and many cut stones, which induced us to imagine that this was once the site of a town. Indeed the place is called *Kafr Joum*. We had with us a firman from the Pasha of Aleppo, desiring the Sheiks of the different villages to supply us with what-ever we might require ; besides an escort of horsemen as a guard. At Khan Touman, we were told, there have been attacks of the plague.

June 4. — At six A. M. we continued our journey in a westerly direction, and a little before nine passed a ruined village : our road then led to the southward of west, across a very extensive plain, in a good state of cultivation : at ten we arrived at the small village Zedany, where there are many cisterns, and a small circular height, on the

SYRIA.

east side of the place, apparently artificial : one hour beyond is Rama-
dan ; and at noon we arrived at Maat-mishereen. From Zedany to this
place our route was nearly in a westerly direction : in these different
places we have heard of a few persons having been attacked by the
plague. We proceeded over some rocky, uncultivated ground, to the
north-west, and in less than an hour crossed a plain in a northerly direction, which is well cultivated, and where there are many plantations
of olive trees ; here are also several artificial heights. We traversed this
valley in its breadth : it runs east and west ; and on the south side is a
well. We entered the mountains ; and after passing a very cragged
road towards the east of north, we encamped in one of the most wild
romantic spots that can be imagined, near a spring of fresh water,
under a rock, and shaded by a single fig-tree. This fountain is called
Ain-el Razee : it is encompassed on all sides by rocks, with scarcely
any verdure, except in the little cavities, and separations between them.
At our entrance into these mountains we passed the small village
Ashat on our left, built on the summit of a circular, isolated rock,
which is so rugged and abrupt, that one would think it inaccessible.
In the early part of this day's journey, we observed several ruined and
abandoned villages : the soil of the plains was of a reddish colour,
and in the large plain, before our arrival at Maat-mishereen, extending south, as far as the eye could reach, we remarked an extraordinary
degree of cultivation.

June 5. — At five A. M. we continued our route in a north-west
direction, over very rough mountains, in several parts of which we
were obliged to dismount ; and in two hours we arrived at a large
village, called Elmanas, on the south side, and near the head of a long
valley, extending from the east to the westward. In this plain are
several artificial mounds, similar to those we have often observed in
the most level parts of the country : on the north side of the valley is
the village Bayardes ; and on the mountains above Hosereè, in this
valley, are a quantity of olive-trees, vineyards, and orchards of pome-
granates. Elmanas is in a very beautiful situation, and surrounded on
all sides by rich gardens ; but unfortunately it is now visited by the

plague. Here we passed the high mountains bounding the plain to the northward, and continuing our road still to the north-west, we soon came in sight of a most magnificent and extensive prospect, consisting of an immense plain, bounded to the north by very lofty mountains. Across the plain flows the Orontes, making a very serpentine course, and entering the valley from the south-west. We descended the mountains, and a little before ten arrived at Salkeen, on the south side of the valley, but far separated from the river, by a ridge of heights running between them: here we were presented with a large piece of snow, which the inhabitants had procured from the neighbouring mountains. We sent the Pasha's firman to the Sheik of the village, which was worded in such particular terms, that he thought proper to accompany us himself, attended by eleven horsemen. We soon entered the plain, and after passing a small encampment of Curds, we joined the banks of the Orontes. Their tents were in general of coarse black cloth, and the walls of reeds, formed into matting. This plain, we were told, in the winter is entirely covered with the numerous tents of the Turcomans, which circumstance renders the road very dangerous and insecure. Towards the north side of the plain, we observed a lake about a mile distant from the Orontes: it is called Bahr Jagira, is formed of several small streams from the neighbouring mountains, and communicates with the river. After passing over an uncultivated plain, covered with thistles, fertile enough, if we may judge from the exuberance of the weeds, we pitched our tents on the east side of the river, and close to a stone bridge of four arches, called Geseer Hadeed : this bridge has gates, coated with iron, so that it still claims, and retains its antient appellation of " *The iron bridge*," Geseer Hadeed in Arabic. The river through the plain of Antioch, part of which we had just traversed, is rapid, and in general about thirty yards in width : in the beginning of July it is fordable in many parts. On the west side of the bridge is the village of Geseer Hadeed, consisting of about twenty houses of mats, inhabited by Curds, and tributary to the Moutsellim of Antioch.

June 6. — A little after five A. M. we passed the bridge, and continued our route in a N. N. W. direction, across an uncultivated plain,
in which we observed two villages on our left, one on an artificial height,
the other on the top of a hill.   Travelling to the W. S. W., along the
south side of a plain, bounded to the north and east by lofty mountains, at a quarter before nine we arrived at Bab Paulos, one of the
antient gates of the city of Antioch : immediately within, is a clear
spring of excellent water, shaded with trees.   A mile before we arrived at the gate, we observed the remains of pavement : thence, to
the distance of nearly six hundred yards, is a paved road, having on
either side most pleasant gardens, abounding in all the fruits of the
country.   This road continues to the entrance of the present Antioch,
about half a mile distant from Bab Paulos : we passed through the
town, crossed the stone bridge towards the western extremity, and
at half-past nine pitched our tent near the road to Beilan, and immediately on the bank of the Orontes.

The plain of Antioch, through which was our route both yesterday
and to-day, is nearly of a square figure, each side about twelve miles in
its length : it is bounded on all sides by lofty mountains : those towards
the north are the highest.   Immediately under these heights is the
lake, which is nearly thirty-five miles in its circuit : there are several
small islands scattered over its surface.   The general direction of the
Orontes through the plain, though its course is extremely irregular, is
from south to north ; then it enters the narrow plain of Antioch, and
flows to the westward, but close to the town : here it is very rapid
in its course.   In many places the water has been raised to different
levels, to work corn-mills, or to turn Persian wheels ; some few of
which there are at Antioch similar to those at Hamah, though by no
means of so magnificent a construction : the wheels themselves indeed are well made, and at least thirty feet in diameter : the conduit
for the water is merely a wooden trough, placed on a wall a few yards
in length, and of very bad work in appearance.

At present the plague rages at Antioch ; and there have been frequent instances of thirty, and once thirty-nine deaths in a day : already

upwards of one thousand persons have perished. Elias, a Christian, to whom we presented a letter from Mr. Barker, made us a visit at our tent, and told us that in consequence of the infection, he had long since cut off all communication with the inhabitants: he was extremely civil, and undertook to supply us with whatever provisions might be required. We had also two letters for the Moutsellim of the town; one from the Pasha of Aleppo, the other from Mr. Barker: these we sent to the governor, who immediately presented us with a sheep.

· June 7. — Antioch (now called Antakiè) is situated on the south bank of the Orontes, and at the foot of some very abrupt lofty mountains, part of which was once included within the walls of the city: its length was about three quarters of a mile, and greatest breadth seven or eight hundred yards. The walls which now exist, though much ruined, mark the antient boundary of Antioch: they were built since the introduction of Christianity: the form of them is nearly of a rectangular figure; of the longest sides, running north-west and south-east, one confined the town on the plain, the other passed along the ridge of precipices above: the short sides were partly in the plain, partly along the slope of the mountains. Though there may have been several sally-ports in different parts of the fortification, it does not appear that there are more than five principal gates to the city: that towards the north, Bab Geniun; the present Bab Paulos, to the east; Bab Hadeed, leading to a deep ravine on the south; a fourth called Bab Lataquie, on the west side; and the fifth, in the north-west angle of the inclosure of the city, called Bab-el-Geseer. The walls are about twenty feet high, and flanked with square towers at intervals: they are built of an excellent hard stone, of which the surrounding mountains are composed, much resembling the stone of the temple of Balbec. The workmanship of the whole is exceedingly good, and in many parts courses of brickwork are introduced between the masonry. In the towers there are in general three floors, one above the other; and the two upper are supported by arches of solid brickwork. The height of the walls along the slope of the mountain is regulated by the direction of the ground. Towards the east angle of the south side there is a deep ravine, formed by two precipices, almost perpendicular; and so anxious were the people of Antioch to place themselves in a complete state of security, that along the ridges of these heights, though in most parts absolutely inaccessible, they have continued their fortifications, and closed the ravine (about twenty-five feet wide) with a solid wall, the greater part of which is still in existence, and was upwards of seventy feet in height. On the north side of the mountain are many excavations and niches in the rock: some for catacombs; others have been formed after the Christian æra, and by the addition of masonry have served as places of devotion: these are on the east side of the deep ravine. Without the gate Bab Hadeed, on the west side, is a bridge of five arches across a valley. The piers are of the natural rock, with arches of masonry turned over them: in many parts, which are not sufficiently inaccessible from their steepness, are the remains of a ditch, on the west side fifty feet in width, and fifteen in depth. On the highest part of the rocks within the fortifications, and rather nearer the west than the east side, is a most magnificent and extensive view. To the east is the great plain of Antioch with its lake, bounded by distant mountains; the Orontes, winding through the plain in front of the city; the high mountains of Beilan; the sea in the south-west; Mount Casius; the irregular valley covered with vineyards behind the heights of the city: these are the chief objects which strike the beholder from the highest point of the antient capital of Syria. Mount Casius is of a conical form. The Orontes, after passing Antioch, takes its course between some low mountains north of Mount Casius; and discharges itself into the sea, about six leagues from Antioch. Antakiè occupies about one-fifth part of the antient city, and is situated towards the western extremity of the walls: the houses have sloping roofs, are covered with tiles, and built in a very slight manner. There are fifteen minarets at Antakiè, and though the place is not extensive, it is considered a populous town, containing perhaps four thousand inhabitants: it is governed by a Moutsellim, tributary to the Pasha of Aleppo. Much cotton is manufactured here, which is grown in the neighbouring villages ; grapes are also dried and preserved, and much wine is made by the Christians ; there are also many tan-yards on the banks of the river. The bridge is at the west end of the town, and consists of four arches. The tiles for the roofs of the houses are made at Antakiè. This forenoon a messenger arrived from Mr. Barker at Aleppo, who mentions in his letter, that in consequence of several recent attacks of the plague, his family had determined to close their gates, and cut off, for the present, all intercourse with the inhabitants.

June 8. — At five A.M. we continued our route, accompanied by five horsemen of the Moutsellim of Antioch. About half an hour from the place of our encampment, about twenty more joined us on the road, saying, that they were the guard of the Moutsellim, and that they expected a present. We offered them four piastres (six shillings). As they were not contented with this, we took leave of each other without any further ceremony. Our route was across a plain, towards the N.N.E. for five hours, until we arrived at a fine oak-tree, near the entrance of the mountains of Beilan. At half-past ten we arrived at Khan Caramout, where there is a narrow pass, and a small village of mountaineers, who claim a tribute from every traveller or caravan they meet. They mount about a hundred horsemen ; and when they are not satisfied with the liberality of passengers, they proceed to violence, and make no scruple to plunder them. As soon as we arrived, a few of these ferocious robbers appeared, and attempted to stop our caravan, which preceded with the baggage : however, the leader of our escort explained to them that our caravan might pass, and we would pay the customary tribute. We sent for the chief of these mountaineers, and drank coffee with him, and a large circle of his people, under the shade of a plane-tree. After some little conversation, we gave him seven piastres, and took our leave, although the chief and his party did not appear well contented with the present ; however, as we had drunk coffee with him, he did not openly object. From hence we were accom-

panied to Beilan by two of the Caramout horsemen.   At Caramout
the Turkish language only was spoken.   One man of the whole
party could converse a little in Arabic.   We now continued our route
to the northward, over very lofty and picturesque mountains, covered
with the arbutus, fir-trees,. woodbines, myrtle, and innumerable
fragrant shrubs, regaling us as well with their charming odour as
their beautiful appearance.   Soon after Caramout we passed on our
left a castle, situated on the top of a precipice, in a most romantic
situation, called Bagras ;   close to it is a village.   Half an hour from
Caramout we joined a paved road, which leads to Beilan ; and in
winter must be very useful, as, on account of the rains, and the
nature of the soil, the ordinary road must be impassable.   After
crossing these rugged yet noble heights, we arrived at Beilan, in
three hours, from Khan Caramout.   On passing through the plain
between Antioch and the heights of Beilan, the lake of Antioch was
on our right, leaving a space of two miles between it and the mountains.   We passed several little streams, which, if the country was
properly cultivated, would assist to fertilise the soil and render it
extremely productive.   The earth appears black, and of an excellent
quality : some parts were cultivated, and the people were employed
in taking in the harvest.   About three hours from Antioch we passed
a small camp or village, of fifty tents, belonging to the Curds, who
plough and.sow the ground in the neighbourhood.   One hour from
Antioch there is much marsh land ; and there is a small river called
Kara-sou, (or " Black water," in the Turkish language,) which
discharges itself into the lake.   This appellation is derived from the
black stones at the bottom, which give a similar appearance to the
water.   Khan Caramout is the Khan of " Black Myrtle," so called
from the quantity of that kind of shrub in the neighbourhood.   Beilan
is situated on either side of a deep, narrow, and elevated valley : a
stream from the mountains above, rushes through the middle of the
town.   There are three or four aqueducts across the valley, which are
still in use, and seem to be of antient construction.   The houses are
built of stone, with flat terraced roofs ; and placed on the steep slope

of the mountains, intermixed with a variety of trees: they form a most agreeable prospect. From Beilan to Scanderoon the descent from the mountains to the sea, in a northerly direction, is very striking: the heights are lofty, picturesque, well covered with wood, and a great part of them planted with vines, disposed in the neatest order, and cultivated with the most careful attention: for the caravans, the distance between Beilan and Scanderoon is three hours. We halted more than two hours at Beilan, and at half-past six arrived at Scanderoon. This wretched town consists of a few houses, and is absolutely built in the marshes; and so impracticable is the ground, that there is only one road by which it can be approached. The marshes extend on all sides, more however to the west than to the eastward: the reeds that grow in this swamp afford nourishment to the buffaloes; and in some parts, where the land will admit, it is cultivated: and here we saw some fields of very indifferent barley, the first time we had seen this grain since our arrival in Syria. It seems that at Scanderoon the sea continually retires, and the marshes increase in proportion. About a century ago the line of shore was a mile more inland than at present, as may be seen from the fact of a ruined square building of stone, where there are iron rings, to which boats and small vessels were formerly attached: indeed one of the merchants mentioned, that in the space of ten years the beach had so advanced into the sea, that in a spot where there was formerly water, there is now a magazine for merchandise. The town is chiefly inhabited by a few Greeks, and some Turks, who find an interest in remaining there on account of the arrival of shipping at the anchorage. Here is a neat Greek church, and amongst the tombs we remarked seven of Englishmen, with Latin inscriptions, who had fallen victims to the unhealthiness of the situation. Few persons escape the malignant fever, which constantly rages there in the summer, occasioned by the excessive heat of the sun, seldom relieved by sea-breezes, and the noxious vapours from the surrounding swamps. There are three European agents now resident at Scanderoon, two French and one Italian: their ghastly pale appearance sufficiently marks the black influence of the climate.

The ignorance and imbecility of the Turkish government cannot be more strongly marked than in the position of Scanderoon. This is one of the finest bays in the world : the marshes might be drained and cultivated; and were the town removed to the heights, about half a·mile from the beach, the inhabitants would breathe a purer air, and merchants might be induced to reside there. In many instances, however, under the impotence of the Ottoman government, where the smallest exertion would establish good order and prosperity, all is misery and confusion : only three hours' distant from Scanderoon is the town of Paias, groaning under the tyranny of Kutchuk Ali, whom the Porte is too weak to subdue : ships dare not anchor near this town, fearful of being seized by the rebel ; he also plunders the caravans that pass through his territory ; and thus commerce is obstructed on every side. Scanderoon may be considered the port of Aleppo ; and though the road between them is so much frequented, we experienced more difficulty and impertinent conduct from these uncivilised inhabitants, than in any of our former journeys in Syria. In the village of Salkeen,· and in the mountains above, pistols were fired across our road, and some armed ruffians extorted our money, claiming the right as a Caphar, a tribute from the Franks. At Antioch, Caramout, and Beilan, we met with the same sort of treatment, although we had strong firmans, and letters from the Pasha of Aleppo. From Beilan to Scanderoon we were accompanied by two horsemen of the Pasha ; and although we had continually an escort, the ruffians on the road made no scruple of showing their impertinence. Scanderoon is tributary to Mustapha, Pasha of Beilan, who maintains a small band of troops to exact tribute from caravans and travellers. After supping with. the Imperial agent, we went on board the brig Mentor, lying about a mile distant from the town. We were happy to find ourselves independent, and in our own ship, relieved from the impositions and villainy of Syria : we had been exposed to dangers arising from the plague, earthquakes, plunderers, and suspecting Agas ; and it may be readily concluded that we rejoiced not a little at our emancipation.

A

LETTER TO THE EDITOR

ON

A REMARKABLE EGYPTIAN BASS-RELIEF,

INSCRIBED WITH

GREEK CHARACTERS,

TOGETHER WITH A POSTSCRIPT, CONTAINING

SOME OBSERVATIONS UPON OTHER EGYPTIAN ANTIQUITIES,

BY EDWARD DANIEL CLARKE, LL.D.

My dear Walpole,

The custom among the *Greeks* of inscribing upon their γραφαὶ the names of the persons represented, (which characterised the works of *Grecian* artists, from the earliest ages until long after the period of the *Roman* power,) was also common among the *Egyptians.* In the. representation transmitted to you by Mr. *Wilkins,* of an antient *Athenian* Tripod Chalice in my possession, you have a remarkable instance of this practice; the names of all the principal *Heathen* Deities being there inscribed in letters which were afterwards gilded; and the gilding remained as fresh when the vase came into my possession, as if it had been recently applied. With respect to *Egyptian* antiquities, there are few documents which afford more illustration than the *Apocalypse;* because the uninterrupted train of symbols there enumerated, are, as to their prototypes, so evidently *Egyptian.* Indeed the language of the book itself, and the peculiarity of its phrases and idioms, remarkably distinguish it from the other *Greek* writings of the New Testament; and in every instance, if we trace the discrepancy to its origin, we must have recourse to *Egypt.* In that book we find allusions to *" written names"* upon the *foreheads,* or *above the heads,* or *upon the thighs* of figures; a practice common to the two countries both of *Greece* and *Egypt.* The *image of the Beast* rising out of the sea, is,

for example, described * as having " UPON HIS HEADS THE NAMES OF
BLASPHEMY." In the vision of the personified appearance of idolatry †,
the woman is represented as having " UPON HER FOREHEAD A NAME
WRITTEN." The rider of the *white horse* ‡ had " A NAME WRITTEN
WHICH NO MAN KNEW ;" also § upon his *vesture*, and upon his *thigh*,
" A NAME WRITTEN :" all of which passages are so many allusions to
the antient custom of inscribing the consecrated idols with the names
of the deities. The *Jewish* High Priest, consistently with this practice,
wore the ineffable name of *Jehovah* upon his forehead. Among the
antiquities discovered in the sepulchres, near the Pyramids of *Egypt*,
are sometimes found a sort of *tablets* made of a *whitish stone* ‖, containing, within a cavity, the carved image, in bass-relief, of some idol ;
the name being inscribed in *Hieroglyphics :* but I possess one of so
curious a nature, that its description here will show how intimately
the customs of the most antient heathen nations corresponded with
the allusions made to those customs in the *Apocalypse.* These *tablets*
appear to me to have been used as portable tabernacles after the
manner of other *painted tablets* in *Russia*, which the inhabitants of
that country still worship under the name of *Obraze* or *Bog.* That
to which I allude, is of *white* or *grey limestone*, five inches and a half
long, by two inches and a half wide. It came from *Egypt*, with
others of the same nature, excepting that the characters upon them
were *Hieroglyphics ;* whereas the characters upon this *tablet* are
Greek letters ; and they protrude in relief upon the surface of the
stone. ¶ The idol represented is that of the *Egyptian Mercury,*

---

* Ἐπὶ τὰς κεφαλὰς αὐτοῦ ὀνόματα βλασφημίας. Apocalyps. cap. xiii. 1.
† Ibid. c. xvii. 5. Ἐπὶ τὸ μέτωπον αυτῆς ὄνομα γεγραμμένον.
‡ Ibid. c. xix. 12. Ἔχων ὄνομα γεγραμμένον ὃ οὐδεὶς οἶδεν.
§ Ibid. c. xix. 16. Ἔχει ἐπὶ τὸ ἱμάτιον καὶ ἐπὶ τὸν μηρὸν αυτοῦ ὄνομα γεγραμμένον.
‖ The *tablet*, or *amulet*, mentioned in the *Apocalypse* for the conquering Christian, (on
which a name was to be written, known to no man but to him who was to receive it,) is
described as being of *white stone :* the words are these : (κεφ. β'. 17.) Καὶ δώσω αὐτῶι ψῆφον
λευκὴν, καὶ ἐπὶ τὴν ψῆφον ὄνομα καινὸν γεγραμμένον, ὃ οὐδεὶς οἶδεν εἰ μὴ ὁ λαμβάνων.
¶ I am indebted for it to the kindness of *Mr. Henslow*, B. A. of *St. John's College,*
Cambridge.

naked, bearing in his right hand *a purse.* His left hand is extended upon his breast. He is placed within an arched niche. Upon his head appears a *diadem* with five rays, fastened by a *fillet* above his forehead. Upon the *fillet* occur the following-characters in *relief*:

$$\sqcap \ \wedge \ \Gamma \ V \ \triangleright$$

These characters, elevated above the surface of the stone, are very distinctly and plainly carved. There is no difficulty whatever in reading them; each letter being one-fourth of an inch in height: the only perplexity is in making out their meaning, and this I think may be surmounted with a little attention. For, from what has been already stated, it will, perhaps, appear evident, that they form together the name of the *Deity* above whose forehead they are inscribed. The great idol of the heathen world, whose worship (alluded to in the *Apocalypse*, as the doctrine of *Balaam* *) proved such an abomination among the *Israelites*, was the god BAAL, or BEL; and it is very remarkable that *Kircher*, in his *Pantheon Hebræorum*, (Syntagma iv.) proves this deity to be the same as GAD, and to have been called *Baalgad*, or *Belgad* †; whose idolatrous worship the *Jews* derived originally from *Egypt.* ‡ Now, if the latter name be written *Belgud*, we have it here upon this *tablet;* for substituting, as was often the case, Π for B, and omitting the vowel in the first syllable, the word *Belgud* would be written exactly as it appears upon the stone; namely, Π Λ Γ Υ ▷ : so that there is every reason to believe we are thus presented with a figure of the remarkable idol mentioned by *Kircher*, which by the symbol placed in its right hand is at once identified with the Hermes of *Greece* and of *Egypt*. Among the earliest characteristics of *painting* and sculpture in *Egypt*, *Greece*, *Italy*, and in other countries, it is curious to observe the long continuance of this practice of inscribing above the γϱαφαὶ, whether they were *bass-reliefs* *, or more literally *pictures*, the explanatory names of the figures delineated. Upon the *idol pictures* of the Greek church in *Russia*, exhibiting the manner of painting as practised at the introduction of *Christianity* into that country, we read in *Greek* characters the names of the *divinities* thereon pourtrayed; and in old illuminated *manuscripts* and *missals* of the *thirteenth, fourteenth*, and *fifteenth* centuries, the same custom may be observed.

P. S. — I will not conclude these observations upon a singular *Egyptian* relique, without also adding a few remarks respecting some other *Egyptian* antiquities as they happen to have been recently suggested to me. And first, as a caution to antiquaries, I will mention a circumstance worthy of their notice. It relates to an inscription found at the back of a signet ring, of great antiquity, which was purchased in the *bazar* at *Grand Cairo*. This signet is an *intaglio;* it represents the figure of *Anubis*, bearing in his right hand a *serpent*, and in his left hand the branch of a *palm-tree;* that is to say, it exhibits the figure, or image, by which the antients typified the *subterraneous sun*, namely, *Pluto* in *Hades;* bearing the signs of *reproduction*, or the *revival of nature*. So far the workmanship is antient; but upon the back of this *signet* appears a *Greek* inscription, legible from right to left, and having also an appearance of antiquity. The legend appears in this manner :

. * " Γραφω. Sculpo, insculpo, fodio, vulnero. Il. p. 599. αἰχμὴ γράψεν οἱ ἄχρις ὀστέον: ubi vides notionem proprium fodiendi. Pind. Olymp. iii. 54. ἔγραψεν ἱερὰν, Scripsit eam cervam sacram Dianæ, inscripsit, dedicavit." Damm. Lex. 2101.

ƎↃↃƎↃ
A ꓭꓩƎꓱA/
ꓵ·A꓿Aꟼꟼ
ↃHꓶ

At what period this was inscribed, whether during *Buonaparte*'s late invasion of *Egypt*, or upon any former invasion of the country by the *French*, is uncertain ; but the whole has been unravelled by the ingenuity of our learned friend, the *Rev. John Palmer*, late professor of *Arabic* in the University of *Cambridge*, and it cannot fail to amuse you ; since it is evident from his observations, that the legend exhibits nothing more than a *French* inscription, written in barbarous modern *Gallo-Greek*, by some ignorant *Greek* lapidary ; it runs thus :

Ce. Sceau. Gen. B. Ar. Française.

or, as it is inscribed :

CЄ. CCЄA'. ΓEN. B. AP.

ΦAPANΓHC.

φαραυγη in modern Greek signifies *France**, which here occurs in the genitive φαραυγης : and the whole, being interpreted into English, means nothing more than this:

THIS SEAL (*Ce Sceau*) BELONGS TO THE GENERAL SECOND IN COMMAND OF THE FRENCH ARMY.

In the description which I have given of the *Egyptian Sphinx* †, I mentioned the remarkable fact of its surface being covered with *red paint ;* not being aware, at the time, that *Zoega* had discovered a passage in *Pliny*, which if restored according to the reading found in some manuscripts of that author, contains an allusion to this *red* colour upon the surface of the statue. *Pliny*, speaking of the *Sphinx,*

---

* Hence the etymology of the word *Frank* (φαραυγ), so commonly applied to a *Christian* in the Levant.

† See Travels. · 8vo. edit. Vol. v. p. 200. London. 1817.

says *, " *est autem saxo naturali elaborata et lubrica.*" Upon this
passage *Zoega* observes †, " *pro lubrica, alii legunt rubrica :*" and he
adds, " *sunt et peregrinatores qui rubri pigmenti reliquias in sphinge
superesse aiunt.*" In fact, I have now in my possession a portion of
the *painted* surface of the stone, which I detached from the neck
of the statue when I was in *Egypt.* The stone itself is *limestone ;*
the same of which the Pyramids were principally constructed. Externally it bears so near a resemblance to the *magnesian limestone* of
Roch Abbey, and of *King's College Chapel,* in *Cambridge,* that these
substances might be easily confounded together ; but the *limestone* of
the *Sphinx* is characterized by a much livelier effervescence in acids.
After it has been for some time exposed to the action of diluted
muriatic acid, a considerable portion of *silica* is deposited in the form
of sand. The supernatant fluid being decanted and filtered, and deprived of its excess of acid, and distilled water added, neither *tincture
of galls* nor *prussiate of potass* occasioned any precipitate. With
respect to the *red paint* conspicuous upon the surface of the statue,
and of which a considerable quantity adheres to the fragment I
brought from *Egypt,* it appears to have been applied after the
manner in which the stuccoed walls of the chambers in *Pompeii*
were painted ; a practice still in vogue among the inhabitants of
Italy ; especially at *Naples ;* where not only the walls but the
floors of the houses often exhibit this appearance. It was a
common ornament among all the *Greeks.* But as *Pliny,* in this
instance, calls the colour *rubrica* instead of *minium;* and as the
Egyptians were famous for their *rubrica,* which has been confounded
with *vermilion,* and with the *minium* of *Pliny,* (a pigment prepared
from *mercury,*) a favourable opportunity was here offered of ascertaining, by chemical experiments, the real nature of the *metallic
oxide* used in painting the *Sphinx.* For this purpose I separated a
small flake of the *pigment,* and having divested it as much as possible

---

* Plin. Hist. Nat. lib. xxxvi. cap. 12. tom. iii. p. 484.   L. Bat.   1635.
† De Origine et Usu Obeliscorum, p. 384. note 8*.   Rome: 1797.

of the adhering *limestone,* I exposed it for some seconds upon *charcoal,* to the action of the *blowpipe:* the *red* substance, after sustaining a very intense heat, proved altogether incapable either of being volatilised or fused. When removed from the *charcoal* its colour was *black.* It was now attracted and taken up by the *magnet.* It also communicated a dingy yellowish-green colour to *borax;* and in some places the *borax* became quite black. Hence it was evidently *iron;* and the substance which *Pliny* calls *rubrica* is, therefore, in this instance, *red ochre.* The practice of painting *sacred images* with *rubrica* and with *minium,* prevailed not only in *Egypt* but in *Greece* and in *Italy.* The best sculptured marbles of *Greece* sometimes retain traces of the red pigment by which they were covered. * Among the *Romans* it was usual on festival days to paint *Jupiter's image* in the Capitol with *minium.* PAUSANIAS says that *Bacchus* was painted Κιννάβαρι.† *Camillus* entering Rome in triumph, and affecting a *god-like* aspect, had his body painted with *minium.* All the ointments used at triumphal feasts were tinged with this colour; as were the robes "worn by kings and heroes old," improperly considered as the *purple* of the ‡ moderns. *Pliny* is at a loss to explain the origin of this custom; but he says

---

* The three fluted columns in the *Forum* at *Rome,* at the foot of the *Capitoline Hill,* still retain, in the fluting, near the tops of the shafts, a considerable coating of a red colouring matter, which has not yet been chemically examined.

† Τὰ κάτω δὲ οὐκ ἔστι σύνοπτα τοῦ ἀγάλματος, ὑπὸ δάφνης τε φύλλων καὶ κισσῶν· ὁπόσον δὲ αὐτοῦ καθορᾷν ἐστιν, ἐπαλήλιπται κιννάβαρι εκλάμπειν. Pausaniæ Arcadica, c. xxxix. p. 681. Lips. 1616.

‡ - - - - - - - καθέζετο
'Επὶ τοῖς βωμοῖσιν ὠχρὸς ἐν φοινικίδι. Aristoph. Lysistrata, v. 1141. L. Bat. 1760.
See also Æschyl. Eumenides, v. 1025.
The φοῖνιξ of the antients *(murice tincta)* was, in fact, our *scarlet;* as appears by the representations upon the *painted vases* of *Greece;* and also by the robes still worn by dignitaries upon solemn occasions, consistently with those antient customs which have been transmitted to modern times. *Milton* was evidently aware that the φοῖνιξ did not correspond with that which is now called *purple.*

- - - - - - - - " Over his lucid arms
A military vest of *purple* flow'd,
Livelier than *Meliboean* or the grain
Of *Sarra.*"

that among the *Æthiopians* their *gods* had this colour, and that their *nobles* had the same. Perhaps we may discover the origin of it among those savage tribes who besmear their bodies and their idols with the blood of their vanquished enemies in token of triumph; as also when human sacrifices are offered to their *gods*. The custom itself, whatever be its origin, is sufficient to explain to us the reason why the sort of *marble* called *Rosso Antico* was held in such high request among the antients, for the images of their *gods* and *deified Emperors*; and how exceedingly costly, owing to its rarity, this kind of *marble* must have been.

Before I conclude this *postscript*, already extended to a very unusual length, I wish to call your attention, for a moment, to another subject connected with the antiquities of *Egypt*. Mineralogists having heard, with astonishment, of a monolithal *soros* discovered by *Belzoni*, in *Upper Egypt*, which is said to be as transparent as *glass*, immediately imagined that the substance thus described must necessarily be *alabaster*. I was one of those, who, at first, entertained this notion. But an integral mass of *alabaster* of the magnitude he mentions, has, I believe, never yet been seen. The same might have been said of *rock crystal*; but to my utter amazement, I have received from Lieutenant *Shillibeer* [*], of the Royal Navy, a fragment of a *soros* of immense size, which was of one entire mass of *rock crystal!* It was discovered in *Peru;* being the tomb of the *Incas* at *Yarabamba.* This piece of *crystal* is now in my possession. It was broken from the *tomb* by the *Baron de Nordenfletch;* and it is as diaphanous as the most limpid glass; a part of the antient sculpture being visible upon the fragment. It is therefore possible that the *soros* discovered by *Belzoni* is also of *rock crystal;* adding one more stupendous example to the number of those marvels which almost induce us to consider some of the works of the antients as results of more than human skill and labour. Without ascribing them to the *Cyclops*, or to a race

---

[*] Author of the Narrative of the *Briton's* Voyage to *Pitcairn's Island;* now of *Jesus College, Cambridge.*

of giants, it is nevertheless impossible to behold them without a mixed sensation of admiration and awe. " SUM EX IIS QUI MIRER ANTI-QUOS: NON TAMEN, UT QUIDAM, TEMPORUM NOSTRORUM INGENIA DESPICIO. NEQUE ENIM QUASI LASSA ET EFFOETA NATURA, UT NIHIL JAM LAUDABILE PARIAT." *

I remain, Dear Walpole,

Cambridge, &c. &c.

June 5. 1819. EDWARD DANIEL CLARKE.

---

* Plin. Epist. lib. vi. 21. p. 444. Amst. 1734.

EGYPTIAN IDOL.

JOURNEY FROM CAIRO TO MOUNT SINAI,
AND RETURN TO CAIRO.

[*COMMUNICATED BY J. FAZAKERLEY, ESQ. M. P.*]

CHAP. I.

Departure from Cairo. — Object of the journey of the Pasha of Egypt to Suez. — Petrified Wood.—Illusion occasioned by the Mirage.—Desolate appearance of Suez.—Preparation of the flotilla against the Wahabee.— Departure for Mount Sinai. — Appearance of the Desert. — Plants. — Variableness of the Climate. — Scarcity of rain in the Desert. — Narratives and Stories of the Bedouins. — Mode of preparing their Food. — Bedouin Women. — Tents of the Arabs. —Approach to the Convent of Sinai. — The Traveller Seetzen. — Excursion to the Top of Mount Sinai. — Legends of the Monks, and of the Mahometans.

AFTER passing some time in Cairo, we were invited by Mehmed Ali, Pasha of Egypt, to accompany him to Suez. He went there to superintend the construction of a flotilla destined to act against the Wahabee, and as we felt a great curiosity to see something of the Desert, this was an opportunity too good to be neglected.

We left Cairo on the thirty-first of January, 1811; our party consisting of Mr. Gally Knight and myself; two Levantine servants, whom we had brought with us from Greece; and for our interpreter with the Arabs, a young merchant of Cairo, who spoke tolerable Italian. Besides these, we took one or two Fellah (or common Arabs of Egypt) to look after our baggage, and help to pitch our tent. We found only two horses and one mule provided for us; but the rest of the party, with the baggage, went on camels, of which there was no want. At length, after the usual loss of time in quarrelling, loading, unloading, and other preparations, we left the town at nine in the morning, and proceeded, with very little interruption until half-past five in the evening, when we pitched our tents, for the first time, in the Desert. Our caravan is numerous; and besides a good deal of merchandise, and many of the timbers, and other things belonging to the vessels at Suez, we have with us a large and brilliant party of the modern courtiers and grandees of Egypt. The Pasha himself went yesterday with a small escort on dromedaries, meaning to reach Suez, without halting for a night. The distance is from seventy to eighty miles: they suppose that he would accomplish it in about fifteen hours.

Very soon after we left Cairo all traces of vegetation disappeared: this part of the Desert is not mountainous nor sandy, but consists of a bed of pebbles, many of that sort which we call Egyptian pebbles; with numberless pieces of petrified wood*, some of which are of a great size, looking like whole trunks of trees. Carriages might pass wherever we have been.

Feb. 1.—We proceeded at two in the morning, and only rested a little once or twice for coffee; either allowing the heavy caravan to pass us, or riding forwards, and waiting until it came up ; and at five in the evening we were too happy to reach a few stunted Acacias, where we had been told that we were to pass the night. The appearance of the Desert is much the same as yesterday. There are some high mountains to the south and south-east.

Feb. 2.—Set off at a quarter before seven. We passed the ruins of an old Turkish fort (Ajerout) and a well of bad water (Bir-el-Suez), and reached Suez at half-past ten. The deception of sight, which the French call Mirage, was very frequent this morning: large pieces of water seemed to be spread before us ; and we were at times within less than a hundred yards of these imaginary lakes before the appearance vanished.

Nothing can look more desolate and deplorable than Suez ; a few houses built of mud and wood, and bounded by the desert and the

---

* Pococke, in his journey from Cairo to Suez, observed " many stones that looked like petrified wood." See also the remarks on the " mineralised wood" found in the desert, in Clarke's Travels, vol. v. 8vo. 161. — E.

sea; not a blade of grass, or the leaf of a tree in sight. Crowds of vultures were feeding on the carcasses of mules,. horses, and camels, as we approached the town.

Feb. 3. — The preparations for the expedition against the Wahabee have given an appearance of life and activity even to Suez. The flotilla consists of three or four vessels from forty to a hundred tons: some Greeks have been brought to manage them; for not only is the navigation of the Red Sea dangerous, but its sailors notoriously inexpert. * These matters are, we find, likely to detain all the world here for some time; and as the place has no charms for us, and the return to Cairo, without an escort or caravan, is thought to be unsafe, we have been employed, since we came, in negotiating the means of making an expedition to Mount Sinai. The Pasha has been very good-natured about it; and this morning he sent for us, and committed us to the care of some chiefs of the tribes who occupy that part of Arabia; telling them that we are his friends, and his guests; and that their heads should answer to him for our safety. The Bedouins put their hands to their foreheads in sign of submission, and we have now nothing to do but to prepare for our journey.

Feb. 4. — We laid in our stock of rice, onions, biscuit, and coffee; and what meat we could find. The Bedouins had sent round a sufficient number of camels and dromedaries to wait for us on the other side of the narrow arm of the sea which runs up to Suez. We put on Turkish dresses; and at five in the evening crossed over, and landed in Arabia. While we were stepping into the boat, an Arab, whom we had dispatched last night with letters and messages to Cairo, came running naked and breathless to the shore : after the

---

* " I observed (probably from inadvertence) no remains of the canals formerly existing between the Nile and the Red Sea; though some, it is said, may be seen near Ajerout, among other places. The precise spot where the Israelites crossed into Arabia is still a matter of dispute among the learned ; and tradition is here so vague as hardly to assist us. The natives point out indifferently either the valley of Bedea, or the passage from Suez, or even the places opposite Aijoun Mousa, or Corondel near the Hamman Faraoun." — Note added after the journal was written.

first confusion of questions and exclamations was a little over, we found that he had been met on the road by a large party (he said ninety or a hundred) who had stripped him to the skin, and were with difficulty prevailed upon to allow him to escape. Our Arabs were much disconcerted by this event: they entered immediately into deep consultation on the prudence of our proceeding further. The Bedouins who had plundered our messenger were well known to belong to a hostile tribe; and it was suspected that they might have information of our march, and be tempted to pursue us. We understood what was going on by means of our dragoman Antonio; but as we could not be judges of the degree of danger or of the manner of avoiding it, we left the decision to our guides, whose fidelity we had no reason to question. At last it was determined to advance; and at eight in the evening we set off; a party of twelve persons, including ourselves, and ten camels. We avoided, as we were told, the usual track, and did not go to some wells (Aijoun Mousa) by which we were to have passed; and where the robbers were supposed to have stationed themselves. We were hurried on, and forbidden to speak, or light our pipes: and scouts were detached in every direction to listen and reconnoitre. In the silence and solitude of the desert, suspicious sounds and appearances are, I suppose, easily detected; and as the vigilance of the Arabs is in constant exercise, their senses are probably acute. We were not relieved from this state of anxiety until three in the morning, when our Arabs with a shout of joy proclaimed our safety, and told us that we were now far within their own territory, where their enemies would not dare to pursue them. A ride of some hours upon a dromedary for the first time, independently of all other reasons, made this news very welcome. We pitched our tent, and lighted a fire, and with our pipes and coffee fancied ourselves in a state of luxury.

Feb. 5. — The sea was close to our tent. We set out at eight; came to a well of tolerable water at one, where we rested about an hour; and at five halted for the night. We have kept all day near the sea. The desert here is rather more sandy than between Cairo and Suez : we have met with scarcely a trace of vegetation ; now and then only a few parched thistles ; and a low shrub resembling what is called, I think, Sea Holly ; about the well, indeed, which we passed this morning were some stunted palm-trees, a number of tamarisks, and a good deal of a plant exactly like the Soda or Barilla which I remember to have seen in Spain.   The camels prefer the thistles.

Feb. 6. — Continued our journey at half-past six.   At half-past ten we halted for an hour ; and saw, across the sea, some high mountains to the south-west, which the Arabs told us were near Cosseir.   They can hardly, I should think, be so distant.   At four we came to water, and a few palm-trees ; the water though drinkable would not keep, so that we did not fill our sacks.   At seven, there was a division in the road, (if the tracks in the Desert deserve such a name,) one path leading, as we are told, to Tor ; the other, which we follow, bends to the eastward, in the direction of Sinai.   At ten we encamped for the night.   In the course of this day's journey we have passed great quantities of a substance which in its appearance resembles gypsum ; and over a good deal of ground looking more like the Fiumaras in Sicily than any thing I have ever seen.   Indeed the whole of the desert through which we have yet travelled is like the dry bed of a body of water : covered every where almost with round pebbles, apparently worn by attrition ; in places looking as if it had been swept, and furrowed by torrents.

Feb. 7. — Set off at a quarter before eight, and at ten, waited for half an hour under the shade of a rock.   The climate is quite in extremes : in the morning before sunrise the cold is so great that large woollen cloaks will not keep us warm, and when the sun has been up an hour or two, we are impatient to obtain some shelter from the heat. *

---

* I have since met with a description of the same sensations in an old traveller. " In the daies that I was in this sea, contained from Toro (Tor) to Suez, I felt by night the greatest colds I can remember to have borne; but when the sunne came the heate was unsufferable." Purchas, ii. 1145. This was in April.

The road for some time to-day led us along a narrow valley worn apparently by water, which stretched towards the east among some high mountains of granite ; the first that we have seen of that stone. This continued from half-past ten until a quarter-past two, when we descended into a valley of sand lying between hills of brown-coloured slate. The rocks, even at ·a great height from the ground, had all the appearance of having been worn by water. *

We stopped near a well, where the water to us seemed excellent : the spot, too, was not without pretensions to beauty : there were some wild acacias about, and many tamarisks, and a profusion of the soda plant. One hails with delight any thing green in this part of the world. We filled our water-sacks, but rain came on, which was looked upon as a sort of prodigy; at least, our Bedouins told us that they had seen none for four or five years. The storm soon blew over : but we pitched our tent for the night. The Arabs first thought of their coffee and pipes, and then, as usual, passed the time in telling stories; or singing them in a sort of recitative. This is their invariable custom when we stop at night, and frequently on the march; and they insist upon it that the camels derive no less pleasure than themselves from this practice. We sometimes make Antonio explain

---

* Upon referring to Niebuhr, and one or two other travellers, while I was writing over this journal, I find that they notice these appearances, and ascribe them to the violence of winter rains. I suspect that they have done this a little inconsiderately; and Niebuhr particularly, in the first volume of his travels, p. 183 , and p. 185., and in the " Description de l'Arabie," p. 347., speaks of torrents of rain quite as a thing of course. That it may rain occasionally in this part of the desert, and more fiequently in the mountains about Sinai, is probable; but when in all February we only met with one shower, and even that appeared to excite surprise, and when Niebuhr and the Prefetto of the Franciscans saw no rain in September, and the first half of October, and Pietro della Valle only a snow storm on Mount Saint Catherine in December; and as neither these travellers nor Shaw, nor Pococke, nor, I believe, any others who have left a description of their adventures, have ever spoken of having seen great rains here, or have been prevented from proceeding by the force of these torrents, I cannot think that these appearances are to be ascribed to the violence of rains. There is no account of travelling being interrupted by rains. Christopher Furer makes no mention of rain in the whole of November.

*3 A 4

these stories to us: they seem to relate to the loves of Bedouins ; the persecution of bad, and the protection of good Genii, with much of magic; and ending generally in some happy spot of verdure discovered in the Desert.

Feb. 8. — We began our journey at five ; and stopped to breakfast at nine. The Arabs prepare their mess by first scraping a hole in the ground, in which they make a fire with camel's dung: when this oven is sufficiently heated, they put into it a thin cake of dough, which they suffer to remain for a very short time, and take it out long before we should call it baked ; they then pull it to pieces, and mix it up with honey and liquid butter, which they carry about with them in leather bags. This seems to be their constant breakfast : they squat round the bowl ; and feed themselves with the fingers of the right hand ; each waiting very politely until it is his turn. They enjoy this much : I have tasted it ; and perhaps one might become reconciled to it.

We set off again at half-past ten ; and in our way, or perhaps a little out of it, went to an Arab encampment, and drank coffee with its inhabitants. One or two of the women were pretty : they show their faces with less reluctance than in the towns ; indeed the Bedouins are accused of being but lax Mahometans ; and here particularly, being placed on a sort of neutral ground between the old orthodox Mussulmans, and the new sect of the Wahabee, and obliged probably to maintain an intercourse with both parties, they profess and appear to care but little about the result or merits of the controversy.

A female slave who had but lately been taken prisoner, came up to us before we left the camp, beseeching us to obtain her freedom, and carry her away with us ; we could only recommend her to the care and compassion of her master. The people call us Sultans ; and the protection of the Pasha of Egypt is so powerful that we pass for persons of great consequence.

Our road led us through narrow valleys, producing a few acacias, between high cliffs, first of slate and afterwards of red and grey granite, frequently marked with perpendicular and horizontal veins of some dark stone. The immense masses of rock which are detached from these cliffs, and lie about the valley, have given to a part of the road the name of the " Broken Mountain." A ridge of dark-coloured rock nearly closed the valley at some distance before us; but through an opening we saw what they told us were the mountains of Horeb and Sinai: these were far off, and beyond them we could faintly distinguish the outline of other mountains, which were, however, so distant as to be almost lost in the clouds.

At five we stopped for the night under some huge cliffs of granite that sheltered us from the wind.

The tents of the Arabs which we have seen this morning are but wretched habitations; the climate alone can make them supportable: they are of black woollen cloth, the produce of their camels or goats; and are so imperfectly stretched, or strained to the ground, as to afford little shelter against wind or rain. You can hardly stand upright in them: one side is always left open for an entrance: mats are strewed within; and the furniture consists of one or two wooden bowls, a coffee-pot, and whatever arms the Arab may possess that are not on his person.

They seemed glad to see us: one or two children only were frightened, mistaking us probably for Turks, who are no favourites. The coffee which they gave us was excellent: the berries were green, but they soon roasted and pounded them. We were told, I know not how truly, that they had previously been boiled, and that this precaution is taken with all coffee before it leaves Yemen, lest the plant should be cultivated elsewhere.

To-morrow we hope to reach the convent of Saint Catherine.

Feb. 9. — Began our journey at five: the high mountains about us were covered with clouds: we rode on till nine; and then breakfasted at the entrance of a pass so craggy and difficult, that we were obliged to abandon our beasts, and scramble through it on foot: the dromedaries followed slowly, and with pain: their soft feet are better suited to sands than to such a road as this.

At one o'clock the great object of our journey, the convent at the foot of Mount Sinai, was in sight: we discovered it at the end of a long valley through a sort of avenue of rocks and precipices, which rise abruptly on three sides of it : half an hour more brought us under the walls, and in parley with the monks : the door is walled up, and opened only for the Archbishop, who compounds dearly with the Arabs for this honour. A rope with a stick fixed transversely to the end of it was let down from a window about forty feet from the ground, and we were soon dragged up by a windlass, and deposited within the holy precincts. There was a crowd of priests about the window, who saluted us with καλῶς ὁρίσετε, Χατζή: thus giving us the title of Pilgrim, one of more estimation in the East than among us, and to which a visit to this shrine entitles the traveller. Our visit was attributed to motives of devotion : wax tapers were put into our hands : the priests began to chaunt ; and we were led off in pro-cession to the church, which is much ornamented in the manner of Greek churches, and very pretty. At one end is a chapel, called that of the " Burning Bush," and said to have been built by the Empress Helena over the spot where God first appeared to Moses. The zealous priests scarcely allowed us to pause here, but hurried us along to the shrine of their patroness, Saint Catherine, whose death at Alexandria, and miraculous removal, first to a mountain in the neighbourhood, and then to the convent, form the subject of a favourite legend with this sect of Christians. We found here only twenty-five monks : in other times not only was the number within the walls far greater, but the valleys and mountains about were crowded with hermitages and devotees.

Feb. 10. — We went to mass ; and after again visiting the different shrines, we received some silver rings which had been in contact with the holy reliques of Saint Catherine.

The order of the convent is not to eat meat: as an indulgence they allowed me to shoot some pigeons that were flying about in the Desert; and in our present situation this was a matter of some interest to us.

In one of the cells assigned to us we found a paper giving the following account of Dr. Seetzen's journey hither from Palestine.

" Le 9 d'Avril, 1807, U. J. Seetzen, nommé Mousa, voyageur Allemand, M. D. et assesseur du Collége de S. M. l'Empereur de toutes les Russies dans la Seigneurie de * — en Allemagne, est venu visiter le couvent de la Sainte Catherine, les monts de Horeb et de Sinai et de la Sainte Catherine, après avoir parcouru toutes les provinces orientales anciennes de la Palestine; scavoir; Auranitis, Trachonitis, Gaulonitis, Paneas, Batanæa, Decapolis, Galaaditis, Ammonitis, Amorrhitis, Moabitis, jusqu'aux frontieres de la Gebalene (Idumæa), et après avoir fait deux fois l'entour de la Mer Morte, traversé le desert de l'Arabie Petreé, entre la ville d'Hebron et le Mont Sinai par un chemin jusqu'à ce temps lá inconnu, après un séjour de dix jours il continuoit son voyage pour la ville de Suez."

This is rather pompous; but Dr. Seetzen is, unquestionably, a traveller of great enterprise: he has been seven or eight years in these countries, and his experience, and habits, and knowledge of Arabic, qualify him in a remarkable degree for the pursuits in which he is engaged. We heard much of him from Dr. Malpurgo, among others, at Cairo, who told us that his ultimate design was to cross Africa, nearly in the latitude of Melinda. He is at this moment said to be on his way to Djedda and Mecca. The Arabs know him well by the name of Mousa.

There is also in one of the rooms a memorandum of two French travellers, which is worth copying for the amusing vanity of the dates.

" Le quintidi, 5ᵉ Frimaire, l'an 9 de la République Française, 1800 de l'ere Chrétienne, et 3ᵉ de la conquête de l'Egypte, les citoyens Coutelle et Rosiéres, membres de la commission des Arts et des Sciences, sont venus visiter les lieux saints, les ports de Tor, Ras Mohammed, la mer de Suez, et l'Accaba, l'extrémité de la

---

* A word here, and some of the following names, are nearly erased in my journal.

presqu'isle, toutes les chaines de montagnes, et toutes les tribus Arabes entre les deux Golfes."

Feb. 11. — We were let down from the convent by the rope, and set out on an expedition to the top of Mount Sinai *; one or two of the priests, and a real pilgrim, a Greek, who had come from Cairo, and taken advantage of our escort from Suez, were with us. Great part of the ascent is made tolerably easy by steps, which are said to be another instance of the Empress Helena's munificence to this sanctuary: it took us about three hours to reach the top. We passed in our way many little chapels dedicated to the Virgin, and various saints, where our party burned tapers and performed their devotions. About three quarters of the way up is the chapel of Elias, and near it a fine cypress, which seems to start from the bare rock. In this chapel we found the name of " E. Wortley Montagu," dated 1761 ; hardly any other European names, and those of very old dates ; one or two in the 15th and 16th centuries. At the top of the mountain is a Christian chapel and a mosque, both in ruins. Near the mosque is preserved the impression of one of the feet of Mahomet's camel in that mysterious journey when at the same instant, one foot was on this spot, another at Cairo, the third at Mecca, and the forth at Damascus. Our Mahometan companions here performed their prostrations, and covered themselves with dust, which with the Arabs is the substitute, in religious ceremonies, for water. It is difficult to imagine a scene more desolate and terrific than that which is discovered from the summit of this celebrated mountain ; a haze indeed limited our prospect, but if that which was concealed resembled in any degree what we saw, we lost little by not seeing more ; for, except a glimpse of the sea in one direction, nothing was within our sight but snow, and huge peaks and crags of naked granite. We found snow soon after we left the chapel of Elias; and Antonio, who had

* Le Sinai des Chrétiens auprès du couvent est presque tout de roc de granite rougeatre, et à gros grains.   Niebuhr. — E.

never been further from Cairo than Alexandria, was as much puzzled with its appearance as he had been with the tides at Suez. The mountain of Saint Catherine looks formidable, higher and steeper, and has more snow than Sinai: we are come to sleep below it in. a small uninhabited convent, called the Convent of the Forty Saints.

A Bedouin has brought us some game: the skin and head are gone; but we suppose it to be part of a gazelle.

A strange scene passed this morning under the walls of the convent at Mount Sinai, showing not in a very favourable light either the manners of the Arabs, or the condition of the priests. We were just preparing to set off, when a great noise out of doors, and much agitation within, induced us to go to the window, from whence we saw below us, a crowd of Arabs brandishing their daggers and guns, and screaming with every appearance of fury. The few priests who ventured to show themselves were imploring mercy; and as the Arabs not unfrequently climb up the rocks which overlook the convent and fire into it, we thought that this was the beginning of an attack. Our coming to the window produced a moment's pause; and fortunately some of our own companions from Suez were among the crowd. By the help of Antonio and the priests we soon found that the Arabs were complaining of some irregularity in the usual distribution of bread and fuel: their animosity was chiefly directed against the priest who superintended these matters; and as they understood that this culprit intended to accompany us to the mountain, it was thought a good opportunity to be revenged. Their passion luckily did not allow them to wait until we were all down and in their power; and one savage more furious than the others, flourished his dagger, and swore by the milk of his mother's breasts (an oath said to be held very sacred among them) that the monk should not escape him. As we remained at the window, he concluded by appealing to us as friends of the Pasha of Egypt to witness the justice of his cause: this alone enabled us to interfere with any chance of success; and after some persuasion and promise, and remonstrance, we obtained a ⹀ truce. The monk was allowed to go with us, on our engaging that he should return with us to the convent before we left the country. All parties were at once at their ease: the obnoxious priest descended without fear; and the Arabs either took no notice of him, or spoke to him as to any of the others: but the priests do not seem to infer from this that the conditions may be evaded, or that the quarrel will not be renewed as soon as we are come back, and the truce is over.

CHAPTER II.

Ascent of the Mountain of Saint Catherine.— View from the Summit. — Valley of Rephidim. — Departure from Mount Sinai.— Different Tribes of the Arabs.— Tor. — Shells, Corals, Madrepores of the Red Sea. — Remarkable sounds issuing from a bank of Sand. — Observations of the stars by the Arabs. — Application of the names Camel and Dromedary. — Arrival at Suez. — Abyssinian Women. — Gazelles, or Antelopes. — Reference made to them by the Arabs when speaking of their Women.

FEB. 12.—At half-past eight we left the convent of the Forty Saints; and began to climb the mountain. In about an hour we came to a small spring named the "Fountain of the Partridge," from having been shown by one of these birds to the priests many centuries ago when they were removing the body of Saint Catherine, and fainting with thirst. We found a good deal of snow, and the climbing was severe; but on the whole we fared better than Pietro della Valle, who went up in a violent snow-storm, and gives a lamentable account of his adventures here. We reached the top at half-past eleven: there is a shed over the spot from whence the Saint was removed: the rock is said to have swelled upon that occasion, and assumed the form of her body: its appearance, whether produced miraculously or by art, gives currency to the story: it was covered with scraps of rag and other such pious offerings. The view from hence is of the same kind, only much more extensive than from the top of Sinai: it commands the two seas of Accaba and Suez: the island of Tiraàn and the village of Tor were pointed out to us: Sinai was far below us : clouds prevented our seeing the high ground near Suez : all the rest, wherever the eye could reach, was a vast wilderness, and a 'confusion of granite mountains and valleys destitute of verdure.

Our Arabs pointed to some mountains towards the south-east at a great distance, and much higher than those about us ; and called them " El Accaba," a well-known ridge near the extremity of the gulf of the same name, over which passes the road from Cairo to Mecca. These mountains are sixteen days from Cairo, and twenty-five from Mecca : the caravan from Damascus joins that of Cairo two days before they reach Mecca : from Damascus to Mecca is a journey of forty days ; this at least is what the natives have just told us. At half past twelve we began to descend, and waiting to dine at " Partridge Fountain," we did not reach the convent of the Forty Saints until three : at four we mounted our dromedaries, and before six were once more drawn up into our old quarters ; welcomed by all the tribe of Caloyers and Papádes, except the old Superior, who was too ill to see us. In our way this evening from Mount Saint Catherine to the convent, we passed by the church of Saint Onofrio, and through the valley of Rephidim, where we saw what is always shown as the rock of Meribah : it is a large mass of reddish granite standing alone, and detached from other rocks in the middle of the valley : there are marks and channels upon it, which look as if they had been worn by water ; and many inscriptions were cut upon its sides in characters quite unknown to us : inscriptions in the same characters, as well as in Arabic and Greek, are numerous on the rocks about.

Feb. 13. — A day of rest. We were shown what professes to be the celebrated firman of Mahomet, granting many privileges, particularly to the priests of this Convent, and generally to Christians ; there is, however, reason to suppose that the original document was taken away by Sultan Selim, the conqueror of Egypt, who thought it too precious and sacred a monument to be left in Christian hands. The original was signed by Ali, and Abubekr, and many of Mahomet's chieftains, the Prophet having consecrated it with his own seal. Selim, at all events, left a firman confirming the same privileges ; and to come to more modern times, we found one also from Buonaparte, when in Egypt, promising friendship and protection to the convent. In the library are many antient and modern Greek books and manuscripts, which have been examined by learned men, and are said to be of little value. It was whimsical that in the midst of them we should find a volume of the Spectator, and one of the British theatre. One of the monks pointed to Wallachia on a modern Greek map of the world, and asked if it was not America? The poor old Superior was so ill that he could not leave his couch: he sent for us this evening, and seemed very wretched; and after complaining much of the intrigues of the Convent, and the treatment which he experienced from the monks, he concluded by entreating us, with much earnestness, to take him with us to Cairo. His own infirmities, however, make this quite impossible, without considering the tribute which the Arabs would certainly exact for his passage.

Feb. 14.—This was our last day: we walked in the morning once more over all the convent *, of which not the least curious circumstance is the enclosure of a Turkish mosque and Catholic chapel within its walls. They took us also to the cemetery, a large vault where the skulls of the deceased fathers are preserved. The monk

---

* After Mr. Davison and Mr. Montagu had quitted the convent, they went into a valley where they found the Manna of the Scriptures. The passage in Mr. D.'s MS. journal deserves to be transcribed; it mentions also a curious custom of the Arabs.

" Nous partimes du couvent; et laissant à main gauche le chemin par lequel nous étions venus, nous cheminames entre des hautes montagnes. Nous nous arretames près le sepulcre de Sheick Saleh, dont nos Arabes approchoient avec grande dévotion. Ayant dit une courte prière, ils retournoient avec une poignée de poussière, qu'ils jettoient sur les têtes de leurs chameaux pour qu'ils participassent à la benediction. Ils y sacrifierent un mouton suivant l'usage et le mangerent. Nous partimes l'après midi et passant une pierre sur laquelle on dit que Mahomet se reposa, nous fumes nous coucher dans une vallée pleine de ces arbres que les Arabes appellent Turfé. Nous vîmes quantité d'une espéce de gomme, que brilloit comme des perles sur les branches. Les gens du païs l'appellent *Men ;* et par plusieurs circonstances qui repondent à la description dans l'écriture on croit que c'est le Manne que les Israelites mangoient pendant les 40 ans qu'ils erroient dans le deseit. Il est de la consistence de miel, et d'un gout un peu fade." — E.

who conducted us burned incense before the bones·only of the more dignified ecclesiastics. The garden, the approach to which·is by a subterraneous passage from the convent, produces fruit-trees and common vegetables; but though much extolled, it owes, I think, its principal merit to the contrast of the surrounding Desert.

We were now obliged to take leave of the old Superior, who to the last seemed to indulge himself in vain speculations of being able to go with us, though he was lying almost lifeless on his couch. All reasoning was quite lost upon him; and, as the only chance of doing him any kindness, we left in his hands our present for the Convent, in hopes, that while he has any thing to give, his monks may be induced to treat him with a little more regard. The chance·is, I fear, a bad one; but it was all that we could do.

About half-past ten we were let down by the rope amid clamorous adieus from the convent window, and were received below by our old friends the Bedouins, who had brought us from Suez, and with whom we set off immediately to pay a visit to Awàtt, ·the best· of them, at his own encampment.

The tribe of Arabs in this neighbourhood is, they tell us, divided into three smaller ones. They seem to give the name of Tor to the whole; and when they speak of the divisions or branches, to·distinguish them as follows *: Souwàllah; chief, Sali; Mizaàni; chief, Gimaàn; and Allahaàt; chief, Ibrahim. The first of· these is the most powerful; and Sali its chief is generally about the person of the Pasha of Egypt, and acts there for the whole. Awàtt is of· the Souwàllah branch; and Diako, the old Arab with a red turban, and the most cunning of our party, belongs to the Allahaàt, The lesser Sheiks, or chiefs of ten or twelve families, are named by the great

---

* Niebuhr, I find, upon referring to him, gives the following names to three tribes; Leghàt, Sauâlha, and Saüd: the two first are evidently the same as those given to me: the third is indeed very different from Mizaani. I probably either misunderstood what was said, or was misinformed: Niebuhr was much more capable of making enquiries from his knowledge of the language; and he is much more likely to be right.

Sheik of the tribe, and their authority is said to depend upon his pleasure. In their dress (for both Awàtt and Diako are in possession of this subordinate rank) there is scarcely any thing to distinguish them from the commonest Arabs ;·their tents only are a little longer than the others ; they are those in which strangers are received. The Sheiks are much consulted in all disputes : it is they who make peace : here, as elsewhere, war has little to do with deliberation, and seems to result accidentally from private injury, avidity for plunder, or any sort of caprice. Of justice· their notions are, I believe, strictly limited to retaliation and compromise. Awàtt some years ago quarrelled with an Arab of his own tribe, and killed him : he fled to Acre until the matter could be, settled, and it ended in his paying thirty camels, and ten slaves to the man's family. There may be, perhaps, a little exaggeration in the numbers, but I have no doubt that something very like this took place. Hassan, a nephew of the murdered man, is with us ; and he and the assassin are better friends, and more constantly together, than any two of our party.

Awàtt, who, in spite of this history, was a favourite, welcomed us cordially when we reached his tents, and did not forget the hospitality of his nation : he gave us fresh dates, which were delicious, and re-commended them by reminding us that such had been the food of his Prophet : he killed a kid also for us ; so that we fared sumptuously, and pitched our tent for the night in the middle of his camp.

Feb. 15. — Our road, after passing a mountain of no great consequence, entered into a narrow defile between two cliffs of granite. About half-past eight the head of our little caravan suddenly stopped ; and on riding up to see what was the matter, I found the people in great confusion about poor François, my Greek servant, who was lying lifeless on the ground. His dromedary had started, as it was supposed, at a serpent which crossed the path, and had thrown him, head foremost, upon the rocks : his turban probably saved his life. By degrees we brought him to his senses, and sup-ported him slowly to some wells, and the shade of some palm-trees which were, very fortunately, near us. Here we determined to pass the day. The Arabs, in their anxiety to discover if any limbs were broken, squeezed and pulled the poor man about with violence enough to dislocate every joint in his body: they prescribed for him a dose of hot coffee and butter; and as this strange medicine appeared at least to be harmless, and might possess some secret virtues, we thought it right to insist on his swallowing it.

The valley, which hitherto had been narrow, opened at this spot into a kind of amphitheatre, with a profusion of palm-trees, and tamarisks, and other shrubs, which the moisture of the wells had encouraged to grow to an unusual size among the rocks. The cliffs that surrounded us here, like almost all that we have seen, look as if they had been worn away by water: even at a great height from the ground they are full of those circular excavations smoothed and rounded out, which one observes in rocks exposed to the action of the sea.

Our Arabs were put out of humour at so long a halt: they contrived, however, to pass the time, and amuse themselves, with firing at a mark, which they generally struck with great accuracy. Their powder is of their own making, and very coarse: their guns are matchlocks.

We thought that we might venture to move François a little this evening: we set off at four, and about six came to an end of this long defile, and entered the plain of Tor, where we soon encamped for the night. The mountains of Upper Egypt are in sight, and the village of Tor is, we are told, within a few hours of our tent.

Feb. 16. — We set off at six, and travelled along the plain till about ten, when we came to a thick grove of palms, and a few mud-huts, which they called "El Waadi." The inhabitants of Tor have most of them taken refuge here, to avoid the soldiers of the Pasha of Egypt on their passage to Djedda. The people of the village are Greeks: one of them, named Malim Elias, and a priest, received us most hospitably: they swept their huts, and prepared for us a mess of something between Vermicelli and the Barbary Couscousou.

The Papàs proposed to cup François, who grew worse after we came

3 c 2

here: he performed the operation by making incisions in the back of his neck with a rusty razor, and then drew the blood into an old wine glass : these simple instruments, and the practice, however barbarous, quite answered their purpose, and the patient was instantly relieved.

The Papàs, whose name is Gerasimus, of the convent at Mount Sinai, says that he has not heard of Mousa's (Seetzen's) death, which within a day or two had been rumoured among the Arabs ; but much of his conversion to Mahometanism at Djedda, and of the magnificence with which he had been treated by the Sheriffe.

The Bedouins of the neighbourhood are come in, and insist upon carrying us to Suez. They say that it is their invariable custom, and undoubted right, to take charge of every traveller who passes here in that direction ; and they swear by their beards that it shall be so now. However, we have no thoughts of giving up our old friends ; and as we are sure to have some Arabs on our side, we are not quite at the mercy of these new rascals.

Feb. 17. — We left El Waadi, and rode to a small Ospizio belonging to the convent of Mount Sinai : it is surrounded by palms, and there are several springs of hot salt-water. This spot is generally supposed to be Elim, famous " for its twelve wells of water, and threescore and ten palm-trees ;" though some of the learned are in favour of Corondel, near the Hammam Faraoun. The Arabs pointed to what they called the impression of the fingers of Moses on the rock, and told us the waters had been turned salt, to mark the indignation of the lawgiver at some insult which he received here. The real wonders of these countries are so striking, that they might well be left to make their just impression ; but the inhabitants seem to think that they have done but little to entertain a traveller, unless they invent a miracle for every spot, and answer every question by relating some extravagant tradition.

We went on to the deserted village of Tor, where every thing is in ruins, and nothing remarkable except an old fort, said to have been built by Sultan Selim.

. The Papàs, Gerasimus, showed us, in the course of the day, certifi-
cates of his hospitality, that he had received from Sir Home Popham,
and other officers who have landed on this coast.

We sent for our tent, and determined to pitch it close to the sea,
near Tor, and to remain here rather than at the village, until François
is well enough for us to continue our journey. Tor and El Waadi
are principally peopled by little colonies of Greek Christians, who
observe in their persons the most ostensible rite of the Jewish and
Mahometan religion ; and who seem to depend for their livelihood,
principally upon their skill in fishing. We found on the shore many
of those beautiful shells for which this sea is famous; and as the
natives observed us gathering them, they proposed to us to go with
them in their boats, and promised to show us what they called trees
growing at the bottom of the sea. These people have a great reputation as divers, and they fully justified it. There was not a breath
of wind : the water was as clear as crystal ; and when we had rowed
out to some little distance from the shore, we saw clearly what they
meant by trees : large clusters of coral, and madrepores of different
forms and colours *, and some of great size, looking like shrubs
growing out of the sand, and among these a profusion of shells, either
scattered over the branches of these marine plants, or lying between
them on the ground. The divers went down, and brought up, without fail, any shell to which we pointed, and broke off branches of the

---

* The following are among the remarks made on this subject by that able naturalist,
Forskal, the companion of Niebuhr. See the F. O. p. 130.
.Corallia.
1. Madrepora solida. Nunquam satis admiranda Coralliorum copia in Mari Rubro.
Montes hi lithophyti vocantur Sjææb. Luxus et lusus naturæ. His in locis observator
curiosus plura detegit paucis diebus, quam toto anno alibi. Usque ad decem orgyas vidi
hæc saxa surgentia; dum aquis extrahuntur, suprema parte inveniuntur mollia; inde
magis magisque cartaliginosa; fundus est lapis solidus. Specimina nullo negotio colli-
guntur. Incolæ paratos lapides habent in mari, quos facilius secant et ædibus struendis
aptant, quam saxa calcarea quæ totos montes adjacentes constituunt. — E.

coral. They walked along the bottom of the sea, and remained
under water for a length of time that astonished us.

Afterwards, when we had landed, and were going by the shore towards our tent, some one cried out, " Water ;" and my Sëis (a groom
who had come with us from Cairo) began to scrape away the sand :
he found the water fresh and good a foot below the surface, and not
a yard from the beat of the sea.

Feb. 18. — We could not venture to set off to-day ; and we passed
the morning very agreeably in another diving expedition.

It is settled that we do not change our dromedaries ; but one of
the Sheiks of Tor goes with us, in order to re-assert before the Pasha
the rights of the Arabs of this village, and, as we should say, to pro-
test against their yielding to our resistance being drawn into a prece-
dent injurious to their privileges.

Feb. 19. — We left Tor at eight, and in an hour came to El Waadi.
About ten we sent on the baggage camels by the straight road, to wait
for us at a spot agreed upon, while we, under the direction of Malim
Elias, went among some mountains to the left, in quest of a spot
where it was said that supernatural noises might be heard.

About an hour and a half to the north of El Waadi, keeping along
the shore of the sea, we came to the foot of a high precipice, and a
bank of fine white sand which went in a rapid slope nearly to the top
of it. It is pretended here, as at the antient Memnon, that the noises
are only heard when the sun is at a particular height ; and the hour
at which we got there was fortunately favourable for the experiment.
Elias crossed himself devoutly, looked a little frightened, and then
scrambled up the bank. When he was about half the way up, he
stopped, and began to slide down again ; during which we distinctly
heard a sound, sometimes like one piece of metal struck against
another ; sometimes the sound was more continued, and reminded us
of the musical glasses. We then went up ourselves, and as we were
sliding down, the same sound was produced, louder or softer, as we
pressed more or less against the sand. We felt too, very sensibly, a

sort of quivering or vibration, proceeding, as it seemed, from something immediately under the 'surface of the sand; and this feeling always accompanied the sound. The sand, on the surface, is light and dry, and in digging as deep as I could with my hands and a dagger, I found only a bed of moister sand. Whether there is any cavity below, or from what causes this phænomenon may arise, I cannot pretend to guess; but I have attempted to set down correctly what we heard and felt. The Greeks and Arabs agree in calling it miraculous, and never expect to hear the sound until Saint Catherine or Mahomet have been invoked. They have, of course, a crowd of legends about saints, and departed priests and demons, and good and evil genii, who celebrate their respective mysteries under this incomprehensible bank of sand.

We made the best of our way to regain the Suez road; and having joined our baggage about sunset, immediately pitched our tent. Diako, who commanded the party which went on to wait for us, had met some Arabs in his way, who informed him that the Maazes (the robbers who had nearly deterred us from leaving Suez) had been to the wells by which we had intended to pass on the first evening of our journey, and though disappointed in the prey which they probably expected, had seized thirty camels and made off with them. Our Sheiks listened with much gravity and interest to this story, and took very deservedly great credit to themselves for the plan they had pursued.

Feb. 20. — We set off at four, and went along a plain of flinty pebbles, in a northerly direction, between a range of high mountains to the east, and a lower range near the sea to the west. At eight we stopped to breakfast, when some strange experiments on the camels were exhibited: proceeding again at a quarter after nine, we reached the end of the plain at twelve, and at three we halted at the opening of a valley near the sea. We began our march once more at half-past, six and it was half-past nine before we were allowed to pitch our tent for the night. We were now close to the sea.

The Arabs make great use of the stars, not merely to guide them in the direction of their march*, but as indications of time. I frequently compared their calculations with my watch, and never found them mistaken in above a quarter of an hour. This habit of observation may be perhaps common with other people destitute of both compass and watch.

Feb. 21. — We started at seven; at nine we halted for half an hour, and again at twelve, at the foot of some mountains, which bounded the plain to the north-east. Our camels and dromedaries were here sent to water at a little distance from the road.

I cannot quite satisfy myself about these two animals. Camels are generally said to have two humps on the back, and a dromedary but one; in this country, however, there are none with two humps, and the natives seem to say camel or dromedary, with reference to no distinction between them but their comparative size and lightness; a dromedary here bearing the same sort of relation to a camel, that with us a hunter does to a race-horse. In the more northern parts of Asia, near the Caspian, and in the Crimea, as well as towards Constantinople, there is, I believe, a breed of camels with two humps: I know not whether there are any dromedaries formed in the same way; but here, as well as in Egypt, the slow camels that march with heavy loads in the caravans, and the dromedaries used for riding, and purposes of expedition, have neither of them more than one hump. If, therefore, the opinion that two humps are essential to a camel is to prevail, it follows that those animals do not exist in Egypt, or in Arabia, which have always been supposed to be in a peculiar degree their native countries. The camel and the dromedary breed together;

---

* " No where could we discover in the face of the heavens more beauties, nor on the earth fewer, than in our night travels through the deserts of Arabia; where it is impossible not to be struck with this contrast: a boundless dreary waste, without tree or water, mountain or valley, or the least variety of colours, offers a tedious sameness to the wearied traveller, who is agreeably relieved by looking up to that cheerful moving picture, which measures his time, directs his course, and lights up his way." Wood's Balbec. — E.

and it is sometimes difficult in their mixed progeny to say to which tribe a particular individual should belong. I think I have observed that " camel" is occasionally used almost as a generic term to express all animals of this description ; " dromedary" is certainly always meant to distinguish a particular class. *

We left our watering place at three; halted for dinner close to the sea at half-past four ; set off again at six, turned into a track among the mountains to the right, and at half-past nine we encamped first beyond the cross paths where we had slept a fortnight before. It was a sort of comfort in this solitude to be able to claim acquaintance even with the rocks. The day after to-morrow we hope to be able to reach Suez.

Honesty is not quite banished from among the Arabs. We picked up this day some cloaks, and a sack of flour, which had been dropped here in our way out, to avoid the trouble of carrying them : we had expressed some surprise at the time, but the Bedouins then told us that this was a common practice, and that as the things were left within the territory of their own tribe, no one would think of taking them. In this instance, they were not deceived; and it seems a proof of their confidence, both in each other's honesty, and in the fineness of the weather ; much rain would, of course, have been fatal to their sack of flour.

---

* The following remark of Forskal, in the Fauna Orientalis, may throw some light on the passage in the text : —

Camelus vulgaris. *Djammel.*

Animal natum ad tolerandos labores, et incommoda orbis meridionalis. Os et gingivæ mira cartilagine inductæ ne noceant spinæ plantarum deserti, quæ omnes fere armatæ sunt, quasque cætera animantia horrent; quarum vero helluo camelus est.

C. Dromedarius. *Hadjın.*

A camelo non specie sed propagatione variat; corpore apto et gracili; imprimis capite, collo, pedibus. Cursu equo citatior.

C. Bactrianus. *Bôcht.*

Gibbo dorsi duplice. Exoticus, et proceribus tantum inter animalia rariora reservatus. — We find in this last paragraph the reason why the camel with two humps is not found in the desert. — E.

Feb. 22. — We set out at half-past six. The cold for the first hour or two was as intense as the heat was afterwards. We are travelling now quite among old acquaintances, and at half-past nine halted at the wells, where we had stopped on the sixth of this month. We continued our journey again at a quarter after ten ; the wind from the south, and very warm.

We narrowly escaped a very disagreeable event this morning. Gally Knight and myself, and one or two Arabs, had gone forward ; and we were smoking our pipes under the shade of a rock, when the rest of the party came up evidently in great agitation. The Arab Awàtt, who seemed to be the most concerned, and whose name was loudly repeated by the rest, came forward and told his story. It appeared that François (destined always to get into scrapes from accident or his own fault) had begun by falling into a passion with his dromedary, and ended by striking Awàtt. The Arab fortunately restrained himself, and did not, as is usual, take immediate vengeance with his dagger or his gun. François was led up to us as a culprit : he was not allowed to quit his dromedary, and his stick was taken from him. The Bedouins looked fiercely at him, and rather suspiciously at us : they hardly gave time to Awàtt to finish his story, (which he himself told with great composure,) but interrupted him at every instant, by shouts and gestures very unpleasantly significant. As soon as he had concluded, the others began to scream all at once, some telling the story fifty times over in fifty different ways ; others describing the blow, and acting the whole scene in pantomime. We were not quite in a disposition to be so much amused at this uproar, as we might have been had we been less interested spectators : however, the barbarians, as they are called, behaved admirably ; and after a little pause, and representing the insult they had received, and appealing with great earnestness to the fidelity and care with which they had conducted us through the Desert, they ended by referring the dispute entirely to our decision. François was made to get down from his dromedary, and rebuked before them all with great solemnity ; and we then turned round to the Arabs, and by means of

Antonio told them how much we were offended with the Greek, and that we hoped he never would forget that he owed his life to their mercy: and when we began to express our concern, that after having travelled so many days and nights with them in peace, and so often eat together in each other's tents, any such misfortune should happen to disturb our friendship, they were soon appeased, and coming up to us, kissed our hands and the crowns of our heads, and called us their Sultans, and said their lives were at our service. Awàtt and François embraced; and the generous savage passed suddenly from rage to the warmest affection and tenderness, vowing that from that moment he should look upon our servant as his brother.

Thus ended this unpleasant affair, which might easily have cost some of us our lives; and had one fallen, the rest would, perhaps, scarcely have been spared. We went on again at half-past six, and did not pitch our tent till a quarter past ten.

Feb. 23. — We halted at nine this morning near the place where we had slept the first night. We set off again at ten; and as we were now near the end of our journey, we did not confine ourselves to any very regular order, and one of the Bedouins challenged me to a race. Either his dromedary was better than mine, or, what is at least as probable, he knew better how to urge its speed; but after galloping a mile or two I was obliged to yield. Indeed, three weeks' experience of the quieter paces of the dromedary are not at all a sufficient preparation for the jolts of its gallop: no motion can be compared to it but that of a ship in a storm; and the effort seems as laborious to the animal as it is inconvenient to its rider. The pace at which we have generally gone,.a sort of amble, is easy and far from disagreeable: the walk is uncomfortable, from the great length of the strides. In point of speed, travellers compare its trot to the gallop of a horse: I never saw them tried together; but I have often put the dromedary to a full trot, and the rate of going can hardly be less than nine or ten miles an hour. This pace is rather rough: it is used by the Arabs in flight or in pursuit; and there are accounts of their keeping it up for eight or ten days together, making

*3 D 2

not less than forty leagues a day. It is not uncommon for these
wonderful animals to go six or seven days without water, and with
scarcely any food : a handful or two of flour and water made into a
ball, or a few thistles, where the Desert produces them, are sufficient
for their support. They are very tractable and gentle : we guide them
either by a string fixed to a slit in the nose, or by a common halter.
When the caravan halts they obey a particular signal ; and crouching
upon the ground, with their legs bent under them, enable you to load
and unload them, and to get off and mount again without trouble.
The Arabs often ride them without any saddle : upon the baggage-
camels there is a sort of wooden frame, like a pack-saddle, which covers
the hump : smaller machines of the same kind were placed on ours,
and with the addition of cushions we had very tolerable seats.

At two we came to the beach opposite to Suez, which after the
scenes that we had been now for some time accustomed to, suggested
ideas almost of luxury. In half an hour a boat crossed over to us,
and took us in a few minutes back to human habitations, and the
business of common life. The Pasha was walking on the shore, surrounded by courtiers of many nations, Arabs, Turks, Copts, and
Armenians : he welcomed us with much good nature, and after joking
a little on our Turkish dresses, which we had put on for the journey
to Sinai, he told us to get a good supper, and be prepared to proceed
to Cairo to-morrow. His Italian physician, Mandrici, gave us wines
and many other things to which we have been long strangers ; and he
seems more rejoiced, even than ourselves, at the thoughts of leaving
Suez. Our Arabs and dromedaries forded the arm of the sea a little
higher up, but came here this evening.

Feb. 24. — The Pasha went on with a small escort on dromedaries,
not meaning to stop until he reaches Cairo. We found our horses
here, and abandoned our dromedaries, to the Arabs, the baggage,
and the servants. This is no longer severe travelling, and hard fare :
we are now in the midst of treasurers, and governors, and soldiers, and merchants who spread their Persian carpets, and feast
splendidly, and set the Desert at defiance. Besides these, two

Abyssinian ladies, who do not seem quite so much at their ease, excite great attention: they are carried together in a large wooden box on the back of a camel: the box sometimes loses its balance, and the distress of its unhappy prisoners is then proclaimed by their screams to the whole caravan. Their guards look fierce; and prohibit all approach: at night, too, when we encamped, the cage was not opened till their tent had been raised over it; and the ladies have not been visible during the whole journey. They are said to be the property of some rich Turk at Cairo. Abyssinian women are much admired in this part of the world; and though formerly Christians might purchase them, this privilege has lately been confined to the true believers. The faces of one or two whom I have seen were not disagreeable: their complexion is of the deepest bronze.

We have also with us some Arabs, coming, as we are told, from parts of the Desert to the westward, who have lately made alliances, or perhaps rather capitulations, with the Pasha: every thing about them indicates their belonging to rich and powerful tribes: their horses are beautiful; their arms of value; and their dress very different from that of any Bedouins we have yet seen. Their complexion is fair, and their manners courteous: they seem glad to talk to us, and speak of their having maintained an intercourse with the English when we occupied Egypt.

Feb. 25. — We set off at half-past five, and halted about eight to breakfast under some of the few wild acacias that are to be found between Suez and Cairo. I begin to suspect that our discipline in Arabia was pretty severe; at least the difference between this journey and that to Sinai strikes us more and more every instant. Our party was then small, and our baggage light; and from a sense of danger, or for the sake of company, we all kept together, making the best of our way, and stopping only when it was necessary to feed or rest. But now, besides our caravan of loaded camels, the line of whose march reaches sometimes above a mile, we have soldiers and rich Turks and Armenians on horseback, glittering in arms and silks, and giving to the Desert an appearance of any thing rather than its common soli-

tude and desolation.   Our own poor Bedouins are almost lost in the
midst of all this new finery.   We pitched our tents at four : Mandrici
invited us to sup with him ; and as our provisions were nearly
exhausted, the offer was most acceptable : his canteen is always
well filled ; and the Champagne soon led to a curious theological
controversy upon the comparative merits of the founders of the
Christian and Mahometan religions.   This was carried on between
our host and an Albanian chief, who had assumed the name of
Buonaparte : the Pasha's first dragoman made them intelligible to
each other, and at the same time to. us ; for Mandrici only under-
stands Italian.   It ended in their mutually professing an entire dis-
belief in either mode of faith ; and in vehement and incoherent
exclamations of blasphemy : this did not much surprise me on the
part of Mandrici ; but I had never before heard a Turk speak with so
little reserve of Mahomet.

Feb. 26. — We began our last day's march at half-past five.   I
happened to be for a little while this morning quite at the head of
the caravan ; and on coming to the brow of a hill saw an immense
herd of gazelles, or antelopes, close below me : they ran off instantly
in all directions.   When an Arab talks of the beauty of a woman, all
his comparisons are drawn from the gazelle : her eye is as large* and
as black ; her limbs as slender and her movements as graceful as the
gazelle's.   We had repeatedly seen these little animals in the desert ;
but never before very near us, or in great numbers.

Our beasts, unlike the dromedaries, were getting very faint, and
our stock of water was quite exhausted, when about twelve we reached
the plain irrigated by the Nile.   There was a rush of man and beast
towards the first reservoir of water: the horses plunged their heads
under ; and many men jumped at once into the tank.   The most
delicious wine is not to be compared to the first draught, after the

---

* " The moon has stolen her charms; and the antelope has borrowed the magic of her
eyes." — See Antar, p. 130., translated from the Arabic by Terrick Hamilton, Esq. — E.

dirty, brackish, and almost putrid water that we have been obliged to drink. The sight, too, of this delightful plain, covered with the brightest verdure, after our parched sands and barren rocks, excited a feeling of pleasure and joy that I never can forget. *

At two we were once more at the gates of Cairo: our own party here rallied round us. Awàtt led the way on his dromedary, shouting as if in triumph, and brandishing a huge pole to the terror of all who met him : he soon cleared the way for us through these narrow and crowded streets, and brought us safely to the Franciscan convent, where the friars, and Mr. Schutz, and our other friends, welcomed us with the greater cordiality, as there had been a report of our having perished in the Desert.

Our faithful guides and companions, the Arabs, soon came to take their leave of us : we tried in vain to persuade them to pass a day or two at Cairo ; but they all, at once, declared that the confinement of the houses and the town would be more than they could bear; and they are gone this very evening without the walls, to return instantly to their Deserts, and to resume their lives of fatigue and wandering, and unmolested liberty.

---

* The same feelings which the author has here described are expressed also by the late Mr. Davison, in the following passage of his manuscript-journey to Sinai : —
" Le dernier jour de notre voyage, en passant une montagne, nous decouvrimes avec une joie inexprimable, les heureuses plaines de l'Egypte ; dont la beauté, la fèrtilité, et les délices formoient un contraste le plus frappant avec le desert sec, sablonneux, et brulant, d'ou nous n'étions pas encore sortis. Le desir de quitter l'un fut aussi grand que l'envie d'atteindre l'autre. Nous n'avions plus la patience de rester en compagnie avec la caravane. Nous partîmes d'un consentement commun ; il sembloit que les drome-daires même prenoient part à notre plaisir. Ils oublioient leur fatigue, et paroissoient de ne faire que commencer un voyage. Ils couroient avec une vitesse que rien ne pouvoit égaler, excepté notre empressement d'arriver au Caire, pour boir un moment plus tôt de l'eau delicieuse du Nil. Nous avions une idée si extraordinaire de notre soif et de la quantité de l'eau qu'il falloit pour l'étancher, que nous nous felicitâmes que c'étoit le temps de l'inundation en Egypte ; comme si cela auroit pu faire quelque difference sensible. Nous arrivames enfin ; nous bumes quelques verres de cette eau charmante avec un plaisir, que ceux qui en boivent tous les jours ne sont guére en etat de concevoir."

ON A LAW OF CUSTOM

WHICH IS PECULIAR TO THE ISLANDS OF THE ARCHIPELAGO.

[*COMMUNICATED BY MR. HAWKINS.*]

In a well-known work of Mr. Guys, containing some original information respecting the manners and customs of the modern Greeks, we have the first intimation of a very singular custom which prevails in the island of Mytilin. It is to be found in the following passage of one of his letters: —

" Il y a dans l'Isle de Métélin, qui est l'ancien Lesbos, un usage bien extraordinaire, quoiqu'il ne soit peut-être pas destituè de raison, et qui pourroit provenir des Lesbiens. Toutes les propriétés et tous les immeubles appartiennent aux filles, et à la fille aînée; ce qui importe l'exhérédation des garçons. Comme dans le cours de mes voyages, je n'ai fait qu'aborder à cette Isle, et que je n'y ai pas fait de séjour, je n'ai pu vérifier le fait par moi-même. Mais on me l'a bien assuré, et le premier Météliniote que j'ai questionné sur celà, m'a dit que le fait étoit vrai, que cet usage étoit très-ancien, et que les garçons consentoient volontiers à tout céder à leurs sœurs, pour leur procurer de meilleurs établissemens. ' Ils pourroient,' ajoûtoit-il, ' s'ils vouloient, reclamer la loi Turque, qui admet tous les enfans au partage des biens paternels ou maternels ; mais ceux qui voudroient ainsi se soustraire à la loi du pays, seroient deshonorés.' "

No farther notice of this very remarkable fact seems to have been taken by any traveller, until the late Earl of Charlemont communicated to the Royal Irish Academy some particulars concerning it, which he had received on the spot from a gentleman who had long resided there as French Consul.

This report, drawn up by his Lordship rather in the form of an amusing narrative than as a plain statement of facts, is unfortunately so deficient in clearness and coherency, as to convey very little precise information, either respecting the custom itself, or the circumstances which are connected with it. By a comparison, however, of these two reports, the state of the case appears to be as follows : —

On the marriage of the eldest daughter, to which the parents have no right to refuse their consent, all the real property becomes vested in her ; and the other daughters, for want of a marriage-portion, are condemned to perpetual celibacy. Should the father, however, by his industry, acquire any more property of this description, a great part of it, if not the whole, must be given as a marriage-portion with the second daughter ; and so on in succession.

It appears by the testimony of both these travellers, that this is a custom of long standing, to which the minds of the natives are habitually reconciled; insomuch that there are few instances of any endeavour having been made to evade its operation by an appeal to the Turkish law.

The perusal of the two accounts above mentioned first directed my attention to this subject of enquiry, when I departed from England in 1793, on my second visit to the Levant. I felt anxious to learn how far this custom was peculiar to the island of Mytilin, and what circumstances, connected with it, had been omitted or disregarded by these travellers.

At the close of the year 1794 I had the good fortune to meet Mr. Guys, at Zante. The misfortunes of his country (Marseilles) had driven him, at an advanced age, to the Levant, where he had spent several years of his early life ; and he had immediately availed himself of the advantage thus afforded by his situation, to resume his former enquiries. I was pleased to see the lively interest with which he pursued this object, and the judicious use which he designed to make of the various information he obtained. Our conversation often turned on the singular custom of Mytilin, which he had first made known to the public, and I promised to communicate to him what farther particulars concerning it, I might have the good fortune to collect.

Accordingly, at the close of the year 1797, I transmitted to Mr. Guys, as the result of those enquiries which it had been in my power to make ; that in a large proportion of the islands of the Archipelago, the eldest daughter takes, as her marriage-portion, the family-house, together with all its furniture, and one-third, or a larger share of the maternal property ; which, in reality, in most of these islands, constitutes the chief means of subsistence. That the other daughters, as they marry off in succession, are likewise entitled to the family-house then in occupation ; and the same share of whatever property remains. Finally, that these observations were applicable to the islands of Mytilin, Lemnos, Scópelo, Skyros, Syra, Zea, Ipsera, Mýconi, Paros, Náxia, Siphno, Santoríni, and Cos ; where I had either collected my information in person, or had obtained it through others.

As the subject is so interesting, I shall here literally transcribe the notes from which the above information was compiled. To begin with Mytilin, which is divided into two dioceses. In the diocese of Methymnæ, which extends over the southern half of the island, the antient usage is preserved ; the eldest daughter, whenever she pleases to marry, taking possession of the family-house and furniture, together with all the family-property. But in the diocese of Mytilin, the natives have been prevailed on, by the present bishop, to adopt some modifications, which mitigate the evils occasioned by this singular usage ; and the rule, as it is now established, is as follows : — If the family-property be valued at more than 1000 piastres, (equivalent in 1797 to about 80l.) the eldest daughter's marriage-portion is one-third of the amount, and the second daughter's portion one-third of the remainder ; and so on, if there be more daughters ; the eldest having the choice of her third, and being allowed to take something more. As for the sons, they have a right to nothing, and the remaining property may be bequeathed in whatever manner the father pleases.

In Paros, the eldest daughter, when she marries, takes possession of the family-house, and one-half, or nearly that proportion, of all the family-property. The other daughters divide the remainder as they marry; leaving a small part to the father, mother, and brothers.

In Naxia, the daughters, when they marry, take the property of the mother, and the sons inherit that of the father; but the eldest daughter, who is always stiled Kura, Mistress, (Κυρα, a corruption of Κυρα,) by her brothers and sisters, takes the family-house, and a much larger portion than the others; leaving however, to the parents what is sufficient for their subsistence, under the title of Γεροντομοιρι.

· In Siphno, the eldest unmarried daughter marries first, and takes the family-house, together with a considerable portion of the property; after which the next unmarried does the same.

In Skyros, the eldest daughter, when she marries, is entitled by the law of custom, to a considerable portion of the family-property.

In Santorin, she is distinguished by her superior dower, but is not always entitled to the paternal house.

In Lemnos, each daughter in succession, when she marries, takes the family-house.

In Scopelo, Syra, and Ipsera, every daughter in succession, has a right to a house, as her marriage-portion. In Scopelo, the eldest takes when she marries, not only the family-house, and all its furniture; but the whole of the maternal property: and if the son-in-law prove avaricious, which is sometimes the case, and there is no other property in the family, the parents are stripped of every thing.

No custom of this kind prevails either at Tinos, Andros, Miconi, or Zea. It is equally unknown at Hydria, Spezze, and Poros, which are peopled with Albanians of the Greek ritual.

My information extends no farther. I lament that it is, upon the whole, neither so precise nor so circumstantial as I could wish; and I still feel how much remains to be supplied by the industry of future travellers. Imperfect, however, as it is, no doubt can remain of the

396 REMARKABLE CUSTOM PREVALENT

existence of this very singular custom in a great many, if not in most, of the islands of the Archipelago, under various modifications; and of its having long prevailed there.

Here, then, two questions naturally arise:—Have the islanders derived this singular usage from some parent-stock of high antiquity, as both Mr. Guys and Lord Charlemont suppose? or is there any thing in the circumstances of their situation, which may have suggested the expediency of its adoption?

In respect to the first head of enquiry, Mr. Guys endeavours to account for the origin of this custom, by recurring to the period of a particular event of the Peloponnesian war; and by supposing that the female part of the population, upon that occasion, were spared by the Athenians, when the males were all massacred; and, lastly, that the females married the new settlers, with the view of securing the possession of the family-property. This, to say the least of it, is but a weak attempt to prove the antiquity of this custom; and scarcely merits the notice which Lord Charlemont has bestowed upon it. Let us see, however, whether his Lordship is more happy in his conjectures.

Three quotations are brought forward by him from Herodotus, Plutarch, and Nicolaus Damascenus, to prove that something of this sort prevailed among the Lycians. According to the two former writers, " The Lycians are called after the names of their mothers, not of their fathers;" according to the latter, " Among the Lycians, the women are regarded with more respect than the men, who are, moreover, distinguished by the names of their mothers; *the property, too, is inherited by the daughters, and not by the sons.*" * The circumstance here last mentioned is the only one which bears directly upon the subject before

---

* Λύκιοι τὰς γυναῖκας μᾶλλον ἢ τὰς ἄνδρας Ἰιμῶσι, ἢ καλᾶνlαι μηlρόθεν· τὰς δε κληρονο-μίας ταις θυγαlράσι λείπᾶσιν, ᾗ τοῖς υἱοῖς. — Nicolaus Damascenus de Moribus Græcorum.

To these authorities may be added that of Heraclides Ponticus, de Politiis Græcorum: Λύκιοι διῆγον ληςεύοντες. Νόμοις οὐ χρῶνlαι ἀλλ᾽ ἔθεσι, και εκ παλαιοῦ γυναικοκραlοῦνlαι. See the note on this passage by the late editor Köhler.

us; and this his Lordship says he at first laid hold of, supposing it possible that some colony might in latter ages have passed over from Lycia to Lesbos, and there have established the custom here spoken of. This supposition, however, being too gratuitous, he has recourse to a passage in Diodorus, which he thinks will go a great way in confirming it. We are told, says he, by Diodorus, that the Pelasgi, who under their leader Xanthus, the son of Triopas king of Argos, first inhabited Lesbos, had previous to their settlement in that island, dwelt for some time in a certain part of Lycia which they had conquered. Now, says he, these Pelasgi may be supposed to have brought hither the usage in question. After this attempt to prove its remote antiquity, which makes even his Lordship smile, as well as his readers; no farther stress is laid on this hypothesis than it deserves: it is termed only " a possible way of accounting for a thing," or, " it may have so happened." Had his Lordship been able to prove the existence of such a custom in Lycia, even so late as the time of the Romans, we might have some hopes of being able to trace its transmission to the islands of the Ægean: for I should here observe, that both Plutarch and Nicolaus Damascenus were merely transcribers and compilers from works of a much older date. Instead of this obvious course, we are at once carried a thousand years still farther back, to the time of the Pelasgian invasion of Lesbos; or, in other words, one difficulty is brought forward to remove another; for if we can suppose that this usage had subsisted from so remote a period in Lesbos, how is it, that neither the three writers above quoted, when they speak of some remarkable usages in Lycia, which bear some analogy to this, should have noticed it, nor that any other writer of antiquity should even have hinted at its existence; when it is well known that most of these writers, especially Plutarch, who treats expressly of the character of the female sex, were fond of noticing every thing that was remarkable in the civil institutions, manners, and customs of different nations. The legitimate inference from all which, is, that the usage here in question did not exist in antient times.

But if we are unable to trace up this singular usage to a period antecedent to the establishment of Christianity, the question may be fairly asked, How can it have originated since? for it is certain that the Justinian Code admits of no modification of the law of succession, which is favourable to such a policy. To remove this difficulty, we must have recourse to the supposition that some method was devised of evading the written law, by substituting a customary one; and I find in the Theodosian Code, (lib. v. tit. xii.) that a long established custom, which was not contrary to the good of the public, was allowed to have the force of law. *

The enquiry into the origin of this custom being thus confined to modern times, and there being no events in the political history of these islands, either during the middle ages or subsequently, which can possibly account for it; it remains for us to ascertain whether there are any peculiar circumstances in the state of society here, which may have suggested the expediency of its adoption.

The obvious tendency of such a customary law, is to prevent the farther partition or accumulation of landed property; but in order fully to comprehend the object of such a permanent restraint on its disposal, it will be necessary to take a view of the natural advantages and disadvantages of these islands.

I shall observe then, in the first place, that these islands are, for the most part, of so limited an extent, that the inhabitants occupy only a single town or village; from whence they visit every day their little farms, or rather plots of vineyards and arable ground. In the next place, that the proportion of arable ground and of vineyards, or of ground adapted to these purposes, is extremely small; the surface of the country being in general so rocky and uneven as to admit of a very thin covering of vegetable mould. Many of the smaller islands have not even the smallest portion of level ground, except that which has been

---

* " Venientium est temporum disciplina instare.veteribus institutis. Ideoque cum nihil per causam publicam intervenit, quæ diu servata sunt, permanebunt."

Interpretatio. Longa consuetudo, quæ utilitates publicas non impedit, pro lege ser-vabitur. .

shaped, by the labour of the inhabitants, into terraces, and is supported by stone walls. The agricultural labours, therefore, of these people are carried on under every possible disadvantage; and their scanty crops, in this dry climate,'make a miserable return for their unwearied industry. To these observations may be added, that little or no wheat is grown in theArchipelago. The bread of the islanders is made of barley; and the remainder of their food consists of pulse and of dried figs: for the more choice articles of food which are obtained here, such as cheese, honey, and wine, must be disposed of to pay the poll-tax, and other government-impositions.

Under these circumstances, it is evident that there can be no such thing as revenue in the shape of rent; and that each spot of arable ground can be cultivated with effect only by its actual proprietor. Here, then, if we except the class of merchants and navigators, all the male inhabitants are necessarily cultivators; and, from the nature of their local circumstances, the majority of them can be occupiers only of as much ground as they can cultivate. It follows, that each portion must be well cultivated, or it would produce nothing, and thus no resource would be left for the discharge of the very heavy pecuniary impositions which are laid upon it; and this, perhaps, will account for the exclusion of the males, above a certain age, from the occupation of land, which is the virtual consequence of the customary law above mentioned.

If, under this view of all the circumstances of their situation, we admit the expediency of fixing the size and extent of each portion of landed property, on the first settlement of an island; the quantity of land so fixed, must be regulated by a calculation of what is sufficient for the decent maintenance of each family, and at the same time for raising as much surplus produce as would discharge the public burdens imposed on it. This quantity being once ascertained and fixed, the population of the island will be regulated by it; and the excess will be under the necessity of migrating, and colonizing on the same principles other islands; until all are inhabited and cultivated. When this however is accomplished, and there are no more unoccupied islands, the supernumeraries must necessarily betake themselves to other modes of industry ; as is actually the case. Numbers of these, in fact, become navigators and merchants : many of both sexes migrate to Constantinople, Smyrna, and Salonica, where they are usually employed in the capacity of menial servants ; and no small proportion of these supernumeraries devote themselves to religion and celibacy.

This mode of accounting for the usage in question, will appear more clear and satisfactory, if we reverse the hypothetical case upon which I have argued. Let us suppose, then, that no restraints whatever have been laid on the disposal of landed property in these islands ; which property is become, in process of time, as unequally partitioned, as it is in other countries ; that is, some of the inhabitants have much more than they can personally cultivate, many less than they can cultivate, and many none at all. In this case, we will admit that the possessions of the great proprietors may be cultivated by the hired assistance of the two other classes : the burden of the territorial impositions being borne by the land-owners, while the poll-tax, with some variation, falls upon all the inhabitants. The result of this state of things must be, first, the same numerical population, although of a very different character ; a few only of the inhabitants being at their ease, without being rich ; but by far the greater part in extreme indigence. Secondly, a very inferior produce; for the soil, under all these circumstances, cannot possibly be so well cultivated : to explain which, it will be proper for me to observe, that in the system of agriculture which alone is practicable here, the hoe, the shovel, and the pruning-hook are much more operative instruments than the plough. In short, the partition of property in such a country as this, seems to be absolutely necessary to its perfect cultivation. The principal articles of produce are, barley, various sorts of pulse, gourds, cotton, silk, wine, figs, a few olives and almonds, honey, and goats' cheese ; all of which are obtained from the cultivation of small portions of land, dispersed over the whole surface of this hilly country, and lying, for the most part, at a great distance from the dwellings of their occupiers. In all the smaller islands, as I have already remarked, the population is assembled in a single town or village, although this town is not always placed in the most central and convenient situation, and sometimes, for its greater security, at one end of the island.

I have here treated the subject purely as a question of political economy, and have given what I conceive to be the most easy and obvious solution of it. But I must again observe, that the introduction and adoption of such an Agrarian law, whether under a heathen or a christian government, can be supposed only to have taken place at the period when each island was newly colonized. In the natural course of events, it must have been transplanted from one island to another by the new settlers, and as, in the infancy of each colony, it was found to be peculiarly well adapted to all the circumstances of their new situation, it must have gradually acquired the force of habit before the natives began to feel its inconveniences. I suspect, therefore, that the more liberal form under which this customary law now appears, in most of the instances which I have cited, has been merely the result of such a feeling.

The history of the Archipelago affords sufficient authority for the supposition that most of these islands have been at some period deserted, and at other times gradually re-peopled. We know that, during a long interval, they were exposed to the depredations of the Saracens, who were succeeded by the Turkish pirates of Pfokia. At length, after the conquest of Constantinople by the Latins, all the larger islands were separately taken possession of by Italian and Catalonian adventurers. These petty sovereigns were finally expelled in the years 1537 and 1538, by Barbarossa. The islands have been subsequently exposed to the insolent rapacity of the Maltese cruisers, and in all the wars between the Turks and the Venetians they have suffered from the alternate exactions of both powers.

Whatever may be the judgment of my readers as to the origin of this Agrarian law, if I may so call it, and as to the period of its introduction, it must be generally admitted that it has derived its existence solely from local causes, some of which are perhaps still uninvestigated. I shall, therefore, conclude with noticing a curious fact, which may be thought to have operated in conjunction with those already mentioned, in producing it. Travellers, from the beginning of the fifteenth century to the present time, concur in remarking, that the female population, in a great many of these islands, is much greater than the male; and, as far as my enquiries extended, a much greater number of female than of male children are born here.

THE LABYRINTH OF CRETE.

[*COMMUNICATED BY MR. COCKERELL.*]

AMONG the antient writers who have mentioned the Labyrinth of Crete, none have given the description of an eye-witness; on the other hand, of the modern travellers who have published their observations upon the same island, Tournefort is the only one who has given a detailed description of that remarkable cavern, at the foot of Mount Ida, and near the site of the antient Gortys, which the modern Cretans suppose to have been the Labyrinth.

Although some reasonable doubt may continue to exist as to the identity of this cavern, we are surprised, that its singularity, and apparent antiquity, combined with the extreme interest attached to a work so celebrated by the antients as the Labyrinth of Crete, have not excited in a greater degree the curiosity of travellers as to the existing excavation.

There is nothing that renders our curiosity upon this subject more reasonable than the unanimity of the antient writers upon the subject of the Labyrinth : they all agree that it was formed by a king, named Minos, who lived several centuries before the Trojan war ; and that the artist was an Athenian, named Dædalus, on his return from Egypt, full of the information derived from the contemplation of the wonderful works of that country.

Hence we cannot help entertaining a hope of finding, in the Labyrinth of Crete, some marks of the earliest imitation, by the Greeks, of the works of that country to which they were indebted for so large a proportion of their Mythology and sacred Architecture ; and it was this sentiment that formed one of my strongest motives for visiting that island, and in particular the place which is still known by the name of the Labyrinth.

We had been detained nearly a month at the capital of Candia, when, with some difficulty, we obtained permission to visit the Labyrinth. The confinement and caution to which we had been obliged to submit, by the jealous and lawless character of the Turkish militia, and by the ceremonious hospitalities of the higher orders, rendered this permission as grateful as our stay had been irksome.

It appeared to us that the disposition of the Turks of this island, so much more savage than in the rest of Greece, had been in a great measure occasioned, or at least strengthened, by the late *French* and *English* expeditions to Egypt. The alarm which these had excited, the reflection on their distance from the capital, and the wretched state of their fortifications, served to increase their apprehensions, and render them particularly averse to the sight of Europeans. We found also among them a ferocious recollection of their long and destructive contest with the Venetians, in an island which was called the grave of the Mussulmauns.

We were easily provided with an escort of Janissaries, from the town of Candia to the Labyrinth ; for they were glad enough to take advantage of the *boyourdi* or passport of the Vizier, to regale themselves at the expense of the unfortunate Greeks ; and, in order to prolong this privilege, we were conducted by a circuitous route of two days, to perform a journey of not more than twenty miles.

We were, however, repaid for this deviation from the direct road by passing over some ruins, which, by the correspondence of the site

3 F 2

with the description of Strabo, we could not doubt must have belonged to the city of Cnossus. At the distance of about three miles
(south-east) from the city of Candia, and at about two miles from the
sea-shore, we found the remains of some antient constructions in the
plain; and along the side of the road, which then led us southward
into some rocky passes, we observed a vast number of catacombs,
which we considered as a confirmation of our conjecture.

Our journey, during the first day, lay through a rocky country, intersected by small plains, naturally fertile, and formerly interspersed
with villages which are now decayed. Early in the second day we
entered the plain of Messaria, the most productive in the island; but
we did not find the country by any means so picturesque as the
scenery we had passed in a former journey, in our road from Canea
to Candia, at the foot of the Sphachiot mountains.

At Agio Deka, which is situated very near the antient Gortys, we
procured guides. Upon the site of the city we observed the ruins of a
theatre, and some other inconsiderable remains; but we found nothing
which could engage us to delay our progress towards the Labyrinth.
We crossed the side of a mountain which forms one of the roots of
Mount Ida; and at the distance of about three miles from Agio Deka
we ascended the steep hill in which the mouth of the excavation is
found. This entrance is not distinguished by any remarkable appearance, and we should easily have passed it as an ordinary cavern.

We examined the surrounding declivity, but could not find the
smallest vestiges of any building which might have been attached to
it; nor indeed would the site have admitted of any such works. The
opening, which is low, and encumbered with earth and fallen fragments, leads by a descent into a double vestibule, which is about 25
feet broad, and 45 feet long; from thence four door-ways conduct into
the interior of the excavation, of which, however, that on the right
hand only is penetrable. Here we established a trusty guard to secure the end of a clue; a precaution, as necessary, as it was classical.

We then proceeded in our examination, each holding his torch, and
our guide always taking every turning to the right. We made the

LABYRINTH OF CRETE.

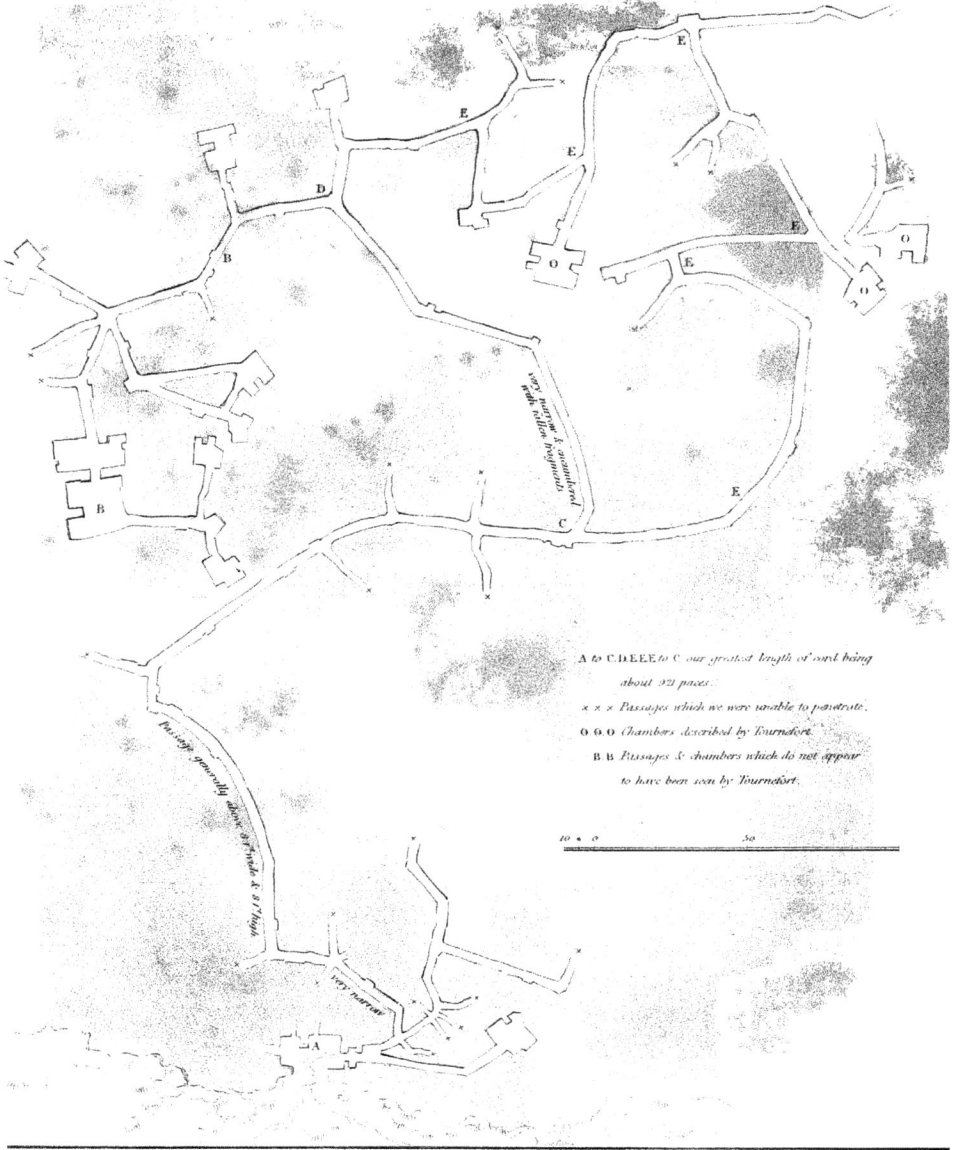

A to C.D.E.E.E to C our greatest length of cord being
about 921 paces.

x x x Passages which we were unable to penetrate.

O. O. O Chambers described by Tournefort.

B. B. Passages & chambers which do not appear
to have been seen by Tournefort.

10 . 0   50

circuit of the first chamber, and of the adjoining passages, till we arrived at that which conducted to the interior: this we found extremely low and narrow, and for some paces we were obliged to crawl on our hands and knees*; but we soon reached the principal way, which is about eight feet wide and as many in height: this we pursued. for some distance without interruption. On the sides we·observed the stones cut into convenient sizes, as if for the purposes of building, and ranged in a careful order; but in the pavement, or path, which is nearly on a level throughout the excavation,.we could not discover any tracks of wheels.

It occurred to us that the intention of the Labyrinth might have been sepulchral; and that in imitation (in some degree) of the Egyptian works, its winding passages might have been designed to protect the bodies deposited in the remote chambers from violation, more effectually than could be done even by the immense masses of the pyramids, or the long passages of the tombs of. the kings at Thebes; we were therefore careful in searching for any vestiges of sarcophagi, or of niches for the reception of coffins; but we could not discover any remains whatever of this kind.

We did not leave a single passage, of those which are still penetrable, unexplored; but we found the greater part of them stopped up by the falling ceiling, or with fragments of stone thrown in; and considering their number †, and that besides, the three principal entrances from the vestibule, are now quite impervious, it may be presumed, a small portion only (although in the whole length and winding of the passages nearly three quarters of a mile) is now accessible.

The designed irregularity of the passages quickly bewilders the traveller in its·present state; but were they all open, the task of un-

---

* Tournefort considers the narrowness of this passage a strong argument against the opinion of Belon and others, that this excavation was a quarry, from the impossibility of drawing any quantity of stone through it; but an observation of the plan will show at ‾once that it was merely a communication between the passages which lead to the entrance, either for ventilation, or to increase the intricacy.

† See the plan.

ravelling the maze would indeed be one of serious difficulty. Three or four door-ways seem often presented to confuse the traveller, and so to bewilder the recollection, by the frequent turnings, as to make it quite impossible to retrace his steps with any certainty.

In proceeding to the part termed Trapezi by the Greeks, and which they consider the most remote chamber, we were sometimes obliged to make our way again on our hands and knees : here we found many Italian names, and some of our own countrymen. There is also a small spring here, and the water that exudes from the rock produces a kind of fungus ; but the chambers are generally remarkably dry : they are considerably higher than the passages, and piers are judiciously left in them to secure the impending rock. In one of these we were much inconvenienced by the number of bats put in motion by the explosion of a pistol, and we had nearly extinguished our lights in the confusion.

In the course of our walk we were a good deal alarmed by the loss of one of our companions, a mad Greek *, who had wandered into one of the passages unperceived, and as our guides declared that there was no termination to the passage, we were in considerable anxiety for some time ; we at length, however, found him in one of the most distant chambers.

At the place marked c in the plan, we were surprised to discover our clue again, not having been aware of the circuit we had been making ; we however followed it until we came to a passage we had left unexplored, and which conducted us to several chambers which I have reason to believe were not seen by Tournefort, or the generality of travellers.

We did not, however, find any difference in the style and manner of the excavation, nor any thing which could in the least convey to us a clear conception of its original intention.

---

* In Turkey, lunatics are treated with a superstitious regard, and when they are harmless they are allowed to go about freely. This poor fellow, attracted, as he assured us, by the likeness of two of our party to St. Michael and St. George, had ran beside our horses all the way from Candia.

We returned, not unwillingly, to the open air, after nearly four hours passed in exploring these passages, sometimes crawling with difficulty along the floor, incumbered with fragments, and always in apprehension of falling into holes, or over the blocks of stone, which in some places are lying on the floor. The object of this excavation is still a matter of conjecture; but the quality of the rock, which is a sandy freestone, very easily cut, and perfectly adequate to the common purposes of building, added to the vicinity of the place to Gortys, inclined us to the opinion that it had served the purposes also of a quarry during the foundation of the city of Gortys; and that the long passages and mazes of this singular form had been given as a secondary object, either for the concealment of property or the security of prisoners. Examples of this combination of purposes occur, both of antient and modern date.

Such are the cemeteries or necropolis of Syracuse, the quarries of Latomiæ; and the Ear of Dionysius, in the same place; the excavations at Agrigentum, Malta, Paris, and one in Maestricht of very considerable extent, which much resembles the Labyrinth of Crete.

Tournefort has supposed it to be a natural cavern, made practicable for the purpose of concealment, or as a place of refuge in times of persecution; but an excavation of this extent would hardly be undertaken for a temporary object; besides, the nature of the rock is such as furnishes no instance of extensive natural caverns; these, if I am rightly informed, are never found but in rocks of calcareous formation.

Whatever may have been the manner in which it was constructed, I am inclined to think that it is the identical Labyrinth alluded to in the writings of antiquity.

I may be allowed perhaps to state a few reasons for this opinion. It must be admitted, indeed, that Strabo and Pausanias* are decidedly adverse to it: they agree in saying that the Cretan Labyrinth was not at Gortys, but at Cnossus; and the evidence of Herodotus

---

* Strabo, lib. x. p. 476. Paus. lib. i. c. 27.

also, who describes the Labyrinth of Egypt as a building, together with that of Pliny *, who compares the Labyrinth of Crete with that of Egypt, tend in some measure to confirm the supposition, that the cavern near the ruins of Gortys was not the Cretan Labyrinth. The observation, too, of Diodorus Siculus †, that not a vestige of the Cretan Labyrinth ·remained in his time, seems more applicable to a building than an excavation in the rock. On the other hand, we find that the Greek word " Labyrinth" was not exclusively employed to signify a building; for Strabo ‡ applies it to some caverns near Nauplia. It is impossible, moreover, for the traveller who has been bewildered in the mazes of the Gortynian cavern, and who has experienced the absolute necessity of a clue to guide him through its windings, not to admit that it is admirably adapted to the Athenian tale of Theseus, released from the Labyrinth by means of a clue supplied to him by Ariadne; while, on the other hand, such a tale seems hardly admissible when applied to a building above ground. Unless, therefore, there was a similar one at Cnossus, it is difficult to believe that the cavern near Agio Deka was not the reputed scene of this story.

We know from Homer, that although Minos, who confined Dædalus and Theseus in the Labyrinth, had his residence at Cnossus, or at least that Cnossus was his foundation, and one of his favourite cities, yet it is evident, likewise, that his dominion extended over the greatest part of Crete, and must certainly have comprised Gortys, which was only twenty miles distant from Cnossus, and which did not become an independent republic, and a rival of Cnossus, until after the extinction of the regal family of Minos. The placing of the Labyrinth at Cnossus, therefore, by Strabo and Pausanias, may have been an error, arising from the circumstances of the king, to whom it belonged, having his residence there; or merely because that city had been called by Homer " the Minosian Cnossus."

---

* He remarks that the Labyrinth of Crete was not a hundredth part of that in Egypt. Lib. xxxvi. c. 13, 14.

† Diod. Sic. lib. i. c. 61.   ‡ Lib. viii. p. 369.

Soon after the age of Strabo and Pausanias it appears to have been equally the custom to suppose Minos to have been the ruler of *Gortys*. Statius calls Minos *Gortynius arbiter*, and Catullus places the scene of the adventure of Theseus, not at Gnossus, but at *Gortys*.

We trace the same opinion prevailing in the 11th and 12th centuries; for Cedrenus describes the place where Theseus was delivered by the clue of Ariadne, as a cavern near Gortys; and Eustathius gives his testimony as to Gortys being the situation of the Labyrinth. Here also the local tradition still continues to place it.

If, therefore, the authorities in the time of the Roman Empire are in discordance as to the position of a place, which is stated by one of them to be no longer in existence, we are the more justified in referring solely to the testimony contained in the story of Theseus and Ariadne, the circumstances of which have such a perfect agreement with the singular excavation still existing near the ruins of Gortys; the extreme antiquity of this excavation can hardly be doubted; and that of the tale of Theseus and Ariadne is equally evident, from its being found designed upon so many antient vases, and from its having been related or sung by most of the early writers.

ON THE SCULPTURES OF THE PARTHENON.

[COMMUNICATED BY MR. WILKINS.]

Pausanias, to whom we are indebted for a variety of information relating to Grecian art, has contented himself with offering a few scanty remarks on one of the noblest productions of the most enlightened age of Greece. His architectural notices, indeed, are every where superficial, but his descriptions of statues and paintings frequently extend to the minutiæ of the composition.

His neglecting the opportunity of signalising the sculptures of the

Parthenon, has been by some attributed to the celebrity of the subjects he so carelessly mentions ; all information relating to them being supposed in the possession, not only of the people amongst whom these objects of admiration were preserved, but of Greece at large.

Such an assumption is wholly inadmissible, so long as analogy is allowed to be one of the tests of fair criticism ; for, laying aside all consideration as to the improbability of a traveller suppressing, in his narrative, all mention of the *chefs-d'œuvre* of the country he visits, merely because these productions and their authors were universally known, we must, in order to admit of the argument, be satisfied that in thus abstaining from eulogy, he was acting upon a general system of silence, in all cases where the celebrity of the object seemed to render description unnecessary.

Numberless instances might be adduced, in proof of the observance of a principle diametrically opposite ; it will be sufficient to mention one ; where, if description could ever be dispensed with on account of the celebrity of the subject, an occasion presented itself—the statue of Jupiter at Olympia ! This most celebrated of the productions of Phidias, the importance of which entitled it to be ranked amongst the wonders of the world, situated in a part of Greece more resorted to than any other spot, is mentioned with all the minuteness of professional description.

The only notice taken by the Grecian traveller of the sculptures adorning the two pediments of the Parthenon, relates to the subjects of the compositions ; if, therefore, any inference is to be deduced from the total absence of remark, either as to the design or execution, it would be more rational to conclude, that, however estimable they appear in the eyes of modern criticism, they excited no strong sensation in the mind of the writer accustomed to the contemplation of works of higher pretensions. What a vast idea of the excellence of Grecian sculpture is conveyed by admitting the existence of such transcendant specimens of the art ! These, indeed, called forth descriptions, not only of the principal features, but of their less important accessories. The short passage in which allusion is made to the sculp-

...s from the ...
...l of Lysicrates.

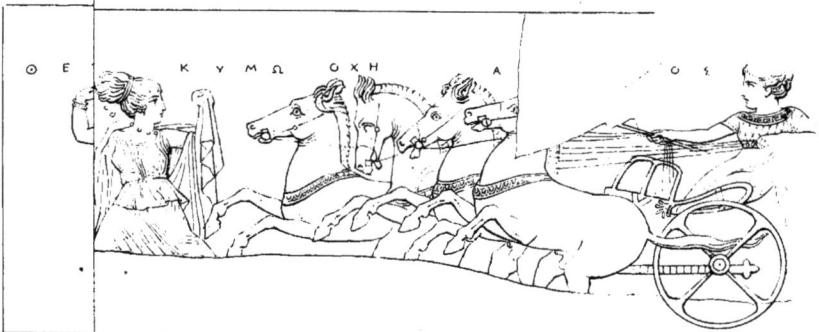

ATHENIAN VASE.

tures in question, furnishes us, however, with a circumstance of some interest — the subjects considered by the Athenians appropriate for the embellishment of this their splendid and noblest temple. " On entering the temple called Parthenon," says Pausanias, " all the circumstances relating to the birth of Minerva occupy the part called the pediment: the rear of the temple displays the contest between Neptune and Minerva for Attica."

Those who have contended that the Athenians regarded, as the entrance of the temple, the front which first presented itself to a spectator on entering the acropolis through the Propylæa, argue in manifest contradiction to the religious observances of the Athenians * ; exemplified in all the other temples of Athens, and particularly in the Erectheum upon the citadel itself.

The entrance into the acropolis was determined by circumstances admitting no alternative. A rock, accessible on one side only, left the projectors of the Propylæa no option as to site, and we enter at the west end. The Parthenon is on our right; and the Erectheum, which lies less out of a direct line drawn from west to east, is on the left. The western fronts of both buildings, therefore, are those more immediately facing us. If, on this account, the eastern front of the Parthenon, from the impossibility of approaching the acropolis at this end, were to be considered as the ὄπισθεν of Pausanias, the same law of necessity must lead us to regard the western end of the Erectheum as the front, properly so called. The plan of the building presents an unanswerable argument in opposition to such an inference — there are three entrances; the west end alone is closed ! †

---

* Πρὸς ἑω τῶν ἱερῶν βλεπόντων. Plut. in vit. Num. 14. The golden shields which Lachares removed fiom the acropolis, were those suspended over the columns in the front of the temple. We know that they were fastened to the Epistylia of the *eastern* front only. The holes recceiving the cramps still remain, and the whole of the area covered by the circular surface of the shields is stiongly marked in the marble.

† There are certainly traces of a narrow aperture also in the west front, in the χρηπις, or plinth, suppoiting the semi-columns; but it appears to have served some temporary purpose, and to have been closed when the building was finished. It was without any architectural decoration, made, without any regard to symmetry, *immediately under* one of the semi-columns.

If any.doubts could reasonably exist as to which was really the principal front of the Parthenon, the drawings by Nointell, of the groups in the pediments, made previously to the Venetian bombardment in 1687, would, by illustrating the observations of Pausanias, be sufficient to dispel them. These drawings, although taken from a disadvantageous and distant point of view, convey a tolerable idea of the whole composition. In some particulars they are erroneous, but the general forms are verified by such of the statues as escaped total destruction during the siege of Athens, which took place about fifteen years after the visit of Nointell.

The two principals in the contest represented in the western pediment, are obviously Neptune and Minerva ; the latter is identified by the ægis, which, in one of the drawings alluded to, is decidedly marked : a fragment of it was recently found in digging below the steps of this front. The figure of Neptune was long regarded by the early writers on the subject of the Athenian temples, who supposed the west end to be the ἔμπροσθεν, as representing Jupiter. Where Wheler supposes the eagle of Jove to have been between the legs of this figure, there was, in fact, the trunk of the olive produced by Minerva in the contention * : a large fragment of it with the feet of the figure, considerably worn by time and accident, is preserved in the British Museum. † The action of Neptune, in opposition to the quiescent Jupiter, in *bas reliefs* representing the birth of Minerva ‡,

---

* In all speculations on the subject of the Athenian remains, we should do well to lay wholly aside the glaring absurdities and blunders of Wheler and Spon. First, conjectures on every subject not admitting of direct proof, are readily accepted : a dissent from them must be supported by argument, which nine-tenths of mankind are too indolent to examine. The hasty opinions of these travellers have involved the subject of Athenian antiquities in difficulties. Chandler and Stuart suffered themselves to be misled by those who preceded them. In their discussions, truth is perpetually struggling against the force of received opinions.

† This fragment is usually viewed, not as it was placed in the pediment, but with the inner side outward. It is not the only piece of the Elgin collection in which the finish all around has led to a similar error of position.

‡ Millin. Gal. Mytholog. plates 36, 37.

pourtrays the whole energies of the Divinity called forth by the nature of the contest.

The other groups, not so immediately recognizable, have given birth to many opinions as to what personages of the heathen mythology they were intended to represent. Names, indeed, have been given to all; but they are supplied from conjecture only, which in most instances has not been happily exercised.

In the description of some of the temples of antiquity, such, for instance, as that of Jupiter at Olympia, we cannot fail to be struck with the architectural symmetry observed in the respective groups in the pediments, in the right and left divisions of the tympanum. We have

Pelops,	opposed to	Oenomaus,
Hippodamia, the wife of Pelops		Sterope, the consort of Oenomaus,
The charioteer of Pelops, supposed to be Sphærus,		Myrtillus, the charioteer of his competitor,
Horses and car of Pelops,		the car and four horses of Oenomaus,
Two grooms of Pelops,		two grooms of his rival,
River Alpheus,		the river Cladeus.

In the two pediments of the temple of Jupiter-Panhellenius at Ægina, recently published in a periodical work *, we have similar examples, of almost perfect equilibrium, preserved in the arrangement of the groups.

How far this formality prevailed in the eastern pediment of the Parthenon we have no means of deciding; the groups remaining appear to have been placed in something like conformity with this practice. Thus we have the chariot and horses of the morn opposed to the equipage of night: the reposing Bacchus †, or Theseus, as

---

* Journal of Science and the Arts, No. 12.

† It is an ascertained fact, that in the statues and bas-reliefs of the deities, the Grecian sculptors frequently followed some one great and celebrated model, with little variation of

this statue has been denominated, and the adjoining group, balance the two sitting figures and the reclining third in corresponding parts of the pediment.

In the west front, this severity of composition seems to have been in great measure abandoned ; nothing appears by way of *pendant* to the figure borne in a chariot, which has hitherto been conjectured to represent Victory conducting the car of Minerva ; unless Amphitrite, in a marine car drawn by dolphins, formerly occupied a larger space on the right of Neptune than Nointell's drawing leads us to imagine. The remaining groups, on the right and left of the principal figures, are more nearly corresponding in attitude and position, making all necessary allowance for the inaccuracy of proportion observable in the production of Nointell's draughtsman.

This abandonment of symmetrical arrangement in the composition admits of a nearer approach to graphical representation, where greater latitude was observed. The comparison, therefore, with an early painting, representing the same subject, may be supposed to offer greater coincidences than would occur where the severities of art prevailed.

A vase of terra-cotta, found in pursuing some excavations immediately under the walls of Athens, was brought to England by Mr. Graham, and is now in the possession of Dr. Edward Clarke of Cambridge. The subject of the representation painted upon it was one predominant in the thoughts of the Athenian people ; proud of the patronage of Minerva, and inhabiting a spot consecrated to this favorite deity. The names being written over the several *dramatis personæ*, afford an illustration of the personages employed in, or spectators of, the fabled contention. The vase was broken into several pieces, and some fragments are wanting, but enough remains for the purposes of elucidation. *

---

attitude. A great coincidence of posture and action may be remarked between the Theseus of the Elgin collection, and the Bacchus on the frize of the monument of Lysicrates : whence I venture to suppose the former to be intended for this divinity.

* The inscriptions were in letters of gold. A recent experiment to unite the several pieces, filling the interior with plaister of Paris, caused the gilding to disappear, and almost

In the centre of the painting are Neptune and Minerva; the latter has not recovered from the effort made in striking the earth, although the olive has been produced. The obliquity of the stroke with the spear, which the attitude of the goddess denotes, causes the olive to appear in the rear of the monarch of the ocean, whose figure at rest seems awaiting the issue. In the sculptured figures of the pediment, the action of producing both prodigies is simultaneous.

To the right of Neptune appear Venus, with Peitho, the ordinary attendant upon the goddess of desire. Love, easily recognised by his youth and his wings, required no superscription. After Love comes Pan, a deity highly reverenced by the Athenians, whose habitation they pretended to be in the side of the acropolis, below the wall at the north-west angle. He appears, not as he is commonly represented, with the feet of a goat, but with gilded horns upon a youthful visage. Cymo, one of the Nereïds, who in that character cannot be considered as out of place in such a composition, follows Pan. She appears to be the harbinger of Apollo, denoting the appearance of the sun rising from the bosom of the ocean, in allusion, perhaps, to the time of the action. The absence of a fragment over the head of Apollo, renders the superscription incomplete, but the initial A, succeeded, after a proportionate interval, by the final ΟΣ, can leave no doubt of the name they assisted in displaying.

Beyond Minerva, on the left, appears the head of a female, whom the inscription above shows to have represented Psamathe, another of the sea-nymphs. The animals beyond are either a representation of Proteus, the son of Oceanus and Tethys, or, as some mythologists imagine, the offspring of Neptune and Phenice, who, thus considered, would be no inappropriate spectator of the scene; or they are acces-

---

obliterated all traces of the letters. I had, however, the good fortune to see the gold in all its original brilliancy, and compared the inscriptions with the printed copy Dr. Clarke had caused to be taken from them. No opportunity, therefore, was left for conjecture on the subject of the inscriptions. The bosses and bits of the horses, the diadems, ear-rings, and buckles of the females, and the wings of Love, were likewise gilt, before the experiment above-mentioned was made.

sories to the group next in succession.   In conformity with a practice
amongst Grecian artists, we have now an episode to the principal
action.   The marriage of Thetis and Peleus seems to have been the
object of the painter.   The lion and serpent, the forms assumed by
Thetis to elude the pursuit of Peleus, are represented in a *bas relief* *,
the subject of which is the successful termination of the suit of the
hero.   The same subject was sculptured on one of the sides of the
celebrated coffer of Cypselus, described by Pausanias †, as an acces-
sorial group to the principal action which represented the marriage of
Jason and Medea.   In this work of art, Thetis is accompanied by only
one of the two emblems which in the Greek vase form the group ; if
these be not introduced, as I have already observed, with a different
intention.

It has been imagined that the figure borne in the car, placed in the
western pediment of the Parthenon, was that of Apteral-Victory, conducting the chariot of Minerva. ‡   This conjecture, which is an
emendation by Visconti, of the original idea of Wheler and Spon, is
equally ill-founded.   It is certain that in the acropolis there was a
statue of Victory represented without wings, but it is no less so that
the Athenian artists usually distinguished Victory by the common
appendages ; witness a group in the frize above the pronaos of the
temple where the genius attendant on Minerva is thus represented. §
The fact however is, that Visconti has mistaken the Amphitrite of

---

* Gal. Mytholog. de Millin. pl. 133.

† Πεποίηται δὲ καὶ Θέτις παρθένος, λαμβάνεται δὲ αὐτῆς Πηλεὺς, καὶ ἀπὸ τῆς χειρὸς τῆς Θέτιδος
ὄφις.   Pausan. v. 18.

‡ This is one of the errors which has originated in the crude conceptions of Wheler,
who imagines the principal female figure to be Victory, leading the triumphal biga of
Minerva, the goddess herself occupying the chariot.   When it was ascertained that the
principal figure was that of the protectress of Athens, the two statues were made to change
characters, as the easiest mode of obviating the difficulty which had now arisen.

§ For the same reason that the Athenians had a statue of Victory, without wings, says
Pausanias, the Lacedemonians possessed a statue of Enyalius, or Mars, with his feet
chained.   The conceit is obvious.   It does not follow that the statues of Mars were always thus represented in Laconia.

Nointell's drawing for the figure formerly placed in the car. This explanation, first offered by Quatremere de Quincy *, is undoubtedly just. The statues having been finished all around, it would have been difficult, without the aid of Nointell's drawing, to determine which side they presented when fixed in the pediment; from this, however, it is obvious, that the Amphitrite, whose *left* arm is thrown back, and whose garment separates over the left thigh, has been reversed, and mistaken for the occupant of the chariot. . The drawing above mentioned represents this figure in an attitude nearly the reverse of the other, the left arm being extended and draped. Although, in all the recent discussions on the sculptures of the Parthenon, the chariot has been usually considered as an accessory of Minerva, there is no antient representation of the goddess of wisdom thus accompanied. In the Iliad †, Minerva goes forth to join the battle in the car of Juno. She again appears conducting the chariot of Diomed, but never in an equipage of her own. In the drawing of Nointell, the figure inclines to the female form, and is attired in a flowing robe. Such is the appearance of Apollo on the vase ; the puer æternus of the poet‡, the Apollo puber of Pliny, the Apollo βούπαις of the Greek Anthology ; and such that of the youthful competitors in the games, represented upon the frize of the Parthenon, whose feminine forms have led a learned antiquary into a similar error with regard to the sex of the objects. §

According, therefore, to the illustration afforded by the vase, we must regard the group as the OXH ΑΠΟΛΛΩΝΟΣ, the equipage of Apollo, conducted by the god of day himself. The figure appearing behind the horses may probably be Pan ; for

---

* Letters to Canova, on the subject of the Elgin marbles.
† Iliad, v. 720. viii. 374.   .
‡ Ovid. Metam. iv. 17 . Puer insidiose. Mart. xiv. 172.
§ Visconti has again erred in mistaking one of these for a female figure of Victory. The tuft of a helmet becomes, in his eyes, the wings of the Genius. Stuart's Athens, ii. pl. xviii.

it is unnecessary to identity that it is deficient in the usual characteristics of this rural deity.   The Egyptians, as well as the Athenians,
says Herodotus *, represented Pan with the head and legs of a goat,
not because they thought the representation correct, believing, as they
did, that in these respects he resembled the other deities.   In the
vase, the head and the legs, so much of them as remains, are human ;
and on the medals of Olympia † the god is represented with all the
members of the *beau ideal*.

The group on the left beyond Apollo probably represented Venus,
attended by Peitho and Love.   Beyond it, is that most absurdly supposed by Wheler to be Hadrian and Sabina.   Chandler, in attempting
to reconcile this anachronism, supposes them " intruders on the
original company ;" their heads, he thinks, were probably " placed
on trunks which before had other owners."   In thus adopting the
absurd notions of pseudo-dilettanti, he is obliged to have recourse to
a supposition wholly at variance with the fact of both figures being
sculptured from single blocks.   The female figure still retains its
coëval head ; the other was, for the first time, separated by the cupidity
of a Turk, in the expectation of selling it to some of the English lately
at Athens, who purchased every fragment with great avidity, and
thus contributed to the destruction of the monuments of Athenian
antiquity.   Visconti supposes this group to be Vulcan and Venus ;
but the helmet of the male figure is incompatible with this conjecture.   The vase again affords us assistance in determining the personages intended to be represented, and no circumstance militates
against our regarding them as Peleus and Thetis.   The reclined
figure, filling up the angle of the pediment, is imagined, with sufficient
reason, to be the river Ilissus, by Visconti ; who supports his opinion
by reference to the description of the temple at Olympia, afforded by
Pausanias.   His criticism, however, upon the action and anatomy of
the statue, is deficient in soundness.

---

* Herodot. ii. 45.   † Gal. Mytholog. i. 72.

The other compartment of the pediment, on the right of the central group, was occupied by marine deities, and partisans of Neptune. Amphitrite, who appears in Nointell's drawing seated with a dolphin at her feet, and accompanied by the Nereïds, doubtless formed a principal part of the composition. The sitting figure with two children, hitherto imagined to be Latona and her infants, may represent Leda with the children of Tyndarus, Castor and Pollux, the tutelary protectors of mariners. The other group may be Thalassa, with Galene. *

It is to be observed that the order is reversed in the two designs. In the pediment of the temple the supporters of Minerva are in the rear of the goddess, and the companions of Neptune are behind him. In the vase, the contrary mode seems to have been observed.

In attempting to elucidate the subject of the sculptures, I have considered the propriety of ranging on the side of Minerva the mythological personages more particularly venerated in the capital of Attica; and mentioned by Pausanias as possessing statues and temples, or consecrated places, among the Athenians. In like manner I have given names to the followers of Neptune, taken from the Memorabilia of Corinth, recorded by the same writer; for there this deity presided.

---

* Τοῦ Ποσειδῶνος δέ εἰσιν ἐπειργασμένοι τῷ βάθρῳ καὶ οἱ Τυνδάρεω παῖδες, ὅτι δὴ σωτῆρες καὶ οὗτοι νεῶν καὶ ἀνθρώπων εἰσὶ ναυτιλλομένων, τὰ δὲ ἄλλα ἀνάκειται Γαλήνης ἄγαλμα καὶ θαλάσσης. Pausan. ii. c. l.

3 H 2

NOTICE OF SOME REMARKABLE ANTIQUITIES,

FOUND AMONG

THE RUINS OF SUSA, IN PERSIA.

" To see old Shushan is neither unworthy our labour, nor out of the way. Shushan is every where famoused. It was one of the three royal palaces the Median monarchs so much gloried in; Babylon, Shushan, and Ecbatan. It is spoken of in the first chapter of Hesther, that there Ahasuerus feasted his lieutenants over a hundred and twenty-seven provinces, a hundred and eighty days, with great cost and triumph. Nehemiah also, and Daniel, remember it to be in Elam, Persia; and notwithstanding the many mutilations and miseries it had from avaricious tyrants, yet was it able to smile upon Alexander, when he extracted thence, to pay his soldiers and fill his bags, 50,000 talents in bullyon, and nine millions in coyned gold." — HERBERT'S TRAVELS, p. 220.

" THE plain, in which once stood the city of Susa, is overspread in various directions with heaps of earth, shaped like tumuli, and with vast mounds ; one, in particular, far surpasses the rest in size, and is called the Kala of Shush. To this spot I first directed my attention. Beneath our feet, and on every side, we beheld fragments of earthen-ware scattered in the greatest profusion ; these, I was told, are to be traced for the distance of seven fursukhs, and are equally numerous. Whether they be coëval with the existence of the city, so as to mark its vastness, or rather its immense population, I cannot pretend to decide. The natives say the ground has been thus strewed ever since the destruction of the city ; and I believe the fragments to be of great antiquity.

" The Kala is between three and four hundred feet high ; its sides are in many places nearly perpendicular, and the top of it is perhaps three acres in extent.   It would appear that a great part of the antient. palace stood originally on an eminence, for the ground below the high mound to the eastward seems to have been occupied by the same building, or range of buildings; and it is a large extent of mounds, which now bears the name of the ' Kala of Shush.'. The rains, by washing down the sides, have exposed, in many of their channels, broken walls and heaps of bricks and stones, in themselves of little interest, but serving to prove this high mound a mass of ruined buildings, and not a mere accumulation of natural earth, as might be supposed from its general outward appearance. The same profusion of broken earthenware, as I had noticed the day before, also exists here; but I could find no fragment sufficiently entire to allow of my distinguishing the original shape of the vessel, or any worthy of being carried away.   Were it in the power of any one to remain several days employed in excavating and digging among these ruins, I am convinced the numerous and interesting treasures of antiquity, which might be discovered, would richly reward the labour of the search.   The Arabs, however, have a great aversion from it, and it was with difficulty that I persuaded them to undertake the little I required; a delay, moreover, in this neighbourhood, sufficient for putting plans of this nature in execution, would be attended with much danger, from the lawless and unsettled state of the country. The Dervish, who dwells at the tomb of Daniel, situated about a stone's throw to the north-west of the Kala, has removed some fragments of antiquity to his own inclosures.   But one stone, from its great size and apparent want of ornament, he has left untouched. This lies on the south-west side of the mound, not far from its foot, and has probably fallen from above to its present situation.   It is a large slab of an inferior species of marble, with the form of an oblong square, and is nine feet in length and four in breadth; its surface is perfectly plain, and has been polished.   I was but ill satisfied with the mere inspection of this stone as it was presented before me; the circumstance of its being single, and there not existing in any other part of the mound remains of stone buildings to which it might have belonged, induced me to conclude that on some part of it there was sculpture; and having accordingly, with the assistance of five or six Arabs, cleared it from the earth, and turned it over, I discovered a long and beautiful inscription in arrow-headed, or Persepolitan, characters, most of them an inch in length, and the whole of very admirable workmanship. There is no other ornament upon the stone, or any sculpture, save this inscription, occupying one half of the side, which had until this moment remained unexposed. The different series of characters are each divided by a thin horizontal line, continued from one side of the stone to the other, a decisive proof that the arrow-headed character was not read, as some have supposed, only perpendicularly. The nature of this stone, or marble, is exactly such as I have seen brought from the Bactiari mountains to Dezfoul, for the purpose of building; and I have little doubt but that the stone I have been describing, as well as all other stones, whether simply for building or sculpture, in the antient Susa, originally came from these mountains. The distance is two days' journey, but there is no spot nearer in the vicinity whence stones of any kind could be procured. It is natural, therefore, to conclude that the greater part of the city was not built of stone, and we may thus, in a great measure, account for its present appearance, and for the few remains which are now to be found. Strabo, when mentioning Susa, says that, ' the building of this city, its palaces, walls and temples, was similar to that of Babylon, of bricks and cement.' L. 15.

" In another quarter of this mound I discovered the fragment of a fluted column, a part of which is buried in the earth, and I have little doubt but that many more are thus concealed. I was finally driven by the heat to the tomb of Daniel, or, as he is called in the East, Danyall, which is but a few hundred feet from the Kala, situated in a most beautiful spot, washed by a clear running stream, and shaded by planes and other trees of ample foliage. The building is of Mohammedan date, and inhabited by a solitary Dervish, who shows the spot where the prophet is buried beneath a small and simple square brick mausoleum, said to be, without probability, coëval with his death.

It has, however, neither date nor inscription to prove the truth or false-hood of the Dervish's assertion.   The small river running at the foot of this building, which is called the Bellarou, it has been said, flows immediately over the prophet's tomb, and, from the transparency of the water, his coffin was to be seen at the bottom ; but the Der-vish and the natives whom I questioned, remember no tradition cor-roborating such a fact; on the contrary, it has at all times been customary with the people of the country to resort hither upon certain days of the month, when they offer up their prayers at the tomb I have mentioned, in supplication to the prophet's shade ; and by becoming his guests for the night, expect remission from all present grievances, and an ensurance against those to come.   I hap-pened to be present on one of these very days ; an unfortunate circum-stance, which prevented my remaining as long as I could have wished ; for notwithstanding the pious motives of this large assemblage, it was but too evident that they had views of another nature directed to-wards my Yakdouns, which, my people assured me, together with all I possessed, would be stolen during the night time.

" In an open court of the building, called Daniel's tomb, I saw three stones of great beauty and interest, and the sight of them served to repay me for the vexation of disappointment, and a considerable de-gree of fatigue.   They have been brought hither, as I have already observed, from the great mound by the Dervish.   Of the three, that most deserving of attention is of no regular shape, and has never been fashioned for the purpose of building ; it is a greenish black species of Egyptian stone, a yard in length, but of an irregular thick-ness, and the whole is finely polished ; on one side of it are five rows of hieroglyphics, another has two rows of the same, and beneath them an inscription in the Persepolitan character, continued to the bottom ; the third side has been completely covered with an in-scription in the same character, though now it is nearly defaced by age.

" The hieroglyphics are beautifully worked in *basso-relievo*, and the inscriptions are as exquisitely engraved.

    " Of the five rows of hieroglyphics on the principal side, the first seems to contain the sun, moon, and a star ; the second, a hare, a dog, and a hawk ; the third row has at the two ends human figures ; one bearing the head of a beast resembling a wolf, the other, excepting the tail of a beast, which is attached to it, is perfectly a human figure ; between the two, are three other signs ; the nature of which I am unable to explain ; but they appear to be a belt, a club, and the head of an arrow : the fifth has a star, and two birds, with some other sign. The characters of the inscriptions are small, but very finely cut ; and are more connected, and partake of more variety in their connection, than those at Persepolis ; they are exactly such as I have seen upon the bricks brought from the remains of antient Babylon."

From the preceding extract, which I have been permitted to transcribe from a manuscript journal, it appears extremely probable that very interesting discoveries might be made by any one who would be permitted to carry on his researches in this part of Persia with leisure and security.

    It is impossible to fix the date of the curious monument to which the following plate* refers ; but it appears to be connected with that part of the Persian history which commences with the reign of Cambyses, and terminates with that of Darius Codomannus, when a great intercourse subsisted between the nations of Ægypt and † Persia. Ægyptian captives and workmen were employed at that time in

---

* For an accurate drawing of the stone the perspective should have been sharper ; but it would have fore-shoitened the subjects of the two sides.

   † The conquest of Ægypt by the Persians, and its subsequent history from that time to the present, afford a valuable illustration of a passage in Ezekiel, c. xxx. v. 13. Ἄρχοντες Μεμφέως ἐκ γῆς Αἰγύπτου οὐκ ἔσονται ἔτι. Sep. Interpr. " Dux de terra Ægypti non erit amplius." Vulg. From the Persians, the Ægyptians were transferred into the hands of the Greeks, the Romans, the Arabs, the Saraccns, the Mamelukes, the Turks. " Cette prophétie," says M. de Sainte Croix, in a remark communicated to Larcher, " est d'une clarté, et d'une évidence à laquelle il n'est pas possible de se refuser."

building. or ornamenting the palaces of *Susa* and Persepolis. * Although the Ægyptians were treated as a conquered people by the Persians, and some insults may have been occasionally offered.to the objects of worship which the former considered as peculiarly sacred, yet it is equally certain that some of the sovereigns of Persia respected the gods of their subjects † ; and that the Magi derived knowledge of various kinds from their communication with them. ‡ In the intercourse between the two nations, their sacred symbols and language became familiar to each other : we observe on the Hæmatite cylinders § found in Egypt, the Tau, the Scarabæus volans, and Isiac figures, accompanied by the arrow-headed character of Persia ‖ ; the same kind of letters, and a collection of hieroglyphics, are found on the vase discovered in Ægypt, and described by Caylus. ¶ An agate seal brought from that country by Denon, and regarded by him as a monument of the Persians under Cambyses, exhibits on one part the Fish-god, or Man-fish, and a human figure, unquestionably Ægyptian **, is sculptured on the side; and learned men have observed a resemblance between the names of some of the Persian and Ægyptian deities. ††

It appears from a passage in Eusebius ‡‡, that the Persians were accustomed to use a symbolical language : with them, as with the

---

* Τεχνίτας εξ Αιγύπτου παραλαβόντας κατασκεύασαι τὰ περιβόητα βασίλεια, τά τε ἐν Περσε-πόλει, καὶ τὰ ἐν Σούσοις. Diod. Sic. l. i. 155. Wess.

† Darius Hystaspis expressed great disapprobation of the impious conduct of his predecessor Cambyses in Ægypt. Diod. Sic. l. l. See also Polyænus, Strat. 1. 7. where mention is made of the reward offered by him for the discovery of a new Apis.

‡ Perhibent veteres philosophum quendam, quem Zoroastrum vocant, initiatum in Ægypto, mysteria illius gentis in Persiam invexisse. Jablons. Pan. Æg. Prol. l. v. 29.

§ See Landseer, Archæol. vol. xviii.

‖ See Caylus, Recueil, tom. iii. pp. 49, 50. tom. iv. p. 22.

¶ Tom. v. 79.　　　　　　　　　** Ouseley's Travels, p. 436.

†† Reland, de Vet. Ling. Pers. and Hyde de Rel. Pers. 91.

‡‡ Euseb. Præ. Ev. l. i. c. 10. Ζωροάστρης δὲ ὁ Μάγος ἐν τῇ ἱερᾷ συναγωγῇ τῶν Περσικῶν φησι κατὰ λέξιν· 'Ο δὲ Θεός ἐστι κεφαλὴν ἔχων ἱέρακος· οὗτός ἐστιν ὁ πρῶτος, ἄφθαρτος, ἀίδιος, κ. τ. λ. The Abbé Foucher supposes that the words 'Ο δὲ Θ. ε. κ. ε. ι. being placed in a parenthesis, may refer to a figure of the Deity placed at the head of a section or treatise, containing the account of the different attributes, an enumeration of which follows in Eusebius.

Ægyptians, the deity was typified by the head of the Hawk * ; and they employed this hieroglyphical mode of description to a very late period ; for, according to Libanius, quoted by the Abbé Foucher, they represented their enemy, the Emperor Julian, by lightning, or by a lion vomiting forth flames. †

From the discovery of these letters at Susa, we derive a strong argument in favour of an interpretation given by Munter ‡ to a passage of Herodotus (l. iv. c. 87.) The historian informs us, that Darius caused to be engraved on one of two pillars erected at the Bosphorus, Ασσύρια γράμματα. He conjectures that the inscription mentioned by Herodotus was in arrow-headed characters ; and since we now find that they were used not only at Babylon, and at Persepolis, but also at Susa, it appears probable that they were familiar to all parts of the Assyrian empire ; and the explanation of Munter may be, therefore, accepted as the true one. §

If some fortunate circumstances should enable future travellers in Persia to procure any of the inscribed monuments of Susa, the acquisition would be of great importance, as it might assist the researches of those orientalists who have already directed their attention to the examination of these characters. According to the opinion of Munter and Grotefend, they should be read in a direction from left to right ; Lichtenstein entertains a different opinion. Professor Heeren, in his late work entitled " Ideen uber die Politik, &c." agrees with Grotefend, and makes some interesting remarks on the history and nature of this species of writing.

This forgery under the name of Zoroaster could have had little success, unless there had been some reason for believing that the symbolical illustration mentioned in the passage from Eusebius had been adopted by that philosopher, or some of the early religious instructors of Persia.

* " The figure of the sacred Hawk, under which semblance Divine Providence was always depicted." Bryant, Ant. My. ii. 400.

† Ac. des Inscr. vol. xxvii. p. 349.

‡ Essai sur les Inscriptions Cuneiformes de Persepolis. An account of this work is given in the Mag. Enc. tom. iii. 1803, by S. de Sacy.

§ I have been informed by the Earl of Aberdeen, that Mr. Payne Knight proposed a similar interpretation of this passage many years ago to him.

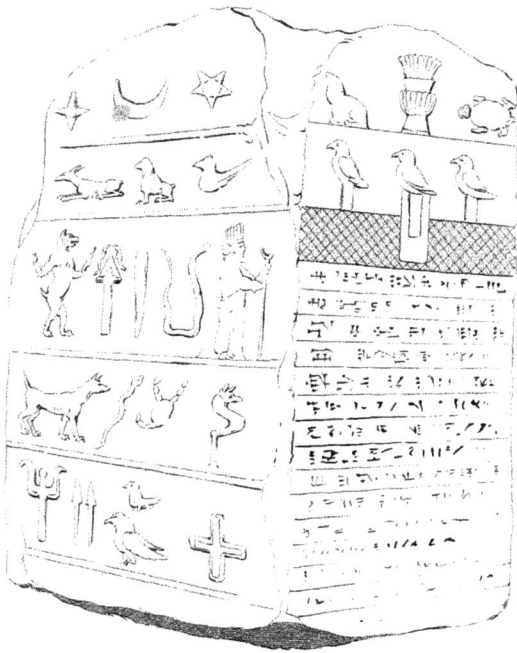

STONE DISCOVERED AT SUSA REPRESENTING HIEROGLYPHIC FIGURES
AND THE ANTIENT CUNEIFORM CHARACTERS OF PERSIA.

London Published May 10th 1819 by Longman Hurst Rees Orme & Brown Paternoster Row

" Independently of the elucidations of Persian antiquities which these monuments promise, they lead us one step farther into the history of the most important of all human inventions, after that of language; viz. the origin of alphabetical writing. The cuneiform character is so simple in its component parts, that it has all the appearance of being a primeval alphabet; it consists only of two elements, the wedge and the rectangle; and with fewer than these it is impossible that an alphabet should be formed. To this, and to the total want of curves, we must attribute the apparently superfluous number of strokes of which some of the letters are composed. It is also quite clear, from the nature of this character, that it has not originated from picture-writing. An alphabet which had been derived from picture-writing, if such a derivation be conceivable, would bear traces of that variety by which this method of representing ideas is characterized. It has also been shewn by Grotefend that it is not syllabic. What, then, remains but to suppose that it was from its first origin alphabetic, though it may have undergone various modifications and improvements? The very multiplicity and superfluity of its strokes seems to shew that it has been formed by a laborious analysis of sound, and with a desire to allow not even a single aspiration to escape without being represented. It appears to be of Asiatic origin; and it is so different not only from the hieroglyphic of Egypt, but also from the alphabetical character as we find it on the Rosetta stone, as to repel the idea of a common origin. The discoveries which have already been made at Babylon and Persepolis prove that it was diffused over a great part of Upper Asia, and adopted by different nations, who formed new letters, but still derived from the same radical elements of the wedge and the rectangle. As it is found in three different states on the walls of Persepolis, its origin must ascend far beyond the time of the Persian monarchy; and, since it can scarcely be doubted that the first and simplest of them is an alphabet of the Zendic language, we are naturally led to seek for its native country in Media, where this language and the doctrine of Zoroaster prevailed. On the other hand, the circumstance that the cuneiform letters are found in the Babylonian inscriptions would seem to point to an Aramæan origin." * — Editor.

Translation of Part of a Persian Manuscript relating to the Tomb of Daniel at Susa, mentioned in the preceding Journal, p. 422.

I am indebted to Sir William Ouseley for the following version from a Persian MS., which he has communicated in a letter to me. It contains some notice of the traditions preserved by the Arabic writers, relating to the prophet and his sepulchre. " The extract," he observes, " may appear of unreasonable length ; yet it is necessary to prefix a few lines."

In the eighteenth year of the Muhammedan era, (of Christ 640,) whilst Omar held the Khalifat, an Arabian army under Abú Músa Alashaari invaded the Persian province of Khúzistán, or Susiana. In the antient capital Susa, (latterly called Sús, or Shúsh,) that General found, besides considerable treasures of various kinds, an extraordinary sepulchral monument, which, according to local tradition, contained the prophet Daniel's body. Of this discovery the most circumstantial account is given by Abu Muhammed Ahmed, whose father, Aasim of Kúfah, flourished within so short a time after the conquest of Susiana, that he might, when young, have conversed with veteran warriors, whose valour had contributed to that event; for he died in the year 117, (A. D. 735). as we learn from Casiri, (Biblioth. Arab-Hisp. Escurial. vol. i. p. 504.)   Ebn Aasim's " Book of Victories," in the original Arabic, is a work extremely rare ; but it was translated into Persian by Ahmed al Mastowfi, about the year 1200, and copies in this language are sufficiently numerous.   From the best of three MSS. preserved in my own collection, I shall here extract what relates to the tomb of Daniel. †

---

* This translation from Heeren is given in the Appendix to the M. Review, vol.-lxxxv.
. ·† In some catalogues of Oriental MSS. we find the Book of Victories described as the Tárikh or Chronicle of Aasim al Kufis, and two ·or three writers have quoted it as his work. On a late occasion (Travels, vol. i. p. 422.) I myself referred to it as such; but subsequent inquiry has convinced me that his son was the author. — O.

Our author informs us that Ahú Músa, having pillaged the territory of Ahwáz, proceeded to Sús, where he slew the governor, a Persian prince, named Shápúr, the son of Azermáhán.

" Then, continues the historian, he entered the castle and palace of that prince, and seized all the treasures deposited there in different places, until he came to a certain chamber, of which the door was strongly fastened, a leaden seal being affixed to the lock. Ahú Músa inquired from the people of Sús what precious article was guarded with such care in this chamber ; they assured him, that he would not regard it as a desirable object of plunder ; but his curiosity was excited, and he caused the lock to be broken and the door opened. In the chamber he beheld a stone of considerable dimensions, hollowed into the form of a coffin ; and in this the body of a dead man, wrapped in a shroud or winding-sheet of gold brocade. The head was uncovered ; Abú Músa and his attendants were astonished ; for, having measured the nose, they found that, proportionably, this dead personage must have far exceeded in stature the common race of men. The people now informed Abú Músa that this was the body of an eminent sage who formerly resided in Irák, (Chaldæa or Babylonia,) and that whenever the want of rain occasioned a famine or scarcity, the inhabitants applied to this holy man, and, through the efficacy of his prayers, obtained copious showers from heaven. It happened once that Sús likewise suffered from excessive drought ; and the people in distress requested that their neighbours would allow this venerable personage to reside a few days among them, expecting to derive the blessing of rain from his intercession with the Almighty ; but the Irákians would not grant this favour. Fifty men were then deputed by the people of Sús, who again petitioned the ruler of Irák, saying, ' Let the holy personage visit our country, and do thou detain the fifty men until his return.' These terms were accepted, and the holy personage came to Sús, where, through the influence of his prayers, rain fell abundantly, and saved the land from famine ; but the inhabitants would not permit him to return, and the fifty men were detained as hostages, in Irák : at length he died. Such, said those who accompanied Ahú Músa, is the history of this dead man. The Arabian general then inquired by what name so extraordinary a person had been known amongst them ; they replied, ' The people of Irák called him Daniál Hakím, or Daniel the sage.'

" After this, Ahú Músa remained some time at Sús, and dispatched to Omar, the Commander of the Faithful, an account of all his con- quests in Khúzistán, and of the various treasures which had fallen into his possession ; he related also the discovery of Daniel's body. When Omar received this account, he demanded from his chief officers some information respecting Daniel, but all were silent except Ali, on whom be the blessing of God ! He declared that Daniel had been a prophet, though not of the highest order ; that in ages long past he dwelt with Bakhtnasser (Nebuchadnezzar), and the kings who succeeded him ; and Ali related the whole history of Daniel, from the beginning to the end, with all the circumstances of his death. Omar then, by the advice of Ali, caused a letter to be written, direct- ing that Abú Músa should remove, with due respect and religious reverence, the body of Daniel to some place where the people of Sús could no longer enjoy the possession of it. Ahú Músa immedi- ately ón receipt of this order obliged the people of Sús to turn the stream which supplied their city with water from its natural course ; then he brought forth the body of Daniel, and having wrapped another shroud over the gold brocade above described, he commanded that ·a grave should be made in the dry channel of the river, and therein he deposited the prophet's venerable remains ; the grave was then firmly secured, and covered with stones of considerable size; the river was restored to its former channel, and the waters of Sús now flow over the body of Daniel."

Such is the extract from Ebn Aasim's MS. Chronicle, or Táríkh, the "⸲Book of Victories." My three copies, fairly written, present various readings in many places, but none throughout this story of Daniel that materially affect the sense.

I am, dear Sir, &c. &c.

W. OUSELEY.

ON THE FOREHEAD

THE LEFT CHEEK

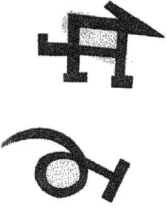

UPON THE RIGHT CH

UPON THE NOSE

UPON THE LEFT SIDE OF THE BREAST

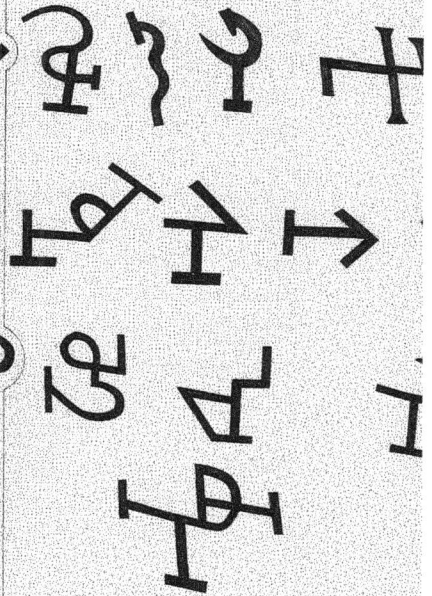

UPON THE RIGHT SIDE OF THE BR

MONOGRAMS AND CHARACTERS ON A BUST OF ISIS.

London, Published May 10th 1819, by Longman, Hurst, Rees, Orme & Brown, Paternoster Row.

FIGURES ON A SUPPOSED HEAD OF ISIS.

The original of the annexed plate was found among the papers of the late Mr. Davison; and was sent to the engraver with the expectation that some referenec to it, or explanation of its subject, might occur among the manuscripts of that gentleman. This, however, has not been the case; and some apology therefore is due to the reader for the insertion of it.

I have reason to believe that the characters are those which were found on a bust supposed- to represent the head of Isis. A controversy about the year 1761 * was excited respecting the genuineness of this head. Mr. Needham, who warmly supported the hypothesis respecting the affinity and intercourse which antiently prevailed between Ægypt and China, found in it an argument to strengthen his own opinion; considering the bust as Ægyptian; and the characters as Chinese. On the other hand, it was contended, that the whole was the work of some impostor. De Pauw alludes to this bust in his Preliminary Discourse to his Essay on the Ægyptians and Chinese, and properly condemns the practice of such frauds, " which," he says, " may one day render the most authentic monuments suspicious." I suppose it to be the same to which Sir W. Jones also refers in the following passage in the Asiatic Researches, ii. 373. " As to the table and bust of Isis, they seem to be given up as modern forgeries ; the fabricator of the letters, if they were really fabricated in Europe, was uncommonly happy, since two or three of them † are exactly the same with those on a metal pillar yet standing in the north of India."

---

* See Monthly Review, vol. xxix. p. 34. The bust was preserved at Turin.
† Among the figures upon the left side of the breast, one of the forms of the first letter in the Phœnician alphabet is represented twice.

NATURAL HISTORY.

MEDICINAL AND ECONOMICAL USES OF CERTAIN PLANTS

SOLD IN THE BAZAR, AND HERB-STALLS AT CONSTANTINOPLE.

[FROM SIBTHORP'S MSS.]

1. Fᴜᴍᴀʀɪᴀ officinalis, κάπνια. The herb is pounded ; and an infusion is made of it, which is drank for exanthematous complaints, and a prurient itching of the skin.
2. Teucrium chamædrys, χαμάιδρυς. A cataplasm of the pounded herb is applied to the rectum for fistula in ano ; an infusion of it is drank for the same complaint.
3. Teucrium polium ; drank in infusion for exanthematous disorders.
4. Sambucus ebulus : the leaves are employed in cataplasms, in swelling of the joints.
5. Plantago major, πεντάνευρον : applied externally as a vulnerary to wounds.
6. Panicum dactylon, άγριάδα : the decoction of the root is much used as a diuretic.
7. Cichorium endivia, ραδίκα : a decoction made of the inside of the root is used in bilious fevers, as a diuretic and deobstruent.
8. Lavendula stoechas : an infusion of it is drank for catarrhs and head-aches.
9. Verbascum sinuatum, φλόμο : the Turks make a bath of the seeds and leaves of this plant, then sit over it, for disorders of the rectum.
10. Matricaria suaveolens, χαμόμιλον : an infusion of the flowers is drank in bilious and nervous fevers ; it is made use of also in deafness to syringe the ears.

11. Peucedanum officinale, μεγαβότανο: the root of this plant is applied in cataplasms to the heads of new-born infants, as a preservative against hydrocephalous and strumous swellings of the neck.

12. Convallaria polygonatum : this root is given to child-bearing women, to produce a large secretion of milk.

13. Artemisia pontica, ἀψίνθιο: taken in infusion for fevers, with Gentiana centaurium ; also in the melancholy, called by the Turks Sefdah.

14. Momordica elaterium, πικρο ἀγγούριο: the fruit powdered is drank in infusion for the jaundice, or snuffed up the nose.

15. Scilla maritima, ἄσκιλλα : made into paste with honey for the asthma, or applied in cataplasms to the joints affected with rheumatic pains.

16. Iris ——, κρίνο: small pieces are cut and applied like pease to issues.

17. Arum maculatum, δρακοντιὸ : the root, powdered with sugar, is taken as a medicine in bilious complaints.

18. Ruta graveolens, ἀπήγανον: is externally applied in rheumatic pains to the joints, feet, and loins.

19. Equisetum fluviatile; taken in infusion for giddiness of the head ; called in Greek ἀλογόυρα.

20. Cistus incanus, λάδανο: infused in the baths to give them a fragrant odour.

21. Tamarix gallica; drank in infusion for head-aches and pains of the stomach.

22. Nymphæa lutea, νούφαρ: a sherbet made of it is drank in colds, as refreshing : the odour or smell is supposed to cure the megrim.

23. Asplenium scolopendrium : the infusion of it is drank in pains of the body.

24. Rumex hydrolapathus, λάπαθο : the root, powdered with milk, is drank for the itch : horses are made to swallow the seeds, to cure them of coughs.

25. Erysimum Barbarea ; is given, in infusion in milk, for depurat-

ing the blood: Sisymbrium nasturtium aquaticum, ὑδροκάρδαμο, and Veronica Beccabunga, are used for the same purpose.

26. Salvia officinalis; taken in infusion for slow fevers, and as a gargle for washing the mouth in the tooth-ache.

27. Melissa Byzantia; taken in infusion in slow fevers and the melancholy, called Sefdah.

28. Papaver somniferum, μάκων: the heads bruised are drank in decoction for coughs.

29. Hyoscyamus albus, ὑοσκύαμος: the fumes of the seeds thrown on hot coals are taken into the mouth to cure the tooth-ache. *

30. Gnaphalium stœchas; taken in infusion for the jaundice.

31. Cannabis sativa; boiled with oil serves as a liniment to remove rheumatic pains. Nerium oleander is used for the same purpose.

32. Malva officinalis, μολόχα †: in the disease of fistula in ano, leeches being first applied, a bath is made of these plants, and the patient sits over it to receive the steam.

33. Tilia alba, φλαμούρια: the flowers are made into a conserve called majiun, and an infusion of the leaves is drank as a purifier of the blood.

34. Santolina anthemoides: the flower is made into a conserve, and the plant drank in infusion to cure strumous disorders of the breast.

35. Eryngium campestre: the roots of this plant, as well as Statice

---

* " I beg leave," says Sir Hans Sloane, " to give an instance of the great virtues of henbane seeds in the tooth-ache. A person, tormented with this pain, had an empiric recommended to him: the quack conveyed the smoke of burning henbane seeds, by means of a funnel, into the hollow tooth, and thereby removed the pain; but at the same time there dropped some maggots from the tooth, as he pretended, into a pail of water, placed underneath for that purpose. One of these I sent to Mr. Lewenhoek, who found it to be entirely like those bred in rotten cheese. Though the smoke of the henbane seeds cured the tooth-ache, it is highly probable the maggots had been conveyed thither, and let drop into the water by some slight of hand." The same empiricism is practised now in the Levant, as well as in this country. — E.

- † Μολόχη pro Μαλάχη dixisse Athenæum observat Eustathius Od: α. 1406. V. Du C. in v. — E.

limonium, are boiled, and the decoction of them drank in the bloody flux.

36. Ligustrum vulgare ; taken in infusion for epileptic fits.

37. Typha major: the cottony substance is applied to burns with oil of Sesamum.

38. Datura stramonium: a drachm of the seed taken, occasions great giddiness of the head.

Birds of Zante.

THE same circumstance, the want of woods and lofty mountains, which explain the reason why so few of the *Feræ* abounding in the neighbouring continent of Greece are to be found in Zante, applies also to the birds of prey ; and the want of rivers and permanent lakes considerably diminishes the number of aquatic fowls. Zante furnishes a breeding-place to a very small number of the species, which are seen in the course of their migration to make this their temporary resting-place. The periods of the greater migrations, such as that of the turtle-doves, are in April and September. Most of the birds that visit Zante during the winter, come at uncertain times, influenced by seasons and weather.

A considerable number of the Falcon tribe pass over from the Morea in October, as the F. Pygargus, Cyanus, Yerakína, Candidus, Pelligri, Turdivorus, and Barbatus : the two last stop only a few days. The Falco Tinnunculus, and the F. Lucaina, which is probably the Buzzard, and Peregrinus, stay here all the year, and breed in the rocks near the sea.

Of the Vultur, the V. Percnopterus is occasionally seen. Of the birds of prey that fly by night, a small number of the Great horned Owl arrive in the middle of August, and retire in October : the Lesser horned Owl, called here αὐτόκουλα, is seen passing at the same period. This species is eaten, and esteemed a delicacy ; a circumstance which is mentioned by Aristotle. The Strix Aluco, and Passerina, reside throughout the year and breed here : the former is rarely seen.

The three sorts of Butcher birds arrive in May, breed here, and retire in September.

Zante is very poor in the order of Picæ. Of the Crow tribe, the noisy Daw, and the almost domestic Pie, are wanting. Neither the Carrion nor the hooded Crow annoy the flocks; the only species that I observed here was the Raven, which breeds in the rocks, and remains throughout the year.

The Roller, the Bee Eater, the Oriole, the Cuckow, the Hoopoe, are summer birds of passage : the four first arrive with the Turtle-Doves ; the Hoopoe a fortnight before them.

The Kingfisher is permanent, and is seen flying throughout the year along the sea-shore.

The island is principally supplied with domestic fowls from the Morea : the Turkies, running in the olive-grounds, become exceedingly fat, and acquire an excellent flavour from the fruit which they pick up. They are sold at six piastres each : a couple of fowls for one piastre.

The persecutions of numerous sportsmen have entirely extirpated the breed of Partridges : the red-legged species is found in Cephalonia, and brought over to Zante, and kept in cages to sing, or rather call.

Quails are found through the summer, and some winter here ; as I observed them in the sedges, near the sea-coast, in January.

Of the Pigeons, a few Stock Doves are kept domesticated : wild Stock Doves breed in the rocks on the coast ; but the greater number arrive in October, spread themselves over the vallies, and retire in the spring. Together with the Stock Doves, great flights of Wood-Pigeons are seen. The Turtle-Doves arrive the beginning of April, and retire early in May ; on their coming to the island they feed on the seed of the Charlock, or Lapsána, and are purged by it, and soon become exceedingly poor. The return of these birds is in August ; but their flocks are then considerably diminished. They may be considered as the first object of pursuit to the Zantiote sportsmen ; great numbers are shot, and several taken in snares; when fat, they are preserved as delicacies.

Of the Larks, the Crested Lark remains throughout the year, and breeds here; the Calandra, the Sky-Lark, Tree-Lark, arrive in October, fly in flocks during the winter-season, retiring in the spring. The Tit-Lark single, or in small flocks, is seen in wet places in the valley throughout the winter.

The Starling is seen in small flocks during the winter, arriving and retiring with the Lapwing.

Of the Thrushes, the Song-Thrush and Blackbird arrive in October, and retire early in the spring, in March : the Solitary Sparrow is confined to the mountains where it breeds and resides throughout the year ; and the Rock-Thrush appears in the autumn.

Of the Grosbeaks, the Hawfinch and Green-finch migrate here during the winter, and retire in April. Of the Buntings, the common Bunting stays through the year, and breeds here ; the Ortolan arrives the latter end of April, breeds, and retires the beginning of June.

Of the Finches, the House-Sparrow, Goldfinch, and Linnet, are permanent : the Chaffinch, which is the most frequent bird in the island, arrives in October, stays the winter, and leaves the island in April.

The slender-billed birds which migrate are very numerous ; the white and yellow Wagtails arrive in October, and stay the winter, retiring in April: they are seen near the town, and in low plashy grounds. The Nightingale arrives in March, is heard part of the summer, and departs in August. The common Wren is seen hopping in the olive-grounds and gardens, throughout the year. The Willow-Wren migrates during the winter months ; at the same season the Redbreast appears, retiring in the spring ; and with it migrates the Katralouthra, the Atricapilla, and the Alessandros. The Wheat-ear, the Stone-chatter, the Bramble-chatter, and the Sycomoura are seen in the summer-months, and retire in autumn. The Beccafico arrives in August, during the season of the figs, and stays a short time : a fortnight before its arrival, the Grape-eater is seen, retiring at the same time. The Whinchat stays the winter, and departs in the spring.

The Great Titmouse, which I saw during the winter-months, I suspect also remains through the year, and breeds here, as well as the Black Titmouse, Κουφανδώνι. The Pratincola is seen in its passage in the month of April. Of the Swallows, the Swift, the Martin, and the common Swallow arrive in March, and retire before September. The Hirundo rupestris is an exception to the Swallow tribe, and is seen during the winter-months. I observed it in December and January flying under the walls of the citadel, and the outskirts of the town.

The Goat-sucker is seen in the summer, and sometimes in the winter ; and the popular report remains of its milking the goats.

Of the Grallæ, from the scarcity of water few are seen, but in their passage. The great species of Crane, called Troumbanos, which is frequent in the lakes of the Morea, may be occasionally noticed. I observed also, in the month of January, the grey Heron. The Stork is rarely seen ; the white and purple Heron, and the Bittern, are observed in the month of April, on their passage. Occasional flights of Woodcocks are found from the beginning of October to the middle of February. During the winter, the common Snipe, and Jack-Snipe, are seen in the vallies. The Curlew, which retires in February, is observed among the rushes, in the plashy plains ; but none of these birds breed here.

The Lapwing arrives the beginning of November, and leaves the island before March. The Stone Curlew is heard piping in the fields in the summer-months, and may be seen sometimes in the winter. The Land-Rail is very rare ; an old sportsman assured me he had never seen but one : the Water-Rail is more frequent, and is sometimes observed in the winter-months.

Yaltarída, Neropoúli, Kousoracos, are species of Grallæ that visit Zante during the winter. The Κοκέλλα arrives in the middle of March, and retires the middle of April.

Of the Anseres, only the Wild Duck breeds here. The Wild Swan is an occasional visitant, as is also the Wild Goose, the Teal, and Wigeon : all these birds are seen in the course of the winter. The Corvorant and Pelican are sometimes observed swimming off the coast; and the common black and white Gulls flying along the shore. The greater Tern is seen sometimes flying near the coast, following the fishing net.

Additional Remarks on. some Parts of the Natural History of Mount Athos, and the Island of Zante.

The Caloyers of Mount Athos not eating flesh, very few domestic animals are kept by them. Bullocks, of an iron-grey colour, I observed feeding in the vales, and browsing on the shrubs : they were kept only to fatten, as objects of profit. A lamb was purchased with some difficulty at Caryes for five piastres, an exorbitant price, when compared with that for which one might have been procured at Lemnos. Dogs were kept as guards to the Kellia and monasteries. The Caloyers seemed fond of cats, but they were all of the male kind: these, with a few horses, mules, and asses, were the domestic quadrupeds of Athos : of the wild, I was told there were no bears or wolves. I procured the following list, though an imperfect one :

Αλουπου *	Canis vulpes
Ελαφι	Cervus elaphus
Ζαρκαδι	Cervus Capreolus
'Αγριοκατζικι	Capra
Αγριογουρουρουνι	Sus Aper ferus
Σκαντζόχοιρος †	Erinaceus Europæus

---

* The word in this form, as well as Αλεπου, is found in Du Cange. But Coray shews that it ought to be written 'Αλωπου, and not 'Αλεπου. I observe the word Αλωπος in the Brevis Historia Animalium, p. 5. edited by Mathæi, at Moscow, 1811, at the expense of the Zosimádes; but it is used as early as the second century of the Christian æra, by Ignatius. See Coray, Ακολουθ. prefixed to the Parallel Lives of Plutarch, part the third. — E.

† Properly Ακανθόχοιρος, and by the barbarous change of θ into τς, Ασκαντσ'χοιρος. Coray.

Ἄσβος	Meles taxus
Κουνάδι	Mustela Martes
Λαγὸς	Lepus timidus
Ἀγριόγαττος	Felis cattus
Βλόυκος	———
Ἀγριοσυνσάπι	———
Πονδικὸς	Mus domestica.

I was favoured with the following list of fishes from the Caloyers.

Λύκνος	Uranoscopus scaber
Σάγγανος	Esox belone
Σκαθάρι	Sparus
Συναγρίδα	Sparus dentex
Λιθινάρι ⎫ Μερτζανι ⎭	Sparus
Σαργὸ	Sparus sargus
Μελανόυρι	Sp. melanurus
Σπάρο	Sp. annularis
Σάλπα	Sp. salpa
Βοῦπα	Sp. Boupa
Μόρμυρο	Sp. mormyrus
Χρύσοφις	Sp. auratus
Φάγγρος	Sp. pagrus
Ρόφος	Sp. orphus
Πέρκα	Perca marina
Λουφάρι	Per. Louphari
Ἥλιο	Labrus Iulis
Χριστόψαρο	Zeus faber
Φρίσσα	Clupea alosa
Σαρδέλλα	——— sardella
Κόλιας	Scomber colias
Σταυρίδι	Sc. trachurus
Τρίγλα ⎫ Βαρβόυνι ⎭	Mullus barbatus

Κέφαλο	Mugil cephalus
Αθερίνα	Atherina hepsetus
Ξίφιο	Xiphias gladius
Μούγγρι	Muræna conger
Δρακίνα	Trachurus draco
Σκορπίνα	Scorpæna porcus
Χάννι	Labrus Chanus
Βαλήνα	
Θύννος	Scomber thynnus
Πελαμίτις	Sc. Pelamitis
Χελιδωνόψαρο	Trigla Gurnardus
Πετεινόψαρο	Trigla hirundo
Γοβιὸ	Gobius
Σμύρνα	Muræna helena
Γάττα	Squalus mustela
Σκυλόψαρο	Squalus catulus.

Mollusca, &c.

Οκτωπόδια	} Sepia octopodia
Σούπια	
Καλαμάρια	
Ἔχινος	Echinus
Ἀστακὸς	Cancer astacus
Κάβουρο	
Πάγουρι	——— pagurus
Φούσκα	——— medusa
Οστρίδια	——— gaideropus
Πεταλίδα	Patella Græca
Πίννα	Pinna marina
Αχιβάδα	Mactra stultorum
Κοκκίλι	Turbo marina.

The shore of Athos is exceedingly rocky ; generally deep : I observed few shell fish cast on it. The Pinna is frequent ; on opening one we observed two shrimp-like crabs within its shell.* The season for the entomologist was past. I saw some species of Lepidoptera, as Pap. Cleopatra, Hyale, Brassicæ, Cardui, Arge, still remaining. The Gnats were very troublesome while we were lying at anchor in the bay of Daphne.

Athos is composed of a variety of rocks of gneiss, of marble of different shades, from grey to white, and of glimmer slate. The hollow of these rocks is filled with the rich earth of decayed vegetables, and offers to the botanist a great diversity of plants, which are sheltered by the shade of the trees, and protected by the superstition of the caloyers from being browsed on by the goats ; so that, at the late season of the year, when we visited it, I was enabled to make a list of 450 plants which I observed on it. I neither visited the northern side of it, nor the higher regions where are the parts which supply the greatest variety of vegetables. I conclude that Athos, more than any mountain in Greece, abounds in plants, particularly those which the botanist terms subalpine, and wood plants. Of the really alpine, Greece furnishes very few ; and if Athos is less high than Parnassus, it is more wooded. It contains a far greater number of trees and shrubs, some of which are not to be found in any other part of Greece. The beautiful Andrachne grows here in greater abundance than either in Crete or Bœotia ; which, if we except Skiatho, are the only *habitats* for it, that I know of. The continual alarms from the pirates prevented my sleeping on shore ; and the little opportunity I had of conversing with the Caloyers did not add much to my stock of knowledge of the economical uses of the Greek

---

* " Cancer Pisum. Crabs of this kind, or allied to them, the antients believed to be the consentaneous inmates of the Pinnæ, and other bivalves, which being too stupid to perceive the approach of their prey, were warned of it by their vigilant friend." Pennant. Dr. Sibthorp refers to Oppian for a description of these Cancri. The passage is in the Halieutics, l. 2. The Cancer is called Πιννοφύλαξ. — E.

plants. The wild cabbage was frequent on the sea-cliffs; our sailors collected quantities of it ; the flavour was bitter, but not unpleasant ; they ate it boiled with oil. They collected also the leaves of the sow-thistle, as a pot-herb. The Donax, which grew in the moist chasms of the rock, supplied them with fishing rods ; and I was informed the Caloyers drew a considerable quantity of oil from the berries of the Bay. Belon figures the Euphorbia Apios, and says, its medicinal virtues were known to the Caloyers. I remember meeting with it in Crete, where a Caloyer told me the upper part, if eaten, proved emetic ; the lower part cathartic.* I observed the apple-like appearance on the Salvia-triloba to be common ; and very perfect specimens of the horn-like figure from the puncture of the Cynips on the Terebinthus.

ZANTE.

PISCES.

Δρόγκος	Muræna conger
Γαλέρα	Ophidium barbatum
Κούκος	Uranoscopus scaber
Δρακίνα	Trachinus Draco
Μελύτζιο	Gadus Merluccius
Μπακαλέος	G. Mustela
Φίλιππος	Blennius Gallongius
Γλιόρδα	B. Pholis
Φιάμμολα	Cepola tænia
Σαμμάμιτα	Callyonymus Zacynthius
Ασγόβιος	Gobius niger
Σκορπίδι	Scorpæna porcus
Σανπίερο	Zeus Faber
Ρόμπος	Pleuronectes rhombus

*. See Dioscorides, l. 4. c. 177.

Πάσσερα	P. passer
Σφύγιο	P. glossa
Σπάρος	Sparus annularis
Τριπούρα	S. auratus
Σαργὸς	S. sargus
Μελανούρο	S. melanurus
Σμαρίδα	S. smaris
Τζερούλα	S. mæna
Ὀρφὸς	S. orfus
Ἐρύθρινος	S. erythrinus
Φάγρος	S. pagrus
Βώπα	S. boops
Σκαθάρι	S. cantharus
Καλόγριτζα	S. chromis
Συναγρίδα	S. dentex
Μορμούρο	S. mormyrus
Σάλπα	S. salpa
Σκάρος	Labrus scarus
Χάννι	L. Channus
Γυφτομανιάτικος	L. furcatus
Πρασινάρι	L. turdus
Τζουγλομίτι	L. tinca
Γιούλος	L. iulis
Χιλούδα	L. lapina
Τζακούλι	L. hepatus
Γύπτος	L. ocellaris
Λαπινάκι	L. melops
Γύπτος	L. fuscus
Συκιὸς	Sciæna umbra
Λαβράκι	Perca lubrax
Πέρκα	P. marina
Γουρουνόψαρο	Gasterosteus ductor
Λίτζα	G. Litza
Τουνίνα	Scomber thynnus

Παλαμίτα	S. Pelamis
Κολιὸς	S. Scomber
Σαυρίδι	S. Trachurus
Χελιδωνόψαρο	Trigla cuculus
Λούτζιον	Esox sphyræna
Βελονίδα	
Τζακουράφα }	E. belone.

INSECTA.

Papilio Atalanta
—— Brassicæ
—— Hyale
—— Urticæ
Cimex hyoscyami
Cimex baccarum
Cancer Pisum

Cancer Rhomboides	ἀναποδοκάβουρα
C. depurator	αμμουκάβουρα
C. araneus	τζαμβλάκος τοῦ πελάγου
C. rostratus	σφαλάγγι τοῦ πελάγου
C. hirtellus	κοκκινοκάβουρα *
C. coccineus	idem.
C. longimanus	σκορπίος τοῦ πελάγου
C. Squilla	γαρίδα *
C. Diogenes	κατζουμάδι
C. Pilosus	καβουρομάνα
C. arctus	μαννόπουλα
C. Mantis	καρδαβίτζα
Oniscus	ψῆρα τοῦ πελάγου

---

* Γαρίδα, cancer; from καρὶς, of the antient Greeks; vid. Du Cange. Κάβουρος, according to Eustathius, is corrupted from κάμμορος. Du C. in v. Καβ.—E.

MOLLUSCA.

Nereis versicolor	·ψῆρα τοῦ πελάγου
Asterias rubens	σταυρὸς τοῦ πελάγου
As. aculeata	idem, and ἀγριοσταυρό
Actinia impudica	μοῦνι τοῦ πελάγου
Ascidia intestinalis	
——— rustica	
Holothuria tubulosa	θαλασσοψωλὴ
Aphrodita squamata	τζικνίδα τῆς βουρλίας
Asterias aranciaca	σταυρὸς τοῦ πελάγου
As. ophiura	ἄστρον τοῦ πελάγου
Echinus esculentus	ἄχινος
——— Sphæroides	κουμαρέλλι
Sepia octopodia	ὀκτωπόδι
S. officinalis	σήπια
S. Lidona	λίδωνα τοῦ πελάγου
S. Loligo	καλαμάρι *

TESTACEA.

Lepas anatifera	ἀμιδάκι τοῦ καραβίου
Pholas dactylus	δάκτυλος and ἀγραμίδα
Solen vagina	σουλήνα
Tellina lævigata	
T. striata	
T. gibbosa	
T. angulata	πλαταμίδα τοῦ ἄμμου
T. lactea	
Cardium rusticum	ἀχιβάδα
C. edule	id.
Mactrastultorum	ἀχιβάδα τοῦ ἄμμου

---

* Τευθίδες τὰ κοινῶς λεγόμενα καλαμάρια., Sch. Opp. Hal. i. 428. — E.

Venus Chione
Venus tellinoides
Arca barbata
A. glycymeris   ἀχιβάδα
A. nucleus   μαμιδάκι
Ostrea Jacobæa   καποσάντα
—— glabra
—— sanguinea
Anomia ephippium   πατελλίδα τῆς οστρέας
Pinna nobilis   πίννα
Cypræa   γουρουνάκι τοῦ πελάγου
Voluta rustica   τούρτουλα
V. cornicula
Buccinum galea
———— testiculus
———— mutabile
Donax trunculus   μύδι τοῦ ἄμμου
Chama Gryphoides
Mytilus edulis   μαβρομύδι
Argonauta Argo   χολακτόποδι
Turbo rugosus   βῆσι τῆς Παναγίας
T. reflexus
T. bidens
T. pictus
T. hæmatostomus
T. politus
T. neritoides   σαλίγγας
Helix albella   σαλιγγοβραικα
H. nemoralis   παμβαλόυτζι
H. subcylindrica
H. cornea
H. lineata
H.᾿ Ianthina   αρμινισταρομάννα

Helix fragilis
Nerita glaucina   γουρουνάκι
Patella vulgata   πεταλίδα
P. inæqualis   Id.
Spondylus gaidaropus γαιδερόποδα
Arca Noæ   σπεττονίκι
Murex trunculus   ἀγριοκαρακάνγιολας
M. reticularis
M. craticulatus

PLANTÆ CULTÆ.

1.	Triticum	πολίτις	Zante
2.	——	ἀσπροσιτάρι	Zante
3.	——	διμηνιό	Lebadea
4.	——	κοκκινοσίτι	Lebadea
5.	——	βλακοστάρι	Lebadea
6.	——	μονολόγι	Lebadea
7.	——	Caracultchuc	Plain of Troy
8.	——	Bogdai	Lemnos
9.	——	Sarabogdai	Troy
10.	——	Devedishi	Troy
11.	——	στάρι	Constantinople
12.	——	στάρι	Athens
13.	——	στάρι	Athens
14.	Hordeum sativum	κρίθι	Athens
15.	Avena sativa	——	Constantinople
16.	——	βρῶμι	Athens
17.	——	βρίζα	Athens
18.	Oryza sativa	——	Lebadea
19.	Holcus	δάρι	Lemnos
20.	——	καλαμβόκι	Peloponnesus
21.	Zea Mays	——	Troy .
22.	——	ἀραποσίτι	Athens

23. Lupinus	λαθού ρι*	Athens
24. Vicia faba	κουκί	Athens
25. Vicia sativa	βίκιον	Athens
26. Ervum lens	φάκη	Athens
27. Cicer ariet.	ροβίθι	Athens
28. Phaseolus vulg.	——	Athens
29. Pisum sativum	——	Lemnos
30. Sesamum off.	——	Constantinople
31. Gossypium	——	Athens
32. Raphanus sativus	——	Athens
33. Hibiscus esculentus	Sultan bamia	Constantinople
34. Cichorium endivia	————	Constantinople
35. Cynara cardunculus	————	Pera
36. Atriplex hortensis	————	Athos
37. Solanum Æthiopicum	————	Constantinople
38. S. Lycopersicum	————	Constantinople
39. Capsicum annuum	————	Byzantium
40. Cucurbita Citrullus	————	Byzantium
41. C. Lagenaria	————	Byzantium
42. C. Melopepo	————	Byzantium
43. Cucumis Melo	————	Troy
44. Trichosanthes Anguina	————	Troy
45. Dolichos Lablab	————	Byzantium
46. Mirabilis Jalapa	————	Byzantium
47. Helianthus annuus	————	Athens
48. Mimosa Nilotica	————	Athens
49. Trifolium Melilotus	————	Pera.

* In Sommavera we find Κουκιά, φακιά, βικιά, λαθήρι.

TRANSLATION OF THE ARABIC INSCRIPTION,

FOUND IN THE INTERIOR OF THE PYRAMID OF CEPHRENES,

March, 1818.

[THE labour, danger, and difficulties which M. Belzoni experienced in his endeavours to open and examine the pyramid of Cephrenes, are stated by him in a letter, which was printed in the Quarterly Review, No. 37. ; In one of his communications addressed to the Earl of Aberdeen, as President of the Society of Antiquaries, he sent a copy of an Arabic inscription which he found on the western wall of the great chamber of the Pyramid. This curious document I have received from the Earl of Aberdeen ; and it is now printed, for the first time, from M. Belzoni's copy, accompanied by the following illustration, with which I have been favoured by Professor Lee.] — *Editor.*.

وفتحهم المعلم أحمد محمد الجمال وذلك وذلك المعلم
عثمان حضر والملك علي محمد اولا ولغلاث

Queen's College, Cambridge; October 24. 1819.
Dear Sir,

I BELIEVE I said, when I last had the pleasure of seeing you in Cambridge, that I was of opinion the order of the words in the inscription, which you had communicated to me, was very much confused. I was led to form this conjecture from the position of the word الاول : which, as it now stands in the inscription, seems to baffle every attempt towards making an intelligible translation. Hence I was also led to suppose, that this was not the only transpósition, which had, by some means or other, found its way into the inscription ; and made it apparently point out persons of whom we have no ac-count in the histories of Egypt. My next endeavour was an attempt to restore the inscription to the order in which it might originally have stood: and then to determine, if possible, both the persons and circumstances to which it alluded. After several trials I fixed upon the. following order, which I now submit, as affording a probable solution of the difficulties, which this curious document appeared to present :

وفتحهم اولا المعلم محمد بن احمد الجار وعلي ذلك حصر الملك عثمان والمعلم (عثمان)

ومحمد لعلاك

TRANSLATION.

" The master*, Mohammed, son of Ahmed the stone-cutter, first opened them †; and, upon this (occasion) were present El Melik Othman, and the master (Othman), and Mohammed Luglák."

Now if we turn to Abdallatif's account of Egypt, we shall find the following remarkable narrative‡, which, I am inclined to think, points out the circumstance alluded to in the inscription. It will be of little consequence whether we adopt the translation of White or De Sacy. I have been inclined to take the latter, as well on account of its superior accuracy, as the valuable notes with which it is accompa-nied.

Quand Mélic-alaziz Othman ben-Yousouf eut succédé à son père, il se laissa persuader par quelques personnes de sa cour, gens dépourvus de bon sens, de démolir ces pyramides ; et l'on commença par la py-ramide rouge, qui est la troisième des grandes pyramides et la moins considerable.

---

* The word معلم here translated " master," appears to be a title of office. " These Mollems," says a late traveller in Egypt, " are, in fact, a kind of clerks to government, in all the principal cities and towns throughout Egypt. They receive the orders of the various governors, and collect the tribute, &c. from the Copts."— Mission. Reg. for Sept.

† Alluding, probably, to the chambers of the Pyramid.

‡ Relation de l'Egypte, p. 177. (page 101 of White's edition.)

3 M 2

Le Sultan y envoya ·donc des sapeurs, des mineurs et des, carriers, sous la conduite de quelques-uns des principaux officiers et des premiers émirs de sa cour, et leur donna ordre de la détruire. Pour exécuter les ordres dont ils étoient chargés, ils établirent leur camp près de la pyramide ; ils y ramassèrent de tous côtés un grande nombre de travailleurs, et les entretinrent à grand frais. Ils y demeurèrent ainsi huit mois entiers, occupés avec tout leur monde a l'exécution de la commission dont ils étoient chargés, enlevant chaque jour, après s'être donné bien du mal et avoir épuisé toutes leurs forces, une ou deux pierres. Les uns les poussoient d'en-haut avec des coins et des leviers, tandis que d'autres travailleurs les tiroient d'en-bas avec des cordes et des câbles. Quand une de ces pierres venoit enfin à tomber, elle faisoit un bruit épouvantable, qui retentissoit a un très-grand eloignement, et qui ébranloit la terre et faisoit trembler les montagnes. Dans sa chute, elle s'enfonçoit dans le sable ; il falloit derechef employer de grands efforts pour l'en retirer ; après quoi, l'on y pratiquoit des entailles, pour y faire entrer des coins : on faisoit ainsi éclater ces pierres en plusieurs morceaux ; puis on chargeoit chaque morceau sur un chariot pour le traîner au pied de la montagne qui est à peu de distance, et où l'on le jetoit.

Après être restés long-temps campés en cet endroit, et avoir consommé tous leurs moyens pécuniaires, comme leur peine et leurs fatigues alloient toujours en croissant, que leur résolution au contraire s'affoiblissoit de jour en jour, et que leurs forces étoient épuisées, ils furent contraints de renoncer honteusement à leur enterprise. Loin d'obtenir le succès qu'ils s'étoient promis, et de réussir dans leur dessein, ils n'en retirèrent d'autre avantage que' de gâter la pyramide, et de mettre dans une entière évidence leur impuissance et leur foiblesse. Ceci se passa en l'année, 593. * (Com. nov. 1196.)

---

* The above date corresponds to A. D. 1196-7, beginning on the 23d of November in the former. In a note by M. de Sacy, p. 223., of the Relation above cited, the date A. D. 1193 is given from the Annales Moslemici of Abulfeda ; but it should be remembered that this is not given as the date of the event : for it will be found by consulting Abulfeda, that the date he gives for the accession of Othman to the throne of Egypt, agrees with that given by Abdallatif.

Hence it appears that a preparation, sufficient to accomplish the event, pointed out by the inscription, was made by Othman ; and that he actually took down a part of the smaller pyramid. It must be confessed, however, that we have no positive account of the opening of the second pyramid, in which our inscription was found: though the probability appears strong to me, that it must have taken place on the above occasion. There is a passage in a work by Makrizi, entitled, كتاب السلوك لمعرفة دول الملوك " An Introduction to a Knowledge of the royal Dynasties," which I have thought may allude to the circumstance in question ; and, as it is dated one year earlier than the account of the partial demolition of the third pyramid, may, if allowed to have any weight, intimate that an attempt was made upon the two larger ones, prior to that time. The passage is this :

دخلت سنة الثنين وتسعين ..... وفي ذي الجة عزم العزيز علي نقض الاهرام ونقل جارتها الي
صور د،بياط فقيل له ان المونة تعظم في هدمها والفايدة تقل من جرها فانتقل رايه من الهرمين
الي الهرم الصغير وهو مبني بالجارة الصوان فشرع في هدمه وفيه سار العزيز الي الاسكندرية

" In the beginning of the year (5)92 ... In the month Dhi 'lhijjat, Alaziz (i. e. Othman) conceived a design of destroying the pyramids, and of carrying the stones to the walls of Damietta : but upon being informed that the expense in demolishing them would be great, and the gain, as regarded the stones, but small, he turned his attention from the two larger pyramids to the smaller one, which was built with granite, and began to destroy it. In the same (month) he returned to Alexandria."

Now as the first pyramid had been opened since the time of * El

___

* It has generally been thought, that El Mamoon opened the first pyramid about A. D. 829, to which the Arabic historians give an universal assent. M. de Sacy, however, doubts the fact, from the manner in which Dionysius of Telmahre speaks of it. " Il me paroît fort douteux," says the learned and ingenious writer, (p. 219.) " que la première ouverture de la grande pyramide soit due au Khalife Mamoun. Mon doute est fondé sur la manière dont Denys de Telmahre, patriarche Jacobite d'Antioche, qui accompagna Mamoun en Egypte, parle de la pyramide, qui étoit déjà ouverte quand il la visita."
The passage alluded to is found in page 556. of the *Relation :*
ܣܘܒ ܚܥܘܕܟܡܗܐ ܐ ܒܚܩܡܐ ܐܘܐ ܚܟܐ ܒܣܡ ܥܕܢܒܝ ܘܚܟܡܚܐ ܐܘܐ ܐܣܪ ܡܟܡܟܡ ܐܟܬܟ
which he translates thus : " Nous avons regardé par une ouverture qui étoit faite de

Mámoon, it is not so likely that the king would make an attempt upon this, as upon the second. There is also another circumstance that appears to add something towards establishing this conjecture, which is the following passage, given in the same book, and under the same date : viz. المحرومي يوسف بن عثمان على بن الله عبد المعلم مات وفيها " And in the same year died the master Abd Allah Ebn Ali Othman Ebn Yusuf El Mahrúmi." Now if this be the person designated in our inscription by المعلم to which I have added عنها in a parenthesis, supposing it to have been omitted for the sake of brevity, we arrive at a great degree of certainty as to the purport and date of the inscription. Still I must not be understood as pronouncing positively on these points ; my object is only to lay before you and your readers the best interpretation of the inscription that has occurred to me.

There is still another name : viz. لغلاك محمد, Mohammed Luglák, of which I am unable to give any account, not having been able to find any in the books I have consulted on this subject. This, however, does not appear to me to present any difficulty, in regard to the interpretation above given, as it is not improbable he may have been some Tartar (for the name is not of Arabic origin) who might have been among the courtiers of Othman.

I know of no circumstance in the annals of Egypt, likely to present a better interpretation of the inscription in question, than that which has already been given ; for, although El Mamoon, as above noticed,

---

l'une de ces édifices et qui est profonde de cinquante coudes." But with every deference to the talents of M. de Sacy, I cannot help thinking that the passage in question, serves rather to establish the general opinion than the contrary; for it does not appear from the Syriac original, that the Patriarch is speaking of an event, that had long taken place, but the contrary. " We saw," says he, " the opening that had been made in the side of one of them, and it was about fifty cubits deep." The time is not mentioned, it is true, when the aperture was made ; but I am inclined to think the Patriarch mentions it as a recent event.

There is a passage in Strabo, (lib. xvii. p. 808. edit. Paris, 1620,) noticed also in Norden, in which it is said, that there was a moveable stone, about the middle of the side of the pyramids, (μέσως πως των πλευρων λίθον ἐξαιρέσιμον,) which opened a passage to the chambers. The taking out of this stone is all Mamoon could have done, and which, I think, it is probable he did.

as well as Ebn Tuloon *, is said to have visited the great pyramid, yet there does not appear any thing in the inscription that points to them. If I may be allowed to hazard a conjecture on the inscription itself, I should say, that the confused order in which it appears, is to me an evidence of its authenticity; for had an Arab been employed to fabricate it in Egypt, I am of opinion, there would neither have been obscurity in its language, nor difficulty in its application. Nor is it improbable, that the confused order already noticed, may have arisen, either from the ignorance of the workman, who engraved it in the pyramid, or from a custom which is found to prevail in the inscriptions of coins, &c. where the order is entirely sacrificed to appearance. It is, however, much to be regretted, that we have not a fac-simile of the inscription, which would probably, on its first appearance, dissipate every doubt and difficulty, that may yet remain. I mention this, because I think there may still be an error in the last word of the inscription; for. if اغلق be the true reading, where we now have لذلك, a key would be afforded towards explaining the silence of the Arabic historians on the event in question; and in that case, I should conclude the inscription to be incomplete. If the word اغلق be substituted for لذلك, it would seem, that the person who opened the pyramid, had already determined again to close it up, which, had it been immediately done, might have been the means of eluding the notice of the historians.

I remain, dear Sir, yours, &c.

SAMUEL LEE.

---

* In a work by Soyuti, entitled, كتاب حسن المحاضرة في اخبار مصر والقاهرة we have the following account: ولما احمد بن طولون .... حفر علي ابواب الاهرام فوجدوا في الحفر قطعة مرجان .... فيئس من فتحها " When Ahmed Ebn Tuloon dug down to the doors of the pyramids, they found a vessel of pearl, &c. ... but he gave up the hope of opening them."
Again,

دخل جماعة في ايام احمد بن طولون الهرم الكبير فوجدوا في احدي بيوته جاما من زجاج غريب اللون فبلغ احمد بن طولون فمنع الناس من الدخول .... " In the time of Ahmed Ebn Tuloon, a number of people entered the great Pyramid, who found in one of its chambers a cup of glass, of wonderful colour. When Ahmed Ebn Tuloon was informed of this, he gave orders that none should enter it."

[For the following literal version of M. Belzoni's copy of the inscription, with the accompanying remark, the editor is obliged to Mr. Usko. — E.]

وفتحهم,   *wa fatahh-hum*, and opened them,

المعلم   *al muâllim*, the master,

محمد بن احمد   *Mohammed ben Ahhmed*, Mohammed Son of Ahhmed,

الحجار   *al-hhuggiar*, the stone-cutter,

وذلك   *wa dhalik*, and likewise

المعلم   *al muâllim*, the Master,

عثمان   *Othman.*

حضر   *hhadera* (There) was present

والملك   *wal malik*, also the king,

علي محمد   *Aly Mohhammed*,

اولا   *awwalan*, at first,

ولغلاك   *wa Leghlak*, and Leghlak.

— — — — — — —

It appears to me that the inscription does not finish here, but is continued to render the sense more complete, and to add the date to it when the opening of the pyramid or pyramids took place ; I say of the pyramids, as the inscription bears at its commencement :—He, the master, opened *them* (هم hum). If any mistake is committed in copying this inscription, the word Leghlak is more liable to it than any other. Let us suppose, then, that Leghlak was written in the inscription اغلاك Oghlak, or Oughlak, (pronounced in English Ooghlak), the copyist might have mistaken the Alif, which is never connected with any letter of the Arabic alphabet at the beginning of a word, for a Lam, which is commonly and usually connected with the following letter. Should we admit it, there would be another difficulty of ascertaining who this Oughlak was. With respect to al Hhuggiar, or as it is more frequently pronounced in common life, al Hhaggiar, there is, I think, no doubt of its signification here, viz. that of stone-cutter. Hhager signifies a stone, in Arabic, and Hhaggiar a stone-cutter. Hagar, in Genes. ch. xvi. v. 15., and ch. xxi. v. 9. &c., and Agar, in the Ep. to Galat. ch. iv, v. 24, 25. are the same words, pronounced with a hard ga, in the same manner as the Arabic ج gim is now pronounced at Mecca and in Egypt.

ACCOUNT OF

A JOURNEY THROUGH PART OF LITTLE TARTARY;

AND OF SOME OF

THE ARMENIAN, GREEK, AND TARTAR SETTLEMENTS

IN THAT PORTION OF THE RUSSIAN EMPIRE.

[*FROM THE JOURNALS OF MR. WHITTINGTON.*]

———

Armenian Settlement of Nachtchivan. — First Appearance of the Town. — Population. — Flourishing state of the Colony. — Rude Statues belonging to the Tumuli on the Stepps. — Religious Ceremonies attending the Elevation of the Cross, over the Dome of the principal Church at Nachtchivan. — Arrival at Taganrog. — Population. — Trade of this Place with Turkey. — Route between Taganrog and Mariapol. — Tents, Dress, Appearance, and Mode of Life of the Calmuks. — Mariapol; a Settlement of Crimean Greeks. — Arrival in the Territory of the Nogay Tartars. — Account of their Habits and Manners. — Striking contrast presented by the Industry and Cultivation visible in a Settlement of Prussian Sectaries.

SATURDAY, June 10. O. S. 1816. — The information which we had received respecting the colonies planted by the Russian government on the northern coast of the sea of Azoff, having determined us to visit that part of Little Tartary, in our way to the Crimea, we this day quitted the city of Old Tcherkask, and after sailing down the Don, as far as Oksai, proceeded along its right bank to the Armenian settlement of Nachtchivan.

Nothing could be more striking than the transition from the deserted and ruinous capital of the Cossacks to the streets of this flourishing little town. The appearance of the houses, which are constructed as in many parts of Turkey, with open wooden corridors, and low tiled roofs, made a pleasing variation to the uniform aspect of Russian architecture ; and the oriental costume of the inhabitants, who filled the market and shops, all active and employed, added forcibly to the effect of the contrast. The Bazar presents a scene really astonishing to one arriving from the vast and lonely Stepps, whose solitary effect had hardly been diminished in our case, by our visit to the empty streets of the two Tcherkasks.* The extensive range of buildings devoted to the shops seems sufficient for a considerable city. Two sides of the large square which they surround have already been completed in brick, and though the others remain still of wood, the whole is filled with a rich display of the merchandise of the East and West ; and being crowded with noisy and anxious bargainers, has a prosperous and cheerful air.

This colony was composed of the Armenians, who were withdrawn from the Crimea by Katharine II., before that peninsula was added to the Russian empire. They were settled on this spot in 1780; and the present generation appear to have no reason to be dissatisfied with the change. The town stands high upon a ridge of shell-limestone, (the last swell of the elevated Stepp,) which forms the right bank of the Don, and overlooks the river with a south-eastern aspect. On the farther side commences the vast plain of Asia, which extends as far as the eye can reach, and which, though low and marshy, does not affect the healthy climate of the place. The winters are severe, but short ; and the broad stream of the Don, which in summer affords the means of commercial intercourse with Taganrog, is occasionally frozen for about two months. When this is not the case, the inhabitants are eager to avail themselves (as an article of summer luxury) of the ice which it brings down with it from more northern latitudes. The town consists of 4600 houses, and contains 6000 male inhabitants. There are from twenty-five to thirty noble families ; and the internal

---

* The removal of the seat of government from Old to New Tcherkask had not been followed, at the time of our visit, by a corresponding movement on the part of the great body of the Cossacks ; so that the modern capital, though the residence of the Ataman and his officers, was but thinly inhabited, and the ancient city, with a considerable population, wore the appearance of poverty and desertion.

government of the place is entirely confided to the Armenians themselves. Provisions are as cheap at Nachtchivan as in the Crimea;
for a pound of meat costs but ten copecks (about one penny), and a
pound of white bread half that sum. The colonists complained in
some degree of the inroads and thefts of the neighbouring Cossacks;
but expressed themselves upon the whole as contented and happy in
their present situation. They have four establishments for the collection of raw silk, but the quantity produced, at the most considerable
of these, appears trifling, not exceeding one hundred weight in the best
years. The white mulberry-tree thrives well in this neighbourhood,
and we even saw it bearing fruit on the marshy islands of Tcherkask.

At the gate of Major Abramoff, an Armenian of noble family, we
observed three of the rude statues, which are collected from the tumuli, or barrows, on the Stepp, and are not uncommonly placed as
ornaments about the houses in this part of Russia. Nothing can be
more uncouth and grim than these representations of the human form.
They are barbarously shaped out of coarse sandstone; but the same
cast of flat Tartar features is observable in all, making it evident that
they are the monuments of some Mongolian tribe. In those which
are transported to towns or villages, the original strange appearance
is not unfrequently increased by the addition of a modern coat of
paint on their faces, hair, and necklaces. Of those at the gate of
Major Abramoff, one is a male, and two are female figures. *

Sunday, June 11. — This was a remarkable holiday for the inhabitants of Nachtchivan. Having just completed their principal church,

* So general has been the removal of these statues, from the stations which they were
formed to occupy, that during the whole of our journey through the Stepps, we saw but
one in its original situation. This figure is placed on the summit of a lofty barrow, not
far from Bakmont, on the road between Kharkoff and Tcherkask. It represents a female
in a sitting posture; but the face is broken, and it is buried to the knees in the earth,
from whence, upwards, it measures about five feet. It fronts the east, and being formed
of white sandstone, is conspicuous from a great distance, over the naked and level Stepp.
There are no others in that neighbourhood; and our driver told us that this was a man
petrified for his sins.

For a good representation of several of these figures, see the plate in vol. i. of P. Pallas's
Travels in the S. of Russia.

in the building of which they have been occupied for many years, they fixed this day for the elevation of the great cross which surmounts the central dome. On arriving at the church we found it already crowded with the inhabitants of both sexes, and the cross deposited in the centre. The women, all enveloped in black ferrigees and white veils, occupied a distinct portion of the aisle from the transepts to the western door. The church itself differs little, externally or internally, from the ordinary modern Russian churches, excepting that the place of the tall pictured screen is supplied by a semicircular curtain, which is occasionally drawn round the altar during the service. The chief priest, when we entered, was occupied in the celebration of the sacrament, but after the usual communion-service was concluded, the ceremony of the day commenced. The officiating priests, habited in rich dresses, formed a ring around the spot where the cross was deposited, while their principal, who wore a splendid mitre, after reading and chanting in the Armenian language, proceeded to wash it all over, first with water and then with wine. A silver vessel, shaped like a dove, was next brought, from which he poured into a plate the precious ointment, which is only made at a convent on Mount Ararat. This he applied with his thumb to the four extremities, and to the intersecting point of the cross, covering the places afterwards with cotton, which the other priests further secured, by binding over it, first paper, and then linen cloths. At particular parts of the ceremony, the noise of the chaunt was heightened by cymbals ; by the chime of a metal cup, which was struck by a boy with a metal clapper ; and by little silver bells attached to a round plate of silver, which, being fixed at the extremity of a long staff, was violently shaken at intervals. After all present had separately advanced, and kissed the cross, it was carried out into the square before the church, and the scene was very pleasing as it was raised by pullies to its place. The whole square was filled with groupes of Armenian figures, all intently watching the ascending cross ; and the loud chaunt of the priests continued in the open air, as it slowly rose and reached its destined situation.

After the ceremony was concluded, an Armenian merchant having asked us to breakfast, we followed him to his house, and were seated upon a divan, beside a low table covered with plates of figs, raisins, parched corn, almonds, and other dry productions of the East. Our meal was rather of a motley description; for we were served in succession with tea, with lemonade, with brandy and water, with liqueurs, until breakfast grew into dinner; and we partook of the usual eastern dishes, pilaff and dolmahs, accompanied by Greek wines, and those of the Don. The women did not dine with us, but sat on a divan in an adjoining apartment, adjusting their heavy dresses of gold brocade. They wore the costume of Constantinople; and their hair, which was dyed black or auburn, hung down their backs in many braids. The men unite the Turkish dress with the European hat, and therefore abstain from shaving the head, except immediately round the forehead and temples. Katarinoff, the merchant with whom we dined, is reputed to possess two millions of rubles; but the plain room in which he received us was ornamented only with two miserable prints of Pitt and Nelson, and with an Armenian almanack, which he said came from Venice. We left Nachtchivan in the evening, and passing through the Russian fortress of Rostoff, traversed the Stepp to Tchaltyr, an Armenian village, where we observed a groupe of female buffaloes with their calves, a sufficient proof that these animals, which at first could ill support the severe winters of this climate, have at length been, to a certain degree, naturalised.

The next day, (June 12.) after a tedious drive across the Stepp, we reached Taganrog. The appearance of this place, at least of its buildings, differs little from the common aspect of the smaller Russian towns; but it is prettily situated on a tongue of land, projecting into the sea of Azoff, at the point of which is a neglected fort. Though the town is placed above a stratum of limestone, and in a country altogether destitute of timber, the Russians have chiefly employed in its construction their usual material, wood, which is procured at great expense from the north, by means of the navigation of the Don. The streets are of great width, and the low houses of a single story by which they are bordered, are only connected with each other by long ranges of wooden paling. A narrow track marks the centre, but the remainder of every street is filled with the luxuriant grass of the Stepp, which at the time we saw it was swarming with green lizards.

The coast presents a cliff of reddish marl; but the usual shell-limestone of this neighbourhood projects at the base. The low line of the opposite Asiatic coast is visible for a great extent, and the fortress of Azoff is sometimes discernible at the distance of thirty versts.

Taganrog contains 8000 houses, and 10,000 male inhabitants. Its trade, which is principally in the hands of Ragusan merchants, is chiefly employed in the interchange of the products of Russia, and even of Siberia, with those of the Levant. The wines of the Grecian Archipelago here find their best market; for the annual average importation of this article is not less than 200,000 vedros, half of which is sent to be consumed in Siberia. The navigation of the Don gives great facilities to this branch of commerce, and brings down the iron and butter, which, together with the corn of Russia, are exported in great quantities to Turkey. We visited the quarantine-establishment, which is the best in Russia, and found its lazaretto entirely occupied by Greek sailors, and by a party of Astrachan Tartars, returning from Mecca.

June 16. — The road between Taganrog and Mariapol, after crossing the Mious, lies over Stepps of the wildest character. The straight black track in the natural soil, which lay in long prospect before us, formed the only variation to the vast field of high and rank grass which surrounded us on every side. Bustards, partridges, and innumerable smaller birds, rose around us as we drove along, and the Stepp seemed alive with myriads of lizards, and of the little animal (Mus Citellus) called Suzlik by the Russians. Among the endless sorts of wild flowers with which the rich soil was every where teeming, we here began to observe the lofty yellow holy-oak, which we afterwards met with in the greatest abundance. In crossing this solitary tract we passed a small Calmuck encampment of two tents. Their form is not unlike that of a bee-hive ; a circular frame of wood rises perpendicularly for two or three feet from the earth, and then closes above into a sort of dome; so that the whole, being covered with mats and felt, contains a chamber of about eight feet in dia-meter. The party we met with consisted of only one family ; the father, mother, and children occupying one tent, and a collection of calves the other. They welcomed us amidst the barking of dogs ; and, conducting us to the smoky interior of their tent, pressed us to repose on a temporary divan of black felt. The features of the fe-male were strongly marked with the characteristics of her race. She was dressed in a loose robe of coarse blue linen, and her jet-black hair hung partly in two tresses, one on each side the face, and partly in a single braid down her back. She wore large silver bracelets, and her nèck and breast were covered with strings of beads. Soon after we were seated, she brought us bread, baked upon the embers, and a small wooden bowl, containing the spirit distilled from a preparation of mare's milk. They told us that the Calmucks prize highly the ad-vantage which their religion (that of the Lhama) gives them over the Nogays, and other Mahometan tribes, by allowing them the use of this ardent beverage, which, on tasting, we found only disagreeable from its great strength. In addition to the care of a few horses, cows, and broad-tailed sheep, this family is accustomed to cultivate annually a small quantity of land, and we saw, not far from their tents, a field of rich barley on the Stepp. They told us that there were other numerous hordes in the neighbourhood, but we were not fortu-nate enough to meet with them. The post throughout the Stepp is served by Cossacks, who dwell in solitary hovels, whither they are frequently sent by way of punishment. Besides these, we passed in the course of the day one or two Russian villages, situated at wide intervals, near the small streams which run towards the sea of Azoff. At one of these, called Gruski Yelenchuck, we saw two specimens of the rude statues before described, in excellent preservation.

Four versts from Mariapol we crossed the Kalmious, by a ferry. The town, which we reached shortly afterwards, is of the same age, and similar origin with Nacht'chivan, being a settlement of Crimean Greeks, who abandoned the peninsula in 1780. Its prosperity, however, has by no means kept pace with that of its sister colony, and seems even to have declined since the visit of Professor Pallas in 1793. The houses resemble those of Nachtchivan in form, but are dirty and in bad repair. The wooden Bazar is ruinous and deserted. No kind of manufacture is now carried on, and the only species of industry displayed in the place is employed on the salting of sturgeons, which are caught in great abundance in the neighbouring sea. The inhabitants, of whom they compute 1500 males, have adopted the Russian costume, but retain the language of the Crim Tartars, making no use of the Romaic.

June 17. — After passing a large Greek village (Mangutch), at the distance of eighteen versts from Mariapol, we found ourselves again on the open Stepp, exhibiting the same wild character as before. We followed for some time the road to Orechoff, and then, turning to the left, proceeded towards the territory of the Nogay Tartars. We saw game, particularly bustards, in great plenty, and the rank luxuriance of the vegetation gave an air of freshness, and even of cheerfulness, to the waste. After driving all day through the high grass, without observing the slightest trace of habitation or cultivation, (for on leaving the road to Orechoff we left also the line of the post,) in the afternoon a Nogay Tartar, handsomely dressed, and well mounted, but unattended, rode up to the side of our carriage, and welcomed us to the territory of his fellow-countrymen. He was going, he said, to visit some hay which was being made for him in a distant part of the Stepp ; and after a short conversation, in the course of which he offered us his fine horse for 800 rubles, suddenly rode off at full gallop. In the evening we reached Obitóchnoe, the capital of the Nogays, and the residence of Count Maison, a French nobleman, now their commandant. He kindly received us into his house, which, to speak the truth, is nearly the only one in the place, and we passed the remainder of the evening in conversing with him on the recent history of the singular people, entrusted to his superintendance.

In consequence of the depredations committed by these wandering tribes, which seemed to be encouraged by their wild and unsettled mode of life, the attention of the provincial government has of late been much directed to the project of inducing them to relinquish their migrations, to build for themselves fixed villages, and to cultivate the Stepp. We listened with much interest to a detail of the measures by which this object, after frequent disappointments, has at last, to all appearance, been accomplished.

Among the devices adopted for the purpose of enticing the hordes of Nogays to make so considerable an infringement on their favourite habits, the first in order was the construction of Mosques ; which having been built at the expence of government, in favourable situations on the Stepp, it was hoped might have had the effect of attracting villages around them. The force of custom, however, was found too strong to be overcome by this inducement ; the tribes moved as before, the Mullahs followed them, and the Mosques were deserted.

The next bait was a fixed bazar ; for Count Maison, having taken advantage of a dispute between the Nogays and some Armenian traders, who followed their migrations, prohibited the latter from attending the Tartar camps, and obliged them to settle near his own house at Obitochnoë. This measure produced a slight effect. The inconvenience of transporting themselves to any great distance from the supplies, which habit had made necessary to them, compelled the Nogays to contract the circle of their movements ; still their general modes of life remained unaltered : they neither built nor settled, but continued to change the situation of their tents, whenever change of pasture became necessary for their herds.

The third measure was of a different nature ; for the government, wearied with the ill success of its ineffectual inducements, suddenly issued an order that a line should be drawn round every Tartar encampment, and that each should be prevented from moving from the

spot, which it at that time chanced to occupy. This command (al_
though on the occasion of a somewhat similar interference in the
reign of Katherine II. the whole nation fled, and took refuge in the
ranges of Caucasus,) was obeyed. The Nogays were content to in_
habit their immoveable camps; and, as their tents decayed, they
were even induced, by the rewards and encouragement of government, to construct houses in their room, and to cultivate a small
portion of land.

There now remained but one step necessary to finish the work
which had been so far successful. In 1812, Count Maison, who,
though a solitary Frenchman, in the midst of ill-satisfied hordes of
the wildest people in Europe, seems, by his address, to have secured
their good-will and respect in a remarkable degree, ventured to order
that every tent which remained should be publicly paid for and de_
stroyed. He was punctually, though unwillingly, obeyed; and had
thus the satisfaction of accomplishing the hazardous undertaking,
which had been entrusted chiefly to his direction and execution. *

The ulterior and more important consequences of this great experi_
ment must remain for some time in uncertainty. Depredations and
murder, which were formerly not uncommon, have already become
rare among the Nogays ; but this is, of course, rather to be attributed
to the stricter superintendance to which they are now subject, than to
any permanent change in their national character. In case the
government should succeed in directing their attention to settled
pursuits of agricultural employment, they will have reason to be
grateful for the interference by which so desirable a change may be
effected ; but at present they seem to have lost the independent
spirit which was engendered by their former mode of life, and to have
fallen into habits of slovenliness and inactivity, from which public

---

* The particular history of these events, and much curious information respecting the
manners of the Nogay Tartars, are well detailed by Professor Degouroff, of Kharkoff, in a
work which deserves to be translated.

encouragements, and the prospect of private gain, are but slowly beginning to rouse them.

The male population, at the time of our visit, amounted to 1700, exclusive of the Myrzas and Mullahs; and the commandant assured me that the number of the whole nation (including the privileged classes, and the women) could not be less than 40,000. They inhabit seventy-three villages*, and cultivate a small quantity of wheat, of which, however, they make little use, living chiefly on preparations of milk in summer, and on flesh in winter. About thirty families have been induced to cultivate potatoes, as an article of food; and four or five have formed gardens. Nearly all the corn which they raise is sent into the Crimea, whence it is exported from the port of Kosloff.

Obitochnoë, so called from the name of the small stream on which it stands, has but few Tartar inhabitants. The house of the commandant, a wretched bazar, and an Armenian church, are the only buildings of the place. Nothing can be imagined more dreary than the appearance of these few ill-constructed edifices, on the surface of the vast Stepp, whose influence is beginning to cover the flat roof of the mud-built Bazar with as rich a crop of grass as that which so widely encircles it. The shopkeepers of this establishment are chiefly Armenians, servants and agents of the merchants of Nachtchivan. They supply the Nogays with tobacco, and with the few manufactured goods which they have learned to use; deriving, as we were told, no small advantage from their traffic. At one of the shops we tasted the drink called koumiss, which is made by fermenting mare's milk, and is a favourite beverage with the Nogays. It retains the appearance of milk, but has a slightly acid flavour, not unlike that of wine-whey. In the spring, and early part of the summer, it possesses no intoxicating power; but after the great heats have rendered the herbs of

---

* Besides these, there is a single village of Russian serfs, the property of the present Ataman of the Don Cossacks, in the vicinity of Obitochnoë.

the Stepp strong and dry, it is said to acquire that property. It is kept in glass bottles, and remains in perfection about a week. The Nogays consider it a stimulant. In the court-yard of the command-ant's house we saw the only remaining specimen of the Nogay tents. It differs from those of the Kalmucks in but one particular; the latter, when transported, being taken in pieces by means of joints, while the more primitive habitation of the Nogays must be placed upon its cart entire.

June 18. — On leaving Obitochnoë, we traversed the Stepp with great rapidity, till, at the distance of fifteen versts, we reached the first Tartar village. It consisted of two rows of low hovels, in all about forty, built at regular intervals so as to form what, had there been a track through the middle, might have been called a wide street. The houses were formed of sun-baked bricks, and were thatched with straw. But the most characteristic feature in the scene was the Taboon, or herd of horses, which was assembled on a rising ground near the village. The groupe consisted of not less than two hundred, and was collected about the spot where several foals were tethered by the foot to a single rope, which was fastened at each end to the ground.

As we drove into the village, we saw the female inhabitants (drest in a bright scarlet costume, with white veils) flying in all directions. The men crowded round us in great numbers, and shewed consider-able curiosity respecting our carriage and its contents, but without rudeness, or any attempt to intrude.

They were coarsely and dirtily habited in the Oriental Caftan and Beniche, which latter was shaped more according to the Persian than the Turkish form. Their flat ugly features, and prominent ears, were surmounted by the close skull-cap of lamb's fur, which seems to have been the model of the tiaras of the Muscovite Tsars. They wore no pistols ; but I observed that some had knives in their girdles, the handles of which were of jasper. They exhibited some symptoms of alarm when we directed our telescope to their Taboon, considering it, at first, as some kind of firelock ; but as soon as we had explained its use, they were anxious to prove it, and delighted with its powers. Upon our expressing our admiration at the beauty and number of their horses, they eagerly assured us that they were able to maintain twice or three times as many, before they were compelled to settle. The value of their finest horses is from 500 to 1000 rubles ; and they told us that a Prussian officer had been with them the year before, and had made large purchases for the use of the cavalry. They spoke with disgust of their houses, which they described as receptacles for filth and vermin, and said that many preferred sleeping on the open Stepp to the confinement of their new habitations. They mentioned the commandant, however, with great affection, calling him " father ;" and his order soon procured us a supply of half-tamed horses, which, driven by a Tartar from the box, conducted us rapidly across the Stepp.

From the neighbourhood of Obitochnoë, we had observed the unusual appearance of a chain of pointed hills rising from the level of the plain ; and we found the next Tartar village situated immediately beneath them. Primitive rock forms the basis of this part of the Stepp, and is very visible in the sides of deep river-courses ; but the Karsak hills form, I believe, the only instance in which it protrudes above the flat alluvial surface, and presents what, in such a country, may be almost considered a bold elevation. We ascended the loftiest of these little eminencies, the height of which is not rated by Pallas at more than eight fathoms above the plain, but which, notwithstanding, commands an undisputed prospect over the surrounding waste. The quartz, of which it is almost entirely composed, is every where pervaded by small black crystals, which, upon analysis, have been found to consist chiefly of iron. The Tartar village, to which we descended, with its slovenly hovels, its Taboon, and its inhabitants, resembled that which we had left behind. Our curiosity led us to the Mosque, which, as may be supposed, partook of the careless character of the place. Its mud walls and straw roof were full of holes, and its wooden minaret, declining far from the perpendicular, seemed to render the office of Muezzin one of no inconsiderable danger.

June 19. — An interval of a few versts, and the river Berda, divide the last village of the Nogays from the first of the Prussian Mennonists. The accompanying change of scene was one of the most extraordinary which occurred in our diversified journey; for the appearance of mercantile activity which enlivens the Bazar of Nachtchivan is hardly more striking than that of agricultural industry and regularity which surrounds the settlements of these German sectaries. Their villages wear a delightful aspect of neatness and comfort. The clean wooden houses, backed by well-built barns and outhouses, are fronted by small paled gardens, and stand embosomed in orchards of cherry-trees. The hospitable interior of these dwellings, is in unison with the promise of the exterior; and the surrounding Stepp, by the exertions of the colonists, has been covered with crops of flourishing corn, which reminded us of the richest parts of the Ukraine. These industrious settlers, who came from the neighbourhood of Dantzig, left the Prussian dominions in consequence of being required to bear arms, which is inconsistent with the religious tenets of their sect. They passed into Russia in the summers of 1803 and 1804, were well received by the government, and were presented with the tract of land which they now occupy, covering about forty square miles to the east of the Moloshnia river. Each of them, who declared himself capable of supporting a farm, received a portion of sixty-four desatines (about 130 acres) of the Stepp. The others settled as servants and labourers. Their whole population amounts to 2621, (of which number 1334 are males,) and has been increased by 700 since their first arrival. Their villages are nineteen in number, but they have, at present, only two places of worship. They seemed well contented with their situation, and spoke highly of the fertility of the natural soil, which returns, in good years, fifteen for one. They experience no annoyance from the neighbouring Nogays, and complain of nothing but of the dryness of the climate, and of the inroads of wolves upon their flocks. The stock of horned cattle and sheep, which they brought with them, has considerably increased, and fetches high prices in the markets of Russia. They make a kind of coarse linen for their own use, and were about to undertake the manufacture of cloth for the same purpose.

They preserve, as much as possible, the usages and language of their country, and, with the exception of a few Russian labourers, have received no mixture of foreigners into their society. There is another colony of Germans, on the west side of the Moloshnia, who bear an indifferent character, and with whom the Mennonists have no intercourse.

At the distance of four versts from Altona, the last German village, we crossed the Moloshnia, a small river, which, like the Berda, and others of this neighbourhood, is choaked at the mouth by the sand which its own stream brings down. Terpenia, which stands on its right bank, is one of eight villages inhabited by the Duchobortzi, or Worshippers of the Spirit, a sect of Russians who reject the use of priests and pictures, and who, after undergoing much persecution, have been collected and settled on this spot, during the reign of the present Emperor. Their population was stated to us at 1500 males. In dress and deportment they did not appear to differ from the common Russians; but on learning that we were travellers from a distant country, they were eager to manifest to us their hospitality and goodwill. They would receive no recompense for the refreshments which we had taken, and even crowded round our carriage with presents of live fowls, sufficient to stock it for several days. We had nothing but money to offer them in return, and this they steadily refused, saying, " God forbid that we should rob a stranger." Their kindness did not even end here; for just as we were about to drive off, the Starista, or chief peasant, a venerable old man, advanced with solemnity, and publicly presented us with bread in the name of the village. We left Terpenia about nine, with the intention of travelling all night, but were detained by an accident at the Russian village of Kisliar till the next morning.

June 20. — After driving all day across the Stepp, in which we passed two villages of Krim Tartars, we reached, in the evening, the Russian station of Tonkoi, or Yenitche. This small groupe of mud cottages is situated upon the Strait, which divides the continental portion of Little Tartary from the slender strip of land, called the Peninsula of Arabat, by which we had determined to enter the Crimea.

The next morning (June 21), as we crossed the ferry, which is not above one hundred yards in width, we had a good opportunity of noting the appearance of the two opposite shores. On the continental side, a cliff rises behind the village, to the height of forty or fifty feet, and running eastward along the sea of Azoff, ends in a cape at the distance of about fifteen versts. To the west, the same cliff continues to edge the strait, and the Sivash, or Putrid Sea, is not visible. The view on the Crimean side, (our first specimen of Crimean scenery,) is singularly dreary. A marsh, partially inundated, stretches onward to the distance of three or four versts, where the ground slightly rises, and is crowned by a few tumuli. The road which leads to Arabat (a distance of 110 versts) along this narrow tongue of land, lies close to the shore of the sea of Azoff, and is composed of the natural soil, which seems to consist chiefly of broken shells. We left a succession of salt lakes on our right, and saw many temporary huts, constructed by the peasants who watch the oxen and broad-tailed sheep, which graze upon this low peninsula. Herons, plovers, and other aquatic birds, superseded the game of the Stepp. At about a third of the distance between Tonkoi and Arabat, we came in sight of the celebrated mountains of the Crimea, rising like a blue cloud before us. Near this spot the peninsula becomes considerably narrower, the two seas are both visible, and the road to Arabat runs between them, along a bank not half a verst in width, the luxuriant herbage of which affords pasture to large droves of Bactrian camels.

From the little village of Arabat, which derives importance from an antient Tartar fortress, commanding this approach to the Crimea, the distance to Kaffa is only thirty versts.*

* Distances. — From Taganrog to Mariapol .... 127 versts.
     Mariapol to Obitochnoë 101
     Obitochnoë to Steinbach 80
     Steinbach to Terpenia 49
     Terpenia to Tonkoi 107
     Tonkoi to Kaffa 140

ON THE SITE OF DODONA.

[*COMMUNICATED BY MR. HAWKINS.*]

Difficulty of collecting from antient Authors any precise Accounts of the Situation of Dodona. — *Reasons for believing it is to be sought on the confines of Thesprotia and Molossia.* — *The Route pursued by Dr. Holland in this Part of Greece seems to trace the Line which separates those two Provinces.* — *A mountainous Ridge, forming a Portion of this Line, is Mount Tomarus, at the foot of which the Temple was placed.* — *Notice by the Antients of some circumstances which marked the Spot where the Building stood.* — *The Mountains of Suli correspond with the Situation of Tomarus.* — *Some Account of the remains of Greek Work in Bronze, which were discovered at Paramythia; forming, probably, part of the consecrated Offerings and Gifts belonging to the Temple of Dodona.* — *Appropriation of the Names Thyamis and Acheron to the modern Calama, and to the River of Suli.*

I⊤ appears extraordinary, when we consider how long the curiosity of the public has been directed to Greece, and how much has been lately added to our knowledge of that part of the world; that no traveller can yet boast of having discovered the site of Dodona. The attempt indeed, to explore this venerable spot, in former periods, would . have been both hazardous and difficult; on account of the anarchical state of the country in which it is situated: but since the power, which was before divided among so many rival chieftains, has been concentrated in the hands of one; the provinces of Epirus have been rendered more accessible : and those travellers who have been induced to put themselves under the protection of Ali Pasha, have had reason to be satisfied with the facilities which were every where afforded to the gratification of their curiosity. It is true that the Pasha is jealous of any political advantages that may be taken of this indulgence; but he has in no instance that I know of, refused his permission to travellers to visit whatever part of his dominions they pleased; and has provided well for their personal safety.

The deficiency however, of our information upon this head, may be satisfactorily accounted for, without imputing any want of zeal, industry, or sagacity to the labours of recent travellers: for, not to dwell upon the entire destruction of the temple at Dodona by *Dorimachus, the antients have left us in a deplorable state of ignorance respecting its precise situation.

This want of information appears to have been felt at a very early period; for Strabo, who is in general our best guide in the geography of these countries, deems it even necessary, before he treats of Epirus, to make some apology for it.† He says, " In former times there was no great difficulty in distinguishing the boundaries of these states, although they were so numerous ‡, so small, and of so little note; for they were well peopled, and each had a kingly government. But now that in most of these states the cities are razed to the ground, and the country stripped of its inhabitants §, were it even possible to ascertain their boundaries, it would be useless to do it; for they have ceased to have any political existence. The work of destruction commenced long ago; yet it may be said that it is still going on in some districts, as a necessary result of the revolts which have taken place there; for the country being in consequence of them occupied in great force by the Romans, their soldiers are quartered upon the inhabitants. ‖ According to the testimony of Polybius, Paulus Æmilius, after the defeat of Perseus and the Macedonians, destroyed

---

* Παραγενόμενος δὲ πρὸς τὸ περὶ Δωδώνην ἱερὸν, τάς τε ϛοὰς ἐνέπρησε, καὶ πολλὰ τῶν ἀναθημάτων διέφθειρε· κατέσκαψε δὲ καὶ τὴν ἱερὰν οἰκίαν. Polyb. lib. iv. c. 67.

† Lib. vii. c. 3. p. 322. The literal sense of this passage being rather obscure, I have endeavoured to convey the sense of it by a free translation.

‡ They amounted to fourteen, according to Theopompus, whose authority is here quoted by Strabo. P. 324.

§ Κατοικιῶν said to be the true reading. See the notes to the French Strabo.

‖ 'Αλλ' ενϛρατοπεδεύσσιν αὐτοῖς Ρωμαῖοι τοῖς οἴκοις, καταϛαϑέντες ὑπ' αὐτῶν δυνάϛαι.

seventy cities of Epirus, (the greater part of them belonging to the
Molossians,) and carried off in slavery one hundred and fifty thousand
of their inhabitants."

Again, at the conclusion of his account of Epirus, (which is little
more than a description of the coast, and a brief enumeration of the
towns contiguous to it,) and previous to his account of Dodona, which
is purely historical; he says : " Formerly, as 1 have already remarked,
the whole of Epirus and of Illyria, notwithstanding the rudeness of
their soil *, and the high mountains with which they are filled, such
as the Tomarus, the Polyanus, and many others, were yet well
peopled ; but now they are, for the most part, a perfect desert ; and
the few inhabitants that remain either live in hamlets, or are dispersed among the ruins. † The Oracle, too, of Dodona has somehow
or other disappeared, as well as the rest." ‡

After the citation of this testimony, which would alone justify our
ignorance at this day of the site of Dodona; I shall again observe,
that neither in the work of Strabo, or in that of any other antient
geographer or historian, have we any precise indication where it is to
be sought for ; nor could the little information which they have transmitted to us, be of any use ; until we had acquired some knowledge of
the interior of the country. § It is with the assistance derived from
this source, that I have again examined and compared the imperfect
notices of the antients, and have endeavoured to form some conjecture
with regard to the site of Dodona, which might lead to its discovery.

It appears to me to result most clearly from the collected testi-

---

* Καίπερ ἐσα τραχεῖα ἡ ὁρῶν πλήρης.

† Here Mr. Gosselin, one of the Editors of the French Strabo, justly observes: " Si
Strabon eprouvoit deja tant de difficultès pour debrouiller la geographie de la Gréce, que
dire après dixhuit siécles de nouvelles destructions, quand les traces de ses anciens peuples,
les ruines de ses anciennes villes, et jusqu' aux denominations des lieux, sont effacées pour
jamais."

‡ 'Εκλέλοιπε δέ πως καὶ τὸ μαντεῖον τὸ ἐν Δωδώνῃ, καθάπερ τἄλλα. P. 327.

§ D'Anville in his map of ancient Greece, particularly notices this want of information
respecting the interior of Epirus.

mony of the antients, that the Oracle of Jupiter at Dodona *was situ-ated on the confines of Thesprotia and Molossia* ; for although it be true that some authors place it in one of these countries, and some in another, while some attribute it indifferently to both *; yet all this is satisfactorily explained by Strabo, who tells us, " Dodona was origin-ally under the sovereignty of the Thesprotians, as well as Mount To-marus, (according to others Tmarus,) at the foot of which the temple is situated ; for both the Tragic poets and Pindar bestow the epithet of Thesprotian on Dodona. Subsequently, however, Dodona passed under the sovereignty of the Molossians ;" for which he accounts in another place by observing, that the preponderance of the latter arose from the consanguinity (συγγένειαν) of their princes who were of the family of the Æacidæ.

Thesprotia, according to the testimony both of Scylax and of Strabo, occupied the very fertile maritime district of Epirus, which extends from the Acroceraunian mountains (now called Tchimára) to the mouth of the Ambracian Gulf; for the most southern extremity of this district, although distinguished by the name of Cassopia, be-longed nevertheless, as Strabo remarks, to Thesprotia. Molossia, on the other hand, occupied the mediterranean tract of country to the eastward, as far as the Arethon or Arachthus, touching only a small part of the sea-coast in the Ambracian gulf, and extending northerly as far at least as the parallel of Thesprotia. This country appears to have been wholly mountainous ; for Strabo, speaking of the Molos-sians, and the neighbouring states on Mount Pindus, represents them as τραχεῖαν οἰκῦντες χώραν. †

Having now acquired some idea of the situation of Dodona, in respect to its longitude ; we must have recourse for more precise in-formation to a traveller, who, in his route from the Ambracian Gulf through the heart of Epirus, appears to have traced out very ac-

---

* It is placed by Herodotus in Thesprotia, attributed by Æschylus indifferently to Molossia and Thesprotia ; again, by later writers, such as Pliny and Stephanus Byzantinus, to Molossia.

† Lib. vii. p. 255.

curately the line of demarcation between the two provinces, in which we are to look for it.

The traveller who conveys to us this valuable information, and whose work is on many other accounts entitled to my warmest commendation, is Dr. Holland. As far as Luro, which lies about twelve miles to the north of Prevesa, and precisely at the north-western angle of the great plains which border on the Ambracian gulf, Dr. Holland travelled through the antient Cassopia; the interval between the sea-coast and the line of his route gradually widening as he advanced. * His course from hence, for several miles, was through a broken irregular country, thickly covered with wood. After this, he says, he entered an open valley, stretching in a northerly direction for ten miles ; a stream descending through it to join the river of Luro. Passing a low ridge beyond this valley, he came to the banks of a stream running in an opposite direction from south to north, to join the river of Suli. Two miles farther on he reached this river, which, descending from the north-west through a valley of considerable width, makes at this place a sudden and remarkable bend towards the north, and enters by a narrow pass the wild and magnificent region of Suli. — From the place where he reached its banks, and crossed the river, to the castle of Suli, and the plains of Paramythia ; the scenery along its course was altogether more singular than any that he had seen in Greece. In the description of his difficult ascent up these mountains, to the new Seraglio of the Pasha, he says, — " In one view you may trace the progress of the river for six or seven miles, between mountains, some of which are upwards of three thousand feet in height; their precipitous sides beginning to rise even from the edge of the water," &c. He continued his route, for about four miles, through this extraordinary valley, by a rugged path, which winds along the declivities, and then turned to the right, to gain by a very circuitous route the insulated heights upon which stood the fortresses, in one of which is the Seraglio. " From the great gallery of this building," he

---

* The sea-coast taking a direction to the north-west.

says, " you look down a precipice, not much less, probably, than a thousand feet in height, into the dark waters of the Acheron below." (How correct he is in the appropriation of this classical name, will be seen hereafter.) " Towards the south, and over the peaked summits which environ the Seraglio, is seen the long chasm-like channel through which it flows; beyond it, the country stretching down to the gulf of Arta ; the gulf itself, and the mountains of Acarnania, in the remote distance. To the west, you look down precipices inter-sected by deep ravines, to that point in the river, where, receiv-ing the stream of Zagouri from the north, it turns at once to the west ; and continuing its course for some way between cliffs of im-mense height, makes a sudden exit from its confined channels into the wide and fertile plains of Paramythia. Its windings through these plains may be traced, while the distant landscape embraces the sea and chains of hills stretching along the coast. The view towards the north is full of the finest mountain-scenery. It is, in fact, a vast amphitheatre of mountains, the space within them being every where intersected by ridges and profound ravines. Through the principal of these ravines flows the river Zagouri," &c. From the place where the river issues from these defiles, Dr. H. computes the distance of Porto Fanári, where it joins the sea, at from sixteen to twenty miles, in a south-westerly direction. Here he crossed the river. " From this place to the city of Paramythia is five hours' journey, (about seventeen miles,) in a northerly direction, along the broad valley through which the river of Paramythia flows, to join that of Suli. This valley, the breadth of which varies from three to five miles, is fertile and well cultivated ; the produce chiefly maize, wheat, rice, to-bacco, &c. *Its boundary on the eastern side is the range of the Suli mountains continued towards the north, and forming a continuous line of precipices of vast height:* on the western side, a chain of hills much less lofty, but terminating somewhat abruptly towards the valley." — " The city of Paramythia is situated near the upper extremity of the plain, on the lower part of the mountains which form its eastern boundary." — " These mountains," he says, " rise to a great height above it."—" The river," he adds, " has its sources in a north-west direction from Paramythia, at the head of the valley," i. e. at the foot of the hills which divide it from that of the Calama." From the spot where he forded the Calama, in his way to Sullopia, " the view up the valley is very striking; its boundaries, particularly on the east side, being formed by the precipices, which may be considered as terminating in this direction the range of the Suli mountains."

After a description so circumstantial as to include every thing which is essential, and yet so clear and comprehensive as to set the whole face of the country before us ; we may be permitted to form a very confident opinion on some points of its antient denomination, which are connected with this enquiry.

The first point, which I think established, is, that the whole line of Dr. Holland's route follows pretty accurately the boundaries of Molossia and Thesprotia, as far as they were contiguous. It has been already shown, that in this line stood Dodona. If we admit this as sufficiently established, it will follow, *that the mountainous ridge, which constitutes a great portion of this line, can be no other than the Tomarus, at the foot of which we must look for the remains of the temple.* Τὸ ὄρος ὁ Τόμαρος, ὑφ᾽ ὦ κεῖται τὸ ἱερόν. *

The spot where the temple stood is farther characterized or designated by the marshes, which, according to Apollodorus, (cited by Strabo †,) were contiguous to it ; " ᾽Απὸ τῶν ἑλῶν τῶν περὶ τὸ ἱερὸν :" and by a remarkable ebbing and flowing source of water, which at midday was constantly dry, and at midnight at its full height, increasing or decreasing every day from one of these extremes to the other. ‡ The waters, too, of this spring had the property of lighting extinguished torches, when held at a certain distance. § This, perhaps, was the same spring as that which, according to Servius ‖, rose at the very foot of the sacred oak ; the ἱερὰ τῦ θεῦ φηγός : which tree we may

---

* ·Strabo, lib. vii. p. 505.   † Lib. vii. p. 327.
‡ Plin. lib. ii. c. 103.   § Mela, lib. ii. c. 3.
‖ In Æn. l. iii. v. 466.

conclude, on the authority of the Prodromus to the Flora Græca, to be of the species distinguished by the name of Quercus Æsculus. As for the broad extended valley to the westward of the ridge of Suli, which Dr. Holland describes as so fertile and well cultivated; it appears to be the same district which, under the denomination of Hellopia, was celebrated for its fertility in very antient times. *

It may be thought by some, that a situation such as that which is here pointed out, does not perfectly accord with the Homeric epithet, δυσχείμερος†, if it be true that Homer speaks here of the Dodona of Epirus, and not of that which was in Thessaly, as some of his commentators have supposed. A situation, however, whether high or low, which was contiguous to the high-lands of Epirus, must have been always characterised by a great severity of cold in winter.

Had the very enterprising and intelligent traveller, whose description of this country I have quoted, examined the base of the whole ridge, from the banks of the river of Suli to Paramythia; (an extent of about seventeen miles,) nothing would have remained to be said upon this subject, for his information would have been decisive of the question: but as he has not done this, we may be allowed to form our own opinion. Nor would it be fair to blame him for this omission; for those who have travelled through countries so misgoverned, well know how many circumstances conspire to thwart the execution of the best laid plans of research. ‡

It appears, however, that Dr. Holland himself had at one time adopted this opinion; for, speaking of his intended excursion down the river Calama, he says, that the principal motive for his journey

---

* Εςι τις 'Ελλοπίη, πολυλήϊος ἠδ' εὐλείμων·
  'Ενθάδε Δωδώνη τις ἐπ' ἐσχατιῇ πεπόλιςαι. — Hesiod.
† Catal. v. 256.
‡ Such, for instance, are, the distance of night-quarters, the shortness of the days at the period of Dr. H.'s journey, the extreme bad state of the roads, the swollen state of the rivers, the miserable condition of the horses, and, lastly, the ill humour and the interested misrepresentations of the guides and guards.

was an idea he then had, that the site of the Oracle of Dodona was to be sought for in this part of Epirus. * Nor does it appear that he had sufficiently examined the country around Paramythia, before he relinquished this opinion; for he says, " In two or three places, within a few miles of the city, there are the remains of ruined walls, indicating the situation of some of the antient towns or castles of Epirus. I had an opportunity of seeing only one of these places, about four miles to the south of the city."

Had Dr. Holland succeeded in the enquiries which he here made, respecting the spot, where, about twenty years before, those celebrated works in bronze were found, which are now in England; it is probable that this would have conducted him to the very site of Dodona: for the discovery was certainly made in the district here spoken of. It may be of some importance, therefore, to this enquiry, to state the circumstances of that event, as far as they are known to me. Shortly after my arrival at Yanina, in the month of June, 1795, I received as a present from a merchant of that city, Demetrio Vassíli, a bronze figure of a Mercury, in the most finished stile of Greek workmanship. I learnt, upon enquiry, that it had been brought thither 'about two years before, together with many other bronze figures of equal beauty, from Paramythia; in which neighbourhood, and at the same period, they were all found : that the person in whose possession they were, being ignorant of their real value, had disposed of them to a brazier, from whose furnace the greater part had been luckily rescued by a Greek, who having seen something of this kind in the museum of a person of rank at Moscow, immediately conceived the idea of converting them into an object of profitable speculation. With this view, he is said to have purchased the whole collection (the Mercury excepted) for a mere trifle above the value of the metal, and to have conveyed them soon afterwards to Moscow. My friends at Yanina highly extolled the beauty of their

* Vide p. 252. of vol. ii. 2d edition.

workmanship, and their fine state of preservation ; and as they appealed as a standard of comparison to the Mercury, I felt the most lively regret at not having visited Yanina a twelvemonth or two earlier.*

The discovery of such a rich deposit of works of art awakened in me, as may be easily conceived, a suspicion that they had belonged to the treasures of the Temple of Dodona, and had been secreted, perhaps, for their security, at the time when it was plundered by Dorimachus. Paramythia was, therefore, that district of Epirus which, above all others, I felt most anxious to explore; and I requested Ali Pasha, who had distinguished me by his hospitable reception, as the first English traveller who had visited his capital ; to grant me an escort thither. He refused however, stating as the true reason why he could not comply with my wishes, that being then on terms of hostility with the Paramythiotes, it was not in his power to ensure my personal safety. He insisted therefore, on my relinquishing all thoughts of this expedition.† Nor was it less mortifying to be obliged to renounce the idea of visiting Paramythia, some time after this, when I had an opportunity of doing it with perfect safety. This was in May, 1798, when I met at Yanina the heads of the principal Mussulman families of Paramythia, who were then ratifying the peace which they had just made with the Pasha ; and, upon that occasion, kindly offered me every accommodation : but I was then on my way to Durazzo ; and a delay, even of a few days, would have prevented me from reaching the place of my intended embarkation in time to effect the passage of the Adriatic ; as was proved by an attempt made by the commander of the French marine force at Corfu to intercept me.

Subsequently to my first visit to Yanina, I learned that there is a

---

* It was at the period of my subsequent visit in 1798 that I purchased that exquisite specimen of the opus cœlatum which represents Paris and Helen. It had been discovered at the same place a year or two before my arrival.

† The distance of Paramythia from Yanina is twelve hours, or from thirty to thirty-five miles directly west.

spot near Paramythia called Aidonà, where there are some ruins in the Hellenic stile, and great sources of water. This name will naturally suggest to my readers an idea of its derivation, corroborative of the opinion which I had formed on other grounds, of its connection with Dodona : but upon looking into the geography of Meletius, I find what I had almost suspected. " Κάςρον τȣ 'Αγίȣ Δονάτου, τὸ ὁποῖον κὰι Παραμυϑία λέγεται, κὰι ὑπὸ τῶν Τούρκων 'Αἰδονά." Aidonà, therefore, may be no other than a corruption of Agios Donatus, under which name two forts in the antient Epirus, are mentioned by Procopius ; although the authority of Meletius is by no means to be trusted, either in this or in any other matter. It is astonishing that this man, who composed for the information of his countrymen a work of general geography, should have known so little of Epirus, although a native of Yanina, as not to be able to point out the true situation of Dodona. And yet he treats largely of the temple, and even says that the city of Dodona was still known under the name of Dodon : ἡ πόλις Δωδώνη, ἐλέγε]ο ἀκόμι κὰι Δώδων. If, at the distance of a century only from the time of Meletius, no place in Epirus is now known by this name ; we may safely conclude that his assertion was merely gratuitous.

It is however, true that some antient authors make mention of Dodona as a city ; and not many years ago an inscription was found in the island of Corfu, which thus designates it. The name of Dodona, too, appears to have been appropriated either to a city or to a district of Epirus ; for some centuries after the destruction of the temple : for it occurs in the Synecdemus of Hierocles ; and one of its bishops, Theodorus, subscribed to the council of Ephesus. Procopius, too, mentions the ravages committed by the Goths in the country around Dodona. *

I had constantly in view, during my first visit to Epirus, the dis-

---

* After speaking of the devastation which they had committed at Corfu, he adds, διαβαινόν]ες δὲ κα) ἐς τὴν ἤπειρον, ἐξαπιναίως ἅπαντα ἐληίζον]ο τὰ ἀμφὶ Δωδώνην χωρία, κα) διαφερόν]ως Νικοπολίν τε κα) ῍Αλχισον. Among the castella refecta veteris Epiri he mentions Ιȣςινιανȣπόλεως κα) Φωτικῆς, φρόυρια δυὸ τȣ ἀγίȣ Δονάτȣ.

3 Q 2

covery of the site of Dodona; and I can truly say that I neglected no means of effecting it. The mountains of Suli appeared to me to correspond best with the situation of the antient Tomarus; but such was the state of hostility at that period, between the natives of this district and Ali Pasha, that I could not court the protection, or experience the hospitality of the one, without forfeiting all claims to the favour of the other; and the protection of the Pasha was then absolutely necessary to the success of my ulterior views in Thessaly.

Having stated my own opinion on the site of Dodona, and the foundation upon which it rests; I shall now revert to that of Dr. Holland, which, with all the respect due to it, will be found to be erroneous. " A careful reference," says he, " to the passages in which it is mentioned by antient writers, has led me to believe that the real situation was to the south or south-east of Joannina, and underneath the great mountain of Tzumerka. * This mountain, the position of which has already been referred to, I consider to have been the Tomarus of antiquity, below which, according to Strabo, stood the temple of Dodona." In another paragraph, he places it eastward of the river of Arta, or the Arachthus: a situation, doubtless, very appropriate to an oracle, as far as regards the wild character of the scenery around it; but I could hear of no ruins there; and the base of Tzumerka extending to a very short distance from Arta, the antient Ambracia; has pent up the channel of this impetuous river within very narrow dimensions. There is, consequently, no room for a marsh; nor does the situation correspond in other respects with what we know of Dodona. It is a singular coincidence, however, that I should once have entertained hopes of finding Dodona in this direction. I had heard, when at Yanina, of some remains of antiquity, under the name of Tomaro-castro; and hastily inferred, from this name, that the mountain on which they were situated might be the antient Tomarus. The distance of this spot from Yanina is about

---

* Ioannina and Tzumerka, according to the Romaic orthography, but Yanina and Jumerka, according to the true pronunciation.

fourteen miles to the southward. I found myself here upon the edge of a declivity which overlooks the deep alpine vale of the Arachthus. The situation derives some interest from a tower of antient Greek construction, which is in tolerable preservation; but there are no other remains of antiquity to be seen here. A small elevated plain extends to the westward, the villages around which are distinguished by the appellation of Tómaro-choria; but my friends at Yanina were of opinion that it arose from the Romaic word Τομάρι, which signifies cordovan·leather, for the manufacture of which these villages were once .celebrated. I climbed the highest eminence above this plain, which lay to the southward of it; but in whatever direction I turned my- eyes, I could discover no other features in the view but those of a mountainous character. After all my enquiries, I could hear of no mountain in the southern parts of Epirus which still bears the name of Tomarus; but on my route to Durazzo, in the year 1798, I observed a very lofty and insulated mountain to the south-east of Berat, which is. called Τομυρ (Tomoor). The situation, however, of this mountain is too far to the northward to admit of the possibility of its being the Tomarus of antiquity.

⸻ To return to the hypothesis which I was examining, that Dodona lay to the eastward of the Arachthus : I find no direct authority for the assertion; but there is much reason to believe, that the deep alpine vale of the Arachthus divided Molossia from the petty states on Mount Pindus, which are mentioned by Strabo and others as lying to the eastward of it; the most considerable of which were the Athamanii. The river itself is described by Strabo as flowing from Mount Tymphé ; and its sources are very correctly placed by him at no great distance from those of the Peneus : it is plain, therefore, that Mount Tymphé can be no other than Jumerka. Now the Tymphœans composed one of the petty states which I have alluded to. Ambracia, too, which is called by Dicæarchus τῆς Ἑλλάδος ἡ πρώτη πόλις, stood on the left bank of the river lower down; and it is likewise placed by two other early Greek

writers beyond the confines of Molossia. * The cause of its having
been subsequently ascribed to Epirus is very clearly explained by
Paulmier. " Inter Epiroticas civitates censebatur ab eo tempore quo
Pyrrhus à Demetrio Poliorceta eam civitatem obtinuerat, auxilii lati
pretium, quod narrat Plutarchus in Pyrrho. Et sic facta est Epiri
urbs primaria, caput regni et Pyrrhi regia."

It is in vain, therefore, to seek for Dodona to the eastward of Ambracia, (the modern Arta,) nor is there a better chance of finding it,
in this parallel of latitude, to the westward of that city. Mela speaks
of the Ambracian Gulf as chiefly distinguished by Actium, Argia
Amphilochis, and Ambracia. † No notice is taken of Nicopolis, for
he seems constantly to have had in his eye the more antient state of
Greece. Would he not have mentioned Dodona, had it been in the
vicinity of those cities? Strabo, too, would not have omitted it in
this part of his geography, had it been so near the gulf. But the
very accurate examination which I made of this part of Epirus en-
ables me to speak with the greater confidence on this point. ‡ ´ I shall
conclude, therefore, what I have to say upon a question which still
remains to be decided by some future traveller, by referring to Polybius, who, in the account which he gives of the irruption of the Aeto-
lians under Dorimachus, speaks of the superior parts of Epirus only,
as the scene of their devastation. " Ἐνέβαλεν εἰς τοὺς ἄνω τόπους τῆς
Ἠπείρου, καὶ τὴν χώραν ἐδήου, θυμικώτερον χρώμενος τῇ καταφθορά."

The subject of the preceding enquiry has naturally led me to consider that of the Thyamis and the Acheron.

---

* Μετὰ δὲ Μολοτίάν Αμβραχία πόλις Ἑλληνίς. Scylax.
Μετὰ τῆς Μολοτῆς δὲ Ἀμβραχία Κορινθίων
Ἀποιχός ἐςίν. Scymnus Chius, v. 452.

† In Epiro nihil Ambracio sinu nobilius est. Facit sinus, qui angustis faucibus, et quæ
minus mille passibus pateant, grande pelagus admittit. Faciunt urbes quæ assidunt ;
Actium, Argia Amphilochis, Ambracia, Aeacidarum regna Pyrrhique.

‡ I made a trigonometrical survey of the gulf from twenty different stations.

There are two rivers of some note, which discharge themselves into the sea opposite to Corfu. The northernmost of these, called the Ca-lamà, is the largest; it rises from a small lake, which lies at the distance of about forty miles north from Yanina. The southern has its source in the mountainous district of Suli, to the west of that city. One of these rivers must be the Thyamis, the other the Acheron. The difficulty lies in the appropriation of their names; for the antient authorities are too confused and inexplicit to enable us to decide. The best information that I can find among them is contained in the following passage of Thucydides, (l. 1.) : " Ὁρμίζονται ἐς Χειμέριον τῆς Θεσπρωτίδος γῆς· ἔςι δὲ λιμήν, καὶ πόλις ὑπὲρ αὐτοῦ κεῖται ἀπὸ θαλάσσης, ἐν τῇ Ἐλαιάτιδι τῆς Θεσπρωτίδος Ἐφύρη. ἐξίησι δὲ παρ' αὐτὴν Ἀχερυσία λίμνη ἐς τὴν θάλασσαν· διὰ δὲ τῆς Θεσπρωτίδος Ἀχέρων ποταμὸς ῥέων ἐσβάλλει ἐς αὐτὴν, ἀφ' οὗ καὶ τὴν ἐπωνυμίαν ἔχει. ῥεῖ δὲ καὶ Θύαμις ποταμὸς, ὁρίζων τὴν Θεσπρωτίδα καὶ Κεστρίνην, ὧν ἐντὸς ἡ ἄκρα ἀνέχει τὸ Χειμέριον." Here we have a promontory of Thesprotia between two rivers, one of which passes through a lake which is not far from the sea; and the other forms the boundary of Thesprotia and Cestrinia. The former answers to the description of the river of Suli, for that alone has a communication with a maritime lake or marsh; consequently the other must be the Thyamis : and this appropriation of the two antient names accords best with the direction in which the writer proceeds in the course of his narrative, which is from south to north. But the limits of Thesprotia are placed by other writers far to the northward of this line. It is therefore probable that Cestrinia, if it formed not like Cassopia a subdivision of Thesprotia, may have been a district which varied its limits, and occupied more or less of the right bank of the Thyamis, according to political circumstances. Pausanias says, that Cestrinus, the son of Helenus, took possession of τὴν ὑπὲρ Θύαμιν ποταμὸν χώραν, " the country beyond or to the north of the Thyamis," which country, according to Stephanus Byzantinus, was a part of Thesprotia. · " Καμμανία μοῖρα Θεσπρωτίας, μετωνομάσθη δὲ Κεςρίνια."

Strabo's account of this part of the coast is shorter and less satisfactory. The order of his description is from north to south : " Ἔπειτα

488 ON THE SITE OF DODONA.

ἄκρα Χειμέριον καὶ Γλυκὺς λιμὴν, εἰς ὃν εμβάλλει ὁ Αχέρων ποταμὸς, ῥεών ἐκ τῆς Αχερυσίας λίμνης, καὶ δεχόμενος πλέιυς ποταμυς, ὥςε καὶ γλυκαίνειν τον κόλπον· ῥει δὲ καὶ Θύαμις πλησίον." There is nothing here which is irreconcilable with the more full account given by Thucydides; but there is an omission of the circumstance of the Acheron flowing into the lake; the position of which is moreover so undetermined as to leave us in doubt whether the Acheron had its source in the lake, or merely flowed through it. Whoever reads this passage of Strabo, as I did, before he has consulted any other antient authority, would immediately conclude that the Acheron took its rise from a lake far inland, and in its long course to the sea was joined by several other rivers : Pliny gives it even a course of 36 M. P. from the lake to the sea.

We must recur, therefore, to a much older writer, whose account of this coast, short as it is, seems to confirm and explain the particulars given by Strabo. Ἐνταῦθα ἔςι λιμήν, ᾧ ὄνομα "Ελεα. Εἰς τοῦτον τὸν λιμένα ποταμὸς ἐξίησιν Ἀχέρων, καὶ λίμνη Αχερυσία, ἐξ ἧς ὁ Ἀχέρων ῥει ποταμός. (Scylax.) And this sense is confirmed by the words of Livy, which are probably borrowed from the lost books of Polybius ; " et Acheronte amne, quem ex Molosside fluentem, in stagna inferna accipit Thesprotius sinus." The result of this enquiry fully establishes the opinion of Dr. Holland, that the river of Suli is the Acheron of antiquity. The Calamà, therefore, can be no other than the Thyamis. *

---

* Dr. Holland seems doubtful whether Arta stands on the site of Ambracia ; the same suspicion is entertained by others, (see the French translation of Strabo,) but its distance from the shore of the gulf is precisely that which is given by Scylax; " ἀπέχει δὲ αὐτη ἀπὸ θαλάτης ςάδια π'. Ἔςι δὲ καὶ ἐπὶ θαλάττης τεῖχος, καὶ λιμὴν κάλλιςος." As for the fortress of Ambracus, to which he is inclined to refer the old walls of Arta, I discovered it in the marshes, a little to the westward of the mouth of the Arachthus, where it is now known by the name of Fidó-castro.

I am sorry to differ on so many points of antient geography from a traveller whose judgment in other respects is so correct; but I cannot help observing in this place, that the ruins at the south-eastern extremity of this gulf, which Dr. H. conjectures to be those of Stratus, belong unquestionably to Argos Amphilochicum ; and that I found the ruins of Stratus precisely where they are placed by Polybius, on the right bank of the Achelous.

LETTER FROM THE EARL OF ABERDEEN

TO THE EDITOR,

RELATING TO SOME STATEMENTS MADE BY M. R. ROCHETTE,

IN HIS LATE WORK,

ON THE AUTHENTICITY OF THE INSCRIPTIONS OF FOURMONT.

Dear Walpole,   Argyll House, Sept. 1819.

I HAVE recently seen a work, by M. Raoul Rochette, on the authenticity of the pretended inscriptions of Fourmont, which, in the form of two letters, he has done me the honour to address to me. * As my communication in your former volume, relative to the marbles brought by me from the neighbourhood of Amyclæ, appears to have procured for me this honour, perhaps the author will forgive me if I direct the short reply which I think it necessary to make to these dissertations, through the medium of your present publication.

It is not my intention to prolong the controversy on a subject, the merits of which have been long since decided to the satisfaction, as I had imagined, of every judicious scholar in Europe. For although I am ready to bear testimony to the learning and ingenuity which M. Rochette has exhibited in supporting his opinions, I cannot admit that any reasonable doubts have been raised in favour of the Abbé Fourmont's veracity, or that we should hesitate to consider his productions as any thing but a tissue of fraud and imposture. The chief object I have in view, is to notice certain misapprehensions into which

---

* Deux Lettres a My Lord Comte d'Aberdeen, sur l'authenticité des inscriptions de Fourmont. Paris, 1819.

the author has fallen respecting what I had myself written, and which, if not corrected, might probably very much mislead those who attempt to form an impartial judgment on this question. The greater part of M. Rochette's work consists of an attempt to answer the objections so ably and so conclusively urged by Mr. Knight, in his Analysis of the Greek Alphabet, against the supposed genuineness of these inscriptions. But as no man is more eminently qualified to do justice to the whole subject, if he think fit, than Mr. Knight, I shall only state my own conviction, without taking the matter out of his hands, that although some unimportant errors may have been detected in his work, there has been absolutely nothing adduced at all calculated to invalidate the main arguments by which he arrived at that conclusion which is now so generally adopted by the learned world.

It appeared to me, that the marbles which I discovered in the neighbourhood of Amyclæ, afforded an additional proof, if any were wanting, of the little reliance to be placed on the assertions of the Abbé Fourmont. M. Rochette entertains a different opinion, and thinks, on the contrary, that they furnish an important testimony in favour of the veracity of this calumniated traveller.

You will recollect that one of his principal discoveries in Greece was the temple of the Goddess Onga, at Amyclæ, in which the marbles in question were deposited. * This temple he described as a species of grotto, about sixteen feet long and ten feet wide in the inside, the pavement of which consisted of a single stone; four other stones composed the four sides of the building. It was covered also by one stone, above which were placed two more, one upon the other, and these formed the roof. The work was rude, and the materials of a black colour. The door was not more than four feet high, and was wrought in the stone which formed the front. The whole rested on three steps, each also of a single stone sixteen inches high, and which, properly speaking, made the foundation of the Temple.

---

* Mem. de l'Acad. des Inscr. et Belles Lettres, tom. xv. p. 402.

Those blocks, which formed the sides and roof, were five feet thick. On the front of this building was inscribed, Ογαι ικετερκερατεες. This strange name of Iketerkerateans, he found it necessary to give to the Lacedæmonians, because he supposes the temple itself to have been built before the age of Lacedæmon ; indeed, it is not clear from his description, if he does not intend to state that the name of Eurotus, the father of Lacedæmon, appears in the dedication. He has been ·thus understood by the Abbé Barthelemy, although M. Rochette denies that such was Fourmont's intention. * I need not repeat how convincingly Mr. Knight has shewn that this singular appellation was stolen from an erroneous reading of Hesychius, as adopted by Meursius, which error was, I believe, first pointed out by Hemsterhusius, and has been since corrected in all the subsequent editions. M. Rochette, indeed, admits that the resemblance of the word in the old copies of Hesychius may have misled Fourmont in reading the inscription, and that, in consequence, he has copied it inaccurately ; but he maintains that this ought not to discredit the discovery, and mentions several instances where Dr. Chandler and others have committed obvious mistakes in their published inscriptions, yet no one ever thought of doubting their authenticity. † It is certainly true that any person in transcribing antient characters may be easily liable to error, but I would suggest to M. Rochette this difference in the cases to which he refers : Dr. Chandler, and others who have communicated these remains to the public, were at once open to correction, on an examination of the originals by succeeding travellers, possessing more industry or a better eye-sight : in addition to which, it may be observed, that they published nothing which, on the face of it, was strange and incredible. In the case under consideration, we have, on the contrary, a subject perfectly new to the literary world, at variance with all history and tradition, the very characters unlike those hitherto used in Greek writing, and the original of this most

---

* Voyages d'Anach. ch. 41. Lettre, p. 28.   † Lett. p. 32, 33.

curious document no where to be found. I do not think it is by a verbal emendation that we ought to establish such a discovery as this ; M. Rochette, however, makes the attempt, and supposes that instead of Iketerkerateans, the true reading ought to be ἐτεοκᾶρες, or antient Carians, and with much ingenuity and research he shews how this people might have been established in Laconia *, although at a period entirely beyond the reach of Lacedæmonian tradition. According to this tradition the Spartans invariably described the Leleges as their predecessors, and as the aboriginal inhabitants of the † land ; a circumstance not a little extraordinary, if they had constantly possessed before their eyes a written monument testifying the contrary. With respect to these genuine or antient Carians, as M. Rochette calls them, *and as they call themselves*, I leave, without further remark, the probability of their writing Greek, a little burlesqued to be sure in appearance, but such Greek in substance as would have been familiar to their latest successors. The fact of their writing at all, some centuries before the Trojan war, and even prior to the supposed introduction of letters into Greece by Cadmus, M. Rochette may, perhaps, think is attended with no difficulty. How much soever this conjecture may prove the superior learning of M. Rochette, it is at least fortunate that the imposition of Fourmont is as clumsy as it is unprincipled.

In my former letter, I observed that this venerable edifice had unfortunately vanished. I added, however, that although the temple of the Goddess had disappeared, yet that the true building, when divested of this antient and venerable character, probably still existed in the shape of a modern Greek chapel, in which M. Fourmont might have seen the marbles in question, and where I found them in the year 1803. M. Rochette considers this as a confession, on my part that there is actually at Amyclæ an antient structure, converted into a Greek church, but of which the original form and character are

---

not destroyed, because the vestiges of an antient worship, and inscription relative to the ministers of that worship, have been discovered in it. * . When I asserted my belief that the temple still existed in the form of a modern Greek church, undoubtedly you must have understood me by the context to have clearly implied that it : never .existed in any other shape. But in consequence of this whimsical mistake, M. Rochette thinks he is justified in accusing me of inconsistency; and even in adducing my testimony in support of the inventions of Fourmont. In point of fact, however, this building is a small Greek chapel, possibly two hundred years old. It is constructed, like other edifices of the same description, of common masonry, composed of small stones and cement; but from being apparently deserted at present, as well as from having been slightly built at first, it is probable that it may not stand a hundred years longer. The interior dimensions assigned by Fourmont may, perhaps, be nearly correct, and the door not much more than four feet high, as stated by him ; but this practice is not uncommon in Greece, and is adopted by the Christian inhabitants in order to prevent the Mussulmans from turning their horses into the churches or houses. Compare this with the temple of Fourmont,—the ten massive stones which had endured from the time of King Eurotas to the visit of the Abbé, undestroyed, and even uninjured, and you will then know what weight to give to the notion of M. Rochette, that this change has taken place in the course of the last eighty years.

.When M. Rochette accuses me of inconsistency, he at the same time lays himself entirely open to a similar charge. For, when, ·in endeavouring to persuade us of the establishment of Priestesses belonging to the temple of the Amyclæan ·Apollo ; he adduces these marbles as an indisputable evidence of the fact †, and says that they afford an invincible argument in favour of the chronicle published by Fourmont; he entirely forgets that, according to Fourmont, they

---

* Lett. p. 29. † Lett. p. 44.

have no connection with the temple of Apollo, but belong to that of the Goddess Onga. On this point in dispute, relative to the priesthood, I must repeat, that I have been able to find no authority whatever for supposing the custody of the Amyclæan temple was ever entrusted to females ; and, consequently, the pretended catalogue of Priestesses, published by Fourmont, even if less absurd in itself, would be liable to suspicion. * M. Rochette is not quite candid in treating this part of the subject : he refers me, with great triumph, to Pausanias for the proof that women were attached by subordinate functions to the temple of Apollo. I only find, however, that there was a building *at Sparta*, and not at Amyclæ, in which the robe or tunic for the covering of the statue was annually woven, and from which circumstance the building received its †name. Now, as this process was, among the Greeks, always performed by females, it would have been very remarkable had they not been employed in the present instance. M. Rochette gives us a list of temples, which might no doubt be easily enlarged, where the priesthood was composed of women ; but the greater part of this list is derived from Pausanias, and I must still be of opinion that his silence respecting this celebrated temple, which he has described at such length, and which he has mentioned so often, is almost decisive of the question. The matter, however, is not of much importance, and I only adverted to it formerly in consequence of a very general notion prevailing on the subject, which, I believe, has no better foundation than the spurious authority of Fourmont himself ; and also as a reason for my not being disposed to consider the marbles, which I discovered in the neighbourhood of Amyclæ, as belonging to the temple of Apollo, although inscribed with the name of a priestess.

While M. Rochette, in one part of his work, confesses the great

---

* Mem. de l'Acad. des Inscr. tom. xxiii. p. 394., accompanied by the elaborate commentary of the Abbé Barthelemy.

† 'Υφαίνουσι δὲ κατὰ ἔτος αἱ γυναῖκες τῷ Απόλλωνι χιτῶνα τῷ ἐν 'Αμύκλαις, καὶ οἴκημα ἔνθα ὑφαίνουσι Χιτῶνα ὀνομάζουσιν. — Pausan. lib. iii. c. 16.

THE INSCRIPTIONS OF FOURMONT.

alteration which has taken place in the appearance of this building,
and says, that the dedicatory inscription to Onga, which he admits
is' not now to be seen, was obviously the first thing that the Greek
Christians would destroy in appropriating it to their own worship;
in another place, he does not scruple to inform us that it actually
exists at the present moment, and precisely as it was described by
Fourmont. * This decisive fact is stated on the authority of a Doctor
Avramiotti, who, in the year 1816, published critical observations on
the travels of M. de Chateaubriand in Greece. I have not seen his
work, but from the specimen afforded us by M. Rochette, it must
indeed be curious, and, of its kind, almost singular. After blaming
M. de Chateaubriand for some other omissions, he continues thus:
" Ma non merita scusa di non aver veduto, cinque cento passi lontan
dal tempio d'Apollo Amicleo, con nessuno suo incommodo, *quel
medesimo magnifico edificio, che ne descrive il Fourmont* negli Atti delle
iscrizioni e belle lettere. E lungo esso sedici piedi, largo dieci; una
pietra ne forma il fondo, due ne formano il capitello; una è posta per
ciascuno dei quatro lati, e tutte sono grezze e nericcie. La sua figura
rappresenta una grotta. Per una porta angusta, non eccedente i
quattro piedi, vi si montava per tre gradini, formati essi pure d'una
sola pietra in tutta l'estenzion della fabbrica. Era questo un tempio
di remota Antichità, consecrato dal re Eurota a Minerva, il cui nome,
che Onga presso i Lacedemoni era, *è scolpito nel frontespizio.*"
M. Rochette thinks the evidence of the Greek Doctor ought to be
received preferably to my assertions; because he speaks, in the
passage above quoted, as an eye witness, and as a person certain of
the fact; because, also, he has been long settled in the country, and
has leisurely examined those objects of which it is insinuated that I
have taken only a superficial and hasty view; and because he
describes the temple as actually existing, conformably in every particular with the account of Fourmont, and says that the name of

---

* Lett. pp. 30. 125.

Onga is inscribed on the front. I cannot help here congratulating M. Rochette on the opportunity afforded him of verifying his conjectural emendation, in order that we may know with certainty to whom we are indebted for this same " magnificent edifice," whether to Fourmont's Iketerkerateans, or to M. Rochette's " genuine Carians." It is a pity the Doctor did not give us the inscription at full length, but I presume that no time has been lost in ascertaining this point. To speak seriously, however, it is really not easy to find words properly to characterise the production of this person ; but as his statement at least brings the whole question within a very narrow compass, I can only say, that I am perfectly contented the judgment of the public should depend on this issue. If any traveller of credit and respectability shall say that he ever saw a building of this description, or any thing which could even fairly be mistaken for it, I will admit my error, and confess that the reputation of Fourmont has, in this respect, been unjustly calumniated. But even if it were possible to produce this, as well as the originals of all his pretended inscriptions, to-morrow, although the Abbé himself would stand acquitted of the fraud, their spuriousness would be equally manifest, for the evidence afforded by their contents is amply sufficient ; and we should then come to the conclusion adopted by Professor Bœckh, of Berlin, who thinks that no man in his senses can believe them to be genuine, but who, not doing justice to the audacity of Fourmont, attributes their forgery to the Spartans themselves, about the first century of the Christian era. *   In the mean time, I will only observe further, that circumstances are much changed since Fourmont visited Greece : few, if any, had then ventured to explore regions which were supposed to be full of difficulty and danger ; the risk of detection was, therefore, slight. Even so late as the year 1803, the

---

* Lett. p. 13.   Quod si jam quæris quid de antiquissimis, qui feruntur, titulis censeam, *insanum* dixerim, qui eos Trojano bello priores cum Barthelemio, Lanzio aliisque putet; neque tamen eos à Fourmonto, sed ab ipsis Spartanis circa primum à Christo nato seculum confictos arbitror.

period of my own journey to Sparta, I believe that not many persons had preceded me in those remote districts of the Peloponnesus. But in the course of the last ten years, the country has been open to travellers of all nations, and has been comparatively much more frequented. There, doubtless, is to be found, at this moment, a very considerable number of active and intelligent men, fully qualified to pronounce between the assertions made by Dr. Avramiotti and myself. Notwithstanding my stay at Sparta scarcely exceeded a week, and although this " eye-witness" is said to be settled at Argos, I am somewhat disposed to believe that he may never have visited the plain of the Eurotas at all, but that he has blindly extracted his description from the Memoirs of the Academy of Inscriptions ; or perhaps from the Travels of Anacharsis, which are well known in Greece, but in which, unfortunately, an undeserved reliance on the veracity of his countryman, has misled the learned author of that most delightful work.

I have no doubt that Fourmont made a large collection of inscriptions, and that he accurately copied the greater part of them. The originals of many which are preserved among his papers, exist at this day in different parts of Greece. But these inscriptions, although unknown to Europe at the time, he did not think it worth while to publish. It was only after having had full time for the work, either from the slender materials furnished by some genuine document, or without any foundation at all, that he has fabricated, and communicated to the Academy of Inscriptions, his pretended discoveries. These, if they had been genuine, would undoubtedly, from their remote antiquity, and from the nature of the subjects, have commanded an interest on the part of that learned body, and of Europe in general, far greater than could possibly have been excited by the communication of any thing which he had really seen in Greece. For it is worthy of notice, that although the authenticity of many of his inscriptions preserved in the King's library has been proved by the copies of other travellers, or by the existence of the originals, this does not apply to any thing which he has himself published ; and indeed it appears that he considered his collection merely

LETTER RESPECTING.

498

as the raw materials from whence he was enabled from time to time to manufacture an occasional discovery for the Paris market. A curious illustration of this is afforded by the marbles in question. The drawings, as they were found by the Comte Caylus, and as published by him, represent instruments belonging to the sacrifice of human victims, instead of the ornaments of female dress ; but the inscriptions are perfectly accurate, both in form and substance; one of them, ΛΑΥΑΓΗΤΑ ΑΝΤΙΠΑΤΡΟΥ ΙΕΡΕΙΑ, being written in the character employed in Greece about the period of the Macedonian conquest; the other, ΑΝΘΟΥCΗ ΔΑΜΑΙΝΕΤΟΥ ΥΠΟCΤΑΤΡΙΑ *, in such as was generally in use under the Roman emperors. The note on the drawing, written by Fourmont, is, *in templo Ongæ;* and the Count informs us he was assured by M. Fourmont the younger, who attended his uncle in Greece, and who seems to have been a companion worthy of him, that " they were found placed one on each side of the entrance of the sanctuary, where, in the antient temples of Greece, the priests were stationed." † Now, it was precisely in this situation, in front of the altar, that they were found by me in the year 1803, in the Greek chapel already so often mentioned. We here see the indi-

* I find in Hesychius that the gloss of ςάlϱια is εμπλέxlϱια, which term signified a person who made ornaments of female dress, and especially of the head dress, either with reference to the net usually worn by women, and frequently represented on antient coins, or perhaps to the different modes of twisting the hair. Στάlϱια has puzzled all the commentators on Hesychius, and Alberti seems to think that the word may have been written erroneously, instead of xoμίςϱια, which, as well as xoμμώlϱια, had the same signification as εμπλέxlϱια. Our inscription, however, together with the objects represented on the marbles, are suf-ficient to authenticate the common reading; and υποςάlϱια will therefore designate a sub-ordinate person engaged in this occupation. Hesych. ed. Albert. in loc. The etymology of the woid is still doubtful. — A.

[It appears from the Etym. M. and from Hesychius, that xoμμώlϱια had, as well as ςτάlϱια, the signification of εμπλέxlϱια: and, by obtaining the meaning of xoμμώlϱια, we shall also find that of ςτάlϱια. Now a passage in Clemens Al. Pæd. l. iii., will illustrate satisfactorily the sense of the word. Κομμῶται δὲ xαὶ xoμμώlϱιαι πεϱὶ τὰς γυναῖxας αμϕιπολέuουσιν· αἱ μὲν xάτοπτϱα, αἱ δὲ τοὺc xεxϱυϕάλους· ἄλλαι τοὺς xτένας. We here find mention of the *mirrors, nets,* or fillets for the hair, and *combs,* as placed under the charge of the Κομμώlϱια : but the same aiticles appear sculptured on the marble, containing the title of ΥΠΟCΤΑΤΡΙΑ. Spanheim translates xoμμῶται by Coiffeurs de Madame. The learned critic, in the Q. Review, vol. 19. refers to the passage in Hesychius. — E.]

† Caylus, Rec. d'Antiquit. t. ii. p. 154.

cation of his project, although he did not venture to carry it fully into execution ; had it been completed, we should doubtless have seen a grave dissertation on the custom of human sacrifices among those antient Iketerkerateans, in honor of this strange deity. The inscriptions themselves, when published, would no doubt have been represented in those whimsical characters which M. Fourmont thought suitable to the remote antiquity of the building ; and some alteration would probably have taken place, in order to render them more accordant with the fact of the existence of this worship, hitherto unheard of. But the appearance of his drawing in its present state, with the absurd anachronism on the face of it, and the total change of the subject of the sculpture, while it sufficiently exhibits his intentions, at the same time convicts him of falsehood and imposture. M. Rochette, although disposed to admit the accuracy of the engraving inserted in your former volume, seems to insinuate the possibility of mistake and error on my part. In answer to this I can only say, that as the marbles are actually in my possession at this moment, either he, or any other person, is perfectly at liberty to examine and verify the truth of the representation.

But we are told that Fourmont, for the purpose of securing to his own country the exclusive glory of his discoveries, by a barbarous precaution, mutilated and destroyed the inscriptions after he had copied them * ; and the evidence of Mr. Dodwell is adduced to prove that the inhabitants of Sparta still preserve a recollection of this fact. Nearly the same account, if I be not mistaken, was given to me by the person mentioned by Mr. Dodwell ; but it appeared at the time, that this history had been derived from what the narrator had heard from others respecting the confessions of Fourmont, rather than from any local knowledge or tradition. I think it extremely probable, however, that Fourmont may have obliterated inscriptions ; and it only remains to be seen with what reasonable or intelligible motive this was done. I confess that what M. Rochette calls his " ill-judged

---

* Lett. p. 10, 11.

3 s 2

patriotism,": seems to me quite inadequate to account for this conduct. He must have known that travellers in those countries were at that, time of very rare occurrence, and that there could be no doubt what-· ever of his being able to present to the public the fruits of his researches, without the risk of the participation of any other person, and even before the objects were again visited. But if he was desirous to preserve these inscriptions entirely from the sight of future travellers, he might easily have brought them with him to France. Their size and weight presented no obstacle, for he describes them as about three feet and a half high, by two feet and a quarter wide. *   A person who, by his own account, employed sixty men for two months, at Amyclæ alone, could have had no difficulty in transporting these marbles a few miles to the sea side. Of their extreme importance to the history and chronology of Greece, he professes himself to have been well aware ; and from their great singularity he must have anticipated universal scepticism, unless he could prove the existence of the originals. For it is worthy of remark, that the only inscriptions said to be destroyed are precisely those whose existence is most doubtful, and which it was most incumbent on him to produce. A great portion of his collection, of different degrees of importance, many of them transcribed by him for the first time, has been since confirmed and copied by succeeding travellers. None of these, however, were ever published by Fourmont himself; and so far from thinking they add any authority to his daring impositions, I cannot but draw a different conclusion from the fact stated. If, therefore, Fourmont went through the farce of defacing any monuments of this description, it was not from " ill-judged patriotism," but in order to obtain the means of inventing, with impunity, what he pretended to have discovered and then destroyed. But whatever may have been the amount of this particular species of barbarism, he seems in other respects, if we are to credit his own relation, to have carried on the work of destruction in a manner quite unparalleled, and under such

---

Mem. de l'Acad. des Inscr. t. xv. p. 398.

circumstances of absurd extravagance as might almost lead us to suspect him of insanity. Mr. Dodwell has furnished us with some curious extracts from his correspondence, which is preserved in the King's library at Paris, and consists of letters from different parts of Greece, addressed to the Comte de Maurepas, M. Freret, the Abbé Sevin, and others. * They are worth inserting as specimens of " ill-judged patriotism ;" although I suspect that this quality will have been better illustrated by their long suppression and concealment, rather than by the publication of the facts contained in them. " Je l'ai fait, non pas raser, mais abattre de fond en comble. Il n'y a plus de toute cette grande ville, une pierre sur une autre, &c. — Depuis plus de trente jours, trente et quelquefois quarante ou soixante ouvriers, abattent, detruisent, exterminent la ville de Sparte, &c. — Je n'ai plus que quatre tours à demolir, &c. — Dans le moment que je suis occupé a la derniere destruction de Sparte, &c. — imaginez vous, si vous pouvez, dans quelle joye je suis. Elle est des plus grandes ; mais elle seroit extrème si on m'avoit laissé faire encore quelque tems. Mantinée, Stymphalus, Pallantium, Tegée, et sur tout Olympia et Nemée, meritoient bien que je les renversasse de fond en comble ; j'en ai l'autorité, &c. — J'ai, chemin faisant, cherché les anciennes villes de ce pays, et j'en ai detruit quelques unes ; entre autres Hermione, Trœzene, Tiryns, la moitié de la citadelle d'Argos, Phliasia, Pheneos, et après avoir percé dans la Magne autant que la prudence l'a pu permettre, je suis depuis six semaines, occupé à la derrière et totale destruction de Sparte, &c. — Sparte est la cinquième ville de la Morée que j'ai renversée, Hermione et Trœzene ont subi le même sort — je n'ai pardonné à Argos, à Phliasia, &c. — Je suis actuellement occupé à detruire jusqu'à la pierre fondamentale du temple d'Apollon Amycléen, &c. — J'en detruirois même d'autres avec autant de facilité, si on me laissoit faire. — Je n'ai point lu que depuis le renouvellement des lettres, il soit venu dans l'esprit de

* Dodwell, Travels in Greece, v. ii. c. 11.

quelqu'un de bouleverser ainsi des villes entières, &c. — Je ne me souviens pas d'avoir vu dans les relations des voyageurs qui m'ont precedé, qu'ils ayent jamais osé abattre des chateaux, ou d'autres grands batimens." In speaking of the destruction of Sparta, the following observations, rightly understood, afford some explanation of his motives. " Si en renversant ses murs et ses temples, si en ne laissant pas une pierre sur une autre au plus petit de ses sacellums, son lieu sera dans la suite ignorée, *j'ai au moins de quoi la faire reconnoitre*, et c'est quelque chose ; *je n'avois que ce moyen là pour rendre illustre mon voyage*, &c."

After this recital, he has the hardihood to sign himself Fourmont Σπαρτιατικος : but, as Mr. Dodwell observes, he should rather have taken the title of *Poliorcetes*, for it would appear that the cities of Greece had not met with such a destroyer since the days of Demetrius. To speak seriously, however, I will frankly confess that these ravages do not excite any regret in my mind, because I do not believe a single word respecting them, and I am persuaded that to you, or to any other person who has been in the country, it would only be an idle waste of time to adduce any proofs of the ludicrous absurdity of the tale. The statement of Fourmont itself is quite sufficient, and I shall detain you with no further remarks, but leave M. Rochette to pronounce such an opinion respecting that statement and its author as he may think fit, whether it be true or false. I must say, however, that his silence concerning these particulars, which must have been in his possession, is scarcely consistent with the candour he professes, especially where so much depends on the credit due to the personal character of the individual in question, and who, M. Rochette would have us believe, was " a laborious, pains-taking man, ignorant of the ways of the world, carrying the bluntness and simplicity of his manners almost to rudeness ; and, in short, much more honest than learned." * I will only further add, in conclusion, that when M. Rochette thinks himself justified in assuming a high tone of in-

---

* Lett. p. 3.

dignation in defence of the " memory and honour of this worthy man," and when he inveighs in strong terms against the arrogance and presumption of those criticks who are prone to believe evil, and who delight to calumniate literary worth, I am surprised that it should not occur to him what may possibly be said of those who virtually assist in the propagation of imposture, for the gratification of exhibiting their own learning and ingenuity in the support of an untenable and exploded paradox.

I remain, dear Walpole, yours, &c.

ABERDEEN.

INSCRIPTIONS,

COPIED IN VARIOUS PARTS OF GREECE,

AND

COMMUNICATED BY LIEUTENANT-COLONEL LEAKE.

I.

THE following inscription is upon a fragment of a large quadrangular Stele at Punta, a low cape at the entrance of the gulf of Arta, oppo‑ site to the modern town of Prevyza. At Punta are many remains of walls óf Roman construction, erected probably by Augustus, when he established the Actian games at this spot, and founded Nicopolis upon the isthmus near Prevyza.

ΕΠΙΕΡΑΠΟΛΟΥΤΩΙΑΠΟΛΛΩΝΙΤΩΙΑΚΤΙΩΙΦΙΑ . . ΜΟΝΟΣ   ΕΠΙΣΤΡΑ
        ΟΣ
ΠΡΟΜΝΑΜΟΝΔΕΑΓΗΤΑΤΟΥΝΙΚΙΑΑΛΥΣΕΙΟΥ   ΩΝΟΣΟΙΝ
ΣΥΜΠΡΟΜΝΑΜΟΝΩΝΔΕΝΑΥΣΙΜΑΧΟΥΤΟΥΑΡΙΣΤΟΚΛΕ   ΧΟΥΤΟΥ
ΟΣΑΣΤΑΚΟΥΦΙΛΟΞΕΝΟΥΤΟΥΗΡΑΚΛΕΙΤΟΥΦΟΙΤΙΑΝΟΣ   ΕΔΟΞΕΤΑ
ΓΡΑΜΜΑΤΕΟΣΔΕΤΑΙΒΟΥΛΑΙΠΡΟΙΤΟΥΤΟΥΔΙΟΠΕΙΘΕΟΣ   ΝΟΥΣΕ
ΜΑΤΡΟΠΟΛΙΤΑΚΟΥΡΟΤΡΟΠΟΥ ΕΔΟΞΕΤΑΙΒΟΥΛΑΙΚΑΙ   ΝΑΝΩΝ
ΤΩΙΚΟΙΝΩΙΤΩΝΑΚΑΡΝΑΝΩΝΙΠΡΟΞΕΝΟΥΣΕΙΜΕΝ   ΓΑΥΣΑΝ
ΚΑΙΕΥΕΡΓΕΤΑΣΤΟΥΚΟΙΝΟΥΤΩΝΑΚΑΡΝΑΝΩΝΚΑΤΑ   ΕΝΑΚΑΡ
ΤΟΝΝΟΜΟΝΑΓΑΣΙΑΝΟΛΥΜΠΙΩΝΟΣΠΑΤΡΗΠΟΠΛΙΟΝ   ΚΑΙΚΑΤ

ΛΕΥΚΙΟΝΤΟΥΣΠΟΠΛΙΟΥΑΚΙΛΙΟΥΣΡΩΜΑΙ   ΕΙΡΑΝΑΣ
ΟΥΣΚΑΙΕΙΜΕΝΑΥΤΟΙΣ   ΜΙΑΚΑΙΦ
ΚΑΙΕΚΓΟΝΟΙΣΕΝΑΚΑΡΝΑΝΙΑΙΑΣΦΑΛΕΙΑΝΚΑΙΑΥΤΟΙΣ   ΝΟΙΣΚΑΙ
ΚΑΙΧΡΗΜΑΣΙΚΑΙΚΑΤΑΓΑΝΚΑΙΚΑΤΑΘΑΛΑΣΣΑΝΚΑΙ   ΝΑΝΩ
ΠΟΛΕΜΟΥΚΑΙΕΙΡΑΝΑΣΚΑΙΓΑΣΚΑΙΟΙΚΙΑΣΕΓΚΤΗΣΙΝ   ΕΠΙΕΡΑΠΟΛ
ΚΑΙΤΑΑΛΛΑΤΙΜΙΑΚΑΙΦΙΛΑΝΘΡΩΠΑΠΑΝΤΑΟΣΑΚΑΙΤΟΙΣ   ΝΟΣΔΕ
ΑΛΛΟΙΣΠΡΟΞΕΝΟΙΣΚΑΙΕΥΕΡΓΕΤΑΙΣΤΟΥΚΟΙΝΟΥΤΩΝ   ΝΑΥΣΙΜ
ΑΚΑΡΝΑΝΩΝΥΠΑΡΧΕΙ   ΡΑΚΛΕΙΤΟ
                                                    ΛΙΟΠΕΙ
                                                    ΙΚΟΙΝΩΙΤ
                                                    ΝΟΥΤ
                                                    ΕΜΜΕ
                                                    ΛΕΟΝΤΙ
                                                    ΑΙΑΣΦ
                                                    ΘΑΛΑ
                                                    ΚΤΗΣΙ
                                                    ΛΟΙΣΓ
                                                    ΥΠΑΡ

'Επὶ Ἱεραπόλου τῷ 'Απόλλωνι τῷ 'Ακτίῳ Φιλ(αί)μονος·
προμνήμονος δὲ 'Αγητάτου Νικία 'Αλυσείου·
συμπρομνημόνων δὲ Ναυσιμάχου τοῦ Αριστοκλέ
ος 'Αστακοῦ, Φιλοξένου τοῦ 'Ηρακλείτου Φοιτιάνος·
γραμματέος δὲ τῇ ἑουλῇ. Προίτου τοῦ Διοπιθέος
Μητροπολίτου Κουροτρόπου· "Εδοξε τῇ ἑουλῇ καὶ
τῷ κοινῷ τῶν Ακαρνάνων, προξένους εἶναι
καὶ εὐεργέτας τοῦ κοινοῦ τῶν 'Ακαρνάνων κατὰ
τὸν νόμον Αγασίαν 'Ολυμπίωνος Πατρέα, Πόπλιον,
Λεύκιον τοὺς Ποπλίου 'Ακιλίους Ρωμαί
ους· καὶ εἶναι αὐτοῖς
καὶ ἐκγόνοις ἐν Ακαρνανίᾳ ἀσφάλειαν καὶ αὐτοῖς
καὶ χρήμασι καὶ κατὰ γῆν καὶ κατὰ θαλάσσην καὶ
πολέμου καὶ εἰρήνης καὶ γῆς καὶ οἰκίας ἔγκτησιν,
καὶ τὰ ἄλλα τίμια καὶ φιλάνθρωπα πάντα, ὅσα καὶ τοῖς
ἄλλοις προξένοις καὶ εὐεργέταις τοῦ κοινοῦ τῶν
'Ακαρνάνων ὑπάρχει.

TRANSLATION.

Philemon having the administration of the sacred things of the
Actian Apollo; Agetatus, son of Nicias, of Alysus, being recorder;

Nausimachus, son of Aristocles, of Astacus (and) Philoxenus, son of Heraclitus, of Phœtiæ, being assistant recorders; Prœtus, son of Diopithes, of Metropolis, being secretary to the council: It was decreed by the council and people of the Acarnanians, that Agasias, son of Olympion, of Patræ, (and) the Romans, Publius (and) Lucius, sons of Publius Acilius, should be public guests and benefactors of the community of the Acarnanians, according to law; and that for them and their descendants in Acarnania, there should be protection for themselves and their property by sea and by land, and in war and in peace, together with the right of acquiring lands and houses, and all other rights of honor and humanity, granted by the community of the Acarnanians to other public guests and benefactors.

NOTE.

Alysus and Astacus were towns of Acarnania, near the coast, lying opposite to Leucas and the Echinades. Phœtiæ and Metropolis were near the banks of the Achelous. In the time of the last Philip of Macedonia, Phœtiæ belonged to the Ætolians (Polyh. l. iv. c. 63.); but it is probable, from this inscription, that Augustus gave the natural boundary of the Achelous to the two provinces, and thus included Phœtiæ, which is on the northern side of the Achelous in Acarnania. I found remains of all these cities.

II.

Of the two following dedications to Aplus, or the Thessalian Apollo, I copied the first from the edge of a quadrangular piece of white marble, in the court of the bishop's house, at Turnavo, a Greek town in Thessaly, eight miles to the N. N. W. of Larissa. The dialect seems to have been peculiar to the adjacent district; at least I never observed it in any of the numerous inscriptions remaining in Thessaly, nor even so near as Larissa, where many still exist. I found the second dedication, which is to Apollo of Tempe, at Tatári, a village situated in the same plain in which Turnavo stands, and not far from the left bank of the Peneus, between Larissa and Tempe.

ΑΠΛΟΥΝΙΚΕΡΔ‚ΙΟΥΣΟΥΣΙΠΑΤΡΟΣ
ΠΟΛΕΜΑΡΧΙΔΑΙΟΣΟΘΥΤΑΣ
ΟΝΕΘΕΙΚΕΙΕΡΟΜΝΑΜΟΝΕΙ
ΣΑΣΚΑΙΑΡΧΙΔΑΥΧΝΑΦΟΡΕΙΣΑΣ

NOTES.

Ἄπλουνι.] The following passage in the Cratylus of Plato, illustrative of this word, has been pointed out to me by the Rev. R. Walpole. Plato, in speaking of Apollo, says : " Κατὰ δὲ τὴν μαντικὴν καὶ τὸ ἀληθές τε καὶ τὸ ἁπλοῦν (ταυτὸν γάρ ἐστιν) ὥσπερ οὖν οἱ Θετταλοὶ καλοῦσιν αὐτὸν, ὀρθότατ᾽ ἂν καλοῖτο. Ἁπλὸν γάρ φασι πάντες Θετταλοὶ τοῦτον τὸν θεόν." — Cratyl. p. 205. ed. Serr.

Κερδῴου for Κερδῴῳ.] This epithet of Apollo is found in Lycophron, v. 208. Δελφινίου παῤ ἄντρα Κερδῴου Θεοῦ, where the Scholiast says that Apollo was called by this name, ὅτι διὰ χρησμῶν τὰ συμφέροντα καὶ ἐπικερδῆ δείκνυσιν

III.

ΑΠΛΟΥΝΙΤΕΜΠΕΙΤΑ
ΑΙΣΧΥΛΙΣΣΑΤΥΡΟΙ
ΕΛΕΥΘΕΡΙΑ

Ἀπόλλωνι Τεμπείτῃ, Ἄισχυλις Σατύρου ἐλευθέριᾳ.

IV.

At Athens.

- ΑΙΑΜΕΝΕΙΣΦΑΟΣΗΡΕΣΙΒΥΡΤΙΝΓΑΙΑΔΕΚΕΥ
ΘΕΙΣΩΜΑΠΝΟΗΝΔΕΑΙΘΗΡΕΛΑΒΕΝΠΑΛΙΝΟΣΠΕ
ΡΕΔΩΚΕΝΠΑΤΡΙΔΕΣΩΙΚΑΙΜΗΤΡΙΛΙΠΩΝΛΥΠΑ
Σ - ΠΑΝΑΝΚΗΣΩΙΧΟΥΑΝΑΡΠΑΣΘΕΙΣΕΠΤΑΕΤΗΓ
- - ΟΝΩ -

Γαῖα μὲν εἰς φάος ἧρε Σίβυρτιν, γαῖα δὲ κεύθει
Σῶμα, πνοὴν δὲ αἰθὴρ ἔλαβεν πάλιν, ὅσπερ ἔδωκεν·
Πατρὶ δὲ σῷ καὶ μητρὶ λίπων λύπας ὑπ᾽ ἀνάγκης
Ὤιχου ἀναρπασθεὶς ἑπτὰ ἔτη γεγονώς.

V.

I found the following upon a solid square block of stone, in a shoemaker's shop, in the town of Dhomoko, the antient Thaumaci.

ΑΓΑΘΑΙΤΥΧΑΙΠΟΛΙΣΘΑΥΜΑΚΩΝ
ΕΔΩΚΕΑΓΕΣΤΩΙΑΓΡΟΛΕΩΝΟΣ
ΚΑΛΛΙΕΙΠΡΟΞΕΝΙΑΝΕΠΙΝΟΜΙ
ΑΝΑΣΥΛΙΑΝΑΣΦΑΛΕΙΑΝΕΝΚΤΗ
ΣΙΝΑΤΕΛΕΙΑΝΠΑΝΤΩΝΚΑΙΠΟΛΕ
ΜΟΥΚΑΙΕΙΡΑΝΑΣΕΝΤΟΝΑΠΑΝΤΑ
ΧΡΟΝΟΝΚΑΙΑΥΤΩΙΚΑΙΕΚΓΟΝΟΙΣΚΑΙ
ΟΣΑΤΟΙΣΑΛΛΟΙΣΠΡΟΞΕΝΟΙΣΠΑΝ
ΤΑΑΡΧΟΝΤΩΝΣΦΟΔΡΙΑΛΕ - - - ΔΑ
ΦΑΝΑΕΝΓΥΟΣΤΑΣΠΡΟΞΕΝΙΑΣ
ΠΟΛΥΜΝΙΑΣΤΟΙ*Σ

VI.

ΑΓΑΘΑΙΤΥΧΑΙΠΟΛΙΣΘΑΥΜΑΚΩΝΕΔΩΚΕΝΠΥΡΡΑ
ΤΙΜΑΓΟΡΟ - - Ρ - - - ΕΙΩΤΑΙΟΝΤΙΕΥΕΡΓΕΤΑ - - -
- - ΣΠΡΟΞΕΝΙΑΝ - - ΟΠΟΛΙΤΕΙΑΝΕΠΙΝΟΜΙΑΝ
ΑΣΥΛΙΑΝΑΣΦΑΛΕΙΑΝΕΝΚΤΗΣΙΝΑΤΕΛΕΙΑΝ
ΠΑΝΤΩΝΚΑΙΠΟΛΕΜΟΥΚΑΙΕΙΡΑΝΑΣΚΑΙΑΥ - - - - -
ΕΚΓΟΝΟΙΣ - ΝΤΟΝΑΠΑΝΤΑΧΡΟΝΟΝΚΑΙΟΣΑ
ΤΟΙΣΑΛΛΟΙΣΠΡΟΞΕΝΟΙΣΠΑΝΤΑΑΡΧΟΝΤΩΝ
- - - - - - ͵ - ΑΙΣΙΡΑΚΟ - ΝΙΚΟΜΑΧΟΥΕΝΓΥΟΣΤΑΣ
ΠΡΟΞΕΝΙΑΣΝΕΟΠΤΟΛΕΜΟΣΕΥΗΘΙΔ - - -

Αγαθᾶ Τύχα· Πόλις Θαυμάκων ἔδωκε Αγέστω
'Αγρολέωνος Καλλιεῖ προξενίαν, ἐπινομίαν,
ἀσυλίαν, ἀσφάλειαν, ἔγκτησιν, ἀτέλειαν
πάντων καὶ πολέμου καὶ εἰρήνης ἐν
τὸν ἅπαντα χρόνον καὶ αὐτῷ καὶ
ἐκγόνοις καὶ ὅσα τοῖς ἄλλοις προξένοις
πάντα. 'Αρχόντων Σφοδρία Λε(ωνι)δαφανα·
ἔγγυος τῆς προξενίας Πολυμνίαστος.

'Αγαθᾶ Τύχα· Πόλις Θαυμάκων ἔδωκεν
Πύρρα Τιμαγόρο(υ 'Η)ρ(ακλ)ειώτα, ὄντι

* Sic in lapide.

εὐεργέτη (τῆς πόλεω)ς, προξενίαν, ἰσοπολιτείαν,
ἐπινομίαν, ἀσυλίαν, ἀσφάλειαν, ἔγκτησιν,
ἀτέλειαν πάντων, καὶ πολέμου καὶ εἰρήνης,
καὶ αὐτῷ καὶ ἐκγόνοις ἐν τὸν ἄπαντα
χρόνον, καὶ ὅσα τοῖς ἄλλοις προξένοις
πάντα· Ἀρχόντων - - - - - αισιρακο - Νικομάχου.
Ἐγγυός τῆς (προ)ξενίας Νεοπτόλεμος Εὐηθίδ(ου).

   2 Καλλιεῖ, Calliensi. Agestus was a citizen of Callium, an important town in Ætolia, situated on the north side of the Spercheius. It was plundered by the Gauls, who marched thither suddenly from their camp before Thermopylæ. B. C. 278. See Pausanias (Phocic. c. 22.)

   2 Ἐπινομία, the right of pasturing cattle.

   6 The word ἐκγόνοις has been substituted for something erased, and καὶ has been added in the margin.

   10 The town of Heraclea, more antiently Trachys, near Thermopylæ, was about twenty-five miles to the southward of Thaumaci. Callium was about the same distance to the westward.

VII.

From Dhadhia, near Mount Parnassus.

Ψ.   Κ   Δ
ΜΟΥΛΔΑΜΑΣΙΠΠ
ΤΟΝΑΡΧΙΕΡΕΑΤΟΥ
ΓΑΛΟΥΘΕΟΥΔΙΟΝΥϹΟ
ΤΟΝΒΟΙШΤΑΡΧΗΝΠΑ
ΤΡΟϹΒΟΙШΤΑΡΧΟΥ
ΓШΝΟΘΕΤΗΝΦШΚΑΡ
ΧΗΝΑΜΦΙΚΤΥΟΝΑΘΕ
ΗΚΟΛΟΝΠΑΝΕΛΛΗΝΑ
ΑΡΧΟΝΤΑΚΑΙΤΑϹΑΛΛΑϹ
ΠΑϹΑϹΕΝΤΗΠΑΤΡΙΔΙ
ΤΕΛΕϹΑΝΤΑΛΙΤΟΥΡΓΙ
ΑϹΚΙΝΤΥΛΙΑΠΛΟΥΤΑ
ΧΗΗΓΥΝΗΤΟΝΙΔΙΟΝ
ΑΝΔΡΑΕΥΝΟΙΑϹΚΑΙΑΡΕ
ΤΗϹΕΝΕΚΕΝΔΙΟΝΥ
ϹΟΥΕΝΤΕΜΕΝΕΙ

Ψηφίσματι κοινῷ δημοσίῳ

Μάρκον Οὔλπιον Δαμάσιππον, τὸν ἀρχιερέα τοῦ μεγάλου θεοῦ Διονύσου, τὸν Βοιωτάρχην, πατρὸς Βοιωτάρχου, Ἀγωνοθέτην, Φωκάρχην, Ἀμφικτύονα, Θεήκολον, Πανέλληνα, Ἄρχοντα καὶ τὰς ἄλλας πάσας ἐν τῇ πατρίδι τελέσαντα λιτουργίας, Κιντύλια Πλουτάρχη ἡ γυνὴ τὸν ἴδιον ἄνδρα εὐνοίας καὶ ἀρετῆς ἕνεκεν Διονύσου ἐν τεμένει.

From this inscription it appears, that the stone upon which it is engraved supported a statue of a high priest of Bacchus, named Marcus Ulpius Damasippus, erected by his wife Quintilia Plutarcha. I found it in a church near Dhadhia, a large village, situated at the foot of Mount Parnassus, on the northern side. The hill upon which the church stands is surrounded by the remains of Hellenic walls, which seem to have belonged to the antient Amphicleia; for the concurring testimonies of Herodotus (l. viii. c. 33.), and of Pausanias (Phocic. c. 33.), place Amphicæa, or Amphicleia, in this vicinity; and the worship of Bacchus, mentioned in the inscription, is described by Pausanias, as existing at Amphicleia, in the following terms : θέας δὲ μάλιστα ἄξιον ἄδυτον· Διονύσῳ δρῶσιν ὄργια ἔσοδος ἐς τὸ ἄδυτον, οὐδὲ ἐν φανερῷ σφισιν ἄγαλμα οὐκ ἔστι· λέγεται δὲ ὑπὸ τῶν Ἀμφικλειέων μάντιν τέ σφισι τὸν θεὸν τοῦτον καὶ βοηθὸν νόσων σφίσι καθεστηκέναι· τὰ μὲν δὴ νοσήματα αὐτοῖς Ἀμφικλεεῦσι καὶ τοῖς προσοικοῦσιν ἰᾶται δι᾽ ὀνειράτων· πρόμαντις δὲ ὁ ἱερευς ἐστι· χρᾷ δὲ ἐκ τοῦ θεοῦ κάτοχος. It appears, therefore, that Damasippus was one of the priests who were inspired by the god to enunciate his oracles. With respect to the remarkable word θεήκολον, we find that at Olympia there was a building called the θεηκολέων, and a sacred officer θεηκόλοτος, who had charge of the sacrifices, μέλει τὰ ἐς θυσίας θεηκολότῳ. Paus. Eliac. prior. c. 15. Facius, however, has supposed that the word should be written θεηκόλῳ, and his conjecture receives the strongest confirmation from our inscription. I copied another at Zante, in honour of a woman who had been priestess * (θεοκολήσασαν) to Diana.

---

* Chandler (Inscr. Ant. p. 86.) has published this inscription with the slight error of ΚΑΙ instead of ΚΛΗ, in the name of the priestess Clenippa.

VIII.

At Amphipolis.

ΕΔΟΞΕΝΤΩΙΔΗΜΩΙΦΙ
ΛΩΝΑΚΑΙΣΤΡΑΤΟΚΛΕ
ΑΦΕΟΓΕΙΝΑΜΦΙΠΟΛΙ(Ν)
.ΠΟΛΙΤΕΩΝΑΕΙΦΥΓ(Ι)
ΗΝΚΑΙΑΥΤΟΣΚΑΙΤΟΣ
ΠΑΙΔΑΣΚΑΙΗΜΠΟΤΑΛ(Ι)
ΣΚΩΝΤΑΙΠΑΣΧΕΙΝΑ(Υ)
ΤΟΣΩΣΠΟΛΕΜΙΟΣΚΑΙ
ΝΗΠΟΙΝΕΙΤΕΘΝΑΝΑΙ
ΤΑΔΕΧΡΗΜΑΤΑΥΤΩΝΔ
ΗΜΟΣΙΑΕΙΝΑΙΤΟΔΕΠ
ΙΔΕΚΑΤΟΝΙΡΟΝΤΟΥΑ
ΠΟΛΛΩΝΟΣΚΑΙΤΟΣΤΡ
ΥΜΟΝΟΣΤΟΣΔΕΠΡΟΣΤ
ΑΤΑΣΑΝΑΓΡΑΨΑΙΑΥΤ
ΟΣΕΣΣΤΗΛΗΝΛΙΘΙΝΗΝ
ΗΝΔΕΤΙΣΤΟΨΗΦΙΣΜΑ
ΑΝΑΨΗΦΙΖΕΙΗΚΑΤΑΔ
ΕΧΕΤΑΙΤΟΥΤΟΣΤΕΧΝ
ΗΙΗΜΗΧΑΝΗΙΟ(Τ)ΕΩΙΟ(Υ)
Ν(Τ)ΑΧΡΗΜΑΤΑΥΤΟΔΗΜ
ΟΣΙΑΕΣΤΩΚΑΙΑΥΤΟΣ
ΦΕΟΓΕΤΩΑΜΦΙΠΟΛΙΝ
ΑΕΙΦΥΓΙΗΝ

Ἔδοξεν τῷ Δήμῳ Φίλωνα καὶ Στρατοκλέα φεύγειν Ἀμφίπολιν πολίτων. ἀειφυγίαν *, καὶ αὐτοὺς καὶ τοὺς παῖδας· καὶ ἐάνποτ᾽ ἀλίσκωνται πάσχειν αὐτοὺς ὡς
πολεμίους καὶ νηποινεὶ τεθνᾶναι· τὰ δὲ χρήματα αὐτῶν δημόσια εἶναι, τὸ δὲ ἐπιδέκατον ἱερὸν τοῦ Ἀπόλλωνος καὶ τοῦ Στρυμόνος· τοὺς δὲ Προστάτας ἀναγράψαι
αὐτοὺς εἰς στήλην λιθίνην· ἤν δέ τις τὸ ψήφισμα ἀναψηφίζει ἢ καταδέχεται
τούτους τέχνῃ ἢ μηχανῇ ἡτινιοῦν, τὰ χρήματα αὐτοῦ δημόσια ἔστω, καὶ αὐτὸς
φευγέτω Ἀμφίπολιν ἀειφυγίαν.

This inscription contains a decree of perpetual banishment by the
people of Amphipolis against two of their citizens, named Philo and

---

* Φεύγειν ἀειφυγίαν, perpetuo exilio mulctari. Φυγὼν δὲ καὶ μὴ θελήσας κρίσιν ὑποσχεῖν,
φευγέτω ἀειφυγίαν. — Plato de Leg. 9, p. 871, ed. Serran.

Stratocles, and their children. If they are ever taken, they are to suffer death as enemies, their property is confiscated to the people, and a tenth of it is to be applied to the service of Apollo and Strymon.. The (magistrates intituled) Prostatæ are to inscribe names of the condemned men upon a pillar of stone; and if any person revokes the decree, or in any manner whatever gives countenance to the banished persons, his property also is to be forfeited to the people, and he himself is to be banished from Amphipolis for ever.

The form of this decree is taken from the laws of the Athenians, of whom the Amphipolitans were a colony. We find all the peculiar expressions of the Amphipolitan decree in one or other of the laws cited by Demosthenes *, in his orations against Aristocrates, Midias, and Neæra. The mode of engraving, and the shape of the characters on the stone, indicate the best times of Grecian art ; and the name of Stratocles, one of the banished men, is found in the first Olynthiac oration, as that of one of the ambassadors who went from Amphipolis to Athens, to invite the Athenians to take possession of Amphipolis. It is not impossible, therefore, that he may be the same Stratocles mentioned in the inscription, and that when the party of Philip gained the ascendancy at Amphipolis, a sentence of banishment may have been pronounced against him.

We are surprised to find at Amphipolis a dialect differing 'so much from the later Attic or Hellenic; for if the conjecture already proposed respecting Stratocles be received, the inscription cannot be

---

* Νηποινεὶ τεθνᾶναι is found in a law quoted in the oration against Aristocrates (p. 639. ed. Reiske), and in Andocides de Myst. p. 47, 48. 'Ωτεψοῦν was the Amphipolitan form for ἡτινιοῦν, which word we find in the following clause of a law cited in the oration against Neæra, p. 1350. 'Εὰν δὲ ξένος ἀστῇ ξυνοικῇ τέχνῃ ἢ μηχανῇ ἡτινιοῦν, γραφέσθω πρὸς τοὺς Θεσμοθέτας : and in the oration against Midias, we find τρόπῳ ἢ μηχανῇ ἡτινιοῦν. The appropriation of the tenth part to the Deity is mentioned by Andocides, in the passage just referred to. His words are precisely those of the inscription, πολέμιός ἐσται τῶν Ἀθηναίων καὶ νηποινὶ τεθνάτω· καὶ τὰ χρήματα αὐτοῦ δημόσια ἔστω καὶ τῆς θεοῦ τὸ ἐπιδέκατον. See also a decree in Plutarch, de decem Rhetor. in Antiph. and Xenophon Hellen. l. 1. c. 7. Επιδέκατον, ἐπίπεμπτον, appear to have been Athenian law terms used only in decrees relating to confiscations. See Harpocrat. in voc.

older than the 107th Olympiad. We find proofs, however, in several inscriptions still existing in Greece, that the Greeks were often accustomed to preserve the use of the antient and obsolete dialects in their public acts. Among other examples of this, I found an inscribed marble in Bœotia, upon which were some verses in Hellenic, followed by a decree in the Bœoto-Æolic dialect ; and inscriptions in both dialects are found in several parts of Bœotia. As the Greek colonies were particularly jealous of preserving the vestiges of their origin, customs were often longer preserved there than in the mother countries ; and it may have been with the same feeling that the Amphipolitans adopted the antient Ionic dialect of Attica for their public acts, although it may have been obsolete at Athens, even when the colony of Agnon went to Amphipolis. *

I copied this Amphipolitan decree from a marble, inserted in a Turkish fountain at Yenikeui, a village situated at six miles from Orfaná, on the road to Serres. At Yenikeui, and on the hill above it, are found many remains of Amphipolis. In the latter ages of the Byzantine empire these remains had given to a Greek village standing on the site, the appellation of Marmári, Μαρμάριον † : the name of Mármara is still attached to the spot, though the village itself has passed away. Yenikeui, or Neochorio, (new village) has been built upon a part of the site, in an unhealthy situation, on the bank of the river, for the sake of the fishery, by which the village is supported. This fishery consists chiefly of the fine eels ‡, for which the Strymon is still as much renowned as it was in antient times. Its profits are

---

* In the 4th year of the 85th Olymp. 437. B. C.
† Cantacuzenus, l. i. c. 53.
‡ Two poets, cited by Athenæus, (l. 7. c. 13.) celebrate the Strymonian eels. Arches-
tratus says :

- - - - ἀρετῆς μέγα κάρτα φέρουσι
Κωπαῖαι καὶ Στρυμόνιαι, μεγάλαι τε γάρ εἰσι
Καὶ τὸ πάχος θαυμάσται.

Antiphanes says :

- - - - ποταμὸς ὠνομασμένος
Στρύμων μεγίστας ἐγχέλεις κεκτημένος. · ·

GREEK INSCRIPTIONS. 513

farmed from the Porte by the Bey of Zikhna, who commands all the surrounding territory.

Thucydides has very accurately described Amphipolis, as situated at twenty-five stades from the mouth of the river Strymon, and as being surrounded on two sides by the river, which, a little above the city, makes a considerable marsh or lake. The position of Amphipolis is one of the most important in Greece. It stands in a pass which traverses the mountains bordering the Strymonic gulf, and it commands the only easy communication from the coast of that gulf into the great Macedonian plains, which extend for sixty miles from beyond Meleniko to *Philippi*. The Strymon, immediately after emerging from a large lake, makes a half circuit in a deep gorge round the hill of Amphipolis, and from thence crosses a plain of two or three miles in breadth to the sea. The name of Amphipolis was given to the place by the Athenian colonists, from its being surrounded by the river. The singularity of the site accounts no less for the name of Ennea Odoi (nine ways), which it bore prior to the time of the Athenian colony*; for all the principal communications between the coast and the plains must have traversed this pass. Near the river's mouth on the left bank are the ruins of a town of the Byzantine empire; built on the site of the antient Eïon. These ruins have often been mistaken for those of Amphipolis.

IX.

I found the following inscription upon a stone in the village of Dhavlia; from another side of the same stone I also copied the inscription which has already been published in the first volume of the present work, from a copy taken by the Earl of Aberdeen.

ΟΔΟΣΔΕΗΕΠΙΤΟΝ   1
ΑΡΧΑΓΕΤΗΝΕΞΕΙΠΛΑ

* Herod. l. vii. c. 114.

VOL. II.   3 u

514 GREEK INSCRIPTIONS.

ΤΟΣΚΑΛΑΜΟΤΣΔΥΟ
ΤΑΔΕΣΗΜΕΙΑΚΑΙΤΟΥ .
ΟΡΟΥΣΤΗΣΜ ΤΡΗΣΕ   5
ΩΣΕΝΧΑΡΑΞΟΥΣΙΚΟ .
ΝΗΕΝΤΟΣΤΗΣΕΙΚΑΔΟΣ
ΤΟΥΔΩΔΕΚΑΤΟΥΜΗ
ΝΟΣΗΜΩΝΟΤΑΝΕΝ
ΧΑΡΑΧΘΩΣΙΝΕΠΕΛΕΥ   10
ΣΟΜΕΝΩΝΑΥΤΟΥΣ
ΠΕΡΙΑΓΡΟΥΔΡΥΠΠΙΟ .
ΚΑΤΑΤΗΝΠΡΟΚΟΜΙΣΘ . .
ΣΑΝΧΕΙΡΑΥΠΟΣΕΡΑΠ .
ΑΔΟΣΖΩΠΥΡΟΥΤΟΥ   15
ΕΓΔΙΚΟΥΚΑΙΤΩΝΠΕΡΙ
ΦΙΛΩΝΑΣΩΣΙΚΡΑΤΟΥΣ
ΚΑΙΔΑΜΩΝΑΖΩΠΥ
ΡΟΥΑΡΧΟΝΤΩΝΚΡΕΙ . .
ΜΕΝΕΙΤΙΛΕΙΠΕΙΤΩ .   20
ΡΙΘΜΩΕΚΤΗΣΑΠΟΦΑ
ΣΕΩΣΤΗΣΕΥΒΟΥΛΟΥ
ΤΕΤΡΑΚΟΣΙΩΝΤΡΙΑΚΟ .
ΤΑΠΕΝΤΕΠΛΕΘΡΩΝ
ΤΟΥΤΟΥΕΧΕΙΝΑΠΑΙΤΗ   25
ΣΙΝΣΕΡΑΠΙΑΔΑΑΠΟ
ΤΗΣΔΑΥΛΙΕΩΝΠΟΛΕ
ΩΣΠΑΡΗΣΑΝ
ΚΟΥΡΡΙΟΣΑΥΤΟΒΟΥ
ΛΟΣΚΕΚΡΙΚΑΚΑΙ   30
ΤΗΝΠΡΩΤΗΝΕΣΦΡΑ
ΓΙΣΑΝΙΚΗΦΟΡΟΣΛΥ
ΚΟΜΗΔΟΥΣΚΕΚΡΙΚΑ
ΑΓΑΣΙΑΣΤΕΙΜΩΝΟΣ
ΚΕΚΡΙΚΑΠΑΙΛΙΟΣ   35
ΔΑΜΟΞΕΝΟΣΕΣΦΡΑ
ΓΙΣΑΤΕΤΑΡΤΗΝΕΙΣΙΔ
ΠΕΜΠΤΗΝΜΗΤΡΟΔ
ΡΟΣΑΠΟΛΛΟΔΟΤΟΥΑΝ
ΤΙΚΥΡΕΥΣΝΕΙΚΑΡΕ   40
ΤΟΣΠΙΣΤΟΥΠΘΟΡΕΥΣ
ΤΥΡΑΝΝΟΣΤΥΡΑΝΝΟΥ
ΕΣΦΡΑΓΙΣΜΑΙΑΚΙΝΔΥ
ΝΟΣΚΑΛΛΙΚΡΑΤΟΥΣΤΙ
ΘΟΡΕΥΣΣΕΞΚΟΡΝΗΛΙ   45
ΟΣΑΣΙΟΧΟΣΕΥΝΟΥΣ
ΕΠΑΙΡΑΚΑΛΛΙΓΕΝΗΣ
ΚΛΕΟΝΕΙΚΟΥΕΣΦΡΑΓΙΚΑ
ΤΙΘΟΡΕΥΣ

" The road to the Archagetes * shall be two calami † in breadth. They shall jointly engrave the landmarks and boundaries of the measurement within the twentieth day of the twelfth month, we coming to them, when they shall be engraved. Concerning the land Dryppium, we adjudge from a view of the writing ‡ exhibited by Serapias, son of Zopyrus the Ecdicus, and by Philon, son of Sosicrates, and Damon, son of Zopyrus, the archons, that if any thing is wanting to the number of four hundred and thirty plethro, settled by the decision of Eubulus, for this, Serapias has a rightful demand from the city of the Daulians. The following were present: I, Curius Autobulus, adjudged and sealed the first seal; I, Nicephorus, son of Lycomedes, adjudged; I, Agasias, son of Timon, adjudged; I, Publius Ælius Damoxenus, sealed the fourth seal in like manner; Metrodorus, son of Apollodotus, sealed the fifth; Nicaretus of Tithorea, son of Pistus, Tyrannus, son of Tyrannus, sealed; Acindynus of Tithorea, son of Callicrates; Sextus Cornelius Asiochus; Eunus, son of Epæras; Calligenes of Tithorea, son of Callinicus, sealed.'

NOTES.

* It appears from the following passage in Pausanias, Phocic. c. 4. that the Archagetes was the tomb of an antient hero of the Daulienses. Ἔστι δὲ τῆς Δαυλίας χώρα καλουμένη Τρωνίς· ἐνταῦθα ἡρῶον ἥρω Αρχηγέτου πεποίηται.

† The Calamus seems to have been a measure of lines peculiar to Phocis, as the *Sphyra*, which occurs in the decree of Eubulus, on the other side of the stone, probably was of surfaces in the same province. Supposing the road to have been about fifteen English feet in width, the Calamus would be nearly of the same length as the Italian *Canna*, a word of the same import as Calamus.

‡ Τὴν ἑαυτοῦ χεῖρα, " his own hand-writing." Hyperides. apud Poll.

REMARKS ON THE PRECEDING INSCRIPTIONS,

BY THE EDITOR

I.

A COPY of this inscription was communicated by M. Pouqueville to M. Boissonade, who published it in his edition of the Epistles of

3 U 2

Holstein, accompanied with a learned commentary. Colonel Leake's copy is more accurate, both with respect to the words themselves and the distribution of the lines. The stone had another inscription, of which part only now remains.

The variation between the two copies is a sufficient reason for inserting in this volume the transcript made by Colonel Leake, even after the recent publication of it by Boissonade.

Pouqueville's copy. L. 1. ΤΟΙ. L. 2. ΠΡΟΜΝΑΜ. Ib. ΑΓΗΤΑ-ΡΟΧΟΥ ΑΛΥΖΕΙΟΥ. L. 6. ΚΟΥΡΟΠΟΥ Ω. L. 12. ΑΥΤΟΣ. L. 14. ΕΙΚΤΙΣΙΝ.

L. 6. The word ΚΟΥΡΟΠΟΥ Ω is inexplicable. M. Boissonade supposes ΚΟΥΡΟΠΟΥ to be the name of the month ; and he adds, " in Ω, latet forte diei notatio."

Boissonade's conjecture respecting the insertion of the month, affords a good explanation of the meaning of the sentence. The word in C. Leake's copy, Κουροτρόπου, if it be a month, is mentioned without reference to any particular day. This, however, is not without example ; in the Testamentum Epictetæ, in Maffei Mus. Ver., there is a similar form, Επὶ Εφόρων τῶν σὺν Ἰμέρτῳ Διοσθύου.* " When Himertus and his colleagues were Ephori, in the month Diosthyon :" and thus, in the present inscription, γραμματέος Πρόιτου, Μητροπολίτου, Κουροτρόπου.

II.

ΑΠΛΟΥΝ we perceive is the Thessalian name of Apollo ; and in this part of Greece † the Pelasgi dwelt, who afterwards founded the cities of Agylla, Tarquinia, and various Etruscan towns. They carried with them into Etruria the same name ; for ΑΠΛΥ, in Etruscan inscriptions,

---

* There is no doubt concerning the meaning of Διοσθύου, as in another part of the inscription we read μηνὸς Διοσθύου.

† Prima di passare in Italia molto avean abitato già nel Peloponneso ; di là passarono in Tessaglia. Lanzi. i. 27.

GREEK INSCRIPTIONS. 517

is Apollo. In Plato the word appears in the Hellenic form, Ἄπλος. Colonel Leake refers to a passage in Lycophron, where the epithet ΚΕΡΔΩΙΟΣ is applied to Apollo. In the present instance we may read ΚΕΡΔΟΙΟΥ; the Bœotians, between whose dialect and the Thessalian there was great affinity, said Πατροῖος, for πατρῶος. Etym. M. 224. 37.

ΣΩΣΙΠΑΤΡΟΣ vocatur in Ep. ad Rom. xvi. 21. qui A. A. xx. 4. est Σώπατρος. Valck. Herod. ed. Wess. p. 418.

L. 2. ΠΟΛΕΜΑΡΧΙΔΑΙΟΣΟΘΥΤΑΣ. Mr. Dobree proposes to divide the line at ΠΟΛΕΜΑΡΧΙΔΑ, and conjectures that some letters preceding ΟΥΤΑΣ may have formed a compound Thessalian word.

If ΙΟΣΟΘΥΤΑΣ be the word on the marble, we may consider it as used for ΙΕΡΟΘΥΤΗΣ.* The first O being written in the Æolian manner for E, as ΟΝΟΙΡΟΣ for ΟΝΕΙΡΟΣ; and the following Σ for P; " Ut *Valesii* et *Fusii* in *Valerios Furiosque* venerunt; ita *arbos, labos, vapos,* etiam et *clamos,* ac *lases,* ætatis fuerunt." † " Arbosem pro Arbore, antiqui dicebant; et Robosem pro Robore." Festus. The Greeks also said πρόσω, transposing the ρ, for πόῤῥω, and ἄρσεν, as well as ἄῤῥεν. ‡

L. 3. ΟΝΕΘΕΙΚΕ. Mr. Dobree refers me to the Cumean marble in Caylus, Rec. t. iii. tab. lvi., where we have ΟΝΤΕΘΗΝ. We may add some instances of the Æolo-Doric use of O for A. The Æolians said πόρνοπας for πάρνοπας: πέποσχε for πέπασχε, occurs in Epicharmus: κοθαρᾶς for καθαρᾶς, in the Tab. Herac.: βροχέως for βραχέως, in Hesychius. Joannes Grammaticus quotes ὄνω for ἄνω, ονέληται for ανέληται. See Greg. de Dial. ed Schaefer. p. 455.

L. 4. ΑΡΧΙΔΑΥΧΝΑΦΟΡΕΙΣΑΣ. Mr. Dobree supposes, with great probability, that Sosipater was ΑΡΧΙΛΥΧΝΗΦΟΡΟΣ. As the in-

---

* The Æolians, in some cases, used T for Θ, as in κατείρωσις; but they also substituted Θ for T; in the Bœoto-Æolic decree of Orchomenus, we read ΑΠΟΔΕΔΟΑΝΘΙ, and the Etruscans retained the same Æolism in *Thelephe* for Telephus, *Adresthe* for Adrastus, as we learn from Lanzi. In the present instance they have made no change of the Θ.

† Quint. i. c. 4. Varro de L. L. 6. 3.

‡ See Maittaire de D. ed. Sturzii. 508.

scription was carefully copied by Colonel Leake, we must retain the letters ΑΥ in ΛΑΥΧΝΟΣ : and as the works on the Dialects give no instance of the Æolian or Doric use of ΑΥ for Υ, we shall endeavour to illustrate this form.

We know how great a degree of Æolism prevailed in the Etruscan language. This Æolism was derived from the Pelasgi, who left Thessaly, and settled in Etruria. Now the Etruscans, as we learn from Lanzi, wrote Laucina for Lucina, Laucil. for Lucilius, Lauchme for Lucumo, Laucania for Lucania.

But the Greek language will furnish us with some instances where ΑΥ is used for Υ.

Θ῾Υμάλωπες, οἱ κεκαυμένοι ἄνθρακες, ἢ ἡμίκαυτα ξύλα, ἢ σπινθῆρες. (Phot. Lex. MS., quoted in the notes to Hesych. in v. θυμάλωψ.)

ΘΑΥμάλωπες, οἱ ἡμίφλεκτοι ἄνθρακες· θάψαι γὰρ τὸ καῦσαι. (Etym. M.)

We may here observe that there can be no doubt respecting the orthography of θαυμάλωπες, in the passage of the Etymolog. as the word is classed with others beginning with ΘΑΥ. But it is singular that θάψαι should remain unaltered, both in the passage now cited, and in Hesychius. The recollection of the manner in which the neoteric Greeks pronounced ΑΥ*, a mode still continued in the present day, led me to suppose that θάψαι had been written by a copyist for θαῦσαι, and this supposition is confirmed by finding in H. Stephens in v. θαυμάλωπες, a reference to the words of the Etym. θάψαι γὰρ τὸ †καῦσαι, with this remark, " nisi forte θαῦσαι scripsit." /

If we turn to the fragments of the Mimes of Sophron, we read, φερὲ τὸ θαύμακτρον, κἀπιθυσιῶμες, " bring the censer, and let us burn incense ;" where, according to the remark of the Critic, who has collected and edited these fragments in the Classical Journal, θαύμακτρον is Doric for θύμακτρον. We may here adduce an illustration of this

---

* Αφθέντης pro αυθέντης scribere amabant, et κλώψιμον pro κλαύσιμον, et alia sexcenta similiter. Salm. His. Aug. Not. p. 467.

† " In the Etym. the true reading is *possibly* θαῦψαι, a mistake for θύψαι. Schol. Acharn. 320. ὁ ἀπολελειμμένος τῆς θύψεως ἄνθραξ." Dobree.

word from Hesychius; not as the passage is given in the printed editions, but as it is preserved in the manuscript, according to the collation by Schow *, Ούη, ΘΑΥματα, ἀρώματα. Musurus altered the second word into θύματα.

It appears also from the observations of the Critic whom I have cited above, that the Tarentines said θαυλακίζειν for θυλακιζειν. Θαυλακίζειν, μετὰ βοῆς ἀπαιτεῖν τι. Ταραντῖνοι. Hesychius. Θυλακίζειν, τὸ ἀπαιτεῖν τι ἐπόμενον μετὰ θυλάκου. Ταραντῖνοι. Id. In these references he supposes that one gloss has been improperly divided by Hesychius, or some of the Mutilators of the Lexicon; and that the passage should be read thus: θαυλακίζειν, θυλακίζειν, τὸ ἀπαιτεῖν τι ἐπόμενον μετὰ θυλάκου. Ταραντῖνοι.

Λυχνηφόρος and λυχνοφόρος were both used. Θεηπολεῖν, θυηπόλος, θανατηφόρος, λαμπαδηφόρος, ξιφηφόρος, ασπιδηφόρος, are found in Æschylus and Plato. The poets used this form to avoid the concurrence of four short syllables. See Blomfield on Sep. C. T. v. 415. Gloss.

The word in Colonel Leake's copy is ΑΡΧΙΔΑΥΧΝ. The substitution of Δ for Λ need not detain us. Τὰ συσσίτια οἱ Λακεδαιμόνιοι ΦΙΔΙΤΙΑ προσαγορεύουσιν, εἴτε ὡς ΦΙΛΙΑΣ καὶ φιλοφροσύνης ὑπαρχόντων, ἀντὶ τοῦ Λ τὸ Δ λαμβάνοντας. Plut. vit. Lycurgi. The change of Λ and Δ occurs in other instances; Μελεταν is meditari †; Οδυσσεὺς is Ulysses; Livius Andronicus used Dacrima for Lacryma; ἄδακρυς is alacris; ὀδωδέναι olere ‡, and odefacit and olfacit are given by Festus. The inhabitants of Perga in Pamphylia used Λ instead of Δ: λάφνη, δάφνη: and some Greeks pronounced λίσκος as well as δίσκος. §

III.

" Æschylis daughter of Satyrus." ΣΑΤΥΡΟΙ, according to the Æolo-Doric form, as ὑπάκοισον for ὑπάκουσον, λιποῖσα, κατθανοῖσα, δίδοι (for δίδου)

---

* Supplem. ad Edit. Hesych. Albertinam. p. 365. The word θαύματα also is found in Hesychius, under Ἰρά. Θυσίαι, θαύματα.

† Servius in Vir. Eclog. 1. 2.

‡ Vict. de Arte Gram. l. 1. See Maittaire de Dial.

§ See Hesych. in. Λάφνη and Λίσκος

καττοὶς νόμοις for κατὰ τοὺς νόμους. See Greg. de Dial. ed. Schaefer. 212. 618.

IV.

L. 2. ΠΝΟΗΝ. See Euripides. Suppl.

ὅθεν δ᾽ ἕκαστον εἰς τὸ σῶμ᾽ ἀφίκετο,
ἐνταῦθ᾽ ἀπῆλθε· πνεῦμα μὲν πρὸς ἀιθέρα,
τὸ σῶμα δ᾽ εἰς γῆν.

L. 3. ΠΑΤΡΙ. So in Anthol. Pal. App. Epig. 375., πατρὶ λίποντ᾽ ἄχεα, and p. 345., πατρί τ᾽ ἐμῷ μέγα πῆμ᾽ ἔλιπον καὶ μητρὶ ταλαινῇ.

L. 4. ΑΝΑΡΠΑΣΘΕΙΣ. " *Rapti* dicuntur quivis mortui, sed peculiariter immatura morte defuncti ; Papinius de Glaucia, " hic finis *rapto.*" In Gruter, *Rapta* sinu matris jacet hic miserabilis infans. — Rein. Ins. 727.

L. 4. ΕΠΤΑ. The compound form is commonly used ; κεῖμαι δ᾽ ἐξαέτις. Πενταετὴς δ᾽ ἱκόμην. Anth. Pal. 345. 368.

V.

L. 3. The privilege of προξενία is thus expressed by the Latins : " Decernunt ut L. fratri hospitium publice fieret." Cicero, Verr. 4.

L. 6. ΕΝ. The Dorians and Laconians use ΕΝ for ΕΙΣ. In the Lacedæmonian decree relating to Timotheus, παρακλαθεὶς δὲ καὶ ἐν τὸν ἀγῶνα, according to the reading of Boethius and Scaliger. Ἐν ἅρματα, in Pindar, Py. Od. 2. 21. *

L. 10. A decree in the Oxford marble XLIX is signed also by the Ἔγγυοι.

VII.

L. 8. ΘΕΗΚΟΛΟΝ. The Greeks seem to have used indiscriminately θεήκολος and θεόκολος. The former occurs in the present inscription ; in

---

7

* See also Valck. on Theocr. 364.

Elis also they said θεηκόλοτος, or, according to the reading of Facius, cited by Col. Leake, θεήκολος. But on a marble found not far from Basilico, we read ΟΙ ΘΕΟΚΟΛΟΙ ΤΟΥ ΑΠΟΛΛΩΝΟΣ, (Marm. Oxon.) and ΘΕΟΚΟΛΗΣΑΣΑΝ, in the Zantiote inscription edited by Chandler. Θεόκολος also occurs in Hesychius.

VIII.

L. 3. ΦΕΟΓΕΙΝ. ΕΟ and ΕΥ were both used in the antient lan_ guage of Greece, in writing the same word; ΟΤΤΕΟ, ΟΤΤΕΥ* oc_ cur in Homer; and ΟΡΣΕΟ, and ΟΡΣΕΥ. †

If Stratocles ‡, mentioned in the inscription, be one of the persons referred to by Demosthenes, in his third Olynthiac oration, which was spoken in the 107th Olympiad, we are able to fix the date of it. The old form of the language might remain in use at that time in Am_ phipolis; while at Athens the new Attic, which began to prevail about the time of Æschines and Demosthenes §, was generally spoken. Col. Leake has referred to inscriptions where the use of the antient dialects is still found, after the Communis Lingua was introduced.

Some of the old forms are retained in the prose and poetry of the Attic Greeks; the Ionic ὑιὸς is in Æschylus, S. C. T. 62., and in Eur. Med. 523. Νηᾶς occurs in the same writer, in Iph. in Au. 248. ‖ 'Ρέε_ θρον, a singular example, is in a senarian Iambic, in the ¶ Persæ: οἴκοισι, in Soph. Œd. T. 249. Τοῖσιν καινοῖσι θεοῖς, in Aristoph. Av. 847. Πόλεος, ὕβρεος, ὄφεος, are found in Eur. Hec. 860. Aristoph. Plut. 1045., and Eur. Sup. 703. 1329.; κακοῖσιν, in Plato Gor. p. 110., and ταύτοισι, ib. p. 28.; προσδέεται, in Xenophon Mem. Socr. iii. 6. 13.; and δέεσ_

---

* Od. ι. 124. χ. 377. ϱ. 121.
† Il. γ. 250. δ. 264.
‡ See Col. Leake's remarks on this marble.
§ See Nicephorus in Schol. on Synesius, in Thom. Magis. note, p. 579.
‖ Matthiæ, Gr. G. Blomfield, p. 96. vol. 1.
¶ Blomfield in Pers. 503.

θαι, Anab. vii. 7. 31. Zeunius has left τοῖς κακονόοις in the text of Xenoph. Cyrop. viii. 2.

·But Ionisms are also found in the writers in the Communis Lingua; and in scholiasts and grammarians. Μετρωτὸν ἔχεεν τὸ ποτὸν, according to a MS., is in Plutarch Mor. t. ii. 618.; and in Xenophon Ephes. 53. ed. Loc. ἐδέετο Αβροκόμης εἰπεῖν. Hermias in Comm. MS. in Plat. Phæd. has μαστίγων δέεται μάλιστα. The Scholiast on Lucian, t. i. 525., τὸ γαρ θεῖον οὐ δέεται θυσιῶν.* The three antient forms, βούλει, ὄιει, ὄψει, are found in the Sep. and N. Test.; Job xxxiv. 12., Luke xxii. 42., Matt. xxvii.

ΑΥΤΟΣ ΚΑΙ ΤΟΣ. We find the short vowels used in these words, although in the same decree the long letters are introduced. The orthography of other Greek inscriptions has the same irregularity. In one of the Oxford marbles, XXIV., we read ΒΟΛΗΣ, ΕΠΙΓΡΑΦΕΝ, ΑΥΤΟΣ, (in the plural), ΠΟΛΕΩΣ, ΤΡΕΣ for ΤΡΕΙΣ: Ο for ΟΥ occurs in inscr. xxi. of the 99th Olympiad; and in the same we have ΧΕΙΡΟΣ.

ΝΗΠΟΙΝΕΙ ΤΕΘΝΑΝΑΙ, " inultum mori, adeo ut reus homicidii non sit interfector." Kuhn. ad Polluc. viii. 70.

ΙΡΟΝ ΤΟΥ ΑΠΟΛΛΩΝΟΣ. Quibus genius Græcæ linguæ perspectus est,iis minime latet,τὸ ἱερὸς passim frequentius cum secundo quam tertio casù construi; ut nimirum quidpiam quod Deo alicui sacrum sit, dicatur ἱερὸν τοῦ θεοῦ potius quam τῷ θεῷ. Reperio Latinos quoque ita locutos. Cic. 1. in Verrem. 18., " illa insula eorum Deorum sacra putatur." Jensii Lec. Luc. 286.

ΟΤΕΩΙΟΥΝ. Ὀτέων τε πόλιν. Odyss. κ. 19.; ὠντινῶν, Schol.; ὀτέοισιν, Il. ο. 491.; οἷστισιν, Schol. " Homer retains, with the rest of the Ionic writers, the ο unchanged in all the cases, e. g. ὅτευ, Od. ρ´. 424., and ὅττευ, ὅττεο, Od. ἀ. 124. χ´. 377. ρ´. 121., for ἧστινος, οὗτινος·" Matthiæ, G. Gram. Blomfield, i. 191. Ὅτεῳ occurs in Il. ο. 664.

" Whoever receives the exiles shall himself be banished." This is

---

* Schaefer ad Greg. de Dial. 431.

also said conformably to an Attic law.   Οἱ νόμοι οὐκ ἐῶσιν ὑποδέχεσθαι τῶν φευγόντων οὐδένα ἢ ἐν τοῖς αὐτοῖς κελευόυσιν ἐνεχέσθαι τὸν ὑποδεχόμενον τοὺς φεύγοντας. Demos. against Polycles.

IX.

L. 3. ΚΑΛΑΜΟΥΣ. Εἶχε μέτρον κάλαμον χρυσοῦν. Apocal. 21. 16.
" Habebat perticam auream, quæ erat mensorium instrumentum."
Grotius.

L. 5. ΟΡΟΥΣΕΝΧΑΡΑΞΟΥΣΙ. The stone on which the boundaries were written was called ὁριαῖος λίθος.

L. 16. ΕΚΔΙΚΟΙ defensores civitatum erant, et imprimis etiam publicas pecunias curabant et persequebantur. Pitiscus in Sueton. 2. p. 906.

L. 25. ΑΠΑΙΤΗΣΙΝ. " Glossæ veteres εἴσπραξιν, ἀπάιτησιν." Vales. on Ammianus Marc. 302.

L. 35. ———— ΠΑΙΛΙΟΣ
ΔΑΜΟΞΕΝΟΣΕΣΦΡΑ
ΓΙΣΑΤΕΤΑΡΤΗΝΕΙΣΙΔ
ΠΕΜΠΤΗΝΜΗΤΡΟΔ.
ΡΟΣ κ. τ. λ.

Perhaps ΕΙΣΙΩΝ *, ΕΙ being written for Ι, as in ΚΡΕΙΝΩ. " I, Publius Ælius Damoxenus sealed. Ision sealed the fourth ; Metrodorus of Anticyra, the fifth."

L. 43. This name occurs in the Anthologia, p. 129. H. Steph.
ἐν πᾶσιν μεθύουσιν 'Ακίνδυνος ἤθελε νήφειν.

---

* ΕΙΣΙΩΝ ΤΡΥΦΩΝΟΣ. Chandler, p. 66.

LETTER FROM MR. COCKERELL,

RELATING TO

THE INSCRIPTIONS ENGRAVED IN THE ANNEXED PLATE.

Dear Sir,   8, Old Burlington-street, June 17. 1819.
I HAVE the pleasure of sending you four inscriptions, collected in Lycia, during my tour on that coast in 1812 ; the character in which they are written is found also at Telmessus and Myra.

No. 1. was copied near the town of Phineka, on the border of the plain, and is remarkable for its termination in Greek: the monument on which it is inscribed is of marble, about 18 feet high, and of the most elegant architecture ; its execution is hardly inferior to that of the best works at Athens. The upper portion, as well as the lower, was calculated for the reception of the dead ; but each had long since been despoiled of its contents.

Nos. 2. and 3. were found at Kakava, on the shore opposite Dolichisté ; they are exceedingly well cut on the face of a rock, and each of the excavated chambers contained six sarcophagi ; the projecting cornice had, in that mild climate, preserved the inscriptions entire, and even the red colour with which the characters were marked.

No. 4. was found on a tomb of the same kind, but which had in addition upon the frize a νεκρόδειπνον, consisting of ten figures about six inches high, in bas relief, and of the best times.

It is remarkable that all the sculpture found on these monuments is evidently by Greek hands, and in the purest style of art ; less rigid, indeed, than that which is commonly understood by the appellation of

ΤΕΙΡ : ΤΡΡΓΡΙΕΙΡ : ΜΤ
ΡΙΜΡΓΙ ΤΥΣΕΔΤΡΕΙΑ : Ι
ΤΕΔΤΕΜΕΡΡΓΓΕΤΤΛΕΤ
ΛΤΙΤΤΟΜΝΗΜΑΤΟΑΓΑ
ΟΙΗΞΑΤΟΣΙΔΑΡΙΟΣΓΑΙ
ΝΙΟΣΥΙΟΣΕΑΥΤΩΙΚΑΙΤΗΙ
ΤΚΙΚΔΙΥΙΔΙΓΥΒΙΑΛΗ

ΓΙΣΛΑΕΥ : ΛΛΤΕΓΡΕΝΑΓΑΙΥΤΤΡΤΕΛΑΜΟΓΑΙΤΡΓΓΕ
ΤΕΔΤΕΜΤΤΒΕΙΤ.

ΞΝΑΓΛΜΤΤΛΓΡΕΞΛΛΓΑΤΛΑΟΓΛΝΕΜΕΤΡΓΓΕΛΓΔΕΤΤΒΕΣΤΤ
ΤΓΤΡΕΚΛΛΤΛΞΤΑΓΡΤΑ.

ΤΞΛΧΥΟΓΧΙΜΤΤΕ : ΓΓΙΝΡΓΡΤΤ : ΤΕΤΤΕΙΡ

Etruscan, but still severe, and having many of the characteristics of that manner.

At Phineka, also, is a tomb of great beauty, on the sides of which, in the solid rock, are figures of low relief in procession, of the most elegant design, and as large as life ; they bear offerings to the tomb, four on one side, and two on the other. To the west of Kakava is another, of fewer figures, but of equal merit.

The bas relief on the side of No. 2. represents a youth, holding in his left hand a piece of drapery, perhaps a net, under which is a partridge : it was probably intended to commemorate some antient sportsman, who had found Kakava not less abundant in that species of game than it is at present; whence, indeed, it derives its modern name, as Meletius tells us.

The architecture of these tombs, excavated in the solid rock, occurs all along the coast of Lycia, and seems peculiar to this country ; some have conjectured them to be funeral piles; but, however this may be, it is evident that they are in imitation of a wooden construction; the cornice is formed of a beam laid on transverse rafters, unsquared, and in their natural state ; and the framing (as it would be technically termed) shows the cross pieces of which it is formed, halved upon each other, and the ends left uncut ; the bottom, or sill, has the form of a piece of ship timber applied to this purpose. There are other examples in the roofs of various tombs, presenting a similar character.; they have the form of a Gothic pointed arch, and are like the section of a boat reversed, thus :

The doors were in pannels, and one of them was made to open by sliding back in a groove ; of all these the execution is very perfect, &c. &c.   Yours faithfully,

C. R. COCKERELL.

REMARKS

ON THE

INSCRIPTIONS DISCOVERED IN ASIA MINOR,

BY COLONEL LEAKE AND MR. COCKERELL.

[BY THE EDITOR.]

The conquest of Thessaly, by Deucalion, forced the Pelasgi to quit that country ; and the traditional accounts of the Greeks had preserved the names of many towns in Asia Minor, which owed their origin to them. Among these Pelasgic settlements, we find Sestos, Abydos, Cume *, Larissa †, Adramyttium ‡, Antandros §. Some of the colonies from Greece had fixed themselves as far as ‖ Tralles ; and a son of Tantalus ¶, a Pelasgic king in the vicinity of Sipylus, founded a town in Phrygia.

One of these colonies, we are informed by Plutarch **, came from Thessaly to Lydia. The time of its arrival may be stated at about the year 1370 B. C. After the Trojan war, an emigration from this part of Asia Minor took place under Tyrrhenus, son of Atys ††; and his followers, who accompanied him to Italy,

---

* Rochette, i. 284. Histoire des Colonies Grecques.
† Ib. i. 284. 289.
‡ Schol. Hom. Il. vi. 396.
§ Herod. lib. vii. 42.
‖ Αἱ γοῦν Τράλλεις τὸ μὲν παλαιὸν Πελασγῶν γέγονεν ἀποικία. Agath. lib. ii. Rochette, i. 183.
¶ Clavier, i. 236. Histoire des premiers temps de la Grece.
** In Romulo.
†† Lanzi, i. 189.

became, according to the opinion of many modern writers, confirmed by the antient testimonies of Herodotus *, Strabo, Pliny, Valerius Maximus, Appian, and Justin, the founders of the Etruscan people. The Etruscans themselves, in the time of Tiberius †, considered their origin to have been Asiatic; for in writing to the citizens of Sardis, they allude to the relation which formerly subsisted between the two countries.

It is impossible to speak with any degree of certainty concerning the nature of the Pelasgic *Greek* ‡, which was in use among the antient Tyrrhenians of Lydia. The Æolic and Ionian colonies, under Penthilus and Neleus, made their settlements at first on the coast of Asia Minor; yet it is very probable that the knowledge of their language was soon spread as far as the neighbouring provinces of Phrygia and Lydia. The general appearance of the two Lydo-Phrygian inscriptions found in this part of Asia, and engraved in the plate facing p. 207., is evidently Greek; yet they present also a variety sufficiently great to confirm the opinion, that the Etruscans were sprung from the early inhabitants of the country where these singular documents were found. We see in them the same use of the Digamma; the same form of letters; the names and verbs §, which occur in the Etruscan language.

It deserves to be here remarked, that the opinion of the *Asiatic* origin of the Etruscans was entertained as a very probable one by Salmasius, long before the question received that full discussion

---

* See Lanzi, Saggio. vol. iii. Circa la Scoltura, x.

† Tacitus, Ann. iv. 55.

‡ I have adopted Lanzi's opinion respecting the language of the Pelasgi: "Esso troppo verisimilmente fu in origine un Greco anticho. i. 27. Congettura Erodoto che fosse barbaro, ma non l'assevera. Questa espressione non esclude un vero Greco, perchè sia misto di vari vocaboli foiestieri e di solecismi. Ib. 441.

§ The rounded form of the M is only found in this inscription, and in the Etruscan alphabet in the Bib. Ital. xviii. The latter also gives the round N. The Π in this shape ∩, is used by the Etruscans (Lanzi, 2.); it occurs also on the antient vase of Mr. Dodwell, and on the votive helmet belonging to Colonel Leake, and found at Olympia.

which has since been bestowed on it by the industry and acuteness of Lanzi, and other Italian antiquaries. In a letter to Peiresc, part of which I extract from the Bib. Ital. t. xviii., Salmasius expresses himself in the following manner: " Les caractères semblent être tout Grecs ; mais de savoir s'ils les ont apportés *tels de la Lydie, ce que je croirois* volontiers ; ou s'ils les ont pris sur les lieux, par le voisinage des Æoliens, ou Arcadiens venus avec Evandre : — c'est la grande question."

The following appears to be the interpretation of the line at * c. d. This, as well as the other, is sculptured on the rock, out of which the Tomb is made, and probably refers to the structure of the Sepulchre.

As the stops after ΜΙΔΑΙ and ΑΝΑΚΤΕΙ plainly mark the termination of the words †, we may consider them as employed for the same purpose through the rest of the inscription.

. ΠΑΠΑ is a common Etruscan ‡ name, written by the Æolians ΒΑΒΑ, as βικρὸν for πικρὸν §, and καββάδιον for καππάδιον. ΜΕΜΕΑΣ is also a proper name, written with ΑΙ, as ὀλέσαις, ποιήσαις, μέλαις, τύψαις. ||

The next name is Πρόιτεςς, or Πρόιταος : if we prefer the first, it is written in the inscription with α, as Ἄρταμις, ἱαρός. The verb follows, to which the preceding are nominative cases.

The scholar will recollect that in one of the Sigean inscriptions, the letter Κ in ΚΑΩΚΑ, is either, as Chishull ¶ expresses himself, " otiosum," or it is wrongly sculptured for Ε. In one of the Oxford

---

* See the plate, facing p. 207.

† A similar mode of punctuation is found on the following antient monuments : on the Sigean stone; on the Athenian inscription, beginning ΕΡΕΧΘΕΙΔΟΣ; on the marble copied at Ægina by Mr. Cockerell ; on the Teian imprecations, edited by Chishull; on the Elean tablet, explained by Mr. Knight; on the Eugubine tables; on a lamina Volsca, mentioned by Lanzi, i. 280 ; and on an inscription copied in the cave of Vari, in Attica, by Mr. Stanhope.

‡ Papa è nome di famiglia Etrusca nota per più lapidi. Lanzi, ii. 144. Βάβυς is a Phrygian name. Athen. l. xiv. p. 624.

§ Plut. Græc. Quæs. t. ii. c. 9. See also Salmas. in H. A. notes, p. 390.

|| Greg. de D. p. 601.

¶ Ant. As. p. 33.

marbles this error may be observed, ΤΡΚΙΣ for ΤΡΕΙΣ. It will also be remembered, that in the Sigean inscriptions, Z and Σ have the same power.* The verb, then, is ΕΦΙΣΑΝ or ΕΚΦΕΙΣΑΝ. But Pheia and Phiaia are verbs in the Eugubine tables, signifying " faciant" and " faciat." †

" Papa, Memeas, Prœteus, made (the tomb)."

Ἐποίησαν in common Greek; or, ΚΦΙΣΑΝ, εκποίησαν, ἐξεπόιησαν, " finished" it; the ε being omitted, as in the Etruscan ΤΕΟΕ (ἔθηκε).

ΑΦΕΣΟΣ, or ΑΕΣΟΣ, may be a name; as well as ΣΙΚΕΜΕΜΑΝ, writ_ ten for ΣΙΚΕΜΙΜΑΣ, like Πολυφὰν for Πολυφὰς ‡ : they precede a verb of which we have only a part, ΕΔΑΕΣ - - - ἐδαίσαν §, referring to some labour ‖ employed in cutting down the rock out of which the tomb is made.

The singular characters represented in the plate accompanying Mr. Cockerell's letter, were found by him on some of the sepulchral monuments belonging to the antient Lycians; the style of architecture, and the form and general appearance of these buildings, may be collected from the description of them contained in his letter, and from the etching presented by him to this volume.

The southern coast of Asia Minor, from Halicarnassus to the bay of Issus, was peopled by numerous Greek colonies. Some of these settlements are referred to a period immediately following the Trojan war. The Pamphylians, we are informed by Herodotus ¶, take their origin from the soldiers who wandered with

----

* ΠΡΟΚΟΝΕΖΙΟ, ΣΙΛΕΙΕΖ. See also the antient alphabets in Astle's Origin and Progress of Writing.
† Lanzi, iii. 820. PHI, in Etruscan, corresponds to ποιῶ: sometimes to " fio." Lanzi.
‡ Lanzi, i. 113.
§ The E being used for the I, as in Ἄνεγμα for Αἴνιγμα. See Hesychius. Δαίζων, κατακόπτων. Hesych. Δαίω, διακόπτω. Etym. M. Δατήριος, " divisor," from δάω, divido. See Blomfield, Gloss. ad v. 708. S. C. T. We have in Strabo, l. xii. 778. Ox. ed. διακοπὴ τοῦ ὄρους, speaking of an opening in a mountain.
‖ See also Colonel Leake's interpretation of ΕΔΑΕ, in p. 212. of this volume.
¶ L. vii. c. 91.

Amphilochus and Calchas ; and the former of these chiefs, together with Mopsus, founded many maritime towns in Cilicia. * Among the colonies of a later period, we may mention those of Nagidos and Celenderis †, established by the Samians ; Aspendus, by the Argives ‡ ; Side, by the Cumeans ; Selge, by the § Lacedæmonians ; Caunus ‖, Physcus, Phaselis, Gagæ, and Corydallus ¶, by the Rhodians ; and Soli, by the Argives. **

The grammarians have preserved a few of the singular forms which were in use among the Dorians who settled on this coast. The Pamphylians said †† φάβος for φάος, ὀρούβω for ὀρούω, βαβέλιον for ἀέλιον, ποιῆαι for ποιῆσαι, μωἶκα for μουσικὰ, and ἀδρὶ for ἀνδρί.

It is much to be regretted that no monuments are yet discovered, which would give additional illustrations of the dialect spoken by the Greeks on this part of Asia Minor. On one of the sepulchral inscriptions in Mr. Cockerell's copy, we have, in Doric, Σιδάριος, the name of the man who constructed the tomb for his wife ; and a similar appellation, though belonging to a woman, occurs in Diodorus Sic. lib. i. 312. ἐπέγημε τὴν ὀνομαζομένην Σιδηροῦν. See Greg. de D. Schaefer, 428.

In addition, however, to the letters and words of the common Greek language, it appears from Mr. Cockerell's plate, and from inscriptions copied by Dr. Clarke, and Captain Beaufort ‡‡, and from various coins § §, that the inhabitants of Caria, Lycia, and Pamphylia were ac-

---

* Cicero de Div. l. i. c. 40.　　　　† Pom. Mela. i. c. 13.
‡ Strabo, l. 14.　　　　　　　　　§ Id. l. 12.
‖ Id. l. 14.　　　　　¶ See Rochette, Histoire des Colonies Grecques, iii. 157.
** Polyb. Exc. Leg. c. xxv. Liv. l. 37. c. 56.　†† Heraclides in Eustath. p. 1654. l. 20.
‡‡ This inscription was found by him in Caria :

ΑΒ✳Ε x x x ΡΓΨΜΑΤ
ΡΡΞWΡϜΛ↑█CΙΕΙΡΜ
ΜΞΤxΤΔΨ x xxΜΕΞΤΕΑ
ΕϷΛϷΛϷΔxΨΙΙ|Ιxxxxﾍ✝ϷΛ
ΛϷΔ↑ϷΔ x x ———

§§ Mionnet. Des. des Medailles, t. iii. 596.　Ν↑ℲΛϟ.　These letters appear on a Pamphylian coin.

customed to employ an enchorial character very different from the language of the Greek colonists.

We find from Strabo *, that four idioms were in use at *Cibyra*; the *Lycaonian* tongue † was different from the Greek ; and although upon the introduction of the latter into Asia Minor, after the time of Alexander, new names were given to different cities and places, yet the original appellations remained. Νιτζίβιον was the *Armenian* name of a town which the Greeks called Antiochia Mygdonia; the Γάλαται, as Salmasius ‡ remarks, were never known by that appel-lation among their own countrymen. The *Carians* § were acquainted with Greek, which they pronounced in a corrupted manner; but their national idiom is mentioned by Strabo and Plutarch. ‖

In Mr. Cockerell's inscriptions we see words belonging to the native language of the inhabitants of this part of Asia, written in *Greek* letters ; there are also characters which probably belonged to some *oriental* dialect. A frequent intercourse existed between parts of Asia Minor and different nations of the East. The citizens of Perga in Pamphylia worshipped Adonis under the name of Aboba; and this is a Syrian appellation. ¶ The Lycian guide, who was to lead Alexander to the frontiers of Persia, was, by his mother's side, a Persian. ** On some of the coins of Cilicia, there is a representation of a bearded head, attired in the Persian manner ††, and of two of the singular characters which were in use in this part of the country. The Carians were δίγλωσσοι ; they understood Persian as well as Greek : Tissaphernes sends a Carian to Mindarus, the Spartan ; the

---

* L. 13.   † See Jablonski, de Lingua Lycaonica.
‡ Præf. ad lib. de annis Climac. p. 16.
§ Βαρβαροφώνους. Strabo's interpretation is κακῶς Ἑλληνίζοντας.
‖ Ὁ προφήτης Καρικῇ γλώσσῃ προσεῖπεν. in. Arist. Some Carian words are given by Jablonski, and his editor, Te Water. See also Strabo, l. 14. p. 946.
¶ Jablonski de Ling. Lyc. § 12.
** Ἡγεμὼν αὐτῷ δίγλωσσος ἄνθρωπος ἐκ πατρὸς Λυκίου, μητρὸς δὲ Περσίδος γεγονώς. Plut. in vit. Alex.
†† Mionnet. t. 3. pl. xxii. " Coiffée à la manière des rois de Perse."

3 Y 2

younger Cyrus, treating with the Greeks, uses Carian * interpreters :
Mardonius commissions one to consult a Greek oracle. Σισόη †, a
Phœnician word, was used by the people of Phaselis ; in consequence
of their vicinity to the Solymi ‡, who spoke Phœnician, they probably
intermixed words of that tongue with their own speech.   The name
of the celebrated mountain Chimæra, in Lycia, on which fire is constantly burning, is Phœnician. §   In Cappadocia, the names of many
of the months were Persian ‖ ; and fire altars, where the ceremonies
were conducted according to the Persian manner, were seen so late
as the time of Pausanias and Strabó. ¶

It would be an useless labour to endeavour to decypher or explain
the characters in use among a people of whom we have no literary
records, and from whose monuments we have not yet obtained a sufficient number of inscriptions to afford us the means of comparing
them with each other, and with the Greek.   The latter appears on
these sepulchres to be united with the language of the Asiatics.   The
vicinity of the two people led to the use of the two idioms ; and the
barbarians ** (for so the inhabitants of this country were called by the
Greeks) prove the intercourse which must have subsisted between
themselves and the colonies established among them, by the style and
mode of structure adopted in forming their tombs.   But the Greek
language was corrupted in consequence of this communication.
When the Ionians arrived in Asia Minor, by intermixing with the
Carians, they vitiated their pronunciation ; they altered the quantity

---

* Valcken. in Herod. Wess. 682.   See also Thuc. 1. 8.

† See Hesychius in the word Σισόη, and the notes.

‡ Γλῶσσαν μὲν Φοινίσσαν ἀπὸ στομάτων ἀφιέντες.   See Heringa, Obs. 157.; and the
passage from Bochart, quoted in the note on Σισόη, in Hesychius.

§ Chamirah, adusta. Spanheim de P. et usu Num. 267. from Le Clerc.   Captain Beaufort, in his Caramania, gives an account of his visit to this " Perpetual Flame."

‖ Freret in Ac. des Insc. t. xix. p. 55.

¶ L. 15. p. 1040. ed. Oxf.

** Βάρβαροι is the term given by Arrian to the citizens of Telmessus and Selge.   Ex.
Alex. l. 1.   We meet with some of the names of these Asiatics in the Greek inscriptions
from Lycia and Pamphylia, published in this volume; ΛΑΣ, ΚΟΥΑΣ, ΟΒΡΑΟΥΓΕΡΙΣ.

of the syllables in some words ; they used φαρμακὸς* with the penultimate long; they also said ἑῶυτος, δεσπότεα, ἀπελέσθαι. † The Scythian,
in Aristophanes, uses a similar barbarism when he pronounces πυλάξη,
παίνεται, κεπαλή.

It may be asked whether the Greek writers make any mention of
the strange idiom which was spoken along the southern parts of Asia
Minor ? — Two passages have occurred, one in Arrian, the other in
Eustathius, (who borrowed his remark from some more antient
author,) in which reference is made to the language of the people of
Side, in Pamphylia, and to that of the inhabitants of Soli, in Cilicia.

" The citizens of Side," says Arrian *, " report of themselves, that
when the first colonists came from Cume into this part of Asia, and
settled there, they straightway forgot the Greek tongue, and uttered a
strange language, not that of the neighbouring barbarians, but a peculiar and new idiom."

" They say † that Soloecism took its rise in this way : some people
of Attica settled at Soli, and vitiated the pronunciation of the genuine
Attic tongue ; and became uncivilised from their dwelling there."

Whether we accept or not of the whole of these statements, we see
plainly that they contain allusions to the language in use among the
people of this part of Asia Minor, and which, as might be expected,
impaired the purity of the pronunciation of the Greeks, who established themselves among them.

---

* Διὰ τὴν τῶν βαρβάρων παροίκησιν ἐλυμήναντο τῆς διαλέκτου τὸ πάτριον, τὰ μέτρα, τοὺς χρό-
νους. Photius Lex. MS.   See Gaisford's Hephæs. 254.

† Salmas. de Hell. c. 7.

‡ Ex. Alex. l. i. p. 26. edit. Steph. 1575. ἀυτίκα τὴν μὲν Ἑλλάδα γλῶσσαν ἐξελάθοντο,
ἐυθὺς δὲ βάρβαρον φωνὴν ἵεσαν, οὐδὲ τῶν προσχώρων βαρβάρων, ἀλλὰ ἰδίαν σφῶν, οὔπω πρόσθεν
ὄυσαν τὴν φωνήν.

§ Eust. in Diony. Per. v. 875. ὡς ἀνδρῶν ποτε Ἀττικῶν οἰκησάντων ἐκεῖ, καὶ τὴν ἐυγενῆ
παρακοπέντων Ἀττικὴν γλῶτταν καὶ ἐξαγροικισθέντων διὰ τὸν ἐν Σόλοις οἰκισμόν.

INSCRIPTIONS,

COPIED IN DIFFERENT PARTS OF ASIA MINOR, GREECE, AND EGYPT,

ILLUSTRATED BY THE EDITOR.

I.

ΑΥΤΟΚΡΑΤΟΡΙΚΑΙΣΑΡΙΘΕΟΥΑΔΡΙΑΝΟΥΥΙΩΘΕΟΥΤΡΑΙΑΝΟΥ
ΠΑΡΘΙΚΟΥΥΙΩΝΩΘΕΟΥΝΕΡΟΥΑΕΓΓΟΝΩΤΙΤΩΑΙΛΙΩΑΔΡΙΑΝΩ
ΑΝΤΩΝΕΙΝΩΣΕΒΑΣΤΩΕΥΣΕΒΕΙΑΡΧΙΕΡΕΙΜΕΓΙΣΤΩΔΗΜΑΡΧΙΚΗΣ
ΕΞΟΥΣΙΑΣΤΟΙΥΠΑΤΩΤΟΔΠΑΤΡΙΠΑΤΡΙΔΟΣΚΑΙΘΕΟΙΣ
ΣΕΒΑΣΤΟΙΣΚΑΙΤΟΙΣΠΑΤΡΩΟΙΣΘΕΟΙΣΚΑΙΤΗΓΛΥΚΥΤΑΤΗ   5
ΠΑΤΡΙΔΙΤΗΠΑΤΑΡΕΩΝΠΟΛΕΙΤΗΜΗΤΡΟΠΟΛΕΙΤΟΥ
ΛΥΚΙΩΝΕΘΝΟΥΣΟΥΕΙΛΙΑΚοΟΥΕΙΛΙΟΥΤΙΤΙΑΝΟΥΘΥΓΑΤΗΡ
ΠΡΟΚΛΑΠΑΤΑΡΙΣΑΝΕΘΗΚΕΝ
ΚΑΙΚΑΘΙΕΡΩΣΕΝΤΟΤΕΠΡΟΣΚΗΝΙΟΝΟΚΑΤΕΣΚΕΥΑΣΕΝ
ΕΚΘΕΜΕΛΙΩΝΟΠΑΤΗΡΑΥΤΗΣΚοΟΥΕΙΛΙΟΣΤΙΤΙΑΝΟΣ   10
ΚΑΙΤΟΝΕΝΑΥΤΩΚΟΣΜΟΝΚΑΙΤΑΠΕΡΙΑΥΤΟΚΑΙΤΗΝΤΩΝ
ΑΝΔΡΙΑΝΤΩΝΚΑΙΑΓΑΛΜΑΤΩΝΑΝΑΣΤΑΣΙΝ
ΚΑΙΤΗΝΤΟΥΛΟΓΕΙΟΥΚΑΤΑΣΚΕΥΗΝΚΑΙ
ΠΛΑΚΩΣΙΝΑΕΠΟΙΗΣΕΝΑΥΤΗΤΟΔΕΕΝΔΕΚΑΤΟΝ
ΤΟΥΔΕΥΤΕΡΟΥΔΙΑΖΩΜΑΤΟΣΒΑΘΡΟΝΚΑΙΤΑΒΗΛΑ   15
ΤΟΥΘΕΑΤΡΟΥΚΑΤΑΣΚΕΥΑΣΘΕΝΤΑΥΠΟΤΕΤΟΥ
ΠΑΤΡΟΣΑΥΤΗΣΚΑΙΥΠΑΥΤΗΣ
ΠΡΟΑΝΕΤΕΘΗΚΑΙΠΑΡΕΔΟΘΗΚΑΤΑΤΑΥΠΟΤΗΣΚΡΑΤΙΣΤΗΣ
ΒΟΥΛΗΣΕΨΗΦΙΣΜΕΝΑ

Copied at Patara by Mr. Cockerell, by Captain Beaufort, and the
Mission of the Dilettanti Society.

L. 1, 2, 3. The same enumeration of the titles of Antoninus, with
the exception of Pius, is given in one of the Farnesian marbles. The
tenth year of his tribunitian power is here mentioned, consequently
we have the date of this inscription; the tenth year of his reign. See
Falcon. Ins. Athl. p. 6. The remaining part may be thus translated:

[To Antoninus Pius] Consul the fourth time, Father of his country; to the Dii Augusti; and to the Dii Penates; and to her beloved country the city of Patara, the (first) mother city of the Lycian nations; Velia Procula of Patara, the daughter of Quintus Velius Ti_ tianus, has dedicated and consecrated both the Proscenium, which her father, Q. V. Titianus, raised from the foundation; and the ornaments upon it, and the things belonging to it, and the erection of the statues of men and of gods, and the building of the Logeion, and the incrus_ tation of it (with marble); which things were done by herself: but the eleventh step of the second Præcinctio, and the curtains of the theatre, raised both by her father and herself, had been already dedi_ cated and delivered over, according to the decree of the most august senate."

REMARKS.

L. 5. ΠΑΤ. Θ. " Θεοὺς πατρώους, intellige, Deos Penates, qui passim cum Diis Patriis junguntur. " Dii Patrii ac Penates." Cic. pro Sulla. See Perizon. on Ælian. 1. p. 264.

L. 6. ΜΗΤΡ. We have in this, and in other inscriptions of Asia Minor, the word Metropolis used not in the original sense of a city, whence colonies were derived, but in that of a city of consequence, in a province. In the same district there were metropoles of various ranks; hence we read Πρώτη Μητρόπολις. * The Asiatic Greeks seem to have borrowed the expression from their neighbours, the Syrians. " Thou seekest to destroy a city and a mother in Israel †," where the Targum of Jonathan, explaining the verse, says: " a city strong, great, and a mother in Israel." On a coin of Laodicea are the words in Greek, " of Antiochus, King;" and in Phœnician, " of the mother Laodicea." Towns ‡, dependent on mother cities, were called " Daughters."

Great disputes often arose between different cities of Proconsular Asia, respecting this title; some assumed the name of " Metropolis

---

* Van Dale, Diss. iii. 239.　　　　† Sam. 2. xx. 19.
‡ Acad. des Ins. Barthelemy, 30. 415.

of Asia," but a rescript of the Emperor Antoninus Pius decreed that the great cities should be considered metropoles separately of their own *nation*, not of the provinces. *   Our inscription uses this expression: ΕΘΝΟΥΣ ΜΗΤΡΟΠ.

L. 7. ΟΥΕΛ. The name Velius occurs in Reinesius Ins. p. 238. and Titianus in an inscription at Ephesus. Chishull. An. As. App. 8.

L. 8. Πρόκλα, Procula, not Procla. Πρόκλος is a corrupted form. †

L. 8, 9. Ανατίθησι και καθιεροῖ τῇ συνόδῳ, " he dedicates and consecrates to the Company." See Chishull, An. As. p. 141., and again, τὸ Ατταλεῖον — ὁ και ζῶν καθιέρωκει τοῖς Ατταλίσταις ανατίθησι.

L. 11. Ἐπισκευάσασα και τὴν θέον και τὰ περι αὐτήν. Chandler, In. Ant. p. 55.

L. 12. ΑΝΔΡΙΑΣ, properly a statue of a man, as in this place; yet in good authors it occurs also, as Θεοῦ ἄγαλμα. Dorville, Mis. Obs. vol. vii. 26.

L. 13. ΛΟΓΕΙ. The Roman pulpitum was wider than the Greek Logeion. " In λογείῳ loquebantur histriones soli apud Græcos; at in pulpito Romano musici, saltantes, et histriones sua artificia præstabant." ‡

L. 14. ΠΛΑΚ. " Incrustationem." The base materials, says Gibbon, speaking of the church of S. Sophia, were concealed by a crust of marble. " Hujusmodi marmoreas crustas πλάκας §vocabant." A remark of Dorville, relating to the theatre ‖ at Tauromenium, will explain the nature of this πλάκωσις. " Nudi hodie parietes olim tabulatis pictis vel crustis marmoreis fuerunt vestiti ;" and we learn from Barthélemy the mode by which these marble ornaments were fastened. " En continuant de travailler à la coupole du Panthéon, on a détaché les marbres qui couvroient les murs de cette espéce d'Attique. Ils étoient attachés par des crampons de bronze." ¶

L. 14. " The eleventh step of the second Præcinctio," points out

---

* Belley ad Mar. Cyzic.   Caylus Rec. t. ii. 214.
† Gataker, Adv. Mis. c. 34. p. 785.
‡ Dorville, Sic. 260.   § Vales. ad Euseb. 205.
‖ Sic. 263.   ¶ Oeuv. div. Part 2.

a different meaning from that usually given to the word ΔΙΑΖΩΜΑ. The theatre of Marcellus had three διαζώματα; there were two at Pola; the theatre of Pompey, and that at Saguntum *, had the same number; at Ferentum there was but one. †

L. 16. ΒΗΛΑ. Ρωμαϊστὶ τὸ Ἱστίον Βῆλον ὀνομάζουσι. ‡ It was a law that the spectators, both at the games of the Circus and at other theatrical exhibitions, should sit with their heads uncovered, γυμνῇ κεφαλῇ, as we learn from a passage in Chrysostom and Basil §, who describe the spectators sitting until mid-day, exposed to rain and heat. At Rome also, in the words of Ammianus, the spectators are said, Sole fatiscere, vel pluviis; expressions, according to Valesius, not easily explained; as Ammianus himself mentions the Vela, the curtains, which might keep off the heat of the sun. The same protection is described by Chrysostom : " Il y a sur les theatres des voiles tendus." See the translation, by Montfaucon. Ac. des Ins. 13. 481.

The mode of fixing the curtains or canopy is described by Em. Marti, in his account of the theatre of Saguntum. Epis. l. iv.

L. 18. The full form is ΠΑΡΕΔΟΘΗ ΤΟΙΣ ΘΕΟΙΣ, which occurs in other inscriptions. ||

II.

- - ΔΡΑΚΑΛΟΝΚΑΙΑ
ΓΑΘΟΝΥΠΑΡΧΟΝΤΑΕΚ
ΠΡΟΓΟΝΩΝΑΡΕΤΗΣΚΑΙ
ΕΥΝΟΙΑΣΕΝΕΚΕΝΤΗΝΔΕΕ - -
ΕΙΚΟΝΑΔΑΠΑΝΗΝΑΥΤΟ -
ΕΠΕΔΕΞΑΤΟΕΚΤΟΥΙΔ -
ΟΥΕΙΣΟΔΙΑΣΑΙ. ¶

At Phineka, on the coast of Lycia. • Copied by Mr. Cockerell.

---

* Em. Marti, Epis. l. iv.   † Montf. An. Ex. vol. iii.   ‡ Plut. v. Rom.
§ Quoted by Valesius, in Amm. Marc. 30. || Mur. Anec. Gr. 7.
¶ A copy of Mr. Cockerell's inscriptions was lent to M. Akerblad, at Rome, who proposed corrections and suppletions of some parts of them. His conjectures are inserted wherever they occur. L. 1. ΑΝΔΡΑ. L. 4. ΤΗΝΔΕΕΙΣ. L. 5. ΑΥΤΟΣ. Ak.

VOL. II.   3 z

REMARKS.

L. 4. A parallel form occurs in an inscription in Van Dale, p. 366. τὸ δὲ εἰς τὸ ἄγαλμα δαπάνημα ποιησαμένου ἐκ τῶν ἰδίων.

L. 5, 6, 7. Perhaps αὐτὸς ὑπεδέξατο ἐκ τοῦ ἰδίου ἐξοδιάσαι, " he undertook to lay out, at his own cost, the expence necessary for the statue or figure." Sometimes ἀνεδέξατο occurs, as in Chandler, In. An. p. 9. τὴν δὲ εἰς ταῦτα δαπάνην ἐσομένην ἐκ τῶν ἰδίων ἀνεδέξαντο ποιήσειν. Ἔξοδος is frequently used in the sense of " *expenditure.*" See the illustration of the Tauromenian inscription in Dorville, Sic. pp. 542. 647. ; and in that found at Alicata we read ἐξοδίαξαι (as δικάξω for δικάσω) " expendere," p. 519. In Gruter. p. cccc. 1. Ἐξοδιάσαι ἐς τὰ προγεγραμμένα ὅσον κα χρέια ᾖ. This verb, according to Maffei, is found in no writer prior to the time of the Septuagint.

Εἰσόδια is explained in Hesychius by ἀνάλωμα, but the general sense of εἰσοδιάζω is directly the reverse ; it means, " to collect money together ;" and answers to the Latin " Redigo." * In the Testamentum Epictetæ, Mus. Veron. xxv. γραφέτω δὲ καὶ τὸν ἔσοδον καὶ ἔξοδον, " reditum et impensam."

III.

ΤΟΜΝΗΜΕΙΟΝΚΑΤΕΣΚΕΥΑΣΕΝΣΥΝΤΩΥΠΟ - - ΡΙΩ †
ΑΥΡΕΠΑΓΑΘΟΣΣΕΛΓΕΤΗΣ
ΠΑΜΦΥΛΙΑΣΕΑΥΤΩΚΑΙΓΥΝΑΙΚΙ
ΑΥΤΟΥΑΥΡΕΠΙΓΟΝΗΤΗΚΑΙΕΥΤΥ
ΧΙΑΝΗΚΥΑΝ - - ΙΔΙΚΑΙΘΥΓΑΤΗΡΑ
ΕΙΑΓΑΘΩ

At Patara, in Lycia ; copied by Mr. Cockerell.

•REMARKS.

L. 5. ΚΥΑΝΙΤΙΔΙ. " For his wife Aurelia Epigone, who is also called Eutychiane, a native of Cyane," a town in Lycia. Epigonus is a Lycian name ; Epigone occurs in Reinesius, Ins. p. 611.

---

* Valck. Theoc. 340.
† L. 1. ΥΠΟΣΟΡΙΩ.   L. 2. ΣΕΛΓΕΙΤΗΣ.   L. 6. ΕΠΑΓΑΘΩ.   Akerblad.

GREEK INSCRIPTIONS. 539

L. 6. The name Ἐπάγαθος, Ἐπαγάθων, and feminine Ἐπαγαθώ, are found in Greek and Latin inscriptions. In the penultimate line, the context would lead us to expect ΘΥΓΑΤΡΙ. The last word, if not a name, must be ΕΠΑΓΑΘΩΙ. " Auspicato." See Dorville, Charit. lib. i. 172.

IV.

```
1   ΑΠΑΝΤΑΠΡΑΞΙΣΕΥΤΥΧΩΣΘΕΟΣΛΕΓΕΙ *
    ΒΟΗΘΟΝΕΞΙΣΜΕΤΑΤΥΧΗΣΤΟΝΠΥΘΕΟΝ
    ΓΗΣΟΙΤΕΛΕΙΟΝΚΑΡΠΟΝΑΠΟΔΩΣΕΙΠΟΝΩΝ
    ΔΥΝΑΜΙΣΑΚΑΙΡΟΣΕΝΝΟΜΟΙΣΙΝΑΣΘΕΝΗΣ
5   ΕΡΑΣΔΙΚΑΙΩΝΕΓΓΑΜΩΝΙΔΕΙΝΣΠΟΡΑΝ
    ΖΑΛΗΝΜΕΓΙΣΤΗΝΦΕΥΓΕΜΗΤΙΚΑΙΒΑΒΗΣ
    ΗΛΙΟΣΟΡΑΣΕΛΑΜΠΡΟΣΟΣΤΑΠΑΝΤΑΟΡΑ
    ΘΕΟΥΣΑΡΩΓΟΥΣΤΗΣΟΔΟΥΤΑΥΤΗΣΕΧΕΙΣ
    ΙΔΡΩΤΕΣΕΙΣΙΝΠΛΗΝΑΠΑΝΤΩΝΕΡΙΕΣΗ
10  ΚΥΜΑΣΙΜΑΧΕΣΘΑΙΧΑΛΕΠΟΝΑΝΑΜΕΙΝΦΙΛΕ
    ΛΑΙΟΣΔΙΕΛΘΩΝΠΑΝΤΑΣΗΜΑΙΝΕΙΚΑΛΩΣ
    ΜΟΧΘΕΙΝΑΝΑΝΚΗΜΕΤΑΡΟΛΗΔΕΣΤΑΙΚΑΛΗ
    ΝΕΙΚΗΦΟΡΟΝΔΩΡΗΜΑΤΟΝΧΡΗΣΜΟΝΤΕ
    ΞΗΡΩΝΑΠΟΚΛΑΔΩΝΚΑΡΠΟΝΟΥΚΕΣΤΑΙΛΑΡ
15  ΟΥΚΕΣΤΙΜΙΣΠΕΙΡΑΝΤΑΘΕΡΙΣΑΙΚΑΡΠΙΜΑ
    ΠΟΛΛΟΥΣΑΙΩΝΑΕΔΙΑΝΥΣΑΣΛΗΨΗΣΤΕΦΟΣ
    ΡΑΟΝΔΙΑΞΙΣΕΤΙΒΡΑΧΥΝΜΕΙΝΑΣΧΙΟΝΟΣ
    ΓΑΦΩΣΟΦΟΙΒΟΣΕΝΝΕΠΕΙΜΕΙΝΟΝΦΙΛΕ
    ΤΩΝΝΥΝΠΑΡΟΥΣΩΝΣΥΝΦΟΡΩΝΕΞΙΣ - ΣΙΝ
20  ΥΠΟΣΧΕΣΙΝΤΟΙΡΑΓΜΑΓΕΝΝΑΙΑΝΕΧΕΙ
    ΦΑΥΛΩΣΤΙΠΡΑΞΑΣΜΕΤΑΧΡΟΝΟΝΕΝ - ΨΗΘΟΙΣ
    ΧΡΥΕΟΥΝΠΟΙΗΣΕΙΣΧΡΗΣΜΟΝΕΠΙΤΥΧΩΝΦΙΛΕ
    ΨΗΦΟΝΔΙΚΑΙΑΝΤΗΝΔΕΠΑΡΑΘΕΩΝΕΧΕΙΣ
    ΩΜΗΝΟΠΩΡΑΝΙΚΛΑΒΗΣΟΥΧΡΗΣΙΜΟΝ
```

Part of an inscription in Senarian Iambics, copied by Mr. Cockerell at Phineka, on the coast of Lycia. They contain the response of an oracle. The Σ is in the form Ϲ, throughout, in the original.

---

* L. 2. ΠΥΘΙΟΝ. L. 6. ΜΗΤΙ ΚΑΙ ΒΛΑΒΗΣ. L. 9. ΑΠΑΝΤΩΝΕΠΙΕΣΗ. L. 10. ΑΝΑΜΕΙΝΑΙ. L. 12. ΜΕΤΑΒΟΛΗ. L. 16. ΑΓΩΝΑΣ. L. 17. ΧΡΟΝΟΝ. L. 18. ΣΑΦΩΣ. L. 19. ΕΞΕΙΣ ΛΥΣΙΝ. L. 20. ΤΟΠΡΑΓΜΑ. L. 24. ΕΙΛΑΒΗΣ. Akerblad.

3 z 2

REMARKS.

L. 2. M. Akerblad alters the last word to ΠΥΘΙΟΝ. There is, however, no necessity for the correction. Spanheim gives two representations of coins, bearing the legend of ΠΥΘΕΟΣ and the figure of Apollo. H. A. v. 70. " The Parian Chronicle, as Porson observes, has Καλλέου, for which Palmer wished to substitute Καλλίου. Dr. Taylor refutes him from the marmor Sandvicense." — I will add a remark of Valesius : " Observavi Græcos fere Αρσενοΐτην dicere pro Arsinoite nomo, seu Præfectura. Sic enim apud Eusebium scribitur etiam in optimis exemplaribus ; et apud Palladium et apud Ptolemæum." *

L. 8. ΑΡΩΓΟΥΣ. Τις θεῶν ἐστιν ἀρωγός ; Eur. Hec.

L. 12. Μοχθεῖν ἀνάγκη. Eurip. Æoli, fr.

L. 15. ΜΗ. — ΘΕΡΙΣΑΙ. Βίον ΘΕΡΙΖΕΙΝ ὥστε ΚΑΡΠΙΜΟΝ στάχυν. Eur. in Hyps. Καρπὸν Δηοῦς ΘΕΡΙΣΑΣΘΑΙ. Aristoph. Plut. 515.

Many parts of these verses are well illustrated in the following remarks, which were communicated to me by Mr. Blomfield.

L. 5. ΕΓΓΑΜΩΝ is for ΕΚ ΓΑΜΩΝ.

L. 7. Ὁ χρόνος ὃς τὰ πάνθ᾽ ὁρᾷ. Eurip. Melan. fr. 25.

L. 9. " There are great labours, but you will overcome them all." ΠΕΡΙΕΣΗ instead of ΕΠΙΕΣΗ. Πλήν, " but," as in Matth. xviii. 7. xxvi. 39. Philipp. iv. 14. It occurs also in the sense of ὅμως, in Xenoph. Anab. p. 85. ed. Hutch.; and in Herodot. vi. 31. Dion. Halic. de Comp. p. 4. Sophocl. Trach. 41. Oed. Col. 1644.

L. 10. ΑΝΑΜΕΙΝΟΝ, ΦΙΛΕ. See l. 18.

L. 11. ΛΟΓΟΣ for ΛΑΙΟΣ.

L. 12. Μοχθεῖν ἀνάγκη. Eurip. Telephus, fr. 18.

L. 13. Νικηφόρον δῶρον. Eur. Iph. A. 1557. At the end of the line read, τὸν χρησμὸν τ᾽ ἔχειν.

L. 14. Οὐκ ἔσται λαβεῖν.

L. 17. Ῥᾷον δὲ διᾶγ᾽ ἢ ἐι χρυσὸν ἔδωκε. Theoc. x. ult.

---

* Vales. ad Soc. E. H. l. 6. 144.

GREEK INSCRIPTIONS. 541

L. 21. ΕΝΙΨΗΘΕΟΙΣ. It should be ἐνίψεις θεούς, "deos inculpabis."
L. 22. "But if you succeed, you will call the oracle a golden one."
Χρυσοῦν ποιήσεις. Qu. χρυσόν? Ananius or Hipponax, apud Athen.
xiv. p. 625. Χρυσὸν λέγει Πύθερμος, ὡς οὐδὲν τἄλλα. Arist. Plut. 268.
ὦ χρυσὸν ἀγγείλας ἐπῶν. Lucretius, "depascimur aurea dicta."
L. 23. Ψῆφον παρὰ θεῶν. Eur. And. 1242.
L. 24. ΩΜΗΝ ΟΠΩΡΑΝ ΜΗ ΛΑΒΗΣ· ΟΥ ΧΡΗΣΙΜΟΝ. "Do not
pluck unripe fruit; it will do you no good."

V.

```
1    ΤΕΡ - ΑΙΟΠΛΑΤΩΝΟΣΠΑΤΑΡΕΙ
     ΚΑΙΞΑΝΘΙΩΠΟΛΕΙΤΕΥΣΑΜΕ
     ΝΩΔΕΚΛΕΝΤΑΙΣΚΑΤΑΛΥΚΙΑΝ
     ΠΟΛΕΣΙΠΑΣΑΙΣΤΗΝΟΣΤΟΘΗ
5    ΚΗΝΙΑΣΩΝΑΝΤΙΓΟΝΟΥ
     ΠΑΤΑΡΕΥΣΑΛΛΩΔΕΜΠΙΕΞΕΣ
     ΤΩΤΕΘΗΝΑΙΕΑΝΔΕΤΙΣΤΙΝΑΘΗ
     ΟΦΕΙΛΕΤΩΙΕΡΑΣΑΠΟΛΛΩΝΙ
     ΔΡΑΧΜΑΣ
10   ΤΗΣΠΡΑΞΕΩΣΚΑΙΠΡΟΣΑΝΓΕ
     ΛΙΑΣΟΥΣΗΣΠΑΝΤΙΤΩΒΟΥΛΟ
     ΜΕΝΩΕΠΙΤΩΗΜΙΣΕΙ
```
At Patara. *

"Jason of Patara, son of Antigonus, (raised) the sepulchre for
Ter - - - son of Plato, who was a citizen of Patara, and of Xanthus,
who was Decurio for the tenth time in the cities of Lycia. Let it
be allowed to no other person to be placed in it. If any one bury
another there, let him pay —— drachmæ, sacred to Apollo. The
levying of this fine, and the laying of the information, belong to any
one who pleases, for half the sum."

REMARKS.

L. 1 and 2. "Patara and Xanthus, two of the greatest cities in
Lycia." Strabo, l. 14.
L. 2. ΠΟΛΕΙΤ ΔΕΚΑ. "Οἱ πολιτευόμενοι, qui Patriæ erant, quod
Romæ Senatores." Reinesius, Ins. 132. They were so called, says

* From Mr. Cockerell. L. 1. ΤΕΡΠΑΙΩ. L. 3. ΔΕΚΑ. Akerblad.

Emmanuel Marti, quod essent *de Curia*, quæ erat instar * Senatus. Valesius † refers to passages in Gregory Naz., Artemidorus, Libanius, Athanasius, where πολιτευόμενοι and πολιτευταί are used in the sense of Decuriones. The Latin versions have sometimes mistaken the meaning. Reinesius gives an inscription where a person is mentioned as Decurio the third time, " D. III." p. 570. From this expression we may be able to explain part of another inscription, No. VIII., in this collection, where mention is made of a person,

```
- - - - - - - - - - - ΔΕΚΑΠΙ
TEΥΣΑΝΤΑ - - - - - - - - - - -
```
read   `- - - - - - - - - - - ΔΕΚΑΠΟΛΙ`
`TEΥΣΑΝΤΑ - - - - - - - - - -`

L. 10. The word πρᾶξις relates to those " qui mulctatitias pecunias exigebant." Budæus. " Πρᾶξις, πράκτορες voces fori Attici." ‡ Εκδικήσουσιν καὶ ἐκπράξουσιν, " they shall bring an action, and demand the money." §

L. 10. Προσαγγελεύς, " an informer, or spy." Προσαγγελία, " delatio." Glossar. Ὁ Μάρκελλος προσήγγειλε τῇ Βουλῇ τὸν ἄνθρωπον, " he charged the man before the Senate." Plut. in v. Marc.

L. 11. Ὑπεύθυνος ἔστω ΠΑΝΤΙ ΤΩ ΒΟΥΛΟΜΕΝΩ γράφεσθαι. Diog. Laer. vol. ii. p. 31.

VI.

TONΔOΠAΛMIΣIPOΦΥΛΑΞ
AMMΩNIOΣEIΣATOBΩMON
AΥTOΣETIZΩAΣTOIΛΥKΥ
ΦENΓOΣOPΩN
HPIONOΦPAΓENOITOTONΩ
MAIAΣKΛΥTEKOΥPE
ΓPMEIHΠENΠOIΣXΩPON
EΠEΥΣEBEΩN

At Patara. ‖

---

* Epist. p. 100.   † In Amm. Marc. p. 320., also in Eus. p. 198.
‡ Span. in Callim. H. Jov. 70.
§ Chishull, A. A. App. p. 9. See also Blomfield, Gloss. to the Persæ. v. 482.
‖ From Mr. Cockerell. L. 3. ΓΛΥΚΥ. L. 5. ΓΟΝΩ. L. 7. EPMEIH. Akerblad.

Some correction is wanting in the first line of these verses. "Ammonius, while he was alive, raised this altar, or sacred building, that it might become a sepulchral monument for his son. O Mercury, illustrious offspring of Maia, convey him, I pray, to the land of the pious."

REMARKS.

L. 6, 7. Ἑρμῆς ὁ πομπός. Œd. Col. 1618.

L. 7. ΠΕΝΠΟΙΣ. The substitution of N for M is not unfrequent in inscriptions in Asia Minor; but it is also found on some antient monuments of Greece; as on the Elean tablet; in the Oxford marbles, No. XXI., ΔΩΔΕΚΟΝΦΑΛΟΝ, ΟΡΘΟΝΦΑΛΟΝ; and ΟΛΥΝΠΙΑΡΑΤΟΣ is given in an inscription copied by Spon, in which occurs ΑΜΦΙΑΝΑΧΣ. The name of the town Olympus, in Lycia, appears on marbles examined by Mr. Cockerell and Captain Beaufort, ΟΛΥΝΠΟΣ. Hence we may explain the cause of a corrupt reading in Cicero. In the third Verrine oration, Servilius is said, " Olynthum urbem hostium cepisse." It was at first probably written OLYNPUM; this was altered into OLYNTHUM; but there is no city of the name of Olynthus in Lycia. It should be Olynpum.

L. 7. ΧΩΡΟΝ. Χῶρον πέμψαν ἐς εὐσεβέων. See the Epigram of Carphylides, quoted in the Museum Criticum, vol. i. p. 227., and Anthol. Palat. 2. App. p. 877. τὴν δ᾽ ἄγ᾽ ἐπ᾽ εὐσεβέων χῶρον.

VII.

ΣΩ - - - - ΗΚΗΠΛΑΤΩΝΙΔΟΣΤΗΣΚΑΙΑΡΣΑΣΕΟΣΜΑ - - - - - ΕΥ - ΒΟΥ
ΗΝΑΝΕΘΕΤΟΗΚΑΤΕΣΚΕΥΑΣΑΜΕΝΗΚΑΙΤΟΗΡΩΟΝΗΜΗΤΗΡΑΥΤ - -
ΕΡΠΙΔΑΣΗΗΚΑΙΣΑΡΠΗΔΟΝΙΣΛΥΣΑΝΔΡΟΤΟΥΤΕΘΗΣΕΤΑΙΔΕΕΝΤΑΥ
ΤΗΤΗΣΩΜΑΤΟΘΗΚΗΑΛΛΟΣΟΥΔΕΙΣΗΟΕΝΘΑΨΑΣΥΠΕΥΘΥΝΟΣ
ΕΣΤΑΙΑΣΕΒΕΙΑΚΑΤΑΧΘΟΝΙΟΙΣΘΕΟΙΣΚΑΙΥΠΟΚΕΙΣΕΤΑΙΤΟΙΣΔΙΑΤΕ
ΤΑΓΜΕΝΟΙΣΚ - - ΞΩΘΕΝΑΠΕΡΑΕΙΤΩΝΤΩΔΗΜΩΧΜ̄

At Patara. *

---

* From Mr. Cockerell. L. 1. ΣΩΜΑΤΟΘΗΚΗ. Ib. ΜΑΡΚΙΟΥΕΥΓΡΙΒΟΥ. L. 6. ΚΑΙΕΞΩΘΕΝ. Akerblad.

" The tomb of Platonis, called also· Arsasis, wife of Marcius Eu-
gribus, which her mother Erpidase called also Sarpedonis, daughter of
Lysander, raised ; who likewise built the Heroum.　No other person
shall be placed in this tomb.　Whoever buries another in it, shall be
charged with the crime of impiety to the Dii Inferi, and shall be subject to the laws decreed against this crime, and shall moreover (pay)
to the people of Aperræ —— thousand denarii.

REMARKS.

L. 1.　ΑΡΣΑΣΕΙΜΑΡΚΙΟΥΕΥΓΡΙΒΟΥ occurs in another inscription
copied by Mr. Cockerell.

L. 4.　ΥΠΕΥΘ.　Ἔστωσαν ὑπεύθυνοι ἀσεβείᾳ, " impietatis rei aguntor."
Chishull, An. As. 159.

L. 5.　Θεοὶ καταχθόνιοι, in Latin, Dii Manes, or Dii Inferi.　The
chief of these was Pluto.

> Tuque o sævissime fratrum
> Cui servire dati Manes.　　　STATIUS.

L. 5.　Ὑποκείσεται τῷ φίσκῳ.　Sepulc. Inscr. Anthol. Palat. vol. iii.

L. 6.　Καὶ ἔξωθεν. ε. " præterea.　Gloss.　In an inscription copied
by Spon, and found at Thyatira, we read, " that whoever puts any
other body in the·tomb shall pay a fine," γενόμενος ὑπεύθυνος ἔξωθεν τῷ
τῆς τυμβωρυχίας νόμῳ.

L. 6.　'Απέῤῥαι in Ptolemy, Apyræ in Pliny. l. 5.　The modern Phineka, " teste Villanovano."　See Hoffman's Lexicon.　Captain Beaufort, in his Caramania, p. 34., points out the situation of the place.

VIII.

ΕΡΠΙΔΑΣΗΗΚΑΙΣΑΡΠΗΔΟΝΙΣ
- ΥΣΑΝΔΡΟΥΑΠΕΡΑΕΙΤΙΣ - ΕΓ -
ΝΥ - ΛΑΡΧΙΕΡΕΙΑΕΝΤΩΕΘΝΙΙΑΥ
- ΑΝΔΡΟΝΔΙΣΦΥΣΕΙΟΣΕΙΟΥ
5　ΑΠΕΡΑΕΙΤΗΝΑΠΟΑΠΟΛΛΩΝΙ
ΑΕΑΝΔΡΑΕΚΤΩΝΠΡΩΤΕΥΣ
- ΩΝΕΚΠΡΟΓΟΝΩΝΑΡΤΑΝ
ΤΩΝΚΑΙΕΝΤΩΛΥΚΙΩΝΕΘΝΕΙ
ΚΑΙΤΗΠΑΤΡΙΔΙΠΑΣΑΣΤΑΣΑ

                :10·· ΧΑΣΤΕΛΕΣΑΝΤΑΚΑΙΔΕΚΑΠΙ
                   - ΕΥΣΑΝΤΑΤΕΙΜΗΘΕΝΤΑΠΟ
                   - ΑΚΙΣΕΦΟΙΣΕΥΕΠΟΙΗΣΕΝΙΑ
                   - ΡΟΝΑΡΙΣΤΟΝΓΕΝΟΜΕΝΟΝ
                   - ΑΡΤΥΡΗΘΕΝΤΑΕΠΙΠΑΣΗΤΗ
          15   - ΟΥΒΙΟΥΚΑΛΟΚΑΓΑΘΙΑΤΟΝ
                     ΕΑΥΤΗΣΠΡΟΠΑΠΠΟΝΜΝΗ
                     ΜΗΣΧΑΡΙΝ

At Patara. *

VERSION.

" Erpidase, who is also called Sarpedonis, of Aperræ, daughter of Lysander, who was priestess in her nation or province, honours her grandfather Lysander, who was grandson of ,——, a citizen of Aperræ, who came from Apollonia; a man descended from those who had the first rank in the state; sprung from ancestors who had been in high office; a man who had in Lycia, and in his own country, gone through all the degrees of magistracy; who had been Decurio for the tenth time; who had been often honoured for the good he had done; an eminent physician; to whom testimony had been borne for ł ., good and honourable conduct in life."

REMARKS.

L. 4. Καίσαρος φύσει. Eus. E. H. l. iv. c. 12. Τοῦ φύσει Ἀττάλου. Ox. Mar. Maitt. ix. 2. The word ΔΙΣ, used in this sense, will be explained in the note to No. XVIII.

L. 6. ΠΡΩΤ. Πρώτους τῆς πόλεως, " chief men of the city;" in our version of the Acts of the Apostles, c. xiii. In Apuleius we have " Fœminas primates." Met. 2.

L. 7. ΑΡΞΑΝ. Honorati sunt, οἱ ἐν ἀρχαῖς γεγενημένοι, οἱ ΑΡΞΑΝΤΕΣ. Vales. in Am. Marc. p. 15.

L. 10. The same expression is found in other inscriptions, πάσας ἀρχὰς τετεληκότα. See Van. Dale. p. 243. One of these Lycian dig-

---

* From Mr. Cockerell. L. 2, 3. ΛΥΣΑΝ. ΓΕΓΟΝΥΙΑ. L. 3. ΕΘΝΕΙ. L. 6. ΑΣ and ΠΡΩΤΕΤΣΑΝΤΩΝ. L. 7. ΑΡΞΑΝ. L. 9. ΑΡΧΑΣ. L. 11, 12. ΠΟΛΛΑΚΙΣ. L. 13. ΤΡΟΝ. L. 14. ΜΑΡ. Akerblad.

nities is mentioned by Philostratus.·, ". In Heraclide Lycio scribit Philostratus ejus majores ´fuisse sacerdótes. Lyciæ, seu Lyciarchas." Vales. Emend. p. 93. The letters ΔΕΚΑΠΙ have been explained in the remarks on No. V. ´

IX.

```
1   ΤΟΜΝΗΜΕΙΟΝΕΠΑΦΡΟΔΕΙΤΟΥ
    ΑΟΥΛΟΥΛΕΟΝΤΟΣΜΟΥΣΑΙΟΥΤΟΥΚΑΙ
    ΙΔΕΟΝΟΣΜΥΡΕΟΣΚΑΙΑΠΕΡΑΕΙΤΟΥ
    ΟΕΩΝΗΣΑΤΟΔΙΑΤΩΝΕΝΜΥΡΟΙΣΑΡΧΕΙΩΝ
5   ΠΑΡΑΤΩΝΣΥΝΑΡΧΙΣΕΟΔΙΣΤΩΚΑΙ
    ΑΛΕΞΑΝΔΡΩΜΥΡΕΙΕΙΣΟΚΗΔΕΥΘΗΣΕΤΑΙ
    ΚΑΙΗΓΥΝΗΑΥΤΟΥΦΑΡΗΣΙΑ
    ΚΑΙΕΥΤΥΧΙΑΚΑΙΟΙΣΑΝΑΥΤΟΣΖΩΝ
    ΕΠΙΤΡΕΨΗΕΑΝΔΕΤΙΣΕΤΕΡΟΣ
10  ΕΝΚΗΔΕΥΣΗΤΙΝΛΟΦΙΛΕ
    ΘΗΚΥΑΝΕΙΤΩΝΙ - ΡΩΥ·-   -
    ΤΗΣΠΡΟΣΑΝΓΕΛΙΑΣΟΥΣΝΕ
    ΠΑΝΤΙΤΩΒΟΥΛΟΜΕΝΩΕΠΙΤΩ
            ΤΡΙΤΩ -
```

At Patara. *· The proper names in l. 2, 3. 5. require correction.

VERSION.

" The monument of Epaphroditus, son of —— Leo Musæus, who is also called ——, a citizen of Myra, and of Aperræ; which tomb he purchased in the Register office at Myræ, from the colleagues of ——, who is also called Alexander ´(τῷ καὶ Α.) a townsman of Myra; in which sepulchre shall be entombed both his wife Pharesia, and Eutychia, and those to whom he shall in his life-time give leave. If any other person shall place a body in it, let him pay to the Senate of Cyane a sum of money. Any one who pleases may lay the information, for a third of the fine."

REMARKS.

L. 4. ῾Ο᾿ ἐωνήσατο διὰ τῶν Αρχείων. Διά, " In." διὰ στόματος ἔχειν, " In ore habere." H. Steph. in v. Διά. Αρχεῖα, the place, where, οἱ δημοσίοι

---

* From Mr. Cockerell. L. 6. Ω for Ο. L. 10. ΤΙΝΑ. L. 11. ΓΕΡΟΥΣΙΑ. · L. 12. ΟΥΣΗΣ. Akerblad.

χάρται ἀπόκεινται. Suidas. Perhaps in the following inscription, edited by Hammer, ΑΡΧΩΝ should be altered to ΑΡΧΕΙΩΝ.

ΚΕΡΑΜΕΥΣΩΝΗΣΑΜΗΝ
ΔΙΑΤΩΝΑΡΧΩΝΤΟΝΠΥΡ
ΓΙΣΚΟΝ. Anthol. Palat. nott. 52. t. iii. p. 1.

L. 5. Παρὰ τῶν σύν. Επὶ κόσμων τῶν σὺν Ἐνίπαντι, " under the Cosmi, who were colleagues of Henipas." Chishull, An. Asiat. p. 129. So in the Testamentum Epictetæ, ἐφόρων τῶν σὺν Ἱμέρτῳ, " sotto gli Efori Imerto e Colleghi." Mus. Veron. 129.

L. 6. Perhaps in his alteration, Akerblad intended to suggest ΕΝ Ω, but ΕΙΣ Ο is an usual form. Εἰς ἣν κηδεῦσαι (σόρον). Chishull, A. A. App. 9.

L. 7. Probably Η is omitted at the end of this line. " Pharesia, who is called Eutychia."

L. 10. Either ὀφειλέτω or ὀφειλήσει; both forms occur.

L. 11. Cyane, a city in Lycia: in Ptolemy, Κύανα.

L. 14. An inscription copied by Mr. C. ; after stating the sum to be paid by any who places another body in the tomb, adds, ΩΝ Ο ΕΛΕΝΞΑΣ ΛΗΝΥΕΤΕ ΤΟ Γ *, " of which, he who convicts him shall receive a third." ΛΗΝΥΕΤΕ is written for ΛΗΜΨΕΤΑΙ, the Ν, as in other instances, being substituted for Μ. Λήμψομαι is an Alexandrian form. See Sturzius de Dial. Maced.

X.

ΔΑΕΚΟΥΑΛΕΩCΚΟΝΩΝΑΚΟ -
ΑΛΕΩCΤΟΝΠΑΠΠΟΝΑΥΤΗCÀ
ΝÉΣΤΗCΕΝΜΝΗΜΗCΧΑΡΙΝ

---

* Chishull, An. As. 131. Λαβέτω τὸ τρίτον μέρος τᾶς δίκας ὁ δικαξάμενος, " let him who brings the action take a third part."

XI.

ΚΟΥΑΣΚΑΙΟΒΡΑΝΓΟΥΕΙΣΥ
ΙΟΙΕΠΙΟΥΑΣΕΩΣΕΠΙΟΥ
ΑΣΙΝΚΟΥΟΥΤΟΝΠΑΤΕΡΑ˙
ΕΥΣΕΒΕΙΑΣΕΝΕΚΕΝΤΗΣ
ΕΙΣΕΑΥΤΟΝ

XII.

ΟΡΕΣΤΗΝΜΙΔΟΥΑΝΕΣΤΗ
ΣΕΝΚΙΔΑΜΟΥΑΣΙΣΟΒΡΑΟΥ
ΓΕΡΕΩΣΤΟΝΘΕΙΟΝΑΥΤΟΥ
ΜΝΗΜΗΣΧΑΡΙΝ

XIII.

ΛΑΝΜΙΔΟΥΘΥΓΑΤΕΡΑΑ
. ΝΕΣΤΗΣΕΝΚΙΔΑΜΟΥΑ
ΣΙΣΟΒΡΑΟΥΓΕΡΕΩΣΤΗΝ
ΘΕΙΑΝΑΥΤΟΥΜΝΗΜΗΣ
ΧΑΡΙΝ

No. X. XI. XII. XIII. from Alaiah *, the antient Coracesium, in Cilicia Aspera. See Beaufort's Caramania.

There is nothing remarkable in these four inscriptions but the names, respecting which there seems to be no doubt in the copies made by Mr. Cockerell. The letters are all perfect, and the names occur more than once. In the first, Däe, daughter of Cualis, erects the statue of her grandfather, Conon †, son of Cualis; in the second, Cuas and Obranguis, sons of Epiuasis, raise the statue of their father, Epiuasis, son of Cuas; in the .third, Cidamuasis, son of Obraugeris, raises the statue of his uncle, Orestes, son of Midas; and the same

---

* From Mr. Cockerell.

† Conon appears to have been a common name in Isauria; it occurs in the following inscription; and the Bishop of Apamia, mentioned by Evagrius, was so called (H. E. l. 3. c. 35.); the appellation was also preserved in the country until the eighth century; it was the original name of the Iconoclast Emperor Leo.

Cidamuasis, in the fourth, commemorates his aunt Las, the daughter of Midas.

XIV.

```
 1   ΟΔΗΜΟΣΕΤΕΙΜΗΣΕΝ
     ΚΟΝΩΝΑΝΙΝΕ ΝΕΟΝΝΕΑΝΙΑΝ
     ΑΕΑΘΟΝΠΡΟΓΟΝΩΝΠΑΝΑΡΕΤΩΝ
     ΚΑΙΔΕΚΑΠΡΩΤΩΝΠΑΤΡΟΣΔΗΜ
 5   ΙΟΥΡΠΕΣΑΝΤΟΣΣΥΝΦΕΡΟΝΤΩΣ
     ΤΗΠΟΛΕΙΚΑΙΠΑΡΑΦΥΛΑΞΑΝΤΟΣ
     ΠΙΣΤΩΣΚΑΙΣΕΙΤΩΝΗΣΑΝΤΟΣ
     ΑΡΕΤΗΣΕΝΕΚΕΝΚΑΙΕΥΝΟΙΑΣ
     ΤΗΣΕΙΣΑΥΤΟΝΤΟΝΔΕΑΝΔΡΙΑ
10   ΝΤΩΝΕΣΤΗΣΕΝΑΝΑΣΑΠΑΤΟΥ
     ΡΙΟΥΗΜΗΤΗΡΑΥΤΟΥ
```

Copied by Captain Beaufort and Mr. Cockerell, at Hamaxia, on the coast of Cilicia. *

REMARKS.

L. 2. NINE. According to Captain Beaufort's transcript, there is a mark in this word after E, as also in Mr. Cockerell's copy; perhaps it is the letter I. The termination of some of the proper names in this part of Asia is very singular. In one inscription we have ὁ δῆμος ἐτείμησεν ΝΙΝΕΙΝ ΚΟΙΤΟΣΤΟΥ ΝΙΝΕΙ ἄνδρα, κ. τ. λ.; in a second, copied by Captain B., ὁ δῆμος ἐτείμησεν ΜΟΥΟΝ † ΝΙΝΕΠΟΣ ΑΝΔΡΑ ἀγαθόν; and although the letters ΕΠ are marked as doubtful in the copy he communicated to me, we have the same word in another which was transcribed by himself and Mr. Cockerell, ΝΙΝΕΠΟΣ. ‡ In a third, we read, γυναῖκα Κόνωνος δὶς τοῦ ΝΙΝΕΙ §, ἄνδρος, (wife of Conon, a grandson of Ninei, a man, &c.) ; in a fourth, ἐτείμησε ΝΙΝΕΙΝ ΚΟΝΩΝΟΣ. In one, copied by Mr. Cockerell, we read, ΑΠΑΤΟΥΡΙΣ (or ΑΠΑ-

---

* L. 3. ΑΓΑΘΟΝ. L. 5. ΔΗΜΙΟΥΡΓΗΣΑΝΤΟΣ. L. 9, 10. ΑΝΔΡΙΑΝΤΑΑΝΕΣ. Akerblad.

† Pamphylia, ante Mopsopia appellata. Plin. l. 5.

‡ As we have Μόψοψ, Μόψοπος, as well as Μόψοπος, Μοψόπου, perhaps we should read ΝΙΝΟΠΟΣ, from ΝΙΝΟΨ. See Ox. Strabo, l. 9. -642.

§ Probably an Asiatic name; the husband and son of Semiramis were Ninus and Ninias.

ΤΟΥΡΙΟΣ) ΜΑΠΕΙ ; and in another, ΕΤΗΚΠΑΣ ΜΑΠΕΙ, seen by him and Captain B. ; and on one found at Selinus, on the coast of Cilicia, ΝΑΝΝΕΙ ΣΥΝΒΙΩ ΑΥΤΟΥ.

L. 3. ΠΑΝΑΡΕΤΩΝ.? παναρετὸς is only found in Suicer. Ecc. Thesaurus.

L. 4. ΔΕΚΑΠΡ. Mention is made in other inscriptions of those who formed part of the body of Decuriones ; and were called, Quinque Primi, Decem Primi. Noris, in his Cenotaph. Pis., Diss. 1. quotes two passages from Cicero relating to them.

L. 5. The father of Conon was ΔΗΜΙΟΥΡΓΟΣ. This office, the title of a chief magistrate, occurs in the inscription communicated by Adler to Barthelemy. Consult also Hesychius on this word, and Thucydides, 1. v. c. 47.

L. 7. ΣΕΙΤ. In the Heraclean tables mention is made of the Σιτα-γέρται ; and in an inscription found by Villoison, in Astypalæa, Demoteles is praised, because ΣΙΤΟΝ ΔΙΕΤΕΛΕΙ ΠΡΟΩΝΟΥΜΕΝΟΣ ΤΩΙ ΔΑΜΩΙ. Proleg. in Hom. 55.

XV.

```
ΟΔΗΜΟΣΕΤΕΙΜΗΣΕΝΝΙΝΕΙΝ
ΚΟΙΤΟΣΤΟΥΝΙΝΕΑΝΔΡΑΑ
ΓΑΘΟΝΑΙΧΙΕΡΑΣΑΜΕΝΟΝΤΩΝ *
ΣΕΒΑΣΤΩΝΚΑΙΠΟΛΛΑΠΕΡΙΤΗΝ
ΠΑΤ ΙΔΑΕΚΠΡΟΓΟΝΩΝΠΕΦΙΛΟ
ΤΕΙΜΗΜΕ - - - - - - - ΕΝΕΚΑΚΑΙ
ΕΥΝΟΙΑΣΤΗΣΕΙΣΑΥΤΟΝ
```

At Hamaxia ; copied by Mr. Cockerell and Captain Beaufort.

REMARKS.

L. 3. ΑΡΧΙΕ. Herodes Atticus is called, in an inscription published by Spon, ΑΡΧΙΕΡΕΥΣ ΤΩΝ ΣΕΒΑΣΤΩΝ, " Grand-prêtre des Empereurs." Ac. des Ins. 30. p. 17. ΣΕΒΑΣΤΩΝ has been sometimes

---

* ΑΡΧΙΕΡΕ; L. 5. ΠΑΤΡΙΔΑ. L. 6. ΜΗΜΕΝΟΝΑΡΕΤΗΣ. Akerblad.

improperly translated, as if it were the genitive of ΣΕΒΑΣΤΑ, Augustalia.

L. 5. ΕΚΠΡΟ. " More majorum.' Ib. ΠΕΦΙΛ. " Liberal, generous, munificent." Φιλοτιμία, proprie quidem notat ambitionem et studium honorum; sed quia ambitiosi magno studio res suas agunt plerumque, et simul crebra utuntur largitione, inde et utramque hanc significationem vocabulum illud accepit." Perizon. Ælian. i. 194.

XVI.

ΑΠΑΤΟΥΡΙΣΜΑΠΕΙΚΑΤΕΣ
ΚΕΥΑΣΕΝΤΟΗΡΩΕΙΟΝΕΑΥΤΩ
ΚΑΙΤΟΙΣΕΑΥΤΟΥΩΣΤΕΕΧΕΙΝ
ΑΥΤΟΝΜΕΡΗΔΥΩΕΙΣΕΡΧΟΜΕ
ΝΩΝΕΚΔΕΞΙΩΝΚΑΙΕ - Τ - - Κ - - ΤΙΟΥ

L. 1. Apaturius, perhaps; as the name occurs in No. XIV.

L. 3. ΩΣΤΕΕΧ. This appropriation of part of a monument or sepulchre is mentioned in an inscription in Maffei. Mus. Ver. " T. Claudius takes half for himself, his wife, his descendants, and freedmen."

` L. 4. ΕΙΣΕΡ. Corresponding to the word " Intro," in Latin. " Cineraria quinquaginta tria intrantibus parte læva, quæ sunt in monumento." Philos. Trans. Abr. ix. 433.

XVII.

```
 1   ΑΓΩΝΟΘΕΤΟΥΝΤΟΣΔΙΑΒΙΟΥΑΥΡΗΛ - -
     ΠΑΙΩΝΕΙΝΟΥΤΟΥΗΣΙΑΝΟΥΚΑΙΕ
     ΠΙΤΕΛΟΥΝΤΟΣΘΕΜΙΝΠΑΜΦΥΛΙΑΚΗΝ
     ΤΟΥΗΣΙΑΝΕΙΟΝΕΠΙΒΑΤΗΡΙΟΝΘΕΩΝ
 5   ΑΘΗΝΑΣΚΑΙΑΠΟΛΛΩΝΟΣΕΞΙΔΙΩΝ
     ΧΡΗΜΑΤΩΝΕΝΕΙΚΗΣΑΝΠΑΙΔΩΝ
     ΠΑΛΗΝΣΥΝΣΤΕΦΑΝΩΘΕΝΤΕΣΑΥΡ
     ΚΟΝΩΝΙΑΝΟΣΝΕΟΠΤΟΛΕΜΟΣ   ·
     ΚΑΙΑΥΡΗΛΙΟΣΕΡΜΙΠΠΙΑΝΟΣΕΡΜΙΠ
10   ΠΟΣΝΕΟΣΣΙΔΗΤΑΙΛΑΒΟΝΤΕΣ
     ΑΘΛΟΝΤΟΤΕΘΕΜΑΚΑΙ
     ΤΟΝΑΝΔΡΙΑΝΤΑΣΥΝΤΗ
     ΒΑΣΕΙ
```

XVIII.

1　ΑΓΩΝΟΘΕΤΟΥΝΤΟΣΔΙΑ - - - -
　ΑΥ - - - ΠΑΙΩΝΕΙΝ
　- - - - - ΥΗΣΙΑΝΟΥ
　ΚΑΙΕΠΙΤΕΛΟΥΝΤΟΣΘΕΜΙΝ
5　ΠΑΜΦΥΛΙΑΚΗΝΤΟΥΗΣΙΑ
　ΝΕΙΟΝΕΠΙΒΑΤΗΡΙΟΝΘΕΩΝ
　ΑΘΗΝΑΣΚΑΙΑΠΟΛΛΩΝΟΣ
　ΕΞΙΔΙΩΝΧΡΗΜΑΤΩΝ
　ΕΝΕΙΚΗΣΕΝΠΑΙΔΩΝ
10　ΠΥΓΜΗΝΑΥΡΗΛΙΟΣ
　ΑΡΤΕΜΩΝΔΙΣΔΙΟΝΥΣΙΟΥ
　ΑΣΠΕΝΔΙΟΣΛΑΒΩΝΑΘΛΟΝ
　ΤΟΤΕΘΕΜΑΚΑΙΤΟΝΑΝΔΡΙΑΝΤΑ
　ΣΥΝΤΗΒΑΣΕΙ

At Side, in Pamphylia.

REMARKS ON INS. XVII.

L. 1. Velleius Paterculus translates ἀρχόντας διὰ βίου, " perpetuos Archontes." As Aurelius Pæoninus was perpetual Agonotheta, we must correct the following remark of Van Dale. " Illud autem Agonothetæ munus æque ac Gymnasiarchæ non perpetuum, sive ad vitam erat, sed semel, bisve, terve," &c.

L. 3. ΕΠΙΤ. ΘΕΜΙΝ. Θέμις is sometimes used for θεσμός. Θεσμοὶ ἱεροὶ, " ritus sacri." Steph. in v. who quotes Τελεῖ τὰ κατὰ θεσμὸν ἱερόν. Dionys. Areop. The Pamphylian Θέμις, in this inscription, may illustrate the unexplained words, ΘΕΜΙΔΟΣ ΤΟ Ε, on a coin of Aspendus, in Pamphylia. *

L. 4. ΕΠΙΒ. This word requires some explanation ; perhaps the following inquiry will help us to the true meaning.

The glossaries interpret the word by " Introitus ;" and ΕΠΙΒΑΣΙΣ by " Incessus, Ingressus ;" in Julius Pollux, Ἐπιβασία is defined ἡ εἰς

---

* Mionnet. Des. des Medailles, t. iii. p. 449.

ἀλλότριον ὃικον ἄναρχος ΕΙΣΕΛΕΥΣΙΣ. Ἐπιβατήριος εὐχὴ dicitur, qua Imperatori primum inaugurato apprecari solebant. Du Cange in v. who cites Cedrenus.

Valesius translates περὶ ἐπιβατηρίου by " adventoria oratione * :" now, " adventoria epistola" was a letter or message sent forward by a person coming from a distance to his friend; he expected his *approach* or arrival to be welcomed by one in return. †

Synesius mentions the πικρὰ ἐπιβατήρια with which he was greeted, πικροῖς ἡμᾶς ἡ πόλις ἐπιβατηρίοις ἐξένισεν.

Captain Beaufort and Mr. Cockerell copied, in this part of Asia Minor, an inscription in which ΕΠΙΒΑΣΙΣ is found. " To the Emperor Cæsar, Trajan, Hadrian, Augustus, father of his country,

ΟΛΥΜΠΙΩΣΩΤΗΡΙ
ΤΟΥΚΟΣΜΟΥ - - - -
ΤΗΣΕΠΙΒΑΣΕΩΣ

Olympian, preserver of the world, on account of his arrival, (perhaps ὑπὲρ τῆς ἐπ.)

Some of the Greek Fathers, in explaining the passage of St. John, ἐσκήνωσεν ἐν ἡμῖν, consider the words as meaning σκῆνος ἀνέλαβεν ἐν ἡμῖν. Theodoret calls this assumption of the body by the Logos, τὴν τοῦ Λόγου ἐπὶ τὸ σῶμα ἐπίβασιν.

But ἐπίβασις, from the explanation already given, (εἰσέλευσις, Ingressus,) corresponds to ἐπιδημία, " adventus ;" now these were religious festivals relating to the ἐπιδημίαι θεῶν ; at certain times the deities *visited* cities under their protection ; " Delum maternam invisit Apollo ;" and the Argives celebrated the *visit* of Diana. (Vales. on Eus. H. E. l. ix. p. 166.) Tyre was said, τῇ τῶν οὐρανίων θεῶν ἐπιδημίᾳ ἀνθεῖν ‡, adventu seu præsentia ; and the Roman coins give " adventus Augusti," ἐπιδημία. We may conclude, therefore, the meaning of the sentence to be, that Pæoninus celebrated, at his own expence, the sacrifice in honour of the visit or manifestation of the gods, Apollo and Minerva.

---

* Emend. p. 30. † Scaliger. Lec. Aus. l. 2.
‡ Marsham, Canon. Chron. p. 53.

On consulting Mr. Blomfield, I received from him the following remarks relating to ἐπίβασις : " When a magistrate goes to a province, or takes upon him an office, he is said ἐπιβαίνειν. See Schleusner, Lex. in v. Hence ἐπίβασις answers nearly to our word *accession;* and τὰ ἐπιβατήρια will be the sacrifices offered at the festival of the accession. So Synesius, quoted by Budæus and Stephens, οὕτω πικροῖς ἡμᾶς ἡ πολις ἐπιβατηρίοις ἐξένισεν, speaking of the reception which awaited him upon his election to his bishopric. This agrees with the gloss which you adduce, Ἐπ. Introitus, and with Cedrenus ; see Facciolati v. Introitus. Thus, in Captain Beaufort's inscription, ἐπιβασέως may allude either to a visit from the Emperor, as you say ; or to the celebration of his accession. Perhaps it was TA THΣ EΠI. which will be equivalent to ἐπιβατήρια."

L. 11. Θέμα. " Having received as a prize, the money and the statue, with the base." In an inscription found at Ephesus (Ins. Ant. Hess. Præf. App. xxxii.) we read of a person τὰ θέματα τοῖς ἀγωνίσταις αὐξήσαντα. The word occurs in another form in Spon, Anti. Mis. 367. ἐνίκα δε θεματικοὺς καὶ ταλαντιαιοὺς ἀγῶνας.* " He was conqueror in games where money was the prize, and the prize not less than a talent." See Pearson's explanation of θέμα. Θεματικοὶ ἀγῶνες and αργυρῖται were opposed to στεφανῖται, in which garlands only, or crowns, were given as the prize. Θέμα was also a sum of money deposited in a banker's hands. †

L. 12. " The statue with the base." The bases were often of different materials from the statues on them. In the Mus. Ver. xxxix. the statue of Jupiter is mentioned, σὺν βάσει ἀργυρεῇ γύψου μέστη. Marmoream basi ænea, also, in Rein. 144.

No. XVIII.

This inscription resembles, in great part, the preceding; and it is fortunate that they are preserved in a perfect state ; the incomplete

---

* Ταλαντ. was not understood befoıe Pearson explained it, ın his notes in Ignat. Epis. ad Polyc.

† Salm. de Trap. Foen. 5C3.

part of the second is easily supplied from the first. There seems to be no variation in the copies made by Captain Beaufort and Mr. Cockerell.

L. 10. ΠΑΙΔΩΝ ΠΥΓΜΗΝ. ' " In the boys' match at cuffs." Bentley, Phal. p. 51.

L. 11. ΑΡ - ΔΙΣ ΔΙΟΝ. " Artemon, grandson of Dionysius." We have already met with ΔΙΣ used in this manner ; see No. VIII. It frequently occurs in other inscriptions in Asia Minor, copied by Mr. C. Baxter was the first who explained the similar form, Ζάβδιλα δὶς Μάλχου, on one of the Palmyrene marbles. Barthelemy * afterwards confirmed the truth of the explanation, by observing that the words in the *Palmyrene* inscription, which corresponded to this expression in *Greek*, the one being a version of the other, gave the meaning proposed by Baxter. In an inscription, copied by Mr. C., we find also the form ΑΡΙΣΤΑΡΧΟΣ ΤΡΙΣ ΝΟΥΜΗΝΙΟΥ, " Aristarchus, great grandson of Numenius."

XIX.

```
CTEΦΑΝΟΟΡΗΤΙΑΡΙC
ΛΗCΤΕCΠΡΟΤΟC
ΠΑΛΟCΕΥΧΑΡΙCΤΩΝ
ΚΥΡΙΑΙCΝΕΜΕCΕ
CΙΝΕΥΧΗΝΕΠΕΝ
ΔΥΤΟΠΑΛΛΙΩΝ
ΖΕΥΓΟCΚΑΙΕΝΟΙ
ΔΙΑΚΑΙΧΟΙΡΟΝΤΑΙC
ΘΕΑΙCΕΥΧΑΡΙCΤΗΡΙΟΝ
ΙΟΗΛΛΔΕΚΑΙΤΩΦΟΙΝΙ
- ΩΝΗΝΚΑΙΘΥCΙΑC
```

At Halicarnassus.

The correction of many words in this inscription is necessary, in order to complete the sense. Letters are marked as doubtful in four of the lines in Captain Beaufort's copy. I have transcribed it, to show

---

* Ac. des Inscr. 26. 590.

4 B 2

that in this part of Asia Minor also the goddesses Nemeses were worshipped. They were venerated at Smyrna *, and the games in honour of them are mentioned in Dio. †

REMARKS.

L. 3, 4, 5. ΕΥΧ. " Εὐχαριστεῖ Διί, non gratias agit, sed donum dat Jovi." Bimard. Diss. 1. 40. ΚΥΡΙΩΝ. ΤΩΝ ΚΥΡΙΩΝ ΝΕΜΕΣΕΩΝ, in Chandler, Ins. Ant. p. 96. ΚΥΡΙΑΝ ΙΣΙΔΑ. Hamilton, Ægyp. 52. The offering was that of two tunics (perhaps ἐπένδυτα) and a pair of cloaks. Ἔνδυτα καὶ πλοκάμους θέτο Γάλλος. Epig. MS. in Spanheim ad Callim. p. 528.

L. 5. Εὐχή. Εὔξασθαι, ut *supplicatio* apud Latinos, non tam precationem, quam gratiarum actionem denotat. Chishull, A. As. 55.

XX.

1　.- ΗΜΟΣΕΤΕΙΜΗΣΕΝ
　ΝΑΝΑΝΤΕΤΕΟΥΣΘΥΓΑΤΕΡΑ
　ΓΟΝΕΩΝΕΥΣΧΗΜΟΝΕΣΤΑ
　ΤΩΝΚΑΙΦΙΛΟΤΕΙΜΩΝΓΥ
5　ΝΑΙΚΑΔΕΚΟΝΩΝΟΣΔΙΣΤΟΥ
　ΝΙΝΕΙΑΝΔΡΟΣΕΥΣΧΗΜΟΝΕΣ
　ΤΑΤΟΥΚΑΙΠΡΩΤΗΣΤΑ
　ΞΕΩΣΑΡΕΤΗΣΕΝΕΚΕΝΚΑΙ
　ΦΙΛΑΝΔΡΙΑΣΤΗΣΕΙΣΑΥΤΟΝ

XXI.

ΟΔΗΜΟΣΕΤΕΙΜΗ
ΣΕΝΝΙΝΕΙΝΚΟΝΩ
ΝΟΣΝΕΑΝΙΑΝΦΙΛΟΛΟ
ΓΟΝΤΑΓΜΑΤΟΣΒΟΥ
ΛΕΥΤΙΚΟΥΕΤΙΚΑΙΠΟ
ΛΕΙΤΗΝΣΙΔΗΤΩΝΓΟΝΕ
ΩΝΕΥΣΧΗΜΟΝΕΣΤΑ
ΤΩΝΚΑΙΦΙΛΟΤΕΙΜΩΝ
ΑΡΕΤΗΣΕΝΕΚΕΝΚΑΙΕΥΝΟΙΑΣ
ΤΗΣΕΙΣΕΑΥΤΟΝ

XXII.

　Ρ-- ----- .
　ΦΙΛΟ - - Ε - - - ΤΕΚΑΙΕ - - - -
　ΚΑΙΔΙΣΔΗΜΙΟΥΡΓΗΣΑΝΤΟ
　ΛΗΝΩΦΕΛΩΣΠΡΥΤΑΝΕΥΣ
　ΤΟΣΑΓΝΩΣΔΕΚΑΠΡΩΤΕΥΣΑΝ
5　ΤΟΣΑΜΕΜΠΤΩΣΑΓΟΡΑΝΟΜΗ
　ΣΑΝΤΟΣΕΚΤΕΝΩΣΣΕΙΤΩΝΗ
　ΣΑΝΤΟΣΣΠΟΥΔΑΙΩΣΣΥΝΔΙΚΗ

---

* Pausanias, in Ach. and Bœot.　　　† Vales. Emen. l. ii. c. 17.

```
        ΣΑΝΤΟΣΠΙΣΤΩΣΓΡΑΜΜΑΤΕΥ
        ΣΑΝΤΟΣΒΟΥΛΗΣΕΠΙΜΕΛΩΣ
   10   ΚΑΙΕΝΕΤΕΡΟΙΣΔΕΙΚΑΝΩΣΠΕ
        ΦΙΛΟΤΕΙΜΗΜΕΝΟΥΑΡΕΤΗΣΕΝΕ
        ΚΕΝΚΑΙΕΥΝΟΙΑΣΤΗΣΕΙΣΑΥΤΟΝ
```

These three inscriptions were found by Captain Beaufort, at Hamaxia, in Cilicia.

Ins. XX. " The people honour Nana, daughter of ――, sprung from parents eminent for their birth and station, and their munificence ; wife of Conon, the grandson of Ninei ? a man of distinguished character, and of the highest rank : — on account of her virtue, and love of her husband."

REMARKS.

L. 3. Such is the meaning of Εὐσχήμων. " Antiquiores et meliores Græci εὐσχήμονα de honesto ac moderato viro dixere ; idiotismus posterioris Græciæ pro divite et honorato, et in dignitate constituto eam vocem usurpat : et sic intelligendus εὐσχήμων βουλευτὴς in Evan. Matt. de Senatore spectabili et honorato vel divite." Salm. de L. H. 100. Τὰς εὐσχημόνας, " honourable women." Acts of the Apostles, c. xiii.
L. 7. Κομήτων πρώτου τάγματος. Euseb. de vita Const. l. iv.

Ins. XXI. " The people honour Ninei, son of Conon, a man of letters and of various knowledge ; of the rank of Decurio ; citizen also of Side, &c."

REMARKS.

L. 3. Appello φιλολογίαν, historiæ et rerum antiquarum cognitionem, literasque humaniores, quas qui tenent, eruditi proprie vocantur. Casaub. in Sueton. vit. Aug.
L. 4. Τοῖς ἐκ τοῦ ἀξιωματικοῦ καὶ βουλευματικοῦ τάγματος. Greg. Naz. in Epis. 22. ad Cæs. See Vales. in Eus. H. E. l. vii. 132.

Ins. XXII. In honour of one who had filled twice the office of Demiurgus ; who was also Prytan, Decaprotos, Ædile, Purveyor of corn, σύνδικος, or defender of the rights of the province, and Secretary of the senate.

REMARKS.

L. 2. ΔΗΜΙΟΥ. See note to No. XIV.

L. 3. The letter H is marked as doubtful in Capt. Beaufort's copy.

L. 4. ΔΕΚΑΠ. See note to Inscr. XIV.

L. 7. Σύνδικ. Syndici, qui a singulis urbibus mittuntur patroni ad causam unius provinciæ tuendam. Budæus. 114.

L. 8. The ΓΡΑΜΜΑΤΕΥΣ, in some of the Asiatic cities, was a situation of considerable importance. Sometimes the same person was Αρχιερεύς, and Γραμματεύς. Il est prouvé par les medailles que dans quelques villes comme a Nysa, le γραμματεύς étoit Eponyme. Belley. Fastes de Cyzique.

XXIII.

ΛΜΑΥΡΗΛΙΟΣΕΥΤΥΧΙΣ
ΝΟΣΕΥΤΥΧΗΣΣΙΔΗΤΗΣΑΝ
ΔΡΩΝΠΥΓΜΗΝΛΑΒΩΝΑ
ΘΛΟΝΤΟΤΕΘΕΜΑΚΑΙΤΟΝ
ΑΝΔΡΙΑΝΤΑΣΥΝΤΗΒΑΣΕΙ
ΑΣΚΗΣΑΝΤΟΣΚΑΙΠΡΟΘΥΜΗΣΑ
ΜΕΝΟΥΤΟΥΠΑΤΡΟΣΑΥΤΟΥΖΩΣΙΜΟΥ

At Side. Copied by Mr. Cockerell.

REMARKS.

L. 1. ΕΥΤΥΧΙΑΝΟΣ?

L. 6. ΠΡΟΘ. We find mention, as late as the time of Basil, of this custom of exhorting those who were about to combat in the games. Γυμνασταὶ καὶ παιδοτρίβαι πρὸς τοὺς ἐν τοῖς σταδίοις ἀγῶνας τοὺς ἀθλοῦντας προάγοντες πολλὰ — διακελεύοντκι. Περὶ Νηστείας.

XXIV.

ΘΕΩΣΕΒΑΣΤΩΚΑΙΣΑΡΙΚΑΙ
ΠΟΣΕΙΔΩΝΙΑΣΦΑΛΕΙΩΚΑΙ
ΑΦΡΟΔΕΙΤΗΕΥΠΛΟΙΑ

At Coryco, on the coast of Lycia. *

* Copied by Captain Beaufort and Mr. Cockerell.

REMARKS.

L. 2. Ὅις Ποσειδῶν Ἀσφάλειός ἐστιν ἡ Βακτηρία. Arist. Achar. 683. See also Plutarch in v. Thes. at the end.
L. 3. ΕΥΠ. Κνίδιοι δὲ αὐτοὶ καλοῦσιν Εὔπλοιαν. Pausan. in Attic. Callirrhoe, addressing Venus, says, πλὴν ὀυ φοβοῦμαι, σῦυ μοι συμπλεούσης. See Chariton. Aphrod. p. 135.

ι

XXV.

ΦΥΛΗ
ΚΑΙΣΑΡΗΟΣΠΑΙΛΙΟΝ
ΑΛΚΙΒΙΑΔΗΝΕΠΙΚΟΙ
ΤΩΝΟΣΣΕΒ - ΦΙΛΟΠΑ
ΤΡΙΝΚΑΙΕΥΕΡΓΕΤΗΝ
ΤΗΣΠΟΛΕΩΣΨΗΦΙ
ΣΑΜΕΝΟΥΚΑΙΕΠΙΜΕ
ΛΗΘΕΝΤΟΣ - ΤΙΒ - ΚΛ -
ΖΩΣΙΜΟΥΟΥΑΛΕΡΙΑΝΟΥ
ΓΡΑΜΜΑΤΕΩΣΤΗΣΠΟΛΕΩΣ

Copied, by the editor, at Nasli Bazar, in Asia Minor; also by Pococke and Mr. Cockerell.

VERSION.

" The Cæsarean tribe honour Publius Ælius Alcibiades, master of the bedchamber of Augustus, lover of his country, benefactor of the city," &c.

REMARKS.

L. 2. A small omicron appears on the stone between the two lines of the Π.
L. 3. ΕΠΙ ΚΟ. " Cubiculi præfectus." See Valckenaer in Herod. p. 6. ed. Wess. In one of the ecclesiastical writers we find Ἐυσέβιον προεστῶτα τοῦ βασιλικοῦ κοιτῶνος. Socr. H. E. l. iii. c. 1. In Ammianus Mar. " Eusebius cui erat Constantini thalami cura commissa." " Blastus, the King's Chamberlain." Τὸν ἐπὶ τοῦ κοιτῶνος. See Acts of the Apos. c. xii. v. 20.

XXVI.

ΔΗΜΑΣΚΑΙ
ΓΑΙΟΣΥΠΕΡ
ΒΟΩΝΙΔΙΩΝΠΑ
ΠΙΑΔΙ - - ΙΣΩΤΗ
ΡΙΕΥΧΗΝΚΑΙ
ΗΡΑΚΛΗΙΑΝΙΚ
ΗΤΩ -

Copied by Colonel Leake in Phrygia.   See p. 215.

REMARKS.

L. 4. " To Papias Jupiter, saviour, &c." The Bithynians, we learn from Arrian, called Jupiter ΠΑΠΑΣ, pater. " Non tantum ΠΑΠΑΣ, ΠΑΠΙΑΣ, ΠΑΠΠΑΣ, sed et ΠΑΣ dicebatur." Valck. in Herod. l. iv. p. 307. Wess. *Ω πάπια, in Aristoph. Vesp. 296, is explained by the Scholiast, ὦ πάτερ.

L. 6. " Herculi Invicto." Reines. Ins. " Passim in antiquis inscriptionibus ' Deus et invictus' Hercules dicitur." Heins. Ex. Sacræ, 340.

XXVII.

ΑΠΟΛΛΟΔΩΡΟΥ
ΙΣΟΤΕΛΟΤΘΥΓΑΤΗΡ   ΜΕΛΙΤΤΑ
ΤΙΤΘΗ

1   ΕΝΘΑΔΕΤΗΝΧΡΗΣΤΗΝΤΙΤΘΗΝΚΑΤΑΓΑΙΑΚΑΛΥΠΤ
    ΕΙΠΠΠΟΣΤΡΑΤΗΣΚΑΙΝΥΝΠΟΘΕΙΣΕΚΖΛΣΑΝΣΕΦΙΛ
    ΟΥΝΤΙΤΘΗΚΑΙΝΥΝΣΕΤΙΜΩΟΥΣΑΝΚΑΤΑΓΗΣ
    ΚΑΙΤΙΜΗΣΩΣΕΑΧΡΙΑΝΖΛΟΙΔΑΔΕΣΟΙΟΤΙΚΛΙΚΑΤΑΓ
5   ΗΣΕΙΠΕΡΧΡΗΣΤΟΙΣΓΕΡΑΣΕΣΤΙΝΠΡΑΤΕΙΣΟΙΤΙΜ
    ΑΙΤΙΤΘΗΠΑΡΑΦΕΡΣΕΦΟΝΕΙΠΛΟΥΤΩΝΙΤΕΚΕΙΝΤΑΙ

In the possession of the Earl of Guildford. Copied by Demetrius Schinas.

REMARKS.

I have not been able to examine the original stone ; but, in the copy sent to me, a letter of this form, Λ, occurs three times, instead of Ω ; in line 2. in ΖΩΣΑΝ ; in line 4. in ΑΧΡΙ ΑΝ ΖΩ ; in line 5. in ΠΡΩΤΕΙ.

L. 1. See a similar line in Boissonade's Commentary on the Actian inscription, published in his edition of Holstein's letters.

L. 4. Ἄχρις ἂν, μέχρις ἂν are often used in this sense; in Menander we read, δεῖ τοὺς πενομένους, ΜΕΧΡΙΣ ΑΝ ΖΩΣΙΝ, πονεῖν. Phil. Lip. p. 82; and in Anthol. H. Steph. p. 20. Ἄχρις ἂν ἧς ἄγαμος, " as long as you was unmarried."

Mr. Blomfield arranges the lines in the following manner; and remarks that a similar mixture of prose and verse is found in other inscriptions.

ἐνθάδε τὴν χρηστὴν τίτθην κατὰ γαῖα καλύπτει.
Ἱπποκράτης καὶ νῦν ποθεῖ σε.
καὶ ζῶσάν σ' ἐφίλουν, τίτθη, καὶ νῦν σ' ἔτι τιμῶ
θύσαν κατὰ γῆς, καὶ τιμήσω σε ἄχρι ἂν ζῶ.
οἶδ' ὅτι καὶ κατὰ γῆς, εἴπερ χρηστοῖς γέρας ἐστιν,
Πρώτη σοι τιμαὶ
ὦ τίτθη, παρὰ Φερσεφόνῃ Πλούτωνί τε κεῖνται.

L. 1. He refers to Anthol. Pal. ed. Jacobs, p. 306. ἐνθάδε τὴν ἱερὴν κεφαλὴν κατὰ γαῖα καλύπτει.

L. 2. He prefers Ἱπποκράτης, and interprets Κ, ΚΑΙ. Of this abbreviated form I find the following instances. Ἀγωνοθετήσαντα δὶς τοῦ τε κοινοῦ τῶν Γαλατῶν Κ δὶς τῶν ἱερων ἀγῶνων. Van. Dale. 292. In another inscription, given by Maffei, Mus. Veron. p. lix., we read, ΓΥΝΑΙΚΟΣΚΤΕΚΝΩΝΑΥΤΩΝΚ; in the Κ, in this instance, there is a horizontal line drawn through the middle. The third instance is of a later date, in Chandler, In. An. p. 18. ΥΠΕΡΕΥΧΗC ΚCΟΤΕΡΙΑC. κ. τ. λ.

XXVIII.

ΟΥΝΟΜΑΘΕΣΜΟΦΑΝΗΝΜΕΠΑΤΗΡΦΙΛΟΣΗΔΑΜΑΜΗΤΗΡ
ΚΙΚΛΗΣΚΟΝΔΥΕΡΟΥΠΡΙΝΘΑΝΑΤΟΙΟΤΥΧΕΙΝ
ΕΠΤΑΔΕΜΟΙΜΟΙΡΑΙΠΕΡΙΤΕΛΛΟΜΕΝΟΥΣΕΝΙΑΥΤΟΥΣ
ΕΚΛΩΣΑΝΤΟΜΙΤΟΙΣΑΤΡΟΠΑΓΡΑΨΑΜΕΝΑΙ
- - - ΚΑΙΠΑΝΤΩΝΜΕΚΑΛΩΝΟΣΑΠΑΙΣΙΦΕΡΙΣΤΟΙΣ
- - ΣΕΝΠΡΟΦΡΟΝΕΩΣΚΛΕΙΝΟΣΕΜΕΙΟΠΑΤΗΡ

ΠΑΣΑΣΓΑΡΛΟΙΒΑΣΤΕΚΑΙΟΣΣΑΜΕΜΗΛΕΘΕΟΙΣΙΝ
ΕΙΝΕΚΕΜΗΣΨΥΧΗΣΟΥΛΙΠΕΜΕΙΛΙΧΙΟΙΣ
ΚΑΙΓΑΡΜΕΥΜ - - - - ΘΥΗΠΟΛΟΙΗΡΕΣΙΩΝΗΝ
ΥΞΑΝΤΕΣ - - - ΙΑΣΑΝΕΥΚΛΕΙΗΝ
ΣΤΕΜΜΑΔΕ - - - - ΔΙΩΝΥΣΟΥΘΙΑΣΩΤΑΙ
ΠΥΡΦΟΡ - - - - - - - ΚΑΤΕΞΕΤΕΛΟΥΝ
- - ΛΟΝΕΕΙ - - - - - - - - - - - - ΣΛΟΓΟΣΑΝΔΡΩΝ
ΠΑΙΔΑ - - - - - - - - - - ΦΙΛΕΟΥΣΙΘΕΟΙ
ΤΟΥΝΕΚΑΜΟΙΠΑΤΕΡΕΣΘΛΕΦΑΝΗΣΕΙΜΗΚΕΤΙΣΕΙΟ
ΤΕΙΡΟΜΕΝΟΣΓΛΥΚΕΡΗΝΤΡΥΧΕΧΡΟΝΩΚΡΑΔΙΗΝ

On a stone in the possession of the Earl of Guildford, brought from Athens. The copy was communicated to me by Demetrius Schinas.

1 Οὔνομα Θεσμοφάνην με πατὴρ φίλος ἠδ' ἅμα μήτηρ
    Κίκλησκον δυεροῦ πρὶν θανάτοιο τυχεῖν·
    Ἑπτὰ· δέ μοι μοῖραι περιτελλομένους ἐνιαυτοὺς
    Ἐκλώσαντο μιτοῖς ἄτροπα γραψάμεναι.

5 —— καὶ πάντων με καλῶν ὅσα παισὶ φερίστοις
    —— σεν προφρονέως κλεινὸς ἐμεῖο πατὴρ·
    Πάσας γὰρ λοιβάς τε καὶ ὅσσα μέμηλε θεοῖσιν
    Εἰνεκ' ἐμῆς ψυχῆς οὐ λίπε μειλιχίοις·
    καὶ γάρ μ' ευμ - - - - - θυήπολοι ἡρεσιώνην

10 υ - αντες - - - - - - - ιασαν εὐκλείην·
    στέμμὰ δε - - ˙ - - - - - - Διανύσου θιασῶται
    Πυρφορ - - - - - - - - - κατεξετέλουν·
    λονεει - - - - - - - - - - - σλόγος ἀνδρῶν
    Παιδα - - - - - - - - - - φιλέουσι θεόι.

15 Τόυνεκά μοι πάτερ ἐσθλὲ Φανησει μηκέτι σεῖο
    Τειρόμενος γλυκερὴν τρύχε χρόνῳ κραδίην.

REMARKS.

L. 1. Thesmophanes belonged to a society under the protection of Bacchus. There were θίασοι, also sacred to Hercules and Apollo, and other deities. Isæus, in his speech on the estate of Astyphilus, mentions one under the care of Hercules. " My father introduced Astyphilus as a boy to the feasts of Hercules, in order to procure his admission into that society." See Sir W. Jones, Isæus. 112., εἰσήγαγεν εἰς θιάσους τοῦ Ἡρακλέους ἵνα μετέχοι τῆς κοινωνίας. In the Anthologia, (ed. H. Steph.) there is an epitaph on a young person who was member of a Thiasus. p. 258.

L. 2. ΔΥΕ. The word is found in Hesychius, but is not cited from any author. Jablonski, Pan. Ægy. l. ii. p. 292. quotes from Proclus, ψυχαῖς δυεραῖς.

L. 4. Μοιρῶν ὡς ἐπέκλωσε μίτος. Rein. Ins. p. 330.

Ib. Ἄτροπα. Μία τῶν μοιρῶν ἄτροπος, ἐπεὶ τὰ παρελθόντα πάντα ἄτρεπτα ἔστι. Auctor. de Mundo.

L. 8. " Mulciber apud vetustissimos Latinos est proprie μειλίχιος θεός." Scal. in Varronem, 37.

L. 9. εἰρεσιώνην. Ἡρίνεος, in Herod. i. 195, for εἰρίνεος.

L. 11. στέμμα. Τοῦσδ' ἐστεφάνωσαν οἱ θιασῶται. Ins. Ant. Chandler, p. 79.

L. 12. κατεκτελέω does not occur in the Lexicons; but we have ἐναποτελέω and συνεκτελέω. Στέμμα κατεξετέλουν, " They offered to me, they gave me a crown." ΤΕΛΕΩ, δῶ, παράσχω. Hesych.

L. 13, 14. Alluding to the opinion respecting the early death of those whom the gods love.

L. 15. The word ΦΑΝΗΣΕΙ requires explanation.

For the following conjectures and remarks I am indebted to Mr. Blomfield.

L. 2. περιτελλομένους ἐνιαυτούς. Il. θ. 404. 418.

L. 5. Qu. ΚΛΑΥΣΕΝ, καὶ πάντων. L. 6. ΠΛΗΣΕΝ, in Mr. Hughes's copy, taken at Athens, and ΚΛΙΗΕΝ in the beginning of line 5.

L. 9. καὶ γάρ μ' Εὐμόλποιο θυήπολοι εἰρεσιώνην καύσαντες (or τεύξαντες) - - - - - - ὤπασαν εὐκλείην.

L. 11. στέμμα δὲ κἀκ μύρτοιο Διωνύσου θιασῶται Πυρφόροι εἰς Ἀΐδαν μνῆμα κατεξετέλουν.

So Meleager. Στοργᾶς λείψανον εἰς Ἀΐδαν.

---

* Or, Π. ἐν τελεταῖς. See Aristoph. Ran. 325—330., and the Scholiast. — B.

L. 13. καλὸν ἐκεῖ βίοτον λαμπρόν τ' ἔχω, ὡς λόγος ἀνδρῶν,

Παῖδα νέον θνήσκειν ὃν φιλέουσι θεόι, or

Παῖδας ἔμεν κατὰ γᾶς οὓς φιλέουσι θεοί, as Mr. Hughes's copy has ΠΑΙΔΑΣΝ - - - ΡΑΣ.

L. 14. Ὃν ὁι θεοὶ φιλοῦσιν ἀποθνήσκει νέος. Menander, in Stob. cxxi.

XXIX.

ΙΣΙ
ΤΗΣΙΠΠΟΣ
ΤΗΣΙΠΠΟΥ
ΧΙΟΣ
ΞΛΑΝΗΦΟΡΟΣ

REMARKS.

L. 1. The dative ΙΣΕΙ occurs in an inscription found at Arta, in 1814. See Boissonade ; Com. on the Actian Inscription.

L. 5. The name is Ctesippus ; and his office was that of Me‑lanephorus. These worshippers, or priests, of Isis, are frequently mentioned in inscriptions. See Le Moyne, in his treatise De Me‑lanephoris.

XXX.

ΣΑΡΑΠΙΔΙΙΣΙΔΙΑΝΟΥΒΙΔΙ
ΔΙΟΓΕΝΗΣΦΑΝΙΟΥΑΛΑΒΑΔΙΔΕΥΣ
ΚΑΤΑΠΡΟΣ - - - ΜΑ

This, as well as the preceding, were found in Delos : both were copied by Mr. Cockerell.

REMARKS.

L. 2. ΑΛΑΒΑΝΔΕΥΣ is the Ethnical name. Steph. in v. A.

L. 3. Πρόσταγμα. Not an uncommon form in inscriptions ; in Latin, the word " Imperio" is used, as Imperio Veneris, Rein. pp. 442. 151. Some command of the Deity, to whom the conse‑cration was made, is supposed to have been given either by dream, oracle, or prophecy.

XXXI.

ΠΙΤΘΕΙΔΑΙΘΕΟΔΩΡΟΝΕΠΕΙΠΟΛΙΝΗΕΞΗΣΕ
ΠΕΥΚΑΛΙΜΟΙΣΑΓΑΝΗΣΜΗΔΕΣΙΠΡΟΣΤΑΣΙΗΣ
ΝΑΙΜΗΝΚΑΙΚΤΕΑΤΕΣΣΙΝΕΠΕΙΛΙΠΕΠΑΣΙΝΕΜΕΣΘΑΙ
ΑΡΓΥΡΟΝΕΣΓΕΝΕΗΝΠΑΣΑΝΕΠΕΣΣΟΜΕΝΩΝ

Copied at Epidaurus by Mr. Cockerell.

REMARKS.

L. 1. ΗΕΞ. This is the correction of Porson and Jacobs. Πόλιν
ἠέξησε scribendum esse docui in Animadv. nec aliter Porsonus. * See
the Adv. p. 40. In Chandler ΗΕΞΗΕΕ, in Mr. Cockerell ΗΕΞΗLΕ.
L. 3. ΚΤΕΑΤΕΙΤΗΝ in Chandler's copy, who corrects it to κτεάτισ-
τον. Κτεάτεσσιν gives a better sense: " Nay, even with his wealth;
since" &c.
L. 4. ΕΠΕΣΣΟΜΕΝΗΝ. Chandler, p. 80.

XXXII.

ΕΠΙΙΕΡΕΩΣΚΡΕΣΦΟΝΤΟΥΕΤΟΥΣPNZ
ΑΓΩΝΟΘΕΤΗΣ
ΤΙΒ - ΚΛΑΥΔΙΟΣΚΡΙΣΠΙΑΝΟΥΥΙΟΣΑΡΙΣΤΟΜΕΝΗΣ
ΙΕΡΟΘΥΤΑΙ
ΑΡΙΣΤΟΒΟΥΛΟΣΑΡΙΣΤΟΒΟΥΛΟΥΝΟΒΙΟΣΑΙΛΙΑΝΟΣ
ΓΡΑΜΜΑΤΕΥΣΣΟΦΟΣΧΑΛΕΙΔΟΦΟΡΟΣΚΛΑΥΔΙΟΣΤΡΟΙΛΟΣ

At Messene. From Mr. Cockerell; copied also by the Earl of
Aberdeen. Cyriacus, of Ancona, transcribed part of the inscription,
as far as ΑΡΙΣΤΟΜΕΝΗΣ. See Reines. p. 286, who explains the numerals PNZ.

XXXIII.

ΑΠΟΛΛΩΝΟΣ
ΔΑΦΝΑΦΟΡΙΩ
ΑΡΤΑΜΙΔΟΣ
ΣΟΩΔΙΝΑΣ

At Chæronea. †

---

* Vol. iii. part 2. 949. Anth. Palat.   † From Mr. Cockerell.

REMARKS.

L. 2. In this word the ἰῶτα is inserted according to the Æolo-Doric custom, as we shall have occasion to observe in the following inscription. 'Απόλλων δαφνηφόρος occurs in Plutarch. v. Peric.

XXXIV.

```
 1    - - ΟΣΜΕΛΑΝΤΙΧΩΑΡΧΟΝΤΟΣ
      ΤΟΝ - ΓΕΓ - ΑΨΑΝΤ - ΕΝΟΠΛΙΤΑ
      ΠΟΛΕΜΑΡΧΙΟΝΤΩΝ
      ΓΑΝΑΞΙΔΝΟΣ - - - ΣΑΩΝ - ΑΟ
 5    ΦΑ - - ΙΝΩ - - ΤΙΜΑΝΔΡΙΑ -
      ΜΟΥΑΓΙΟΝΤΟΣΓΑΔΩΝΟΣΠΟΛΥΚΡΙΤΙΩ
      ΓΡΑΜΜΑΤΙΔΔΟΝΤΟΣ
      ΧΑΦΙΣΟΔΩΡΩΣΑΜΙΩΝΙΩ
              ΞΙΣ      ΚΟΔΙΩΡΟΣ
10    ΑΡΧΙΑΣ       ΟΝΑΚΙΟΣ
      ΟΡΙΣ         ΡΟΥΛΙΟΣ
      ΣΑ  Χ  ΣΚ    ΙΓΙΤΟΝΙΟΣ
      ΠΟΙΔΙΚΟΣ - ΙΩ    ΟΥΣ - ΧΙΟΣ
      ΤΡΙΑΚΑΔΙΩΝΕΓΑΜΝΟΝΔΑΟ
15    ΑΓΑΘΟΝΛΙΩΝΙΟΣ
      ΑΝΤΙΓΕΝΕΙΣΑΝΤΙΓΩΝΙΟΣ
      ΟΑΛΩΝΙΔΑΣΜΝΑΣΙΩΝΙΟΣ
      ΔΙΩΝΤΑΝΑΚΩΝΙΟΣ
      ΜΝΑΣΙΩΝΚΑ  ΙΗΟΣ
20    ΜΕΝΕΚΡΑΤΕΙΣΜΟΛΩΝΙΟΣ
      ΗΛΗΜΩΝΝΙΩΝΙΟΣ
      ΕΥΟΦΕΛΙΝΟΣΑΓΟΛΛΟΔΩΡΙΟΣ
      ΑΜΦΙΤΙΜΟΣΕΥΙΣΤΙΟΣ
      ΕΥΦΡΟΝΙΣΚΟΣΟΝΑΣΙΜΑΣ
25    ΕΙΡΩΙΛΛΕΙΓΡΥΚΙΧΙΟΣ
      ΑΜΗ  ΝΣ    ΤΩΝΙΟΣ
      ΚΛΙΩΝ  ΩΡΟ  ΩΡΙΟΣ
      ΜΕΛΑΜΒΙΟΣΚΛΕΟΠΟΛΕΜΙΟΣ
      ΑΡΧΙΓΠΟΣ  ΕΛΙΤΩΝΙΟΣ
30    ΚΑΡΙΣΑΝΔΡΟΣΞΕΝΟΚΡΑΤΙΟΣ
      ΤΗΛΙΔΩΡΩΝΚΛΙΩΝΙΟΣ
      ΕΥΦΑΜΙΔΑΣΣΙΑΝΟΡΙΔΑΟ
      ΑΡΓΟΥΝΙΩΝ  ΝΙ  ΣΝΙΔΑΟ
```

At Topolias, in Bœotia ; copied by Mr. Cockerell. *

---

* L. 4. ΠΑΝΑΞΙΩΝΟΣ.   L. 5. The name ΦΙΛΙΝΟΣ is found on an Orchomenian marble seen by Dr. Clarke.   L. 6. Perhaps ΠΑΚΩΝΟΣ, a name which occurs on the

REMARKS.

Many letters appear to be wanting in this inscription. The Archon was Melantichus, a name found in Murat. ii. DCXLIX., but it is difficult to give a meaning to the second line; the Polemarchs were probably Panaxio, the son of Saonidas, and Philinus, the son of Timandrias. Pado, son of Polycritus, was head or leader of some musical exhibition ; Cephisodorus, son of Samio, was secretary. There is no adjective to denote the office filled by the names which follow in a long list.

The mode of writing the cases in these names deserves to be remarked. There is no doubt that ΜΟΛΩΝΙΟΣ, line 20, is the genitive of ΜΟΛΩΝ ; that ΚΛΙΩΝΙΟΣ, in line 31, is the genitive of ΚΛΙΩΝ (the Æolic ΚΛΕΩΝ.) ΝΙΩΝΙΟΣ, in l. 21, is in the same case, from ΝΙΩΝ, (ΝΕΩΝ), a name found in Demosthenes ; ΜΝΑΣΙ-ΩΝΙΟΣ, l. 17, is from ΜΝΑΣΙΩΝ, found in l. 19 ; and ΠΟΛΥΚΡΙΤΙΟΥ, l. 6, is the genitive of Polycritus, as ΔΑΦΝΑΦΟΡΙΩ was written in the preceding inscription for ΔΑΦΝΗΦΟΡΟΥ. The l is also redundant in l. 12, which may be read ΣΑΜΙΧΟΣ ΚΛΙΟΓΙΤΩΝΙΟΣ, or ΤΙΜΟΓΙ-ΤΩΝΙΟΣ, or ΘΙΟΓΙΤΩΝΙΟΣ. The same remark applies to l. 26, where we may read ΑΜΙΝΙΑΣ ΛΑΜΠΩΝΙΟΣ, a name occurring on another Bœotian marble, or ΠΛΑΤΩΝΙΟΣ ; and to l. 29, ΑΡΧΙΠΠΟΣ ΜΕΛΙΤΩΝΙΟΣ ; and to line 3.

L. 22. and 28. ΑΠΟΛΛΟΔΩΡΙΟΣ, ΚΛΕΟΠΟΛΕΜΙΟΣ. In an inscription found at Thebes, we read Διονύσιος Ἡρακλίδαο, Ὑπατόδωρος Ἀριστείδαο, Καφισόδωρος ΑΠΟΛΛΟΔΩΡΙΟΣ, Νίκων ΜΕΛΑΝΤΙΧΙΟΣ. Murator. t. ii. p. DXCV. ; and in another, ΖΩΙΛΟΣ ΑΛΕΞΑΝΔΡΟΥ, ΕΡΜΟΓΕΝΗΣ ΑΠΟΛΛΩΝΙΟΣ.

Instances of a redundant use of the I are not unfrequent in Æolo-

---

very antient vase of Mr. Dodwell; he was Μουσάγων, written here Μουαγίων; the I being inserted as in other parts of the inscription. In Muratori we read, ΜΟΥΣΩΝ ΕΝΑΡΧΟΝΤΙ ΜΗΤΡΟΔΩΡΩ, t. ii. DCLI. Some of the Dorians wrote Μωίκὰ for Μου-σικά. Etym. M. 391. and Μούα was in use; " In quibusdam dictionibus solebant Bœoti pro σ, h scribere, Muha pro Musa dicentes." Priscian. p. 25. L. 8. Perhaps ΣΑΜΙ-ΩΝΙΟΣ for ΣΑΜΙΩΝΟΣ. L. 10. Archias, son of Pythonax, a name found in Demos-thenes. L. 14. ΕΠΑΜΙΝΩΝΔΑΟ. L. 16. ΑΝΤΙΦΩΝΤΟΣ. L. 19. ΚΑΛΛΙΚΛΙΟΣ. L. 30. K is probably correct; as in the Cumean marble, ΥΠΑΡΚΟΙΣΑΣ for ΥΠΑΡΧΟΥ-ΣΑΣ.

Doric inscriptions. In one copied in Thessaly by Colonel Leake, and printed in this volume, we read the name ΠΟΛΥΜΝΙΑΣΤΟΣ; on another, found by him and Mr. Cockerell, in Bœotia, and published by the former in the Class. Journ. with an explanation, ΤΙΟΥΧΑΝ occurs for ΤΥΧΑΝ. Δαμοθέτου, in Chishull, An. As. p. 88, is Δαμιοθέτου, in a Doric decree, p. 118. An Agrigentine marble has ἔμειν, ἀναθέμειν, γεγόνειν (for γεγονέναι,) and the Dorians said βοαθησιῶ, προλειψιῶ, ἐμμενιῶ, πραξίομεν, χαριξιόμεθα. * Οἱ Δωριεῖς ἄσσον ἄσσιον φασὶ, καὶ μᾶλλον μάλλιον. Eustat. 1643. l. 32.

XXXV.

```
1   ΒΟΙΩΤΩΝΤΑ - - ΟΔΑΝΕΘΕΙΚΑΝ
    ΤΗΣΧΑΡΙΤΕΣΣΙΚΑΤΤΑΜΜΑΝΤΕΙΙΑΝ
    ΤΩΑΠΟΛΛΩΝΟΣΑΡΧΟΝΤΟΣ
    ΣΑΜΙΑΟΙΣΜΕΙΝΙ - - ΤΑΟΕ - - ΗΩ
5   ΑΦΕΔΡΙΑΤΕΥΟΝΤΩΝ
    ΜΕΛΑΝΝΙΟΣΝΙΚΟΚΛΕΙΟΣΕΡΧΟΜΕΝΙΩ
    ΗΣΧΡΙΩΝΟΣΘΕΡΣΑΝΔΡΙΧΩΚΟΡΩΝΕΙΟΣ
    ΑΡΝΟΚΛΕΙΟΣΑΝΙΙΟΧΙΔΑΟΑΝΘΑΔΟΝΙΩ
    ΑΡΙΣΤΩΝΟΣΜΕΝΝΙΔΑΟΘΕΙΣΠΙΕΙΟΣ
10  ΠΡΑΞΙΤΕΛΙΟΣΑΡΙΣΤΟΚΛΙΔΑΟΘΕΙΒΗΩ
    ΟΙΟΜΝΑΣΤΩΕΡΜΑΙΚΩΤΑΝΑΓ ΙΩ
    ΓΟΥΘΩΝΟΣΚΑΛΛΙΓΙΤΟΝΟΣΩΡΩΠΙΩ
    ΓΡΑΜΜΑΤΕΥΟΝΤΟΣ
    ΔΙΟΚΛΕΙΟΣΔΙΟΦΑΝΤΩΠΛΑΤΑΕΙΟΣ
15  ΜΑΝΤΕΥΟΜΕΝΩ
    ΔΙΝΙΑΟΕΡ - - ΤΙΩΝΟΣΟΣ - - ΠΙΕΙΟΣ
    ΟΙΠΡΟΠΙΟΝΙΟΣ
    ΕΥΜΕΙ - - - ΑΟΕΡΧΟΜΕΝΙΩ
    ΑΤΕΥΟΝΤΟΣ
20  ΩΛΑΜΠΡΙΑΟ - - - - - ΟΤΩΕΡΧΟΜΕΝΙΩ
```

At Orchomenus. † The inscription relates to a consecration of a

---

* Maitt. on Oxf. Marb. p. 623. He makes a remark which has been confirmed by many inscriptions recently discovered. Hæc vocum monstra a communi formatione et usu adeo aliena, oscitantibus marmorariis imputarem, nisi sæpius repeterentur; et si forsan plura superessent monumenta gentium illarum Dialectis exarata, permulta hujusmodi occurrerent a consuetá Græcorum lingua haud minus discrepantia.

† From Mr. Cockerell. Copied also by Col. Leake. L. 4. ΤΑΟΘΕΙΒΗΩ. L. 8. ΑΝΤΙΟΧΙΔΑΟ. L. 11. ΘΙΟΜ ―――― ΤΑΝΑΓΡΙΩ. L. 16. ΕΡΜΟΤΙΩΝΟΣ ΘΕΙΣ. L. 18. ΕΥΜΕΝΙΔΑΟ. L. 20. ΛΑΜΠΡΙΑΟ. Akerblad.

Tripod to the Graces, who were particularly reverenced at Orchomenus. (Theoc. Idyll. xvi. 104.)

REMARKS.

L. 2. Κατὰ τὴν τοῦ θεοῦ μαντέιαν. Plato. " Ex Dei Oraculo." H. Steph.

L. 4, &c. Samias, son of Ismenias, Theban, was Archon; * Melas, son of Nicocles, of Orchomenus ; Æschrio, son of Thersandrichus, of Corone ; Arnocles, son of Antiochidas, of Anthedon ; Aristo, son of Menidas, of Thespiæ; Praxiteles, son of Aristoclidas, of Thebes; Theomnestus, son of Hermaïcus, of Tanagra; Pytho, son of Calligiton, of Oropus, raised or placed the tripod ; Diocles was secretary ; Dinias was augur; Eumenidas was expounder of the oracle; and Lamprias was priest.

L. 1. In Col. Leake's copy, ΒΟΙΩΤΟΙΤΟΝΤΡΙΠΟΔΑΑΝΕΘΕΙΚΑΝ.

L. 4. Ismenias occurs in another inscription copied at Orchomenus : it was the name also of a celebrated Theban musician. See Vales. Em. lib. ii.

Ib. In Col. Leake's copy, ΘΕΙΒΗΩ. In an Orchomenian inscription, copied by Dr. Clarke, we have ΘΕΙΒΕΙΟΣ, where the ΕΙ is used both for Η and ΑΙ.

L. 5. This word appears without any variation in the two copies of the marble. Perhaps it is synonymous with ΑΦΙΔΡΥΩ, " erigo, colloco," alluding to the placing or raising the Tripod. The Greeks said, ἱερῶ and ἱερατεύω, probably also ἱδρυω and ἱδρατεύω ; the second ι in ἱδριατεύω is inserted as in other words in the Bœotian dialect, already referred to. The Ε is substituted for Ι in ἀφεδριατεύω, according to the Æolo-Doric custom ; ΑΠΥΔΕΔΟΣΘΑΙ is found in the Cumean inscription for ΑΠΟΔΙΔΟΣΘΑΙ. Caylus, Rec. t. ii.

L. 17. Read ΘΙΟΠΡΟΠΙΟΝΤΟΣ, according to the Bœotian dialect, for ΘΕΟΠΡΟΠΕ. Θεόπροπος had two meanings † ; in one sense it was synonymous with Προφήτης, as in the present instance. It was the business of the " propheta" to interpret and put into writing the answer

---

* ΜΕΛΑΝΟΣ υἱός. Ælian. Π. Ι. l. 3. † Larcher, Herod. vol. iv. p. 331.

of the oracle. *   Col. Leake's copy gives the termination ΟΝΤΟΣ, which confirms the proposed reading; and in l. 7., ΘΕΡΣΑΝΔΡΙΑΟ. See Class. Jour. vol. xiii.

L. 19. Read ΙΕΡΑΤΕΥΟΝΤΟΣ.

XXXVI.

ΑΛΥ

E:II:ΣIΔHPIAEΞOΓHΣ:III:
ΚΛΡΚΙΝΩ ΙΙΞΥΛΙΝΑΤΑ
ΔΕΕΞΑΛΕΙΠΤΡΟΝ·I ΚΙΒ
5   ΩΤΟΙ III·ΙΚΡΙΑΓΕΡΙΤΟΕ
ΔΟΣΕΝΤΕΛΗΘΡΟΝΟΣ I:
ΔΙΦΡΟΣΙΒΑΘΡΑ·IIII·ΘΡΟΝ
ΟΣΜΙΚΡΟΣ:I.ΚΛΙΝΗΣΜΙ
ΚΡΑ:I:ΒΑΘΡΟΝΑΝΑΚΛΙΣ
10   ΙΝΕΧΟΝ:I:ΚΙΒΩΤΙΑΜΙΚ
ΑΡΑ·III:ΒΑΘΡΟΝΥΓΟΚΡΑΤ
ΗΡΙΟΝ:I:ΚΙΒΩΤΙΟΝΠΛΑ
ΤΥ·I ΕΝΤΩΙΑΜΦΙΠΟΛΕΙ
ΩΙΤΑΔΕΧΑΛΚΙΟΝΘΕΡΜ
15   ΔΝΤΗΡΙΟΝ I:ΧΕΡΟΝΠΤ
ΡΟΝ:I:ΦΙΑΛΑ:II ΠΕΛΕΚΥΣ:I:
ΟΧΑΟΣ·I ΜΑΧΑΙΡΙΑ·III
ΛΙΝΑ:II:ΧΑΛΚΙΟΝΕΙ
ΟΤΗΡΙΟΝ:I:ΑΡΥΣΤΙΧΟ
20   Σ:I:ΗΘΜΟΣ:I:

From Ægina. †

The quæstors at Athens (ΟΙ ΤΑΜΙΑΙ ΤΗΣ ΘΕΟΥ ΚΑΙ ΤΩΝ ΘΕΩΝ) gave an account every year to their successors, of the sacred offerings, or vessels, or ornaments, which had been entrusted to their care by those who preceded them. The weight, the number, the nature of these sacred articles, are recorded in some imperfect but antient inscriptions published by Chandler. Among these ἱερὰ χρήματα, are, ΣΤΕΦΑΝΟΙ, ΦΙΑΛΑΙ, ΑΠΟΡΑΝΤΗΡΙΟΝ, ΘΥΜΙΑΤΗΡΙΟΝ, ΚΑΡΧΗΣΙΟΝ, ΟΙΝΟΧΟΑΙ, ΚΡΑΤΗΡ, ΜΑΧΑΙΡΑ. (Chandler, p. xv. p. xvii. p. xviii.)

---

* See Valck. in Herod. p. 555., also, Chishull, Mil. Ins. in An. As.
† Copied by Mr. Cockerell.   L. 5. ΠΕΡΙ.   L. 11. ΥΠΟΚ.   L. 15. ΘΕΡΜΑ;   L. 17. ΜΟΧΛΟΣ.   L. 18. ΚΛΙΝΑ.   L. 19. ΛΟΤΗ.. Akerblad.

The inscription before us contains an inventory; or list, of various vessels, instruments, and offerings belonging to a temple at Ægina, in which may be seen some of the preceding articles. It is of antient date, as we may infer from the mode of dividing the words in general with the vertical stops, found only in monuments of remote times. The numerals are placed in the same manner as in the inscriptions given in Chandler. The Κιβωτοὶ and Κιβώτια are mentioned in the Ægina marble; and in Chandler's work the contents of these sacred chests, κιβωτὸι, are noticed.

REMARKS.

L. 1, 2. ΑΛΥΣΙΕ or ΑΛΥΣΕΕ, " two chains." " Three irons from within a window." ΟΠΗΣ. ὀπὴ, θυρίς. Hesych. 'Εκ, used as ἀπὸ, to denote the removal from the inside of a place. Matth. G. G. § 574.

L. 3. Read ΚΑΡΚΙΝΩ. ΙΙ. It is uncertain whether we are to refer the word to Καρκῖνος, an instrument or machine, of a shape like the claws of a crab, Καρκῖνος λίθους ἑλών· εἴποις δ' ἂν καὶ μηχανὴν λιθαγωγόν, (Jul. Polluc. l. x. 1332.), or to κάρκινος, forceps. The former is defined, Instrumentum fabrile, quo saxa tollebant, vel comprehendebant; a cancrinis pedibus ita dictum, nimirum qui ad quid tenendum certe aptissimi. Jungerm. in Polluc.

L. 4. " A pot to hold ointment." 'Εξάλειπτρον is rendered, in our English version of Job, " a pot of ointment." xli. 31.

L. 5. " The scaffolding round the statue complete;' or, " the wooden rails round it." As we do not know on what occasion or for what purpose this ἀναγραφὴ was made, we cannot give the precise meaning of ἴκρια. 'Εδος is sometimes a " temple." (D'Arnaud de Diis Paredris.)

L. 8. 10. Both ΣΜΙΚΡΟΣ and ΜΙΚΡΟΣ appear in this inscription. In line 10. ΜΙΚΑΡΑ requires some alteration. Probably ΜΙΚΕΡΑ was a Greek word. See Blomfield, ad v. 446. Pers. Gloss.

L. 7. " A seat with a back; one chair; four stools." The θρόνος is often mentioned in Pausanias. See also Herod. i. 14. I have adopted the definition in Hesychius, θ. ἀνάκλιτος δίφρος. Quatremére,

4 D 2

in his work on the " Jupiter Olympien," gives a representation of the sacred Thronus.

L. 8. ΚΛΙΝΗ, " one small pulvinar or Lectisternium." Κλίνή τε ἱερὰ τῆς Ἀθηνᾶς, Paus. Arcad. ; and in his Phocica, speaking of a temple of Æsculapius, κλίνη δὲ ἐν δεξίω κεῖται τοῦ ἀγάλματος. " The devotion of the Pagans inclined them to think that the gods ought not to want any thing conducive to their ease and satisfaction." Seller, Antiq. of Palmyra. 367.

The *Sella* of the Latins was likewise part of the furniture of a temple. " De sellâ Cæsaris bene tribuni." says Cicero, ad Att. l. xv. Ep. 3. " The tribunes have done well in not suffering the chair of Cæsar to be placed in the theatre." Among other honours decreed to him before his death, it was ordered that a gilt chair should be placed for him in the senate-house, and at the public games. This chair resembled those on which the statues of the gods were placed. Dio and Suetonius, therefore, consider the honour intended for him as one of a sacred kind. See Mongault's note on the passage of Cicero.

L. 9. ΒΑΘΡΟΝ, " a stool or small seat, with a back to it." See the description of the δίφρος Πτολεμαϊκὸς in the Monum. Aduli. Chishull, An. As. καὶ τὸ ἀνακλιτὸν τὸ ὄπισθεν τοῦ θρόνου, " the back of the chair." Ἀνακλιτοὶ δίφροι, vocantur sellæ, quæ anaclinteria habent, aut pluteos dorsuales quibus sedentium dorsum acclinari posset. *

L. 11. ΥΠΟΚ. Ἐπίστατον, in the oldest of the two Sigean inscriptions, is explained in the more recent one by ὑποκρητήριον, a word which occurs in no writer. The diminutive ὑποκρητηρίδιον is in Herod. l. i. c. 26. The word means " a stand," on which a cup is placed; " basis," in Latin. †

L. 13. ΑΜΦΙΠΟΛΙΩΙ, the ΕΙ in the original being written for Ι, as in other monuments ; Εἰδίαν γᾶν, in the Tab. Herac. ΔΙΕΙΤΡΕΦΕΣ, in an antient inscription in Spon ; and ΑΝΑΚΤΕΙ, on the Lydo-Phrygian

---

* See Salmas. in his Confut. anim. An. Cercoetii. de Pallio. 128.
† Chishull, An. As. 35.

sepulchre. See this volume, p. 207. We have περιπολίῳ, in an inscription edited by Chishull, An. As. 159. ἐκ τῶν ἐν τῷ περιπολίῳ τῆς θεοῦ, " ex iis qui in sacro Deæ circuitu degunt ;" and perhaps Αμφιπ· was the place round or near the temple, where those in waiting on the Deity resided. 'Αμφιπολεύω ἱερὸν Διός, " in Jovis templo ministro." Herodotus.

L. 14. In some parts, the numeral seems to be omitted, as in this line, after XAΛKION ; and in line 9., after BAΘPON. Among the gifts noticed in the Attal. Mon. in Chishull, p. 142, is χάλκιον τετραχοιαῖον, " vas æreum capacitate quatuor congiorum."

L. 16. Of the different offerings in the antient temples, none seem to have been more numerous than φιάλαι. It is not easy to render the word in English ; for sometimes it appears that the ἔκπωμα was borne upon a φιάλη. Xenoph. Cyr. lib. i. c. 3. Here, therefore, it is a salver, or waiter ; " Assiette," Larcher, Herod. lib. iii. The word, when it occurs in the Septuagint, is translated in our version " Basin ;" but the expression in the Apocalypse, c. xvi. ἐκχέατε τὰς φιάλας suggests a different form.

L. 18. Perhaps XAΛKIONEIΣ
ΠΟΤHPION. So in the offering, or gifts, mentioned in Chishull, Pseph. Att. 142. λεκάνην ἐς ποτήρια, " pelvem ad pocula ;" or ΛOTHPION. λευτήρια etiam inter pocula recenset Epigenes apud Athen. l. xi. p. 486. *

L. 19. " One pitcher ; one strainer."

XXXVII.

MΥΣΤΩNHГHTHPA
ΠOΛΥZHΛONΠATPOΣ
EΣΘΛOΥΞEINAГOPOΥ
MHTPOΣΘEPMIΠΠIΔOΣ
ГNZAΘEOIΣINEIΣEΘEAIN
ΦPΩN

At Eleusis. †

* Note to Hesych. in v. Λουτ. † Copied by Mr. Cockerell. L. 5. EN.

574 GREEK INSCRIPTIONS.

Part of a metrical inscription in honour of Polyzelus, Hierophant, son of Xeinagoras and Thermippis.

REMARKS.

L. 1. " Mystagogi proprie dicebantur qui Mystas, hoc est, initiatos deducebant." * Ἡγητῆρα περίπλοον, in Crinagoras, is thus explained by Salmasius ; " περιηγήτην, qui per singula ducit memorabilia quæque ostendens et describens." In the marbles of Cyzicus, and in an inscription copied at Smyrna, there is mention of the ΜΥΣΤΑΡΧΗΣ, and ΠΑΤΡΟΜΥΣΤΗΣ.

L. 5. ΘΕΑΙΝ. Ceres and Proserpine. Παρὰ τῷ ταῖν θεαῖν ἱεροφάντῃ. Eunapius, in v. Max. Sometimes a different declension occurs ; μεγαλαῖν θεαῖν στεφάνωμα of Soph. Œd. C. 673, is quoted by Plutarch, Sympos. iii. c. 1. ; μεγάλων θεῶν σ. Τὼ θεώ, τοῦτ᾽ ἐστι τὰς θεὰς, τὴν Δήμητρα καὶ τὴν Κόρην. Eust. ad Il. θ. 723. See Blomfield ad Pers. v. 186., App. ad Notas.

XXXVIII.

ΑΓΑΘΗΙΤΥΧΗΙ
ΑΠΟΛΛΩΝΙ
ΠΡΟΣΤΑΤΗΡΙΩ - - ΙΟΤΡΟΓΑΙΩΙ
ΑΓΥΕΙ

From Athens. †

These three titles are found in Sophocles, Aristophanes, and Demosthenes : in the Electra of the first, v. 637. Φοῖβε προστατήριε ; in the Plutus of the second, Ἄπολλον ἀποτρόπαιε ; in the Oration of the third, πρὸς Μακαρ᾽ Ἀπόλλωνι Ἀγυιεῖ. Πρεστατήριος. " Tutelaris." See Blomfield, Gloss. ad v. 445. Sep. C. Th.

XXXIX.

1   ΑΓΑΘΗΙΤΥΧΗΙ
ΗΠΑΤΡΙΣΟΥΛ
ΠΙΑΝΜΑΡΚΕΛΛΑΝ
ΙΕΡΑΣΑΜΕΝΗΝ

* Vales. Am. Mar. 287.   † Copied by Mr. Cockerell.

```
 5 ·  ΤΗΣΑΡΤΕΜΙΔΟΣ·
       ΑΡΧΙΕΡΕΙΑΝΤΗΣ
       ΑΣΙΑΣΝΑΩΝΤΩΝΕΝ
       ΣΜΥΡΝΗΑΓΩΝΟ
       ΘΕΤΙΝΤΡΙΣΤΗΣ
10     ΠΑΤΡΙΔΟΣΙΕΡΕΙ
       ΑΝΔΙΑΒΙΟΥΤΗΣ
       ΜΗΤΡΟΣΤΩΝ
          ΘΕΩΝ
```

At Thyatira. *

REMARKS.

L. 4. Sometimes with a dative, as ἱερασάμενος τῇ Πάτριδι. Van Dale. 231.

L. 6. The distinction, according to Valesius, between Ἀρχιερεὺς, the Pontiff, Sacerdos; and ἱερεὺς, Flamen, was this; the temples and shrines of the province were under the care of the former; the latter attended only to the sacred rites and ceremonies belonging to the worship of the deities in different towns.

L. 7. " The temples of Asia at Smyrna." Other inscriptions mention the temples of Asia at Sardes; one copied by Spon records the Ἀρχιερεὺς τῆς Ἀσίας ναῶν τῶν ἐν Περγάμῳ.

L. 8. Female Agonothetæ, ἀγωνοθετούσαι, are mentioned in Pausanias. Eliac.

L. 11. ΔΙΑΒΙΟΥ. The Latin form, abridged, is FLPP, Flamen Perpetuus. Vales. ad Euseb. 174. ·

XL.

```
ΜΥΡΙΧΟΣΠΟΛΥΚΡΑΤΙΟΣΙΑΡΩΝΥΜΟΣΔΙΟΓΙΤΟΝΟΣ
ΑΝΔΡΕΣΣΙΧΟΡΑΓΕΙΣΑΝΤΕΣΝΙΚΑΣΑΝΤΕΣΔΙΟΝΥΣΟΙ
ΑΝΕΘΕΙΚΑΝΤΙΜΩΝΟΣΑΡΧΟΝΤΟΣΑΥΛΙΟΝΤΟΣΚΛΕΙΝΙΑΟ
ΑΙΔΟΝΤΟΣΑΛΚΙΣΘΕΝΙΟΣ
```

At Orchomenus. †

This inscription relates to an offering or consecration of a tripod, by

---

* From Mr. Cockerell. ·　　　　　† Copied by Mr. Cockerell and Col. Leake.

Myrichus and Hieronymus, who had been Choregi, or " Furnishers of a chorus *," and had been victors in a Dionysiac contest.

REMARKS.

L. 2. The victory gained by the Choregus is expressed in various ways ; χόρω δ᾽ εκτήσατο νίκην 'Ανδρῶν. Theoc. Epig. 12. Sometimes the elliptical form occurs, νικᾶν 'Ανδρῶν, or παιδῶν. † In Spon, as in the present instance, we read ΘΡΑΣΥΛΛΟΣ ΑΝΕΘΗΚΕΝ ΧΟΡΗΓΩΝ ΝΙΚΗΣΑΣ ΑΝΔΡΑΣΙΝ, and in Lysias, ('Αποл. Δωροδ.) ἀνδράσι χορηγῶν εἰς Διονύσια ενίκησα καὶ ἀνήλωσα σὺν τῇ τοῦ τρίποδος αναθέσει π. δ. where τρίποδος αναθέσει explains ἀνέθεικαν in our inscription.

XLI.

```
ΝΟΣΣΟΣΜΥΡΜΙΔΟΝΟΣΚΟΥΡΑΝΔΙΟΣΑΝΘΕΤΟΠΑΙΔΑ
ΑΡΤΕΜΙΝΕΥΟΛΒΩΙΤΩΙΔΕΠΑΡΑΠΡΟΠΥΛΩΙ
ΦΟΙΒΩΙΑΓΥΕΙΤΑΝΔΕΝΕΜΩΝΧΑΡΙΝΟΥΠΕΡΙΚΡΑΤ
ΔΑΦΝΑΣΕΥΣΑΜΟΥΣΚΛΩΝΑΣΑΝΑΣΤΕΦΕΤΑΙ
ΑΛΛΑΣΤΟΙΤΙΜΑ - - - - - - - - - - - ΕΠΙΤΩΙΔΕ
ΩΣΑ - - ΤΑΜΕΓΑΛΑ - - - - - - ΕΠΕΥΣΕΒΙΑΙ
```

From Halicarnassus. In the possession of the Earl of Guildford. Copied by Demetrius Schinas.

REMARKS.

L. 1. Διὸς κόρης 'Αρτέμιδος. Eur. Iphig. Au. 1543. Ἄρτεμι, παῖ Διός. 1570.

L. 3. ΝΕΜΩΝΧΑΡΙΝ. Ἀπονέμουσα χαρίτας. Mon. Att. Chishull. 142. ; at the end of the line, read ΚΡΑΤΙ.

L. 4. Δαφνῆς κλῶνα. Meleager, in Anthol.

XLII.

```
ΙΔΡΙΝΑΘΗΝΑΙΗΣ
ΠΑΝΤΩΝΔΙΟΝΥΣΙΟΝ
ΕΡΓΩΝ
```

HΞΕΙΝΗΠΑΤΑΡΩΝΓΗΜΕ
ΛΑΒΟΥΣΑΚΡΑΤΕΙ
ΤΜΩΛΟΥΑΠ - - - ΕΛΟΕΝ
ΤΟΣ
ΕΧΩΔΕΚΛΕΟΣΚΑΙΕΝ
Α - ΤΟΙΣ
ΩΔΕΙΩΜΕΓΑΛΗΝ
ΑΜΦΙΒΑΛΩΝΟΡΟΦΗΝ

Copied by Capt. Beaufort at Patara.

REMARKS.

L. 1. 3. Ἀθην· — ἔργων. Ἔργα δ᾽ Ἀθηναίη γλαυκώπιδι ἰσοφαρίζοι. Il. I. ;
also in Anthol. Palat. Appen. ii. 861.

ἔργα δ᾽ Ἀθαναία τερπνὰ σαοφροσύνας.

L. 6. Probably ΑΜΠΕΛΟΕΝΤΟΣ, as it is corrected in Beaufort's
Caramania. " Tmolus croco florentissimus et *vitibus* consitus dicitur." Plin. H. N. v. 24.

L. 9. ΑΣΤΟΙΣ. " I have glory also among the citizens of Patara,
having placed a large roof round the Odeum."

XLIII.

```
 1    ΑΝΤΙΟΥΑΡΧΟΝΤΟΣΑΓΩΝΟΘΕΤΟΥΝ - - -
      ΠΟΠΛΙΟΥΚΟΡΝΗΛΙΟΥΤΟΥΠΟΠΛΙΟΥΥΙΟΥΙ
      ΜΑΙΟΥΤΩΝΤΗΣΤΙ - Ω - ΣΩΤΗΙ - ΩΝΠΡΩ
      ΛΠΟΤΟΥΠΟΛΕΜΟΥΙΕΡΑΤΕΥΟΝΤΟΣΔΕΤΟ
 5    ΟΣΤΟΥΣΩΤΗΡΟΣΘΕΩΜΝΗΣΤΟΥΤΟΥΠΑΡΑ
      ΜΟΝΟΥΟΙΔΕΕΝΙΚΩΝ
         ΣΑΛΠΙΣΤΗΣ
      ΟΝΗΣΙΜΟΣΔΕΞΩΝΟΣΚΟΡΩΝΕΥΣ
         ΚΗΡΥΞ
10    ΦΙΛΟΚΛΗΣΝΙΚΟΚΛΕΟΥΣΘΗΒΑΙΟΣ
      ΕΝΚΩΜΙΩΙΛΟΓΙΚΩ
      ΠΟΛΥΞΕΝΟΣΚΑΦΙΣΟΤΙΜΟΥΑΚΡΑΙΦΙΕΥΣ
      ΕΠΩΝΠΟΙΗΤΗΣ
      ΠΡΩΤΟΓΕΝΗΣΠΡΩΤΑΡΧΟΥΘΕΣΠΙΕΥΣ
      ΡΑΨΩΔΟΣ
```

In the church of Carditza, on the site of the antient Acræphia, in
Bœotia ; copied by Mr. Hawkins.

REMARKS.

L. 1. The first word is part of the Archon's name. The Agonotheta was Publius Cornelius; the third line is imperfect in many letters; in the fourth we find that the priest was Soter Theomnestus, son of Paramonus. A name before Soter requires correction.

L. 7. The form of this word varies; here, and in an inscription copied by Dr. Clarke, it is σαλπιστής; in one at Orchomenus, of antient date, transcribed by the same traveller, we read ΣΑΛΠΙΓΚΤΑΣ. " Sincerior scriptura," says Dorville, " σαλπιγτὴς, συριγκτὴς, ut optimus codex in Theoc. Idyll. viii. 9." Charit. p. 660.

L. 11. ΕΝΚΩΜ; a singular expression : there is, however, mention in an inscription found at Thebes, and published in Muratori, DCLI., of two persons who were distinguished, the one by his encomium on the Emperor, the other by his praise of the Muses. Ζωσιμὸς ἐγκωμιό-γραφος εἰς τὸν Αυτοκράτορα ; and Publius Maximus wrote ἐγκώμιον εἰς Μούσας. Λογικὸς is " eloquens."

XLIV.

```
 1   ΠΡΟΦΗΤΗΣΛΛΛΑΚΑΙΚ
     ΙΑΡ - ΙΣΜΑΡΚΟΥΟΥΛΠΙΟΥ
     ΒΙΑΝΟΥΔΑΜΑΤΟΣΚΥΡΕΙΝ
     ΒΙΑΝΟΣΦΙΛΕΑΣΛΑΒΩΝ
 5   ΤΗΣΠΑΤΡΙΔΟΣΤΗΝΠΡΟΦΗΤΕ
     ΑΝΑΚΛΗΡΩΤΕΙΕΤΩΝΩΝΕΙΚΟ - · ΕΠ
     ΩΝΣΤΕΦΑΝΗΦΟΡΟΣΓΥΜΝΑΣΙΑΡΧΟΣ
     ΠΑΤΕΡΩΝΤΕΝΟΥΣΝΑΥΑΡΧΩΝΚΑΙΚΙ - ·
     ΤΩΝΠΑΤΡΟΣΦΑΔΑΜΑΜΗΤΡΟΣΔΕΦ -
10   ΒΙΑΝΗΣΓΛΑΦΥΡΑΣΑΡΧΙΕΡΕΩΝΤΩΝΣΕ
     ΒΑΣΤΩΝΠΟΙΗΣΑΝΤΩΝΘΕΩΡΙΑΣΕΠΙ
     ΜΕΡΑΣΔΕΚΑΚΑΙΜΟΝΟΜΑΧΙΑΣΑΠΟΤ
     ΜΟΥΣΕΠΙΗΜΕΡΑΣΔΕΚΑΔΥΩΚΑΙΑΡΧΙΕΡ
     ΩΝΤΗΣΙΩΝΙΑΣΠΟΙΗΣΑΝΤΩΝΔΕΚ - · Ε
15        ΣΕ   ΚΑΙΔΗΜΟΘΟΙΝΙΑ   \ΙΓΥΜΝ
               ΟΣΕ            ΠΟΛ
```

Found at Ieronda *, the site of the temple of the Didymean Apollo.

---

* Copied by Mr. Whittington.

It appears from a remark in the Ant. Asi. p. 93., that Chishull had seen the present inscription, or received a copy of it from some traveller; for he quotes the beginning ΠΡΟΦΗΤΗΣΑΜΑΚΑΙΚΡΙΤΑΡΧΗΣ ΦΛΑΒΙΑΝΟΣΛΑΒΩΝΠΑΡΑΤΗΣΠΑΤΡΙΔΟΣΤΗΝΠΡΟΦΗΤΕΙΑΝΑΝΑΚΛΗΡ ΩΤΕΙ. It is fortunate that the original was sufficiently perfect to preserve Κριτάρχης; (see the first and second lines). The word is not found in any other inscription, or in any writer.

REMARKS.

L. 1. ΚΡΙΤ. Κριτὴς, " Conjector," ὀνειροκρίτης. See Blomfield ad Pers. Gloss. v. 23. Phileas was not only " Propheta," expounder of the oracle, but also head of the Oneirocritics, or dream interpreters, of the τεράτων καὶ ἐνυπνίων ἐξηγηταί.

L. 3. The name Damas occurs in an inscription copied by Dr. Askew, at Athens (Corsini, In. Att. p. x.); and on a marble of Eleusis we have the genitive, ΑΡΧΙΑΣΔΑΜΑ. ΥΟΣ is written in this form in other inscriptions. ΚΥΡ is here the name Quirinus.

L. 8. ΠΑΤΕΡΕΣ, " majores," as Patres in Latin. Perhaps ΚΡΙΤΑΡΧΩΝ in this and the following line. In l. 9. correct, ΦΛ.

L. 10. We have already seen a female in the high office of Ἀρχιέρεια τῆς Ἀσίας ναῶν. No. 38.

L. 11. Θεωρία. Omnis generis spectacula hâc voce complectitur Aristotel. Polit. vii. See Stoeber ad Th. Mag. 447.

L. 14, 15. I supply ΚΑΙΕ
ΠΙΔΟΣΕΙΣΚΑΙΔΗΜΟΘΟΙΝΙΑΣΚΑΙΓΥΜΝ
ΑΣΙΑΡΧΙΑΣ. οἰνοδοσίας καὶ γυμνασιαρχίας occurs in an inscription copied by Capt. Beaufort in Asia Minor; ἐπίδοσις is Congiarium.

VERSION.

Quirinus Flavianus Phileas having received from his country by lot the office of Propheta and Critarcha at the age of twenty-seven, (erected this). He was crown-bearer and gymnasiarch; he sprung from ancestors who were commanders of fleets and ——. His father, Flavianus Damas, and his mother, Flaviana Glaphyra, were pontiffs of the Augusti; they represented shews for ten days, and —— gladiatorial exhibitions for twelve; they were pontiffs of Ionia, and gave presents and feasts to the people, and gymnastic entertainments.

XLV.

```
 1    ΥΔΡΟΦΟΡΟΣΑΡΤΕΜΙ
      ΔΟΣΠΥΘΙΗΣΜΑΛΙΑΡΟΥ
      ΦΕΙΝΑΠΑΤΡΟΣΛΕΥΚΙ
      ΟΥΜΑΛΙΟΥΣΑΤΟΡΝΙΝΟΥ
 5    ΠΡΟΦΗΤΟΥΚΑΙΣΤΕΦΑ
      ΝΗΦΟΡΟΥΚΑΙΤΑΣΕΝΠΑΙ
      ΣΙΤΕΤΕΛΗΚΟΤΟΣΛΕΙ
      ΤΟΥΡΓΙΑΣΠΑΣΑΣΜΗΤΡΟΣ
      ΙΟΥΛΙΑΣΛΟΥΚΙΑΣΠΑΠΠΟΥ
10    ΛΕΥΚΙΟΥΜΑΛΙΟΥΡΗΓΕΙ
      ΝΟΥΧΕΙΛΙΑΡΧΟΥΚΑΙΣΤΕΦΑ
      ΝΗΦΟΡΟΥΚΑΙΠΑΙΔΟΝΟΜΟΥ
      ΚΑΙΓΥΜΝΑΣΙΑΡΧΟΥΠΑΝ
      ΤΩΝΤΩΝΓΥΜΝΑΣΙΩΝΠΡΟ
15    ΓΟΝΩΝΚΑΙΣΥΝΓΕΝΩΝΣΤΕ
      ΦΑΝΗΦΟΡΩΝΚΑΙΠΑΣΑΙΣ
      ΕΝΤΕΛΕΣΙΛΙΤΟΥΡΓΙΑΙΣ
      ΤΗΝΠΑΤΡΙΔΑΚΕΚΟΣΜΗΚΟ
      ΤΩΝΤΕΛΕΣΑΣΑΘΗΝΥΔΡΟΦΟ
20    ΡΙΑΝΕΥΑΡΕΣΤΩΣΤΟΙΣΠΟΛΕΙ
      ΤΑΙΣΩΣΥΠΕΡΑΥΤΗΣΠΑΣΗΣ
      ΕΥΧΑΡΙΣΤΟΥΤΙΜΗΣΔΙΑΨΗΦΙΣ
      ΜΑΤΩΝΑΞΙΩΘΗΝΑΙΠΡΟΦΗΤΕΥ
      ΟΝΤΟΣΜΗΤΡΟΔΩΡΟΥΤΟΥΜΗΤΡΟ
25    ΔΩΡΟΥΣΤΕΦΑΝΗΦΟΡΟΥΝΤΟΣΕ
      ΡΗΝΑΙΟΥΤΟΥΜΕΝ ⌐Κ - - -
```

Found at the same place as the preceding. *

VERSION.

Malia Rufeina, Water-bearer of the Pythian Diana; her father was Lucius Malius Saturninus, expounder of the oracle, and crown-bearer, and had filled every office in his country; her mother was Julia Lucia; her grandfather was Lucius Malius Regeinus, military tribune,

---

* Copied by Mr. Whittington and Mr. Cockerell.

GREEK INSCRIPTIONS. 581

and crown-bearer, and superintendant of the education of the youth, and head of all the gymnastic establishments; her ancestors and relations were crown-bearers, and adorned their country by the discharge of all the important offices in the state; she filled the place of Water-bearer in a manner highly pleasing to her citizens; so that, in consequence, she was thought worthy of being honoured by public decree with every mark of splendid distinction. Metrodorus, son of Metrodorus, being at the time Propheta, and Eirenæus, son of Meniscus, Stephanephorus.

REMARKS.

L. 6. For the office of Stephanephorus, see Selden ad Mar. Arun. ii. p. 165.

L. 6. In Mr. Whittington's copy, and in Mr. Cockerell's, we find

```
- - - - ΤΑΣΕΝΠΑΙ
ΣΙ - - - - - - - - - -
```
read
```
- - - - ΤΑΣΕΝΠΑΤΡΙ
ΔΙ - - - - - - - - - -
```

So in Reines. p. 508., τὰς μεγίστας ἄρχας καὶ τὰς λοιπὰς λειτουργίας τῇ πάτριδι ἐκτελέσαντος.

L. 17. Ἐντελέστατοι, ἐντιμότατοι. Hesych. See also Blomfield ad Agam. v. 104.

L. 25, 26. ΕΙΡΗΝΑΙΟΥΤΟΥΜΕΝΙΣΚΟΥ. In Mr. C.'s copy.

XLVI.

ΠΡΟΦΗΤΗΣΚΛΑΥΔΙΟΣ
ΔΑΜΑΣΥΠΕΣΧΕΤΟΔΕΥ
ΤΕΡΑΝΠΡΟΦΗΤΕΙΑΝΕΤΩΝ
ΩΝΟΓΔΟΗΚΟΝΤΑΕΝΟΣΚΑΙ
ΑΝΕΝΕΩΣΑΤΟΤΑΠΑΤΡΙΑΕΘΗ
ΚΑΙΤΟΥΣΤΕΚΟΣΜΟΥΣΕ -
ΤΩΠΕΡΩΙΕΠΙΔΩΔΕΚΑΗΜΕΡΑΣ
- - - - ΤΕΛΕΣ - - ΚΑΙΤΟ - -

From the same place as the preceding. Copied by Mr. Whittington.

REMARKS.

L. 2. ΥΠ. " undertook the office of Propheta the second time." ὑπέστη, ὑπέσχετο· Hesych. ὑπέστη ταύτην τὴν λειτουργίαν. Lysias contra Philoc. L. 7. Perhaps we may supply the deficient parts of this inscription from one found at Cyzicus, and preserved in Caylus, Recueil, t. ii. 197. ΤΑΣ ΣΥΝΤΕΛΟΥΣΑΣ ΤΟΥΣ ΚΟΣΜΟΥΣ ΠΑΡΑΤΗ ΜΗΤΡΙ ΤΗ ΠΛΑΚΙΑΝΗ, which the Abbé Belley translates " les vierges chargées de l'entretien des ornemens de la mere Placiène ;" i. e. Cybele worshipped at Placia. In our inscription, in the last line, we may read ΣΥΝΕΤΕ-ΛΕΣΕΝ, or ΕΠΕΤΕΛΕΣΕΝ, referring to ΚΟΣΜΟΥΣ.

XLVII.

ΟΔΗΜΟΣ
ΔΙΟΝΥΣΙΟΝΑΣΙΛΙΔΟΝ
ΚΑΙΤΙΤΟΝΜΑΡΚΕΛΛΟΝ
ΚΑΙΘΕΟΓΕΝΗΝΔΙΟΝΥΣΙΟΥ

In the wall of the castle at Brusa.   Copied by Mr. Whittington.

REMARKS.

L. 4. Add this to the termination of substantives in ΗΝ; as ΔΗΜΟΣΘΕΝΗΝ (Thucyd. l. 4.) ΣΩΣΘΕΝΗΝ, Act. App. xviii. ΙΕΡΟΚ-ΛΗΝ, ΗΡΑΚΛΗΝ, Maitt. Ox. Marb. We also find in Chishull, 149. Μενεκρατου, Ευκρατου.

XLVIII.

1   ΥΚΛΗΝΙ - Α - ΧΑΟΥΤΑΜΙ - - ΣΑΝ
     ΕΠΙΣΤΕΦΑΝΗΦΟΡΟΥΑΝΤΙΟΧΟΥΑ - ΕΧΙΝ
     ΚΑΙΠΑΡΕΔΡΕΥΣΑΝΤΑΤΗΝΠΡΩΤΗΝΕΞΑΓ
     ΝΟΝΟΠΡΟΦΗΤΗΣΜΟΣΧΙΩΝΗΦΑΙΣΤΙΩΝΟ -
5   ΚΑΙΗΥΔΡΟΦΟΡΟΣΤΡΥΦΩΣΑΑΠΟΛΛΩΝΙΟΥΚΑΙ - -
     ΠΕΡΙΤΟΜΑΝΤΕΙΟΝΠΑΝΤΕΣΚΑΙΟΙΤΟΙΕΡΟΝΚ - -
     ΚΟΥΝΤΕΣΚΑΙΟΙΠΡΟΣΧΩΡΟΙΕΣΤΕΦΑΝΩΣ -
     ΚΑΙΕΤΕΙΜΗΣΑΝΕΙΚΟΝΙΓΡΑΠΤΗΙΕΠΙΧΡΥΣ -
     ΔΙΚΑΙΟΣΥΝΗΣΕΝΕΚΕΝΚΑΙΕΥΣΕΒΕΙΑΣ -

At Ieronda. *

---

* Copied by Mr. Cockerell.

REMARKS.

L. 1.. and 2. in Mr. Whittington's copy, stand thus:

- - - ΛΗΝΤΑ - Ν - - ΡΟΥ - ΑΙ - ΞΑΝ - - -
ΕΠΣΤΕΦΑΝΗΦΟΡΟΥΑΝΤΙΟΧΟΥΑ

L. 3. Akerblad proposed ΕΞΑΓΩΝΩΝ, the meaning of which is not very evident. Perhaps ΤΗΝΠΡΩΤΟΝΕΞΑΜΗΝΟΝ. See Chandler, pp. 83, 84. βουλεύοντος τὰν πρῶτον ἐξάμηνον.

VERSION.

The expounder of the oracle, Moschio, son of Hephæstio ; and the Water-bearer, Tryphosa *, daughter of Apollonius, and all belonging to the oracle, and those who inhabit the sacred precincts, and those of the neighbouring territory, have crowned and honoured with a painted and gilded statue ——, who was quæstor (l. 1.), during the time that Antiochus, son of ——, was crown-bearer, and was † assessor for the first six months ; — on account of his justice and piety.

XLIX.

ΝΕΤΑΝΙΚΗΝ
ΟΥΚ - - ΙΔΑΜΟΣΘΕΝΕ
ΡΑΠΑΣΗΣΑΡΕΤΗΣ
ΕΝΓΥΝΑΙ - ΙΝΕΙΝΕΚΕΝΠΡΟΣ
5 ΔΕΞΑΜΕΝΟΥΤΟΑΝΑΛΩΜΑ
ΤΟΥΠΡΟΣΦΙΛΕΣΤΑΤΟΥΠΑΤΡΟΣ
ΑΥΤΗΣΤΙΒΚΛΑΥΕΥΔΑΜΟΥ
ΤΟΥΣΠΑΡΤΙΑΤΙΚΟΥΑΡΧΙΕ - - - Σ
ΤΩΝΣΕΒΑΣΤΩΝΚΑΙΤΩΝ
10 ΘΕΙΩΝΠΡΟΓΟΝΩΝΑΥΤΩΝ
ΑΡΙΣΤΟΠΟΛΕΙΤΕΥΤΟΥ

Found at Amyclæ, on a large cippus, by the Earl of Aberdeen. The upper part of the stone is broken.

---

* The name occurs in St. Paul's Ep. to Rom. xvi.

† The Paredri, in the Temple of Apollo, are mentioned in the Milesian inscriptions, in Chishull, l. 4. ταμιευόντων καὶ παρεδρεύοντων. Akerblad's conjectures are, in L. 1. ΤΑ-ΜΙΕΥΣΑΝΤΑ. L. 4. Σ at the end. L. 5. ΚΑΙ ΟΙ. L. 6. ΚΑΤΟΙ. L. 7. ΑΝ at the end.

584 GREEK INSCRIPTIONS.

REMARKS.

L. 2, 3. " Daughter of Demosthenes." L. 4. ΓΥΝΑΙΞΙΝ. L. 8. ΑΡΧΙΕΡΕΩΣ.

L. 5. The same expression occurs in three inscriptions given by Muratori, and found at Sparta. ii. p. DXLVI. p. DXLVIII. and i. p. DXLIX. We·read in Dio, τό τε ανάλωμα τὸ τῆς ἀρχῆς αὐτὸς ἀναλώσειν ὑπεδέξατο. See Casaub. in Hist. A. S. p. 58.

L. 8. Damocratidas is called also " High Priest of Augustus, and of his deified ancestors." ΑΡΧΙΕΡΕΩΣ ΤΟΥ ΣΕΒΑΣΤΟΥ ΚΑΙ ΤΩΝ ΘΕΙΩΝ ΠΡΟΓΟΝΩΝ ΑΥΤΟΥ. Murat. t. ii. DXLVI.

L. 11. Τῆς Ἀριστοπολιτείας τέιμας. Muratori, t. ii. DLIII. Πολιτευσά-μενον ἄριστα. Maffei, Mus. Ver. XLIII.

L.

```
1    ΑΥΡΗΛΙΟΣΠΙΓΡΗΣ
     ΤΟΥΤΕΛΕΣΦΟΡΟΥ
     ΟΛΥΜΠΗΝΟΣΚΑ
     ΤΕΣΚΕΥΑΣΑΕΑΥΤΩΚΑΙ
5    ΓΥΝΑΙΚΙΜΟΥΑΥΡΗΛΙΑΘΕΟ
           ΔΟΤΗΔΙΟΥ
     ΟΛΥΜΠΗΝΗΚΑΙ
     ΤΕΚΝΟΙΣΗΜΩΝΑΥΡΗΛΙΟΙΣ
     ΕΝΤΕΙΜΩΚΑΙΝΕΙΚΟΣΤΡΑ
10   ΤΩΚΑΙΗΦΑΙΣΤΙΩ - -
        ΚΑΙΤΗΕΣΟΜΕΝΗ
     ΕΚΑΣΤΟΥΓΥΝΑΙΚΙΚΑΙ
     ΤΟΙΣΕΞΑΥΤΩ - ΤΕ
     ΚΝΟΙΣΚΑΙΕΓΓΟΝΟΙΣ
15   ΕΞΩΝΕΙΑΡΡΕΝΕΣΓΕ
     ΝΩΝΤΑΙΚΑΙΤΗ
     ΕΣΟΜΕΝΗΕΚΑΣΤΟΥ
     ΓΥΝΑΙΚΙΕΙΔΕΘ
     ΛΕΙΑΙΓΕΝΩΝΤΑΙΚΑΙΤΩΕΣΟ
20   ΜΕΝΩΕΚΑΣΤΗΣΑΝΔΡΙΚΑΙΕΙΤΙ
     ΝΙΕΝΓΡΑΦΩΣΕΠΙΤΡΕΨΩΕΙΔΕΤΙΣ
     ΤΟΛΜΗΣΗΒΙΑΣΑΣΘΑΙΚΑΙΚΗΔΕΥΣΗ
     ΤΙΝΑΔΩΣΕΙΤΩΙΕΡΩΤΑΤΩΦΙΣΚΩ
     ΧΕΚΑΙΤΗΠΑΤΡΙΔΙΜΟΥΑΛΛΑΧΕ
25   ΟΔΕΕΛΕΝΞΑΣΑΜΦΟΤΕΡΩΝΤΟΤΡΙ
     ΤΟΝΛΑΒΕΤΩ -
```

Copied at Phineka, on the coast of Lycia, by Mr. Cockerell. L. 13. ΑΥΤΩΝ. Ak.

VERSION.

I, Aurelius Pigres, a citizen of Olympus, son of ——, who was son of Telesphorus, built this tomb for myself, and my wife Aurelia Theodote, a citizen of Olympus, daughter of Dius; and for our children, Aurelius Entimus, Aur. Nicostratus, Aur. Hephæstio, and for the future wife of each, and their children and descendants; out of whom, if they be sons, (I allow the use of the tomb) to the wife also of each of them; if they be daughters, to the husband also of each of them; and to whomsoever else I shall by writing give leave. But if any one shall dare to violate it, and to place any other person in it, he shall pay to the treasury of the emperor 5000 denarii, and to my country another 5000; and let the man who convicts him receive the third part of both the fines.*

NOTES.

L. 1. The name Pigres occurs in various epigrams in the Anthologia, p. 431. ed. Steph. See also Xenophon's Anabasis, l. 1.

L. 5. "ΕΑΥΤΟΣ esse omnium personarum, tam in singulari quam plurali numero viri docti ostenderunt." Mis. Ob. vol. iii. 142.

L. 8. So in the Actian inscription copied by Col. Leake, ΠΟΠΛΙΟΝ ΛΕΥΚΙΟΝ ΑΚΙΛΙΟΥΣ.

L. 20. ΕΚΑΣΤΗΣ.

L. 22. Many of the inscriptions on the tombs of Asia Minor conclude with specifying the fine to be paid by those who violate them. We find in Muratori some Iambic verses on the same subject.

λοιπὸν φυλάσσου, μὴ τιν᾽ ἐνθήσης τάφῳ,
δίκην θ᾽ ὑφέξης παρανόμου τυμβωρύχου,
φίσκῳ τε δώσης * Β καὶ τῇ πόλει * Α.

"Take care then that you place no one in the sepulchre, and undergo the punishment due to the lawless violator of the tomb; and pay to the treasury 2000 denarii, and to the city 1000." Dor. Char. i. 105.

---

* The sigma, throughout the inscription, is in the form Ϲ, and the numeral in l. 25. is Χ, with a horizontal line through the middle.

The opening and robbing of tombs seem to have been practised to a great extent in the third, fourth, and fifth centuries of the Christian æra. Many epigrams in Greg. Naz. allude to this profanation; and it appears that the plunderers sold the ornaments. Τοὺς δ᾽ ἀπέδοσθε πολλάκι, " often you sold them," says Gregory Naz.: addressing these Τυμβώρυχοι. " *I* never," he observes elsewhere, " made a profit from the tombs; I swear by justice and the dead." οὐδ᾽ ἀπὸ τύμβων Ἔργον ἔγειρα· Δίκην ὄμνυμι καὶ Φθιμένους. He protests, in another place, against the practice of some Christians who plundered them for the sake of raising the Basilicæ of the martyrs. See Murat. Anecd. Gr. The most formidable denunciation against these Latrones Bustuarii, as A. Marcellinus calls them, is contained in an Athenian inscription, copied by Muratori, from a MS. in the Bibliotheca Ambrosiana; see his Anec. Gr. p. 7. It begins, παραδίδωμι τοῖς καταχθονίοις θεοῖς. The person who pulls off any of the ornaments of the tomb, or opens it, or moves any part of it, shall be exposed, ΦΡΙΚΗΙ, ΚΑΙ ΠΥΡΕΤΩΙ, ΚΑΙ ΤΕΤΑΡΤΑΙΩΙ, ΚΑΙ ΕΛΕΦΑΝΤΙ.

L. 23. Ἱερώτατον ταμεῖον is rendered " Fiscus Imperatoris," in the Mis. Obs. vol. iv. 353. " Recte," says the editor; " nam omnia tum dicebantur ἱερὰ et ἱερώτατα, quæ spectabant ad personam principalem."

LI.

```
 1   ΑΥΤΟΚΡΑΤωΡΚΕΟΑΡΖΗΝωΝΕΥΟΕΒΗΟΝΙΚ - -
     ΠΟΛΕΟΥΧΟΟΜΕΓΙΟΤΟΟΑΕΙΟΕΒΑΟΤΟΟΑ - -
     ΦΙΛΟΤΙΜΗΟΑΜΕΝΗΙΑΥΤωΝΕΥΟΕΒΙΑωΟΕΝ
     ΠΑΟΑΙΟΤΑΙΟΠΟΛΕΟΙΝΚΑΙΕΝΤΑΥΤΗΤΗΑΥΤωΝ
 5   ΠΟΛΙΕΔωΡΗΟΑΤΟΧΡΗΜΑΤωΝΔΟΟΙΝΤΑΟΥΝΑ
     ΓΟΜΕΝΑΕΚΤΟΥΠΡΑΚΤΙΟΥΦΗΜΙΤΟΥΕΝΤΑΥΘΑ
     ΒΙΚΑΡΑΤΟΥΤωΝΚΑΘΟΟΙωΜΕΝωΝΒΑΛΛΙΟ
     ΤΡΑΡΙωΝΔΙωΝΑΝΑΝΕΟΥΝΤΕΤΑΤΙΧΗΠΡΟΟ
     ΟωΤΗΡΙΑΝΤΗΟΑΥΤΗΟΠΟΛΕωΟΚΑΙΕΥΧΑΡΙΟ
10   ΤΟΥΝΤΕΟΑΝΕΘΗΚΑΜΕΝΤΟΔΕΤΟΤΙΤΛΟΝ
     ΕΙΟΜΝΗΜΟΟΥΝΟΝΑΕΙΔΙΟΝΤΗΟΑΥΤωΝ
                - ΒΑΟΙΛΙΑΟ -
     ΑΝΕΝΕωΘΗΔΕΟΠΥΡΓΟΟΟΥΤΟΟΠΡ - -
     ΤΟΝΤΟΟΤΟΥΜΕΓΑΛΟΠΡSΚΟΜS - - - -
15   ΔΙΟΓΕΝ - - - ΕΤΟΥΟ : ΦΙΒ : ΕΝΙΝΔΟΙΔ  -
```

The marble bearing this inscription originally came from the New Chersonesus, and is now in the villa of the governor of the Crimea. The copy given by Pallas, in the second volume of his Travels, being incorrect, it was thought proper to insert that lately made by by Mr. Whittington.

The first part of the inscription, which terminates in line 12, commemorates a gift of money by the Emperor Zeno, to the city. The 6th and 7th lines require explanation. ΑΥΤΩΝ, in line 3. and 11., refers in an unusual manner to ΖΗΝΩΝ in the singular number. The three last lines bear a different date. " The tower was repaired under the —— of the noble Count Diogenes." The date and year of the indiction follow. The termination of the second line contains the abridged forms of Μεγαλοπρέπους Κόμητος. Probably the same Diogenes is mentioned in an inscription found at Megara, and edited by Chandler, p. 79. It begins, Ἔργον καὶ τοῦτο τοῦ μεγαλοπρε- πεστάτου Κόμητος Διογένους τοῦ παιδὸς Ἀρχελάου.˙ Diogenes was general in the reign of Anastasius, in the year 494 of the Christian æra.

LII.

ΙΛΙΕΙΚΑΙΠΟΛΕΙΚΟΙΝΩΝΟΥΣΑΙΤΗ - ΟΣΙΑΣ -

This line is part of an inscription cited by Boissonade, in his illustration of the Actian marble, printed in his edition of Holstein's letters. It is quoted from the Voyage de la Troade, t. iii. p. 30., in which work it is translated " Iliensi et urbi participes sacrorum." ΤΗΣΟΣΙΑΣ. As Ἵππαρχος immediately follows, Boissonade objects to that version, and proposes " Populo Iliensi et urbi participi sacrorum." ΚΟΙΝΩΝΟΥΣΑΙ, in the dative.

We ought to read ΘΥΣΙΑΣ; the mistakes of Ο and Θ are frequent. Paul Rycaut, (Greek Church, p. 76.) published ἐπιτελέσασαν τὰ τῆς θεοῦ μυστήρια καὶ τὰς οὐσίας, instead of θυσίας. See Gregor. de Dialectis, ˉed. Schaefer. p. 232. Little doubt will remain on the mind of the reader respecting the proposed alteration, when he is informed that in the vestibule of the Public library at Cambridge, there is a small column brought from the plain of Troy, by Dr. Clarke, bearing an

4 F 2

inscription, (the letters of which are throughout perfect,) in honour of Pytha. It begins,

AIKOINΩNOTΣAITHΣΘTΣIAΣ
KAITOTAΓΩNOΣKAITHΣ
ΠANHΓTPEΩΣ
ΠTΘAN.

LIII.

TAΦΓIΙΙOIANEΘENTOIDIFITONΦODINΘOΘEN

Inscribed, in very antient characters, on a brass helmet found in the Alpheus, near Olympia, in 1795, by Mr. Morritt; and now in the possession of Mr. P. Knight.

NOTES.

Mr. Blomfield and Mr. Dobree consider the line as expressing an offering or dedication to Jupiter, TOIΔIFI ; and I find from a remark in Professor Porson's hand-writing, in the possession of Dr. Clarke, that he was of the same opinion.

ANEΘEN is found in an epigram of Simonides, corrected by Mr. Blomfield on the Persæ, p. 208. *

According to this mode of interpretation, the line, if we suppose the name at the beginning to be ᾿Αργεῖοι, would be read in common characters,

Τοὶ ῎Αργεῖοι ἄνεθεν τῶι Διὶ τῶν Κορινθόθεν.

The scholar will recollect, in an antient inscription copied by Pausanias †, Τῷ Διὶ τ᾿Αχαιοὶ τ᾿αγάλματα ταῦτ᾿ ἀνεθῆκαν, where the first words are parallel to TAPΓEIOITΩIΔII.

The Greeks said, Ζεὺς, Ζέος, Ζέι, Ζέα ‡ ; and Δεὺς, as well as Ζεύς. See Hesychius. Now Ζεὺς was written antiently ΖεFς §, as Ατρεὺς, ΑτρεFς, and βασιλεὺς, βασιλεFς ; hence in the genitive, ΖεFος or ΔεFος,

---

* " In Simonid. ap. Plutarch. t. ii. p. 870. ὅπλ᾿ ἀνέθεντο Λατοῖ. Manifesto legendum, ὅπλ᾿ ἄνεθεν Λατοῖ. ᾿Ανέθεσαν. B."

† L. 5. 25. Not, as it is given in Facius, τῷ Διὶ τ᾿Αχαιόι.

‡ Sex. Emp. adv. Math. i. 177.

§ Heyne, Excur. iv. ad Il. 19. p. 770.

from ΔεϜϛ (Δεὺς), and ΔεϜι, in the dative. But ΔεϜι is ΔιϜι.* Ἀινιγμα was written Ἀνεγμα by the Tarentines †; and another substitution of the ε for ι occurs in Νεώβη for Νιώβη ‡; and in Latin, " E loco fuit I, ut Menerva, et Magester, et Dijove." Quint. l. i. c. 4. § 17.

It has been objected § to ΔIFI, as derived from ΔIΣ, " that in no dialect or modification of the Greek tongue was the digamma ever employed in the flexion of any word ending in IΣ; the second case having been progressively in words of this declension IΣTOΣ, ITOΣ, IOΣ, EΩΣ, HΩΣ." We may propose another reading, TOIΔIEI— adding the lower horizontal line to what appears to be F.

It is well known that the Greeks formerly wrote EI for the long I ‖ ; but it is equally certain that they used EI also for the short vowel. That very antient inscription, copied by Colonel Leake in Asia Minor, gives ANAKTEI; EIΔIAN, for ἰδίαν, occurs in the Heraclean Tables; and the *word* ΔII *itself* was written ΔIEI. ΔIEITPEΦEΣ is found on a marble seen by Spon, of considerable antiquity, as AMΦI-ANAXΣ, OΦΣIAΔEΣ, HAΓNON, are sculptured on it; and Montfaucon gives in his Diar. Ital. p. 422. ΔIEI TΨIΣTΩ ETXHN. See also Muratori, Ins. XIII. ¶

LIV.

AΓAΘHITTXHI
ATTOKPATOPIKAIΣAPIMAPKΩIATPHΛIΩI
ΣEOTHPΩIAΛEΞANΔPΩIETΣEBEIETTTXEI

ΣEBAΣTΩI	ΣEBAΣTHI
MHTPIATTOT	ΛHTTHTΩN
ΣTPATOΠEΔΩN	HΣKAIAIΩNIOT
ΔIAMONHΣATTΩNK	MΠANTOΣATTΩNOIKOT
EΠIMHOTIOTONΩP	TEΠAPXOTAIΓTΠTOT

---

* " TTΔETC, TTΔEFOC, TTΔEFIΔHC, so ΔETC, ΔEFOC, (ΔιFoϛ) ΔEFI (ΔIFI)." From Mr. Blomfield.

† Hesych. in v.

‡ Eurysus, apud Clem. Alex. Strom. i. 321. See Maitt. de Dial., ed. Sturzii.

§ See the communication respecting this inscription, in the Classical Journal, vol. i. 329.

‖ EI pro omni I longa scribebant more antiquo Graecorum. Pris. l. i. 561.

¶ We find the same permutation in the antient Latin: SVFEIS is SVIS in Oscan. Lanzi.

A dedication to the Emperor Alexander and his mother.　Hamilton's Ægyptiaca. p. 282.

Heliogabalus adopted his cousin, and declared him Cæsar, at the age of twelve years.　The young prince, on that occasion, took the names of Alexander and Severus. *　On the death of Heliogabalus, A. C. 222.　Alexander was proclaimed Emperor.　His mother was Mamæa, whom he honoured with the title of Augusta, " mother of her country and of the armies.".　This appellation occurs in the inscription.

We are able to supply the deficient parts of it from another, preserved in Spon. Mis. Erud. Ant. 369.

ΥΠΕΡΣΩΤΗΡΙΑΣΚΑΙΝΙΚΗΣΚΑΙΑΙΩΝΙΟΥΔΙΑΜΟΝΗΣΤΩΝΚΥΡΙΩΝΑΥΤΟΚΡΑΤΟΡΩΝ
——ΚΑΙΙΟΥΛΙΑΣΣΕΒΑΣΤΗΣΜΗΤΡΟΣ ΣΤΡΑΤΟΠΕΔΩΝ ΚΑΙ ΤΟΥΣΥΜΠΑΝΤΟΣΑΥ
ΤΩΝΟΙΚΟΥ.

In the third line, therefore, after ΣΕΒΑΣΤΩΙ insert ΚΑΙ.　L. 4. read ΚΑΙ ΑΗΤΤΗΤΩΝ " invincible armies."　L. 5. ΥΠΕΡΝΙΚΗΣ. L. 6. ΚΑΙΣΥ - - -

LV.

ΒΑΣΙΛΕΩΣΠΤΟΛΕΜΑΙΟΥ
ΘΕΟΥΝΕΟΥΔΙΟΝΥΣΟΥ
ΦΙΛΟΠΑΤΟΡΟΣΚΑΙΦΙΛΑ
ΔΕΛΦΟΥΚΑΙΤΩΝΤΕΚΝΩΝ
ΤΟΠΡΟΣΚΥΝΗΜΑΠΑΡΑΤΗΚΥ
ΡΙΑΙΙΣΙΔΙΚΑΙΤΟΙΣΣΥΝΝΑΟΙΣΘΕ
ΟΙΣ

From the temple at Philæ.　See Hamilton's Ægyptiaca. p. 52.

The inscription records the homage of Ptolemy Auletes, before the presiding Isis.　This sovereign assumed the appellation of the " Young Bacchus."　The same title was claimed by Mithradates Eupator. †

---

* Herodian. l. 5.　　　　　† Dorville. Mis. Obs. vol. vii. 50.

'REMARKS.

L. 2. NEOΥ. Ex diis gentium, alii seniores, juniores alii dicebantur: οἱ μὲν παλαιότεροι, οἱ δὲ νεώτεροι τῶν θεῶν, ut scribit Menander Rhetor. *
L. 4. ΤΕΚΝΩΝ. The usual form employed by the Ptolemies; ἐρρώμεθα καὶ αὐτοὶ καὶ τὰ τέκνα ἡμῶν. Macc. iii. 7.

LVI.

ΠΤΟΛΕΜΑΙΟCΗΡΑΚΛΕΙΔΟΥ
ΕΠΙΣΤΡΑΤΗΓΟCΤΗCΘΗΒΑΙΔΟC
ΗΛΘΟΝ

From the same temple.

I, Ptolemy, son of Heracleides, commander in chief of the Thebaid, came (to worship Isis.) Ἐπιστρατηγὸς, " summus Dux." Sic enim interpretor : ut ἔπαρχος summum præfectum notat ; nam ἐπὶ respondet Latinorum " super." Dorv. Mis. Ob. vol. vii. 50.

LVII.

ΓΑΙΟCΙΟΥΛΙΟCΠΑΠΕΙCΕΠΑΡΧΟC
ΗΚΩΚΑΙΠΡΟCΚΕΚΥΝΗΚΑΤΗΝΚΥΡΙ
ΑΝΙCΙΝCΥΝΙΟΥΛΙΩΙΤΩΙΥΙΩΙΚΑΙΥ
ΠΕΡ - ΑΙΩΝΟCΤΟΥΝΕΩΤΕΡΟΥΥΙΟΤΕ
ΤΙΔΕΚΑΙCΥΝΤΟΙCΦΙΛΟΙCΚΑΙCΥΝ
ΑΠΟΔΗΜΟΙCCΥΜΜΑΧΩΙ - - - - - -

From the same temple.

" I, Caius Julius —, chief prefect, am just arrived ; and have done homage to the powerful or presiding Isis, with my son Julius, and in behalf of my younger son Plato ; (I have worshipped also) with my friends, and with those who are travelling in this country, Symmachus," &c.

REMARKS.

L. 2. ΗΚΩ, used here in the Attic sense, ἀντὶ τοῦ ἀρτίως ἦλθον. See

---

* Vales. Euseb. 25.

Budæus, p. 770. and p. 1083., who refers to the first line in the Hecuba of Euripides.

L. 4. Perhaps ΠΛΑΤΩΝΟϹ.

LVIÏI.

ΣΠΤΟΛΕΜΑ‥ΣΠΤΟΛΕΜΑΙΟΥΚΑΙΚΛΕΟΠΑΤΡΑΣΘΕΩΝΕΠΙΦΑΝΩΝΚ‥ΕΥΧΑΡΙΣΤΩΝ
ΣΙΛΙΣΣΑΚΛΕΟΠΑΤΡΑΗΤΟΥΒΑΣΙΛΕΩΣΑΔΕΛΦΗΘΕΟΙΦΙΛΟΜΗΤΟΡΕΣ
ΑΟΝΑΝΤΑΙΩΚΑΙΤΟΙΣΣΥΝΝΑΟΙΣΘΕΟΙΣΑΥΤΟΚΡΑΤΟΡΕΣΚΑΙΣΑΡΕΣΑΥΡΗ…ΙΑΝΤΩ
              ΝΕΙΝΟΣ
ΕΣΣΕΒΑΣΤΟ‥‥ΕΝΕΩΣΑΝΤΟΤΗΝΣΤΕΓΑ‥ΤΡΙΔΑΕΤΟΥΣΤΕΤΑΡΤΟ

On the frize of the portico of a temple at Antæopolis. See Hamilton's Ægyptiaca. p. 268. The imperfect parts may be supplied thus :

βασιλευΣ ΠΤΟΛΕΜΑΙΟΣ ΠΤΟΛΕΜΑΙΟΥ ΚΑΙ ΚΛΕΟΠΑΤΡΑΣ ΘΕΩΝ ΕΠΙΦΑΝΩΝ Καὶ ΕΥΧΑΡΙΣΤΩΝ
καὶ βαΣΙΛΙΣΣΑ ΚΛΕΟΠΑΤΡΑ Η ΤΟΥ ΒΑΣΙΛΕΩΣ ΑΔΕΛΦΗ ΘΕΟΙ ΦΙΛΟΜΗΤΟΡΕΣ τὸ προν
ΑΟΝΑΝΤΑΙΩ ΚΑΙ ΤΟΙΣ ΣΥΝΝΑΟΙΣ ΘΕΟΙΣ
                      ΑΥΤΟΚΡΑΤΟΡΕΣΚΑΙΣΑΡΕΣΑΥΡΗλιος καὶΑΝΤΩΝΕΙΝΟΣ
ἐντυχειΣ ΣΕΒΑΣΤΟΙ ωΕΝΕΩΣΑΝΤΟ ΤΗΝ ΣΤΕΓΑσΤΡΙΔΑ ΕΤΟΥΣ ΤΕΤΑΡΤΟυ

The sovereigns recorded in the first inscription, as having raised or consecrated the Pronaon to Antæus, are Ptolemy and Cleopatra, children of Ptolemy Epiphanes, and Cleopatra.

The latter inscription relates to the " Emperors, Aurelius Cæsar, and Antoninus Cæsar, ——, Augusti, who repaired the roof in the fourth year."

The person called Antoninus is better known by the name of Lucius Verus. On the death of Antoninus Pius, M. Aurelius, who succeeded him, made Lucius Verus partner in the empire, and added to those two names that of Antoninus. After this name, either ΕΥΤΥΧΕΙΣ or ΕΥΣΕΒΕΙΣ may be inserted, as in another inscription. Æg. p. 282. 'Αλεξάνδρῳ ΕΥΤΥΧΕΙ ΕΥΣΕΒΕΙ ΣΕΒΑΣΤΩΙ.

" Repaired the roof." If ΣΤΕΓΑΣΤΡΙΣ be the word in this place, it occurs in an unusual sense.

. In the first inscription, the Ptolemies are called ΕΠΙΦΑΝΕΙΣ and ΕΥΧΑΡΙΣΤΟΙ. The proper meaning of the former word is stated in a note of Valesius on Eusebius. 25. " Non intellexerunt interpretes vim Græci vocabuli ; neque enim ἐπιφανὴς, nobilissimum, hic significat, neque illustrem. *Præsentem* potius vertere debuerant. Sic enim Latini vocant; quoties de Diis loquuntur. " Per te præsentem conspicuumque Deum." Ovid. l. 2. Trist.

ΕΥΧΑΡ. " Liberal, munificent," ex usu seculi Alexandrini. Heyne, in the xviith. vol. of the Archæol.

LIX.

On the temple of Ombos, on the cornice above one of the doors, in capital letters, nearly three inches in length. Ægyptiaca. p. 75.

ΥΠΕΡΒΑΣΙΛΕΩΣΠΤΟΛΕΜΑΙΟΥΔΙΟΥΚΑΙΒΑΣΙΛΙΣΣΗΣΚΛΕΟΠΑΤΡΑΣΤΗΣΑΔΕΛΦΗΣ
ΘΕΩΝΦΙΛΟΜΗΤΟΡΩΝΚΑΙΤΩΝΤΟΥΤΩΝΤΕΚΝΩΝΑΡΩΗΡΕΙΘΕΩΙΜΕΓΑΛΩΙ
ΑΠΟΛΛΩΝΙΚΑΙΤΟΙΣΣΥΝΝΑΟΙΣΘΕΟΙΣΤΟΝΣΗΚΟΝΟΙΕΝΤΩΙΟΜΒΙΤΗΙΤΑΣΣΟΜΕΝΟΙΠΕΖΟΙ
ΚΑΙΙΠΠΕΙΣΚΑΙΟΙΑΛΛΟΙΕΥΝΟΙΑΣΕΝΕΚΕΝ - - - ΕΙΣΑΥΤΟΥΣ

REMARKS.

L. 1. ΥΠΕΡ. sometimes ΥΠΕΡ ΣΩΤΗΡΙΑΣ, which the Latins express in their inscriptions, Pro Salute.

Ib. ΔΙΟΥ. The use of ΔΙΟΣ, in prose inscriptions, is very rare : it occurs on a coin given by Cuper, ΑΝΤΙΝΟΟΣ ΔΙΟΣ.

L. 2. ΑΡΩΗΡΕΙ. The copies of Plutarch have a different orthography, Ἀρούηριν ὃν Ἀπόλλωνα. de Is. et Os. Boubier, in his correction of the inscription at Apollinopolis parva, reads the dative, ΑΡΩΗΡΙΔΙ ΘΕΩΙ; but the termination of the word in Mr. Hamilton's copy is plainly ΡΕΙ. The Egyptian word Aruer is explained by Jablonski, Pan. Aeg. l. ii. p. 225. " virtus effectrix vel causalis."

L. 3. ΣΗΚΟΣ. " Potest vel delubrum vel sacellum significare." Jablonski, Pan. Aeg. l. iv. 267. Mr. H. says the temple is divided into two separate Adyta ; the ΣΗΚΟΣ here erected or consecrated by the foot and horse soldiers, in the Ombite district, was one.

L. 3. ΤΑΣΣΟΜΕΝΟΙ. Τοῖς πέζοις τοῖς τεταγμένοις ὑπὸ Τίμωνα. Mar. Oxon. p. 57.

LX.

On the entablature of the temple at Cous or Apollonipolis parva. Ægyptiaca. p. 178.

ΒΑΣΙΛΙΣΣΑΚΛΕΟΠΑΤΡΑΚΑΙΒΑΣΙΛΕΥΣΠΤΟΛΕΜΑΙΟΣΘΕΟΙΦΙΛΟΜΗΤΟΡΕΣ
ΕΥΣΕΒΕΙΣΚΑΙΤΕΚΝΑΑρωηΡΕΙΘΕΩΙΜΕΓΙΣΤΩΙΚΑΙΤΟΙΣΣΥΝΝΑΟΙΣΘΕΟΙΣ

It is evident (as Zoega remarks) from Alexandrine coins, that the Ptolemies erected temples, constructed on Egyptian and Greek models. They raised obelisks also, inscribed with hieroglyphics; and the Zodiacs of Tentyra display, in the clearest manner, a mixture of the mythology and arts of Greece with the religion and arts of antient Egypt.* " The Greek inscriptions which are discovered on the temples," says Mr. Hamilton, " induced us to conjecture that perhaps many of these buildings may be attributed to the Ptolemies. One of them had felt it his duty to bring back from his campaign in Syria, the statues of gods and goddesses, of which the Persians had plundered the temples of Egypt; and we know that these sovereigns long indulged a peculiar partiality for the religion of their subjects. The Greek writers assure us that several of them built rich and magnificent temples." pp. 19. 75. Zoega considers this inscription at Apollinopolis parva as confirming the fact, of the erection by the Ptolemies, of buildings constructed on the Egyptian model. It is, he says, sculptured " in fronte templi, loco maxime conspicuo; quare ab ipsis conditoribus ibi collocatum reor; non ut alia sunt hujusmodi, ob ædificium ornamentis auctum, vel ad devotum numini animum demonstrandum posteriùs adjectum." 543.

Some of the temples raised by the Ptolemies were inscribed with hieroglyphical characters; for when the Serapeum was destroyed, they were found engraved † on the stones of it. A compliance with

---

* Visconti's letter to Larcher, on the Zodiacs of Tentyra.

† Ἐν δὲ τῷ ναῷ τοῦ Σαράπιδος λυομένου καὶ γυμνουμένου ηὑρητο γράμματα ἐγκεχαραγμένα τοῖς λίθοις, τῷ καλουμένῳ ἱερογλυφίκῳ. Sozom. l. vii. c. 15.

GREEK INSCRIPTIONS. 595

the religious feelings of their subjects might lead them to adopt the Egyptian style in their sacred buildings; particularly as we find that it was used by them on other occasions. The ship of extraordinary magnitude, constructed by Ptolemy Philopator, was ornamented with columns strictly *Egyptian*. " The capitals," according to the description of Callixenus *, " were rounded; about that part called the Calathus, there were no volutes, as in Greek buildings; or rough leaves (as those of the acanthus); but there were the calyces of the *river-lotus*; and the fruit of the budding *palm*." The lower part of the capitals had a distribution of ornaments similar to the leaves and fruit of the *Egyptian bean*, entwined, as it were, together.

LXI.

ΕШΡΑCΕΚΑΜΒΥCΗCΜΕΤΟΝΔΕΤΟΝΛΙΘΟΝ
ΒΑCΙΛΕΟΣΕ - - - - ΟΥΕΙΚΟΝΑΕΚΜΕΜΑΓΜΕΝΟΝ
ΦШΝΗΔΟΔΥΜΟCΗΝΓΙΑΛΑΙΜΟΙΜΕΜΝΟΝΟC
ΤΑΠΑΘΗΓΟΟCΑΗΝΑΦΕΙΛΕΚΑΜΒΥCΗC
ΑΝΑΡΟΡΑΔ - ΝΥΝΚΑΙΑCΑΡΗΤΑΦΘΕΓΓΜΑΤΑ
ΟΝΟΦΥΡΟΜ - ΙΤΗCΠΡΟCΘΕΛΕΙγΑΝΟΗΤΥΧΗC.   Ægyptiaca, p. 173.

This is one of the numerous inscriptions which are sculptured on the legs and feet of the vocal statue of Memnon. It is well restored in the following manner in the Anthologia Palatina. The metrical inaccuracies prove it to be of late date.

Ἔθραυσε Καμβύσης με τόνδε τὸν λίθον
βασιλέως ἑωου εἰκόν᾽ ἐκμεμαγμένον.
Φωνὴ δ᾽ ὀδυρμὸς ἦν πάλαι μοι Μέμνονος
τὰ πάθη γοῶσα, ἣν ἀφεῖλε Καμβύσης·
ἄναρθρα δὴ νῦν κάσαφη τὰ φθέγματα
ὀλοφύρομαι, τῆς πρόσθε λείψανον τύχης.

---

* Athen. l. r. 293. ed. Schweig. ἐισὶ δ᾽ αὐτῶν αἱ κεφαλαὶ τῷ σχήματι περιφερεῖς. — περὶ τὸν προσαγορευόμενον κάλαθον, οὐχ ἕλικες, καθάπερ ἐπὶ τῶν Ἑλληνικῶν, καὶ φύλλα τραχέα περίκειται· λωτῶν δὲ ποταμίων κάλυκες καὶ φοινίκων ἀρτιβλάστων καρπός. — κιβωρίων ἄνθεσι καὶ φύλλσις ὡσανεὶ καταπεπλεγμένοις. The round capital is found among aichitectural remains in Egypt, presenting the form of a bulb. The Lotus heie mentioned is the Nymphæa Lotus; the Egyptian bean is the Nymphæa Nelumbo.

4 G 2

The statue is supposed to address the spectator. " Cambyses *broke this stone which you see before you, representing the image of the Eastern king † (Memnon)." 'Εκμεμάχθαι εἰκόνα (expressam esse imaginem) occurs in Lucian ; but here the word is used in an active sense, as in Nicander. Ther. γενεὴν ἐκμάσσεται ἵππου. ‡ It has been supposed by some, that the noise which issued from the vocal statue of Memnon was occasioned by an artifice of the priests in Egypt, who intended, by a pretended miracle, to oppose the progress of Christianity in that country. But we learn from this inscription, that sounds also proceeded from it at the time when Cambyses invaded Egypt. According to de Pauw, subterraneous grottoes, or galleries, passed probably under the statue ; and to make Memnon resound, nothing more was necessary than to strike the rock with an instrument of metal ; when the passages could no longer be preserved, the phænomenon ceased. A different explanation has been recently proposed ; see De Humboldt's Travels, vol. iv. p. 560.

The accounts of those who record their visit to the statue agree in saying, that the noise was heard early in the morning ; this is stated by Pausanias, Pliny, and Strabo. The latter suspected that the sounds were made by some one near the statue. In the following inscriptions, which are copied by Mr. Hamilton, from the legs and feet of the figure, the early part of the morning is mentioned by all the writers.

1   CAMILLUS HORA PRIMA SEMIS AUDIVI MEMNONEM
2   AUDIT MEMNONEM HORA PR.
3   AUDIVI MEMNONEM ANTE SECU HORAM

      ΚΛΑΥΔΙΟϹΕΜΙΛΙΟϹ
      ΑΡΑΒΑΡΧΗϹΚΑΙΕΠΙϹΤΡΑΤΗ
      ΓΟϹΘΗΒΑΙΔΟϹΗΚΟΥϹΑ
      ΑΝΑΠΛΕΩΝШΡΑϹΓ
      ΚΑΤΑΠΛΕΩΝШΡΑϹΒ

* Διέκοψε, Paus. l. i., speaking of this statue.   † Ηώω Μέμνονι. Philos. V. A. vi.
‡ Ἐκ· ἐκτυπόι. Schol.

LXII.

On a small votive helmet, found near Olympia, and now in the possession of Colonel Leake.

Ύφ ϴ ϚƎΟ ꞁΑΜ Ϛ Ο|Ο Ϙ

This inscription records the name of the workman ; Κῶος μ᾽ ἐπόει. The antient offerings are frequently represented as addressing themselves to the spectators. The Sigean stone furnishes us with a parallel form, ΜΕΠΟΕΙΣΕΝ, " Æsop made me;" on the tripod of great antiquity, seen by Herodotus at Thebes (l. 5.) was written, Αμφιτρύων μ᾽ ἀνέθηκε ; and on the cornucopia, dedicated by Miltiades, Ζηνὶ μ᾽ ἄγαλμ᾽ ἀνέθηκαν. Paus. l. vi. c. 8. See Chishull, An. As. 33. The Α is here used instead of Ε, according to a well-known form ; as ναώριον for νεώριον, in the Corcyrean inscription. Mus. Ver. xxxii. ; and the Æolo-Doric ποέω is retained. The Latins, whose language was derived from the Greek, preserved the same mode of writing the word in " poeta." The tense ἐπόιει is also a common tense, applied to works of art.

The three last letters are doubtful.

LXIII.

ΤΟΝΑϴΕΝΕΟΝΑϴΛΟΝΕΜΙ

Inscription on a vase found at Athens by Mr. Burgon. The form of the letters is very antient, and they are written from right to left. *

Two examples, and of considerable antiquity, may be cited to show that the Greeks wrote Ε for ΑΙ ; the well-known inscription which records the names of some who died in the beginning of the Pelopon-

---

* See Clarke's Travels, vol. vii. Preface ; where this inscription is given according to a fac-simile, accompanied with some remarks by Mr. Knight and Mr. Blomfield.

nesian war, gives ΑΛΚΜΕΟΝΙΔΕΣ; and the Sandwich marble has ΑΛΚΜΕΩΝΙΔΗΣ. Mr. Kidd (Dawes, Mis. Crit. p. 121.) cites ὁ νοσῶν δὲ μανικῶς Ἀλκμέων᾽ ἐσκέψατο, from Timocles. in Athen. vi. 223.

LXIV.

On a marble forming part of the Elgin collection, and now in the British Museum, are three Orchomenian inscriptions. They are printed in the first volume of this work, and in the Travels of Dr. Clarke, to whom Mr. Dobree has lately communicated a valuable illustration of one of them. * It is here inserted with their permission.

```
      ΑΡΧΟΝΤΟΣΕΝΕΡΧΟΜΕΝΥΘΥΝΑΡΧΩΜΕΙ
      ΝΟΣΑΛΑΛΚΟΜΕΝΙΩΕΝΔΕΦΕΛΑΤΙΗΜΕ
      ΝΟΙΤΑΟΑΡΧΕΛΑΩΜΕΙΝΟΣΠΡΑΤΩΟΜΟ
      ΛΟΓΑΕΥΒΩΛΥΓΕΛΑΤΙΗΥΚΗΤΗΠΟΛΙΕΡ
  5   ΧΟΜΕΝΙΩΝΕΠΙΔΕΙΚΕΚΟΜΙΣΤΗΕΥΒΩ
      ΛΟΣΠΑΡΤΑΣΠΟΛΙΟΣΤΟΔΑΝΕΙΟΝΑΠΑΝ
      ΚΑΤΤΑΣΟΜΟΛΟΓΙΑΣΤΑΣΤΕΘΕΙΣΑΣΘΥ
      ΝΑΡΧΩΑΡΧΟΝΤΟΣΜΕΙΝΟΣΘΕΙΛΟΥΘΙΩ
      ΚΗΟΥΤΟΦΕΙΛΕΤΗΑΥΤΥΕΤΙΟΥΘΕΝΠΑΡΤΑΝ
 10   ΠΟΛΙΝΑΛΛΑΠΕΧΙΠΑΝΤΑΠΕΡΙΠΑΝΤΟΣ
      ΚΗΑΠΟΔΕΔΟΑΝΘΙΤΗΠΟΛΙΤΥΕΧΟΝΤΕΣ
      ΤΑΣΟΜΟΛΟΓΙΑΣΕΙΜΕΝΠΟΤΙΔΕΔΟΜΕ
      ΝΟΝΧΡΟΝΟΝΕΥΒΩΛΥΕΠΙΝΟΜΙΑΣΦΕΤΙΑ
      ΠΕΤΤΑΡΑΒΟΥΕΣΣΙΣΟΥΝΙΠΠΥΣΔΙΑΚΑ
 15   ΤΙΗΣΦΙΚΑΤΙΠΡΟΒΑΤΥΣΣΟΥΝΗΓΥΣΧΕΙ
      ΛΙΗΣΑΡΧΙΤΩΧΡΟΝΩΟΕΝΙΑΥΤΟΣΟΜΕΤΑ
      ΘΥΝΑΡΧΟΝΑΡΧΟΝΤΑΕΡΧΟΜΕΝΙΥΣΑΠΟ
      ΓΡΑΦΕΣΘΗΔΕΕΥΒΩΛΟΝΚΑΤΕΝΙΑΥΤΟΝ
      ΕΚΑΣΤΟΝΠΑΡΤΟΝΤΑΜΙΑΝΚΗΤΟΝΝΟΜΩ
 20   ΝΑΝΤΑΤΕΚΑΥΜΑΤΑΤΩΝΠΡΟΒΑΤΩΝΚΗ
      ΤΑΝΗΓΩΝΚΗΤΑΝΒΟΥΩΝΚΗΤΑΝΙΠΠΩΝΚ
      ΚΑΤΙΝΑΑΣΑΜΑΙΩΝΘΙΚΗΤΟΠΛΕΙΘΟΣΜΕ
      ΑΠΟΓΡΑΦΕΣΘΩΔΕΠΛΙΟΝΑΤΩΝΓΕΓΡΑΜ
      ΜΕΝΩΝΕΝΤΗΣΟΥΓΧΩΡΕΙΣΙΗΔΕΚΑΤΙΣ
```

---

* Mr. Dobree was informed by one of the gentlemen of the British Museum that in the third line of the first inscription, the word appeared to be ΧΡΙΟΣ. This, according to the Bœotian dialect, is ΧΡΕΟΣ. It is followed by Ἀπέδωκα.

```
25  *   *   ΗΤΟΕΝΝΟΜΙΟΝΕΥΒΩΛΟΝΟΦΕΙΛ
    *   *   ΛΙΣΤΩΝΕΡΧΟΜΕΝΙΩΝΑΡΓΟΥΡΙΩ
    *   *   ΠΕΤΤΑΡΑΚΟΝΤΑΕΥΒΩΛΥΚΑΘΕΚΑΣ
    *   *   ΝΙΑΥΤΟΝΚΗΤΟΚΟΝΦΕΡΕΤΩΔΡΑ
    *   *   ΤΑΣΜΝΑΣΕΚΑΣΤΑΣΚΑΤΑΜΕΙΝΑ
30  *   *   ΤΟΝΚΗΕΜΠΡΑΚΤΟΣΕΣΤΟΕΥΒ - - -
    *   *   ΤΟΝΕΡΧΟΜΕΝΙΟΝ
```

The latter part of the inscription Mr. Dobree would read in this manner : —

```
21   ΚΗ or ΚΗ, Η
22   ΜΕΙ
25   ΕΜΠΡΑΤΤΗΤΟΕΝΝΟΜΙΟΝΕΥΒΩΛΟΝΟΦΕΙΛ
26   ΕΤΩΑΠΟΛΙΣΤΩΝΕΡΧΟΜΕΝΙΩΝΑΡΓΟΥΡΙΩ
27   ΜΝΑΣΠΕΤΤΑΡΑΚΟΝΤΑΕΥΒΩΛΥΚΑΘΕΚΑΣ
28   ΤΟΝΕΝΙΑΥΤΟΝΚΗΤΟΚΟΝΦΕΡΕΤΩΔΡΑΧ
29   ΜΑΣ - - - ΤΑΣΜΝΑΣΕΚΑΣΤΑΣΚΑΤΑΜΕΙΝΑ
30   ΕΚΑΣΤΟΝΚΗΕΜΠΡΑΚΤΟΣΕΣΤΩΕΥΒΩΛΥ
31   ΚΑΤΤΩΣΤΩΝΕΡΧΟΜΕΝΙΩΝΝΟΜΩΣ.
```

The whole of the inscription, according to his interpretation, is to be read in the common language, thus : —

Ἄρχοντος ἐν Ὀρχομενῷ Θυνάρχου, μη
νὸς Ἀλαλκομενίου, ἐν δὲ Ἐλατείᾳ Με
νοίτου Ἀρχελάου, μηνὸς πρώτου· Ὁμο
λογία Ἐυβούλῳ Ἐλατειαίῳ καὶ τῇ πόλει Ὀρ
χομενίων. Ἐπειδὴ κεκόμισται Ἔυβου
λος παρὰ τῆς πόλεως τὸ δάνειον ἄπαν
κατὰ τὰς ὁμολογίας τὰς τεθείσας Θυ
νάρχου Ἄρχοντος μηνὸς Θειλουθίου,
καὶ οὐκ ὀφείλεται αὐτῷ ἔτι οὐδὲν παρὰ τὴν
πόλιν, ἀλλ᾽ ἀπέχει πάντα περὶ παντὸς,
καὶ ἀποδεδώκασι τῇ πόλει οἱ ἔχοντες
τὰς ὁμολογίας· Ἔιναι πρὸς δεδομέ-
νον χρόνον Ἐυβούλῳ ἐπινομίας, ἔτη
τέτταρα, βουσὶ σὺν ἵπποις διηκο
σίαις ἔικοσι, προβάτοις σὺν αἰξί χι
λίαις. Ἄρχει τοῦ χρόνου ὁ ἐνιαυτὸς ὁ μετὰ

Θύναρχον ἄρχοντα Ὀρχομενίοις. Ἀπο
γράφεσθαι δὲ Ἐύβουλον κατ᾽ ἐνιαυτὸν
ἕκαστον παρὰ τὸν ταμίαν καὶ τὸν νομώ
νην τά τε καύματα τῶν προβάτων καὶ
τῶν αἰγῶν καὶ τῶν βοῶν καὶ τῶν ἵππων, κἂν
τινα ἄσημα ὦσι, καὶ τὸ πλῆθος· μὴ
ἀπογραφέσθω δὲ πλείονα τῶν γεγραμ
μένων ἐν τῇ συγχωρήσει. Ἐὰν δέ τις
ἐμπράττῃ τὸ ἐννόμιον Εὔβουλον, ὀφειλ
έτω ἡ πόλις τῶν Ὀρχομενίων ἀργυρίου
μνᾶς τετταράκοντα Εὐβόυλῳ καθ᾽ ἕκασ
τον ἐνιαυτόν· καὶ τόκον φερέτω δραχ-
μὰς - -ʹ - - τῆς μνᾶς ἑκάστης κατὰ μῆνα
ἕκαστον, καὶ ἔμπρακτος ἔστω Εὐβούλῳ
κατὰ τοὺς τῶν Ὀρχομενίων νόμους.

MR. DOBREE'S NOTES.

L. 13. I put a comma after ἐπινομίας. " Let Eubulus have a right
of pasturage for a given time; that is to say, the right of grazing, for
four years, 220 head of cattle, including horses, and 1000 sheep, including goats;" i. e. a horse to reckon as an ox, and a goat as a
sheep.

L. 19. Νομώνης is the contractor who farms the public pasture-land.
Thus, τελώνης, ἐργώνης, in Chandler's Marm. Ox. XLIX. Eubulus enters
his cattle at the offices of the treasurer and of the contractor, that
their accounts may check each other.

L. 20. Καῦμα, or ἔγκαυμα, is a burnt-in mark. See Scaliger on
Varro de L. L. p. 107. ed. 1619., and the notes on Hesychius, vv.
κοππατίας et τρυσίππιον. Eubulus is to register, 1. the marks of his
cattle, horses, &c. specifying any that may be unmarked; 2. the
number of each sort.

L. 22. Ἰῶνθι is for ὦσι (ἔωσι), I being put for E, as in ΑΓΩΝΟΘΕΤΙ-
ΟΝΤΟΣ and ΔΟΚΙΕΙ, in other Orchomenian inscriptions, and ΙΟΣΑΣ

'(ΙΩΣΑΣ) for ὄυσης, in one at Thebes, which Pococke has given with his characteristic inaccuracy. p. 50.

The following list of examples showing the nature of the dialect in use among the people of Bœotia may be here added to Mr. Dobree's notes. I have selected them from various inscriptions found in that country.

I for EI, as in ΠΛΙΟΝΑ; Υ for Ω *, in ΕΥΒΩΛΥ; H for ΑΙ, in ΚΗ; ΔΙΑΚΑΤΙΟΣ for διακόσιος, presents A for O, according to the Dorian use of ΥΠΑ for ΥΠΟ, and Τ † for Σ. ΕΙ occurs for H in ΜΕΙΝΑ, the ac_ cusative of the Æolic ΜΕΙΣ, and also for ΑΙ in an inscription copied by Dr. Clarke at Orchomenus, where we read ΑΘΑΝΕΙΟΣ, ΘΕΙΒΕΙΟΣ; I for E in ΠΟΛΙΟΣ; Υ for ΟΙ ‡ in ΤΥ (τοὶ), E for O in the name of the town of Orchomenus, which substitution is also found on their money; and A for E in ΑΓΧΙΑΡΟΣ; ΟΥ § for Υ in ΣΟΥΝ. ‖ In the words ΗΓΥΣ, (ΑΙΞΙ in the common dialect) ΙΩΝΘΙ, and ΑΠΟΔΕΔΟΑΝΘΙ, the forms are singular. In the last there are no less than four changes arising from the dialect: 1. in the use of Θ for Τ. Lanzi quotes ΑΓΑΘΑΙ ΘΥΧΑΙ; a lamp in Passeri bears the words ΑΡΘΕΜ. ΙΕΡΟΣ; and the name of the people of Crete, Ἱεραπύτνιοι, is written on a coin in Vaillant's collection, ΙΕΡΑΠΥΘΝΙΩΝ ¶, which word is also given by Gruter in his Inscriptions with Θ. 2. In the termination, αντι for ασι, as in ἱστάκαντι, πεφύκαντι, πεποιήκαντι. 3. In the use of O for Ω. ** 4. In the omission of Κ. ††

---

* In Sappho, χελύνη for χελώνη. Greg. de Dial. ed. Schaef. 586.
† Ποτιδᾶν, Ποσειδῶν, Epichar. in Athen. l. vii.
‡ Ἐμὺ, ἐμόι. Apoll. Dyscolus, in Maitt. 555.
§ Ἰαρὸς and τάμνειν. See Greg de Dial.
‖ Illud ΟΥ pro Υ, in multis scriptum est. Valck. Theoc. 279.
¶ The Tuscans, who had many Æolisms in their language, said Thelephus for Te- lephus, and Atresthe for Adrastus. Lanzi, i. 247. 255.
** The Dorians said ΟΤΕΙΛΗ. Greg. de Dial. 618.¹
†† The Æolians wrote πεποιηός. Maittaire de D. 162. Τεθνηότος occurs in Hom. Il. ϱ. 435 ,; βεβάασι for βεβήκασι. Il. β. 134. In Herodotus the κ is omitted, as in ἑστεώς. L. 3. See Maitt. 161.

ΠΑΣΙΚΛΕΙΝ and ΔΑΜΟΤΕΛΕΙΝ, in the first of the three inscriptions, are the accusatives of Pasicles and Damoteles *; ΠΕΤΤΑΡΑ is the origin of the Oscan, petorritum, " a four-wheeled carriage."† ΕΠΑΣΙΝ has been lately well explained by Boissonade, in his notes on Herodian; the word is found in an inscription copied at Orchomenus by Col. Leake and Mr. Cockerell; and in the same we read ΤΙΟΥΧΑΝ for ΤΥΧΑΝ. The digamma occurs in various words; in ΕΑΡΝΩΝ, ΕΕΛΑΤΙΗ, ΕΙΚΑΤΙ, ΕΥΚΙΑΣ; and on an Orchomenian marble seen by Dr. Clarke ‡, ΑΥΛΑΕΥΔΟΣ, ΚΟΜΑΕΥΔΟΣ.

LXV.

ΒΑΣΙΛΕΩΣ ΔΙΝΩΝΟΣ -

" I saw at Athens, in the possession of Mr. Fauvel, an inscription brought from the island of Samothrace, consisting only of these words. They were inscribed on a cippus, on which was sculptured the entrance of a temple; and on each side the representation of a lighted torch, being emblematical of the mysteries for which that island was celebrated. It would have been difficult to identify the name of this monarch, had it not been explained by Livy, who states (lib. xlv. c. 5.) that the chief magistrates of Samothrace were styled kings, although it does appear to have ever been an independent state. This is an additional confirmation of the close connection in early times of the offices of chief priest and king, the titles of which were, in truth, nearly synonymous. Thus the king archon, at Athens, continued to preside over sacrifices, and to regulate religious ceremonies, &c. The word which appears strictly to signify the kingly office, and which did not bear the evil interpretation given to it in more recent times, is ΤΥΡΑΝΝΟΣ." — Extracts from Lord Aberdeen's Journal.

---

* " In inscriptionibus sæpe invenias Ἐυσεβῆν aliaque hujus commatis." Th. Mag. See the note, p. 424. Μενεκλῆν, Διοκλῆν, are given in the Oxford Mar. ed. Maittaire. Ind. v. contracta.

† Menage, in Jur. Civ. Amæn. p. 7., and Hemster. in Polluc. l. ii. 1059.

‡ Travels, vol. vii. p. 200.

LXVI.

It appears very probable, from the recent discoveries of M. Caviglia in Egypt, that a temple once stood on the platform in front of the Sphinx, and centrally between the paws. The large block of granite, 14 feet high, and two tablets of calcareous stone, which were found there, formed part of it. The inscription sculptured on the second digit of one of the paws, describes the Sphinx, (according to the proposed reading of Dr. Young,) as " the attendant or minister of Latona." Τῇ δὲ θεᾷ Λητοῖ πρόσπολον ἀγυοτάτην. We find that a temple, sacred to this goddess, stood in a district of Memphis. *

On the granite block were represented two *Sphinxes* on pedestals. It appears, therefore, that this symbolical figure was connected with the worship of *Latona*, as it was with that of her daughter. " Utrumque Dianæ latus duæ Sphinges muniunt." † But Jablonski, in his chapter on Latona, or Buto, does not mention the Sphinx.

The skilful restoration of the inscription, by Dr. Young, may be seen in the Quarterly Review, vol. xix. p. 412. In the copy sent from Egypt, the first line is CONΔΕΜΑCΕΠΙΑΓΥΟΝΓΕΥΣΑΝΟΙΟΝΙΕΝΕΟΝΤΕC, which Dr. Young reads, Σὸν δέμας ἔκπαγλον τεῦξαν θεοὶ αἰὲν ἔοντες. The reader will recollect that the three last words terminate a line in Homer; and τεῦξαν θεοὶ occurs in an epigram in the Anthol. ed. Steph. 315.

In line 5. the copy presents ΘCCANEI OPACΘAI, which Dr. Young reads θέσαν εἰσοράασθαι. In an inscription in Falconer (In. Athlet. p. 149.) we find θῆκεν ὁράασθαι.

---

* Λητοῦς πόλις, μοῖρα Μεμφίδος, καθ' ἣν αἱ Πυράμιδες καὶ Λητοῦς ἱερόν. Steph. Byz.
† Claudius Menetreius de Diana Ephesi Statua Symbolica.

Printed by A. and R. Spottiswoode,
Printers-Street, London.

APPENDIX.

—◆—

INSCRIPTIONS *relating to the incorporated bodies of* ACTORS *and* MUSICIANS *established on the Coast of Ionia and the Hellespont, under the protection of the Attali.*

THE Marble containing these inscriptions was found at Sedgikeui, a village situate a short distance to the south of Smyrna; it was brought to England in the year 1732, and has been lately presented to the University of Cambridge. A copy was taken by Maittaire, and printed at the end of his edition of the Arundel marbles. They are now published according to an accurate transcript made from the original stone by Dr. E. D. Clarke, (to whom this valuable relic was presented for the University by his friend Mr. Harvey, of Jesus College) in the types which he invented to imitate the lithography of the antient Greeks.

That the reader may understand more readily the general purport of them, we may observe, that Eumenes mentioned in line 3, was king of Pergamus, and died 158 B. C. He was deified by his brother Attalus: hence the inscription mentions the Ἱερεύς, who officiated at the sacred ceremonies and festivals celebrated in honour of him; that, the persons called Διονυσιακοὶ τεχνῖται engaged for certain sums * to represent dramatic and musical † entertainments of various kinds: that they answered, according to Plutarch, ‡ to the Latin Histriones; that, during the reigns of Eumenes and Attalus they received great protection, being established at Lebedus; § and formed themselves into different bodies or companies, which assumed the fol-

---

* Montfaucon Di. It. 412, publishes a Corcyrean inscription, in which "Aristomenes gives to the city of Corcyra 60 minæ of Corinthian money for the purpose of hiring the players; εἰς τὰν τῶν τεχνιτᾶν μίσθωσιν.

† Ita vocantur actores cantoresque scenici. Wytt. in Plut. Anim. vol. I. 619.

‡ Διὰ τί τοὺς περὶ τὸν Διόνυσον τεχνίτας Ἱστριώνας οἱ Ῥωμαῖοι καλοῦσι; in Rom. Qu. 289.

§ Strabo. lib. xiv. p. 922.

* A

lowing appellations : τὸ κοινὸν τῶν περὶ Διόνυσον τεχνίτων· κοινὸν τῶν Ατταλιστῶν· κοινὸν τῆς Εχίνου Συμμορίας. Their Scenic exhi. bitions were not only performed in Ionia, and thence, as far as the Hellespont ; but also in Greece, at Nemea, and in the Isthmus of Corinth. Many individuals bequeathed money to these Societies, and shewed to them various acts of liberality and kindness ; in return, they were honoured by a commemoration of thanks registered on marble, as in the inscriptions before us, and in the Attalic monuments published by Chishull. It appears also, that these Societies had their own Priests.

Crato son of Zotichus is the person commended in these decrees ; he is honoured by a statue ; and by being allowed the privilege of wearing a crown for life ; and after his death, (which took place at Pergamus,) particular days were in memory of him,· called by his name.*

```
ΕΓΙΙΕΡΕΩΣΣΑΤΥΡΟΥΚΑΙΑΓΩΝΟΘΕΤΟΥΚΑΙ
ΙΕΡΕΩΣΒΑΣΙΛΕΩΣΕΥΜΕΝΟΥΝΙΚΟΤΕΛΟΥΣ
ΕΔΟΞΕΝΤΩΙΚΟΙΝΩΙΤΩΝΓΕΡΙΤΟΝΔΙΟΝΥΣΟΝΤΕΧΝ:
ΤΩΝΤΩΝΕΓΙΩΝΙΑΣΚΑΙΕΛΛΗΣΓΟΝΤΟΥΚΑΙΤΩΝΓΕΡ:
ΤΟΝΚΑΘΗΓΕΜΟΝΑΔΙΟΝΥΣΟΝΕΓΕΙΔΗΚΡΑΤΩΝΣΩΤΙΧΟΥ
ΑΥΛΗΤΗΣΕΥΕΡΓΕΤΗΣΕΝΤΕΤΩΙΓΡΟΤΕΡΟΝΧΡΟΝΩΙΤΗΙΣ
ΓΑΣΑΝΣΓΟΥΔΗΝΚΑΙΓΡΟΝΟΙΑΝΕΙΧΕΝΤΩΝΚΟΙΝΕΙΣΥΜΦΕ
ΡΟΝΤΩΝΤΕΙΣΥΝΟΔΩΙΚΑΙΤΙΜΗΘΕΙΣΑΞΙΩΣΩΝΕΥΕΡΓΕΤΗ
ΚΕΝΥΓΕΡΤΙΘΕΤΑΙΤΕΙΕΥΝΟΙΑΙΚΑΙΦΙΛΟΤΙΜΙΑΙΤΕΙΕΙΣΤΟΥΣ
ΤΕΧΝΙΤΑΣΓΑΝΤΑΓΡΑΤΤΩΝΤΑΣΥΜΦΕΡΟΝΤΑΔΕΔΟΧΘΑΙ
ΤΩΙΚΟΙΝΩΙΤΩΝΓΕΡΙΤΟΝΔΙΟΝΥΣΟΝΤΕΧΝΙΤΩΝΕΓΑΙΝΕΣΑΙ
ΜΕΝΚΡΑΤΩΝΑΣΩΤΙΧΟΥΑΥΛΗΤΗΝΕΥΕΡΓΕΤΗΝΕΓΙΤΩΙΤΗΝ
ΑΥΤΗΝΕΧΕΙΝΑΙΕΙΓΡΟΑΙΡΕΣΙΝΤΗΣΕΥΕΡΓΕΣΙΑΣΤΗΣΕΙΣ
ΑΓΑΝΤΑΣΤΟΥΣΤΕΧΝΙΤΑΣΓΡΟΣΔΟΥΝΑΙΔΕΑΥΤΩΙΓΡΟΣ
ΤΑΙΣΓΡΟΥΓΑΡΧΟΥΣΑΙΣΤΙΜΑΙΣΑΝΑΚΗΡΥΞΙΝΤΕΣΤΕΦΑ
ΝΟΥΤΟΥΕΚΤΟΥΝΟΜΟΥΗΜΓΟΙΗΣΕΤΑΙΑΙΕΙΕΝΤΩΙΘΕΑΤΡΩΙΟ
ΕΚΑΣΤΟΤΕΓΙΝΟΜΕΝΟΣΑΓΩΝΟΘΕΤΗΣΚΑΙΙΕΡΕΥΣΒΑΣΙΛΕΩΣ
ΕΥΜΕΝΟΥΕΝΤΗΙΒΑΣΙΛΕΩΣΕΥΜΕΝΟΥΗΜΕΡΑΙΟΤΑΝΗΤΕΓΟΜΓΗ
ΔΙΕΛΘΗΙΚΑΙΑΙΣΤΕΦΑΝΩΣΕΙΣΣΥΝΤΕΛΩΝΤΑΙΟΜΟΙΩΣΔΕ
ΚΑΙΓΑΡΑΤΟΝΓΟΤΟΝΓΙΝΕΣΘΩΤΗΙΑΥΤΗΙΗΜΕΡΑΙΜΕΤΑΤΑΣ
```

* Ἐπωνύμους ἡμέρας Κράτωνος. Chishull, p. 142.

ΣΓΟΝΔΑΣΥΓΟΤΩΝΑΡΧΟΝΤΩΝΗΑΝΑΓΓΕΛΙΑΤΟΥΣΤΕΦΑΝΟΥ
ΓΑΡΑΤΙΘΕΣΘΑΙΔΕΚΑΙΕΝΤΑΙΣΘΕΑΙΣΚΑΙΕΝΤΑΙΣΓΟΜΓΑΙΣΓΑ
ΡΑΤΟΝΑΝΔΡΙΑΝΤΑΤΟΝΚΡΑΤΩΝΟΣΤΟΝΕΝΤΩΙΘΕΑΤΡΩΙΤΡΙΓΟ
ΔΑΤΕΚΑΙΟΥΜΙΑΤΗΡΙΟΝΚΑΙΤΗΣΕΓΙΘΥΜΙΑΣΕΩΣΤΗΝΕΓΙΜΕΛΕΙ
ΑΝΚΑΘΕΚΑΣΤΟΝΕΤΟΣΑΙΕΙΓΟΙΕΙΣΘΑΙΤΟΝΑΓΩΝΟΘΕΤΗΝΚΑΙ
ΙΕΡΕΑΒΑΣΙΛΕΩΣΕΥΜΕΝΟΥΓΙΝΟΜΕΝΟΝ

ΕΔΟΞΕΝΤΩΙΚΟΙΝΩΙΤΩΝΣΥΝΑΓΩΝΙΣΤΩΝΕΓΕΙΔΗΚΡΑΤΩΝ
ΣΩΤΙΧΟΥΚΑΛΧΗΔΟΝΙΟΣΑΥΛΗΤΗΣΕΥΝΟΥΣΩΝΔΙΑΤΕ
ΛΕΙΤΩΙΚΟΙΝΩΙΤΩΝΣΥΝΑΓΩΝΙΣΤΩΝΚΑΙΛΕΓΩΝΚΑΙ
ΓΡΑΤΤΩΝΑΙΕΙΤΑΣΥΜΦΕΡΟΝΤΑΤΟΙΣΣΥΝΑΓΩΝΙΣΤΑΙΣ
ΙΕΡΕΥΣΤΕΑΙΡΕΘΕΙΣΓΡΟΤΕΡΟΝΤΗΝΓΑΣΑΝΕΓΙΜΕΛΕΙΑΝ
ΕΓΟΙΗΣΑΤΟΤΑΣΤΕΘΥΣΙΑΣΣΥΝΕΤΕΛΕΣΕΝΓΑΣΑΣΟΣΙ
ΩΣΜΕΝΤΑΓΡΟΣΤΟΥΣΘΕΟΥΣΚΑΙΤΟΥΣΒΑΣΙΛΕΙΣΚΑΛΩΣ
ΔΕΚΑΙΕΝΔΟΞΩΣΤΑΓΡΟΣΓΑΝΤΑΣΤΟΥΣΣΥΝΑΓΩΝΙΣΤΑΣ
ΟΥΤΕΔΑΓΑΝΗΣΟΥΤΕΦΙΛΟΤΙΜΙΑΣΟΥΘΕΝΕΛΛΕΙΓΩΝΚΑΙ
ΝΥΝΔΕΑΓΩΝΟΟΕΤΗΣΓΕΝΟΜΕΝΟΣΚΑΛΩΣΤΩΝΑΓΩΝΩΝ
ΓΡΟΣΤΑΣΚΑΙΤΟΙΣΝΟΜΟΙΣΑΚΟΛΟΥΘΗΣΑΣΑΙΕΙΜΝΗΣΤΟΝ
ΤΟΙΣΕΓΙΓΙΝΟΜΕΝΟΙΣΚΑΤΕΛΙΓΕΝΤΗΝΑΡΧΗΝΙΝΑΟΥΝΚΑΙ
ΟΙΣΥΝΑΓΩΝΙΣΤΑΙΕΜΓΑΝΤΙΚΑΙΡΩΙΦΑΙΝΩΝΤΑΙΤΙΜΩΝΤΕΣ
ΤΟΥΣΕΞΕΑΥΤΩΝΔΕΔΟΧΘΑΙΤΩΙΚΟΙΝΩΙΤΩΝΣΥΝΑΓΩΝΙΣ
ΤΩΝΣΤΕΦΑΝΟΥΝΚΡΑΤΩΝΑΣΩΤΙΧΟΥΚΑΛΧΗΔΟΝΙΟΝΔΙΑ
ΒΙΟΥΕΝΤΕΤΩΙΚΟΙΝΩΙΔΕΙΓΝΩΙΤΩΝΣΥΝΑΓΩΝΙΣΤΩΝΚΑΙΕΝ
ΤΩΙΘΕΑΤΡΩΙΓΟΙΟΥΜΕΝΟΥΣΤΗΝΑΝΑΓΟΡΕΥΣΙΝΤΗΝΔΕΤΟ
ΤΟΚΟΙΝΟΝΤΩΝΣΥΝΑΓΩΝΙΣΤΩΝΣΤΕΦΑΝΟΙΚΡΑΤΩΝΑΩΣΤΙΧΟΥ
ΚΑΛΧΗΔΟΝΙΟΝΣΤΕΦΑΝΩΙΤΩΙΕΚΤΟΥΝΟΜΟΥΑΡΕΤΗΣΕΝΕΚΕΝ
ΚΑΙΕΥΝΟΙΑΣΗΣΕΧΩΝΔΙΑΤΕΛΕΙΕΙΣΤΟΥΣΣΥΝΑΓΩΝΙΣ
ΤΑΣΤΗΣΔΕΑΝΑΓΓΕΛΙΑΣΤΗΣΤΟΥΣΤΕΦΑΝΟΥΕΓΙΜΕ
ΛΕΙΣΘΑΙΤΟΥΣΑΡΧΟΝΤΑΣΤΟΥΣΚΑΤΕΝΙΑΥΤΟΝΑΙΡΟΥ
ΜΕΝΟΥΣΙΝΑΔΕΚΑΙΤΟΙΣΑΛΛΟΙΣΓΑΣΙΝΦΑΝΕΡΑΗΙΕΙΣ
ΤΟΝΑΓΑΝΤΑΧΡΟΝΟΝΗΤΩΝΣΥΝΑΓΩΝΙΣΤΩΝΕΥΧΑΡΙΣ
ΤΙΑΑΝΑΓΡΑΨΑΙΤΟΨΗΦΙΣΜΑΤΟΔΕΕΙΣΣΤΗΛΗΝΛΙΘΙΝΗΝ
ΚΑΙΣΤΗΣΑΙΓΡΟΣΤΩΙΔΙΟΝΥΣΙΩΙΕΝΤΩΙΕΓΙΦΑΝΕΣΤΑ
ΤΩΙΤΟΓΩΙΑΝΑΘΕΙΝΑΙΔΕΑΥΤΟΥΚΑΙΕΙΚΟΝΑΕΝΤΩΙΔΙΟΝΥ
ΣΙΩΙΓΡΑΓΤΗΝΤΕΛΕΙΑΝΕΓΙΓΡΑΨΑΝΤΑΣΤΟΚΟΙΝΟΝΤΩΝ
ΣΥΝΑΓΩΝΙΣΤΩΝΣΤΕΦΑΝΟΙΚΡΑΤΩΝΑΣΩΤΙΧΟΥΚΑΛ
ΧΗΔΟΝΙΟΝΑΡΕΤΗΣΕΝΕΚΕΝΚΑΙΕΥΝΟΙΑΣΤΗΣΕΙΣΑΥ
ΤΟΥΣ

ΤΩΝΕΝΙΣΩΜΩΙΚΑΙΝΕΜΕΑΙΤΕΧΝΙΤΩΝ

ΕΓΕΙΔΗΚΡΑΤΩΝΣΩΤΙΧΟΥΓΕΡΓΑΜΗΝΟΣΑΥΛΗΤΗΣΚΥ
ΚΛΙΟΣΓΡΟΤΕΡΟΝΤΕΓΟΛΛΑΣΚΑΙΜΕΓΑΛΑΣΓΑΡΕΣ
ΧΗΤΑΙΧΡΕΙΑΣΚΑΤΙΔΙΑΝΤΕΤΟΙΣΕΝΤΥΓΧΑΝΟΥΣΙΝ

4 APPENDIX.

I.

Ἐπὶ Ἱερέως Σατύρου καὶ Ἀγωνοθέτου κ[αι
Ἱερέως βασιλέως Εὐμένου Νικοτελο[υς
Ἔδοξεν τῶι κοινῶι τῶν περὶ τὸν Διόνυσον τεχν[ι
τῶν τῶν ἐπ' Ἰωνίας καὶ Ἑλλησπόντου καὶ τῶν πε[ρι
τὸν καθηγεμόνα Διόνυσον· Ἐπειδὴ Κράτων Ζωτίχο[υ
αὐλητὴς ἐνεργέτης ἔν τε τῶι πρότερον χρόνωι τ[ην
πᾶσαν σπουδὴν καὶ πρόνοιαν εἶχεν τῶν κοινεῖ συμ[φε
ρόντων τεῖ συνόδωι· καὶ τιμηθεὶς ἀξίως ὧν εὐεργέτ[η
κεν ὑπερτίθεται τεῖ εὐνοίαι καὶ φιλοτιμίαι τεῖ εἰς τοὺς
τεχνίτας πάντα πράττων τὰ συμφέροντα· Δεδόχθαι   10
τῶι κοινῶι τῶν περὶ τὸν Διόνυσον τεχνίτων ἐπαινέσαι.
μὲν Κράτωνα Ζωτίχου αὐλητὴν ἐνεργέτην ἐπὶ τῶι τὴν
αὐτὴν ἔχειν ἀιεὶ προαίρεσιν τῆς εὐεργεσίας τῆς εἰς
ἅπαντας τοὺς τεχνίτας· προσδοῦναι δὲ αὐτῶι πρὸς
ταῖς προυπαρχούσαις τιμαῖς ἀνακήρυξίν τε στεφά   15
νου τοῦ ἐκ τοῦ νόμου, ἢμ ποιήσεται ἀιεὶ ἐν τῶι θεάτρωι ὁ
ἑκάστοτε γινόμενος ἀγωνοθέτης καί ἱερεὺς βασιλέως
Εὐμένου ἐν τῆι βασιλέως Εὐμένου ἡμέραι, ὅταν ἡ τε πομπ[η·
διέλθηι καὶ αἱ στεφανώσεις συντελῶνται· ὁμοίως δὲ
καὶ παρὰ τὸν πότον γινέσθω τῆι αὐτῆι ἡμέραι μετὰ τὰς   20
σπονδὰς ὑπὸ τῶν ἀρχόντων ἡ ἀναγγελία τοῦ στεφάνου·
παρατίθεσθαι δὲ καὶ ἐν ταῖς θέαις καὶ ἐν ταῖς πομπαῖς πα
ρὰ τὸν ἀνδρίαντα τὸν Κράτωνος τὸν ἐν τῶι θεάτρωι τρίπο
δά τε καὶ θυμιατήριον· καὶ τῆς ἐπιθυμιάσεως τὴν ἐπιμέλει
αν καθ' ἕκαστον ἔτος ἀιεὶ ποιεῖσθαι τὸν ἀγωνοθέτην καὶ   25
ἱερέα βασιλέως Εὐμένου γινόμενον.

II.

Ἔδοξεν τῶι κοινῶι τῶν συναγωνιστῶν· Ἐπειδὴ Κράτων
Ζωτίχου Καλχηδόνιος αὐλητὴς εὔνους ὤν διατε
λεῖ τῶι κοινῶι τῶν συναγωνιστῶν καὶ λέγων καὶ
πράττων ἀιεὶ τὰ συμφέροντα τοῖς συναγωνισταῖς   30

ἱερεύς τε αἱρεθεὶς πρότερον τὴν πᾶσαν ἐπιμέλειαν
ἐποιήσατο, τάς τε θυσίας συνετέλεσεν πάσας, ὁσί
ὡς μὲν τὰ πρὸς τοὺς θεοὺς καὶ τοὺς βασιλεῖς, καλῶς
δὲ καὶ ἐνδόξως τὰ πρὸς πάντας τοὺς συναγωνιστὰς
οὔτε δαπάνης οὔτε φιλοτιμίας οὐθὲν ἐλλείπων· καὶ   35
νῦν δὲ ἀγωνοθέτης γενόμενος καλῶς τῶν ἀγώνων
προστὰς καὶ τοῖς νόμοις ἀκολουθήσας ἀιείμνηστον
τοῖς ἐπιγινομένοις κατέλιπεν τὴν ἀρχήν· ἵνα οὖν καὶ
οἱ συναγωνισταὶ ἐμπαντὶ καιρῶι φαίνωνται τιμῶντες
τοὺς ἐξ ἑαυτῶν· Δεδόχθαι τῶι κοινῶι τῶν συναγωνισ   40
τῶν στεφανοῦν Κράτωνα Ζωτίχου Καλχηδόνιον διὰ
βίου, ἔντε τῶι κοινῶι δείπνωι τῶν συναγωνιστῶν, καὶ ἐν
τῶι θεάτρωι ποιουμένους τὴν ἀναγόρευσιν τηνδε· το
τὸ κοινὸν τῶν συναγωνιστῶν στεφανοῖ Κράτωνα Ζωτίχου
Καλχηδόνιον στεφανῶι τῶι ἐκ τοῦ νόμου ἀρετῆς ἕνεκεν   45
καὶ εὐνοίας ἧς ἔχων διατελεῖ εἰς τοὺς συναγωνισ
τάς· τῆς δὲ ἀναγγελίας τῆς τοῦ στεφάνου ἐπιμε
λεῖσθαι τοὺς ἄρχοντας τοὺς κατ' ἐνιαυτὸν αἱρου
μένους· ἵνα δὲ καὶ τοῖς ἄλλοις πᾶσιν φανερὰ ἦι εἰς
τὸν πάντα χρόνον ἡ τῶν συναγωνιστῶν εὐχαρισ   50
τία ἀναγράψαι τὸ ψήφισμα τόδε εἰς τὴν στήλην λιθίνην
καὶ στῆσαι πρὸς τῶι Διονυσίωι ἐν τῶι ἐπιφανεστά
τωι τόπωι· ἀναθεῖναι δὲ αὐτοῦ καὶ εἰκόνα ἐν τῶι Διονυ
σίωι γραπτὴν τελείαν ἐπιγράψαντας· τὸ κοινὸν τῶν
συναγωνιστῶν στεφανοῖ Κράτωνα Ζωτίχου Καλ   55
χηδόνιον ἀρετῆς ἕνεκεν καὶ εὐνοίας τῆς εἰς αὐ
τούς.

Τῶν ἐν Ἰσθμῶι καὶ Νεμέαι τεχνιτῶν.
Ἐπειδὴ Κράτων Ζωτίχου Περγαμηνὸς αὐλητὴς κύ
κλιος πρότερόν τε πολλὰς καὶ μεγάλας παρέσ
χηται χρείας κατ' ἰδίαν τε τοῖς ἐντυγχάνουσιν

VERSION.

" When Satyrus was priest (to the Society of Actors,) and when Nicoteles was Agonotheta and priest of King Eumenes; the Society of those Actors, who are established in Ionia and as far* as the Hellespont, and of those who are under the protection of Bacchus, decreed.—Whereas Crato son of Zotichus, a performer on the flute, a benefactor, hath both in former times paid every regard and consideration to the interests of this body; and having been honoured for the benefits which he conferred, still continues to shew good will and a friendly disposition to the Actors, doing whatever is advantageous to them; it is agreed by the Community, to commend Crato son of Zotichus, performer on the flute, Benefactor, because he continues to entertain those same sentiments of benevolence, which he has shewn towards all the Actors; and that in addition to the honours already bestowed on him, there shall be granted to him a proclamation of a crown given according to the law, which proclamation the person who happens to be at the time Agonotheta and Priest of King Eumenes, shall cause † to be made always in the theatre, on the day of King Eumenes, when the procession passes by, and the ceremony of coronation takes place: and likewise on the same day after the libations are offered, during the feast there shall be made a declaration of the Crown by the Archons; and at the time when the shews are exhibited and the procession passes by, there shall be placed by the statue of Crato, which is in the Theatre, a tripod and censer: and he who happens to be Agonotheta and priest of King Eumenes, shall have charge of the incense every year."

II.

" It is agreed upon by the Society of the Συναγωνισταί, or those who are engaged together in Dramatic and Musical exhibitions:—Whereas Crato son of Zotichus, a citizen of Chalcedon, performer on the flute,

---

* See the citation from Strabo in the note on line 4.

† Ἀργεῖοι σφέων εἰκόνας ποιησάμενοι. Herod. I. 31. " caused statues to be made." Matthiæ Gr. Gram. Blomfield's Transl. p. 714. 2.

continues to be well disposed to the Society, both by word and deed consulting the interests of it : and when he was chosen priest formerly, shewed all possible attention; and performed all the sacrifices, religiously, in what relates to the Gods and to the Kings, and splendidly and honourably in what concerns the Society, deficient in no degree either in expence or liberality ; and latterly when he was Agonotheta, by his proper conduct as president of the games, and by his obedience to the laws, has left his magistracy a subject of perpetual remembrance to his successors; in order therefore, that the Corporation of Joint Actors may at all times appear to honour those who belong to their body, it has decreed to give to Crato of Chalcedon, son of Zotichus, a crown for life, making at the same time this declaration, both at the common supper of the members, and in the theatre : " the society of the actors crown Crato, of Chalcedon, son of Zotichus, with a crown, given according to the law, on account of his virtue, and the good will which he continues to entertain towards them :" The magistrates chosen every year shall have the charge of the proclamations of the crown; and that the gratitude of the members be for ever manifest to all persons, they have ordered this decree to be written on a marble stele, and to be fixed in the most conspicuous place near to the temple of Bacchus ; and a painted statue of him, at full length, to be placed in the said temple, bearing this inscription :—The society of Joint Actors crown Crato son of Zotichus, of Chalcedon, on account of his virtue, and his good will towards them.

" The actors at the Isthmus and at Nemea, decree,

" Since Crato of Pergamus, son of Zotichus, a player on the flute, who performs publicly, and gives lessons in his art in different towns, hath formerly conferred many and great services, both privately on those who are acquainted with him, (and) "

NOTES.

Line 1. τῶν τεχνίτων is understood after ἱερέως· ἐπὶ ἱερέως τῶν τεχνίτων Κρατίνου καὶ ἀγωνοθέτου καὶ ἱερέως Θεοῦ Εὐμένου Ἀρισταίου. Chish. An. As. p. 146.

2. Εὐμένου. The same form (Κναξάρου) occurs in Xenophon, and in the Milesian inscriptions in Chishull, Μενεκράτου, Εὐκράτου. p. 149.

4. In Strabo. σύνοδος τεχνιτῶν καὶ κατοικία τῶν ἐν Ἰωνίᾳ μέχρι Ἑλλησπόντου. Lib. xiv. 922.

5. Maittaire prints καθηγημόνα; the marble has καθηγεμόνα; so in Van Dalen, 252, ἱερεὺς τοῦ Καθηγεμόνος Διός.

5. Maittaire prefers Ζωτίκου. But the name of Crato's father is also written Ζωτίχος in Chishull; and we have Ἀμύντιχος, Θυώνιχος, Πύρριχος, Λεόντιχος, Βοσπόριχος, Σωτήριχος. Greg. de D. ed. Schaef. 291.

7, 8. The old orthography κοινεῖ, τεῖ, and the more recent forms are mixed in this inscription.

9. ὑπερτίθεται. Maittaire translates it, "superat omnes." I have given a different meaning, which is suggested by ὑπερθέσιμος in the Ecclesiastical writers. Nicephorus explaining a passage of Evagrius (τὰς καλουμένας ὑπερθεσίμους) says, οὗτοι δὲ πολλάκις καὶ δυὼ καὶ τρεῖς ὑπερθέμενοι τῶν ἡμερῶν. "They protract or prolong their fast for two or three days." Ii sæpius in biduum et triduum jejunium proferunt. See Vales. anim. in l. 1, His. Ecc. Evag. p. 65.

18. Perhaps there was an ἐπώνυμος ἡμέρα, called after Eumenes, as there were ἐπώνυμοι ἡμέραι Κράτωνος.

19. πότον. during the time of supper. δεῖπνον in the second inscription. In the anecdote of Archelaus, in Plutarch, we read αἰτηθεὶς παρὰ πότον, which is elsewhere given, αἰτηθεὶς παρὰ δεῖπνον. P. Leop. Em. l. iii. chap. 14.

21. A similar expression occurs in an inscription given in Chandler, p. 9. ἀναγγεῖλαι αὐτὸν τὸν στέφανον τοῖς Λευκαθέοις μετὰ τὰς σπόνδας.

24. Ἀναγγελία, ἐπιθυμίασις, συναγωνισταὶ are not found in the Lexicons. The first word occurs on another marble. See Greg. de D. ed Schaefer, 618.

32. τάς τε θυσίας πάσας συνετέλεσεν πρεπόντως. Chandler, p. 9.

41. Throughout the inscription we find Καλχηδών, not Χαλκηδών, as the copies of Strabo give the word.

43. Maittaire refers to Demos. de Cor. ἀναγορεῦσαι τὸν στέφανον ἐν τῷι θεατρῶι.

47, 48. τῆς δὲ ἀναγγελίας ἐπιμελεῖσθαι τοὺς καθ᾽ ἕκαστον ἔτος τιμωμένους προστάτας. Chandler. M. An. p. 9.

53. Maittaire doubts whether εἰκόνα γραπτὴν τελείαν may not refer to a " full-length portrait." I have preferred the meaning of " Statue :" on account of ἐπιγράψαντας; as inscriptions were placed on statues, rather than on pictures. Εἰκόνι γραπτῃ ἐπιχρυσῃ occurs on a marble at Ierondas, copied by Mr. Whittington; see Ins. No. 48. in this volume; where the words evidently point to a *statue*; the *picture* was not gilded. Εἰκόνα χρυσῆν ἐφ᾽ ἵππου. Pseph. Sig. Chishull, 57. Εἰκόνα γραπτὴν ἀναθεῖναι. Mis. Obs. vol. III. p. 197.

59. "Κύκλιοι αὐληταὶ erant tibicines circumforanei qui publice in variis locis artem exercebant et docebant." H. Steph. in Th. quoted by Maittaire.